TECHNOLOGY AND LITERATURE

Whereas previous books have explored how literature depicts or discusses scientific concepts, this book argues that literature *is* a technology. It shows how literature has been shaped by technological revolutions, and reveals the essential work that literature has done in helping to uncover the consequences of new technologies. Individual chapters focus on how specific literary technologies – the development of writing, the printing press, the typewriter, the computer – changed the kinds of stories it was possible to tell, and how one could tell them. They also cover the way in which literature has engaged with non-literary technologies – clocks, compasses, trains, telegraphs, cameras, bombs, computer networks – to help its readers to work through the new social configurations and new possibilities for human identity and imagination that they unveil. Human life is inescapably mediated through technology; literature demonstrates this, and thus helps its readers to engage consciously and actively with their technological worlds.

ADAM HAMMOND is the author of *The Far Shore: Indie Games, Superbrothers, and the Making of Jett* (2021) and *Literature in the Digital Age* (2016), and coauthor of *Modernism: Keywords* (2014). His work has appeared in *Wired* and the *Globe and Mail* and has been profiled on BBC and CBC Radio.

CAMBRIDGE CRITICAL CONCEPTS

Cambridge Critical Concepts focuses on the important ideas animating twentieth- and twenty-first-century literary studies. Each concept addressed in the series has had a profound impact on literary studies, as well as on other disciplines, and already has a substantial critical bibliography surrounding it. This series captures the dynamic critical energies transmitted across twentieth- and twenty-first-century literary landscapes: the concepts critics bring to reading, interpretation, and criticism. By addressing the origins, development and application of these ideas, the books collate and clarify how these particular concepts have developed, while also featuring fresh insights and establishing new lines of enquiry.

Cambridge Critical Concepts shifts the focus from period- or genre-based literary studies of key terms to the history and development of the terms themselves. Broad and detailed contributions cumulatively identify and investigate the various historical and cultural catalysts that made these critical concepts emerge as established twenty-first-century landmarks in the discipline. The level will be suitable for advanced undergraduates, graduates, and specialists, as well as for those teaching outside their own research areas, and will have cross-disciplinary relevance for subjects such as history and philosophy.

Titles in the Series

Law and Literature
Edited by KIERAN DOLIN
University of Western Australia

Time and Literature
Edited by THOMAS M. ALLEN
University of Ottawa

The Global South and Literature
Edited by RUSSELL WEST-PAVLOV
University of Tübingen

Trauma and Literature
Edited by ROGER KURTZ
The College at Brockport, State University of New York

Food and Literature
Edited by GITANJALI SHAHANI
San Francisco State University

Animals, Animality, and Literature
Edited by BRUCE BOEHRER, MOLLY HAND AND BRIAN MASSUMI
Florida State University, University of Montreal

Terrorism and Literature
Edited by PETER HERMAN
San Diego State University

Climate and Literature
Edited by ADELINE JOHNS
University of Surrey

Orientalism and Literature
Edited by GEOFFREY NASH
SOAS, University of London

Decadence and Literature
Edited by JANE DESMARAIS AND DAVID WEIR
Goldsmiths, University of London and Hunter College

Affect and Literature
Edited by ALEX HOUEN
University of Cambridge

Sound and Literature
Edited by ANNA SNAITH
King's College London

Magical Realism and Literature
Edited by CHRISTOPHER WARNES AND KIM ANDERSON SASSER
University of Cambridge and Wheaton College, Illinois

Surrealism
Edited BY NATALYA LUSTY
University of Melbourne

Globalisation and Literary Studies
Edited by JOEL EVANS
University of Nottingham

War and Literary Studies
Edited by ANDERS ENGBERG-PEDERSEN AND NEIL RAMSEY
University of Southern Denmark and University of New South Wales

Diaspora and Literary Studies
Edited by ANGELA NAIMOU
Clemson University, South Carolina

TECHNOLOGY AND LITERATURE

EDITED BY

ADAM HAMMOND

University of Toronto

CAMBRIDGE
UNIVERSITY PRESS

CAMBRIDGE
UNIVERSITY PRESS

Shaftesbury Road, Cambridge CB2 8EA, United Kingdom

One Liberty Plaza, 20th Floor, New York, NY 10006, USA

477 Williamstown Road, Port Melbourne, VIC 3207, Australia

314–321, 3rd Floor, Plot 3, Splendor Forum, Jasola District Centre, New Delhi – 110025, India

103 Penang Road, #05–06/07, Visioncrest Commercial, Singapore 238467

Cambridge University Press is part of Cambridge University Press & Assessment, a department of the University of Cambridge.

We share the University's mission to contribute to society through the pursuit of education, learning and research at the highest international levels of excellence.

www.cambridge.org
Information on this title: www.cambridge.org/9781108472586

DOI: 10.1017/9781108560740

First published 2024

A catalogue record for this publication is available from the British Library

Library of Congress Cataloging-in-Publication Data
NAMES: Hammond, Adam, 1981– editor.
TITLE: Technology and literature / edited by Adam Hammond.
DESCRIPTION: Cambridge ; New York, NY : Cambridge University Press, 2024. | Series: Cambridge critical concepts | Includes bibliographical references and index.
IDENTIFIERS: LCCN 2023027871 (print) | LCCN 2023027872 (ebook) | ISBN 9781108472586 (hardback) | ISBN 9781108560740 (ebook)
SUBJECTS: LCSH: Literature and technology.
CLASSIFICATION: LCC PN56.T37 T44 2024 (print) | LCC PN56.T37 (ebook) | DDC 809/.93356–dc23/eng/20230804
LC record available at https://lccn.loc.gov/2023027871
LC ebook record available at https://lccn.loc.gov/2023027872

ISBN 978-1-108-47258-6 Hardback

Contents

Figures

Contributors

CHRIS BARRETT is Associate Professor of English at Louisiana State University and the author of *Early Modern English Literature and the Poetics of Cartographic Anxiety* (2018).

SUSAN BROWN is Canada Research Chair in Collaborative Digital Scholarship, University of Guelph, and leads the Orlando Project in literary history, the Canadian Writing Research Collaboratory, and the Linked Infrastructure for Networked Cultural Scholarship.

JASON CAMLOT is Professor and Research Chair at Concordia University. His recent books are *Phonopoetics* (2019) and the coedited collections *Collection Thinking, Unpacking the Personal Library* (2022), and *CanLit Across Media* (2019). He directs SpokenWeb.

DANIEL CARTER is Associate Professor of Digital Media Innovation in the School of Journalism and Mass Communication at Texas State University.

BECI CARVER is a lecturer in twentieth-century literature at the University of Exeter. Her first book, *Granular Modernism*, was published in 2014, and she is now finishing a second, *Modernism's Whims*.

DAVID CICCORICCO is Associate Professor of English at the University of Otago in Dunedin, New Zealand. He is the author of *Reading Network Fiction* (2007) and *Refiguring Minds in Narrative Media* (2015).

MAXWELL FOXMAN is Assistant Professor of Media Studies/Game Studies at the University of Oregon at the School of Journalism and Communication.

ALICE HALL is a lecturer in contemporary and global literature at the University of York. She is the author and editor of four books on modern literature, disability, and embodiment.

ADAM HAMMOND is the author of *The Far Shore: Indie Games, Superbrothers, and the Making of Jett* (2021) and *Literature in the Digital Age* (2016), and coauthor of *Modernism: Keywords* (2014). His work has appeared in *Wired* and the *Globe and Mail* and has been profiled on BBC and CBC Radio.

PETER C. HERMAN teaches at San Diego State University. His most recent book is *Early Modern Others: Resisting Bias in Renaissance Literature* (2023).

NATALIE M. HOUSTON is Associate Professor of English, University of Massachusetts Lowell. She uses computational methods in her current research to analyze nineteenth-century poetic style and its relationship to the literary canon.

LISE JAILLANT is Reader (Associate Professor) in English and Digital Humanities at Loughborough University. Her latest monograph, *Literary Rebels: A History of Creative Writers in Anglo-American Universities*, was published in 2022.

JENNIFER A. JANECHEK is a science and technology writer. Her work on telephony has appeared in *Texas Studies in Literature and Language* and *The Conradian*.

NICOLA KIRKBY is a Leverhulme Early Career Fellow in English at Royal Holloway, London. Her research on literary technology includes her forthcoming book *Railway Infrastructure and the Victorian Novel.*

ANN LARABEE is Professor Emerita of English and American Studies at Michigan State University and the author of *The Wrong Hands: Popular Weapons Manuals and Their Historic Challenges to a Democratic Society* (2015).

SCOTT LIGHTSEY teaches at Georgia State University. His work focuses on networks of literary and technological history, and he is the author of *Manmade Marvels in Medieval Culture and Literature* (2007).

I. J. MACRAE is Associate Professor of English at Wilfred Laurier University, Ontario.

BONNIE MAK is a historian of information practices, with interests ranging from antiquity to the twenty-first century. She is Associate Professor at the University of Illinois Urbana-Champaign and the author of *How the Page Matters* (2011).

PAULA McDOWELL is Professor of English at New York University and is the author of *The Invention of the Oral: Print Commerce and Fugitive Voices in Eighteenth-Century Britain* (2017) and the editor of *Reading McLuhan Reading* (2021).

SIMON READER is Associate Professor of English at the City University of New York, College of Staten Island. He is the author of *Notework: Victorian Literature and Nonlinear Style* (2021).

DARREN WERSHLER is Professor of English, Affiliate Professor of Communication Studies and Cinema, and Acting Director of the Technoculture, Art and Games Research Centre at Concordia. With Lori Emerson and Jussi Parikka, he is an author of *THE LAB BOOK: Situated Practices in Media Studies* (2022).

AARON WORTH is Associate Professor of Rhetoric at Boston University and the author of *Imperial Media: Colonial Networks and Information Technologies in the British Literary Imagination, 1857–1918* (2014).

Timeline

- *c.* 5000 BCE: Writing in the Western tradition begins as an instrument of clerks and accountants in Mesopotamia
- *c.* 1000 BCE: First evidence of written words being graphically divided by spaces, vertical strokes, or raised dots
- *c.* 750 BCE: The Greeks modify the Phoenician alphabet, rendering its sounds from a Semitic language (Phoenician) into Indo-European Greek
- *c.* 150 BCE: Roman scribes abandon word-division in favor of spaceless *scriptio continua*
- 200: Invention of paper in China
- *c.* 700: Irish and Anglo-Saxon scribes reject *scriptio continua* when copying texts in Latin, inserting spaces between words
- *c.* 1000: Invention of printing with movable clay type in China
- *c.* 1100: Developed centuries earlier in China, the magnetic compass is first mentioned in England
- 1199: Invention of paper in Europe
- *c.* 1300: Mechanical clocks spread rapidly in Europe
- 1377: The *Jikki*, the earliest surviving text printed with movable metal type, is printed in Korea
- *c.* 1436: Gutenberg invents his printing press
- 1476: Introduction of movable type printing in England
- 1539: Juan Pablos of Italy sets up a printing press in Mexico City, the first in the Western hemisphere
- 1557: The Worshipful Company of Stationers receives a royal charter; its membership has the sole right in England to print, publish, or traffic in the printed word
- 1610: Publication of Galileo's astronomical treatise *Sidereus Nuncius*
- 1695: Lapse of the Licensing Act sees the proliferation of printed texts in England
- 1702: First daily newspaper, the *Daily Courant*, is published in London

- 1710: First copyright law, the Statute of Anne, passed in 1695, comes into force in Great Britain
- 1798: Nicolas Louis Robert invents a machine for the mechanical creation of paper at the Essonnes Mill in France
- *c.* 1800: The Earl Stanhope invents an iron hand press
- *c.* 1810: Friedrich Koening and Andreas Bauer create the first steam-powered cylindrical press
- 1814: *The Times* of London installs a steam-powered press
- 1839: Louis Daguerre discovers he can record light onto a silver-coated photographic plate
- 1844: F. B. Morse sends the first long-distance telegraph from Baltimore to Washington with the message "What hath God wrought!"
- 1856: Submarine telegraph line laid under the Gulf of St. Lawrence to Newfoundland
- 1857: Édouard-Léon Scott patents the phonautograph, precursor of the phonograph
- 1876: Alexander Graham Bell transmits the first telephonic message
- 1895: Gugliemo Marconi broadcasts the first radio signal
- 1895: Discovery of X-rays by Wilhelm Conrad Röntgen
- 1900: Haida poets Ghandl and Skaay recite works to John Swanton
- 1906: Reginald Aubrey Fessenden produces the first true "radio broadcast," a Christmas program sent to United Fruit Company ships in the Atlantic and Caribbean Seas
- 1935: First Penguin paperback appears
- 1939: US paperback revolution begins with the launch of Pocket Books
- 1945: Vannevar Bush's "Memex" reading device is conceptualized
- 1962: Marshall McLuhan's *Gutenberg Galaxy* is published
- 1964: Joseph Weizenbaum's experimental *ELIZA* program is developed
- 1967: Formal release of the first ASCII standard for the digital representation of roman letters, numbers, and other functions on the modern US keyboard
- 1971: Project Gutenberg online text repository founded by Michael S. Hart
- 1976: Text adventure computer game *Adventure* is released

Introduction

Adam Hammond

The notion that we live in a technology-obsessed society has become axiomatic, requiring no demonstration or corroborating evidence. And yet who can resist, in our technology-obsessed society, going ahead anyway, needlessly but irresistibly employing high-tech means of demonstrating what is already absolutely clear? In this case, as always, Google – today's definitive tech-startup-turned-tech-behemoth; purveyor of universally employed search engines, web browsers, mobile operating systems; pioneering developer of such futuristic devices as augmented-reality glasses, quantum computers, and self-driving cars – is there to oblige. A quick search of their Ngram Viewer (Figure 0.1), which instantly scans the contents of millions of digitized Google Books, shows the meteoric rise in employment of the word "technology" over the past four centuries.

The *OED* informs us that the word "technology" entered the English language in the early seventeenth century. Its etymons are the Greek *τέχνη* – "art" in the practical, hands-on sense of craft creation, *τέχνη* being the root of the Greek *τέκτων*, "carpenter" – and *λογία*, from *λόγος*, *logos*, "word" or "discourse."[1] In the first two centuries of its employment in English, usage of "technology" hewed close to this etymology. It was used to refer to treatises or discourses on the arts, particularly the practical arts; the terminology of particular branches of knowledge, particularly technical language; and systematic treatments of grammar.[2] Employed in these senses, the word was not used frequently enough to appear as more than a minuscule blip on the chart produced by the Ngram Viewer.

Around the turn of the nineteenth century, an expanded modern sense of technology began to develop. The word was now used to refer to "the branch of knowledge dealing with the mechanical arts and applied

[1] *OED*, "techno-, comb. form." "Technology" notably shares this root with "text," etymologically derived from another craft, weaving.

[2] *OED*, "technology," 1, 2, 3.

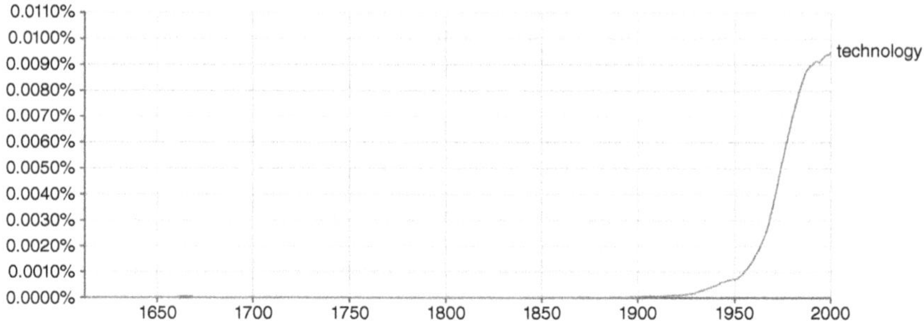

Figure 0.1 Google Books Ngram Viewer chart for "technology," 1600–2000, English corpus.

sciences" as well as "the application of such knowledge for practical purposes, esp. in industry, manufacturing." As such, "technology" became synonymous with "mechanical (or useful or practical or industrial) arts." Later in the nineteenth century, the word came also to refer to "the product of such application": Technology was not only the branch of knowledge or the process employed to produce objects – not only *logos* – but the object itself, synonymous now also with "machine," "machinery," and "mechanism."[3] Drawing on the word's etymological connection to hands-on production, these uses distinguished technology from science – whose Latin root is *scientia*, "knowledge" – on the basis of *application*. Science was theoretical and abstract; once its concepts were put to work in the realm of practical production and concrete objects, they became technology. If science could be "pure," technology could not, since it depended by definition on its use in the real world.

Although the vastly expanded modern sense of "technology" entered the language with the onset of industrialization, the Ngram Viewer shows that it did not attain broad currency until the next century. Compare technology's sudden upward trend in the twentieth century with the graphs for "science," the discipline on which its definition depended, and our own discipline, "literature" (Figure 0.2). Throughout the twentieth century, science and literature remained relatively stable, both very frequently employed. Technology doesn't register in the graph until the 1910s, but following an explosion of employment beginning in the 1950s, it catches up with both terms by the late 1980s and, if the finer movements of the

[3] *OED*, "technology," 4a, 4b, and 4c.

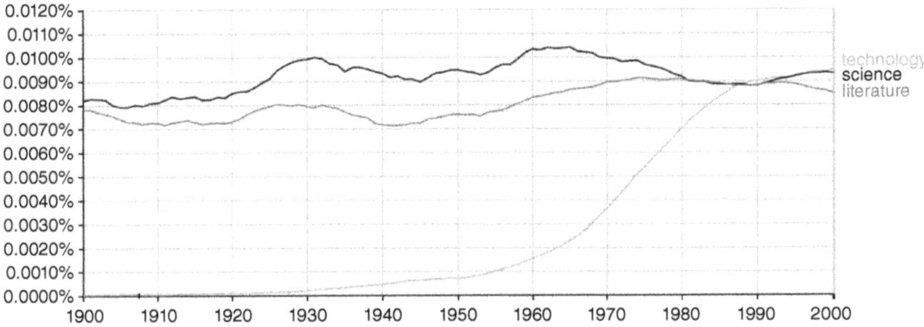

Figure 0.2 Google Books Ngram Viewer chart for "technology," "science," and "literature," 1900–2000, English corpus.

graphs can be trusted, leaves literature behind, keeping pace with and occasionally surpassing science.

What explains our increasing obsession with technology – our growing interest in applied as opposed to abstract science? As the word rode its upward slope in the second half of the twentieth century, numerous theories were advanced. In his under-appreciated *Television: Technology and Cultural Form* (1975), Raymond Williams explains the shift in terms of a social phenomenon he calls "mobile privatization."[4] In the course of the nineteenth and early twentieth centuries, he argues, populations became increasingly mobile – moving from the country to the city – yet also increasingly isolated in a home-centered lifestyle. Technology – particularly communications technology – filled the need to connect the isolated household with the dispersed kinship network. As populations became increasingly atomized and increasingly mobile, the mediating function of technology increased proportionally, and our fascination grew through intimacy; whereas "science" remained in the laboratory and the classroom, technology came to mediate the most basic activities of everyday life. In an analogous argument in *The Machine in the Garden: Technology and the Pastoral Ideal* (1964), Leo Marx explains the rising interest in technology as a response to the increasing sense of alienation from nature that accompanied urbanization.[5] Drawing on contemporaneous philosophers such as Herbert Marcuse and Martin Heidegger and sociologists such as Lewis

[4] Raymond Williams, *Television: Technology and Cultural Form* (London: Routledge, 1990), 26ff.

[5] Leo Marx, *The Machine in the Garden: Technology and the Pastoral Ideal in America* (New York: Oxford University Press, 1964). Marx defines his position in "American Literary Culture and the Fatalistic View of Technology," *The Pilot and the Passenger: Essays on Literature, Technology, and Culture in the United States* (New York: Oxford University Press, 1988), 179–207.

Mumford and Jacques Ellul, Marx describes a process by which "technology" – which by this time could be used to refer to anything from a body of knowledge (as in the Massachusetts Institute of Technology) to an industrial process to the machines such processes produced – became conventionalized as the opposite of the natural. As such, Marx argues, technology became an object of paranoid fascination that could be used to explain the repressed, dehumanized, dissatisfied condition of the 1960s. Toward the end of the century, Bernard Stiegler offered an explanation that resisted the narratives of rapid change and sudden transformation presented by Williams and Marx. In *Technics and Time, 1: The Fault of Epimetheus* (1994), Stiegler rejects the notion of a split between technology and nature, arguing for an "originary technicity" of the human, by which we have always depended on and "co-evolved" with our tools.[6] Whatever the rising *interest* in technology, he argues, we are no more "technological" today than at any other point in our history.

More common than such explanations of the *causes* of the rising interest in technology, however, have been investigations of its *effects*. Since the word attained its modern sense, commentators have been less interested in why we are so fascinated with technology than in predicting where our fascination will land us. As early as the mid-nineteenth century, long before the word "technology" entered widespread use, bold predictions of the social effects of new machines began to circulate. In his essay "Signs of the Times" (1829), Thomas Carlyle argued that in the "Mechanical Age," industrial processes had come to regulate not only "modes of action" but also "modes of thought and feeling": "Men are grown mechanical in head and in heart as well as in hand."[7] In an early example of what would come to be known as technological determinism, Karl Marx wrote in *The Poverty of Philosophy* (1847) that "The hand-mill gives you society with the feudal lord; the steam-mill society with the industrial capitalist."[8] Such determinist accounts dominated discussion of technology in the period of its rapid rise in the second half of the twentieth century. In works such as *Understanding Media* (1964), Marshall McLuhan advanced an influential theory whereby shifts in communications technologies alter subjective "sense ratios" and thereby alter the fundamental categories of individual thought and identity. For McLuhan, media technologies "work us over

[6] Bernard Stiegler, *Technics and Time 1: The Fault of Epimetheus*, trans. George Collins and Richard Beardsworth (Stanford, CA: Stanford University Press, 1998).

[7] Thomas Carlyle, "Signs of the Times," *The Edinburgh Review* 49 (1829): 439–459.

[8] Karl Marx, *The Poverty of Philosophy* (London: Martin Lawrence, [1847] n.d.), 92.

completely"; in particular, the shifts from orality to writing and writing to print brought about corresponding shifts from "tribal" identity and magic to individualism and rationality, which, he prophesied, the new technology of television would reverse.[9] Elizabeth Eisenstein's *The Printing Press as an Agent of Change* (1979) developed McLuhan's notion, changing focus from the psychological to the world-historical to argue that the defining functions of print – the standardization, preservation, and dissemination of knowledge – made the Protestant Reformation, the Renaissance, and the Scientific Revolution inevitable.[10] Such determinist accounts of the effects of communications technologies remain widespread, from Friedrich Kittler's pronouncement that "media determine our situation" to Marc N. B. Hansen's more modest reworking, "media *are* our situation."[11]

Increasingly, however, leading thinkers have pushed back against what they regard as a simplistic and misleading account of the social effects of technology. In *Television*, Williams argues that determinism overlooks the crucial role of human intention in the development and implementation of communications technologies. Technology, in his view, does not emerge autonomously but is always "looked for and developed with certain purposes and practices in mind."[12] McLuhan's procedure of working backward from present effects to technological causes, Williams argues, serves to "ratif[y] the society and culture we now have" and to "desocializ[e]" all "media operations."[13] In *The Nature of the Book* (1998) and elsewhere, Adrian Johns has mounted a similarly forceful argument against Eisenstein's determinist account of the "print revolution." Focusing on the new social and economic structures that needed to be developed before print could contribute to any "revolution," Johns argues that "the nature of the printed book emerged from social machinery as much as from technological."[14] In *The Letters of the Republic* (1990), Michael Warner argues against the "retrodetermination" of McLuhan and Eisenstein on the basis that its appeal

[9] Marshall McLuhan, *Understanding Media: The Extensions of Man* (New York: McGraw Hill, 1964) and Marshall McLuhan, Quentin Fiore, and Jerome Agel, *The Medium Is the Massage: An Inventory of Effects* (New York: Random House, 1967).

[10] Elizabeth L. Eisenstein, *The Printing Press as an Agent of Change* (Cambridge: Cambridge University Press, 1979).

[11] Friedrich Kittler, "Preface to *Gramophone, Film, Typewriter*," in *Literature, Media, Information Systems: Essays*, ed. John Johnston, trans. Stefanie Harris (Amsterdam: G+B Arts, 1985), 28. Mark B. N. Hansen, "Media Studies," in *The Routledge Companion to Literature and Science*, ed. Bruce Clarke and Manuela Rossini (London: Routledge, 2011), 360.

[12] Williams, *Technology*, 14.

[13] Ibid., 127.

[14] Adrian Johns, "The Coming of Print to Europe," in *The Cambridge Companion to the History of the Book*, ed. Leslie Howsam (Cambridge: Cambridge University Press, 2015), 119.

to "the agency of print upon culture" falsely presupposes that technology and culture are "distinct entities."[15] Warner argues instead for a model of "*reciprocal* determination" that takes into account both the social effects *of* new technologies and the social effects *on* technological development, "always with an eye to their changing mutual determination."[16] In a late essay, Leo Marx warned of the growing tendency to seek solutions to social problems in technology rather than in deliberate human action, declaring technology a "hazardous concept" that in practice "relieves the citizenry of onerous decision-making obligations and intensifies their gathering sense of political impotence."[17] For Marx as for Williams, Johns, and Warner, this dangerous situation results from an attitude that "consign[s] technologies to the realms of things" rather than approaching them through the "human relations" that structure their uses and ends.[18]

As this summary suggests, literary scholars have contributed tremendously to contemporary understanding of the origins and tendencies of our technological society. They have perhaps been able to take this leading role because their object of study, literature, has been so profoundly shaped and affected by developments in communications technology. As writers from Marshall McLuhan to Benedict Anderson have noted, the book, still the most familiar literary medium, was the first mass-produced industrial commodity. With the successive inventions of writing, the scroll, the printing press, the steam press, electronic media, and the digital computer – some of the most significant technological developments in history – literature and the literary experience have changed palpably. Further, literature is not only conspicuous in its technological mediation, but is also productively understood *as* a technology. For Walter Ong, all writing must be seen as technological because it requires, at minimum, the use of numerous "artificial" tools and implements such as styli, paper, and ink.[19] Clare Pettitt sees literature as "a tool for the organization of the experience of human life, and for the invention of meaning."[20] Nicholas Dames argues that the genre of the novel in particular is "a machine

15 Michael Warner, *The Letters of the Republic: Publication and the Public Sphere in Eighteenth-Century America* (Cambridge, MA: Harvard University Press, 1990), 9, 6. Emphasis in original.

16 Ibid., xii.

17 Leo Marx, "Technology: The Emergence of a Hazardous Concept," *Technology and Culture* 51.3 (July 2010): 576–577.

18 Ibid., 576.

19 Walter J. Ong, *Orality and Literacy: The Technologizing of the Word* (London: Routledge, 2012), 80–82.

20 Clare Pettitt, "'The Annihilation of Space and Time': Literature and Technology," in *The Cambridge History of Victorian Literature*, ed. Kate Flint (Cambridge: Cambridge University Press, 2012), 571.

constructed to make its reader feel through an only slightly variable, and possibly perfectable, series of events."[21] Literary studies have been so attuned to technology because literature is so inescapably technological: produced by machines, distributed by machines, read through machines, itself a machine.

The emphasis on technology is not new in literary studies, but it has become a particular focus in recent years. If Thomas Carlyle can be seen as representing a first phase of interest in literature and technology, Walter Benjamin and other modernists as initiating a second, and Leo Marx, Marshall McLuhan, and Raymond Williams as constituting a third, the advent of our own digital age has brought renewed attention to the subject. Perhaps the most conspicuously technological approach to literature has been that of Digital Literary Studies, a subdiscipline of the Digital Humanities that uses quantitative methods and computational models to study literary history and style, produce archives and digital editions, and theorize new digital literary genres. Literature and Science, a relatively new "interdiscipline" concerned with overlaps and resonances between the two fields,[22] has likewise demonstrated an interest in technology, despite privileging traditional scientific disciplines. Another thriving discipline concerned with literary technology is Book History, practitioners of which – Eisenstein, Warner, and Johns among them – have made major contributions to historical understandings of the relationship between technology, literature, culture, and society. Media Studies, descended from McLuhan's technology-focused approach, has emerged as an important sister discipline to literary studies. "Mainstream," historically focused literary studies has experienced a technological turn of its own. In their 2008 *PMLA* report on the state of my own discipline, Modernist Studies, Douglas Mao and Rebecca Walkowitz point to exemplary work such as Todd Avery's *Radio Modernism* in order to argue that "attention to [modernist] technologies" – particularly the role that mass communications play in promoting global and transnational ways of thinking and writing – represented a vibrant new direction in the field.[23] In the ensuing years, this trend has only continued, and the pattern has been repeated in every historical field of literary studies.

[21] Nicholas Dames, *The Physiology of the Novel: Reading, Neural Science, and the Form of Victorian Fiction* (Oxford: Oxford University Press, 2007), 57–58.

[22] Cf. Martin Willis, *Literature and Science: A Reader's Guide to Essential Criticism* (London: Palgrave, 2015), 1.

[23] Douglas Mao and Rebecca Walkowitz, "The New Modernist Studies," *PMLA* 123.3 (May 2008): 742–745.

While the recent interest in literature and technology has been intense, it has been dispersed between fields that are seldom in conversation, and none of these fields has individually taken on the subject in its full breadth. Within Digital Literary Studies, the question of technology has proven divisive; in particular, the much-debated "hack versus yack" controversy has pitted keen users and developers of new digital technologies (generally those practicing computational text analysis, who "build code") against those who wish to theorize and often resist digital technologies (generally those who come from a Media Studies background, who "break code"). Book History has arguably made the greatest contribution to the analysis of literature and technology of any single discipline, yet technology is only one focus among many – with activities such as critical editing and analytic bibliography only incidentally concerned with the subject – while the history of *literary* books is a consistent but not an exclusive focus. While Science and Technology Studies and its more recent offshoot Technology Studies have proven fruitful sources of theoretical models for studying the social lives of literary texts, the disciplines themselves are not concerned with literature.[24] The interdiscipline of Literature and Science, as its name implies, has tended to focus on science rather than technology. Although Bruno Latour and others have disputed the notion of a clear separation between science and technology, preferring the hybrid term *technoscience*, the scholarship emerging from Literature and Science demonstrates the continued relevance of the distinction. Critics such as Charlotte Sleigh and Martin Willis have argued that Literature and Science too often treats science as prior to and separate from literature: On the one hand, this scholarship dutifully notes the "science bits" in literary texts in order to present "a one-way process by which literary writers reflect the metaphors of science";[25] on the other, it calls for a "dialogue" between literary and scientific texts that it thereby posits as belonging to separate spheres.[26] Whereas a focus on *science* and literature leads inevitably to such oppositions, the focus on *technology* and literature does not. This is because while literature is not a science, it *is* a technology. The study of Literature and Science, a separate discipline, tends to lead away from literature itself. Because literature can be understood as a technology – and since it is produced, distributed, and mediated technologically – the study of literature

[24] Rather than analyze literature, Science and Technology Studies applies hermeneutic methods informed by literary studies and literary theory, treating scientific works and the discipline of science itself as texts.

[25] Charlotte Sleigh, *Literature and Science* (London: Palgrave Macmillan, 2011), x.

[26] Willis, *Literature and Science*, 1.

and technology brings ever closer focus to the culture, nature, and reception of literary texts.

Cambridge Critical Concepts: Technology and Literature does not, then, announce the creation of a new field. Instead, it gathers technologically focused work from a variety of subfields of literary studies – work that, although collectively constituting the most exciting and progressive research in the field today, has yet to be placed in conversation.

Part I, "Origins," draws together scholars of literature, Book History, and Media Studies to tell the story of how literature "co-evolved" with communications technologies – how new technologies such as the scroll, the printing press, and the digital computer reshaped the literary communications circuit, and how these technologies were in turn shaped by the needs and desires of writers, printers, publishers, booksellers, and readers. As becomes clear from I. J. MacRae's "Orality and Writing" (Chapter 1), in tracing the mutual impact of literature and key literary technologies, the chapters in this section resist the widespread tendency to read media history as a teleological progression that naturalizes and justifies our present-day media environment. Pushing against standard scholarly accounts of the triumph of print that have served to provide "an intellectual bulwark for imperialism and colonialism" — what he calls "romances of technological ascension" – MacRae positions orality and oral performance as rich and generative technologies whose complex affordances are impossible to render in other media: Writing and printing, he argues, "impact literature and culture" primarily "by leaving things out: gestures, colors, coughs, shouts, and murmurs, the sound of falling rain: the entire three-dimensional world of human experience."

Several chapters from Part I take on another technology too often left behind in scholarly accounts of technological progress: the human body. In "Manuscript" (Chapter 2), Bonnie Mak presents the human hand – which "supports the production and circulation of ideas in manuscript, printed, digital, and other forms" – as central to all textual transmission, "whether it be scribes who took dictation in antiquity, stonecutters who fashioned the inkstones to the world of scholarship and art in China, or the legions of students and overseas workers who manually transcribe and encode literary, medical, and other texts in service of their digital use." Writing on "The Hand Press" (Chapter 3), Paula McDowell similarly argues for approaches that consider the human body as an essential literary technology; indeed, her approach to the long history of the hand-operated press makes us question any neat separation of body and machine. Hand-printed works, she argues, are the product neither of a human or a of mere tool, but the two formed into a hybrid: "neither a printing press nor a hand can produce a printed text," McDowell argues, "but together, machine and worker can and do." In "Typewriters" (Chapter 5), Darren Wershler makes the case for the typewriter as an "assemblage": a series of technologies, techniques, and discourses that work together to shape the expressive pathways in which humans express and constitute their subjectivities. The history of hand-made literature shows us that technology is not categorically exterior to the human, but is rather an essential, defining dimension of it.

The chapters in Part I also explore the way that literary technologies have increasingly served to break down another border: that between literature and the other arts. In "The Mechanical Press" (Chapter 4), Simon Reader shows that any scholarly investigation of the literary legacy of steam-driven presses must leave behind narrow disciplinary boundaries: "Literary scholars wishing to assert the importance of machine printing," Reader argues, "must necessarily place texts in relation not only to other works of literature but also to competing media: journalism, advertising, and other products of the print industry." Lise Jaillant's "Literature in the Electric Age" (Chapter 6) focuses not on a particular literary technology, but on the shifts in the literary field that occurred in response to the threat of obsolescence at the hands of competing media such as film and television. Adapting marketing techniques from those media, and capitalizing on new formats such as the paperback, the literary field broadened to expand its appeal to an ever-widening "middlebrow" reading public. By the 1930s, Jaillant argues, these developments in format and marketing had effectively broken down any rigid dividing line between "literary" and "nonliterary" reading publics, so that advertisements for a bestseller such as Pearl S. Buck's *The Good Earth* and James Joyce's modernist classic *Ulysses* could appear side by side. Closing Part I, Maxwell Foxman argues in "Digital Text" (Chapter 7) that developments in the digital representation of texts have continued to challenge divisions long held to be immutable – not least those separating content, author, and reading. As we arrive in the digital present, Foxman argues, we are left questioning all our traditional beliefs about what text is.

Part II, "Developments," draws on period-focused literary scholarship as well as Media Studies, Literature and Science, Disability Studies, and Postcolonial Studies to investigate how literary texts have served to frame public understanding of new nonliterary technologies such as clocks, telescopes, steam engines, and computer networks. Drawing on Williams, Johns, and Warner, the chapters in this section show how the appropriation of such technologies as literary devices has shaped public perception of their human impact – and altered our sense of "the human" itself.

Alice Hall begins the section with "Prostheses" (Chapter 8), which covers a wide range of historical periods to outline the difference that literature can make in challenging dominant technological narratives and reframing them in terms of human uses. Taking as emblematic a pair of short stories by William Faulkner and Flannery O'Connor, Hall argues that these works do more than simply register shifts in prosthetic technology; they also challenge normalizing discourses through forms that "resist any urge toward stable order, whether narrative, social, or bodily." "Language and storytelling are important to our understanding of prosthesis," Hall argues, "because anxieties, hopes, and fantasies about enablement, modification, and enhancement, as well as the powerful fiction of the 'normate,' are reinforced but also renegotiated in literary and cultural spaces."

A series of chapters on the late medieval and early modern period follows; these treat literary engagements with clocks, compasses, and telescopes. In each case, what we learn from the literary record challenges some aspect of received wisdom about the progress of technology. In Scott Lightsey's "Clocks" (Chapter 9), the contemporaneous literary record shows that clocks pointedly did *not* impose a secular conception of time that regulated human life; instead, the population of medieval Christian Europe continued to reckon time through cycles of light and dark and according to the liturgical calendar. Drawing on readings of Christine de Pizan, Philippe de Mézières, Jean Froissart, and Geoffrey Chaucer, Lightsey argues instead that clocks were primarily received in the time of their invention as mechanical wonders and primarily employed as displays of wealth. In "Compasses" (Chapter 10), Chris Barrett reads the literary engagements of John Milton, John Donne, and others with two kinds of compasses – those that trace circles, and those that point to magnetic north – to demonstrate how the devices served both to amaze and also to reorient the colonial geographic imagination of early modern readers: As she argues, "With the era of European exploration (and its associated colonial projects), the compass became virtually synonymous, for professional pilots and lay people alike, with navigation – and wonder." In "Telescopes" (Chapter 11), Peter C. Herman argues that the lesson of works such as Aphra Behn's *The Emperor of the Moon* is that we must remain skeptical of the notion that any technology can relieve us of the burden of sustained critical engagement. "The telescope does not automatically reveal the truth," Herman concludes: "The image it presents must be interpreted."

Chapters on nineteenth- and twentieth-century literary engagements with technology reveal similar tensions and ambivalences. In "Steam Engines" (Chapter 12), Nicola Kirkby argues that, for authors of the long nineteenth century, "steam engines occupy an odd vanishing point that falls somewhere between ubiquity and obscurity, material presence and absence." In "Wires" (Chapter 13), Aaron Worth shows how telegraph and telephone wires were conceived not only as nerves connecting the globe, but also, acting as the circulatory system of Empire, as veins or arteries – "metaphorical carrier[s] not only of information but also of blood." In "Cameras" (Chapter 14), Beci Carver reads work by William Empson, William James, W. H. Auden, and others to argue that cameras served "not only to make the visible world familiar, as early inventors hoped they might do, but also to make it *strange*." In his investigation of "Phonographs" (Chapter 15), Jason Camlot traces the twofold nature of the literary engagements with sound recording: On the one hand, they "suggested a direct, unmediated experience of events from the past"; on the other, in drawing attention to the material limitations of this new technology, which "worked to shape the real-time sonic events it recorded," these engagements "revealed how indebted our sense of reality is to mediating factors."

The closing chapters of Part II outline the stakes of literary engagements with technology for authors, readers, and for literary studies itself. In the expansive "Waves and Rays" (Chapter 16), Jennifer A. Janechek shows how telephony, wireless telegraphy, X-rays, and radio broadcasting combined to inform an emerging "vibratory narrative aesthetic" in the modernist novel – one that sought not to "allegorize or simulate electronic transmission, but rather [to] take advantage of the principles already energizing it." "No longer beholden to the representation of reality," Janechek writes, "the novel could conceivably foster direct sensory experience, becoming a connective technology in its own right." In "The Bomb" (Chapter 17), Ann Larabee shows how the threat of nuclear apocalypse galvanized literary criticism's sense of its social mission. Although she reads "nuclear criticism" as a failure, she reads John Adams's and Peter Sellars's opera *Doctor Atomic* as exemplary of the "new critical and creative forms" that might "bring the humanities and sciences together to address threats such as nuclear weapons." In "Networks" (Chapter 18), David Ciccoricco reads fiction by William Gibson and Porpentine as serving to train its readers in the ambivalent business of navigating their own networked realities. "Just as metaphor itself relies on distance between source and target," Ciccoricco argues, "figurations of networks are vital to the project of maintaining a critical distance from the social and political networks that we propagate and that in turn interpenetrate our experience."

A short concluding Part III, "Applications," draws on the field of Digital Literary Studies to investigate the new interpretive possibilities presented by digital technologies of reading. Exploring and unpacking a series of computational approaches to investigating hundreds or thousands of literary texts at one time, Natalie M. Houston argues in "Distant Reading" (Chapter 19) that these techniques, "changing the scale at which texts are analyzed," serve to "transform the object of study and thereby the kinds of questions that can be explored" in literary studies. In "Visualization" (Chapter 20), Daniel Carter speaks with leading practitioners in the field to unpack the ways in which new techniques in digital data visualization are allowing scholars "to perform conventional work in new ways." Applying these techniques to literary data for which they are not designed, however, also reveals a productive push and pull: As one of Carter's interview subjects, Alex Christie, puts it, "We're reading the literature on the technology, but we're also seeing where the literature we're trying to model pushes against the edges of the technical frameworks we have in hand." Susan Brown closes the volume with "Digital Editions" (Chapter 21), which gestures back to preceding sections of the volume to outline the future of literary form. Often positioned as the dangerous other to the printed book, auguring its obsolescence, Brown argues that digital editions are and will remain in dialogue with printed books. Yet Brown offers a sketch of a future for the digital edition – one of new "conventions and infrastructure to pry editions away from the legacy of print towards the wide range of affordances offered by digital instantiations of texts." The digital edition of the future, she argues, carries with it the promise of another "sea change."

It is a fitting image with which to end the volume, for the history of literature and technology is one of a series of sea changes. Neither side of the exchange is fixed, nor does each remain distinct or pure in relation to the other. Literature, a technology, has been shaped by shifts in communications technology; literature in turn has shaped our understanding of the possibilities and perils of new technologies, while these technologies have shaped our understanding of ourselves. In these shifting seas, through processes of adaptation, reconfiguration, and survival, literature and technology have continued their mutual churn. It is the only constant in this story.

PART I

Origins

CHAPTER I

Orality and Writing

I. J. MacRae

In the Second Book of *El Ingenioso don Quijote de la Mancha*, published in 1615, Cervantes has the Don take a stroll into Barcelona, where he comes immediately upon a printing house, enters, and takes a tour. The Don is a "gentleman" who "spent times of leisure – which meant most of the year – reading books of chivalry with so much devotion and enthusiasm" that "his fantasy filled with everything he had read in his books," and "he lost his mind."[1] Enchanted by writing, he forgets to manage his estate, and sells "acres of arable land in order to buy books of chivalry to read." A man made of writing, who grounds his identity in reading, he is undone by misreading in the end. The Don's fundamental mistake is to believe what he reads, to be a naïve reader, to take fiction as fact. He is what Marshall McLuhan would call a "typographic man,"[2] which for Cervantes means shallow, vain, rigidly principled, inflexible, a fool – someone easily duped. The Don is not *literate* in the full sense of the word, which is not to say he cannot read (he can), but this does mean he is unable to deploy the full cultural resources of texts, is unschooled in the practices of reading and interpretation, cannot properly manage the relationship between the world and the text. The Don, in other words, is a man "prepared to pay the price" for the technology of reading, to suffer what Robert Bringhurst calls "a kind of ritual mutilation of the intellect, a sort of cerebral circumcision" – a perspectival winnowing that might come with utter absorption in a limited discourse, in books and not life.[3] Writing, Bringhurst observes, as Cervantes well understood, has great value, but comes with genuine cost.

Cervantes uses his fiction to conduct an extended inquiry into the problems and possibilities of print technology. And so he brings the Don

[1] Miguel de Cervantes, *Don Quixote*, trans. Edith Grossman (New York: Ecco, 2005), 20.
[2] Marshall McLuhan, *The Gutenberg Galaxy: The Making of Typographic Man* (Toronto: University of Toronto Press, 1962), 17, 245.
[3] Robert Bringhurst, *The Tree of Meaning: Thirteen Talks* (Kentville, NS: Gaspereau Press, 2006), 164.

"home" to the printing house, source of his identity and seat of his illusions, as if to unravel his origins and so to determine his ends. In the print shop, Don Quixote "saw them printing in one place, correcting in another, typesetting here, revising there, in short, all of the procedures that can be seen in large printing houses."[4] Cervantes pays close attention to a set of intellectual and material technologies involved in the transcription of written works, the materialization of the word, the fixity of the text, and its reification into an unvarying and iterable product, dependent now upon a series of tools, techniques, and inventions that exist "outside" the author (paper, ink, metallic type, casting processes, the producers and technicians who manufacture and operate these tools, those who distribute and market and sell the product). It's an exemplary accounting of the work of art in the age of mechanical production.[5] The book is a commodity newly capable of movement into economic and cultural spheres well beyond any spatiotemporal unity of the oral utterance – the close, intimate, participatory lifeworld where speakers and listeners are copresent, where the technology (if we may call it that) of orality tends to reside.

Quickly, the Don comes across a book in correction he knows well: "[I]t was called the *Second Part of the Ingenious Gentleman Don Quixote de la Mancha*, written by somebody from Tordesillas." This is not the Second Book we are reading, however, but a pirated text written by an imposter and published as a profit-making scheme in an era before copyright. "I have already heard of this book," says the Don, before condemning it to ashes.[6] It is a vertiginous experience for the Don, who confronts the source of his own identity, sees himself being written, and understands himself as being read – iterated, depersonalized, sent out to the community in a mediatized form that belongs to a larger – soon a mass – culture. The ramifications, limitations, and possibilities of print technology have at last become clear to the Don. In transposing chivalric codes from obsolete romances into lived experience, he has entered into the heart of an anachronism, misjudging the temporality of texts and the role writing may play in the construction of memory, perception, and identity. This revelation of identity is a disaster for the Don, a reversal of fortune and a scene of suffering, from which he will not recover. It is also a cathartic moment in the Aristotelian sense, however, if we as readers recognize with pity and

[4] Cervantes, *Don Quixote*, 872.

[5] Walter Benjamin, "The Work of Art in the Age of Mechanical Reproduction," in *Illuminations*, trans. Harry Zohn (New York: Harcourt & Brace, 1968), 217–251.

[6] Cervantes, *Don Quixote*, 875.

fear the implications of what it means to be a human grappling with print technology, and if we move to purge naïve, mimetic readings from our own relationships with inherited narratives of oral and print technologies.

In Cervantes's calibrated, ironic understatement, the Don leaves the print shop "showing some displeasure." It is the same critique Flaubert furnishes in *Madame Bovary* (1857), in which Emma reads sentimental romances and believes this phantasmagoria of sensation and feeling shall be her destiny. Both are veiled critiques of reading practices of "true" believers, of naïve readers, ideologues, and pedants, but also of sacred texts and orthodox traditions – any culture of the one "true" book, any hegemonic tradition that stifles interpretation and critique, any text interpreted in terms of a singular truth.

This image of the Don reading himself being written and read in a printing house, which is both palace of mirrors and shop of horrors, distills several of this chapter's central themes. What might it say about the technology of print, its possibilities and its limits, the play of imagination and desire in "typographic man" (should such a thing even exist)? What might it say of the particular gap, dichotomy, or dissonance between orality and writing as critical categories, a particular interpolation or cultural politics of representation that I take to be a piece of bad faith, but also bad history?

Don Quixote constitutes a negative example and does negative work; we need to read as the Don does not. It may be useful to be reminded of this now, as we set out to consider two weighty and long-standing literary-critical categories, in that received tradition concerning the differences between oral and written cultures seems to be one of literate culture's stranger and more profane fictions, a semantic or philosophical complex that amounts to a collective narrative fantasy. I want in this chapter to read the past productively, with an eye to moving beyond simple oppositions and binary taxonomies, and toward a more complex grammar of "unequal proximities."[7]

1 What Is Water? (Orality and Writing)

The late David Foster Wallace once told an old joke, derived from inherited oral tradition, in a quintessential theater of orality, a strictly regulated ceremony marked by often unconscious convention, with attendees in full regalia coming forward as their name is uttered in oral–aural (mouth-to-ear)

[7] Alan Lawson, "The Anxious Proximities of Settler (Post)colonial Relations," in *Literary Theory: An Anthology*, 2nd ed., ed. Julie Rivkin and Michael Ryan (Malden, MA: Blackwell, 2004), 1210–1223.

communication with the community, which they are reentering now after a hiatus, prepared to take on a new title and a new identity.[8] "How's the water?" an old fish asks two young fish. The youngest fish, puzzled, takes a moment and asks: "What the hell is water?" There is no place "outside" the problem, no vantage point from which to gain a "proper" (rational, analytical, objective) understanding of the inquiry. The same question, modified for our purpose, holds here: What the hell is language? How do we understand language as technology? How do those two formidable, foundational, capacious categories known as *orality* and *writing* come to complement, critique, interact, and exchange with one another? Given the diversity of cross-cultural covenants, disciplinary tensions, and generic dispensations at work (and play) in these fields, to what extent are orality and writing even useful as critical taxa – to what extent do such terms obscure ground they are meant to reveal? With respect to the creative use of language, to literature and questions of literary form broadly defined, how might the terrains these terms map onto overlap, and do they do so with any meaningful equivalencies? How do current understandings of these oft-paired terms fit, as a "powerful form of symbolic structuration," as a strategy within the larger politics of colonialism and imperialism?[9] Dear reader, rest assured, there are many myths – untested and often unconscious assumptions, deeply held prejudices – at work within these familiar, entirely quotidian categories, in which a good deal of canonical discourse, from Plato and Rousseau to Walter Ong and the Toronto School, remains regrettably ethnocentric, arrogant, condescending, self-congratulatory, even racist.

We might recognize that we can't get out of this water in which we swim. There is no place to stand to fully understand what *orality* and *writing* might mean, how they work and serve as both a medium of and vehicle for our thoughts and feelings, our identities and cultures, our social relations and systems of governance, the ways we work in the world. It's an old paradox, that the present interpellation is constituted by the medium it seeks to interlocute; as Barbara Johnson comments, "An essay about writing, therefore, is an unclosable loop: it is an attempt to comprehend that which it is comprehended by."[10] And a piece of writing about orality,

[8] Also known as a graduation ceremony, a Convocation Address. David Foster Wallace, "This Is Water." Kenyon College Convocation Address, 2004: http://bulletin-archive.kenyon.edu/x4280.html (accessed July 25, 2023).

[9] Lawson, "Anxious Proximities."

[10] Barbara Johnson, "Writing," in *Literary Theory: An Anthology*, 2nd ed., ed. Julie Rivkin and Michael Ryan (Malden, MA: Blackwell, 2004), 339.

for readers whose patterns of recognition are deeply conditioned by habits of literacy, is another difficult line to cross. The terms and conditions we have inherited for understanding orality and writing as technologies are woefully inadequate to the task.

This chapter defines technology as "the application of scientific knowledge for practical purposes, especially in industry," with respect to the "tools and equipment developed from the application of scientific knowledge," and in terms of the "branch of knowledge dealing with" applied science.[11] Technology is not just theory or science, but is concerned with how knowledge and tools become operative in the world and in human lives, as "codified ways of deliberately manipulating the environment to achieve some material objective."[12] In literary terms, how do we manipulate words in the oral and written spheres, and to what ends? How have ideas about orality and literacy been constructed and *applied*?

These questions raise significant concerns with far-reaching implications that have been taken up by ancient and contemporary thinkers to different ends for millennia. I will go over some of this genealogy here, recognizing that such large areas of cultural activity cannot be covered in their entirety; that other thinkers and subjects could be brought to bear. These are what philosopher Cornelius Castoriadis would call "genuine questions" for which there are no finished or final answers, yet the discourse in which they are constituted goes some way toward instituting our own society, our sense of ourselves as individuals in relation to *others*, how we understand and categorize differences between *us* and *them*.

Given this range of concern, this chapter will necessarily be interdisciplinary and comparative, moving across commonly held boundaries of language, culture, period, and political jurisdiction, and the disciplines of literary criticism and linguistics, philosophy, archaeology, anthropology, and classical and media studies. I want to consider how these concepts (orality and writing) have been constituted in discourse, how these terms have been formed and translated, and to address some of the ideologies that underpin these distinctions. I will offer both context and canon in the construction of these terms, presenting leading figures and supporting ground; consider the history of the alphabet and the concept of orality; then stage a refutation, before concluding with a new dispensation. A whistle-stop tour in places, with other thinkers we will linger. This aims

[11] *OED*, "technology, n."

[12] Quoted in Jack Goody, *The Interface between the Written and the Oral* (Cambridge and New York: Cambridge University Press, 1987), 132.

to be a reflexive study, which looks into the speaking mirror that dawns on the Don in the printing house in Barcelona, the *espejo hablado* that the final Aureliano translates in Gabriel García Márquez's *Macondo.* We will sound the canon, from Homer and Plato to Havelock and Ong, from Parry and Lord to Sapir and Whorf, with attention to the Toronto School of Communication Theory and the work of Innis and McLuhan. But we will also tune to less familiar, possibly more germane voices – a surprising number from the Pacific Northwest, including Bringhurst, Julie Cruikshank, Skaay, Ghandl, Angela Sidney, and Ted Chamberlin – as we take up questions of Indigeneity and orality in positing a genuinely plurivocal, polyphonic idea of the Humanities, one in which oral tradition as social activity is a necessary and vital "part of the equipment for living."[13] In so doing, we need to enlarge the idea of the historical document, and consider materials once thought largely suspect, in focusing attention outside areas of standardized historical inquiry. The challenges are significant and current. As Ong has observed in *Orality and Literacy: The Technologizing of the Word*, "Not only are the issues deep and complex, but they also engage our own biases."[14]

At the root of most contemporary understandings of orality and writing is the assumption that these are different, opposed, indeed dichotomous categories. Most often they are studied in contrast to one another, as a twinned pair, a binary system, a hierarchical opposition not subject to dialectical synthesis. Their history is of being defined together and in contrast to one another; as Alan Rumsey explains, "like most technical terms, orality has taken on a specific sense in linguistic anthropology through the way it is contrasted with something else – in this case with literacy."[15] Emphasizing this distinction in fortifying this view, Ong's foundational work focused on the "differences between writing and orality" and sought analytical tools "[f]or understanding orality as contrasted with literacy."[16] The present chapter, structured in accordance with this widely held convention, looks also to subvert it.

Orality involves speaking and listening, the mouth and ear, the use of the organ of the mouth to compose speech, what Ong usefully called the "oral–aural" channel. Orality implies a dialogue that is voiced, immediate,

[13] Julie Cruikshank, *The Social Life of Stories: Narrative and Knowledge in the Yukon Territory* (Vancouver: University of British Columbia Press, 1998).
[14] Walter J. Ong, *Orality and Literacy: The Technologizing of the Word* (New York: Methuen, 1982), 3.
[15] Alan Rumsey, "Orality," in *Key Terms in Language and Culture*, ed. Alessandro Duranti (Oxford: Blackwell, 2001), 166.
[16] Ong, *Orality and Literacy*, 28.

embodied, present-tense, participatory, performative. Orality is a social activity dependent upon a listener or audience, in which context is crucial, and gestures of face and body and registers and rhythms of voice are significant. For Édouard Glissant, orality "is inseparable from the body in movement."[17] As Marcel Jousse notes in an early, perceptive study, we can differentiate between the *spoken* – any utterance that comes from the mouth – and the *oral*: a (literary) utterance formalized in a specific manner, one that is subject to tradition.[18] I am interested in orality in this second sense, as oral narrative or poetry, which Paul Zumthor defines as "any poetic communication where transmission and reception at least are carried by voice and hearing," and which carries a knowledge "at least partially mediated by tradition."[19] In Ruth Finnegan's view, oral narratives constitute a much more "complex and variegated" concept and category of language and thought than is generally recognized.[20]

As speaking involves a listener or listeners, and a voice as fleeting and evanescent as air, so writing implies reading, and a reader, abstracted now, not necessarily present, but imagined and distant from the producer of the text, no longer capable of responding to the writer directly. Writing in the Western tradition begins as an instrument of clerks and accountants in Mesopotamia in *c.* 5000 BCE. It was a good method for keeping records of transactions, for counting grain and wine and sheep. Only later, as chirography developed, did it become a means for recording stories. Whether or not consciousness and its operations has a history (a question at the crux of disagreements in the field), alphabetic writing certainly does; and this series of technological innovations, the most obvious hinge between orality and literacy, lies at the heart of Western concepts of writing, and of literature more generally. ("Literature" derives from *littera*, Latin for "letter," and carries the Middle English sense of "knowledge of books" – which is only one way to figure the problem. The concept engages our biases.)

As Caleb Crain sketches a brief history of early alphabets, "In the fourth millennium BCE, the Sumerians developed cuneiform, and the Egyptians hieroglyphs. Both scripts began with pictures of things, such as a beetle or

17 Édouard Glissant, *Caribbean Discourse: Selected Essays*, trans. J. Michael Dash (Charlottesville: University of Virginia Press, 1992), 237.

18 Marcel Jousse, *The Oral Style*, trans. E. Sienaert and R. Whitaker (New York: Garland, [1925] 1990).

19 Paul Zumthor, *Oral Poetry: An Introduction*, trans. Kathryn Murphy-Judy (Minneapolis: University of Minnesota Press, 1990), 23.

20 Ruth Finnegan, *Oral Poetry: Its Nature, Significance, and Social Context* (Cambridge: Cambridge University Press, 1992), 8.

a hand, and then some of these symbols developed more abstract meanings, representing ideas in some cases and sounds in others."[21] A welter of scripts developed in the Near East, some a combination of *logographic* and *alphabet* representations (the first of things, concepts, ideas, words; the second of sounds, the voice – phonetics). The Narmer Palette from Egypt, of *c.* 3000 BCE, depicts the *rebus* technique, in which pictures or symbols suggest the sounds of syllables or words, thereby combining and bridging logographic and alphabetic systems.[22] Four major script groups (Sumerian, Egyptian, Chinese, Mayan) developed, and though the question of diffusion is complex, and they may have all developed separately, there is also the possibility of diffusion from a common source in Sumer to Egypt and then China, with the Mesoamerican development almost certainly unique. In each tradition, writing depends on a host of subtechnologies, craftspeople, and functions, each with its own "discrepant history," and which may include "styli or brushes or pens, carefully prepared surfaces such as paper, animal skins, strips of wood, as well as ink or paints, and much more."[23] Paper, for example, was invented by the Chinese in *c.* 200 CE, and was in Baghdad by *c.* 800 CE and in Europe in *c.* 1100 CE.

Any good encyclopedia entry will tell you that what is known as the Proto-Canaanite alphabet, for inscriptions older than around 1050 BCE, is the oldest verified alphabet. Made up of twenty-two consonants, with vowel sounds implicit, its innovation lies in its phonetic nature, with one sound or phoneme represented by one symbol, which meant only a few dozen symbols had to be learned. (By contrast, Egyptian hieroglyphs required a prolonged period to learn and master.) The Phoenician alphabet, a Northern Semitic language used in what is now Syria, Lebanon, and northern Israel, appears in around the eleventh century BCE. These were seafaring and merchant peoples, and they brought their tools with them as they traded, to keep track of their deals. Their alphabet was taken up with regional variation in parts of Northern Africa and Southern Europe, and was found to be of genuine mercantile utility. In *c.* 750 BCE, the Greeks adopted the Phoenician alphabet, rendering its sounds from a Semitic language (Phoenician) into Indo-European Greek. The Greeks added vowels to facilitate the writing of their language, eventually leading

21 Caleb Crain, "Twilight of the Books: What Will Life Be Like if People Stop Reading?" *New Yorker* (December 24, 2007).

22 Dominic Wyse, *How Writing Works: From the Invention of the Alphabet to the Rise of Social Media* (Cambridge: Cambridge University Press, 2017), 57.

23 Ong, *Orality and Literacy*, 82.

to the alphabet as we know it today, and to twenty-six letters. The alphabet is often celebrated as a singular achievement, a culmination of culture, which makes widespread, near universal literacy possible in the West. And yet as David Olson explains, the technology of the alphabet was developed through a centuries-long historical process that is multilingual, multicultural, entirely dependent upon translation, and not attained through a relentless drive to perfect a technology, but as "the by-product of attempts to use a script for a language for which it is ill-suited."[24]

So how are the tools of writing and orality different, how do they interact in specific cases, and do they entail different epistemes, even different modes of civilization and consciousness, as has long been posited in the Western tradition? Are reading and writing crucial elements of the line drawn between the raw and the cooked, the civilized and barbaric, the mythopoeic and the rigorously rational, the informational and the performative, in a series of dichotomies that defines a structuralist way of thinking, as put forward comprehensively in an influential series of texts by Claude Lévi-Strauss?[25] That is, does writing enable a "good" kind of thinking, "proper" thinking, *our* kind of thinking, and orality some other, vestigial, weak, fuzzy, intuitive, emotional, less rational kind?

2 "Writing Heightens Consciousness" (Received Tradition)

The celebration of writing at the expense of orality has a long history. In *Writing and Script*, published by Oxford University Press in 2009, for example, we read that "Writing, though not obligatory, is a defining marker of civilization. Without writing there can be no accumulation of knowledge, no historical record, no science (though simple technology may exist)."[26] Primers such as this abound, with fictions masquerading as fact – romances of the modern mind. More substantially, Foucault posits the "end of the eighteenth century" as coinciding with the period when writers begin to recognize the possibilities of writing itself as the subject of writing, in a self-reflexive turn that opens the book to its own system of self-presentation, as in the work of Diderot, Hölderlin, Sade, and later Flaubert; this is the period when "works of language became what they are

[24] David R. Olson, *The World on Paper: The Conceptual and Cognitive Implications of Writing and Reading* (Cambridge: Cambridge University Press, 1994), 88.

[25] See, for example, *Structural Anthropology* (New York: Basic Books, 1963) and *The Raw and the Cooked* (New York: Harper & Row, 1969).

[26] Andrew Robinson, *Writing and Script: A Very Short Introduction* (Oxford: Oxford University Press, 2009), 1.

now for us, that is literature."[27] Rousseau's *Essay on the Origin of Language* (1781), which figures the alphabet as appropriate "to civilized peoples," focalizes and canonizes this line of thinking. It descends at least from Plato's *Republic*, with his attack on oral poetry and the banishment of poets from his ideal polis, a position that reads today as censorious, anti-humanist, and in need of explication, as Havelock argued.[28] I think we can see narrow, ethnocentric notions of history, science, knowledge, and literature at work in these figures.[29]

The apotheosis of this line of thinking is surely Walter J. Ong's many contributions to the field, including *The Barbarian Within* (1962), *Rhetoric, Romance, and Technology* (1971), *Interfaces of the Word* (1977), *and Orality and Literacy: The Technologizing of the Word* (1982). This latter widely translated, highly influential text summarizes and codifies his thoughts on the matter, sits at the heart of most current understandings of the problem, and defines the terms of the present chapter. An ordained Roman Catholic priest, member of the Society of Jesuits, past President of the Modern Language Association, expert on the Liberal Arts writ large, Ong was a deeply learned, highly persuasive speaker and scholar who wrote far-reaching, synoptic arguments on the subject of "primary orality, that of persons totally unfamiliar with writing." He posited the condition of "pristine oral culture" in order to understand "subsequent writing culture" – our own.[30] "In an oral culture," Ong argues, "knowledge, once acquired, had to be constantly repeated or it would be lost: fixed, formulaic thought patterns were essential for wisdom and effective administration."[31] Oral tradition is the product of memory, and therefore must be memorable, and so is inherently conservative. In Ong's view, "oral societies live very much in a present which keeps itself in equilibrium or homeostasis by sloughing off memories which no longer have present relevance." In contrast to written cultures, "The oral mind is uninterested in definitions." In a chapter titled "Some Psychodynamics of Orality," Ong lays out his program, that oral cultures are "additive" rather than subordinative; redundant or "copious" ("repetition of the just-said, keeps both speaker and hearer surely

[27] Michel Foucault, "Language to Infinity," in *Language, Counter-Memory, Practice: Selected Essays and Interviews*, ed. Donald F. Bouchard, trans. Donald F. Bouchard and Sherry Simon (Ithaca, NY: Cornell University Press, 1977), 59–63.

[28] Eric A. Havelock, *Preface to Plato* (Cambridge, MA: Harvard University Press, 1963).

[29] The idea that oral traditions accumulate no knowledge and hold no history or science would be a surprise to the Inuit, Haida, or Maori, whose political and spiritual economies depend upon a fine-grained knowledge of their physical and cultural worlds.

[30] Ong, *Orality and Literacy*, 2.

[31] Ibid., 24.

on the track"); agonistically inclined ("orality situates knowledge within a context of struggle"); and empathetic and participatory, rather than objective, distanced, or rational.[32]

In enabling thought to break free from the conservative patterns of orality, literate consciousness entails a "Completely new experience for the human mind." Ong's thesis in *Orality and Literacy* is that "writing restructures consciousness,"[33] in that it "[p]ermits the full realization – a higher realization – of the human subject, consciousness, and intellect"; "writing provides for consciousness as nothing else does."[34] In this view, alphabetic writing materializes and objectifies thinking, enabling a more rational, distanced approach to language and thought, leading to the development of a linear, causal form of argumentative logic that is simply not possible in oral tradition. The technology of writing gives rise to a literate mindset characterized by highly abstract and analytical thinking, introspection and objectivity, and to explosive, accelerating growth in accumulated knowledge. Ong writes, persuasively and perniciously, that literacy "is absolutely necessary for the development not only of science but also of history, philosophy, explicative understanding of literature and of any art, and indeed for the explanation of language (including oral speech) itself."[35] Further, the ability to write is "utterly invaluable and indeed essential for the realization of fuller, interior, human potentials"; "Writing heightens consciousness." Understanding the changes that the technology of writing has wrought is clearly a holistic, comprehensive exercise: "We have had to revise our understanding of human identity." Such work is not easy, of course: "We – readers of books such as this – are so literate that it is very difficult for us to conceive of an oral universe of communications or thought, except as a variant of a literate universe."[36]

The point of departure for such thinking, as Ong's colleague Eric Havelock has made clear, is that "an oral state of mind and an oral condition of culture" does indeed exist.[37] Havelock and Ong both emphasize a distinctive mode of consciousness, a "mentality" shared by "oral" peoples everywhere. Together they articulate a positivist, linear, developmental teleology in which first alphabetic writing and then Gutenberg's movable

[32] Ibid., 31–77.
[33] Ibid., 78.
[34] Ibid., 82.
[35] Ibid., 15.
[36] Ibid., 2.
[37] Eric A. Havelock, *The Muse Learns to Write: Reflections on Orality and Literacy from Antiquity to the Present* (New Haven: Yale University Press, 1986), 52.

type are seen as advancements, evolutionary leaps forward that entail not only a profound transformation of society and consciousness, but also a chiasmus, a break in consciousness and culture, not just in the media of communications.

Havelock examines the crux of writing among the Ancient Greeks, in particular the questions of orality and writing in Homer and Plato. A classicist by training, in a series of influential works including *Preface to Plato* (1963), *Prologue to Greek Literacy* (1973), *The Origins of Western Literacy* (1976), *The Literate Revolution in Greece and Its Cultural Consequences* (1982), *The Orality of Homer and the Literacy of Plato* (1984), and *The Muse Learns to Write* (1986), he focuses on the "[c]risis that occurred when Greek orality transformed itself into Greek literacy."[38] For Havelock, because the alphabet was easier to learn and read, it made possible the scientific, technological, and philosophical developments of Western civilization. It did so by efficiently producing and reproducing the literate mindset, with its linear, logical, syllogistic method for accumulating and disseminating knowledge and information. For Havelock, "The formulaic style characteristic of oral composition represented not merely certain verbal and metrical habits but also a cast of thought, or a mental condition."[39] Conceptual thought doesn't achieve "fluency" until it becomes literate, Havelock argues: "[T]he transition from the oral to the written" is also "from the concrete to the abstract." In Havelock's view, the Greek alphabet is "an explosive piece of technology, revolutionary in its effects on human culture."[40]

Havelock makes the case, contentious at first among classicists, that Plato's rejection of poetry, literature, and the imaginative arts in the final Book X of the *Republic*, is a sustained attack on and rejection of oral culture, a rebellion against the centrality of the oral-mythical complex in Greek culture, particularly its role in education (pedagogy) and cultural memory (history). Havelock argues that Plato's denunciation of orality was part of a larger philosophical project, which entailed the displacement of the Greek poetic tradition and its role in the collective life of the *demos*, and was a means to promote the ascendancy of the emergent technology of alphabetic writing and its associated logico-rational complex.[41]

[38] Ibid., 1.

[39] Havelock, *Preface to Plato*, x.

[40] Eric A. Havelock, *The Literate Revolution in Greece and Its Cultural Consequences* (Princeton: Princeton University Press, 1982), 6.

[41] Plato's theory of ideal forms is in this sense made possible through and enabled by the abstracting, distancing powers of alphabetic writing.

Poetry, in Plato's view, poses a danger to abstract (literate) thought, to "rational" man, and hence to the good society and to systems of good governance. So-called oral cultures are composed of barbarians best kept outside the gates of his ideal city. Poetry for Plato is a form of *mimesis*, of imitation or representation – but an imitation of appearances, not of knowledge, understanding, or useful truths: The poet can imitate without being knowledgeable. Poetry exercises the emotions, and appeals to nonrational parts of the soul, and is therefore deleterious and licentious – all of which has serious psychological and social effects. Plato's tripartite argument against (oral) poetry is neatly summarized by Nickolas Pappas: The good life requires the rule of reason; poetry imitates appearances, and appeals to the worst parts of the soul; poetry should be banned from the good city.[42] By contrast, writing, for Plato, in an argument Havelock and Ong develop at length, turns language itself into an object of study, a representation that can be examined at a distance from consciousness. The materialization of the word as an external object allows thought to think of itself, as if for the first time.

Havelock and Ong, along with Marshall McLuhan, were building on the important early work of Harold Innis, who analyzed sociopolitical and ideological aspects of technologies of communication in *Empire and Communications* (1950) and the *Bias of Communication* (1951). Innis was at the University of Toronto from 1920 to 1958, along with Havelock (1929–1947) and Marshall McLuhan (1946–1980). Before arriving at the University of Toronto, McLuhan taught at Saint Louis University (1938–1944), where he supervised Ong's MA in English. Hence the "Toronto School" of Communication Theory, in what amounts to an act of retrospective canonization.[43]

Innis was a careful scholar who died young, wrote quickly on these themes, and was mindful not to overgeneralize his conclusions. His scholarship is marked by a modesty and discretion his interlocutors would sometimes relinquish. A political scientist, he was at the forefront of the "staples theory" in Canadian economic history, in which one central

[42] Nickolas Pappas, *Routledge Philosophy Guidebook to Plato and the Republic* (London: Routledge, 1995), 179.

[43] There were certainly allegiances, as this chapter outlines, but certainly also no such group existed at the time, and Innis and McLuhan, who met in 1949, maintained separate spheres and kept at a distance in Toronto. See Menachem Blondheim and Rita Watson, *The Toronto School of Communication Theory: Interpretations, Extensions, Applications* (Toronto: University of Toronto Press, 2007) and Derrick de Kerckhove, "McLuhan and the Toronto School of Communication," *Canadian Journal of Communication* 14.4 (1989): 73.

commodity dominates and organizes an undifferentiated colonial economy. Late in life, after meeting McLuhan, Innis turned his attention to communications media as the central figure of his analysis – the staple that determines an entire social-economic formation. In considering the clay tablets of Mesopotamia, papyrus in Egypt and the Graeco-Roman world, parchment in the early Middle Ages, and paper in the West, Innis proposed a topos of empire based on media, some of which travel well and facilitate governance in space ("light" media), some more durable that promoted governance over time (stone tablets: "heavy" media). Innis's work provides a working model for the periodization of history based on communications media, and remains a foundational work in media studies. It articulates both the characteristics of media and their effects as agents of change in society, and analyzes the sociopolitical and ideological aspects of shifts in technologies of communication. His grounding precept is that the medium of communication is not neutral, not a passive transmitter of data, but itself has important effects, what Innis refers to as *biases*.

Marshall McLuhan shared this insight, that the technological form of media is more important than its contents, and rephrased it in aphorism: *The medium is the message*. Ong and Havelock made the biases of orality and writing their principal subject. In taking up the relationship between media, consciousness, and cognition with respect to both the individual and society, McLuhan envisioned a media "environment" or "ecology" in which media, including writing and orality, were "extensions" of man. The scope of McLuhan's ideas was exciting, and his metaphors were simulating; he became well known, though it was not always clear exactly what he meant. Like Ong, he introduced conclusions without fully developing them, without always articulating their history or detailing their substance. His notions of "oral" man and "literate" man, however resonant conceptually, were far from carefully developed, and are recognized today to "have limited theoretical use."[44] These are not precise figures, as David Olson argues, and "do not show how media actually produced these effects."[45] And it is upon such shaky foundations that current ideas remain precariously perched.

It is important that these thinkers are closely allied (Havelock is the most-cited author in *Orality and Literacy*) and reached similar (noncoincidentally parallel) conclusions on a number of important matters. They cited and reviewed each other's work, gave innumerable lectures,

[44] Olson, *The World on Paper*, 37.
[45] Ibid.

public talks and papers, and produced an extensive, widely read, generally accepted corpus. Their collective output forms a sort of canon, helping to establish and demarcate the borders of a discursive field, to regulate its modes of representation, its boundaries and its limits. The work identifies and articulates a certain family of resemblances, discursive modalities that bound the range of what can be thought and said with respect to questions of literary and orality as technologies – particularly for readers who may only dabble in such expansive fields, and thereby tend to recycle apparently consensual meanings, as many of us do. One might call their combined project aggregative, copious, even agonistic. The nature of Ong and Havelock's work in particular produces and reproduces various forms of colonial-imperial power, and is itself an instrument and effect of such power. But it also, as Foucault's work makes clear, "undermines and exposes" such power, "renders it fragile and makes it possible to thwart," by making it visible and hence available to criticism.[46]

3 Linguistic Determinism (Context)

The work of Havelock, Ong, and others was achieved through a period of intense interest and activity on a number of fronts, and was prefigured by a series of important works, particularly in anthropology and classical studies. Havelock notes a number of groundbreaking texts published within twelve months of each other in 1962 and 1963, including Lévi-Strauss's *The Savage Mind*, Goody and Watt's article "The Consequences of Literacy" (1963), McLuhan's *The Gutenberg Galaxy* (1962), and his own *Preface to Plato* (1963).[47] This is the period in which Benjamin Lee Whorf's original and influential work (1956) was in circulation, as well as the structuralist theories of Claude Lévi-Strauss and the work of Russian formalist Vladimir Propp. This too is the period when Milman Parry and Albert Lord's work became well known – particularly Lord's groundbreaking *The Singer of Tales*,[48] which persuasively argued that Homer's *Iliad* and *Odyssey* were orally composed works that only later were transcribed in writing.

Parry studied and recorded the singers or *guslar* of south Slavic oral poetry in the 1930s in Yugoslavia, in what is now Bosnia, with the help of his student Albert Lord and field assistant Nikola Vujnović (also a *guslar*, from Hercegovina); their combined program is known as the "Parry–Lord"

[46] Michel Foucault, *The History of Sexuality*, trans. Robert Hurley (New York: Vintage, 1990), 100–101.
[47] Havelock, *The Muse Learns to Write*, 24.
[48] Alfred Lord, *The Singer of Tales* (Cambridge, MA: Harvard University Press, 1960).

or "Oral Formulaic Hypothesis." This project made clear that oral composition in Homer is a process facilitated by regular metrical lines and the extensive use of fixed expressions, what Parry calls "formula," which function as mnemonic devices and provide an adaptive flexibility in oral composition, particularly given rigid and fixed metrical constraints (the six-footed dactylic hexameter). Parry defines formula in Homeric poems "as a group of words which is regularly employed under the same metrical conditions to express a given essential idea."[49] This potent and apparently transportable meme helped codify Havelock and Ong's thought on the conservative rigidity and homeostatic traditionalism of oral poetry. The concept does fit well and partially solves the "Homeric question" that had long perplexed scholars (how were these poems composed?), yet it does little justice to Ruth Finnegan's "complex and variegated" oral traditions more generally. Put differently, the oral formulaic theory works well in Homer's case, but has less purchase when abstracted, decontextualized, universalized, and applied to distant and distinct traditions. Another pillar of the oral–literary dichotomy, this idea continues to underlie fixed ideas of oral tradition as formulaic, rigid, conservative, vestigial, and all-too-prone, in some vulgar Darwinian drama, to being eclipsed (rendered extinct) by writing.

Benjamin Lee Whorf and Edward Sapir's work also circulated in this period, particularly Whorf's innovative collected essays, *Language, Thought and Reality*.[50] As linguists and anthropologists who recorded and interpreted Indigenous oral traditions in the field, Sapir and Whorf believed that patterns embedded in language determine the way one thinks, acting as a code woven into language and thus into consciousness. Proponents of this theory of linguistic determinism argue that differences between languages influence consciousness and culture, and thus the ways in which societies are organized. Sapir was Whorf's teacher, and also a student of Franz Boas. As he argues, people "are very much at the mercy of the particular language which has become the medium of expression for their society," such that "the 'real world' is to a large extent unconsciously built up on the language habits of the group."[51] This formal determinism, a rigid homology between linguistic form and conscious process known as the Sapir–Whorf

[49] Milman Parry, *The Making of Homeric Verse: The Collected Papers of Milman Parry*, ed. Adam Parry (Oxford: Oxford University Press, 1971), 272.

[50] Benjamin Lee Whorf, *Language, Thought, and Reality: Selected Writings of Benjamin Lee Whorf*, ed. John B. Carroll, Stephen C. Levinson, and Penny Lee (Cambridge, MA: MIT Press, 1956).

[51] Edward Sapir, *Selected Writings in Language, Culture, and Personality*, ed. David G. Mandelbaum (Berkeley: University of California Press, 1949), 162.

Hypothesis, continues to undergird much contemporary understanding of orality (it certainly informed McLuhan's thinking). "We cut nature up, organize it into concepts, and ascribe significances as we do," Whorf proposes in his version of the theory, in "an agreement that holds throughout our speech community and is codified in the patterns of our language."[52] The overall effect of these theories has been negative, leading to the denigration and dismissal of oral traditions as primitive, undeveloped, neither literary nor historical, and certainly not scientific. Such understandings work to reduce, simplify, and overdetermine what is a marvelously complex field.

What was "sad" for Lévi-Strauss in his memoir *Tristes Tropiques* (1955; he refused to translate the title) is the recognition of the use of writing as an institution of the state, as a tool to impoverish, subjugate, and enslave peoples without writing.[53] Underlying this insight is the familiar assumption that such a sharp dichotomy exists, and is determinative of culture. It is not simply the technology of print that compels large-scale social change, however; print is imbricated in a matrix of factors that are themselves saturated in relations of power. (It is writing's attachment to the crude institutions of colonial and imperial power that Ong and Havelock tend to overlook.) Imperialism entails the proliferation of information; yet writing alone is not responsible for the archive. The resources of empire allow printed texts to be stored and to circulate. This attention to quantity says nothing of quality.

One finding from this brief survey of inherited tradition, and as is made clear in Lévi-Strauss's work, is that this way of thinking about orality and writing as an oppositional dichotomy provides an instructive case of a structuralist way of thinking. It is a means of looking at elements of a diverse ensemble primarily as they relate to an abstracted, overarching whole; of trying to tease out an underlying, coherent system (the "true" meaning of orality) from a series of disparate traditions; of a search for unities, commonalities, and morphological "laws" (of symmetries and synchronies) at the expense of atomization, heterogeneity, discrete and disjunctive elements (of diachronies and difference).

More usefully, Vladimir Propp's *Morphology of the Folktale*, published in Russia in 1928 and translated into English in 1958, also began to circulate in this period.[54] This seminal structuralist text informed the work of

[52] Whorf, *Language, Thought, and Reality*, 213–214.

[53] Claude Lévi-Strauss, *Tristes Tropiques* (Paris: Plon, 1955).

[54] Vladimir Propp, *Morphology of the Folktale*, trans. Laurence Scott (Bloomington: Indiana University Research Center in Anthropology, Folklore, and Linguistics).

Lévi-Strauss and Roland Barthes. Propp studied a specific genre of stories, the Russian folktale or magic tale, and articulated the morphology, shape or structure of the tale, the ways in which meaningful literary patterns are made. As Propp knew, in terms of literary technology, form *is* meaning, and meaning is made by the deliberate manipulation of form; in this sense, literature is *applied* form. This holds true in oral as well as written traditions; and yet the relationship between meaning and form in oral narratives is something most outsiders struggle to hear, let alone articulate. As such, the language becomes artless, gibberish, not at all literary. By partitioning oral texts into smaller structural units, Propp was able to articulate literary form in oral traditions. His work makes clear that when we recognize the morphology of a literary work, and think through its meaningful patterns, we begin to understand oral narrative as literature.

4 Refutation

No one is arguing print technology and writing do not impact literature and culture. They do, and mainly at first by leaving things out – gestures, colors, coughs, shouts and murmurs, the sound of falling rain: the entire three-dimensional world of human experience, the setting for storytelling performance. Paralinguistic cues, nonlexical properties such as stress and intonation – speech act and discourse properties – that are inherent in oral performance are recast in writing as syntactical and lexical cues, but always incompletely. What is gained in durability and transportability is lost "in comprehensiveness," says Olson.[55]

One reason it is hard for us literates – or anyone else for that matter – to conceptualize a "pure" or "pristine oral culture" is because such a thing does not exist; it is a simple myth. In accounting for some factors while neglecting others, such large-scale hypotheses "confound" the field.[56] Their proselytizers tend to forget they are (only) hypotheses. They are useful as metaphors, less so as applied theory.[57] The conceit has obvious limitations; it provides a vastly oversimplified picture of historical growth, with Western literacy sitting on the highest branch of the evolutionary tree. Embedded within these ideas is a series of assumptions about language, culture, literature, orality, even consensual reality itself. As Ted

[55] Olson, *The World on Paper*, 111.

[56] Brian Stock, *The Implications of Literacy: Written Language and Models of Interpretation in the Eleventh and Twelfth Centuries* (Princeton: Princeton University Press, 1983), 5.

[57] The lack of specificity we find at times in Ong, Havelock, and McLuhan remains startling. See Stock, ibid., for a meaningful counterexample.

Chamberlin observes, despite their contributions to media studies, the Toronto School "has a lot to answer for in the characterization of oral cultures as more or less backward."[58]

One of the telling elements absent from Ong's discourse is the presence of actual oral poets or their texts. Oral tellers are abstracted as categorical imperatives, an absolute and unconditional category, not individualized or specified in terms of artists or their texts. Beyond Homer, they are rarely named. The Indigenous traditions of North America are hardly considered in any meaningful specificity. It is far easier to abstract a communicative practice and talk about someone we never have to meet.

In the first instance, oral tellers don't go around repeating one another, or themselves; their performance is never perfectly reiterable. They are not bland copyists, but generate original creative works. These texts are often carefully composed products of long-standing traditions, drawing upon a stock fund of images, narratives, and cultural resources, as do painters and poets in any tradition. These artists are individuals, not anonymous representatives of a collective; their work is inflected with the creative and critical stuff of the individual maker. Their stories are often extremely concise, certainly not copious. The use of verbal formulae and meter as mnemonics to facilitate composition does not mean that such thinkers are repetitive, conservative, or traditional, or that to retain information in oral tradition one must have fixed thoughts. Nor does it mean oral cultures live only in the present, or that any such thing as an oral culture in fact exists.

Much recent thinking recasts the orality–literacy dichotomy as a false binary. Bringhurst puts it bluntly: "Cultural historians often use these terms, *oral* and *written*, as if they were opposites or alternatives. They are not."[59] As Perry concludes, "The myth of a 'primary orality' is highly questionable."[60] For Zumthor, "It is not productive to think about orality in a negative fashion, by contrasting it with writing. Orality does not mean illiteracy, nor should it be perceived as a lack."[61] As Brian Stock makes clear – and Stock's treatment of orality and writing in early Medieval Europe is a model of care and attention – "It is only the rise of literacy that gave prevalence to an anachronism, and archaism, linked to cultural

[58] J. Edward Chamberlin, "A New History of Reading: Hunting, Tracking, and Reading," in *For the Geography of a Soul: Emerging Perspectives on Kamau Brathwaite*, ed. Timothy J. Reiss (Trenton, NJ: Africa World Press, 2001), 151.

[59] Bringhurst, *Tree of Meaning*, 178. Emphasis in original.

[60] Antonio Perry, "Writing," in *Key Terms in Language and Culture*, ed. Alessandro Duranti (Oxford: Blackwell, 2001), 272–273.

[61] Zumthor, *Oral Poetry*, 17.

values, and oral tradition became identified with illiteracy.... There is in fact no clear point of transition from a nonliterate to a literate society."[62]

Rather than existing alone and apart, as separate solitudes, oral or written modes in fact operate together, in "mixed" states that involve longer-term historical processes and complex conditions of transformation and assimilation. As Rumsey explains, even the most literate of readers and writers reads and writes with relation to an "extended series of oral speech acts."[63] We "literates" are so deeply immersed in orality that only with difficulty and at significant cost (to others, if not ourselves) have we imagined a way "out" of, beyond, or apart from oral tradition. Even in our own apparently highly literate cultures, our classrooms and courtrooms remain quintessential theaters of orality, as do our churches and parliaments, wedding ceremonies and theaters, staff meetings and backyard palavers, United Nations assemblies, convocations, and family affairs. We literates remain resolutely and resiliently immersed in oral tradition, which governs much of what is meaningful and valuable in our daily lives. Orality is not some vestigial state "back then" and "over there," with those "others"; we remain resolutely, persistently, tenaciously oral, here and now. There is no evolutionary hard line, no rupture of *before* and *after*, *them* and *us*, oral and literate; we may step across this line by dissolving it. (The category holds less water than we think.) Working definitions of orality and writing retain descriptive and explanatory purchase, yet their tenets must be critically examined.

At the same time, even for the most avowedly oral people, other communicative channels are always present. These forms of inscription, which include poles, chests, blankets, masks, winter counts, *quipus*, stained glass, architecture, clothing, birchbark scrolls, canoes and spoons and dishes and so on, cannot be "read" (interpreted) without speech and a community of speakers (a culture). We all read the wind, water, each other's voices, facial gestures, body language, the songs of birds and the tracks of animals – the discourses of the natural world. Any "developments" in consciousness that alphabetic literacy apparently entails have long been prefigured by such reading habits. In the field where people live, not in the tower where theorists perch, "in their actual contexts of use, no single channel of communication or mode of inscription is ever self-sufficient."[64] Defining the technology broadly, "In an anthropological sense, writing includes all

[62] Stock, *The Implications of Literacy*, 12, 9.
[63] Rumsey, "Orality," 166.
[64] Ibid., 166.

social practices that use systems of graphic (sometimes also material) signs, which are recurrent, combinable and conventionally linked to a linguistic content."[65] In this sense, writing and orality complement one another and are fully copresent, deeply integrated, capable of couplings, feints and ruses, of dalliances and antagonisms. They are component parts of larger economies of inscriptive practices present in any society at any given time. In that "a circulation of graphic messages does in fact exist in all cultures," it is clear that "The myth of a 'primary orality' is highly questionable."[66] As Rumsey concludes, it is "misleading to use the term orality in reference to an entire society, culture, or communicative regime."[67]

The ways academics have misread oral traditions, and substituted romances of technological ascension and cultural priority in place of genuine understanding, have provided an intellectual bulwark for imperialism and colonialism by undervaluing and denigrating oral traditions, and the associated systems of governance and structures of meaning-making and cultural memory, which continue to orient many Indigenous legal, spiritual, and literary traditions. "The question is not what you look at," Thoreau taught us, "but what you see."[68] In this case, we have failed to see what is right before our eyes.

5 A New Dispensation

So then, if you will, what the hell is orality? In a volume dedicated to technology, we might say that speech itself is entirely natural, part of the genetic inheritance of our species. As Ong observes, "oral speech is fully natural to human beings,"[69] in that all otherwise capable humans may talk. In Bringhurst's view, "for human beings, language is as natural as walking."[70] Orality in this primary sense is natural, not a technology at all; it is a property or power – the ability to vocalize – that belongs also to birds and bees, wolves, and whales. And literature is "natural" to language, and seems to be found wherever language is found. But that which is perfectly natural is also always cultural and historical, and oral traditions themselves are "not natural products," as Cruikshank argues: "They have

65 Perry, "Writing," 272.
66 Ibid., 272–273.
67 Rumsey, "Orality," 167.
68 Henry David Thoreau, *The Journal: 1837–1861*, ed. Damion Searls (New York: New York Review of Books), 65.
69 Ong, *Orality and Literacy*, 81.
70 Bringhurst, *Tree of Meaning*, 164.

social histories, and they acquire meaning in the situations in which they are used"; and these "[m]eanings shift depending on how cultural understandings are shared by tellers and listener."[71]

An oral narrative belongs to the language and culture of which it is a part, and to the speaker who inflects it with markers of individual identity, and to a specific audience that is intended receiver of the utterance. One can speak alone, but no one has learned a language alone; language belongs to the collective. So too is it shaped by individual subjectivity, perception, desire; it is never the fully objective recorder of the "datum of experience," as Whorf has it.[72] By someone's spoken accent alone, we tend to glean (and often misread) something of their lot in life. The common ground between oral and written technologies is this quality of the solo *voice*. As Octavio Paz emphasizes, "I shall repeat, yet again, that the written line, even that of the concrete poem, is a metaphor of speech."[73] As Bringhurst has it, "*All literature is oral.* Writers are simply that unusual or deviant class of storytellers and singers who take their own dictation."[74] For Foucault, "writing refers not to a thing but to speech."[75] The creative artist's voice comes first, and it is the performance of voice we need to consider, by whichever channel, written or spoken.

But what does the voice carry, if not narrative? Narrative is how we recollect the past, evaluate the present, and imagine a future. This attention to situating ourselves in time through narrative appears to transcend cultural difference. In this sense, there *are* commonalities across cultures, as Paul Ricœur's work makes clear: We are beings in time, we are in the world, and we are with others.[76] We don't control our origins, we can't get away from this, and narrative, whether oral, in alphabetic writing, or through some combination of signs, is the way we represent the human experience of time, which is the human experience of being in its most encompassing expression. The way one does this is culturally informed, not universal. The challenge is to learn to listen to these stories, to become fluent in these oral–aural technologies, to recognize their forms, which may challenge our own identities; how we make sense of sound.

[71] Cruikshank, *The Social Life of Stories*, 40.
[72] Whorf, *Language, Thought, and Reality*, 1.
[73] Octavio Paz, "The New Analogy: Poetry and Technology," *Convergences: Essays on Art and Literature*, trans. Helen Lane (1970; Orlando, FL: Harcourt & Brace, 1987), 128.
[74] Bringhurst, *Tree of Meaning*, 178. Emphasis in original.
[75] Foucault, "Language to Infinity," 56.
[76] Paul Ricœur, *Memory, History, Forgetting* (Chicago: University of Chicago Press, 2004).

The crucial issues become those of translation and transcription, and how to move between contexts and mediums – transforming the oral poem into text, putting performance on the page. For those of us locked or lost in libraries, the text is the hinge that opens these cultural spaces, the space of transition between orality and writing, where the voice slips across media and the practices of orality articulate with alphabetic writing. How can we learn to read the oral text as performance, animating it, making the verbal structure sing? This is the problem we need to teach, practice, edit for, learn to read, encourage in our students. It is in the narratives themselves where voice, performance, and narrative converge.

We in the West don't generally have a name for this type of performance, which is not verse and not prose, but something different. We don't have a genre for it, lack widespread understanding of it, and are generally unaware of practitioners at the level of those operating in precolonial Indigenous America. It is understatement to say our criticism of the genre is impoverished. This is a genre in search of readers. These oral narratives are more complex and subtle than we have imagined, and collectors and recorders did not always recognize what they were hearing. The colonial situation brought Euro-Westerners into contact with Indigenous languages they did not speak, and with literary forms of which they had little experience. Many early ethnographers did not transcribe stories directly, but rewrote their own versions, in which much of the form, and some of the bawdy bits, formulaic introductions, repetitions, and so on have been lost. These paraphrases, by Boas, Knud Rasmussen, and others, are not the genuine article. It is little wonder that few faithful texts survive, and a wonder that some do. Faithful versions allow us to encounter, still, the morphology of the story. What is left on the page is available for study; there is work to be done. This is one way to decolonize the academy, to understand where we are and how we got here, and to articulate a truly "Canadian" or "American" literature, creating a polyphonic literary culture that might allow us to make better sense of our difficult relations and to find more ethical disciplinary paths forward.

We know that when oral literature is transcribed as text, a good deal is left behind. The printed text will forever lack "voice"; the text is a skeletal, ossified form. Alphabetic writing is a relatively recent invention; literature is age-old. As Olson observes, "The history of literacy, in other words, is the struggle to recover what was lost in simple transcription."[77] Much of the music of the moment is left out of transcription – nuance, gesture,

[77] Olson, *The World on Paper*, 111.

meter, pitch, tone, the speaker's often expert effects in acting and mimicry. What remains is the skeleton of voice, the "frozen form of spoken words."[78] Rabelais was already aware of this, transforming this sense of loss into a moving image in the *Fourth Book of Pantagruel* (1552), when the ship's crew encounters frozen words out at sea on the Arctic Ocean. The mighty Pantagruel hears them first, and "According to his command we listened, and with full ears sucked in the air as some of you suck oysters, to find if we could hear some sound scattered through the sky." Pantagruel throws handfuls of frozen words onto the deck, where they land in multicolored hues like "rough sugar-plums," and begin to pop as they thaw like "chestnuts when they are thrown into the fire."[79]

The task of the recorder of the oral teller, the translator, those involved at the printing press, and finally the reader, is to breathe life into the oral performance, to thaw the frozen words that writing shapes on the page, making them pop like warm chestnuts in our minds. To do this with any reasonable competency requires a toolkit of cultural and historical competencies, which the implied listener of the poem, its first audience, would have already had in hand. This might include knowledge of stock literary characters, local gods and monsters, geographic referents, systems of belief, and the circulation of political and spiritual power, how material culture signifies and how genealogies are constructed, not to mention the body of work the teller is known for, and her or his affiliation and relation to the audience assembled. In short, an audience would know the familiar forms and themes of oral narrative in the tradition at hand, the grammar of storytelling in a specific culture. No wonder we often fail to cross this line.

Perhaps the relationship of artist to community in oral performance was something like it is in literary culture today, and not everyone would have the specialized ability to compose these texts or to articulate their full or formal sense. Listeners, then as now, would have taken what they could. The tellers knew they were telling stories, of course; they knew what they were doing. This does not mean they left behind treaties on composition or outlined the principles of literary theory as known to them or their culture. This did not mean these principles did not exist.

In metered verse on the page, the patterns readers most readily recognize are visual and acoustic. We hear rhyming schemes and accented lines,

[78] Bringhurst, *Tree of Meaning*, 175.

[79] François Rabelais, *The Histories of Gargantua and Pantagruel*, trans. Thomas Urquhart of Cromarty and Peter Antony Motteux (Project Gutenberg), chs. 55–56, www.gutenberg.org/files/1200/1200-h/1200-h.htm.

hexameters and sestinas. This is what Robert Frost called the "sound of sense," the "abstract vitality of our speech," the fusion of which (of sound and sense) we hear and find pleasurable if the poem is any good.[80] In oral narratives – and this is the trick – with nothing written, there are no line endings to rhyme, no blank space on the page to surround the text, to section off stanzas and quatrains and line endings – nothing that allows us to visualize the poem's morphology, to see where rhythm and rhyme might be heard. This level of form, the design of language in space, the visual element of the text, is not available to the oral poet. This does not mean form is absent.

Two accomplished Haida poets, Skaay and Ghandl, who told their stories to the young Harvard-trained linguist John Swanton in 1900, can help us here. They spoke to another Haida named Robert Moody, ensuring their narratives were not dumbed-down for an outsider audience. Moody was bilingual and repeated the tale, so that Swanton could confirm he had heard the sounds of the language correctly. Swanton transcribed these stories phonetically – some 41,000 lines, when we have about 27,000 from Homer – before performing, with Moody's assistance, an interlinear translation into English. He did not know Haida, but knew he was onto something. These narratives have been rendered again into English, edited and interpreted in three volumes by Robert Bringhurst, in a crucial work that guides us here.[81]

In Skaay's story "Goose Food," a young man out hunting geese falls in love with a woman swimming with her sister in a lake behind the town.[82] They marry and live together, first on land and then, after she is insulted and leaves, in the sky. Both are of good family, both become heartsick and hungry in places they do not belong, both return alone to their own world having suffered longing and loss. The structure of the story is finely balanced, with ten tools collected and then deployed in pairs by the young man as he moves into the sky; tension builds and is released as balance is restored. The story is about transgression and limits, about love and loss, and the price one pays when recognizable limits are breached. It is love that motivates the man's dangerous journey into a strange land in a retelling

80 Robert Frost, letter to John Bartlett, July 1913, in *Collected Poems, Plays, and Prose*, ed. Mark Richardson and Richard Poirier (New York: Library of America, 1995), 655.

81 The three volumes are Robert Bringhurst, *A Story as Sharp as a Knife: The Classical Haida Mythtellers and Their World* (Vancouver: Douglas & McIntyre, 1999); Ghandl of the Qayahl Llaanas, *Nine Visits to the Mythworld*, ed. and trans. Robert Bringhurst (Vancouver: Douglas & McIntyre, 2000); and Skaay of the Qquuna Qiighawaay, *Being in Being: The Collected Works*, ed. and trans. Robert Bringhurst (Vancouver: Douglas & McIntyre, 2001).

82 Skaay of the Qquuna Qiighawaay, "Goose Food," trans. Robert Bringhurst, in Bringhurst, *A Story as Sharp as a Knife*, 29–50.

of the Swan Maiden tale, of a hunter's necessary care and attention for his prey, as in *Swan Lake*. The hunt should end (for the hunter) in the killing of that which he depends on, has observed intimately, has treated with great attention, and in this sense loves. If it doesn't, the world will turn out of balance and trouble will ensue. The story's morphology offers a structural metaphor for ecological relation, respect, balance, and interdependence.

In "Goose Food," literary form is not audible or metrical, but is found at the larger level of storytelling units. The principal unit of repetition or pattern is a *unit of meaning* (not of sound), an event or incident or element that returns, in a semantic series marked by repetition with critical difference. You hear the sounds, certainly, but you need to work to find the patterns and make meaning of them, which is to recognize the sophisticated morphology of the poem and how form creates meaning. These repetitions form a structure, a pattern that can be discerned, and which must be grasped in the mind. Form (as an ideal, immaterial property of the text) is itself an abstraction, a shape that shimmers behind the work. Dell Hymes was expert in uncovering these structures in oral narratives, the way groups of meaning, incident, and imagery echo with repetition and variation across a text, building and resolving tension in units much larger than the line, and without using techniques such as end rhyme, or prefound forms such as the stanza or sestina.[83] Bringhurst recognizes such patterns as *noetic*, "of or pertaining to the mind or intellect; characterized by, or consisting in, mental or intellectual activity."[84] They are made, he says, of "syntactic rhymes and recurrent shapes of incident and event."[85] He considers "some of the symmetries" of "Goose Food": "It begins at a lake – a patch of water surrounded by land," and

> ends with the same man marooned on a reef – a patch of land surrounded by water – where the man himself is squawking like a loudmouthed gull. At the centre of the story is a pole that links earth and sky. Either side of the pole is a series of tests and exchanges, and framing these sequences are the two domestic scenes. The first is in the groom's father's house, where a vegetarian bride, who cannot speak directly to her mother-in-law, is offered food she cannot eat. The second is in the bride's father's house. There the omnivorous groom, who cannot speak directly to his father-in-law, tries to eat the same restricted diet as the birds.[86]

[83] See Dell Hymes, *"In Vain I Tried to Tell You": Essays in Native American Ethnopoetics* (Philadelphia: University of Pennsylvania Press, 1981) and *Ethnography, Linguistics, Narrative Inequality: Toward an Understanding of Voice* (London: Taylor & Francis, 1996).
[84] *OED*, "noetic, adj."
[85] Bringhurst, *Tree of Meaning*, 221.
[86] Bringhurst, *A Story as Sharp as a Knife*, 51.

There are verbal insults thrown by humans at animals on land and in the sky, though the geese in each case "respond with perfect courtesy." This is narrative music, says Bringhurst, "played by calling images into the mind with spoken words."[87] The effect is that of "a complex narrative crystal, or a piece of conceptual music," the patterns are fractal and cladistic, consistent and predictable.[88] Beside them the end-rhymes of a poem seem superficial, of the page and not of the mind. As in biology, when simple patterns are repeated at different scales, they quickly become complex.

Bringhurst observes that his translations are cataloged under "Haida Indians-Folklore" when what they are is literature. Skaay and Ghandl are individual artists and creators. Skaay was blind and Ghandl was disabled; they may have had more time than most to think through these stories. The mind and language of either is certainly not copious, redundant, homeostatic, agonistic, or aggregative. This is not verbal "magic," with the word taken for the thing, what Lévi-Bruhl identified as the workings of the primitive mind.[89] It is not a meaning made "tribally" or by some anonymous static collective. These are powerful, discrete, deeply metaphoric works of art. They use words of power with precision and great care.

Swanton's context was of a once vibrant culture in ruins. Skaay and Ghandl spoke to an anthropologist, not a crowd. Julie Cruikshank has spoken with Indigenous women in the Yukon Territory for over forty years.[90] Her long-term relations with Angela Sidney, Annie Ned, and Kitty Smith have been remarkably productive. For these multilingual speakers of Athabascan languages, English is just one more Indigenous language in the North. These dialogues illustrate that oral traditions are not an evolutionarily extinct product, but a still-active process, a way of making meaning that is both highly personal and cultural determined, and a means of connecting seemingly unrelated events. Questions such as who had the right to tell a particular story, Cruikshank observes, are of continuing interest to people living on the Yukon River. These stories link people to land through language and lineage, and are "updated" regularly to reflect new conditions and different audiences – pipelines, roadbuilding, world wars, disease, land claims, motherhood, the movements of game. Translating them is one challenge of literary-critical studies in the new dispensation.

Peter, servant to the Capulets in *Romeo and Juliet*, wanders the street with a list of names for the party in hand, wondering "What names the

87 Ibid., 54.
88 Ibid., 53.
89 Cf. Lucien Lévy-Bruhl, *How Natives Think*, trans. Lilian A. Clare (London: Allen, 1926).
90 Cf. Cruikshank, *The Social Lives of Stories*.

writing person hath here writ," for he cannot read. He asks a stranger on the street if he can read. "Ay," says Romeo, "mine own fortune is my misery" (1.2.58). Upon this chance meeting, Shakespeare hangs the plot of his play. Again at a crucial early moment of transition between media, we find the dual valence of writing and reading – reading will bring Romeo great joy and suffering. "Can you read anything you see?" presses Peter. "Ay," says Romeo, "I know the letters and the language" (1.2.61). We may not know the letters of oral tradition (though much is gained in translation), but we also don't know much of the *language*, the grammar of storytelling, the toolkit of strategies and techniques, the know-how and local knowledge, that constitutes any specific oral tradition. For each specific culture, we etics need to learn differently and distinctly if we are going to activate the potentials of ethical, nonappropriative, cross-cultural research and teaching. In the Americas, in universities and cultures founded upon genocidal and ecocidal colonial programs such as my own, these imperatives are essential; they can help renew literary curricula, make our programs more adaptive and responsive to place. We have yet to build adequate or appropriate bridges of translation, interpretation, and transcription – to make connection with and forge a meaningful relation to – Indigenous oral and settler-colonial languages and literature formations. The (false) dichotomy between orality and writing as technologies is at the root of this misunderstanding. As such, our ability to learn from difficult colonial contexts is compromised: We don't quite know, in literary terms most specifically, where we are, and our relations remain incomplete. What we need are new taxonomies that don't divide and categorize, but cut across. Form – Propp's morphology, the meaningful structure of a literary work, not the desiccated structuralism of an abstracted theoretical program – is the first and most obvious means across.

CHAPTER 2

Manuscript

Bonnie Mak

A "manuscript" is written by hand. A poem hastily scribbled with crayon on a napkin is a manuscript, as is a tax record carefully inscribed on clay. Manuscripts can be constituted of pages that have been bound together or loose sheets of any size. They can be made of palm leaves, bark, wax, bone, bamboo, papyrus, paper, or silk. They might be parchment fragments that reinforce the spine of a printed book or strips of linen that are wrapped around a mummy. Although the term "manuscript" has become associated with particular genres or formats – for example, the unfinished draft of a novel or correspondence between lovers – manuscripts themselves do not abide by these categories. They might be personal notes not intended to be read by anyone or ceremonial objects produced by many hands and designed for public display. Manuscripts can represent various stages of formality and publication, and transmit multiple texts simultaneously.[1] For instance, the *Book of Kells*, a lavishly decorated manuscript copy of the Gospels from the early Middle Ages, was also considered an appropriate place to register property transactions.[2] Meanwhile, an elaborate hand-drawn building plan of St. Gall monastery, dedicated to the abbot in the ninth century, carries a twelfth-century copy of the *Life of Saint Martin* of Sulpitius Severus on its reverse. Manuscripts may even carry printed graphics, such as in the case of

[1] Lately, Kathryn M. Rudy, *Piety in Pieces: How Medieval Readers Customized Their Manuscripts* (Cambridge: Open Book Publishers, 2016) and Catherine Brown, "Manuscript Thinking: Stories by Hand," *postmedieval: a journal of medieval cultural studies* 2 (2011): 350–368. On scribal publication, see Brian Richardson, *Manuscript Culture in Renaissance Italy* (Cambridge: Cambridge University Press, 2009); Harold Love, *Scribal Publication in Seventeenth-Century England* (Oxford: Clarendon Press, 1993); and O. A. W. Dilke, *Roman Books and Their Impact* (Leeds: Elmete Press, 1977).

[2] Important materials, such as charters that documented the rights and privileges of a monastic community and inventories of valuables, were often safeguarded in liturgical books. See Jessica Berenbeim, *Art of Documentation: Documents and Visual Culture in Medieval England* (Toronto: Pontifical Institute of Mediaeval Studies, 2015) and Michael T. Clanchy, *Early Medieval England* (London: The Folio Society, 1997), 309–312.

postcards and tax forms.[3] Plains artists in nineteenth-century America drew illustrated histories in printed ledger books; names of kin are still written by hand onto the flyleaves and printed title pages of family bibles. Once prized locally as objects of symbolic and economic import, such diverse materials are now held in institutional repositories, and may furthermore be transcribed or digitized by hand for widespread use. A single manuscript can therefore perform across what are currently considered documentary and literary realms, and accrue a rich multimedia life with varied readership over time. The manuscript is a site of complex and intersecting temporalities, traversing social class, gender, geography, language, literacy, material, and medium, and comes to rest equally in archives, museums, libraries, businesses, private domiciles – and even dumpsters.[4]

But refusal to heed these divisions that mark the modern world has come at a cost. Indeed, the manuscript is often dismissed as unruly and prone to error in relation to the purported stately precision of its printed counterpart in the West. As art historian and librarian L. M. J. Delaissé observes, "The possibility of introducing unlimited variety into the execution of a manuscript apparently led people to think that each was a *unicum*, unworthy of being called a book, whereas the mechanical process of printing, in assuring the uniformity of a number of copies, became, perhaps unconsciously, a condition for this status."[5] The ability of the printing press to generate materials that are ostensibly graphically consistent was conjoined in the imagination with notions of accuracy and authoritativeness.[6] This particular conception of mechanical reproducibility,

3 For example, Michael Johnston and Michael Van Dussen, eds., *The Medieval Manuscript Book: Cultural Approaches* (Cambridge: Cambridge University Press, 2015); and Michèle Barrett and Peter Stallybrass, "Printing, Writing and a Family Archive: Recording the First World War," *History Workshop Journal* 75 (Spring 2013): 1–32.

4 Among others, Anna Kłosowksa, "Premodern Trans and Queer in French Manuscripts and Early Printed Text," *postmedieval: a journal of medieval cultural studies* 9.3 (Fall 2018): 349–366; Elaine Leong, *Recipes and Everyday Knowledge: Medicine, Science, and the Household in Early Modern England* (Chicago: University of Chicago Press, 2018); Andrea Brigaglia and Mauro Nobili, eds., *The Arts and Crafts of Literacy: Islamic Manuscript Cultures in Sub-Saharan Africa* (Boston: de Gruyter, 2017); The Multigraph Collective, "Manuscript," in *Interacting with Print: Elements of Reading in the Era of Print Saturation* (Chicago: University of Chicago Press, 2017), 185–203; Christopher Hager, *Word By Word: Emancipation and the Act of Writing* (Cambridge, MA: Harvard University Press, 2013); and Peter F. Kornicki, "Manuscript, Not Print: Scribal Culture in the Edo Period," *The Journal of Japanese Studies* 32 (2006): 23–52.

5 L. M. J. Delaissé, "Towards a History of the Medieval Book," *Codicologica* 1 (1976): 75. On how printing precedes manuscript, and the notion of the manuscript as "always-already nostalgic," see Peter Stallybrass, "Printing and the Manuscript Revolution," in *Explorations in Communications and History*, ed. Barbie Zelizer (New York: Routledge, 2008), esp. 114–115.

6 David McKitterick, *Print, Manuscript and the Search for Order, 1450–1830* (Cambridge: Cambridge University Press, 2003), esp. 222ff; Adrian Johns, *The Nature of the Book: Print and Knowledge in the*

which depends on a depreciation of the manuscript, became adopted as a standard by which other modes of communication came to be judged. The preferential attention bestowed upon printing technologies has thus operated to define other traditions of transmission. Namely, because oral and handwritten modes of transmitting knowledge do not function in the same manner that printing does, they have been made subordinate in this configuration of history. As a consequence, their distinctive characteristics, including the complex ways that they invoke embodied performance and remembering, can be too easily cast as a problematic or faulty way of making knowledge visible.[7]

Naturalized over centuries, the contributions of manuscript are now taken for granted. Yet handwork has played a profound role in the development of knowledge practices.[8] It is by hand that techniques for arranging information were – and often still are – refined, from the strategic layout of words, diagrams, and musical notation, to the cycles of remembering, circulating, and revising. For instance, handwritten narratives were shared through the early modern global networks of the Society of Jesus, and translated into printed tables and statistics for further dissemination.[9] These maneuvers in which the technological hand of the printer takes up

Making (Chicago: University of Chicago Press, 1998); and Elizabeth L. Eisenstein, *The Printing Press as an Agent of Change: Communications and Cultural Transformations in Early Modern Europe*, 2 vols. (Cambridge: Cambridge University Press, 1979). For the relationship between printing and (state) authority in eighteenth-century Russia, see Simon Franklin, *The Russian Graphosphere, 1450–1850* (Cambridge: Cambridge University Press, 2019), esp. 231ff. I am grateful to my colleague, John Randolph, for bringing this work to my attention.

7 Cf. Roberta Magnani and Diane Watt, "Towards a Queer Philology," *postmedieval: a journal of medieval cultural studies* 9.3 (Fall 2018): 252–268; Michael T. Clanchy, *From Memory to Written Record, England 1066–1307*, 3rd ed. (Chichester: John Wiley & Sons, 2013); Walter J. Ong, *Interfaces of the Word* (Ithaca, NY: Cornell University Press, 2012); Mary J. Carruthers, *The Book of Memory: A Study of Memory in Medieval Culture*, 2nd ed. (Cambridge: Cambridge University Press, 2008); Jocelyn Penny Small, *Wax Tablets of the Mind: Cognitive Studies of Memory and Literacy in Classical Antiquity* (London: Routledge, 1997); and Frances A. Yates, *The Art of Memory* (Chicago: University of Chicago Press, 1966).

8 For example, Aileen Douglas, *Work in Hand: Script, Print, and Writing, 1690–1840* (Oxford: Oxford University Press, 2017); Lisa Nakamura, "Indigenous Circuits: Navajo Women and the Racialization of Early Electronics Manufacture," *American Quarterly* 66.4 (December 2014): 919–941; and Jonathan Goldberg, *Writing Matter: From the Hands of the English Renaissance* (Stanford, CA: Stanford University Press, 1990).

9 Markus Friedrich, "Circulating and Compiling the *Litterae annuae*. Towards a History of the Jesuit System of Communication," *Archivum Historicum Societatis Iesu* 77 (2008): 3–39; and Markus Friedrich, "Communication and Bureaucracy in the Early Society of Jesus," *Schweizerische Zeitschrift für Religions- und Kulturgeschichte = Revue suisse d'histoire religieuse et culturelle* 101 (2007): 49–75. For a similar dynamic, see Hugo Blotius and his *Tabula peregrinationis* in, Paola Molino, "Istruzioni per un viaggio in Italia: *Hodoeporicum Hugoni Blotii earum rerum quas in Italia vidit et observavit*," *Biblos Wien* 55.1 (2006): 124–137; and Justin Stagl, *A History of Curiosity: The Theory of Travel, 1550–1800* (Chur: Harwood, 1995).

and obscures the manuscript have helped define the look of information and power today. Similarly, hands now digitize manuscripts and encode text, and the design of an algorithm is often first sketched out by hand before being implemented – these are writing hands that remediate the written hand.[10] However, in service of a broader narrative of progress, the aesthetic of information in the twenty-first century cannot accommodate the visible presence of the hand; the human hand is not perceived as a modern technology. Strategically excluded from the recent history of knowledge practices, it has instead been cast as orthogonal or even in opposition to the production and transmission of information. Nevertheless, the hand supports the production and circulation of ideas in manuscript, printed, digital, and other forms.[11] The hand-drawn cartoon is mimeographed; a hand that inscribes on bone may also photograph, calibrate, or code. The writing hand is transmedial and transmaterial.

Let us for a moment, then, suspend any assumptions about handwriting that have been influenced to a large degree by notions of mechanical objectivity and modernity's attitudes about the past. After all, the somatic experience of handling manuscripts has impressed itself upon literary practice and the imagination for millennia, affecting language, writing, and interpretation.[12] In the tradition of a *florilegium* or commonplace that gathers together excerpts from diverse sources, the following discussion offers a

10 For example, Kathryn Cunningham, Sarah Blanchard, Barbara Ericson, and Mark Guzdial, "Using Tracing and Sketching to Solve Programming Problems: Replicating and Extending an Analysis of What Students Draw," in *Proceedings of the 2017 ACM Conference on International Computing Education Research* (Tacoma, WA, 2017), 164–172. I am grateful to my colleagues Vetle Torvik and Matthew J. Turk for clarification on this point. See also Jack Linchuan Qiu, *Goodbye iSlave: A Manifesto for Digital Abolition* (Urbana: University of Illinois Press, 2016); Bonnie Mak, "Archaeology of a Digitization," *Journal of the Association for Information Science and Technology* 65.8 (August 2014): 1515–1526; Benjamin Shaykin, *Special Collection* (2013); and Andrew Norman Wilson, *ScanOps* (2012). In general, Bruno Latour, "Visualization and Cognition: Thinking with Eyes and Hands," *Knowledge and Society: Studies in the Sociology of Culture Past and Present* 6 (1986): 1–40.

11 Similarly, see Patricia Jane Roylance, "Winthrop's Journal in Manuscript and Print: The Temporalities of Early-Nineteenth-Century Transmedial Reproduction," *PMLA* 133.1 (2018): 88–106; Johanna Drucker, *Graphesis: Visual Forms of Knowledge Production* (Cambridge, MA: Harvard University Press, 2014); Lisa Gitelman, *Paper Knowledge: Toward a Media History of Documents* (Durham, NC: Duke University Press, 2014); Elaine Treharne, "Fleshing Out the Text: The Transcendent Manuscript in the Digital Age," *postmedieval: a journal of medieval cultural studies* 4.4 (2013): 465–478; Anna Chen, "In One's Own Hand: Seeing Manuscripts in a Digital Age," *Digital Humanities Quarterly* 6.2 (2012), n.p.; and Thomas S. Mullaney, "The Moveable Typewriter: How Chinese Typists Developed Predictive Text during the Height of Maoism," *Technology and Culture* 53.4 (October 2012): 777–814.

12 Michael Camille, "Sensations of the Page: Imaging Technologies and Medieval Illuminated Manuscripts," in *The Iconic Page in Manuscript, Print, and Digital Culture*, ed. George Bornstein and Theresa Tinkle (Ann Arbor: University of Michigan Press, 1998), 40.

selection of vignettes that may illuminate the ways in which manuscript technologies continue to configure the organization and transmission of ideas.[13] The assembled examples demonstrate how the materiality of manuscripts – and attentiveness to its conditions – bear upon the practices of writing, transmission, and reception. As we shall see, a detail as minute as the direction of a pen-stroke in the Middle Ages still contributes in a fundamental way to the broad infrastructures of knowledge exchange in the twenty-first century. Meanwhile, the manuscript and its organizational devices – of space between words, of tables, indexes, and citations – provide graphic evidence of the changing demands of readership as well as a shift toward the regularization of how information should be conveyed. More than simple vehicles for communication, manuscripts operate to configure knowledge. The decisions related to the visualization of information made by writers, scribes, editors, designers, and compilers over time have contributed to the ways in which we now suppose ideas should be expressed and comprehended. Such histories furthermore govern how works are transmitted and read today in printed, digital, and other forms.

From at least as early as antiquity, attention to materiality could affect the composition and internal structure of texts. Wax tablets were employed from the classical to the early modern period for ephemeral compositions, such as letters, school exercises, drafts, and accounts. Physically similar to small picture frames or writing slates, these devices were usually made of wood with a layer of tinted wax flattened into the central void. Multiple tablets could be strung together with leather or wire, and then closed

[13] On *florilegia* and the activity of assembling various sources in general, see Stephen G. Nichols and Siegfried Wenzel, eds., *The Whole Book: Cultural Perspectives on the Medieval Miscellany* (Ann Arbor: University of Michigan Press, 1996); Neil Hathaway, "*Compilatio*: From Plagiarism to Compiling," *Viator* 20 (1989): 19–44; Alastair J. Minnis, "Late-Medieval Discussions of '*Compilatio*' and the Rôle of the *Compilator*," *Beiträge zur Geschichte der deutschen Sprache und Literatur* 101.3 (1979): 385–421; A. A. Goddu and Richard H. Rouse, "Gerald of Wales and the *Florilegium angelicum*," *Speculum* 52.3 (July 1977): 488–521; and B. L. Ullman, "Tibullus in the Mediaeval Florilegia," *Classical Philology* 23.2 (April 1928): 128–174. Also, Alberto Cevolini, ed., *Forgetting Machines: Knowledge Management Evolution in Early Modern Europe* (Boston: Brill, 2016); Seth Lerer, "Bibliographical Theory and the Textuality of the Codex: Toward a History of the Premodern Book," in *The Medieval Manuscript Book, 17–33*; Arthur Bahr, *Fragments and Assemblages: Forming Compilations of Medieval London* (Chicago: University of Chicago Press, 2013); Jeffrey Todd Knight, *Bound to Read: Compilations, Collections, and the Making of Renaissance Literature* (Philadelphia: University of Pennsylvania Press, 2013); Karen Fresco and Anne D. Hedeman, eds., *Collections in Context: The Organization of Knowledge and Community in Europe* (Columbus: Ohio State University Press, 2011); the special issue of *English Manuscript Studies, 1100–1700* 16 (2011), ed. Richard Beadle and Colin Burrow; Ann M. Blair, *Too Much to Know: Managing Scholarly Information before the Modern Age* (New Haven: Yale University Press, 2010); and Ann Moss, *Printed Commonplace-Books and the Structuring of Renaissance Thought* (Oxford: Clarendon Press, 1996).

together at the hinge-point to protect the writing surface. An implement such as an iron stylus or sharpened bone was used to inscribe letter-forms into the wax. Such manuscripts were perceived as flexible and customizable, with material properties that could be directed with intention. In the first century CE, the Roman rhetorician, Quintilian, relates that a young man who was unable to shorten his lengthy compositions was finally corrected of the habit by modifying the size of the wax tablets on which he wrote.[14] This example demonstrates how the materiality of the tablet could be deliberately used to impose discipline upon a writer and the composition of the text. Manuscripts are therefore designed not merely to transmit text, but also to control its transmission. But the dynamic is not so simple, for what was perceived as a material limitation of writing could eventually become known as fundamental to its process. For instance, Quintilian indicates that composing with a stylus on a wax tablet is superior to using ink on parchment because the hand need not be lifted from the surface of the page, a movement that he says interrupts the flow of thought.[15] Compare Quintilian's sentiments with those of Samuel Taylor Coleridge, almost two millennia later, who suggests that the perfect inkstand enables dipping the pen "without requiring any effort or interruptive act of attention from the writing."[16] Coleridge signals, then, that there might be ways that a pen could be lifted from the page without being disruptive. After centuries of habituation, the material pragmatics of writing with pen and ink came to shape how texts were thought to be produced. Once perceived as an unavoidable distraction, the regular pauses to refresh the pen were later reimagined as essential to composition. One hand rewrites the other.

When ancient Greek and Latin texts came to be written down more formally, long works were subdivided into individual papyrus rolls called "books." A single bookroll might measure around 9 to 12 inches (22 × 30 cm) in height, and was created by connecting some twenty sheets of papyrus in a long series. Although more sheets could be added, this length of about 20 feet (6 m) was sold by stationers as a basic unit.[17] The first sheet was called the

[14] *Inst.* X.3.32.

[15] *Inst.* X.3.31. Notably, he concedes that writing with ink is better for those with poor vision.

[16] S. T. Coleridge, "Substance of a Dialogue, with a Commentary on the Same," *Blackwood's Edinburgh Magazine* 10.56 (October 1821): 256. See discussion in Susan Zieger, Ch. 3, "Ink, Mass Culture, and the Unconscious," in *The Mediated Mind: Affect, Ephemera, and Consumerism in the Nineteenth Century* (New York: Fordham University Press, 2018), 87–128.

[17] Edward Maunde Thompson, *An Introduction to Greek and Latin Palaeography* (New York: Burt Franklin, 1912, repr. 1965), 25–26; and Frederic G. Kenyon, *The Palaeography of Greek Papyri* (Oxford: Clarendon Press, 1899), 18. In general, William A. Johnson, *Bookrolls and Scribes in Oxyrhynchus* (Toronto: University of Toronto Press, 2004).

protocol – often bearing details of its manufacture – and was of better quality to withstand the wear and tear of being the outermost part of the roll. The last sheet was called the *eschatocol*; this was of lesser quality because it would be protected as the innermost part of the roll and might even be trimmed off as excess. Text was written with a brush on the papyrus in regular columns that ran in a series from left to right across the length of the roll. Overly lengthy works in overly lengthy scrolls were to be avoided. For instance, although his book "had not yet grown too long nor undergone many windings of its scroll," the fifth-century writer, Rutilius Namatianus, worries in a fairly common trope that any longer and the reader might "shrink from handling an undivided work." He confesses to have split his "nervous modesty" or "author's angst" across two shorter bookrolls, realizing too late that it might have been better to have had to face the trauma only once in a single roll.[18] In the *Historia Augusta*, we learn that despite the custom of many history writers to devote a bookroll to the life of each emperor, the biographies of the three Gordians were combined to fit together in one.[19] These passages suggest how some ancient authors might have fashioned or refashioned texts according to the material performances of reading and writing. As paleographer E. Maunde Thompson observes,

> Although the authors themselves may not originally have divided their writings into separate portions to suit the ordinary length of a conveniently-sized roll, yet the practice of the scribe would eventually react on the author. Thus we find the works of Homer divided into books of a length which could be contained in an ordinary roll; and we know that in the course of time authors did regularly adapt the divisions of their works to the customary length [of the rolls].[20]

A material sensibility has thus exerted significant influence upon the composition and circulation of texts over time. The division of the "book," once identified with the physical dimensions of the manuscript roll, is still used as a structural articulation in the modern editions of ancient works in printed and digital platforms. In this way, the form of the manuscript roll acted upon classical tradition and its dissemination, and the conditions of

[18] *Nondum longus erat nec multa volumina passus, iure suo poterat longior esse liber: taedia continuo timui incessura labori, sumere ne lector iuge paveret opus … partimur trepidum per opuscula bina ruborem, quem satius fuerat sustinuisse semel.* II.1–4, 9–10. Translations drawn from *Rutilius Namatianus' 'Going Home': De reditu suo*, trans. Martha A. Malamud (New York: Routledge, 2016); and *Minor Latin Poets*, Vol. II, trans. J. Wight Duff and Arnold M. Duff (London: Heinemann, 1934).

[19] SHA 20.4–5.

[20] Maunde Thompson, *An Introduction to Greek and Latin Palaeography*, 45–46.

this materiality continue to influence scholarship and inform twenty-first-century perceptions of the past.

Another example of the entwined dynamic of material form and textual content comes from Asia, where – among other approaches – Chinese characters could be written with a brush on long, narrow strips of bamboo. A strip or "slip" of bamboo, often around 9 inches (23 cm) long and less than half an inch (1 cm) wide,[21] was held steady against the body with the left hand, while the right hand was used to write a single column of text down its length. Writing on individual slips minimizes the risk of smudging wet ink with a sleeve because the hand need not cross over freshly written text, an issue to which right-handed writers of English are less attuned than their left-handed counterparts. In preparation for dissemination, the slips were laid out in a series from right to left, the columns running in the opposite direction of our examples from ancient Greece and Rome. The arrangement in which each new column of text is set to the left of the preceding one persists today in some sinographic visualization practices in handwritten, printed, and digital forms, especially in places such as Hong Kong and Taiwan.[22] The slips were joined together in two or three places with threads of hemp, silk, or leather, the result somewhat resembling a vertical window blind. Thus connected, the slips could then be rolled into a bundle for storage or transport. Bamboo bundles were often of standard sizes that reflected the relative importance of the text, and the number of slips for some documents was even regulated by law.[23] The longest work up to the first century BCE, the *Shiji* (or *Records of the Grand Historian*), was composed of over 500,000 characters, which might have been written on 14,000 to 21,000 slips of bamboo. Divided into nearly 700 bundles, the entire text on bamboo likely weighed in the range of 100 lb (45 kg).[24] Such heavy piles of bamboo bundles had to be moved by ox- or horse-drawn

[21] Some of the variations and variables are listed in Yi Xumei and Lu Xiuwen, "The Calligraphy and Printing Cultural Heritage of Gansu – The Development of the Engraved Printing Process and Papermaking: An Archaeological Approach," in *The History and Cultural Heritage of Chinese Calligraphy, Printing and Library Work*, ed. Susan M. Allen, Lin Zuzao, Cheng Xiaolan, and Jan Bos (Boston: K. G. Saur, 2010), 45–70.

[22] Thomas S. Mullaney, "Quote Unquote Language Reform: New-Style Punctuation and the Horizontalization of Chinese," *Modern Chinese Literature and Culture* 29.2 (Fall 2017): 240. I am grateful to Anatoly Detwyler for clarification on this point. Endymion Porter Wilkinson notes that this columnar arrangement of text affected the shape and orientation of certain Chinese characters, in *Chinese History: A New Manual*, 4th ed. (Cambridge, MA: Harvard University Press, 2015), §69.1.2 See also Shun-chiu Yau, "La verticalisation en écriture chinoise archaïque, excursion au-delà des 'six principes,'" in *Écritures archaïques: systèmes et déchiffrement*, ed. Centre de recherches linguistiques sur l'Asie Orientale (Paris: Langages croisés, 1995), 197–212.

[23] Tsuein-hsuin Tsien, *Written on Bamboo and Silk: The Beginnings of Chinese Books and Inscriptions*, 2nd ed. (Chicago: University of Chicago Press, 2004), 116.

[24] Wilkinson, *Chinese History*, §59.1.5, §69.1.3.

cart, and it was logistically difficult to transport numerous pieces together. Bundles therefore more commonly circulated as individual treatises or in small groups, and were only later brought together as "chapters" of a larger whole.[25] In the specific case of the *Shiji*, historian Endymion Wilkinson suggests that most of the sections were composed so that they would be meaningful when read in isolation. Understanding that the text was likely distributed in discrete bundles helps to shed light on the considerable repetition of content in the *Shiji*, and explains "why different aspects of the same event are sometimes scattered among different chapters or even told in a different way." Wilkinson also notes that the broad adoption of paper as a writing material in the fifth century CE had "important consequences for book culture," because it enabled long works to circulate in their entirety, rather than in sections: "By no coincidence, literary collections or collected works of an individual began to become more common in the centuries after paper was introduced."[26] Materiality and textuality thus emerge as crucially linked. Although fundamental to the processes of production and reception, their complicated relationship also has the potential to generate competing tensions. That is, the particular structure of the composition might reflect an attentiveness to the circumstances of near-contemporary dissemination. Meanwhile, later reception may be influenced by those same conditions as well as the subsequent agenda of scholars and critics who chose to collect the texts and assign them a particular coherence.[27] The material form of the manuscript had the capacity not only to divide texts conceptually and physically – as we have seen in the examples of the bookroll and the bamboo bundle – but also to consolidate them.

Quite apart from the intentions of writers, disparate texts could be fused into a single entity by other hands. The example of miscellanies from medieval Europe demonstrates this dynamic.[28] A miscellany is a collection of several texts, often from different writers. Paleographer Armando Petrucci argues that the activity of recopying third- and fourth-century

[25] Martin Kern, "Early Chinese Literature, Beginnings through Western Han," in *The Cambridge History of Chinese Literature*. Volume 1: To 1375, ed. Kang-i Sun Chang and Stephen Owen (Cambridge: Cambridge University Press, 2011), 64.

[26] Wilkinson, *Chinese History*, §59.1.5, §69.3.

[27] On the significance of coherence in literary studies and New Criticism generally, see, for example, Terry Eagleton, *Literary Theory: An Introduction*, 2nd ed. (Hoboken, NJ: John Wiley & Sons, 2011), 40–43.

[28] On miscellanism as a deliberate choice, see Jason König and Tim Whitmarsh, "Ordering Knowledge," in *Ordering Knowledge in the Roman Empire*, ed. Jason König and Tim Whitmarsh (Cambridge: Cambridge University Press, 2007), 3–39, esp. 31–34, and König's chapter, "Fragmentation and Coherence in Plutarch's *Sympotic Questions*," 43–68, esp. 43–45. Also n. 13 in this chapter. For a useful summary of recent work on multitext codices, see the introduction to Karen Pratt, Bart Besamusca, Matthias Meyer, and Ad Putter, eds., *The Dynamics of the Medieval Manuscript: Text Collections from a European Perspective* (Göttingen: V&R unipress, 2017), 11–39.

"libraries" of Greek, Coptic, and Latin texts worked to inscribe them in the imagination as unitary traditions. Their material configuration as assemblages had consequences for how the texts would be further transmitted and received. Readers "must inevitably have ended up considering the individual texts contained in the book that they had in their hands as a single whole; they then used them and memorized them as a whole, that is, in their unitary sequence."[29] As the miscellanies were thus recopied, they gained a textual and organizational integrity over time as collections – as *corpora*. The materiality of the manuscript, particularly when manifested under two covers in the form of the codex, generated a physically bounded space that would come to be mapped as the conceptual space of a unified idea.[30]

Although manuscripts are sometimes dismissed as capriciously variable, whether in terms of textuality, materiality, or both, a closer examination reveals that this was not always the case, and especially not when regularity mattered. Around the fourth century, the Gospels in Latin were organized into the now-customary order of Matthew, Mark, Luke, and John, permitting a more effective application of the Eusebian Apparatus. The Eusebian Apparatus includes a prefatory set of Canon Tables that highlight different kinds of agreement across the four Gospel texts, using section numbers as reference points. These section numbers are repeated in Matthew, Mark, Luke, and John as marginal notations, and point back to the Canon Tables. For such cross-referencing devices to be maximally effective, texts should remain in a specific arrangement; the Apparatus and similar finding aids are better able to index certain passages if those sections are not continually in flux. Visualizing information with such devices not only influences the layout of the page, but can also operate to formalize a particular sense of textual authority. With the aid of the Eusebian Apparatus, the four Gospel texts came to be harmonized in a unified representation of the Christian message well before the advent of the printing press. As theologian Thomas O'Loughlin notes, the Apparatus "allows one to build up a composite picture of events on the assumption that each can add details to the others; likewise, it can create the illusion that the texts do not contradict each other."[31] For example, was it to the region of the

[29] Armando Petrucci, "From Unitary Book to Miscellany," in *Writers and Readers in Medieval Italy: Studies in the History of Written Culture*, ed. and trans. Charles M. Radding (New Haven: Yale University Press, 1995), 18.

[30] James J. O'Donnell, "Retractions," in Nichols and Wenzel, *The Whole Book*, 171.

[31] Thomas O'Loughlin, "Harmonizing the Truth: Eusebius and the Problem of the Four Gospels," *Traditio* 65 (2010): 12.

Gadarenes (Matt. 8:28) or the Gerasenes (Mark 5:1, Luke 8:26) that Jesus traveled, and did he meet a single possessed man from town (Luke 8:28) or from the tombs (Mark 5:1), or two from the tombs (Matt. 8:28)? The presence of an apparatus of order can moderate the skepticism that may arise in a reader who is confronted with varying accounts of the same story. Because the Eusebian Apparatus emphasizes agreement across the texts, apparent discrepancies are perceived as contributing to a fuller picture of the Gospels rather than undermining their authority. Significantly, such apparatus may encourage an intellectual slip that associates the textual integrity required to support indexing devices with textual coherence or even authoritativeness.[32] Indeed, the Eusebian Apparatus that accompanies the medieval *Book of Kells* is unfinished; the decorated Canon Tables in the opening pages of the *Kells* manuscript refer to sections that have not been marked in the text.[33] The copying of a partial Apparatus suggests that the urgent challenge of resolving textual inconsistencies to bolster the authority of the Gospels had been addressed at least for one audience – the incomplete nature of the device in *Kells* perhaps reperforming or indexing a concluded act of authorization. Given the formidable effect of organizational devices on transmission and interpretation, it is worth considering whether the recent tendency to characterize them as "paratextual" has obscured their full contribution to the traditions of literature and knowledge.

By understanding manuscripts as technologies that can discipline the transmission of ideas, we may begin to read the layout of their pages as the product of a design calculus that involves the hands of scribes, artists, and their audiences.[34] Paleographer Malcolm Parkes proposed to study manuscripts as evidence of knowledge practice. Not limited to observation and description, his "grammar of legibility" concerned itself with the broader social and cultural implications of the layout of a manuscript. He observes that the arrangement of word, sentence, paragraph, and page developed in stages, coinciding "with changing patterns of literacy, whereby new generations of readers in different historical situations imposed new demands on the written medium itself."[35] An analysis of the visual grammar of the

[32] Similarly, on the use of tables of contents for establishing legitimacy, see Andrew M. Riggsby, "Guides to the Wor(l)d," in *Ordering Knowledge* (Cambridge: Cambridge University Press, 2007), 88–107.

[33] O'Loughlin, "Harmonizing the Truth," 20; on the *Book of Kells*, 25–27.

[34] On the manuscript page in particular, see, among others, Daniel Wakelin, *Designing English: Early Literature on the Page* (Oxford: Bodleian Library, University of Oxford, 2017); and Bonnie Mak, *How the Page Matters* (Toronto: University of Toronto Press, 2011).

[35] M. B. Parkes, *Scribes, Scripts, and Readers: Studies in the Communication, Presentation, and Dissemination of Medieval Texts* (London: Hambledon Press, 1991), xv.

manuscript can therefore offer insights into the milieux in which it was produced and used.

One of the defining features of a manuscript and key to its grammar of legibility is the presence of handwriting. Handwritten letter-forms may be used to transmit a verbal message – but they, and the manuscript in which they reside, constitute an interface of communication that is constituted of particular dimensions and qualities. The shape of letter-forms in particular has been of interest to a variety of scholars, from epigraphers and paleographers to calligraphers, book artists, and graphic designers.[36] Their examination of handwriting has resulted in the classification of scripts, or particular styles. Scripts are identified by the regular manner in which strokes are inscribed upon the writing surface, as well as distinctive features, such as unusual letter-shapes, abbreviations, or ligatures that combine multiple graphemes. The shape of letter-forms is produced in part by technical aspects related to – for instance – the angle of the pen nib, the consistency of the ink, and the texture of the material substrate; however, the choice to emulate a script might be influenced by social, cultural, and political factors. Handwritten scripts can exhibit sufficient regularity that noteworthy aspects of letter-forms, such as curved ascenders or wedge-shaped finials, have been used to develop a history of textual transmission that includes centers of production, genealogies of influence, and networks of trade and expertise.

Over time, particular scripts have come to be associated with specific places, communities, contexts, or ideologies.[37] For example, it is well known that the humanist scholars of the late medieval period were concerned with handwriting reform. Their innovations influenced the design of typefaces through the following centuries, and even now contribute to the "look" of our printed and digital texts. The humanists were active

[36] Among others, Albert Derolez, *The Palaeography of Gothic Manuscript Books: From the Twelfth to the Early Sixteenth Century* (Cambridge: Cambridge University Press, 2003); Johanna Drucker, "The Art of the Written Image," in *Figuring the Word: Essays on Books, Writing, and Visual Poetics* (New York: Granary Press, 1998), 57–75; Armando Petrucci, *Public Lettering: Script, Power, and Culture*, trans. Linda Lappin (Chicago: University of Chicago Press, 1993); James J. John, "Latin Paleography," in *Medieval Studies: An Introduction*, 2nd ed., ed. James M. Powell (Syracuse, NY: Syracuse University Press, 1992), 3–81; and Stanley Morison, *Politics and Script: Aspects of Authority and Freedom in the Development of Graeco-Latin Script from the Sixth Century BC to the Twentieth Century AD* (Oxford: Clarendon Press, 1972).

[37] For example, Xigui Qiu, *Chinese Writing*, trans. Gilbert Louis Mattos and Jerry Norman (Berkeley: Society for the Study of Early China and the Institute of East Asian Studies, University of California, 2000); Bernhard Bischoff, *Latin Palaeography: Antiquity and the Middle Ages*, trans. Dáibhí ó Croínin and David Ganz (Cambridge: Cambridge University Press, 1990); Michelle P. Brown, *A Guide to Western Historical Scripts from Antiquity to 1600* (London: British Library, 1990); and E. A. Lowe, *Codices Latini Antiquiores: A Palaeographical Guide to Latin Manuscripts Prior to the Nineteenth Century*, 12 vols. (Oxford: Clarendon Press, 1934–1972).

readers and writers: They disseminated their compositions for copying and review; they reacted to the work of their peers, appending handwritten annotations or formulating separate responses for broad circulation.[38] In 1366, the humanist Petrarch, at sixty-two years of age, marveled over the clarity of the rounder letter-forms of the Carolingian hand that had been developed in the latter part of the eighth century.[39] He called them *castigata et clara*, plain and clear, in contrast to the angular and compressed Gothic script of his time. He described the latter as painterly – pleasing to the eye from a distance, but confusing when examined up close – as if Gothic letter-forms had been designed for something other than reading.[40] The revival of the older Carolingian letter-forms by humanists in the fifteenth century has generally been understood to be the graphic representation of a new scholarly identity associated with a return to the study of Greek and Latin classics. However, Latinist B. L. Ullman notes that the complaints about the clarity of scripts came especially from a community of aging scholars who had devoted a significant part of their lives to reading and writing. Surviving correspondence indicates that such readers commissioned the recopying of texts that were already in their possession in larger and more legible letter-forms in the style of the Carolingian hand. From this perspective, the manuscript – and the handwriting in it – can be appreciated as a customizable and assistive aid for failing eyesight. As Ullman observes, "Thanks to the improvement of eyeglasses in modern times, we determine our need for them and their strength by the ability to read the telephone book. In 1400 it was easier to change handwriting than to change glasses."[41] Likewise, in today's world of digital devices, readers often choose to adjust the size of text to make it more legible – now with a simple keystroke or gesture of the hand.

In addition to being an adaptable technology for the near-sighted, the manuscript was also deployed to support different practices of reading.

38 For example, Albert Rabil, Jr., ed., *Knowledge, Goodness, and Power: The Debate over Nobility among Quattrocento Italian Humanists* (Binghamton, NY: Center for Medieval and Early Renaissance Studies, State University of New York at Binghamton, 1991). In general, see, for example, Brian Richardson, *Manuscript Culture in Renaissance Italy* (Cambridge: Cambridge University Press, 2009); and Anthony Grafton, *Commerce with the Classics: Ancient Books and Renaissance Readers* (Ann Arbor: University of Michigan Press, 1997).

39 On Petrarch and his views on handwriting, see Albert Derolez, "The Script Reform of Petrarch: An Illusion?" in *Music and Medieval Manuscripts: Paleography and Performance. Essays Dedicated to Andrew Hughes*, ed. John Haines and Randall Rosenfeld (Burlington, VT: Ashgate, 2004), 3–19 and Armando Petrucci, "La scrittura di Francesco Petrarca," *Studi e testi* 248 (1967): 1–155.

40 *Fam.* XXIII.19.8.

41 B. L. Ullmann, *The Origin and Development of Humanistic Script* (Rome: Edizioni di storia e letteratura, 1960), 12–14, n. 9.

For instance, the layout of words – whether separated or not – can be understood as a design choice related to modes of reading. There is evidence of words being graphically divided by space, vertical stroke, or raised dot from as early as the tenth century BCE.[42] However, words are not generally separated in the papyrus scrolls that transmit ancient Greek and Latin writing; these manuscripts exhibit a preference for the form of *scriptio continua*, or continuous script, in which individual words are not visually distinguished from each other. Perhaps more surprisingly for the modern reader, the scribes of Rome abandoned word-division after a period of six centuries in favor of continuous script by the second century CE.[43] Given the consciousness of multiple strategies for organizing text on the page in antiquity, the use of *scriptio continua* can be read in relation to broader activities of reading and writing. The unseparated words of continuous script constitute a graphic device that reflects "the mechanics and aesthetics" of reading aloud.[44] As classicist Gregory Nagy argues in his study of the Bacchylides papyri, *scriptio continua* facilitates the observation of meter, or colometry, which is critical to understanding oral performance. The continuous script in these manuscripts is, then, a form of graphic instruction that seeks to embody "the mellifluous metrical and accentual patterns of pronounced text" rather than elements of grammar.[45] Because the metrical unit of the *colon* is a clause composed of around eight to seventeen syllables, its terminus may or may not coincide with a word ending.[46] The visual separation of words, then, is not key to the observation of the *colon* and the communication of meter, and was therefore not a significant consideration in the layout of the page.

As the cultures of reading and writing changed, so too did the interface of the manuscript's page. The spread of Christianity in particular created a wider audience for the written word. No longer the preserve of a specialized elite, manuscripts were redesigned to accommodate those who were developing skills in literacy. At stake was the effective transmission of the

42 In general, see Stephan Hillyer Levitt, "Word Separation and India," *Annals of the Bhankdarkar Oriental Research Institute* 83 (2002): 37–48; Paul Saenger, *Space between Words: Origins of Silent Reading* (Stanford: Stanford University Press, 1997); and Alan R. Millard, "*Scriptio continua* in Early Hebrew: Ancient Practice or Modern Surmise?" *Journal of Semitic Studies* 15 (Spring 1970): 2–15.

43 Saenger, *Space between Words*, 10. On *scriptio continua* in Chinese writing, see Wilkinson, *Chinese History*, §70.9.

44 Gregory Nagy, "Reading Greek Poetry Aloud: Evidence from the Bacchylides Papyri," *Quaderni Urbinati di Cultura Classica*, n.s. 64.1 (2000): 7.

45 Saenger, *Space between Words*, 11.

46 According to the commentator, Joannes Siculus, in Maunde Thompson, *An Introduction to Greek and Latin Palaeography*, 70.

Christian message. Visualizing text in a way that assisted sense-making became a priority, and the strategies developed in the manuscripts of the early medieval period are still in service today. For instance, whereas a page might have previously been filled from margin to margin with lines of text, scribes began to subdivide these lines according to metrical unit. In this technique of *per cola et commata*, each new verse begins on a fresh line, with the remainder being inset from the margin on subsequent lines until the end of the unit.[47] The ventilated layout deploys blank space to mark conceptual pauses; this graphic arrangement was designed to facilitate the performances of reading and sense-making. Indeed, in the sixth century, Cassiodorus declares that the layout of *per cola et commata* was of great utility to the "simple brothers" of his monastery who might, thus assisted, "pronounce the holy texts without error."[48]

Although readers of *scriptio continua* in antiquity may have determined syntax and meaning through a familiarity with tradition, their later counterparts came to rely on the division of words on the page. Word-separation helps to convey sense by visually isolating and distinguishing elements of grammar. Irish and Anglo-Saxon scribes in the seventh and eighth centuries rejected the custom of *scriptio continua* when copying texts in Latin, preferring instead to insert spaces between words. In doing so, they drew upon the work of ancient grammarians, whose treatises offered strategies by which different parts of speech could be identified and their syntactical function recognized – a great boon to those acquiring Latin as a second language. They also inserted punctuation marks – tools that had been used on occasion in antiquity – to characterize the grammatical function of words within the sentence. When copying in their native language, however, Irish scribes employed a different method of visualization, choosing to organize text according to stressed syllables rather than parts of speech. In this arrangement, multiple words might be combined into a single unit. The difference in the two contemporaneous practices suggests that Old Irish was a language that was spoken and heard, while Latin was comprehended chiefly through its graphic expression by these readers and writers of the early Middle Ages.[49]

47 M. B. Parkes, *Pause and Effect: An Introduction to the History of Punctuation in the West* (Berkeley: University of California Press, 1993), 15–16.

48 *Simplices fratres*; *pronuntiare sacratissimas lectiones ... inculpabiliter. Inst.* I, *praef.* 9; I.12.4. Translation in Cassiodorus, *Institutions of Divine and Secular Learning, and, On the Soul*, trans. James W. Halporn (Liverpool: Liverpool University Press, 2004).

49 M. B. Parkes, "The Contribution of Insular Scribes of the Seventh and Eighth Centuries to the 'Grammar of Legibility,'" in *Scribes, Scripts, and Readers: Studies in the Communication, Presentation, and Dissemination of Medieval Texts* (London: Hambledon Press, 1991), 4–5. For

Further efforts to refine the techniques of visualizing information on the page included the development of minuscule letter-forms. These smaller letters were to be employed in conjunction with the majuscule or capital letters that scribes had been accustomed to using. The arrangement of the majuscule and minuscule forms was furthermore regularized, setting the logic for our use of upper- and lower-case letters today. Scribes additionally established a hierarchy of letters, a visual system in which larger letter-forms were used to demarcate the beginning of different subdivisions of text – a precursor to the modern convention of section headings.

The scribal work of copying manuscripts in the early medieval period was an activity that was predominantly located in monasteries and therefore governed by devotional practice.[50] In a departure from the solitary living that typified much of early Christian spiritualism, monks and nuns began to reside in community around the fifth century. Their lives were organized according to a set of precepts, some of which were laid out in texts such as the influential *Rule of St. Benedict*, which circulated in manuscript in Latin and vernacular translations, and is still read widely in printed and digital forms.[51] The *Rule* established reading as an important spiritual activity; reading offered a way to contemplate the divine. Devotional reading was a slow, meditative, and difficult act that was intended to involve the whole body and all its senses. As words were read, eyes and fingers tracked across the page, the mouth enunciated, the ears strained to hear the resultant murmurs, and the torso swayed. This embodied notion of reading prompted the use of figurative language related to mastication, ingestion, and digestion, as well as – in some cases – their literal exercise. In the twelfth century, Hugh of St. Victor noted that the lessons in Scripture "like so many sweetest fruits, we pick as we read and chew as we consider them."[52] Monastic reading and meditation,

example, the seventh-century Bangor Antiphonary (Milan, Bib. Ambrosiana MS C.5.inf.), and the eighth-century Cambrai Homily (Cambrai, Bibl. mun. MS 679, ff. 37–38).

[50] For some exceptions, see Armando Petrucci, "Literacy and Graphic Culture of Early Medieval Scribes," in *Writers and Readers in Medieval Italy: Studies in the History of Written Culture*, ed. and trans. Charles M. Radding (New Haven: Yale University Press, 1995), 77–102. In general, see Jean Leclercq, *The Love of Learning and the Desire for God: A Study of Monastic Culture*, trans. Catharine Misrahi, 3rd ed. (Fordham, NY: Fordham University Press, 1982).

[51] See, for example, Urbana, University of Illinois Library, Pre-1650 MS 0098, a thirteenth-century vernacular copy for nuns, possibly at the Abbey of Sainte-Glossinde in Metz.

[52] *Didascalicon* 5.5. Translation in Hugh of St. Victor, *The Didascalicon of Hugh of St. Victor: A Medieval Guide to the Arts*, trans. Jerome Taylor (New York: Columbia University Press, 1961, repr. 1991).

for Hugh, were carnal activities. As historian and philosopher Ivan Illich explains, reading translates into body movements: "The reader understands the lines by moving to their beat, remembers them by recapturing their rhythm, and thinks of them in terms of putting them into his mouth and chewing."[53] Indeed, the embodiment of Scripture in manuscript opened up performative possibilities in which the divine word could be written and ingested to be retained or recalled. For example, Ezekiel is commanded to eat a scroll transmitting the words that he was to preach to the Israelites (Ezek. 2:9–10, 3:1–3). A similar understanding of ingestion as a mode of "investing the body with traces of the divine" is exhibited in the practice of drinking Qur'anic verses that had been written on paper or painted on the inside of a bowl and then dissolved in water.[54] In both Christian and Islamic traditions, parts of devotional manuscripts were often kissed or rubbed to the point of obliteration in an attempt to absorb any spiritual residue that might be conducted through the interface of word, image, or surface.[55]

Materials for reading were necessary in order to follow the vision of spiritual life that had been laid out in the *Rule*. A monastery might rally the resources to produce texts for its own use, setting some of its inhabitants to that work. Recent studies have drawn attention to the contribution of women to the transmission of knowledge, and especially in monastic *scriptoria*, where the activity of copying texts was shared among multiple hands.[56] The format of the codex or book form is conducive to such piecework because it is composed of a series of folded booklets. Known as quires or gatherings, these booklets could be handed out to different workers. Certain scribes might be responsible for copying the main text; anything

[53] Ivan Illich, *In the Vineyard of the Text: A Commentary to Hugh's Didascalicon* (Chicago: University of Chicago Press, 1993), 54.

[54] Finbarr Barry Flood, "Bodies and Becoming: Mimesis, Mediation, and the Ingestion of the Sacred in Christianity and Islam," in *Sensational Religion: Sensory Cultures in Material Practice*, ed. Sally M. Promey (New Haven: Yale University Press, 2014), 475.

[55] In addition to Flood, "Bodies and Becoming", see Kathryn M. Rudy, "Kissing Images, Unfurling Rolls, Measuring Wounds, Sewing Badges and Carrying Talismans: Considering Some Harley Manuscripts through the Physical Rituals They Reveal," *Electronic British Library Journal* (2011): 1–56; and Jeffrey F. Hamburger, *The Visual and the Visionary: Art and Female Spirituality in Late Medieval Germany* (New York: Zone Books, 1998). On seeing and touching in the Byzantine tradition, Roland Betancourt, "Tempted to Touch: Tactility, Ritual, and Mediation in Byzantine Visuality," *Speculum* 91.3 (July 2016): 660–689; and Robert S. Nelson, "To Say and to See: Ekphrasis and Vision in Byzantium," in *Visuality Before and Beyond the Renaissance: Seeing as Others Saw*, ed. Robert Nelson (Cambridge: Cambridge University Press, 2000), 143–168.

[56] For example, Jeffrey F. Hamburger and Eva Schlotheuber, "Books in Women's Hands: Liturgy, Learning and the Libraries of Dominican Nuns in Westphalia," in *Entre stabilité et itinérance: livres et culture des ordres mendiants, XIIe–XVe siècle*, ed. Nicole Bériou, Martin Morard, and Donatella

that required red ink would be passed to the rubricator. Decoration or illustration was the particular skill of another worker, and the application of gold leaf might be the expertise of yet another. A corrector would check the text for errors. Catchwords were added at the end of each quire to ensure that the pieces would be assembled in order. The catchword repeats the first word of the following quire so that the gatherings can be matched together by casting the eye quickly over the end of one quire and the beginning of the next. Details about ideal scribal activity in the monastery can be gleaned from Cassiodorus, who offers guidelines in the sixth century for the copying of both sacred and classical texts.[57] According to Cassiodorus, copying texts was a way to engage closely with the sacred word and promote its dissemination. He discusses how to balance personal judgment and authority in textual transmission, noting that although a word or idiom in the exemplar might seem wrong, it should not be changed if found in multiple instances of the text.[58] However, if there are words in the exemplar that make no sense, "they must be courageously corrected" in accordance with more trustworthy sources.[59] Reading and writing in the monastic *scriptorium* might therefore involve thoughtfully emending texts with the aid of more authoritative copies.

Scribes were acutely aware of the corporeal toll associated with the practice of copying manuscripts. Surviving colophons – inscriptions that were often added at the end of a piece – indicate that the work could be backbreaking. The same hand that copied a sacred text might also append a complaint about flickering or low light that was hard on the eyes, the injustice of working with poor materials, or the cramping of hand and body.

Nebbiai (Turnhout: Brepols, 2014), 127–155; Felice Lifshitz, *Religious Women in Early Carolingian Francia: A Study of Manuscript Transmission and Monastic Culture* (New York: Fordham University Press, 2014); Cynthia Cyrus, *Scribes for Women's Convents in Late Medieval Germany* (Toronto: University of Toronto Press, 2009); Alison Beach, *Women as Scribes: Book Production and Monastic Reform in Twelfth-Century Bavaria* (Cambridge: Cambridge University Press, 2004); and Rosamond McKitterick, "Nuns' Scriptoria in England and Francia in the Eighth Century," *Francia* 19.1 (1992): 1–36. See the seminal work, David N. Bell, *What Nuns Read: Books and Libraries in Medieval English Nunneries* (Kalamazoo, MI: Cistercian Publications, 1995). In the domestic sphere, see, for example, Anne Lawrence-Mathers and Phillipa Hardman, eds., *Women and Writing, c.1340–c.1650: The Domestication of Print Culture* (Woodbridge: York Medieval Press, 2010). On medieval scribal activity, Christopher de Hamel, *Scribes and Illuminators* (Toronto: University of Toronto Press, 1992); and on the *scriptorium* in general, Florence Edler de Roover, "The Scriptorium," in *The Medieval Library*, ed. James Westfall Thompson (New York: Hafner, 1939, repr. 1957), 594–611.

57 There is some debate as to his historical importance. See Mark Vessey's introduction to, Cassiodorus, *Institutions*, 4–6; and James J. O'Donnell, *Cassiodorus* (Berkeley: University of California Press, 1979), 239ff.

58 *Inst.* I.15.5.

59 *Inst.* I.15.11.

In a colophon to Gregory the Great's *Moralia*, an extended commentary on the Book of Job, a tenth-century scribe named Florentius describes the burden of writing, "It makes the eyes misty. It twists the back. It breaks the ribs and belly. It makes the kidneys ache and fills the whole body with every kind of annoyance." He concludes by asking readers to respect his handiwork in the massive manuscript of 500 folios: "Turn the pages slowly, and keep your fingers far from the letters, for just as hail damages crops, so a useless reader ruins both writing and book." Literary scholar Catherine Brown calls this colophon a "bravura performance"; the passage was reused by Florentius elsewhere and copied liberally by his contemporaries into other manuscripts.[60] Hand in hand – inscribed and reinscribed – the embodied and material costs of literary tradition may thus be communicated through time. Indeed, the body is central to textual transmission, whether it be scribes who took dictation in antiquity, stonecutters who fashioned the inkstones that are indispensable to the world of scholarship and art in China, or the legions of students and overseas workers who manually transcribe and encode literary, medical, and other texts in service of their digital use.[61] The production and circulation of texts has been and continues to be shaped by these agents and their working conditions. To understand the extent of the influence of materiality in and on the traditions of knowledge means grappling with its social, political, and economic implications.

As the written word was further integrated into the activities of devotion and administration, the role of the manuscript began to change – and so too its design.[62] A wider audience meant that measures had to be taken to ensure the continued intelligibility of the word on the page. According

[60] Madrid, Biblioteca Nacional de España, MS 80, f. 500v. See Catherine Brown, "Remember the Hand: Bodies and Bookmaking in Early Medieval Spain," *Word & Image* 27.3 (2011): 272. In general, see Matthew Fisher, *Scribal Authorship and the Writing of History in Medieval England* (Columbus: The Ohio State University Press, 2012); and Michael Gullick, ed., *Pen in Hand: Medieval Scribal Portraits, Colophons and Tools* (Walkern: Red Gull Press, 2006).

[61] For example, Nancy K. Turner, "The Materiality of Medieval Parchment: A Response to 'The Animal Turn'," *Revista Hispánica Moderna* 71.1 (2018): 39–67; Dorothy Ko, *The Social Life of Inkstones: Artisans and Scholars in Early Qing China* (Seattle: University of Washington Press, 2017); Sarah Kay, "Legible Skins: Animals and the Ethics of Medieval Reading," *postmedieval: a journal of medieval cultural studies* 2 (2011): 13–32; and Bruce Holsinger, "Of Pigs and Parchment: Medieval Studies and the Coming of the Animal," *PMLA* 124.2 (March 2009): 616–623.

[62] In general, see Michael T. Clanchy, *From Memory to Written Record: England, 1066–1307*, 3rd ed. (Chichester: Wiley-Blackwell, 2013); Patrick J. Geary, *Phantoms of Remembrance: Memory and Oblivion at the End of the First Millennium* (Princeton: Princeton University Press, 1994); Rosamond McKitterick, *The Carolingians and the Written Word* (Cambridge: Cambridge University Press, 1989); and Brian Stock, *The Implications of Literacy: Written Language and Models of Interpretation in the Eleventh and Twelfth Centuries* (Princeton: Princeton University Press, 1983).

to art historian Michael Camille, "once the letter had to be recognizable as a part of a scanned system of visual units, possibilities for its deformation and play became limited."[63] For example, imagery was no longer to be incorporated as part of the letter-form itself, but instead carefully inserted into a free-standing initial or "exiled" from the center of the page into the margins, thus contributing to a certain kind of legibility. The visual design of the page witnessed significant developments through the twelfth century in particular, when readers began to make more specific demands of their texts. New schools and universities in urban settings attracted a diverse body of students who intended to pursue professions in civil and canon law, medicine, and theology. These students were drawn from linguistically varied backgrounds, and sought to familiarize themselves quickly with the Latin texts of the scholastic tradition. Depending on their curriculum, students might be required to navigate multiple texts and their commentaries; having such materials cross-referenced and at hand for consultation could expedite study. Moreover, the ability to locate relevant passages efficiently became advantageous as the students prepared for their daily drill sessions and exercises in debate. There was little time for the leisurely tasting and chewing that characterized the meditative reading of monastic life. In this environment, aids for the swift acquisition of knowledge, navigation of text, and the rapid identification of relevant materials emerged as priorities. Authoritative sources were brought together by compilers and rearranged in a way that would be optimally useful for their readers. For instance, Peter Lombard emphasizes his contribution to easy searching, having organized his compilation of biblical texts in the twelfth century with chapter-headings and subdivisions so that readers could find relevant passages "without effort."[64] Texts began to be organized systematically with devices such as commentary, subject indexes, chapter titles, running headlines, paragraph marks, and foliation

[63] Michael Camille, *Image on the Edge: The Margins of Medieval Art* (Cambridge, MA: Harvard University Press, 1992), 20.

[64] Richard H. Rouse and Mary A Rouse, "*Statim invenire*: Schools, Preachers, and New Attitudes to the Page," in *Renaissance and Renewal in the Twelfth Century*, ed. Robert L. Benson and Giles Constable with Carol D. Lanham (Cambridge, MA: Harvard University Press, 1982), 206; Minnis, "Late-Medieval Discussions of *Compilatio*," 393–394; and Henri Cloes, "La systématisation théologique pendant la première moitié du XIIe siècle," *Ephemerides Theologicae Lovanienses* 34 (1958): 281. On the organizational system of Peter Lombard's *Sentences* in particular, see Marcia L. Colish, *Peter Lombard* (Leiden: Brill, 1994); Ignatius Brady, "The Distinctions of Lombard's *Book of Sentences* and Alexander of Hales," *Franciscan Studies* 25 (1965): 90–116; and Ignatius Brady, "The Rubrics of Peter Lombard's *Sentences*," *Pier Lombardo* 6 (1962): 5–25. Recently on compilation and glossing, see Rolf H. Bremmer Jr. and Kees Dekker, eds., *Practice in Learning: The Transfer of Encyclopaedic Knowledge in the Early Middle Ages* (Walpole, MA: Peeters, 2010).

or page numbers. Other developments included the use of alternating blue and red initials at the beginning of lines, as well as an enhanced hierarchy of letters, both graphic techniques serving to facilitate navigation. As Illich suggests, the calculated layout of letter-sizes in the manuscripts of the mid-twelfth century "reflects the new pleasure of projecting mentally organized and quantified patterns of 'knowledge' onto the empty space of the page." But there were important implications of this shift for the transmission of knowledge, for "this visual architecture … makes it increasingly necessary, when reading, to have the book under one's eyes."[65] Because readers were more likely to encounter the word with the eye, designers could cultivate increasingly complicated architectures on the page, which would eventually come to define how information was expressed and visualized. It is thus in the manuscripts of the twelfth century that much of the foundation was laid for an understanding that knowledge could be made visual for transmission, and its acquisition might be achieved through a close engagement with the written document.

An illustrative example of the sophisticated layout of the page comes from the glossed books of the twelfth century. Legal and biblical texts could be understood in various ways, and readers often sought aid to their interpretation from authoritative sources. In the early medieval period, individual words or passages might be glossed – or explained – with notes inserted between the lines or in the margins. These commentaries began to grow in length and complexity; some such commentaries were collected in the twelfth century, regularized, and arranged together in an order that reflected that of the main text. The gloss soon became a canonical text in its own right, and was mandatory reading for any scholar. But the layout of a glossed text required meticulous planning, for each page should transmit two separate texts that must remain distinct, and "run in parallel from page to page without one becoming out of step with the other."[66] Lines were ruled on the page to mark out separate columns for the main text and the gloss to be inserted. In the case of biblical material, the convention was to rule three columns so that the gloss surrounded the main text on both sides. Complications arose when the gloss was too short or too long in comparison to the main text, and failed to fit neatly in its column. To solve the visual imbalance caused by a gloss that was too short, scribes might stretch out the last lines to fill the width of a column, much like

[65] Illich, *In the Vineyard of the Text*, 98–99.

[66] Christopher de Hamel, *Glossed Books of the Bible and the Origins of the Paris Booktrade* (Woodbridge: D. S. Brewer, 1984), 14. See also Beryl Smalley, *The Study of the Bible in the Middle Ages*, 2nd ed. (Notre Dame, IN: University of Notre Dame Press, 1964).

the modern use of "justification" that aligns both the left and right ends of each line of text. In the case of a gloss that was too long for the allotted space, scribes could inscribe the commentary in an L-shape around the main text, or subdivide the commentary itself into narrower parallel columns that could still be placed in the correct position in relation to the main text. These subdivided columns offered opportunity for aesthetic variation; unconventional shapes could be used to fill out the width of the gloss column while also enabling the commentary to remain in step with the main text.[67] In addition to the alignment of the commentary with the main text, explicit visual cues aided the performance of indexing. For example, scribes used red ink to underline the *lemmata* – the verbal callouts repeating the terms from the main text that were being explicated in the gloss – lending a hand to their reading audience. This visual link permitted readers to move between the two texts without losing their place, and worked in tandem with the careful placement of the commentary in relation to the main text. Quotations were marked off graphically, and the names of the sources were written with red ink in the margin. The citational relationship was furthermore emphasized with matching symbols that helped to link the names of the sources with their corresponding quotations, an obvious antecedent of the modern footnote. As the example of the glossed books of the twelfth century suggests, the elaborate layout of text points to – and is a product of – contemporaneous practices of knowledge that increasingly relied on an engagement with the page for the transmission of information. Such complex architectures would eventually begin to foreclose on other modes of knowledge exchange.

The shift toward a methodical and regular arrangement of information on the page was also bolstered by institutional and commercial interests. By the thirteenth century, the Catholic Church had begun to recognize the value of sermons as way to maintain the faith. Ordinary parish priests were enjoined to preach, and some religious orders had begun sending their members beyond the walls on the monastery to conduct their work in diverse communities. Away from the infrastructure of the Church, these preachers might only have their key texts on which to rely for teaching and ministry. A compilation of materials that was organized for consultation, and arranged in a concise and portable format, was an asset for the purposes of composing a sermon on a particular topic. The Church was concerned about ensuring quality and maintaining a consistent message in such practices; it was felt that the preaching of correct doctrine should be

[67] de Hamel, *Glossed Books*, 16.

executed by competent and well-trained representatives.[68] For this reason, efforts were made to regularize the training of preachers, preaching tools, and the instructional programs that were to be carried out on parishioners. One of the ways to control the activities related to preaching was to control the content and form of the page.

The standardization of material was also favored by the expanding commercial market for manuscripts. Parkes observes that by the thirteenth century, an organized book trade catering to academic readers in Paris and elsewhere "consciously strove to achieve uniformity in matters of format and features of layout."[69] At some universities, students would rent parts of an unbound text from booksellers or stationers to copy or have copied. Separate portions of an authorized text – checked and controlled by university officials – were divided into pieces, called *peciae*.[70] Each *pecia* was a sheet of parchment, usually folded twice to make a gathering of four folios or eight pages. The *peciae* of a key text could be doled out to different scribes or rented by different students to expedite reproduction and thereby increase profit. As in the *scriptorium*, this arrangement capitalized on the format of the quire. With a standardized text divided into materially standardized *peciae*, sections could be copied out of order. Blank space could be left in the copy to be returned to when the corresponding *pecia* was available, and scribes would be able to estimate how much space to leave blank. If one exemplar could be used to serve multiple customers, profit could be maximized with minimal effort and investment. Then as today, reproducibility was an advantage for those involved in the commercial production of books.

As the foregoing examples have made evident, the manuscript is a responsive device for the graphic presentation of information. For millennia, it has enabled the transmission of ideas, and in so doing has also laid the foundation for how those ideas should be visualized – whether certain texts ought to be organized in columns; whether images or numerical data

68 Richard H. Rouse and Mary A. Rouse, *Preachers, Florilegia, and Sermons: Studies on the Manipulus Florum of Thomas of Ireland* (Toronto: PIMS, 1979), 50; also 57–59.

69 M. B. Parkes, "The Influence of the Concepts of *Ordinatio* and *Compilatio* on the Development of the Book," in *Medieval Learning and Literature: Essays presented to Richard William Hunt*, ed. J. J. G. Alexander and M. T. Gibson (Oxford: Clarendon Press, 1976), 137.

70 In general, Mary A. Rouse and Richard H. Rouse, "The Book Trade at the University of Paris, ca. 1250–ca. 1350," in *Authentic Witness: Approaches to Medieval Texts and Manuscripts* (Notre Dame, IN: University of Notre Dame Press, 1991), 259–338; Graham Pollard, "The *Pecia* System in the Medieval Universities," in *Medieval Scribes, Manuscripts & Libraries: Essays Presented to N.R. Ker*, ed. M. B. Parkes and Andrew G. Watson (London: Scolar Press, 1978), 145–161; and Jean Destrez, *La pecia dans les manuscrits universitares du XIIIe et du XIV siècle* (Paris: Éditions Jacques Vautrain, 1935).

are appropriate, where, and in what configuration. The act of visualizing information in the manuscript has served to conjoin certain kinds of materials, and, more significantly, associate them with particular forms and aesthetics. Over time, these identities have been codified into the different genres that now constitute our documentary and literary traditions. Attentiveness to the materiality of the manuscript offers us a longer view of these traditions and the circumstances of their construction. Thus equipped, we may begin to understand that the manuscript is itself shaped by contemporary perspectives – then and now – with respect to how knowledge has come to look and be transmitted.

Handwork and handiwork are rewritten as each technological age grapples with establishing its own infrastructures of difference. It is consequently not only the artifact of the manuscript that shapes literary tradition and knowledge practice, but also the remediations, refractions, and reconsiderations of handwork. Indeed, the manuscript yields indications of desires through time; a digitized medieval manuscript of today cannot be read simply as a product of the Middle Ages, for it also carries traces of the intervening years and reveals the urges of the twenty-first century. In this way, the manuscript is always a palimpsest – if not of text or image, then of readerly or writerly projections of the past, present, and future.

CHAPTER 3

The Hand Press, 1450–1800

Paula McDowell

In 1678, Joseph Moxon (1627–1691) published *Mechanick Exercises, or, The Doctrine of Handy-Works ... of the Smiths Trade.*[1] The same year, he became the first tradesman to be elected to the Royal Society. In 1683–1684, he published a second volume, *Mechanick Exercises: Or, the Doctrine of Handy-Works. Applied to the Art of Printing* (Figure 3.1).[2] The first detailed account of the inside of a printing house as seen through the eyes of a master printer and the first comprehensive printing manual in any language, this nearly 400-page work was published in twenty-four parts and dedicated to a lord bishop, a member of the Privy Council, and a secretary of state. Lavishly illustrated with copperplate engravings depicting printing tools and methods, this guide to "*Typographie*" is an impressive "Piece of *Typographie* itself."[3] Attempting to justify the work's price ("2 *d.* for each Printed Sheet. And 2 *d.* for every Print taken off of Copper Cuts"), Moxon advised customers that *Mechanick Exercises*, vol. 2, consisted of "all new matter, not Collected, or Translated from any other Authors, and the drafts of the Cuts all drawn from the Tools and Machines used in each respective Trade."[4]

Mechanick Exercises: ... Applied to the Art of Printing epitomizes a "technology" in several senses of this term. Today, we commonly think of a technology as a "practical or industrial art; a branch of the mechanical arts or applied sciences; a technological discipline," or the application, study, or product of this.[5] But in Moxon's day, a technology was "a discourse

[1] Moxon, *Mechanick Exercises, or, The Doctrine of Handy-Works ... of the Smiths Trade*, 3rd ed. (London: Printed for *Dan. Midwinter* and *Tho. Leigh*, at the *Rose and Crown* in St. *Paul's Church-Yard*, 1703). The work was originally published in fourteen parts in 1678–1680.

[2] Moxon, *Mechanick Exercises: Or, the Doctrine of Handy-Works. Applied to the Art of Printing.* The Second Volume (London: Printed for *Joseph Moxon* on the West-side of *Fleet-ditch*, at the Sign of *Atlas*, 1683–1684).

[3] Moxon, *Mechanick Exercises*, A2.

[4] Ibid., 8.

[5] *OED*, technology, *n.* 5, from 1858.

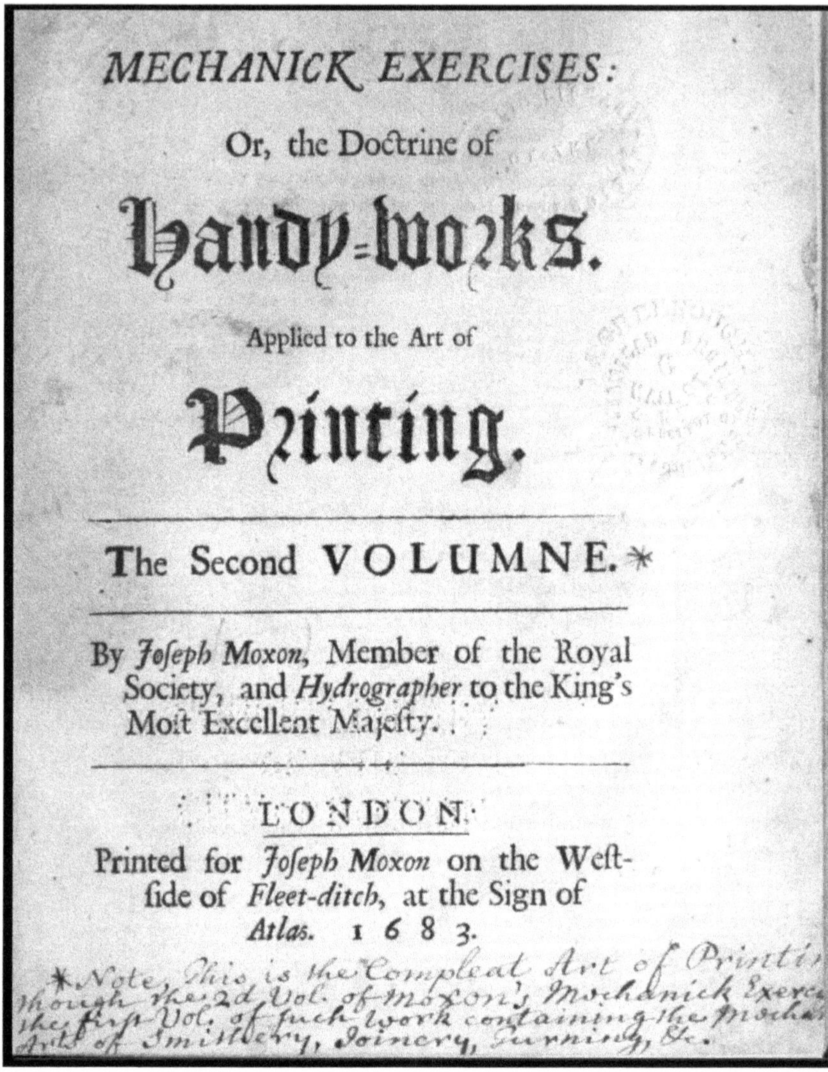
MECHANICK EXERCISES:

Or, the Doctrine of

Handy-works.

Applied to the Art of

Printing.

The Second VOLUMNE. *

By *Joseph Moxon*, Member of the Royal Society, and *Hydrographer* to the King's Most Excellent Majesty.

LONDON:

Printed for *Joseph Moxon* on the West-side of *Fleet-ditch*, at the Sign of *Atlas*. 1683.

*Note, This is the Compleat Art of Printi
though the 2d Vol. of Moxon's Mechanick Exerc
the first Vol. of such work containing the Mecha
Arts of Smithery, Joinery, Turning, &c.

Figure 3.1 Title page of Moxon, *Mechanick Exercises: … Applied to the Art of Printing* (1683), Boston Public Library, Rare Books Department.

or treatise on an art or arts; *esp.* … a treatise on a practical art or craft."[6] The founding charter of the Worshipful Company of Stationers, the livery company that oversaw printing in England from 1577, refers to the

[6] *OED*, technology, *n.* 1, from 1612.

"Art and Mystery" of printing (an "art and mystery" is "the art and craft of a trade").[7] A third meaning of technology is "technical language or nomenclature."[8] Moxon appended to his work a glossary of printing terms (a "Dictionary of … Words and Phrases … mentioned in these Exercises"), encapsulating a technology in this third sense.

Mechanick Exercises describes the "Tools and Machines" of hand press printing. But for Moxon, the most important tool of printing was the human body. The term "Handy-works" in the title of his work is a crucial reminder that printed texts in the hand press period were "the product[s] of the manual or creative labour of a person or other agent … a thing or things collectively made by a person's hands."[9] Reading Moxon's text today challenges us to scrutinize what we mean by technology, for the nomenclature of hand press printing often makes it difficult to distinguish between "human" and "tool" (or, from another perspective, between animate and inanimate tools). A hand press is by definition "a press operated by hand; *esp.* a printing press so worked, as distinguished from one operated by steam or electrical power."[10] A hand is "the terminal part of the human arm beyond the wrist, consisting of the palm, four fingers, and thumb, and used for grasping, holding, and manipulating things."[11] To pay attention to *both* elements in the compound term "hand press" is to foreground the central ontological challenge at the heart of printing history: "Press" is a verb as well as a noun. Neither a printing press nor a hand can produce a printed text, but together, machine and worker can and do.

In her pioneering study of the advent and implications of printing in Western Europe, Elizabeth L. Eisenstein explains her decision to focus on the larger social and cultural consequences of printing rather than on the human agents involved: "[I]n the end, practical considerations became paramount. I decided that cataloguing would be simplified if I referred to the tool rather than its user."[12] Almost as soon as Eisenstein's work was published, a reviewer praised it as a major contribution to early modern history, yet also (somewhat paradoxically) accused the author of taking "the printing press itself entirely out of history. For Eisenstein, print seems to be an independent force in human affairs, a cause but never a

7 *OED*, mystery, *n.* 2, 2. c. "art and mystery."
8 *OED*, technology, *n.* 2, from 1658.
9 *OED*, handiwork, *n.* 1.
10 *OED*, hand press, *n.*
11 *OED*, hand, *n.* I. 1. a.
12 Elizabeth L. Eisenstein, *The Printing Press as an Agent of Change: Communications and Cultural Transformations in Early Modern Europe*, 2 vols. (Cambridge: Cambridge University Press, 1979), xv.

result of historical processes. She refuses to see it as a tool … exploited by forces outside itself."[13] Today, printing historians agree that human agents significantly shaped the "consequences" of print, and that the latter varied greatly, both within Europe and across the globe. (Indeed, Eisenstein herself states that printing was "of no more consequence than any other inanimate tool. Unless it had been deemed useful to human agents it would never have been put into operation.")[14] Printing technology was both a cause of effects and itself an effect of human agency. In addition, as Eisenstein emphasizes in the opening pages of her nearly 800-page book, "the effects produced by printing are by no means self evident…. To track them down and set them forth … is much easier said than done."[15]

The first section of this chapter introduces *Mechanick Exercises: … Applied to the Art of Printing* and the technology of hand press printing with metal type, which remained remarkably stable from the 1480s to 1800. The second section turns to the eighteenth century, a pivotal period in the history of the press, to show how the consequences of printing were shaped chiefly by legal, political, sociocultural, and economic factors rather than by any significantly new developments in the technology itself. In 1694, there were only twenty-four legal master printers in all of England, almost all of them in London; a century later, there were hundreds of presses located throughout Great Britain, and printing had affected Britons at every social level.

Since *The Printing Press as an Agent of Change* was published four decades ago, scholars such as Adrian Johns have emphasized that "print culture" did not emerge directly from the press; rather, "the very identity of print itself has had to be *made*."[16] Moxon contributed to the cultural work of constructing an "identity" for print and printing – as did the later authors whose arguments concerning print, printing, and "print culture" I discuss in the third section of this chapter. From the eighteenth century onward, writers as diverse as Daniel Defoe, Dugald Stewart, and Nicolas de Caritat, Marquis de Condorcet in the eighteenth century and Marshall McLuhan and Walter J. Ong in the mid-twentieth century theorized the "implications" of the introduction and spread of printing. In so doing,

[13] William Bouwsma, "Review of Eisenstein, *The Printing Press as an Agent of Change*," *American Historical Review* 84 (1979), 1357.

[14] Eisenstein, *The Printing Press as an Agent of Change*, 703.

[15] Ibid., 7.

[16] Adrian Johns, *The Nature of the Book: Print and Knowledge in the Making* (Chicago: University of Chicago Press, 1998), 2, emphasis in original in all instances, unless otherwise stated; see also Michael Warner, *The Letters of the Republic: Publication and the Public Sphere in Eighteenth-Century America* (Cambridge, MA: Harvard University Press, 1992).

they have all indirectly shaped our own ideas of what "print," "printing," and "print culture" mean.[17]

From the later nineteenth century, another set of authors theorized a coevolutionary relationship between the human body and its tools.[18] In 1877, philosopher Ernst Kapp argued that humans use tools to project their organs, and in 1949, paleontologist Kenneth Oakley argued that "employment of tools appears to be [humans'] chief biological characteristic, for considered functionally they [tools] are detachable extensions of the forelimb."[19] Whereas other mammals developed "specialized bodily equipment" (such as claws), "in the process of evolution man avoided any such specializations" and came to rely on "extra-bodily equipment of his own making."[20] In 1964, McLuhan argued in *Understanding Media: **The Extensions of Man*** (my emphasis) that communications technologies, too, are "extensions" of our senses and limbs.[21] But whereas Oakley emphasized humans as agents ("man the tool-maker"), McLuhan countered that our tools also make us (in his phrase, "work us over").[22] Influenced by McLuhan and by paleoanthropologist André Leroi-Gourhan, philosopher Bernhard Stiegler has recently pushed these debates further, arguing that "man the tool maker" is "primordially" technical or technological himself. In Mark Hansen's paraphrase of Stiegler, "the human evolves by exteriorizing itself in tools.... Technology on this account is not something external and contingent, but rather an essential – indeed, *the* essential – dimension of the human."[23]

Assessing the still-vexed (and controversial) question of the relationship between humans and their tools, media philosopher John Durham Peters has lately proposed that the spread of actor-network theory since the 1980s

17 For an argument that the term print culture was largely a post-1960s invention, see Paula McDowell, "Toward a Genealogy of 'Print Culture' and 'Oral Tradition.'" *This Is Enlightenment*, ed. Clifford Siskin and William Warner (Chicago: University of Chicago Press, 2010), 229–246.

18 For a nineteenth-century example, see Ernst Kapp, *Elements of a Philosophy of Technology: On the Evolutionary History of Culture*, ed. Jeffrey West Kirkwood and Leif Weatherby, with an afterword by Siegfried Zielinski; trans. Lauren K. Wolfe (1877; Minneapolis: University of Minnesota Press, 2018).

19 Kenneth P. Oakley, *Man the Tool-Maker* (Chicago: University of Chicago Press., 1959), 1.

20 Ibid., 1–2.

21 Marshall McLuhan, *Understanding Media: The Extensions of Man*, orig. 1964 (London and New York: Routledge, 2001), passim.

22 McLuhan uses this phrase frequently; e.g. see Marshall McLuhan, Quentin Fiore, and Jerome Agel, *The Medium Is the Massage: An Inventory of Effects* (Harmondsworth: Penguin, 1967), 148.

23 Mark B. N. Hansen, "Memory," in *Critical Terms for Media Studies*, ed. W. J. T. Mitchell (University of Chicago Press), 64–87, at 65; for Stiegler, see esp. *Technics and Time*, vol. 1: *The Fault of Epimetheus*, trans. Richard Beardsworth and George Collins (Palo Alto, CA: Stanford University Press, 1998).

has "overs[een] a kind of truce." Actor-network theory's "interest in the agency of things and the thingliness of agents" is "sociological enough to allow for the wisdom of people and technical enough to demonstrate the constraints of design."[24] Like all new technologies, the introduction and spread of printing with movable type enabled some new possibilities and constrained others. For Moxon, printing technology was not a *thing* but an *action*, enabled and constrained by the capacities of the human body. Printing was above all a "*Mechanick Exercise*": a physical activity and habitual occupation "relating to or involving manual labor or skill."[25] Using Moxon's text as our guidepost to consider "the Art and Mystery of Printing" and the question of its effects, this chapter similarly foregrounds the human body in the story it tells about an artisanal technology and its products.

1 What Was Printing Technology?

Moxon's project in *Mechanick Exercises: … Applied to the Art of Printing* was ideological as well as technical. He aimed to elevate the status of the master printer to that of a man of "Science" and printing itself to a "Science, nay Science of Sciences." He divided "*Typographie*" into "several Trades," including "Founders," "Printers," and "other Trades they take into their Assistance."[26] But by far the most important tradesman in his view was the "Master Printer," or "Typographer" – and by these terms, he urged, "I do not mean a *Printer*, as he is Vulgarly accounted."[27] The master printer made the "Art of Printing" possible through the organization of others. He was "the Director of all the Work men … the Base on which the Workmen stand."[28] (In Moxon's text, the Master Printer is always male, an ideological but not factual representation I will discuss later.)

Before outlining aspects of the printing trade, Moxon paused to consider the origins of letterpress printing. While he acknowledged that the first inventors of printing were "in *China* and other Eastern Countries, who (by general assent) have had it for many hundreds of years," he erroneously implied that all "Eastern" printing was block printing. He wrote: "their Invention is very different from ours; they cutting their Letters

24 John Durham Peters, "'You Mean My Whole Fallacy Is Wrong': On Technological Determinism," *Representations* 140 (2017) 10–26, at 20.

25 *OED* mechanic, *adj.*, A. I. 1.

26 Moxon, *Mechanick Exercises*, pp. 5, 7; font reversed.

27 Ibid., 6.

28 Ibid., 9.

upon Blocks in whole Pages or Forms, as among us our Wooden Pictures are Cut; But *Printing* with single Letters Cast in Mettal, as with us here in Europe, is an Invention scarce above Two hundred and fifteen years old."[29] In fact, the Chinese developed printing with movable clay type by the eleventh century, and the earliest surviving text printed with movable metal type, the *Jikki*, was printed in Korea in 1377.[30]

Similarly, in outlining the origins of metal type printing in Europe, Moxon got some things right and some things wrong. Today, Johannes Gutenberg (d. 1468) of Germany is generally given credit as the first European to manufacture and use metal type. But Moxon recounted a story he had heard that "*Lawrensz Jansz Koster* [Laurens Janszoon Coster] of Harlem was the first Inventor of Printing" and that his "Companion, *John Gutenberg*, stole his Tools away while he was at Church."[31] In reality, Gutenberg was a skilled goldsmith who approached Johann Fust, a Mainz-based businessman, to develop a series of printing-related projects. An enterprising merchant as well as skilled technician, Gutenberg's many innovations included the development of oil-based printing ink and a new method for delivering ink to paper, as well as a process for manufacturing metal type. But his greatest innovation was arguably not so much any one particular technological breakthrough as his combination of several innovations and his own business acumen into a practical system that enabled the mass production of printed books.[32] Gutenberg brought together new materials and techniques with the new financing structures necessary to fund a business that required substantial up-front investment. By about 1450, he was able to print broadsides and longer works, and by 1454 the 1,200-page folio Gutenberg Bible was in production.

By Moxon's day, type was increasingly cast by specialists, and most printers purchased a "body" of type as a finished product. Type was phenomenally expensive, and by the eighteenth century, government press agents knew that the quickest way to shut down an offending printing house

29 Ibid., 1; font reversed.

30 For concise overviews of the complex history of printing in the Far East, see J. S. Edgren, "China," P. F. Kornicki, "Japan," and Beth McKillop, "Korea," in *The Book: A Global History*, ed. Michael Suarez and H. R. Woudhuysen (Oxford: Oxford University Press, 2013), 573–622. On China, see also Kai-Wing Chow, "Reinventing Gutenberg: Woodblock and Movable-Type Printing in Europe and China," *Agent of Change: Print Culture Studies after Elizabeth L. Eisenstein*, ed. Sabrina A. Baron, Eric N. Lindquist, and Eleanor F. Shevlin (Amherst: University of Massachusetts Press, 2007), 169–192.

31 Moxon, *Mechanick Exercises*, vol. 2, 2. Emphasis in original.

32 For this argument, see Stephen Fussel, *Gutenberg*, trans. Peter Lewis (orig. *Johannes Gutenberg*, 1999; repub. London: Haus Publishing, 2019) and James Mosley, "The Technologies of Print," in Suarez and Woudhuysen, *The Book: A Global History*, 130–153.

was simply to damage or remove the cases of type.[33] Individual type pieces were sorted into slots in two cases (the "upper" and "lower" case). The compositor (typesetter) plucked letters and spacing from the cases with one hand and arranged them in an iron composing stick held carefully in the other hand (Figure 3.2). Lines of type were transferred to a galley (a tray), tied up with string and locked into a chase (a frame). Once the chase (or "form[e]") was assembled, it was carried to the press, inked, and rolled under the platen of the press to form an impression on paper. The process of imposition, or the layout of type pieces in a spatial arrangement, was (and still is) a complex art. This was especially true as multiple future "pages" were often printed simultaneously on a single large sheet of paper that was later folded so that the pages appeared in the correct order.

Setting type requires intense focus and a high degree of mental and manual coordination, and in a business environment it also required a daunting degree of speed. Moxon emphasized that typesetters needed to develop a kind of somatic memory that would allow them to make complex decisions and movements "very quick." In the following passage, he describes the compositor "reading his Copy" and almost "instant[ly]" pulling pieces of type. Each piece of type has a characteristic "posture and position" that allows it to be "immediately" identified and "seiz[ed]":

> [A]s his Eyes are very quick in reading his *Copy*, and in shifting its Visual Ray to the several *Boxes* he is to have a *Letter* out of, so is his choice what *Letter* to take up very sudden; for though the Box be full of *Lette[r]s*, yet in an instant he resolves and pitches his Fingers upon that one, which for its posture and position his Fancy reckons lyes most commodious for his immediate seizing.[34]

In several such passages in *Mechanick Exercises*, the compositor's body parts appear to merge seamlessly with the parts of the "body" of type. Type pieces, like typesetters, have "feet," "toes," "cheeks," "shoulders," and "faces," and animate and inanimate "body" parts working together comprise the technology in question:

> When he *Composes* the Letters he holds the *Composing-stick* in his Left Hand, placing the Second Joynt of his Thumb over the moving *Cheek* of the *Stick*, and the end of the Ball of his Thumb reaches down to the bottom of

[33] For women printers affected by this practice, see Paula McDowell, *The Women of Grub Street: Press, Politics, and Gender in the London Literary Marketplace, 1678–1730* (Oxford: Clarendon Press, 1998), 65–66.

[34] Moxon, *Mechanick Exercises*, 213.

Figure 3.2 The "handy-work" of typesetting: balancing type in a composing stick. Moxon, *Mechanick Exercises: ... Applied to the Art of Printing* (1683), plate 24, Boston Public Library, Rare Books Department.

> the *Cheek* and *Stick*; so that with the end of the Ball of his Thumb he gently presses the *Letter* close to the *Cheek*, and keeps the *letters* tight and square together, as he places them in the *Stick*.[35] (See Figure 3.2, top)

Then as now, insertable parts were often gendered. In the following passage describing letter founding (versus composing), "Male" and "Female" parts appear to copulate, with the typecaster functioning as a kind of pimp:

> When his *Stick* of *Letters* is thus transfer'd to the *Male-Block*, He claps the middle of the *Male-Block* into his left-Hand, tilting the *Feet* of the *Letter* a little upwards, that the *Face* may rest upon the *Tongue*, and then takes about the middle of the *Female-Block* in his right-Hand, and lays it so upon the *Male-Block*, that the *Tongue* of the *Male-Block* may fall into the *Tongue* of the *Female-Block* [etc.].[36]

Compositors needed to read manuscripts well enough to "get [themselves] into the meaning of the *Author*." But in Moxon's view, they should also take care to amend the author's "deficien[cies]" where "Necessary" to protect the printer's reputation: "[I]t is Necessary that the *Compositers* Judgement should know where the Author has been deficient, that so his care may not suffer such Work to go out of his Hands as may bring Scandal upon himself, and Scandal and prejudice upon the *Master Printer*."[37] Good compositors should also have aesthetic judgment and taste to lay out the text in a pleasing spatial arrangement "graceful to the Eye, and pleasant in Reading."[38] The compositor should therefore be something of a "Schollar," but the "Corrector," or proofreader, should also be multilingual, "well skilled in Languages ["besides the English Tongue"], especially in those that are used to be Printed with us, viz. the *Latin, Greek, Hebrew, Syriack, Caldae, French, Spanish, Italian, High Dutch, Saxon, Low Dutch, Welch, &c.*"[39]

While type was increasingly manufactured by specialists, Moxon held that "an understanding Press-man" should know not only how to *operate* a press but how to *build* one: "how to give a strange Joyner and Smith instructions how to make a *Press*, and all its parts" and "Set up and Fasten a *Press* when it is made."[40] Wooden screw presses had long been used to make oil and wine, and by the fifteenth century, high-pressure versions were developed that had

[35] Ibid., 213.

[36] Ibid., 191. For more on this aspect of Moxon's text, see Lisa Maruca, "Bodies of Type: The Work of Textual Production in English Printers' Manuals," *Eighteenth-Century Studies* 36 (2003), 321–343, esp. 328–329.

[37] Moxon, *Mechanick Exercises*, 219.

[38] Ibid., 220.

[39] Ibid., 197, 260.

[40] Ibid., 270.

sufficient force to make crisp impressions on paper. Moxon recommended that press frames should be made of "Good, Fine, Clean, Well-Seasoned *Oak*," and he described additional parts of the press such as the press stone, carriage, tympan and frisket, platen, spindle, and bar. As with the nomenclature of type pieces, parts of the press commonly shared names with workers' body parts. Moxon observed that "the *Press* is a Machine consisting of many Members," and he discussed inanimate parts such as the "Toe," "Eye," and "Shank" of the spindle, the "Ear of the Frisket," and the "Feet," "Cheeks," "Head," "Ribs," and "Joynts" of the press.[41] Coordinating these "Members" typically required two human bodies: a "puller, who placed the paper on the tympan, wound the carriage under the platen, and pulled the bar; and the beater, who worked out the ink and applied it to the forme."[42] (A "printer's devil," or third worker, might assist.)

The habitual and strenuous actions of the puller and beater required intense physical conditioning and the acquisition of somatic memory. Recalling the title of *Mechanick Exercises*, these occupations exemplify "Exercises" in both dominant meanings of that term: a "habitual employment or activity" and an "exertion of the muscles, limbs, and bodily powers."[43] The puller, especially, must work "with various Set and Formal Postures and Gestures of his Body" until his "constant and methodical posture and gesture" becomes "habitual to him, and eases his Body."[44] The word "manual," as in "manual labor," stems from the Latin *manu*, or hand. Moxon aimed to elevate printing to the status of a "science," but *Mechanick Exercises* never downplays the "Physical," bodily aspects of hand press printing. The essence of printing technology as Moxon depicts it is "*Handy-works* and Physical Operations" (my emphasis). In fact, in the process of setting in motion the mechanical parts of the press, the "*Press-mans* Hands" seem to acquire minds of their own. In the following passage, each "Hand" appears to work independently *and* with its partner, anticipating its next task, before the task 'at hand' is "half performed":

> Thus you see both the *Press-mans* Hands at the same time alternately ingaged in different Operations: For while his Right Hand is imployed in one Action his left is busie about another, and these exercises so suddenly varied, that they seem to slide into one another Posture; beginning when the former is but half performed.[45]

41 Ibid., 39–40, 321.
42 Mosley, "The Technologies of Print," 139.
43 *OED*, exercise, *n.* 2 and *n.* 7.
44 Moxon, *Mechanick Exercises*, 320.
45 Ibid., 325.

Some eighty years after Moxon published his guide to printing house practice, Denis Diderot and Jean le Rond d'Alembert's coedited *Encyclopedia, or a Systematic Dictionary of the Sciences, Arts, and Crafts* (1751–1775) depicted the ideal printing house as a clean, orderly, genteel space, sparsely populated with silent workers absorbed in their individual tasks. Yet both representations are ideological, for both Moxon and the encyclopedists depict the printing house as an all-male space. In fact, the domestic (versus industrialized) nature of the early modern print trades meant that male and female family members often worked alongside one another. Daughters, as well as sons, grew up in family printing houses, and sometimes took them over from their parents. Apprentices and servants were also household members, and businesses were commonly passed down through intermarriage. In Moxon's lifetime, twenty-five-year-old Tace Sowle succeeded to the London printing business of her mother Jane Sowle (the widow of printer Andrew Sowle) and went on to become the leading Quaker printer of her generation (fl. 1691–1749). Although Tace eventually married, she retained control of her press. She printed the major works of the founders of Quakerism, including George Fox, Margaret Fell Fox, and William Penn. (Ironically, her own name, Tace, stems from the Latin *taceo*, to be silent.) For more than half a century, this woman who spent her entire life in a printing house served the largest Nonconformist sect in England not only as the primary printer but also as the primary publisher, warehouser, collecting agent, and adviser on market demands.[46]

Another contemporary London printer, Elinor James (*c.* 1645–1719), was also a prolific author herself. The wife and later widow of printer Thomas James, Elinor James wrote, printed, and distributed more than 100 broadsides and pamphlets between 1681 and 1716. In one of her broadsides, she described herself as "in the element of Printing above forty years."[47] James's papers comment on national and local political issues and also on issues pertaining to her trade. In one of her many petitions to parliament, she urged that printing should not be a free trade because it was not a "Trade" at all: "Printing is not a Trade as other Trades are, but is an Art and Mystery that ought … not to be made so common, as that it should

[46] For further information on Tace Sowle and Jane Sowle, see Paula McDowell, "Sowle, Tace (1666–1749)" and "Sowle, Andrew (1628–1695) and Jane Sowle (c. 1631–1711)," *Oxford Dictionary of National Biography*, Oxford University Press; online ed., January 2008.

[47] *Mrs. James's Advice to All Printers*, *c.* 1715, in *Elinor James: Printed Writings*, ed. Paula McDowell (Aldershot: Routledge, 2005), 258.

be slighted and trampled under Foot."[48] The topical, occasional nature of James's hastily produced papers suggest that she may have "written" these works not with a pen but rather directly at her press with type. The male, homosocial world of the printing house that Moxon depicts must be recognized as a fiction, not reality. In addition to women printers (and their daughters and female servants), other women worked in different areas of the printing trades as engravers, illustrators, binders, and manufacturers of supplies such as type, paper, and ink.[49]

2 Eighteenth-Century Developments

In Moxon's day, the English book trade was small, closely knit, and highly centralized. But in the eighteenth century, the English press underwent some of the most important transformations in its history. Between the introduction of movable type printing in England in 1476 and the collapse of prepublication censorship after the lapse of the Licensing Act in 1695, printing deeply affected English life. But in the eighteenth century, printing technology and its products affected social, political, and literary life at every level.

When we talk about the "proliferation" or "saturation" of print, we need to talk about perceptions as well as data. Well before the eighteenth-century explosion of print, Desiderius Erasmus (1466–1536) complained about printers producing too many "foolish, ignorant, malignant, libelous, mad, impious and subversive" books.[50] But in quantitative terms alone, the phenomenal proliferation of printed texts in England after 1695 is "indisputable."[51] Significantly, this proliferation was triggered not by new technological developments but rather by legal, political, economic, sociocultural, and other factors. In 1557, the Worshipful Company of Stationers received its royal charter, granting its highly restricted membership the sole right in all of England to print, publish, or traffic in the printed word. But in 1695, the Licensing Act of 1662 was allowed to lapse owing to parliamentary negligence, and the period that followed

[48] Elinor James, *To the Honorable House of Commons. Gentlemen, Since You Have Been Pleased to Lay Such a Heavy Tax upon Paper*, n.d. (*c.* 1696–1698), in McDowell, *Elinor James*, 97–98.

[49] For examples, see McDowell, *The Women of Grub Street*; for a window into an exponentially expanding area of scholarship, see Cait Coker and Kate Ozment, eds., *Women in Book History Bibliography*, womensbookhistory.org.

[50] Qtd. in Ann Blair, *Too Much to Know: Managing Scholarly Information before the Modern Age* (New Haven: Yale University Press, 2010), 55–56.

[51] Multigraph Collective, *Interacting with Print: Elements of Reading in the Age of Print Saturation* (Chicago: University of Chicago Press, 2018), 242.

was one of anarchic expansion in the printing trades. The Company's historic monopoly over printing was undermined, and an older, guild-based model of trade was increasingly displaced by a more openly competitive commercial model.

In the eighteenth century, printing was not a new technology, but the uses of printing changed. The period saw an explosion of cheap print (pamphlets, broadsides, almanacs, and job printing),[52] together with the proliferation of newspapers and periodicals. In Moxon's day, there were only a few sources of regularly printed news. The chief newspaper was the government-published *London Gazette* (from 1665), in which Moxon advertised his work. But in 1702, the first daily newspaper, the *Daily Courant*, was published, and by 1712 there were "about twenty single-leaf papers … regularly published in the capitol each week."[53] Regularly published political journals made state affairs a matter of open discussion, and "public opinion" was established as a political force. Paper remained expensive, as most paper was imported, but between 1690 and 1800, the number of paper mills in Britain quadrupled. Encouraged by the increasing availability of paper and by new fixed mail routes, magazines and essay journals flourished. In the inaugural issue of *The Tatler*, Richard Steele (aka "Isaac Bickerstaffe") announced that his innovative paper would be published "every *Tuesday, Thursday*, and *Saturday*, in the Week, for the Convenience of the Post."[54]

The eighteenth century saw the development of the modern literary marketplace and a professional literary culture that was satirized as "Grub Street." The growing circulation of manuscripts, as well as printed texts, complicates any over-easy alignment of print with "publication" and manuscripts with the "private sphere." But for authors looking to reach a wider readership or to earn money by writing for "the public," the dramatic spread of printing "restructur[e]d rather than merely modif[ied]" the world of letters.[55]

Eighteenth-century readers increasingly encountered textual illustrations as well as visual materials such as maps, charts, atlases, diagrams, and

[52] On job printing, see Lisa Gitelman, "Print Culture (Other than Codex): Job Printing and Its Importance," in *Comparative Textual Media: Transforming the Humanities in the Post-Print Era*, ed. N. Katherine Hayles and Jessica Pressman (Minneapolis: University of Minnesota Press, 2013), 183–197.

[53] Michael Harris, *London Newspapers in the Age of Walpole: A Study of the Origins of the Modern English Press* (Cranbury, NJ: Associated University Presses, 1987), 19.

[54] Richard Steele, *The Tatler*, no. 1, 12 April 1709.

[55] Alvin Kernan, *Samuel Johnson and the Impact of Print* (Princeton: Princeton University Press, 1989) 9.

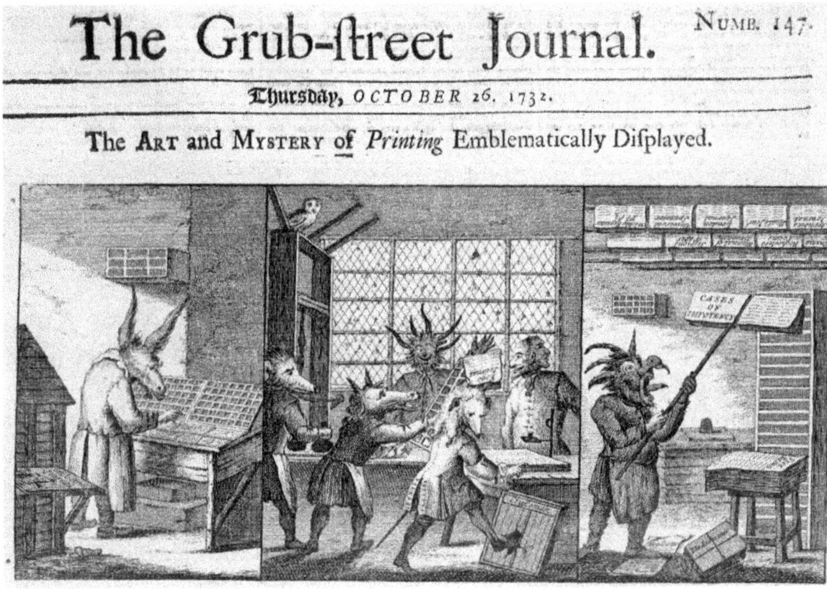

Figure 3.3 "The Art and Mystery of *Printing* Emblematically Displayed," *The Grub-Street Journal*, no. 147, October 26, 1732.

satirical prints. In 1732, the editors of the *Grub-Street Journal* printed a satiric engraving titled "The Art and Mystery of Printing Emblematically Displayed" (Figure 3.3). This engraving depicts the inside of a printing-house, with animals and monsters setting type, inking forms, pulling at the press, and hanging up freshly printed sheets to dry. On the left, a donkey compositor stands hunched over his cases of type (both "upper" and "lower" case). His long ears allow him to hear an "abundance of news," and his loud braying voice lets him spread it. On the right, a printer's devil hangs up a sheet of *Cases of Impotency*. This printing house appears to specialize in printing "rabble-rousing" political journals and scandalous publications, such as Lord Rochester's pornographic poems and excerpts from the Sessions Papers describing salacious criminal trials.

The eighteenth century also saw the rise of the novel and the development of circulating (lending) libraries. In the 1790s, the Minerva Press Library in London, established by publisher John Lane, advertised more than 20,000 titles. In the judgment of Martinus Scriblerus, Alexander Pope's fictional pedant in his mock-epic poem *The Dunciad*, "Providence … permitted the invention of Printing as a scourge for the sins of the learned," rather than as a tool for the betterment of humankind.[56] But significantly, in declaiming "against the Multitude of Writers whereof the whole Multitude of Writers most reasonably complains," authors such as Pope who excoriated the new literary marketplace also chose to exploit print themselves.

As William St. Clair has shown, intellectual property laws "had immense effects on the nature of the texts ... available for reading in the English-speaking world during the first three centuries of the age of print." After 1695, publishers worked to pass the first copyright law, the Statute of Anne (8 Ann. c. 21), which came into force in 1710. The decades from 1710 to 1774 were a "high monopoly period" characterized by the cartel-like power of major publishers.[57] But copyright laws were almost impossible to enforce, and in 1774, a decision in the House of Lords put a decisive end to the idea of perpetual copyright. Thousands of books previously subject to monopoly power were now available for reprinting, and new publishing opportunities fueled another major period of expansion in the trade. Publishers began producing series of "classic" literary works, and competitive markets led to lower prices, larger sales, and expanding readerships. By the turn of the nineteenth century – more than 300 years after William Caxton introduced a printing press to England in 1476 – Britain could finally be characterized as a "print society."

3 Theorizing the Impact of Print

Within decades of Gutenberg's inventions, presses were set up in major European cities such as Rome (1467), Venice (1469), Paris (1470), Kraków (1475), and London (1476), and the spread of printing in Europe coincided with the beginnings of exploration and colonization overseas. In 1539, Juan Pablos of Italy set up a press in Mexico City, the first in the Western hemisphere; he was sent there by Juan Cromberger of Spain. In 1556, Portuguese colonizers set up a press in Goa, on the southwest coast of India. Nearly a century later, English colonizers in Cambridge, Massachusetts printed the first book printed in British North America, *The Bay Psalm Book* (1640). The "meaning" of print was different in every geographical area and sociopolitical context. Many early presses were established by missionaries, for

[56] Alexander Pope, *The Dunciad in Four Books*, 1743, ed. Valerie Rumbold (New York: Longman – Pearson Education, 2009), 70.

[57] William St. Clair, *The Reading Nation in the Romantic Period* (Cambridge: Cambridge University Press., 2004), 53.

instance, and religious agendas (and the colonizers' preferred languages) shaped uses of and responses to printing. Once again, the "impact" of printing was determined by factors other than the technology itself.

Similarly, printing spread at different rates in different nations, geographical areas, and religious, political, and cultural communities. Printing spread slowly in China, for instance – a phenomenon attributable to a variety of factors. Most obviously, the vast number and complexity of characters in the Chinese language made producing a complete set of type a monumental task. Furthermore, as Kai-Wing Chow has pointed out, by the eleventh century, China already had an economically viable printing tradition that did not require movable type.[58] The continuing respect accorded to block printing (xylography) and the abundance of cheap labor and wood for carving made it more practical and economical for Chinese printers to continue to use this method. Along similar lines, the Arab Muslim world was long a "culture of the book," but printing "did not become a normal method of transmission … until the second half of the nineteenth century."[59] Some Muslims viewed printing as a threat to traditional systems of Islamic learning and print itself as a type of graphic image that was "potentially idolatrous,"[60] while others deemed calligraphic scripts aesthetically superior to early letterpress printing.

In the Anglophone world, too, multiple factors determined the reach of printing technology and its products – and especially which texts were available to non-elite readers. St. Clair describes the "historically specific techno-economic conjunctures" that shaped the availability of printed texts in Britain from the introduction of printing to the mid-nineteenth century.[61] Too often, we forget that the single most important factor shaping the "consequences" of printing is literacy. Before 1900 in Britain, there was little support for state-sponsored public education, and in rural areas as much as half the population could not read. In 1723, the philosopher Bernard Mandeville argued that schooling made sense for those likely to obtain careers where literacy was necessary. But for those "born to poverty, and the drudgeries of life,"[62] spending years learning how to read and write was a waste of time that should be devoted to the larger social good. Still,

58 Kai-Wing Chow, "Reinventing Gutenberg," in Baron et al., *Agent of Change*, 169–192.

59 Geoffrey Roper, "The Printing Press and Change in the Arab World," in Baron et al., *Agent of Change*, 250–267, at 265.

60 Baron et al., *Agent of Change*, 161.

61 St. Clair, *Reading Nation*, 24.

62 Mandeville, "An Essay on Charity, and Charity-Schools," 1723, repr. in *The Fable of the Bees, or Private Vices, Public Benefits*, ed. Philip Harth (Harmondsworth: Penguin, 1970), 261–325, at 294–295.

the spread of print itself encouraged new readerships, and over the course of the eighteenth century, older assumptions about literacy as an occupational tool were increasingly challenged by arguments anticipating our modern assumption that literacy is a universal good.[63]

For Moxon's partial contemporary Thomas Hobbes (1588–1679), "the Invention of *Printing*, though ingenious, compared with the invention of *Letters*, is no great matter."[64] Hobbes chose to circulate most of his writings in manuscript, and he viewed print chiefly as a way to circulate a few of his manuscripts more widely (rather than as medium with a profoundly different character). As Adrian Johns has suggested, the commercial and cultural success of printing could come only after the technology and its products had acquired an "air of intrinsic reliability."[65] Printers such as Moxon and market-oriented authors such as novelist and journalist Daniel Defoe (1660–1731) had the most to gain by encouraging the idea of the trustworthiness of print. Seventy-five years after Hobbes dismissed printing as essentially a new form of writing, Defoe declared that "the *Printing Art* has out-run the Pen, and may pass for the greatest Improvement of its Kind in the World."[66]

Defoe was the most prolific print author of his generation, and not coincidentally, he was also an ardent propagandist for print. In a 127-page work titled *An Essay Upon Literature: Or, an Enquiry into the Antiquity and Original of Letters* (1726), he contributed to the cultural elevation of the "Art of Printing" (291). Drawing on *Mechanick Exercises*, he mentioned pioneers in the history of printing (such as Caxton), and he noted developments in printing technology and related trades. But ultimately, Defoe was less interested in printing technology per se than in the question of its effects. As its full title suggests, Defoe's *Essay upon Literature* addresses the origins of "Letters," or writing. Although he advanced a scripture-based argument for the origins of letters (i.e., God gave writing to Moses at Mount Sinai), he also forged a new, stadial model of human communications that made room for the modern invention of printing. In Defoe's view, printing triggered massive, beneficial sociopolitical shifts and ushered in a new "Age" in the history of humankind.

63 Paula McDowell, "Why Fanny Can't Read: *Joseph Andrews* and the Irrelevance of Literacy," in *A Companion to the Eighteenth-Century English Novel and Culture*, ed. Paula R. Backscheider and Catherine Ingrassia (Maldon, MA and Oxford: Blackwell Publishing, 2005), 167–190.

64 Thomas Hobbes, *Leviathan* (London: Andrew Crooke, 1651), ch. 4, "Of Speech," par. 12, p. 24.

65 Johns, *Nature of the Book*, 3.

66 Daniel Defoe, *An Essay upon Literature: Or, an Enquiry into the Antiquity and Original of Letters*, 1726, repr. in *A General History of Discoveries and Improvements (1725–6) and An Essay upon Literature (1726)*, ed. P. N. Furbank (London: Pickering, 2001), 227–308, at 301.

In the later eighteenth century, Enlightenment moral philosophers developed this new model of human history. They proposed that human societies naturally progress through a succession of "stages" or "ages," each with its own institutions, economy, and social arrangements. Around the 1790s, we begin to detect the idea of communications technologies (especially the invention and spread of printing) as part of this unfolding sequence. Some stadial theorists suggested that shifts in communication practices and tools themselves triggered stages in human history. Edinburgh philosopher Dugald Stewart declared that "the invention of printing" was the "single event, independently of every other" that was "sufficient to change the whole course of human affairs." Anticipating our modern idea of "communications" media, Stewart asserted that "the means of communication afforded by the press, have, in the course of two centuries, accelerated the progress of the human mind."[67]

Meanwhile, across the English Channel, the fugitive philosopher Nicolas de Caritat, Marquis de Condorcet was penning his *Esquisse d'un tableau historique des progrès de l'esprit humain*. After he died in prison in suspicious circumstances, this work was published as *Sketch for a Historical Picture of the Progress of the Human Mind* (1795). Like Stewart, Condorcet divided human history into "ages," then systematically linked stages of social development to stages in the development of communications. As in Defoe's *Essay*, so in Condorcet's stadial history each new invention or major discovery seems to trigger or enable a new "age" or "stage." The "Seventh Stage" includes "the progress of science … to the invention of printing," and the "Eighth Stage" addresses human development "from the invention of printing to the time when philosophy and the sciences shook off the yoke of authority."[68] To be sure, fifteenth-, sixteenth-, and seventeenth-century authors such as Martin Luther, John Foxe, and Moxon also lauded printing technology. But by the later eighteenth century, meditations on the world-historical force of this still "new" communication technology are recognizable as a genre: a grouping of a distinct kind of text that I have called "histories of mediation."[69]

[67] Dugald Stewart, *Elements of the Philosophy of the Human Mind*, 1792, pt. 1, in *Collected Works*, ed. Sir William Hamilton, 11 vols. (Edinburgh: Thomas Constable, 1854–1860), 2: 242, and "Account of the Life and Writings of Adam Smith, LL.D," wr. *c.* 1790; read 1793, in *Works*, 10: 54.

[68] Condorcet, *Sketch for a Historical Picture of The Progress of the Human Mind [or Spirit]*, 1795, trans. June Barraclough, with an introduction by Stuart Hampshire (London: Weidenfeld and Nicolson, 1955), 89, 100.

[69] See Paula McDowell, "Defoe's *Essay Upon Literature* and Eighteenth-Century Histories of Mediation," *PMLA* 103, no. 3 (May 2015): 566–583.

Today, stadial models of communications developments have been naturalized to the point that we commonly speak of moving "from" one communications culture or era "to" another. In 1962, McLuhan popularized the term "print culture" as one among a series of such terms, including "oral culture," "scribal culture," the "Gutenberg era," and the "electronic age." Meanwhile, McLuhan's former student Walter J. Ong associated the spread of printing in Western Europe with cognitive, as well as sociopolitical, shifts. In a series of erudite works such as *Ramus, Method, and the Decay of Dialogue: From the Art of Discourse to the Art of Reason* (1958) and *Orality and Literacy: The Technologizing of the Word* (1982), Ong posited a relationship between the spread of letterpress printing and "new habits of organizing thought."[70] Just as a compositor lays out type on a page, he pointed out, so writing and printing commit words to visual space. Ong linked the development of typography to an epochal "shift in sensibility," as humans moved from "orality" to literacy. Words became things we see, not hear. In his view, the spread of printing technology "heightened the value of the visual imagination and … memory over the auditory imagination and … memory and made accessible a diagrammatic approach to knowledge."[71]

Like Ong, McLuhan held that printing had profound implications for the human psyche. In his bestselling books *The Gutenberg Galaxy: The Making of Typographic Man* (1962) and *Understanding Media: The Extensions of Man* (1964) – now often considered the founding texts of modern media studies – he argued that "technological environments are … active processes that reshape people."[72] Tools are "extensions" of our limbs and senses; in turn, "when the perverse ingenuity of man has outered some part of his being in material technology, his entire sense ratio is altered."[73] Both McLuhan and Ong especially valued oral/aural communication, and lamented what they saw as print's displacement of ancient rhetorical arts. But McLuhan claimed that the real problem in this was a lack of sufficient reflection on *any* of the social and cognitive consequences of technological change. "The theme of this book," he insisted in *The Gutenberg Galaxy*, "is

[70] Ong, *Ramus, Method, and the Decay of Dialogue: From the Art of Discourse to the Art of Reason*, Cambridge, MA: Harvard University Press, 1958; with new preface, 1983; with foreword by Adrian Johns (Chicago: University of Chicago Press, 2004), 313.

[71] Ong, *Rhetoric, Romance, and Technology: Studies in the Interaction of Expression and Culture* (Ithaca, NY: Cornell University Press, 1971), 167.

[72] Marshall McLuhan, *The Gutenberg Galaxy: The Making of Typographic Man* (Toronto: University of Toronto Press, 1962), Preface, n.p. See also *Understanding Media: The Extensions of Man* (1964; New York: Routledge, 2001).

[73] McLuhan, *Gutenberg Galaxy*, 265.

not that there is anything good or bad about print but the unconsciousness of the effect of any force is a disaster."[74]

Writing *The Gutenberg Galaxy* and *Understanding Media* in the late 1950s and early 1960s, before the publication of the detailed historical studies of printing that we rely on now, McLuhan drew heavily on literary works in forming his notions of the social, cultural, and (in his view) cognitive consequences of print. He especially drew on Pope's *Dunciad*, which he called one of "four massive myths of the Gutenberg transformation of society."[75] "It is to *The Dunciad*," he pronounced, "that we must turn for the epic of the printed word."[76] As we have seen, Pope satirized the emergence of "Grub Street" and the then-new practice of authors selling their works to the public for pay. The opening lines of the 1728 *Dunciad* announce Pope's mock-epic subject in brief: "BOOK and the man I sing, the first who brings / The *Smithfield* muses to the ears of kings."[77] The central action of *The Dunciad* is a giant yawn, as the Goddess Dulness spreads her hypnotic fog over Britain and puts everyone to sleep. Not coincidentally, McLuhan's dominant metaphor for what he called humankind's condition of "helpless unawareness" of the "effects inherent in our own technologies" was that of being asleep, hypnotized, or drugged.[78]

Pope never wrote about "print" or "printing" abstracted from particular human users. Nonetheless, McLuhan was not unjustified in describing *The Dunciad* as one of the "myths of the Gutenberg transformation of society." He suggested that Pope was prophesying some kind of total shift – not just satirizing particular people and practices relating to the spread of print. In later editions of *The Dunciad*, especially, Pope suggested that new human uses of printing technology were contributing to a total, hegemonic takeover of culture and institutions (political, educational, literary, and so on). As his fictional commentator Martinus Scriblerus observes, "the Crowd assembled in the second book, demonstrates the design to be more extensive than to bad poets only.... And the third book ... seemeth to embrace the whole world."[79] Yet Pope was no technological determinist. In Book III of *The Dunciad*, the mock-hero's vision of a future of Dulness passes

74 Ibid., 248.
75 Ibid., 147.
76 Ibid., 255.
77 Pope, *The Dunciad. An Heroic Poem. In Three Books* (Dublin [*sic, recte* London], Printed, London Reprinted for A. Dodd, 1728), ll. 1–2.
78 McLuhan, *Understanding Media*, 325; *Gutenberg Galaxy*, 350.
79 Pope, *The Dunciad*, ed. Rumbold, 73.

through ivory gates – an allusion to Virgil that suggests this nightmarish vision need not necessarily come to pass. Similarly, McLuhan insisted that "far from being deterministic … the present study will, it is hoped, elucidate a principal factor in social change which may lead to a genuine increase of human autonomy."[80] By recognizing our mutual constitution *of and by* technologies, he argued, we may be able "to emancipate ourselves from" our technologies' "subliminal operation."[81]

Since Eisenstein published *The Printing Press as an Agent of Change* forty years ago, historians and media theorists have relentlessly (and now routinely) critiqued technological determinism in assessing the consequences of printing technology. But as John Durham Peters has shrewdly observed, "it is a lot easier … to denounce technological determinism than to write a really good history of technics and civilization." Most importantly, Peters asks: "[A]t a time when the meaning of technics is indisputably one of the most essential questions facing our species, do we really want to make it an intellectual misdemeanor to ask big questions about 'technology' and its historical role, however ill-defined the category is?"[82]

*

The greatest printing feat of the Enlightenment was arguably the production of Diderot and d'Alembert's *Encyclopedia*.[83] The first reference work of its kind to include detailed entries on the mechanical or "useful" arts, the *Encyclopedia* includes entries for letter founding, presswork, papermaking, and other printing-related trades. Totaling twenty-eight volumes, including eleven volumes of lavishly engraved plates, the *Encyclopedia* is a monumental tribute to the arts of "*Typographie*." Nonetheless, some eighteenth-century purchasers complained about the printing of the work. They detected printers' inky fingerprints on their copies, and they did not want to see this kind of evidence of the makers' hands.[84] Today, the discovery of a printer's fingerprint on a text printed during the hand press period is a poignant (and exhilarating) reminder of hand press printing as an artisanal craft. Moxon's *Mechanick Exercises: … Applied to the Art of Printing* foregrounds "handy-work" as the essential element of the technology of the hand press. But to detect evidence of actual early modern

80 McLuhan, *Gutenberg Galaxy*, 3.
81 Ibid., 246.
82 Peters, "'You Mean My Whole Fallacy Is Wrong,'" 24.
83 On the printing of the *Encyclopedia*, see Robert Darnton, *The Business of Enlightenment: A Publishing History of the Encyclopédie 1775–1800* (Cambridge, MA: Harvard University Press – Belknap, 1979).
84 See Darnton, *Business of Enlightenment*, 228 n. 85.

printworkers' hands today, we need to closely examine original copies of the material texts that they produced.

In keeping with the Enlightenment goal of public science, Moxon published his argument for printing as "the Science of Sciences" in order to bring hitherto "conceal'd" craft knowledge into the open.[85] But ultimately, Moxon's pride in his profession made him emphasize to his genteel readers that book learning was no substitute for unwritten trade knowledge and "hands-on" experience. It was through making, rather than reading, that printers' bodies in a sense became their books, imprinted with irreplaceable somatic knowledge. Accordingly, it is time for us bring this chapter to a close; for ultimately, as this seventeenth-century master printer advised his readers, "the Art and Mystery of Printing" can only be learned through "*Practice and Exercise*": for "*Hand-Craft* signifies … *Craft* of the Hand, which cannot be taught by Words."[86]

[85] Moxon, *Mechanick Exercises*, 81.

[86] *Mechanick Exercises, or, The Doctrine of Handy-Works … of the Smiths Trade*, 3rd ed. 1703, Preface, n.p., font reversed.

CHAPTER 4

The Mechanical Press, 1800–1900

Simon Reader

In 1800, the fundamentals of printing technology had remained more or less unchanged for three centuries. Europeans still relied on the hand press to reproduce the printed word. They made paper from rags and by hand. They used relief and intaglio plates to create images in multiple. However, by 1900, print would become a fully mechanized and omnipresent part of everyday life in Europe and the colonized world. Machines would make paper. Machines would print words and images. In an interval of one hundred years, print was transformed, with shapely black letters covering territory at incredible speed, driven by the same technology that also propelled trains and ships. In the words of Aileen Fyfe, this was an era of "steam-powered knowledge."[1] Developments in printing occurred in tandem with other technologies – paper production, typecasting, wood engraving, and lithography – and along with mandated increases in public education in Britain. Thus the mass production of printed materials met a growing market of diverse consumers. Literary scholars addressing these developments face the challenge of connecting significant material transformations to their elusive effects on texts, writers, and readers.

The general tendency of such scholarship has been to complicate the thesis that more printing automatically improves democratic engagement. That thesis received its most detailed exposition in Elizabeth Eisenstein's *The Printing Press as an Agent of Change* (1979), the two volumes of which stop their survey before the nineteenth century begins.[2] They do not, therefore, take into account the full effect of mass production. Literary critics have been keen – especially after the interventions of Michel Foucault – to poke holes in triumphant narratives linking printing and politics, such as

[1] Aileen Fyfe, *Steam-Powered Knowledge: William Chambers and the Business of Publishing* (Chicago: University of Chicago Press, 2012).

[2] Elizabeth Eisenstein, *The Printing Press as an Agent of Change* (New York: Cambridge University Press, 1979).

the one Eisenstein offers, and to mitigate overstatements about the effects of this technology. Christian Thorne satirizes such triumphant narratives as follows: "Europe was once full of imbeciles; then came the printing press, and there were imbeciles no more; for with print came mass literacy, and with literacy came learning and with learning – it is here that the story gets hazy – came democratic self-fulfillment in some guise or another."[3] When it comes to studies of the machine press, an invention of direct service to industrial capitalism in the nineteenth century, the causal argument linking printing and democracy becomes more and more difficult to make. Quantity of print does not guarantee quality of citizenship.

While narratives of displacement should be treated with some skepticism, it is fair to say that machine printing presented a certain challenge to the supremacy of the book, that is, the bound codex so important to European culture in the Renaissance and Enlightenment.[4] From the nineteenth century on, the book would compete for public love with its younger and somewhat grubbier relations: the newspaper, the magazine, the advertisement, the poster, and even the wallpaper. None of these were invented in the nineteenth century, of course, but their production benefited greatly from the period's new technologies. The story of the machine press in this period arguably has journalism or advertising as a protagonist rather than literature, strictly speaking. As Matthew Rubery points out, "[w]hat we think of as the age of the novel was thought of by John Stuart Mill as 'the age of newspapers.'"[5] Print becomes inextricably tied to capitalist production and trade. The general claim in this chapter, then, is that a focus on technology reconfigures the questions scholars ask of literary texts from this period, bringing issues of media and the marketplace to the fore. Literary scholars wishing to assert the importance of machine printing must necessarily place texts in relation not only to other works of literature but also to competing media: journalism, advertising, and other products of the print industry. Much of the literary criticism about this period that takes technology as a starting point involves tracing these relationships.

I will proceed by outlining the basic technological innovations of printing in the nineteenth century. Then I will consider the ways in which these

[3] Christian Thorne, "Thumbing Our Nose at the Public Sphere: Satire, the Market, and the Invention of Literature," *PMLA*, 116.3 (2001): 531.

[4] See John Barnard, D. F. McKenzie, David McKitterick, and I. R. Willison, eds., *The Cambridge History of the Book in Britain I–V* (Cambridge: Cambridge University Press, 1999–2009).

[5] Matthew Rubery, *The Novelty of Newspapers: Victorian Fiction after the Invention of the News* (New York: Oxford University Press, 2009): 4.

innovations have been theoretically deployed to address a topic at once central and strangely orthogonal to literary studies: reading. What follows here pertains mainly to Great Britain. This is in part because of the limits of my expertise; readers interested in other histories will find a great deal of work by scholars on these subjects in North American and other contexts.[6] However, many studies of the printing press and its effects on literature and culture have been largely focused on Britain, and even on London in particular. As the center of industrial capitalism in the nineteenth century, Britain witnessed extraordinary developments in the manufacture of print and paper alongside all other products. In one sense, print may be considered a commodity like any other, but it also plays a special role in the sale and circulation of every other commodity: Blank forms, postage, ledgers, advertisements, instruction manuals, packaging, and even paper currency itself all grease the wheels of trade.[7] As we will see, the ubiquity of print and its commercialization was met with resistance from certain quarters as the nineteenth century drew to a close, with the glut of print becoming for some late Victorians a sign of cultural degeneration rather than progress.

1 Press, Paper, Prints

The wooden hand press remained dominant from the time of Gutenberg to the first decades of the nineteenth century. Compositors would painstakingly arrange type by hand in a flat surface. Printers inked the type, laid a page over it, and pressed this with a flat wooden plank. The process was slow going, advancing one sheet at a time. In or around the year 1800 (the precise date is not known), the Earl Stanhope invented a hand press made entirely out of iron, an advance that improved accuracy but did nothing for speed.[8] With the rise of steam-powered technology in other domains, however, the race was on to find a way to join this apparatus to the trade of printing. The solution came from Friedrich Koenig, who, with his engineer Andreas Bauer, created the first steam-powered *cylindrical* press about

[6] For other European contexts, see Guglielmo Cavallo and Roger Chartier, eds., *A History of Reading in the West*, (Cambridge: Polity Press, 1999); for the United States, see David D. Hall, *Cultures of Print: Essays in the History of the Book* (Amherst: University of Massachusetts Press, 1996); for considerations of print history across global contexts, see Sabrina Alcorn Baron, Eric N. Lindquist, and Eleanor F. Shevlin, eds., *Agent of Change: Print Culture Studies after Elizabeth L. Eisenstein* (Amherst and Boston: University of Massachusetts Press, 2007).

[7] Michael Twyman, *Printing 1770–1970: An Illustrated History of Its Development and Uses in England* (London: Eyre & Spottiswoode, 1970), 6.

[8] P. M. Handover, "British Book Typography," in *Book Typography 1815–1965*, ed. Kenneth Day (Chicago: University of Chicago Press, 1966), 141.

a decade into the nineteenth century. After Koenig, the presence of cylinders in printing machines would be the norm for nearly all such technology down to the present day, from the printing plant of the *New York Times* in twenty-first-century Queens, to the dusty inkjet printer sitting beside your desk at home. With the cylinder, paper could be fed continually over a bed of type rather than one sheet at a time.

The newspaper industry undoubtedly drove demand for and benefited the most from these advances. Indeed, it would be several decades before book presses fully embraced steam-powered cylinders in their operations.[9] November 1814 represents a watershed moment in this history, for this is when the *Times* newspaper of London installed steam-powered presses in its offices. The managers took this action in the dead of night, fearing reprisal by workers resisting automation.[10] (The trades of printing, typemaking, compositing, and other related industries had long been fiercely protected by proto-unions: guilds called "Chapels" that represented the interests of the laborers. There is a long history of such workers resisting – often successfully – the implementation of technological change.)[11] It seems, however, that no open protest occurred as a result of the new presses being installed. The public felt the significance of the change, with John Walter writing that the "combination of the cylinder and steam-power [is] the greatest improvement connected with printing since the discovery of the art itself."[12]

In describing the effects of these changes, accounts of printing technology in the nineteenth century often replicate the Victorian obsession with statistics. In turn, cultural critics seeking less numerical approaches to this history can occasionally belittle the use of numbers as a way of understanding it.[13] However, some of these figures are worth noting, even if they are constantly being adjusted and disputed by material historians. The hand press produces about 250 printed sheets of paper per hour. The early Koenig presses: 1,100 per hour. The cylindrical technology evolved until the presses comprised six or more giant cylinders in the same machine,

[9] Fyfe, *Steam-Powered Knowledge*, 7.

[10] David Finkelstein and Alistair McCleery, *An Introduction to Book History* (London: Routledge, 2013), 61.

[11] S. H. Steinberg, *Five Hundred Years of Printing* (Baltimore, MD: Penguin Books, 1974), 278. See also Finkelstein and McCleery, *An Introduction to Book History*, 61; Twyman, *Printing 1770–1970*, 10.

[12] Steinberg, *Five Hundred Years of Printing*, 280.

[13] William R. McKelvy, "'This Enormous Contagion of Paper and Print': Making Literary History in the Age of Steam," in *Bookish Histories*, ed. Ina Ferris and Paul Keen (New York: Palgrave Macmillan, 2009), 62.

with paper being fed from multiple entry points. With these advances, particularly those developed by Applegarth and Cowper, the number jumped to about 4,000 printed sheets per hour. By the end of the nineteenth century, a newspaper could print 24,000 copies of a twelve-page paper in an hour. Printers now measured paper in tons and miles rather than pounds and sheets.[14]

Over the course of the nineteenth century, presses took many different forms as competing inventors adapted Koenig and Bauer's patent in different directions. While very little remains in the way of technological artifacts from this period, textual and visual sources provide clues as to the range of inventions that could properly be called machine presses. Harold E. Sterne's *Catalogue of Nineteenth Century Printing Presses* includes beautiful etchings of approximately 150 more or less distinct machines that worked on cylinder and steam.[15] These ranged from the massive vertical cylindrical presses (which resemble giant, intricate insects) used to generate *The Times*, to the relatively small Treadwell press, which introduced a smaller-scale alternative to the Koenig for booksellers satisfied with reaching a smaller public.

The production of type also benefited from machine technology. Hand casting of type pieces was a slow process given the volume of characters needed to set any particular page. Working manually, 3,000 to 7,000 pieces of type could be cast by hand in a day.[16] The machine typecaster more than doubled these figures, producing between 12,000 and 20,000 pieces of type per day. The rates, predictably, continued to increase over the course of the century, so that by 1878 the Wicks Rotary typecaster generated 60,000 pieces of type in a single hour. The linotype machine, invented by Ottmar Mergenthaler in 1884, revolutionized the work of typecasting and compositing by combining these operations. At a linotype machine, a single operator would punch in complete lines of text, which would then be immediately cast from molten metal within the same device.[17] Generally speaking, type became increasingly aestheticized over the course of the nineteenth century, with typefaces being developed specifically for use in books, newspapers, and advertisements.[18] The look of newsprint changed dramatically, as columns of typographically neat print

[14] Steinberg, *Five Hundred Years of Printing*, 280; Twyman, *Printing 1770–1970*, 51–52.
[15] Harold E. Sterne, *Catalogue of Nineteenth Century Printing Presses* (Cincinnati, OH: Ye Olde Printery, 1978).
[16] Steinberg, *Five Hundred Years of Printing*, 281.
[17] For an entertaining overview of linotype technology, see *Linotype: The Film*. Dir. Douglas Wilson. (New York: FilmBuff, 2012).
[18] Handover, "British Book Typography," 140–141.

lay beside the distinct typefaces used for headlines and advertisements. Certain faces, such as Antique and Egyptian, arose directly in response to the demand for increasingly novel print in advertising.[19]

The accelerated production of type and print naturally increased demand for paper. In 1798, Nicolas Louis Robert invented a machine for the mechanical creation of paper at the Essonnes Mill in France. Robert created "the first successful model of a machine that made paper in an endless strip, or web."[20] Yet it was in England that this machine would be implemented on a large scale. The first mechanical paper makers established a mill in 1803 at Frogmore, Hertfordshire.[21] They were brothers: Henry and Sealy Fourdrinier, stationers and paper manufacturers from London. John Gamble, another entrepreneur, established a mill at St. Neots, Huntingdonshire. These machines increased the rate of production by a factor of ten. While 60 to 100 lb of paper might be made by hand in a paper mill in a single day, the new machinery produced up to 1,000 lb of paper in the same interval.[22] The price of paper dropped as a result, by about 25 percent by 1824 and 50 percent by 1843 (compared with the prices at the beginning of the century).[23] A pound of paper cost 1s 6d in 1800, 6½d in 1860, and 1d in 1900.[24] Yet the increased speed and volume of production meant an increasing – and increasingly unmet – demand for the raw material of paper: rags.

At the beginning of the nineteenth century, all paper was made from rags. This was still the case in 1849. The hunt for rags was big business; their circulation came with baroque regulations, taxes, and tariffs. Rags were rare and paper expensive. Gleaners of rag would go so far as to track warring armies in order to pillage soldiers' clothing when the smoke cleared. As William St. Clair writes, "the battlefields of Europe were picked over before the blood was dry for every scrap of cloth that could be sold in the rag fairs and on the international markets."[25] Newspapers occasionally printed apologies for curtailed editions owing to shortages of the materials needed for the production of paper.[26] As the book and news industries

19 Ibid., 140.
20 Philip Gaskell, *A New Introduction to Bibliography* (New Castle, DE: Oak Knoll Press, 1995), 216.
21 Steinberg, *Five Hundred Years of Printing*, 278.
22 Ibid.
23 Ibid.
24 Ibid.
25 William St. Clair, *The Reading Nation in the Romantic Period* (New York: Cambridge University Press, 2004), 178.
26 Nicholas Basbanes, *On Paper: The Everything of Its Two-Thousand-Year History* (New York: Alfred A. Knopf, 2013), 175.

demanded more and more paper to fuel their enterprise, alternative materials were sought for its manufacture.

There followed a period of wild experimentation in the middle of the century, during which paper might be made from "old ropes, mill-sweepings, and straw," with some proposals for rag substitutes including "coconuts, nettles, [and] rhubarb."[27] The challenge lay in the fact that not all organic materials have the chemical composition necessary for the production of paper. By the early 1860s, substitutes had emerged, principally in the form of esparto grass (native to southern Europe and North Africa) and wood chips. By the latter third of the nineteenth century, almost all paper derived from a mix of rags and these other substances.[28] The production of paper thus increased by a factor of sixty between 1800 and 1900. S. H. Steinberg records, "Annual paper production in the UK was 11,000 tons, all handmade, in 1800; it rose to 100,000 in 1860 when 96,000 tons were machine-made, and to 652,000 tons in 1900, when, again, only 4,000 tons were handmade."[29] As is often the case with mass production, an increase in quantity comes with a decrease in quality. Paper made from grass and wood chips disintegrates much more quickly than paper made from rags. As such, many of the paper products from the nineteenth century are more fragile than their older counterparts.

Technologies of the image ("prints" in the art-historical sense) made unimaginable strides in the late eighteenth and early nineteenth centuries, from the innovations of wood engravings in the late eighteenth century to the capacity to reproduce photographic images in the last third of the nineteenth. The full explication of these inventions (particularly of photography) remains well beyond the scope of this chapter, but two innovations are worth singling out briefly: the wood engraving and the lithograph. Charlotte Brontë begins *Jane Eyre* with Jane reading from Thomas Bewick's *A History of British Birds* (1797), a book famous for featuring the novel technology of wood engraving, an enormous improvement on its ancestor, the woodcut. The difference between cuts and engravings lies in the side of the wood used. Woodcuts follow the grain of a wooden plank and as such cannot easily render a curved line; wood engravings use the end of a wood block, where the grain does not impede the free movement of the tool. This latter technique thus allows for an astounding, almost photographic level of detail. The images in Jane's book catalyze her interest in its verbal

[27] Twyman, *Printing 1770–1970*, 50.
[28] Gaskell, *A New Introduction to Bibliography*, 222.
[29] Steinberg, *Five Hundred Years of Printing*, 278.

descriptions: "the letterpress thereof I cared little for, generally speaking; and yet there were certain introductory pages that, child as I was, I could not pass quite as a blank. They were those which treat of the haunts of sea-fowl; of 'the solitary rocks and promontories' by them only inhabited."[30] The level of realism made possible by Bewick's technique might be said to mirror the psychological detail with which Brontë renders her characters.

Lithography, especially as a way of disseminating photographs, would become the dominant medium for printed reproduction by the end of the nineteenth century. It was deployed in books, magazines, and newspapers, and also on commercial packaging such as boxes and tin cans. Lithography ("writing on stone") involves drawing directly onto a flat stone using a greasy crayon and treating the surface with chemical compounds, such that ink applied to the stone adheres only to the initial crayon image. A paper print can then be made. Lithography enabled high-quality and high-volume reproductions, and had become mechanized by 1875. More advances followed with the invention of offset lithography, which involves transferring the image from the stone to a rubber blanket that could bend around a cylinder and allow for rapid printing to paper or (as the inventor of offset lithography applied it) to tin cans. This technology remains in wide use today.

2 Reading

Scholars conventionally use the term "print culture" to describe the array of effects – social, political, economic, and aesthetic – produced by the technological advances described in the previous section. However, the term has recently come under critique by scholars such as Lisa Gitelman, Andrew Piper, and the Multigraph Collective, among others, because of its limitations and problematic connotations.[31] Animating these critiques is a desire to understand the printed word as one technology interacting with many others in a variegated media landscape, whether we are speaking of the sixteenth century or the nineteenth. Advances in printing, for example, need not entail the displacement of oral culture. As the Multigraph Collective explain, "To speak of shifting from an oral to a textual culture

[30] Charlotte Brontë, *Jane Eyre* (New York: Harper, 1899), 2.

[31] Lisa Gitelman, *Paper Knowledge: Toward a Media History of Documents* (Durham, NC, and London: Duke University Press, 2014), 7–9; The Multigraph Collective, *Interacting with Print: Elements of Reading in the Era of Print Saturation* (Chicago: University of Chicago Press, 2018), 10; Andrew Piper, *Dreaming in Books: The Making of the Bibliographic Imagination in the Romantic Age* (Chicago: University of Chicago Press, 2009), 128.

overlooks the extent to which conversations, lectures, sermons, and public readings persisted in the age of print and gained currency from their relationships with print."[32] It is not just oral culture that remains vibrant in the age of print, but also handwritten products. Piper, emphasizing the importance of manuscripts in eighteenth- and nineteenth-century German intellectual circles, describes "the *simultaneity* of various writing technologies within what we have traditionally called 'print culture.'"[33]

The resistance to the term "print culture" is generally accompanied by an explicit or implicit critique of the idea that society actually improved because of developments in printing technology. As Ina Ferris and Paul Keen note, "history unfolds in ways that are more complicated and generate more unintended consequences than progressivist narratives of the power of print can accommodate," pointing out the way that the printed word is "invoked as often in terms of disease as enlightenment."[34] With these words, Ferris and Keen call attention to the ways that the historical record is often ambivalent on the question of printing technologies' effects on people: Some commentators view it as a cause of cultural degeneration, while others see it as the vehicle for progress and democratic advancement. Given these caveats, then, how do scholars understand the effects these technologies had on readers, writers, and citizens in the nineteenth century?

In many ways, it is easier to describe the minutiae of printing techniques and to recite statistics than it is to interpret the effects these changes had on reading and readers. One conceptual advantage of the term "print culture" is that it widens the playing field of cultural analysis to include objects and activities that extend beyond the literary per se: As an object of study, it encourages investigations not only into the specifications of extinct machinery but also into the forms of attention, education, and entertainment this machinery sponsored. The desire to illuminate the history of reading has been acutely felt by historians and literary critics in recent decades. For those studying nineteenth-century Britain, this means coming to terms with the reality that most people in this period read more advertisements than they did pages of *Middlemarch*. As William St. Clair writes, "any study of the consequences of the reading of the past ought to consider the print which was actually read, not some modern selection, whether that selection is derived from judgments of canon or from other modern criteria."[35]

[32] Multigraph, *Interacting with Print*, 10.
[33] Piper, *Dreaming in Books*, 127.
[34] Ina Ferris and Paul Keen, "Introduction," in *Bookish Histories*, ed. Ina Ferris and Paul Keen (New York: Palgrave Macmillan, 2009), 4.
[35] St. Clair, *The Reading Nation*, 3.

St. Clair's monumental study *The Reading Nation in the Romantic Period* is the counterpart to another foundational text in the history of reading, Robert Altick's *The English Common Reader*.[36] Both of these works and many others that have followed take seriously the historical realities of print in the nineteenth century by focusing less on the "canon" of literature as it would be subsequently formed and more on the actual printed objects that captured people's attention. The methodology of the Stanford Literary Lab continues this work in a different vein by considering the range of titles readers actually purchased rather than the prestigious few that appear in our late twentieth-century and early twenty-first-century survey courses. For the Literary Lab as for St. Clair and Altick, making reading a primary object of study entails moving away from highly prized literary objects and toward the acts and events that characterize the world of readers in the larger culture.[37]

Reading, however, is very difficult to pin down – a fact that confronts any literary critic who aims to describe and interpret it. In her book *How To Do Things with Books in Victorian Britain*, Leah Price admits to an enormous "frustration" with the lack of empirical data about the mysterious act of textual absorption.[38] In response, she proposes to examine the uses to which books were put in the nineteenth century *other* than reading. "Reading elicits the most curiosity and leaves the least evidence," she writes: "any reception historian will sooner or later be maddened by the low proportion of traces left in books that are verbal. For every pencil mark in the margin, ten traces of wax or smoke; for every ink stain, ten drink spills."[39] Reading is hard to grasp: We may describe every aspect of a typecasting matrix or the chemical composition of a paperback, but just how and where these material contingencies eventuate in "reading" is difficult to say.

What we do know is that by the first third of the nineteenth century, drastic increases in the urban population drove the demand for more and more printed products. Men, women, and children were reading more than they ever had before.[40] They read books, newspapers, and periodicals,

[36] Robert Altick, *The English Common Reader: A Social History of the Mass Reading Public 1800–1900* (Chicago: University of Chicago Press, 1957).

[37] Mark Algee-Hewitt, "Stanford Literary Lab," Stanford Literary Lab, 2018, https://litlab.stanford.edu/ (accessed July 15, 2023).

[38] Leah Price, *How to Do Things with Books in Victorian Britain* (Princeton: Princeton University Press, 2012), 19.

[39] Ibid.

[40] St. Clair, *The Reading Nation*, 11.

to be sure, but the explosion of commerce and industry also "created the need for letterheads, invoices, receipts, statements, bills of lading, and other business printing which had in the past often been written by hand."[41] Add to these still more forms of printed matter such as postage stamps, checks, and even paper currency, and a heterogeneous picture of reading begins to emerge.

Thinkers of the day debated the value of reading and tried to determine the influence it exerted on people, particularly working-class people. The debates over the relationship between information overload and democratic engagement, so alive in the digital age, were already in full force by the last decades of the nineteenth century. This period saw the rise of panicked articles, diatribes, and lectures "devoted to answer the questions of how, why, and what readers were and should be reading," often announcing that the fate of society itself rested on the distribution and allocation of readerly attention.[42] In these assessments, reading is not an unqualified good. A quotation from *Macmillan's Magazine* of 1859 encapsulates the point: "it is this habit of ceaseless reading … that bodes so much danger to our modern system of enlightenment."[43] Thus the industrial age gave rise to fears among certain cultural conservatives (a term that meant something very different in the Victorian period from what it means now) that readers were becoming machines themselves, devouring print without reflecting adequately upon it. In addition, this led to utopian and dystopian fictions based on precisely these problems, projecting what Patrick Brantlinger calls "overbooked" or "bookless" futures.[44]

George Gissing spells out these complications with darkly comic verve in *New Grub Street* (1891), a triple-decker novel about the death of the triple-decker novel and the competitive literary marketplace in London at the end of the nineteenth century. In this world, hack writers of trendy articles vie for public attention with novelists of high ethical motivations, the latter of whom seek to preserve the tradition of Dickens or George Eliot or the Brontës in a world where piecemeal sensation defines the rhythm of the marketplace. In a particularly funny scene, the character Whelpdale – a former writer who has established a business to assist clients

[41] Twyman, *Printing 1770–1970*, 14.

[42] Kelly Mays, "The Disease of Reading and Victorian Periodicals," in *Literature in the Marketplace: Nineteenth-Century British Publishing and Reading Practices*, ed. John O. Jordan and Robert L. Patten (Cambridge and New York: Cambridge University Press, 1995), 166.

[43] Ibid., 170.

[44] Patrick Brantlinger, *The Reading Lesson: The Threat of Mass Literacy in Nineteenth Century British Fiction* (Bloomington: Indiana University Press, 1998), 192.

in publishing and editing novels – announces to his friends his plans to start a magazine called "*chit-chat*":

> I would have the paper address itself to the quarter-educated; that is to say, the great new generation that is being turned out by the Board schools, the young men and women who can just read, but are incapable of sustained attention. People of this kind want something to occupy them in trains and on 'buses and trams. As a rule they care for no newspapers except the Sunday ones; what they want is the lightest and frothiest of chit-chatty information – bits of stories, bits of description, bits of scandal, bits of jokes, bits of statistics, bits of foolery. Am I not right? Everything must be very short, two inches at the utmost; their attention can't sustain itself beyond two inches. Even chat is too solid for them: they want chit-chat.[45]

Confronting the "quarter-educated" readers of Britain, the writers depicted in *New Grub Street* have to develop saleable products if they are to survive. Gissing contrasts characters such as Whelpdale with those still holding tenaciously to the aesthetic and ethical protocols of the realist novel. Yet these highfalutin writers are doomed to failure in Gissing's universe. In a world where print is so common as to have become a background hum of daily life, present in nearly every private room and public space, seizing the attention of a reader increasingly means offering immediate, tantalizing gratifications.

The spread of sensational publications went hand in hand with a documentary doubling of events in the world, as the speed and volume of news production gave rise to a way of life in which less time separated events and printed accounts of those events. Print increasingly mirrored phenomena as they transpired, such that ideas of what the "present" meant were in large part defined by news media. Print journalism both responded to and produced a market for novelty, catering to a reading population eager to believe that dramatic changes to the world lay around every corner.[46] These forms embody the strange hybrid of documentary and suspense that Mark Seltzer sees as a signature aspect of modern life; what he calls "the official world."[47] As Seltzer puts it, "[a] modern world is a self-conditioning and self-reporting one. If, prior to the nineteenth century, society could not describe itself,

[45] George Gissing, *New Grub Street* (New York: Oxford University Press, 2016), 407. On "*chit-chat*" as a parody of the real publication *Tit-Bits*, see Richard Menke, "Touchstone and Tit-Bits: Extracting Culture in the 1880s," *Victorian Periodicals Review* 47.4 (2014), 559–576.

[46] On the role of "present" in Victorian literature and culture, see Richard Altick, *The Presence of the Present: Topics of the Day in the Victorian Novel* (Columbus: The Ohio State University Press, 1957).

[47] Mark Seltzer, *The Official World* (Durham, NC, and London: Duke University Press, 2016).

now it cannot stop describing itself."[48] This aspect of nineteenth-century journalism has only increased in the last two hundred years.

Advertising made up no small share of printed matter in this period and no doubt contributed – then as now – to a sense of discomfort with what reading had become. Advertisements became bigger, more lurid, decked out in seductive typefaces, taking over the visual field of urban areas.[49] John Parry's famous 1835 watercolor, "London Street Scene," depicts a brick wall almost entirely covered by overlapping printed advertisements for politicians, plays, variety shows, haberdashers, and shaving products. Human figures stand or sit in the foreground as if they are themselves merely illustrations in the folds of a giant magazine, small elements in a massive print collage. Advertisers also distributed vast quantities of ephemera in the form of bills or pamphlets, and they would clog the streets in order to "thrust bills into the hands of passers-by at street-corners, railway stations, and other vantage points."[50] These forms of printed matter and slips circulating beyond the book or the newspaper suggest a kind of half-reading incited by this explosion of the ornate but disposable printed word, which captures visual as much as verbal interest.

The expanded presence of advertising and ephemera may be usefully viewed as part of what Rolf Engelsing famously (and controversially) terms the transition from intensive to extensive reading.[51] Engelsing describes "a late eighteenth-century shift from the rereading of a few prized texts to the consumption of many ephemeral ones."[52] Just as rag paper was more durable than the wood chip and esparto grass products of the later nineteenth century, so too was there an awareness of greater disposability of print.[53] People collected more and more print, but the general trend involved spending less time with any one collection of words. The trend continues to this day. To citizens of the twentieth and twenty-first centuries, the label "well-read" usually refers to the quantity of material a person has absorbed, rather than the quality of any particular act of reading.

These alterations in the volume of print and its uncertain effect on reading incited untold amounts of political angst. William Hazlitt, the late Romantic essayist, saw that revolutionary politics may be keyed to

48 Ibid., 6.

49 Twyman, *Printing 1770–1970*, 10–14.

50 Ibid., 12.

51 Rolf Engelsing, "Die Perioden der Lesergeschichte in der Neuzeit," *Archiv für geschichte des Buchwesens* 10 (1970): 945–1002.

52 Price, "Reading: The State of the Discipline," *Book History* 7 (2004): 317.

53 Price, *How to Do Things*, 219–257.

the circulation of print: "the French Revolution might be described as the remote but inevitable result of the invention of the art of printing."[54] Compared with the handmade books of previous eras, Hazlitt opined, the mass printed ones of his day had "a million times the range and power."[55] For Hazlitt and others in the early nineteenth century, machine print carried with it a certain democratic and even a radical potential. But some later Victorian artists, writers, and bookmakers took the opposite view, investing in the potentially radical possibility of returning to an earlier moment of printing technology.

By the latter third of the nineteenth century, the correlation of the volume of print with the quality of a democracy, suggested by Hazlitt, met opposition from Victorian sages such as John Ruskin and William Morris, who also sought to enhance democratic potentials but by means of a different relationship with books and print. In *Sesame and Lilies*, a set of two lectures delivered in Manchester in 1864, Ruskin implicitly laments the surplus of printed matter in his time: "[t]here are good books for the hour, and good ones for all time," he writes: "we none of us need many books, and those which we need ought to be clearly printed, on the best paper, and strongly bound."[56] Ruskin and his followers advocated *quality* of printing and reading over *quantity* of either as the best way to improve and democratize society.

In an age of mass production, handmade products of all kinds take on an alluring aura. Thus a movement took shape in late Victorian socialist culture that advocated returning to an earlier moment where social harmony prevailed as a direct result of nonalienated labor. For thinkers such as Morris – the poet, novelist, essayist, craftsman, and printer – this social idealism found an emblem in the handprinted book itself. In her study of Morris and like-minded printers, *Slow Print: Literary Radicalism and Late Victorian Print Culture*, Elizabeth Carolyn Miller outlines the contours of this counter-movement against the machine press: "The print community that emerged in British radical circles during these years directed itself, for better or worse, to a small-scale audience, a political and aesthetic counterculture, a public that defined itself against mass-oriented, mainstream print culture."[57]

[54] Andrew Franta, *Romanticism and the Rise of the Mass Public* (Cambridge: Cambridge University Press, 2007), 137.

[55] Ibid., 137.

[56] John Ruskin, *Sesame and Lilies* (New Haven and London: Yale University Press, 2002), 11.

[57] Elizabeth Carolyn Miller, *Slow Print: Literary Radicalism and Late Victorian Print Culture* (Palo Alto, CA: Stanford University Press, 2013), 3.

Miller writes "for better or worse" in order to emphasize the democratic contradictions faced by mass-produced print and the countermovements against it. Voluminous print and innumerable readers might seem to be a good thing for democratic engagement, but this also leaves the population vulnerable to manipulation and commercial bombardment. Small-scale printing, these artisans believed, restored humanity and humility to the practice of distributing letters and images. However, their valorization of the handmade risked consolidating cultural power in the hands of an aesthetic elite. Like the contemporary "slow food" movement that Miller's title evokes, the nostalgic Luddism of Morris and his peers may have served to harden lines of privilege rather than to break them down. Not everyone has the leisure to grow turnips one by one – or to print sheets one at a time.

In her recent essay "The Printing Press as Metaphor," Elyse Graham cautions against using the printing press to analogize contemporary digital technology, identifying the ways in which this metaphor supports "market imperatives."[58] In the contemporary world, however, it may be impossible to look back on earlier technological eras without the mediation – literal and figurative – of our screens. Whether or not the machine press offers an appropriate historical antecedent to the internet, the ready mixture of printed forms that we find in its products – books, advertisements, journalism, and highly detailed images – presents opportunities for aesthetic and formal analyses that go beyond material description or even the literary per se. It should also strike us that the discourses and debates about the effects of these technologies on democracy remain strikingly familiar, with overstated optimism on the one hand meeting skepticism and resistance on the other.

[58] Elyse Graham, "The Printing Press as Metaphor," *Digital Humanities Quarterly* 10.3 (2016): www.digitalhumanities.org/dhq/vol/10/3/000264/000264.html (accessed July 15, 2023).

CHAPTER 5

The Typewriter

Darren Wershler

"Typewriter" makes it all sound so simple. But the truth of the word is much more complex.

Many scholarly books and articles have been written on various aspects of typewriters and typewriting over the last few decades. A brief chapter like this can't do justice to the wealth of history and theory contained in these rewarding texts, but the ones that have had the greatest influence on my own thinking about typewriting, both before and after I wrote *The Iron Whim*,[1] are worth listing before going any further: Scott Bukatman's "Gibson's Typewriter+";[2] Vilém Flusser's "The Gesture of Writing";[3] Lisa Gitelman's *Scripts, Grooves, and Writing Machines*;[4] Christopher Keep's "The Cultural Work of the Type-Writer Girl";[5] Friedrich Kittler's *Gramophone, Film, Typewriter*,[6] and "Dracula's Legacy";[7] Thomas S. Mullaney's *The Chinese Typewriter*;[8] Jennifer Wicke's "Vampiric Typewriting: *Dracula* and Its Media";[9] and, from several decades earlier, Marshall McLuhan's "Into the Age of the Iron Whim," his chapter on

[1] Darren Wershler, *The Iron Whim: A Fragmented History of Typewriting* (Ithaca, NY: Cornell University Press, 2007).

[2] Scott Bukatman, "Gibson's Typewriter+," *South Atlantic Quarterly* 92.4 (1993): 627–645.

[3] Vilém Flusser, "The Gesture of Writing," *Flusser Studies* 08 (May 2009): www.flusserstudies.net/pag/08/the-gesture-of-writing.pdf (accessed July 15, 2023).

[4] Lisa Gitelman, *Scripts, Grooves, and Writing Machines: Representing Technology in the Edison Era* (Stanford, CA: Stanford University Press, 1999).

[5] Christopher Keep, "The Cultural Work of the Type-Writer Girl," *Victorian Studies* 40.3 (Spring 1997): 401–427.

[6] Friedrich A Kittler, *Gramophone, Film, Typewriter*, trans. Geoffrey Winthrop-Young and Michael Wutz (Stanford, CA: Stanford University Press, 1999).

[7] Friedrich A. Kittler, "Dracula's Legacy," in *Literature, Media, Information Systems: Essays* (Amsterdam: G+B Arts International, 1997), 50–85.

[8] Thomas S. Mullaney, *The Chinese Typewriter: A History* (Cambridge, MA: MIT Press, 2017).

[9] Jennifer Wicke, "Vampiric Typewriting: *Dracula* and Its Media," *ELH* 59.2 (Summer 1992): 467–493.

the typewriter in *Understanding Media*.[10] In a theoretical context, Kittler's work casts a long shadow over the subject, but there are also significant problems with his arguments that scholars could address in a productive fashion. Gitelman and Mullaney are the exemplary media historians in this list, and their work should serve as inspirations for how scholars might add depth, nuance, and fine detail to our understanding of specific temporal and geographic aspects of typewriting.

What's left to do at a cultural moment when representations of typewriters still abound, but most people have never touched one? Turning typewriting into a hauntological thematics for literary and cultural interpretation might be amusing,[11] but would leave the analysis on the symbolic level. Precisely in order to avoid this problem, most extant typewriting theory relies on some mixture of discursive analysis and material media history for its methodology. What I want to argue is that this powerful combination could be expanded to take the relatively recent refinements of cultural technique theory into account. To do the topic justice, we need a circuit of sorts that considers typewriting's various aspects. In this chapter, I'm going to sketch out a framework that might help scholars interested in the subject to delineate the cultural significance of any particular instance of typewriting.

No matter how smoothly its components fit together, "the typewriter" is always an assemblage. Its various interlocking components include the *material technologies* at work in the act of typewriting; a set of *cultural techniques* that manage the production and operation of those technologies, and of the writing that they produce; and the *discourse* that determines what it is possible to say (or not say) about any of the above. With a sense of the way these components are articulated at a particular time and place, it's also possible think about the *subjects that are produced* as a result of being trained by specific institutions to use the technologies and techniques that typewriting affords.

[10] Marshall McLuhan, "Into the Age of the Iron Whim," in *Understanding Media: The Extensions of Man*, 2nd ed. (New York: Signet Classics, 1964), 227–232.

[11] Derrida's notion of hauntology from *Specters of Marx* (New York: Routledge, 2012) has developed a certain currency in the early twenty-first century, especially following the popularity of the work of Mark Fisher (see esp. Mark Fisher, *K-Punk: The Collected and Unpublished Writing of Mark Fisher, 2004–2016* (New York: repeater, 2018), 715 et passim; and *Ghosts of My Life: Writings on Depression, Hauntology and Lost Futures* (Alresford: Zero Books, 2014, 107 et passim)). In practice, the theoretical concept of hauntology loses efficacy by becoming a thematics in which critics list cultural objects and describe their hauntological feel. For a more nuanced media-historical take, see Jeffrey Sconce, *Haunted Media: Electronic Presence from Telegraphy to Television* (Durham, NC: Duke University Press, 2000).

1 Discourse Analysis

For most literary scholars, discourse analysis is the most familiar of the analytic methods I've just mentioned – and it was really the only one I was taught when writing *The Iron Whim* as a doctoral student in an English department (albeit a heavily "theoretical" one) at the turn of the millennium. In the work of Michel Foucault, discourse is the system of regularities that defines what it is possible to say or not say about a subject at a given time and place. While discursive analysis moved humanists (including literary scholars) away from a strict focus on sign systems to the matter of how and why that content was produced, and according to which modalities of power, it doesn't go far enough into the externalities of discourse to allow us to say everything we need to say about typewriting. This is Kittler's insight at the end of *Discourse Networks 1800/1900*: "discourse-analytic studies had trouble only with periods whose data-processing methods destroyed the alphabetic storage and transmission monopoly, that old-European basis of power. Foucault's historical research did not progress much beyond 1850."[12] Foucault has plenty to offer about the techniques of power-knowledge that produce discursive regularities, and some about the nondiscursive (material) environments in which such processes occur,[13] but only a few lines about the role of material technologies in the flurry of typewriting's production.

In a discursive analysis of typewriting, the arrangement of letters on the typewriter keyboard is a good a place to start. Most people who have ever typed already know something about that discourse, because they have been trained to recite its visible aspects like a kind of technological catechism. Since it first appeared on the Scholes and Glidden Type-Writer in 1874, the order of the top row of keys on most English-language typewriter keyboards has been Q-W-E-R-T-Y-U-I-O-P, or QWERTY for short. The logic of QWERTY is so ingrained, even today, that it has become a metonymy for the discursive formation of typewriting itself in its mature modern form (viz. the title of Torbjörn Lundmark's *Quirky Qwerty: A Biography of the Typewriter & Its Many Characters*).[14] When referring to QWERTY, many sources even deign to call it "universal," despite plenty of evidence to

[12] Friedrich A Kittler. *Discourse Networks 1800/1900*, trans. Michael Metteer, with Chris Cullens (Stanford, CA: Stanford University Press, 1990), 369.

[13] Gilles Deleuze, *Foucault*, trans. and ed. Seán Hand (Minneapolis: University of Minnesota Press, 1988), 31.

[14] Torbjörn Lundmark, *Quirky Qwerty: A Biography of the Typewriter & Its Many Characters* (New York: Penguin, 2002).

the contrary. Indeed, the Herkimer County Historical Society's *The Story of the Typewriter* (an early popular history of the machine) smugly declares that "The universal keyboard has a hold similar to that of language itself."[15] In order to understand why such claims appear in the first place, it's necessary to employ a tool that allows us to identify something else about them: the statements that combine to form a discourse.

One of Foucault's own examples of a discursive statement, conveniently, is the keys on the top row of a French typewriter keyboard. The letters marked on a keyboard, he writes, are not statements, either on their own or listed in series: "at most they are tools with which one can write statements."[16] The same series of letters, listed in a typewriting manual, is the statement of the order adopted by a given sort of typewriter, a statement that outlines the order that the keys have been placed in according to a certain logic (whether or not that logic is faulty is irrelevant).[17] Deleuze provides a helpful gloss on this passage. He refers to both the keyboard and the letters on the keys themselves as points in space, or "visibilities." The statement is the thing that "actualizes relations" between those points in order to make a specific kind of sense out of them. This statement may strongly resemble the visibilities that it connects "to the point of being virtually identical" with them, but it's not the same thing. The purpose of the statement is to diagram the network of rules, possible positions, correlations, ordering processes, functions, and transformations that determine what, for example, typewriting can (and can't) say at a given place and time.[18]

Foucault's example has everything to do with why the notion of a "universal keyboard" in popular typewriting histories is far from universal, but part of an historically and geographically specific argument about technology, progress, and modernity. That is, QWERTY is yet another entry in the discourse of US technological exceptionalism. The order of top-row keys that Foucault describes in *The Archaeology of Knowledge* is not QWERTY, of course, but AZERT,[19] because he has in mind a French typewriter. Neither set of keys constitutes a word, nor are they entirely random sequences, nor can one be swapped for the other. Both are statements from different discourse networks – we might as well call them QWERTY and AZERT.

[15] Herkimer County Historical Society, *The Story of the Typewriter 1873–1923* (Herkimer, NY: Herkimer County Historical Society, 1923), 68.

[16] Michel Foucault, *The Archaeology of Knowledge and the Discourse on Language*, trans. A. M. Sheridan Smith (New York: Pantheon Books, [1969] 1972), 85.

[17] Ibid., 88.

[18] Deleuze, *Foucault*, 79.

[19] Foucault, *Archaeology*, 86.

Some of the statements that a discursive analysis might extract from either sequence are similar: Owing to mechanical limitations, it was once necessary to order keys in a certain way to keep type lugs from jamming together when typing at high speed; typing at high speed is an inherently good thing because it is efficient. Such statements are part of the discursive formation of typewriting in general, and pertain to the thinking that makes the machine itself a necessity. However, although some objects, people, and institutions may be common to both networks, the articulations between them are different, reflecting different regimes of power, intellectual and theoretical traditions, different canons, different national histories, and different institutions that use different sets of techniques for the training and production of subjects. Other statements produced in QWERTY and AZERT will differ considerably. French and English have different frequencies of letter appearance, which will affect choices in keyboard layouts, as will differing manufacturing philosophies of various companies in respectively French- and English-speaking nations. One of the remaining tasks for scholars working with discourse analysis is to parse these differences. Rather than an overarching mythology, we need a range of historically and geographically specific archaeologies of twentieth-century typewriting – for example, QZERTY in Italy (there is a growing critical literature on Olivetti, a major producer of typewriters), Katakana in Japan, QWERTZ in Switzerland and central Europe, and so on, in as much detail as the archives will allow. Crucially, we also need to think beyond the logic of QWERTY and company, to understand that what it has excluded also turns out to be enormous (see the next section, "Material Technological History").

Discursive analysis is helpful when thinking about typewriters and typewriting because it can track the shifts that occur across epistemological breaks. What typewriting meant when it was at the height of its influence is not what it means at the time of this writing. A combination of nostalgia (typing hipsters in coffee shops) and the ever-increasing distance from the mundane operation of typewriters accentuates this difference. One of the central arguments in *The Iron Whim* is that the discursive relationship between typewriting and writing the truth has changed in significant ways. From the perspective of the US cultural elite, typewriting was often associated with a mechanical inferiority of imagination and fallibility, as epitomized by Truman Capote's famous dismissal of Jack Kerouac's prose as typing rather than writing.[20] But over the course of the

[20] Wershler, *The Iron Whim*, 243.

twentieth century, snobbery like Capote's, which implicitly supported an older, romantic notion of the individual writer as a special sensitive soul rather than a worker crafting text, became the exception rather than the rule. More often than not, twentieth-century literary and popular culture position typewriting as part of the discourses of modernity and technological progress. From this perspective, typewriting becomes a powerful technique for the production of various kinds of truth. As a quick example, think about every movie you've ever seen where a solitary figure sits down at the typewriter to document "what really happened" as the story begins to unfold. The opening of *Lemony Snicket's A Series of Unfortunate Events* is stereotypical in this respect,[21] as is Jack Torrance's infamous novel typescript in Stanley Kubrick's *The Shining*,[22] which tells the terrifying truth about his mental state.

There are two probable reasons for the persistence in typewriting discourse of the notion that typewriting produces truth. One is the relative certainty of mechanical operation versus the inscrutability of computing. Normative typewriting practices strongly connote the idea that writing is a logical, intentional act, because of the relative simplicity of the mechanism: Pressing a key moves a lever or two, which brings an inked key down on a sheet of paper, producing a letter. For Italian Futurists Bruno Corradini and Emilio Settimelli, a functioning typewriter was the epitome of empirical reason by virtue of its construction:

> if one key is pressed it must write in lower case; if the shift and another key are pressed, it follows that it must write in upper case; when the space-bar is pressed, it must go back. For a typewriter to have its E pressed and to write an X would be nonsensical. A broken key is an attack of violent insanity.[23]

On many machines, the typing process was observable, and the result of the key press was immediately verifiable. Indeed, since at least 1875, when typewriter marketing discourse began to use the word "visible" to describe machines where typists could actually see the words they were typing on the page as they typed them (the Fitch, patented in 1875, and the Horton, in 1883;[24] and then a long string of successful Underwoods after the no. 1

[21] Brad Silberling, dir., *Lemony Snicket's A Series of Unfortunate Events*, screenplay by Robert Gordon (Dreamworks Pictures, 2004).

[22] Stanley Kubrick, dir., *The Shining*, screenplay by Stanley Kubrick and Diane Johnson, (The Producer Circle Company/Peregrine Productions/Hawk Films, 1980).

[23] Bruno Corradini and Emilio Settimelli, "Weights, Measures and Prices of Artistic Genius," 1914, repr. in *Futurist Manifestoes*, ed. Umbro Appolonio, trans. Robert Brain, R. W. Flint, J. C. Higgitt, and Caroline Tisdall (New York: The Viking Press, 1973), 136.

[24] "Some Unsuccessful Typewriters," *The Illustrated Phonographic World*, 10.4 (December 1894): 90–91.

in 1897, along with machines manufactured by various competitors with the word "visible" in their names), this verifiability had been a strong selling point. By contrast, processing on a computer takes place on a scale too small and too fast to be observed with the naked eye. Further, the relationship between a keystroke and its result is anything but fixed. Whether typing the W key produces the letter W on screen, moves your avatar slightly forward, or closes your document window depends on the software the computer happens to be running at the time.

Another reason that typewriting discourse associates typing with the production of truth has to do with the structure of dictation. I deal with this subject extensively in *The Iron Whim*,[25] building on the philosophical model that Avital Ronell describes in *Dictations: On Haunted Writing*.[26] The scene of typewriting needs to be treated as an assemblage because for much of its early history, typewriting was not a solo act: A writer spoke, and an amanuensis (or amanuenses) typed their words into a machine (or machines). Later, as Lisa Gitelman has detailed, electromechanical media such as the telegraph and phonograph added the possibility of time-axis manipulation to the typewriting assemblage by recording and storing the speech of the dictator.[27] This did away with the need for copresence during typewriting, because the dictating voice could operate at a different time and place, and be played (and played back) by the amanuensis at their convenience. The person in the dictating position or the typing position could change, and the machine could be swapped out, but the flow of writing from the assemblage would continue, and writing would still appear, with no evidence of such changes to the assemblage in the final product.

Time-axis manipulation in typewritten dictation is the relative beginning of the infamous "haunted" quality of typewriting discourse. As John Durham Peters explains in *Speaking into the Air,* "The word, voice or image of a person dead or distant channeling through a delicate medium: this is the project common to electronic media and spiritualist communication. Indeed, all mediated communication is in a sense communication with the dead, insofar as media can store 'phantasms of the living' for playback after death."[28] Unsurprisingly, then, in many well-documented cases, it was not uncommon for the amanuensis to continue receiving dictation even after the writer they worked with had died. The example I discuss at length in

[25] Wershler, *The Iron Whim*, 73–118.

[26] Avital Ronell, *Dictations: On Haunted Writing* (Lincoln: University of Nebraska Press, 1989).

[27] Gitelman, *Scripts, Grooves*, 188, 192.

[28] John Durham Peters, *Speaking into the Air: A History of the Idea of Communication* (Chicago: University of Chicago Press, 2012), 140.

The Iron Whim is the relationship between Henry James and his best-known amanuensis, Theodora Bosanquet, who continued to transcribe messages from James after his death, along with texts from the ghosts of his brother William James, George Meredith, Thomas Hardy, and John Galsworthy, among other spirits.[29] Even among late-twentieth-century solitary typists, the discourse of mediumship remains strong. From William S. Burroughs to Paul Auster, typists and their characters often describe themselves as receivers of texts from elsewhere. So paradoxically, typewritten texts feel objective and true because they aren't really "ours." They originate with some external authority, the muses of the electromechanical age: aliens, ghosts … or, in more mundane circumstances, your boss, who is dictating a letter to you.

What these examples show is that a Foucauldian discursive-analytic approach to typewriting has been rewarding because the typewriting assemblage is shot through with power relations. Most typewriting scholars have noted at some point that the word "typewriter" itself is a constant reminder of this fact, because it used to refer to the typist, not the machine, and for most of the twentieth century, the typist was a woman, while the person composing the writing and dictating it, either in person or via some sort of intermediary recording device, was a man. Many sorts of resistances, ambivalences, and complexities occur in this scenario, but the scene of typewriting is never free from some form of agonism.

It's one thing to recognize, as Deleuze does, that in Foucault's thinking, technology is social before it is technical,[30] but it's another thing to give the nondiscursive aspect of technology short shrift. Producing an "archaeology of the present" also requires attention to the material functions of technological media in operation:[31] data storage, calculation, transmission, and playback.

2 Material Technological History

Lisa Gitelman's concise definition of media as "socially realized structures of communication, where structures include both technological forms and their associated protocols, and where communication is a cultural practice" means that for any given instance of typewriting, we also need to consider the operation of particular material technological forms arranged

[29] Wershler, *The Iron Whim*, 95–104.
[30] Deleuze, *Foucault*, 40.
[31] Kittler, *Discourse Networks 1800/1900*, 369.

in specific material formats as well as discourse.[32] That being said, writing a material media history of the typewriter *in general* is next to impossible because in terms of its material technology, "the typewriter" is not a coherent object.

To complicate matters, as I've already pointed out, typewriting is an assemblage that can and does connect to other technological forms, with their own histories and discourses. Most histories of the typewriter necessarily include reference to a range of other technologies that bear a family resemblance to typewriting: pantographs and other scribing devices,[33] movable type, mechanical automata, jacquard looms, punch card machines, coding devices, Linotypes, and so on.[34] Though they are part of the story of typewriting, these technologies also have histories of their own, and it would be a mistake to relegate them solely to the history of typewriting, as though typing were their culmination.

This is one of the major shortcomings of Kittler's work on the typewriter, which he conflates first with the ENIGMA coding device and then with computing. As I explain in *The Iron Whim*,[35] what Gitelman calls technological form, or what Manuel De Landa calls the engineering diagram of the typewriter – a series of fixed mechanical levers and keys – is totally different than that of the Enigma cryptographic machine, which is based on a series of movable electrical rotors. The presence of a keyboard as an interface for the Enigma, or a computer, for that matter (which again has an entirely different engineering diagram), is provisional; other interfaces for the Enigma were possible, and other interfaces for computers could and can work just fine, as we are discovering with touchscreens and speech recognition. While the presence of a keyboard on an encoding machine or a computer is not insignificant, conflating them into the history of typewriters on that basis returns the analysis to the level to the discursive (i.e., what it's possible to say) rather than taking technological form and material format into account with a greater degree of precision.

32 Lisa Gitelman, *Always Already New: Media, History and the Data of Culture* (Cambridge, MA: MIT Press, 2006), 7.

33 See Wershler, *The Iron Whim*, 36–37 on the relationship between early typewriting devices, pantographs and polygraphs. A polygraph was originally a form of pantograph that allowed for an author to scribe one letter and have the machine simultaneously write many faithful copies. Later, the term becomes associated with lie detector machines that transcribe the inner truth of a subject onto paper via an inked lever. This connotation likely persists as part of typewriting discourse to describe how the levers of the typewriter truthfully transcribe the thoughts of the writer.

34 See, for example, Gitelman on the deep interrelationships between typing and phonography, which were "partners for a time" (Gitelman, *Scripts Grooves*, 188).

35 Wershler, *The Iron Whim*, 270–73.

When we do start thinking about the technological form and specific material formats of specific typewriters rather than "the typewriter," it becomes evident that from its relative beginnings to its relative demise, the history of typewriter design is a long and wide tangle of competing technological systems for text input, paper advancement, key punching, inking, and so on that never really stopped changing. There are quite a few popular works cataloging the technological history of the typewriter,[36] produced chiefly for collectors as aids in the process of discernment and collection-building, or as part of corporate history and business literature.[37] A significant number of them were privately published and can be difficult to obtain. These texts make a good starting point for research into a materially informed analysis of particular moments in typewriting history, but collectively, they point to how much work remains to be done rather than to the exhaustion of the subject. Wolfgang Ernst's repeated exhortations to observe technological device in operation,[38] and to incorporate other technological recording devices as agents into the media-archaeological process,[39] need to guide further media-historical and media-archaeological research.

The admirable example to hold up in terms of what is possible for contemporary scholars of typewriting is Thomas Mullaney's theoretically and methodologically exemplary book *The Chinese Typewriter: A History.*[40] Mullaney begins with the observation that in typewriting discourse, the supposed universality of the typewriter keyboard holds up "only to the degree that Chinese script was effaced or erased from the story."[41]

[36] Here are the standard popular reference works: Michael H. Adler, *The Writing Machine* (London: Allen & Unwin, 1973); Wilfred A. Beeching, *Century of the Typewriter* (London: Heinemann, 1974); Bruce Bliven Jr., *The Wonderful Writing Machine* (New York: Random House, 1954); Richard N. Current, *The Typewriter and the Men Who Made It* (Urbana: University of Illinois Press, 1954); Herkimer County Historical Society, *The Story of the Typewriter*; Torbjörn Lundmark, *Quirky QWERTY: A Biography of the Typewriter and its Many Characters* (New York: Penguin Books, 2002); G. Tilghman Richards, *The History and Development of Typewriters* (London: Her Majesty's Stationery Office, 1964); Thomas A. Russo, *Mechanical Typewriters: Their History, Value and Legacy* (Atglen, PA: Schiffer Publishing Co., 2002); *The Typewriter: An Illustrated History* (Mineola, NY: Dover Publications, 2000), repr. of *The Typewriter: History and Encyclopedia* (New York: Typewriter Topics, 1924).

[37] Cornelius E. DeLoca, and Samuel J. Kalow, *The Romance Division: A Different Side of IBM* (Wyckoff, NJ: The D&K Book Company, 1991).

[38] See, for example, Wolfgang Ernst, "Media Archaeography: Method and Machine Versus the History and Narrative of Media," in *Digital Memory and the Archive* (Minneapolis: University of Minnesota Press, 2013), 55–73.

[39] Wolfgang Ernst, "Toward A Media Archaeology of Sonic Articulations," *Digital Memory and the Archive*, 178.

[40] Thomas S. Mullaney, *The Chinese Typewriter: A History* (Cambridge, MA: MIT Press, 2017).

[41] Mullaney, *The Chinese Typewriter*, 9.

(Mullaney is apparently considering *QWERTY is Dead* as the title for his forthcoming book on Chinese computing.)[42] What follows is a rigorous documentation and theorization of how the Chinese script demanded not just a different keyboard configuration, but a fundamental reorganization of the manufactural infrastructure that produced typewriters. This concern with infrastructure is one of the ways in which Mullaney incorporates a greater concern with material media into his analysis.

Crucially, Mullaney also did something that is becoming an increasingly important component of writing material media histories: He built a research collection.[43] Apparently now the largest Chinese and Pan-Asian typewriter and information technology collection in the world,[44] Mullaney's collection appeared at the Museum of Chinese in America as the Exhibit "Radical Machines: Chinese in the Information Age" from October 18, 2018 to March 24, 2019, and has been touring since.[45] This is no mean feat; though once common, research collections fell out of favor with many academic disciplines for most of the twentieth century, and contemporary universities are poorly equipped to understand their relevance, let alone house or fund them. For humanists and social scientists, working with research collections almost always involves devoting large amounts of time to enterprises their colleagues find mystifying. Building, maintaining, and circulating a collection requires a scholar to move beyond signs and paper archives to confront the materiality of the objects they require. Machines need to be cleaned, repaired, and operated upon, processes that provide checks and balances for archival work. But circulating a collection does another kind of work entirely: It helps to build cultural imaginaries.

As Mullaney assembles this history of exception, he also crafts a theoretical mechanism to deal with it. He describes the "technolinguistic imagination" as "a rich ecology of both machines and ways of thinking about machines," where the imaginary portion of the assemblage functions as a kind of "conceptual algorithm" that shapes how its thinker considers

42 "As the first-ever history of Chinese computing in the 20th and 21st centuries, *QWERTY is Dead* will explore the circuitous pathways and eccentric personalities of this unknown chapter in the history of global information technology": https://history.stanford.edu/people/thomas-mullaney.

43 For more on research collections, see Darren Wershler, Jussi Parikka, and Lori Emerson, "Lab Apparatus. Research and Teaching Collections as Part of the Material Apparatus of the Hybrid Lab," in *The Lab Book: Situated Practice in Media Studies*, (Minneapolis: University of Minnesota Press, 2022).

44 "1/25 – 4/16 – Radical Machines: Chinese in the Information Age," *Vanguard Culture* (January 23, 2017).

45 www.radicalmachines.org/; www.mocanyc.org/event/radical-machines/.

a given cultural object, often to the exclusion of other possibilities.[46] Mullaney's technolinguistic imaginary bears a family resemblance to psychoanalytic Marxist arguments about the relationship of the imaginary to ideology. But in its continual insistence that the imaginary is a crucial component of the material infrastructure that allows cultural objects to function in the first place, and on the strange continuity of the networks of prototypes, parallels, clones, and failures that surround and inform all technological objects, it's closer to a Kittlerian discourse network on the media-archaeological formulation of imaginary media.[47]

What has been missing from most theory about typewriting is some uptake on how best to articulate the nondiscursive field to the discursive. In his writing about Foucault's archaeology and the typewriter keys, Deleuze makes the crucial connection, but does not expand on it: "already we feel that AZERT, on the keyboard, represents the focal point of power or of power relations between the letters of the French alphabet, depending on which one crops up, and the typist's fingers, depending on which one is used."[48] This is precisely the sense that Bernhard Siegert invokes when he writes about technique being "the exteriority/materiality of the signifier."[49] As a result, we need to consider how to describe the interface between discourse, signification, materiality, and cultural technique.

3 Cultural Technique

While the method in Kittler's best-known books could be described as discourse analysis informed by material media history, the latter part of his work, increasingly influential at the time of this writing, focuses on cultural technique. As Geoffrey Winthrop-Young helpfully summarizes, "cultural technique" is a complex term that focuses on the articulation of basic mental and physical skills to media technologies.[50] A 2012 special issue of *Theory Culture & Society*,[51] plus Bernhard Siegert's recent eponymous book on cultural technique, provide more detailed accounts. It's worth noting that the German version of cultural technique theory doesn't take into account older traditions of thinking about technique and everyday

46 Mullaney, *The Chinese Typewriter*, 42, 43.
47 Ibid., 22, 23, 26.
48 Deleuze, *Foucault*, 12.
49 Bernhard Siegert, *Cultural Techniques: Grids, Filters, Doors, and Other Articulations of the Real* (New York: Fordham University Press, 2015).
50 Geoffrey Winthrop-Young, *Kittler and the Media* (Cambridge: Polity Press, 2011), 3.
51 Geoffrey Winthrop-Young, Ilinca Iurascu, and Jussi Parikka, eds., "Cultural Techniques," special issue of *Theory Culture & Society* 30.6 (November 2013).

practice in sociology and cultural studies,[52] but we can and should do so, in part as a way of mitigating its apolitical if not conservative tendencies.[53]

Cultural technique theory posits that chains of simple operations can coalesce over time and through repeated use into a more powerful technique.[54] Thomas Macho notes that "cultural techniques are always older than the concepts that are generated from them,"[55] meaning that everyday practice is as important an object of inquiry as expertise. For Siegert, cultural technique is a way of enfolding such "operative chains" into "a more or less complex actor network,"[56] which also includes technological objects, signs, discourse, and disciplinary procedures, so it becomes a kind of container for everything I'm discussing in this chapter. Siegert includes the typewriter in his list of "media, symbolic operators, and drill practices" that now fall under the rubric of cultural technique, but doesn't provide much more on the subject, so there is plenty of work to do in terms of defining the details.[57]

There are a number of significant cultural techniques associated with typewriting that have received considerable scholarly attention. I've already mentioned Avital Ronell's theorization of the basic structure of dictation, which mostly holds for typewriting. Cornelia Vismann's book *Files* provides a wonderful account of the production and circulation of information genres in modern bureaucracy.[58] But entire other books could be filled with accounts of the role of typewriting and attendant techniques in this scene. We need accounts of carbon-copying and other early techniques of duplication, such as mimeography; something on the related technique of form-filling; discussions of the relative origins of the typing pool and the spatiality of office organization; and more attention to the role of typewriting in techniques such as motion studies and workplace efficiency, to name a few.

[52] See, for example, Jacques Ellul, *The Technological Society*, trans. John Wilkinson (New York: Vintage Books, 1964); Martin Heidegger, *The Question Concerning Technology and Other Essays*, trans. William Lovitt (New York: Harper & Row, 1977); Marcel Mauss, *Sociology and Psychology: Essays*, trans. Ben Brewster (London: Routledge and Kegan Paul, 1979); Lewis Mumford, *Technics and Civilization* (Chicago: University of Chicago Press, [1934] 2010).

[53] Jonathan Sterne, "Is It Time Yet to Talk About the Conservatism of German Media Theory?" *Super Bon!* (blog), November 13, 2019, https://superbon.net/2019/11/13/is-it-time-yet-to-talk-about-the-conservatism-of-german-media-theory/ (accessed July 15, 2023).

[54] Siegert, *Cultural Techniques*, 11.

[55] Quoted in ibid., 11.

[56] Ibid., 11.

[57] Ibid., 2.

[58] Cornelia Vismann, *Files: Law and Media Technology*, trans. Geoffrey Winthrop-Young (2000; Stanford, CA: Stanford University Press, 2008).

Cultural technique also offers an intriguing starting point for a posthuman poetics of typewriting, organized not around the author-function but as a kind of inventory of operations and effects in particular material and cultural circumstances. British poet Bob Cobbing's rarely seen lecture notes, *Changing Forms in English Visual Poetry: The Influence of Tools and Machines*,[59] provide an inspirational glimpse of what such an approach might produce. In an attempt to understand the technical processes behind the production of mid- to late twentieth-century concrete and visual poetry, Cobbing focuses on technical operations such as the "misuse" of mimeography and photocopying, repeated enlargement and reduction on a photocopier, mimeography, and so on. This approach could be extended into the vast repertoire of operations that poets and artists have used to create work, such as monospacing, overtyping, silkscreen stencil-cutting, typing onto unusual paper formats such as long, narrow scrolls or textured paper, the use of multiple colored ribbons, rotation of paper on the platen, erasure, custom or altered keyboards and keys, using a finger to create drag on a typewriter ribbon, the use of toy typewriters, typewriter destruction, and many other techniques. Further, this method would work well for both documentation and as a primer for research-creation in performance art pieces involving typewriters, the percussive use of typewriting in music, and typewriter sculpture.

The major cultural technique of typewriting – the production of typing subjects – is complex enough that it merits separate consideration.

4 Cultural Technique and the Production of Subjects

Not only do cultural techniques precede their respective media forms;[60] Siegert contends that "Humans as such do not exist independently of cultural techniques of hominization."[61] So it should come as no surprise that, as Lisa Gitelman observes, "typewriters helped negotiate new forms of human subjectivity";[62] new kinds of authors and new kinds of workers that existed as components of the larger electromechanical world rather than masters of it.

Subject production in modernity is a large and complex cultural technique with a long history. Foucault contends that during the seventeenth

[59] Bob Cobbing, ed., *Changing Forms in English Visual Poetry: The Influence of Tools and Machines* (London: Writers Forum, 1997) includes works by dom sylvester houédard, Peter Mayer, John Furnival, Jennifer Pike, Robin Crozier, and Clive Fencott.

[60] Siegert, *Cultural Techniques*, 11.

[61] Ibid., 9.

[62] Gitelman, *Scripts, Grooves*, 185.

and eighteenth centuries, a series of precise, cost-effective techniques of power emerged, and that they have persisted and become more elaborate. They exercise themselves through social institutions, where they gain access to the bodies, attitudes, and behaviors of individuals in order to exact productive service out of them.[63] As a result of these techniques, subjects produced by the state learn to govern themselves. Julien Offray de la Mettrie's 1748 essay *Man a Machine* posits a body that would be both intelligible and manipulable, a body that power can transform and improve, but also a body that can use things for its own ends.[64] The blueprint for such bodies lies in the writing automata that were one of the ancestors of the typewriter,[65] a series of material technological devices that embody the dream of what these new techniques of power wished to produce.

Unlike the monolithic forms that preceded them, these techniques do not treat the body as an undivided whole. Instead, they focus on micromovements, gestures, attitudes, and the relative speed and efficiency with which these were accomplished. They exercise themselves continually and constantly and are interested in process as well as results. Taken together, they constitute what Foucault calls "discipline." Discipline functions by controlling the distribution of subjects in space and time – that is, in a grid – continually devising ever-more precise techniques that allow it to operate on increasingly finer levels, with new combinations and permutations.[66] The result is a regime of recombinatorial body parts rather than whole sovereign subjects, which creates both possibilities (industrial and aesthetic) and problems.

Siegert also has plenty to say about the grid as a major cultural technique,[67] and the grid is central to the function of typewriting. In monospaced type, the only kind of type for much of the history of typewriting, each letter occupies the same amount of space: one cell in an implicit grid. This grid not only remakes the page, but also the body and soul of the typist, the scene of writing, and then the world around it in the image of its own logic. When Frank Gilbreth and Lillian Moller began their workplace efficiency motion studies for clients including major typewriter manufacturer

63 Michel Foucault, "Truth and Power," in *Power: Essential Works of Foucault 1954–1984*, vol. 3, ed. Paul Rabinow, trans. Robert Hurley et al. (New York: The New Press, 1994), 125.

64 Julien Offray de la Mettrie, *Man: A Machine*, trans. Gertrude C. Bussey et al. (La Salle, IL: Open Court Classics, [1748] 1987).

65 Wershler, *The Iron Whim*, 52–55.

66 Michel Foucault, *Discipline and Punish: The Birth of the Prison*, trans. Alan Sheridan (New York: Vintage Books, [1975] 1979), 136–137.

67 Bernhard Siegert, "(Not) in Place: The Grid, or Cultural Techniques of Ruling Spaces," in *Cultural Techniques*, 121–146.

E. Remington & Sons, one of their major tools was a grid screen that helped them abstract and break down worker operations in a single task.[68]

Over the course of typewriting's history, other techniques emerged to aid in this process. One of the major ones is all-finger touch typing, which had its relative beginnings around 1881,[69] but was hotly contested by alternative techniques such as two-finger hunt-and-peck for many years. Still, in all-finger touch typing, the interface between technique, the symbolic, material technology, and discourse is on full display: Bodies accommodate to machines (this is true of all technologies, where the use does not emerge until long after the material device is "invented"). The arrangement of the keys itself is also part of this history. On a cultural level, we have elevated sections of this ongoing fascination to odd levels, as in the QWERTY vs Dvorak "debate."[70] In light of Mullaney's arguments about the exclusion of the Chinese typewriter from typewriting history altogether, perhaps the interesting question to ask is not which configuration was "better" but what the discursive stakes were for staging such arguments in the first place.

What remains to be done in this area is to identify and study the ways that specific techniques and particular technologies in the typewriting assemblage in particular times and places made particular kinds of subjects. Crucially and once again, because techniques involve applications of power, some subjects have been excluded from extant histories. Who does not appear in existing accounts, and why? As Lisa Gitelman points out, "For the most part, secretarial typing forms the classic case of the sexual division of labour."[71] As a result, untangling the power relations in various historical statements about women and typewriting has been an ongoing task from typewriting's inception, and it is far from complete. We also badly need intersectional accounts of typewriting history that consider LGBTQ+ and BIPOC typing subjects, both in terms of their production and their various resistances to typewriting regimes. It will also be interesting to conduct comparative analyses of the ways in which subject production shifts with the move from typewriting to computing, and then to touch and voice interfaces in the context of an increasingly visual networked digital milieu. Matthew Kirschenbaum's *Track Changes*,[72]

[68] Wershler, *The Iron Whim*, 144–151.

[69] Ibid., 231–232.

[70] For the best account, see S. J. Liebowitz and Stephen E. Margolis, "The Fable of the Keys," *Journal of Law & Economics* xxxiii (April 1990). See also Wershler, *The Iron Whim*, 158–165.

[71] Gitelman, *Scripts, Grooves*, 187.

[72] Matthew G. Kirschenbaum, *Track Changes: A Literary History of Word Processing* (Cambridge, MA: Harvard University Press, 2016).

a history of literary word processing, has begun this project already, and Marcin Wichary's forthcoming *Shift Happens*,[73] a book that proposes to relate 150 years of the design history of the keyboard, also looks promising.

It's also worth considering how typewritten autoethnography or typewritten phenomenology in a post-typewriter world might serve as an interesting technique for producing knowledge. Sociologist David Sudnow's book-length essay, *Talk's Body*,[74] describes a personal phenomenology of "keyboarding" based on his everyday practice of working on a swivel chair with a piano on one side and a typewriter on the other.[75] For Sudnow, the dominant technique is that of jazz, but other typing assemblages with other techniques have produced other models. Vilém Flusser's "The Gesture of Writing," a performative account of Flusser philosophizing about what typewriting means as "gesture" while he is typing, addresses many of the theoretical issues that have come up in this chapter, but works particularly well with formulations of technique.[76] From this side of the discontinuity that separates us from the regime of typewriting, though, such practices will look different and produce different results.

5 The Ends of Typewriting

What does typewriting look like after the typewriter's demise?

The discourse network Kittler dubbed "1900" altered the way in which culture is produced, circulated, stored, and received. But what happened when it ended? For Kittler, this happened somewhat apocalyptically, with the advent of computing, when "As one knows without saying, we do not write anymore,"[77] because the volume and sophistication of computerized communication outscales human missives by magnitudes.

Alan Liu has done the difficult work of describing the lineaments of discourse network 2000,[78] dominated by the techniques and technologies of computing, especially the form of the database. But again, there is more to write about the details, in large part because it is difficult to find ways to describe the formation from the inside. Various entities can

73 Marcin Wichary, "*Shift Happens*," *Medium* (August 14, 2017), https://mwichary.medium.com/shift-happens-5b049f5a93a8 (accessed July 28, 2023).
74 David Sudnow, *Talk's Body* (Harmondsworth: Penguin Books, [1979] 1980).
75 Wershler, *The Iron Whim*, 172–176.
76 Flusser, "The Gesture of Writing."
77 Kittler, *Literature, Media, Information Systems*, 147.
78 Alan Liu, "Transcendental Data: Toward A Cultural History and Aesthetics of the New Encoded Discourse," in *Local Transcendence: Essays on Postmodern Historicism and the Database* (Chicago: University of Chicago Press, 2009), 209–238.

and do persist across the divide between discourse networks (such as the QWERTY keyboard, which is still standard for many computers), but because the set of cultural relations that invest them with meaning shifts as a new order emerges, they are transfigured in ways that are sometimes subtle and sometimes drastic.

There are also questions about how technique is affected when it crosses discursive breaks. For example, what are the differences between touch typing on a typewriter and on a computer, using word-processing software? Perhaps the break between 1900 and 2000 is not so decisive; maybe we need to think also about the long continuities as well as abrupt breaks. Typewriting is no longer a dominant discursive formation, but it has a strong presence as residual media, in Raymond Williams's sense.[79]

We do different things with keyboards on screens and virtual keyboards than we did with typewriters – swiping, pinching, thumb typing – and, because of their networked digital aspect, they certainly do different things with *us*, recording, transmitting, and aggregating our smallest micromotions and the durations of all our hesitations. New techniques will bring new orders and new kinds of subjects. What kinds of subjects do such techniques produce, and at the behest of which disciplinary regimes? Ponder this, the envoi of Flusser's typescript:

> to write is structurally the gesture of a historical and scientific being-in-the-world. Should this gesture fall into disuse, (and there are many symptoms at present which seem to suggest this), the universe of history and science will fall into oblivion, or at least it will cease to be the universe we live in. Because that universe is a "fiction", (the result of the technique of writing), and materializes only in the form of surfaces covered by letters. Thus if the art of writing is lost, it will not be missed by future generations. But for us, who are programmed by it and for it, not to be able to write means that life is not worth living.[80]

[79] Raymond Williams, "Dominant, Residual, and Emergent," in *Marxism and Literature* (Oxford: Oxford University Press, 1977), 121–127.
[80] Flusser, "The Gesture of Writing," 18.

CHAPTER 6

Literature in the Electric Age

Lise Jaillant

In 1894, *Scribner's Magazine* published an essay on "The End of Books," by Octave Uzanne, a French writer and bibliophile. Uzanne imagined a world where print has been replaced by audio. Writers have morphed into "tellers," and readers have become hearers who listen to recordings using portable devices that look like Walkmans. "Hearers will not regret the time when they were readers," Uzanne wrote. "With eyes unwearied, with countenances refreshed, their air of careless freedom will witness to the benefits of the contemplative life." Many American readers found Uzanne's vision exciting. The obsolescence of print would completely change the rules of the literary world. Women would no longer admire charming writers, turning instead to famous tellers. "All shuddering with emotion, they will sigh, 'Ah, how this Teller's voice thrills you, charms you, moves you! What adorable low tones, what heart-rending accents of love! ... There is no ravisher of the ear like him!'"[1]

New technologies do not necessary replace older ones, as media scholars have shown. At the roots of the "myth of the disappearing medium" is a good story: "it is a striking tale about the transformative power of technology, easy to remember and to spread," as Andrea Ballatore and Simone Natale point out.[2] Uzanne was of course proven wrong, and print did not disappear at the turn of the twentieth century. Yet he rightly anticipated a world where print was no longer the dominant medium and had to compete against cheap, attention-grabbing entertainment. The rise of radio, cinema, and later television transformed literature, publishing, and the reading experience – a transformation at the heart of this chapter. The first section focuses on the rise of a celebrity culture associated with book publishing. In the 1920s and 1930s, a younger generation of publishers started

[1] Octave Uzanne, "The End of Books," *Scribner's Magazine* 16 (1894), 225–226.

[2] Andrea Ballatore and Simone Natale, "E-Readers and the Death of the Book: Or, New Media and the Myth of the Disappearing Medium," *New Media & Society* 18.10 (2016), 2380.

using techniques inspired by the movie industry to market writers as literary stars. The second section shows that these innovative marketing techniques targeted a changing readership, including "middlebrow" readers. The final part turns to the anxieties of cultural degeneracy that new formats and media (paperbacks, television) generated in the 1940s and 1950s. This chapter mentions technological advances, such as the new machines and processes used in the mass production of books. However, its main focus is on the cultural impact of technological change, with the appearance of new cultural forms that would have been unthinkable in earlier periods.

1 Book Publishing, Celebrity Culture, and New Marketing Techniques

Imagine you are a male student living in New York City in the early twentieth century. Would you spend your evenings reading books? Or would you rather go out to the theater and get a chance to meet young actresses? For Bennett Cerf, who later became a distinguished publisher, the choice was clear. His time at Columbia University triggered not a passion for books, but for the stage. His interest in show business was always closely intertwined with his fascination for celebrity. On May 27, 1919, the twenty-one-year-old Cerf wrote in his diary, "met Edna Hibbard, who is playing one of the leading roles in 'Tumble In.' My first date with a gen-u-ine actress, + I enjoyed the experience. She is very pretty, but when she told me she was 25 years old, all was not so well!"[3] After graduation, Cerf started working in the financial sector, but found his job tedious.[4] His friend Richard Simon, who later established the publishing company Simon & Schuster, introduced him to the publisher Horace Liveright.

In Cerf's account of his first meeting with Liveright, the publishing field appears much more glamorous than Wall Street. The two men had lunch at the Algonquin Hotel and saw the celebrated group of writers and critics that gathered there regularly. Liveright then offered Cerf the opportunity to accompany Theodore Dreiser to a baseball match. Cerf eagerly accepted: "I'd never met an important author in my life, and at this time Theodore Dreiser was a giant."[5] Although there is no evidence that Cerf

[3] Diary, May 27, 1919, box 11, Cerf Papers, Rare Book and Manuscript Library, Columbia University (hereafter referred to as CP).

[4] "The market has lapsed into utter lethargy. Boredom has me in its clutches." Diary, May 16, 1923, box 11, CP.

[5] Reminiscences of Bennett Cerf, Oral History Research Office collection, Columbia University (hereafter referred to as OHRO), n.d. [c. 1967], session 2, p. 72.

admired Dreiser's writing, he was undoubtedly impressed to meet a star author. In spring 1923, Cerf left his job and started working for Liveright. In exchange for investing some of the money inherited from his mother, the young man was made vice president of the firm.

Liveright was one of the first literary publishers to produce celebrities by using marketing and communication techniques inspired by the movie industry. Indeed, the invention of a new technology (the moving picture) gave rise to an associated business in Hollywood and elsewhere, but it also impacted older cultural industries – such as publishing. With the help of Edward Bernays, the inventor of modern public relations, Liveright organized the first book-launch parties, he advertised books on huge billboards, and he asked movie stars for testimonials.[6] His unconventional book promotion was inseparable from his love of celebrity. In 1924, he started investing in Broadway plays. Biographers would later mythologize Liveright's wild parties, where young actresses rubbed shoulders with intellectuals. But many of the plays backed by Liveright were failures, and in 1925, growing financial difficulties forced him to sell the profitable Modern Library series to Cerf and Donald Klopfer.

Before Cerf took it over, the Modern Library was a successful but relatively unglamorous series of reprints. When it was created in 1917, it published European contemporary texts in cheap editions. Liveright was never really interested in this project.[7] For him, it was far more exciting to sell potential bestsellers than to deal with a series of classics. After Cerf left the Liveright firm to become the co-owner of the Modern Library, he included a growing number of American writers, such as Willa Cather, William Faulkner, and Ernest Hemingway. In the 1930s, Cerf made the series even more "modern" by participating in the new celebrity culture. A 1934 advertisement asked: "Have you read OF HUMAN BONDAGE? Somerset Maugham's great story which is the moving picture of the year?" A photo showed the actress Frances Dee "enjoying the complete Modern Library edition." Of course, the use of movie stars to promote products was nothing new. But publishers had traditionally been reluctant to hire actresses to promote books. Many thought that books were different from beauty cream or soap. In contrast, Cerf saw the emerging celebrity culture as an opportunity to sell more books. Movie tie-ins and the use of celebrities in advertisements became defining features of the publishing business.

6 Walker Gilmer, *Horace Liveright: Publisher of the Twenties* (New York: David Lewis, 1970), 26.

7 When the co-founder of the Modern Library, Albert Boni, left the firm, the number of new titles dropped significantly. There were only five new titles in 1923 and seven in 1924. This decline was reversed after Cerf and Klopfer took control of the Modern Library.

Publishers not only employed movie stars to advertise books, but they also transformed writers into literary celebrities. Faye Hammill argues that "the high-profile authors of the twenties and thirties were constructed in relation to new models of fame emerging from Hollywood. Literary celebrity was increasingly predicated on forms of public performance."[8] Large-scale magazines such as *Vanity Fair*, *Vogue*, and *Time and Tide* promoted this model of celebrity authorship inspired by the movie industry. Hammill gives the example of the British writer E. M. Delafield, whose best-known work, *Diary of a Provincial Lady*, began as a serial in *Time and Tide* in December 1929 before appearing in book form. Its enormous commercial success made its author internationally famous and gave rise to three sequels, *The Provincial Lady Goes Further* (1932), *The Provincial Lady in America* (1934), and *The Provincial Lady in Wartime* (1939). The fact that Delafield was a regular broadcaster on BBC radio highlights the overlaps between various media. In short, radio and film opened up new markets for writers and reinforced the new model of literary celebrity.

In the United States, Bennett Cerf used his knowledge of the entertainment industry to market difficult writers as literary stars. For example, he reinforced Gertrude Stein's image as an atypical celebrity who could reach a broad audience.[9] The year 1933 was a turning point in Stein's career. As an American expatriate in Paris, she was well known for her association with the modern artistic scene. Yet no publisher showed interest in her esoteric writings. That changed when Stein decided to write about her famous friends in *The Autobiography of Alice B. Toklas*. The book was published in September 1933 by Alfred Harcourt. That same month, Cerf added *Three Lives* to the Modern Library and, shortly thereafter, he issued another difficult text by Stein (*Four Saints in Three Acts*) under his new Random House imprint.

In summer 1934, Stein confirmed that she would come to America for a lecture tour. Cerf immediately started working on a large-scale publicity campaign. He later recalled that "it was a front-page story …; the papers … all sent down their cleverest reporters to meet Gertrude Stein.… Gertrude proceeded to handle this bunch of fresh photographers and newsmen as the master she was. She was the publicity hound of the world – was simply great.

[8] Faye Hammill, *Women, Celebrity, and Literary Culture between the Wars* (Austin: University of Texas Press, 2007), 2.

[9] See Lise Jaillant, "Shucks, We've Got Glamour Girls Too! Gertrude Stein, Bennett Cerf and the Culture of Celebrity," *Journal of Modern Literature* 39.1 (2015): 149–169.

She could have been a tremendous hit in show business."[10] Here, Stein is presented as a star with a natural talent for attracting attention. Like Hollywood executives, Cerf stayed in the shadows so that media attention seemed the result of the star's charisma rather than the product of the star machine.

Cerf used not only print but also broadcasting to boost Stein's celebrity. On the evening of Stein's arrival in New York, the movie company Pathé recorded a short film in her suite at the Algonquin Hotel, and the film was then shown in theaters across the country. In this recording, Stein explicitly presented her writings as fun and enjoyable. In November 1934, Cerf also organized a coast-to-coast radio broadcast on NBC. He was proud to be Stein's publisher, but he admitted: "as I've always told you, I don't understand very much what you're saying." Stein replied: "Well, I've always told you, Bennett, you're a very nice boy but you're rather stupid."[11] Cerf presented himself as an ordinary reader baffled by Stein's difficult writing style, which was a clever way to side with the audience. He used the same strategy two years later, when he wrote the blurb for another book by Stein, *The Geographical History of America*: "I must admit frankly that I do not know what Miss Stein is talking about. I do not even understand the title. I admire Miss Stein tremendously, and I like to publish her books, although most of the time I do not know what she is driving at" (inner dust jacket). Thanks in part to this unconventional blurb, Stein's difficult book was widely reviewed.

Notably, the actress Miriam Hopkins – a close friend of Cerf – was also present at the NBC radio interview. Cerf first met Hopkins when he was working for Liveright. By the early 1930s, Cerf had developed an extensive network of contacts in the film industry. He was still very close to Hopkins, who had scored her breakthrough in Ernst Lubitsch's *Trouble in Paradise* (1932).[12] Although she worked primarily in the movie industry, she had also appeared in the radio production "Seventh Heaven," broadcast on NBC in October (the month before Stein's interview). It is highly probable that Cerf knew some people at NBC through his connection with Hopkins. Cerf understood that there was no gap between different media: film, radio, and print. Techniques used in Hollywood to produce stars such as Hopkins could also be applied to the publishing business to create interest in writers and their books.

[10] Reminiscences of Bennett Cerf, OHRO, October 23, 1967, session 6, p. 278.

[11] Ibid., p. 282.

[12] See Allan R. Ellenberger, *Miriam Hopkins: Life and Films of a Hollywood Rebel* (Lexington: University Press of Kentucky, 2018).

2 A Changing Readership: The Rise of the "Middlebrow"?

Innovative marketing techniques were designed to make books competitive in a marketplace saturated with other forms of entertainment. In this struggle to grab the public's attention, book publishers cunningly targeted readers who wanted to appear sophisticated and intellectually superior to the masses. The rising prosperity of the middle class finds its roots in economic and technological transformations associated with the Second Industrial Revolution. This changing readership was often described as "middlebrow," a term that appeared in the 1920s in Britain. "The BBC claim to have discovered a new type, the 'middlebrow,'" declared the satirical magazine *Punch*: "It consists of people who are hoping that some day they will get used to the stuff they ought to like."[13] In its original sense, "middlebrow" described someone with high cultural aspirations, but who lacked the formal education to understand difficult art and literature.

The term can be applied to middle-class audiences and also to cultural institutions, as I have shown in my monograph *Modernism, Middlebrow and the Literary Canon*.[14] The Modern Library, for example, published difficult modernist texts by Gertrude Stein, James Joyce, and Virginia Woolf alongside crime fiction and popular novels. The series can be seen as a "middlebrow" institution that made complex literature available to a wide audience. Catering to the vast audiences eager to acquire taste and distinction, middlebrow institutions offered clear steps and "how to" guides to master high cultural expectations. They often used celebrity appeal and page-turners to make education more palatable. The celebrity of modernist writers – who were often discussed in mainstream media – thus attracted the attention of book clubs. Virginia Woolf's *Flush*, for example, was one of the "dual" selections of the Book-of-the-Month Club in October 1933 – and Stein's *The Autobiography of Alice B. Toklas* was the September 1933 selection of the Literary Guild.[15]

For readers who lived away from major cities, book clubs offered a chance to follow the latest literary trends. In the United States, bookstores were mostly concentrated in urban centers on the East Coast. In his 1931 survey of the book industry, O. H. Cheney criticized the overconcentration and inadequacy of the distribution system. Over 33,000,000 people were

[13] Quoted in "middlebrow, n. and adj.," *OED Online*, May 2018, Oxford University Press: www.oed.com/view/Entry/252048?redirectedFrom=middlebrow (accessed May 16, 2022).

[14] Lise Jaillant, *Modernism, Middlebrow and the Literary Canon: The Modern Library Series, 1917–1955* (London: Routledge, 2014).

[15] Karen Leick, *Gertrude Stein and the Making of an American Celebrity* (New York: Routledge, 2009), 6.

without access to "an adequate book outlet," Cheney wrote.[16] The Book-of-the-Month Club, created in 1926, transformed the way Americans consumed literature. Recent books, which had so far been a luxury, became available to a large audience via mail order. The success of the club led to the creation of many imitators on both sides of the Atlantic.

In 1929, the popular novelists Hugh Walpole and Arnold Bennett established the Book Society in Britain. The club rapidly acquired a large membership of over 10,000 members in the mid-1930s. In *Fiction and the Reading Public* (1932), Q. D. Leavis decried the Book Society as one of the "middlemen" responsible for promoting second-rate literature. It set up "a middlebrow standard of values," Leavis wrote, and it also organized "middlebrow taste."[17] Like the Modern Library, the Book Society published all kinds of texts – including Vita Sackville-West's *The Edwardians*, a novel originally issued by Virginia Woolf's Hogarth Press. Nicola Wilson has criticized Leavis's rigid vision of cultural categories, with the Hogarth Press categorized as highbrow and the Book Society as middlebrow.[18] In fact, the British literary field featured significant overlaps between cultural categories, and the Hogarth Press did not hesitate to collaborate with the Book Society to increase its sales and visibility among middle-class audiences.

Like book clubs, literary prizes played a central role in widening the market for literary texts. The Prix Femina Vie Heureuse, created in France in 1904, is an example of a women-only prize that expanded outside its country of origin toward the Anglophone world. The development of new technologies facilitated rapid communication across borders, and made the rise of international literary prizes possible. The first wireless telegraph point-to-point service connected Britain with Continental Europe in 1920. Eight years later, Woolf was awarded the Femina for *To the Lighthouse*, a difficult novel that employs the new technique of stream-of-consciousness. Each year, the prize selected one text from a selection of three established by the English Committee. During a ceremony at the French Institute in London, Hugh Walpole presented the award to Woolf, and spoke of the modern development of the novel as a sort of spiritual detective tale in which an idea instead of a crime is pursued.[19] Once again, the middlebrow sphere of Walpole and the highbrow sphere of Woolf found common ground.

16 O. H. Cheney, *Economic Survey of the Book Industry, 1930–1931, as Prepared for the National Association of Book Publishers* (New York: Bowker, 1949), 278.

17 Q. D. Leavis, *Fiction and the Reading Public* (London: Chatto and Windus, [1932] 1939), 24.

18 Nicola Wilson, "Virginia Woolf, Hugh Walpole, the Hogarth Press, and the Book Society," *ELH* 79.1 (2012): 237–260.

19 "Men and Women of To-day," *Courier and Advertiser* [Dundee, Scotland], May 5, 1928, 10.

Reporting on the Femina Prize, the *Illustrated London News* included a picture of Woolf as part of a page of personalities titled "The World of Women." She appeared alongside Princess Mary and the Duchess of Bedford, thus signaling the distinction and taste attached to modern literature. The same page also featured photos of Storm Jameson and Stella Benson, whose novels had also been selected by the Femina's English Committee. Jameson was described as the London-based "managing director" of the American publishing firm Alfred A. Knopf Inc., a description that echoed the caption for Woolf ("She is the wife of Mr Leonard Woolf, with whom she conducts a publishing business"). In both cases, the novelists were presented as businesswomen who challenged conventional norms. Woolf was also featured in a page on the "feminine achievements in 1928" published in the *Aberdeen Press and Journal*.[20] Middlebrow institutions made *To the Lighthouse* desirable to aspirational readers, eager to emulate role models such as Woolf and other successful women.

Literary prizes not only popularized difficult texts, but also brought prestige to bestselling page-turners and facilitated their international circulation. In 1938, Pearl S. Buck won the Nobel Prize for Literature, seven years after the publication of *The Good Earth*. Buck often wrote about China, where she had grown up as the child of American missionaries. *The Good Earth*, her novel about a Chinese rural family before World War I, sold 300,000 copies in its original edition and won the Pulitzer Prize. It began to appear in Chinese in the magazine *Eastern Miscellany* within eight months of its publication in the United States. As Richard Jean So puts it, "the velocity by which books traveled internationally was staggering and unprecedented."[21] Technical advances in China – such as the spread of mechanized printing – led to an expansion of book publishing and a boom in translation. Promoted by the Nobel and other international prizes, literature circulated through global channels, rapidly reaching a wide audience.

The popularity of Buck's novel – at home and abroad – was not an obstacle on the path to literary glory. Far from decrying *The Good Earth* as a potboiler, critics praised Buck's ability to appeal to a large readership. When the novel was included in the Modern Library in 1934, the *Washington Post* declared: "If you haven't read *The Good Earth*, this edition

[20] "Feminine Achievements in 1928," *Aberdeen Press and Journal* [Aberdeen, Scotland], December 31, 1928, 2.

[21] Richard Jean So, *Transpacific Community: America, China, and the Rise and Fall of a Cultural Network* (New York: Columbia University Press, 2016), 67.

is an excellent means. Otherwise you will remain in the sorry plight of your grandfather who missed *Quo Vadis* – the only other American best-seller as popular as Mrs Buck's splendid story."[22] An advertisement in the *American Mercury* described the Modern Library edition as "a real 'scoop' – the book that made Pearl Buck, overnight, one of the outstanding writers of our time."[23] This announcement appeared next to an advertisement for the Random House edition of James Joyce's *Ulysses,* which had just been legalized in the United States. In the interwar period, there were no rigid boundaries between highbrow literature and novels that we now see as middlebrow.

Following the announcement of the 1938 Nobel Prize, many critics celebrated Buck's achievement. "She deserved it," declared the *New York Times.*[24] As Buck was only the third American to win the prize after Sinclair Lewis and Eugene O'Neill, articles often expressed patriotic pride. Although Buck had learned to speak Chinese before English, she was co-opted into the emerging canon of American literature. Amid this praise, other critics argued that the Nobel Committee had chosen Buck for political rather than literary reasons. As "a liberal, sympathetic study of China," *The Good Earth* appealed to the Swedish Academy at a time of political trouble in the Far East, wrote *Life* magazine. Sweden "chose the book to show its own support of a liberal, pro-democratic point of view and its own sympathy toward hard-pressed China."[25] Amid rising political tensions, the Swedish Academy was seen not as a neutral committee, but as a biased player in the field of international relations.

With the rise of a new generation of American critics in the late 1930s and 1940s, middlebrow institutions (including literary prizes that endorsed popular authors) became increasingly criticized. In the work of Dwight Macdonald and the New York Intellectuals, mass culture was manufactured by a small elite of cultural producers and sold to the masses in an effort to control and manipulate them.[26] Macdonald was especially critical of middlebrow institutions that mixed High and Low cultures. In *Masscult and Midcult,* he attacked Pulitzer Prize winners such as Hemingway's *The Old Man and the Sea* ("written in that fake-biblical prose Pearl Buck used in *The Good Earth,* a style which seems to have a malign fascination for

[22] Theodore Hall, "No End of Books," *Washington Post,* February 17, 1934, 17.
[23] Advertisement for the Modern Library, *American Mercury* 24 (1934), 122.
[24] "Nobel Prize Winner," *New York Times,* November 11, 1938, 24.
[25] *Life,* November 21, 1938, 18.
[26] See Hugh Wilford, *The New York Intellectuals: From Vanguard to Institution* (New York: St Martin's Press, 1995).

the midbrows").[27] Drawing on Marx's analysis of the destructive power of capitalism, Macdonald condemned the disappearance of cultural categories and value judgments. No art form was sacred anymore, and all that was solid had melted into air.

3 Cultural Anxieties: New Formats and Media

Shortly before World War II, the development of the paperback – first in Britain with Penguin and then in the United States – contributed to rising cultural anxieties. An oft-repeated story is that the idea for Penguin Books came to the publisher Allen Lane in 1934 when he was returning to London and could find nothing to read on the train; the railway stands offered only magazines and reprints of low-quality fiction. The following year, Lane launched a series of sixpenny books produced and advertised on a mass scale. Each title would have to sell at least 17,000 copies to break even, a huge number at a time when few British people bought books.[28] This large print run allowed Lane to drive a hard bargain. He initially contracted with the printing firm of Hazell, Watson and Viney to produce a dummy and specimen pages for the first ten titles. But the actual printing order went to a rival firm (the Athenaeum Printing Works) with slightly more advantageous terms. Producing large quantities of books quickly and cheaply was made possible by the development of new, high-speed presses. Initially, Lane ordered 20,000 copies of each of the ten titles to be ready on July 30, 1935. Last-minute fears caused him to reduce his order to 10,000 – but following the immediate success of Penguin, he rushed to the printer and went back to his original order.

Lane chose titles that would appeal to discerning readers and packaged them with a stylish cover, sewn binding, and good-quality paper. Among its first titles was Ernest Hemingway's *A Farewell to Arms*, a 1929 novel first published by Scribner's in the United States and Jonathan Cape in Britain. It is surprising that Cape agreed to let Penguin reprint a bestselling novel that was still available in its Florin Books series.[29] Apparently,

27 Dwight Macdonald, "Masscult and Midcult," in *Masscult and Midcult : Essays against the American Grain*, ed. John Summers (New York: New York Review Books, 2011), 38.

28 Raymond N. MacKenzie, "Penguin Books," in *British Literary Publishing Houses, 1881–1965*, ed. Jonathan Rose and Patricia Anderson (Detroit: Gale Research, 1991). See also Jeremy Lewis, *Penguin Special: The Life and Times of Allen Lane* (London: Penguin, 2006); Vike Martina Plock, "Virginia Woolf, Penguin Paperbacks, and Mass Publishing in Mid-Century Britain," *Book History* 25.1 (2022): 238–268.

29 *A Farewell to Arms* was published by Cape in November 1929. 15,000 copies were printed that year. The novel was reprinted in the Florin Books series in 1932. See Production Ledger, Archives of Jonathan Cape Ltd, University of Reading.

Cape believed that paperbacks would never work in Britain and that Penguin would soon disappear. For Cape, selling the reprint rights to Penguin would bring in some money before the demise of this new competitor. Hemingway's novel had been a success in Britain, but also in the United States. In 1932, it was included in the Modern Library with an introduction by Ford Madox Ford. There was a first printing of 7,000 copies, followed by several printings of 2,000 copies.[30] By the standards of the Modern Library, *A Farewell to Arms* was a bestseller. However, these figures were soon dwarfed by the sales of paperbacks on both sides of the Atlantic.

In a 1954 article, the publisher Kurt Enoch outlined the conditions that made the paperback revolution possible in the United States: rapid technological advances and the use of magazine distribution channels to sell books. Four categories of new technologies were associated with the phenomenal growth of the paper-bound book: new presses, binding, glue, and materials used for covers. First, paperbacks were printed on high-speed magazine presses and on special book presses printing from rubber plates at the rate of 18,000 impressions of 128 pages, or 12,000 copies of a 192-page book, per hour. Second, the expensive process of sewing (used for the early Penguins) was replaced by "perfect" binding, a form of bookbinding in which the leaves are bound by gluing. Third, new types of glue made this binding almost as strong as the traditional forms. And fourth, new materials improved the paperback covers, which became glossy, dust-repellent, and even washable. However, "these technical advances in inexpensive mass production," wrote Enoch, "would have been useless without the vehicle of magazine distribution which makes possible the immediate marketing of the huge quantities of every new title."[31]

The US paperback revolution started in 1939 with the launch of Pocket Books.[32] The driving force behind the company was Robert de Graff, who had a long experience in the reprints sector. In the 1920s and 1930s, de Graff worked for Doubleday, Page's Garden City Publishing Company, and Blue Ribbon Books. These companies published clothbound reprints and sold them for one or two dollars across America – including in small

30 Box 85, Random House Records, Rare Book and Manuscript Library, Columbia University (hereafter referred to as RH).

31 Kurt Enoch, "The Paper-Bound Book: Twentieth-Century Publishing Phenomenon," *Library Quarterly* 24.3 (1954): 215. Enoch had a long association with paperbacks – from Albatross Modern Continental Library when he was still living in Germany in the 1930s, to the New American Library created with Victor Weybright in 1948 after his move to the United States.

32 Timothy D. Murray, "Pocket Books," in *American Literary Publishing Houses, 1900–1980. Trade and Paperback*, ed. Peter Dzwonkoski (Detroit: Gale, 1986); Dictionary of Literary Biography, vol. 46.

towns and rural areas. They targeted a much larger audience than the Modern Library, which was once described as "essentially a big town series,"[33] limited in its appeal to readers in major cities such as New York and Chicago. Yet de Graff thought that the market for reprints could be even wider. He looked toward Europe, where paperbacks already had a long history, with Tauchnitz in Germany and its successor, Albatross Modern Continental Library. American publishers were of course aware of these European paperbacks, but many thought that cheap books had to be of the sort that would compete with the pulp market and mass-circulation magazines. In contrast, de Graff believed that quality paperbacks could find a mass audience in America, as they had in Europe.

His paperbacks sold for 25 cents; "kind to your pocket – and to your pocketbook," declared a promotional leaflet. The price was made possible by low royalties paid to authors, only 1 cent per copy. Pocket Books combined low cost and small size with literary quality. The mass American reading public wanted "the best in books – books that have stood the test of time."[34] With this philosophy in mind, De Graff selected titles that were recognized as classics, and looked toward the Modern Library for inspiration. Among the first sixteen Pocket Books, six titles were available in the Modern Library, including *The Good Earth* and Edna Ferber's *Show Boat*.

At first, Bennett Cerf did not mind sharing the market with Pocket Books: The enterprise looked more like an experiment than a serious competitor. But he soon became worried. "There are thousands of books that have been best sellers and that are not in the Modern Library series," he wrote to de Graff. "Why not go after some of them instead of going after all the titles that we already have?"[35] A highly placed executive at Simon & Schuster – Pocket Books' partner firm – even predicted the end of the Modern Library.[36] Why would anyone buy books at 95 cents when cheaper alternatives were available? Yet, Cerf's fears, and his competitor's hopes, proved unfounded. Both the paperbacks and the hardcover Modern Library thrived in the 1940s and 1950s, owing to rising economic prosperity and a boom in the number of university students.[37]

33 James L. Crowder to Bennett Cerf, October 11, 1930, box 764, RH.

34 "The "'Inside' Story of Pocket Books," Box 98, RH.

35 Bennett Cerf to Robert de Graff, September 20, 1939, box 98, RH.

36 Cerf to Wallis E. Howe, Jr. ["Avon Publications, Inc."], March 29, 1954, Box 25, RH.

37 Gordon Neavill has shown that the sales of the regular Modern Library were multiplied by five between 1940 and 1948, despite the competition of paperback series. Gordon Neavill, "Publishing in Wartime: The Modern Library Series during the Second World War," *Library Trends* 55.3 (2007), 588.

Pocket Books and other paperback series initially adopted the conservative taste that already characterized Penguin's publishing practice in Britain. They refused to publish controversial texts and their covers were far from racy. Advising an author who was eager to see his novel appear in paperback, Cerf warned: "Pocket Books people have proven themselves to be pretty prudish and straight-laced in the past."[38] But with rising competition, paperback companies devised new ways to attract readers, including sexy covers and lurid blurbs. Allen Lane was horrified by this evolution. This led to a conflict with the American branch of Penguin, whose managers were pushing for more controversial books with sensational covers. When Victor Weybright, who was running the American house, suggested adding the salacious Southern writer Erskine Caldwell to the list, Lane responded that they should change the name of the imprint to Porno Books.[39] He objected to the content as well as to the covers of novels by Caldwell, James M. Cain, James T. Farrell, and William Faulkner.

Allen Lane was not the only one to find the new paperbacks distasteful. The New York Intellectuals were particularly critical of Signet, the paperback series of the New American Library. Founded in 1948 after Weybright's split with Lane, the New American Library promised "Good Reading for the Millions!" and selected texts by Faulkner and James Joyce alongside crime fiction. This mix of high and low culture infuriated the poet Delmore Schwartz. In "Masterpieces as Cartoons," an essay published in *Partisan Review*, Schwartz wrote:

> even when a reader goes from James M. Cain to William Faulkner and James Joyce because they are available in pocket book form for twenty-five cents, most readers who come to Faulkner and Joyce by means of pocket books do not know the difference between James M. Cain and James Joyce or Dashiell Hammett and William Faulkner; and some of the time they do not remember the names of the authors, no matter how many of their works they read.[40]

For Schwartz, the failure to distinguish between great modernist writers and hard-boiled hacks such as Cain or Hammett exemplified the disappearance of clearly defined taste levels and the triumph of a relativist mass culture.

38 Cerf to Stephen Longstreet, February 26, 1942, box 146, RH.
39 J. E. Morpurgo, *Allen Lane, King Penguin: A Biography* (London: Hutchinson, 1979), 227.
40 Delmore Schwartz, "Masterpieces as Cartoons" (1952), in *Arguing Comics: Literary Masters on a Popular Medium*, ed. Jeet Heer and Kent Worcester (Jackson: University Press of Mississippi, 2004), 52–53.

For many people, the lurid packaging of paperbacks also contributed to a pornographication of culture. In February 1949, shortly after Random House had invested in a new paperback company, Bantam, Robert Haas wrote to his colleague Bennett Cerf to complain about the new series' covers. "They've really gone too far," declared Haas, giving the example of Raoul Faure's *Lady Godiva*, based on the medieval legend of an English noblewoman who rode naked and covered only in her long hair. The Bantam edition featured a blonde beauty on a horse, observed by a man behind a window. "I felt the jacket and front matter took it straight into the pornographic category," Haas declared.[41] Women in various states of undress, watched or touched by men, became a feature of paperback covers from the late 1940s onward.

The contrast with previous covers is particularly striking in the case of Ernest Hemingway's *A Farewell to Arms*, of which Bantam published yet another edition in January 1949. The book did "sensationally well," said Ian Ballantine, the president of Bantam.[42] By June, total net sales had reached 308,010.[43] At 25 cents, the first US paperback edition of the novel was just a quarter of the price of the Modern Library edition. "Would you dare love like this?" asked one advertisement, next to an illustration of a man holding a woman in a nightdress. The Hemingway novel was available in low price drug stores and promised the right mix of entertainment and titillation. "They stole love from a world afire," declared the front matter of the Bantam edition. On the back cover, the publisher praised Scribner's for its original edition of the novel, and even included an image of the modernist dust jacket, its modest design a far cry from the sexy cover of the paperback.

The contrast between the two covers fueled fears of cultural degeneracy, and Hemingway's novel was added to the list of banned books issued by the National Organization for Decent Literature (NODL). This infuriated James Rorty, another figure of the New York Intellectual scene. He criticized both the NODL for its censorship and the paperback imprints for using "the same kind of covers, of mostly bosomy and dishevelled females, which are employed by the publishers of the cheap sex magazines to exploit the lowest common denominator of the commercial market for concupiscence." Advertising serious texts with sexy covers was "fraudulent," misrepresenting both the intent and the content of the books. Although Rorty recognized

41 Robert Haas to Bennett Cerf, February 16, 1949, box 12, RH.
42 Ian Ballantine, "Confidential Report to the Board of Directors," January 28, 1949, box 11, RH.
43 Bantam Books, Cumulative Sales Figures, box 11, RH.

that paperback publishers had made reading available to the masses, his preference was for modestly packaged books offered at a cheap price.[44]

The rise of television triggered similar concerns of cultural decline and criticisms of low-quality content. Bennett Cerf was, once again, at the forefront of this media revolution. He became famous in the 1950s not as president of Random House but as a panelist in the popular TV show *What's My Line?* Every Sunday night, millions of Americans tuned in to CBS to watch Cerf and other panelists try to guess the occupation or the identity of the contestant. As Evan Brier puts it,

> definitions of mass culture are frequently contested, but there seems little question that television in the mid-1950s is an example of it: a moment that in retrospect seems singular, when an unthinkably large audience of culture consumers, made possible by the combination of the postwar economic boom's expanded middle class, the prewar technology of the cathode ray tube, and the paucity of viewing choices in the precable television age, could and routinely did tune in to the same show.[45]

With many intellectuals criticizing the conformity and mediocrity of mass culture, Cerf's roles as the publisher of James Joyce's *Ulysses* and panelist in *What's My Line?* seemed entirely incompatible.

In November 1957, Cerf justified his positioning between "high" and "low" cultures on *The Mike Wallace Interview*, an eclectic prime-time TV show. Mike Wallace invited generals, politicians, businessmen but also actors, writers, stripteasers, and even publishers. In his interview with Cerf, Wallace asked a series of probing questions, such as: "Why does a man of your stature, and I put this to you very sensibly, with your dissatisfaction with television's mediocrity which you have stated, to some extent … why do you lend yourself for seven years to *What's My Line?*, a television parlor game, what do you get out of it?" Cerf complained that he had never said that all TV programs were mediocre. He saw no contradiction in publishing writers such as William Faulkner while also participating in mass culture. In fact, Random House sold Faulkner's books as mass culture products. For Cerf, broadcasting – and especially TV broadcasting – did not endanger the book trade. On the contrary, it was opening new markets for books.

Cerf eagerly took part in radio and television programs not only because he was a self-confessed "ham" – and not only because he was paid a lot

[44] James Rorty, "The Harassed Pocket-Book Publishers," *The Antioch Review* (December 1, 1955), 416.

[45] Evan Brier, *A Novel Marketplace: Mass Culture, the Book Trade, and Postwar American Fiction* (Philadelphia: University of Pennsylvania Press, 2010), 2.

of money to participate in *What's My Line?* – but also because he was an excellent businessman. Broadcasting reached the great mass of people who never read a book, and these people could be persuaded that reading was essential to middle-class status. The growing importance of mass media meant that the role of the publisher was changing. Publishers had traditionally been associated with a gentle and reclusive lifestyle. In the age of mass media, print had not disappeared. Techniques used across media – radio, movies, and television – could also apply to print, and transform writers and even publishers into instantly recognizable celebrities.

CHAPTER 7

Digital Text

Maxwell Foxman

Few question the profound impact of digital technology on text. Computers and smartphones place countless literary genres "in front of the reader … that, in the world of the scribal and a fortiori printed cultures, were distributed among distinct objects."[1] Email, social media posts, hypertext, and traditional novels are among the deluge of documents that flood a single e-reader or smart device. Such convergence has "ruptured" the ways we write, disseminate, relate to, and even organize texts.[2] Nowhere is this more evident than in universities, where the rise of digital humanities and the inclusion of audio, visual, multimedia, and interactive formats – ranging from online fan-fiction to video games – have become commonplace in literary curricula, leading to a reassessment of the very materials that comprise books and book culture. The upshot is an exciting, messy, and even playful "grayness" that shrouds our understanding of what qualifies as a document or text.[3] Not only is the term "digital" used to describe an almost incalculable array of media, objects, and activities – including social networks, calculators, televisions, refrigerators, and cars – but when they all are also suffused with words, "digital text" as a concept may simply serve too many purposes.

As such, this chapter seeks to transcend a penumbra of terms and theories to comprehend what "digital text" is and how its origins have led to so many rich meanings. In order to derive a substantive definition, a disambiguation of the expression is required. Peters qualifies what digital is in his critical assessment of the term. Based on its etymological root – the Latin *digitus*, finger – he suggests three key and interrelated elements of digital media: They count, point, and manipulate. When counting, the digital

[1] Roger Chartier, "Languages, Books, and Reading from the Printed Word to the Digital Text," *Critical Inquiry* 38.1 (2004): 142.

[2] Ibid., 142.

[3] Lisa Gitelman, *Paper Knowledge: Toward a Media History of Documents* (Durham, NC, and London: Duke University Press, 2014), 116.

is symbolic, setting "artificial thresholds" by which all natural signals are reduced.[4] These thresholds allow phenomena to be distilled to numeric form. Although such translation occurs organically – for instance, counting on hands – computers and related devices are able to do this more easily than humans. Translating phenomena into symbolic form for counting also leads to the "indexical" or "pointing" character of the digital. Digital media "point beyond themselves and exclude something significant in the process."[5] Real-world data need to be categorized to be intelligible to a computer. In other words, indexes specify rules for both the technology and the user to interpret information they are given. Who and how such categories are determined are central to Peters' third notion: that digital media "manipulate our many social worlds."[6] As an example, he demonstrates how Google Maps navigates users through physical space primarily via its exclusive algorithms and corporate bylaws.

Peters' tripartite definition draws guidelines by which to frame digital media, but is not exclusive to it. Alphabetic writing can also be considered "predominantly digital,"[7] in that each character is symbolic and discrete. What makes digital technology culturally distinct is the "degree and scale to which … large reservoirs of computing power have begun to be consolidated in the hands of increasingly powerful data-rich institutions."[8] Counting, pointing, and manipulating ultimately establish ways to comprehend, incorporate, and even subvert digital text.

The effects of digitization on the content and structure of texts have brought about dynamic approaches to literature. In particular, digital media is untethered "from any specific material support, making it accessible through a variety of interfaces (including the computer, cell phone, tablet, and dedicated e-reader) each of which influences our reading."[9] Its liquidity and modifiability have contributed to a profusion of formats: hypertext, hypermedia, interactive fiction, cybertext, and ergodic literature are just a few of the many new genres. However, Borsuk's comment also underscores how the very materiality of digital texts impacts content: Whether on a smartphone or game console, its technical underpinnings are integral to comprehension.

4 Benjamin Peters, "Digital," in *Digital Keywords*, ed. Benjamin Peters (Princeton and Oxford: Princeton University Press, 2016), 96.
5 Ibid., 99.
6 Ibid., 103.
7 Grant Kien, "The Digital Story: Analyzing Binary Code as a Cultural Text" (Master's Thesis: York University, 2002), 30.
8 Peters, "Digital," 105.
9 Amaranth Borsuk, *The Book* (Cambridge, MA: The MIT Press, 2018), 203.

Many of these new formats also require the active participation of readers, engendering novel modes in which audience, text, and authors inform one another. Cover's study of narrative control in interactive fiction articulates an "author-text-audience" relationship, which he sees as an "ongoing struggle" between producers and consumers.[10] Similarly, Hillesund contends that all texts go through "cycles" of "interrelated elements or phases, such as writing, distribution and reading."[11] Thus, the very traits associated with digital technology – its exactness, its ability to index, and its capacity to manipulate the social imaginary – have created dynamic interplay between content, authors, and readers alike, upending traditional beliefs of what text is.

Predicated on Peters' thesis, the following sections examine how digital technology operates with text. They show how efforts to encode and standardize language – from Morse Code to the American Standard Code for Information Interchange (ASCII) – have relied on the ability of computers to *count* or render content symbolically readable. These efforts *pointed* or demarcated the boundaries of digital text, which authors and readers explored and experimented with in the 1990s and 2000s. Finally, those who currently *manipulate* or control the platforms by which digital texts are distributed chart their future course. These three concepts shape the unique playfulness of the medium. Digital technology has prescribed the rules by which readers, writers, and publishers play with, experiment with, and ultimately understand text.

1 Counting: A History of Digitizing Texts

> All real signals can be reduced, with certain loss, into digital symbols. Anything one wants to describe — say, content (sensory experience), space (coordinates), time (intervals), or instructions (programming, algorithms) — can be expressed in the irreducibly countable alphabet of that one binary difference, 0 or 1.[12]

The essence of digitization is counting, or translating phenomena in the outside world into numerical code. Three pivotal and complementary inventions based on the reduction of natural language to countable

[10] Rob Cover, "Audience Inter/active: Interactive Media, Narrative Control and Reconceiving Audience History," *New Media & Society* 8.1 (2006): 155.

[11] Terje Hillesund, "Digital Text Cycles: From Medieval Manuscripts to Modern Markup," *Journal of Digital Information* 6.1 (2005): https://journals.tdl.org/jodi/index.php/jodi/article/view/62/65 (accessed July 15, 2023).

[12] Peters, "Digital," 95.

symbols exemplify this premise: Samuel Morse's trail-blazing telegraph, Emile Baudot's automated printing telegraph, and ASCII for computers. The telegraph is perhaps the archetypical invention premised on the notion of counting language. It embodies the threshold described by Peters, turning voltage "on" or "off" for messaging, as the earliest versions sent a signal from one machine to another based on a completed electrical circuit. In telegraphy, there is no middle ground; this binary logic led Jennings to favor the term "discrete" rather than "digital" to describe it, since operators and readers "do not rely on finely measuring the voltage; its mere presence or non-presence suffices."[13] The telegraph "recorded its signals on a narrow strip of paper with a pen, making little wiggles when the voltage of the wire changed."[14] This inscribed code, or "encoding," is foundational to the ease by which digital media "counts" the real world because it reduces data to a common language (binary code in the case of computers) that devices can share. Cramer suggests that this supports multimodality: "the possibility to losslessly translate information from one sign system to the other, forth and back, so that the visible, audible or [tactile] representation of the information becomes arbitrary."[15]

Computers are particularly adept at encoding, decoding, and transmitting these arbitrary sign systems. But, as with the telegraph, humans play an integral part in the process, setting up and translating encoded messages into something meaningful. However, "meaning" is based on cultural and social conditions. For instance, Morse initially planned to decrypt telegraph messages via a numeric codebook: "the receiver and the sender both would have a giant dictionary of words, each word numbered."[16] This system would have been bewildering for most users, requiring significant memorization. It was only later, with his assistant Alfred Vail, that Morse developed a code explicitly based around the Roman alphabet. The simplified method afforded rapid and easy transmission of information, which enabled the proliferation of the technology and eventual growth of a telegraph labor force and consumer culture.

Easy communication between systems requires that the "storage" of digital code and its legible "representation" remain separate processes.[17]

13 Tom Jennings, "An Annotated History of Some Character Codes or ASCII: American Standard Code for Information Infiltration," *American Standard Code for Information Infiltration* 1.11 (2004).

14 Ibid.

15 Florian Cramer, "Digital Code and Literary Text," *Beehive Hypertext/Hypermedia Literary Journal* (2001): www.dvara.net/Hk/digital_code_and_literary_text.pdf (accessed July 15, 2023).

16 Jennings, "An Annotated History of Some Character Codes or ASCII."

17 Hillesund, "Digital Text Cycles."

As opposed to traditional books, in which written language contains all layers of comprehensible information, computers translate code into coherent messages. The machine acts as an intermediary for human reinterpretation. The best way to achieve this is to make the encoding predictable. For instance, in Morse code the shortest piece of data is the letter "E," the most probable letter in any English word. A predictable encoding system that allows for seamless feedback between machines and humans would come to define digital communication. Claude Shannon's information theory, which was foundational to cybernetics and computation, depends on removing meaning from communication in order to treat language as formulaic and countable symbols.

Shannon's concept was also based, in part, on telegraphy, especially the work of Emile Baudot, who upgraded Morse's thirty-year-old system by automating the translation of language into countable code. In 1874, with demand for communication over telegraph wires escalating, Baudot sought to squeeze "even more capacity out of a telegraphy line."[18] His invention permitted concurrent automatic messaging among four operators, who would send messages at exact intervals in rotation. To facilitate the process and reduce delay, Baudot manufactured a device resembling a piano made up of five keys that could be simultaneously pressed down at fixed moments in time to represent thirty-two Roman letters and symbols. Not only was the implementation of Baudot's code quite literally digital, it was also binary. Rather than the traditional long and short "dits and dahs" of Morse code, each combination of five depressed keys corresponded to an individual letter of the alphabet or symbol (i.e., piece of information). When printed out, the codes were easy to decipher because of the five discrete units or "bits" in the system, where each bit is either on or off. "Baudot code" (Figure 7.1) allowed for up to 360 words to be transmitted per minute,[19] which generated more volume and faster messages than Morse's traditional system.

The Baudot code's logic of discrete units to represent letters was embraced as the norm, and the bit system was soon adopted worldwide, first by the British Post Office and later as the international telegraph standard (ITA2). A century later, Baudot's concept spawned ASCII; instead of five, it is a seven-bit code that allows for the representation of 128 unique characters. IBM engineer Bob Bremer is credited with originating ASCII when he introduced the idea to the American National Standards Institute

[18] Tom Standage, *The Victorian Internet: The Remarkable Story of the Telegraph and the Nineteenth Century's Online Pioneers* (London: Phoenix, 1998), 192.

[19] Ibid., 193.

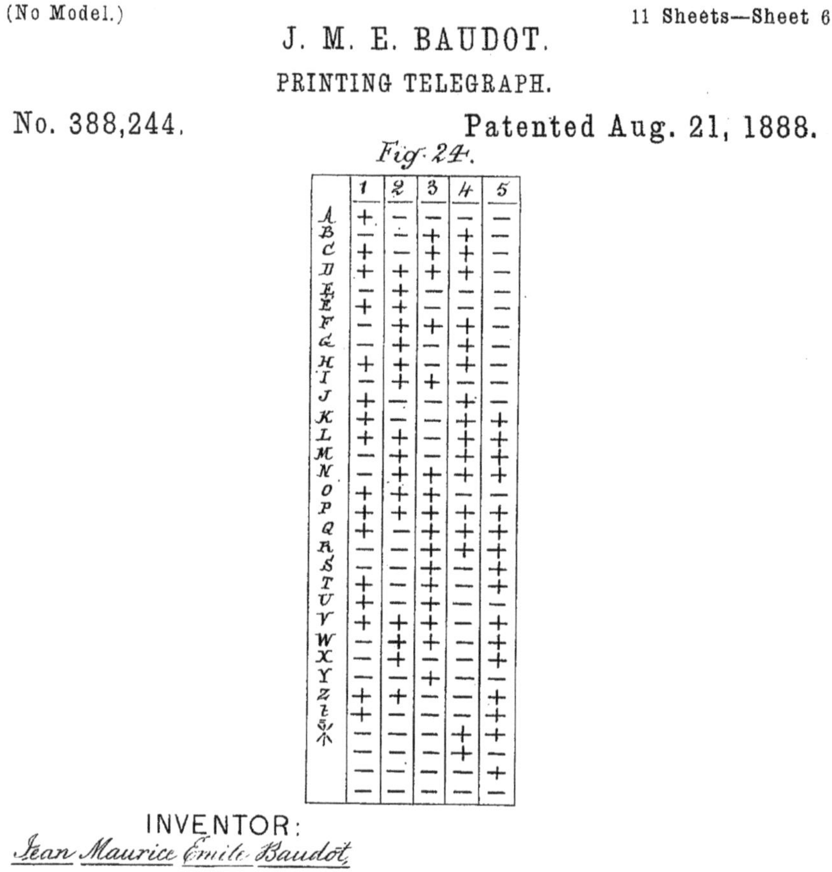

Figure 7.1 Baudot code from the 1888 patent. A plus sign ("+") indicates a pressed key. Source: Wikimedia Commons.

(ANSI). The code sought to make electronic text compatible among the myriad (and competing) commercial, military, and education computer systems across the United States. Because of hardware limitations, ANSI's task force concentrated on a seven-bit framework and, in 1967, released a formal version of code composed of Roman letters, numbers, and other functions that are reflected on the modern US keyboard.

ASCII's legacy is significant. By standardizing text across computers, communication via the ARPAnet (and later the Internet) became significantly easier. The "Unicode" system that succeeded ASCII is 16 bits and 65,536 characters, which means it can contain "all characters and ideographs in all written languages of the world."[20] However, the first 128 characters of Unicode are the same as ASCII. Simply put, ASCII forms the basis for how to understand digital text.

Conceptually, ASCII epitomizes both the value of and social circumstances by which digital texts are "counted." On the one hand, almost any textual symbol can be encoded, and with Unicode thousands have been. Through this universal set of rules, digital text can be rendered and efficiently read. On the other hand, circumstantial factors and constant haggling forged these supposedly universal rules. Fischer describes painstaking negotiations surrounding the establishment of ASCII, including the integration of the US military's FIELDATA standard, European practices, existing computer and corporate criteria, and even conventions taken from typewriters.[21] The X3 committee tasked with devising the code failed numerous times before members agreed upon guidelines, which included much-debated final symbols such as the exclamation point ("!") and a broken vertical line ("¦") to appease members of IBM's Fortran team and international programmers (27). Further, the first ASCII standard was almost immediately modified: During the 1960s, computer hardware rapidly improved to handle eight-bit requirements, expanding the possibilities of what could be included.

The adoption of ASCII and eventually Unicode underscores the importance of "counting" as a construct in the origination of digital text. By taking the multitude of mathematical, symbolic, and linguistic choices associated with language and reducing them to 128 discrete symbols, hardware manufacturers, programmers and computer users could occupy a common playing field.

2 Pointing: Playing with the Rules

Digital media thus have meaning insofar as they index the world.[22]

By the 1980s, ASCII was the formal standard for digital text, but its enduring legacy in popular culture stretches into the realm of art – specifically, in "ASCII art," which Danet calls "one of the best known forms of play with computers."[23] ASCII art or "text-based art" consists of "pictures or visual

[20] Charles Petzold, *Programming Windows, Fifth Edition* (Seattle, WA: Microsoft Press, 1999), 15.
[21] Eric Fischer, "The Evolution of Character Codes, 1874–1968," 2002: http://dump.deadcodersociety.org/ascii.pdf (accessed July 15, 2023).
[22] Peters, "Digital," 99.
[23] Brenda Danet, *Cyberpl@y: Communicating Online* (London and New York: Routledge, 2001), 194.

Figure 7.2 An example of ASCII art.
Source: Wikimedia Commons.

images created with letters, numbers, and other typographic symbols on the computer keyboard" (see Figure 7.2).[24] These range from elaborate tapestries of text to short snippets of expression, such as emoticons (e.g., :-), :-(, :-/). Textual art preceded ASCII; designers even employed Baudot's five-bit system to create artwork. However, the code rose to prominence alongside Usenet newsgroups and the World Wide Web in the 1990s, on which millions of textual images were shared, stored, and used for a wide variety of purposes, such as signature files and greetings.[25] Danet delineates a dazzling and extensive ASCII typography, including representational images, shapes, greetings, humor, miniature drawings, and calligraphy made entirely of text.

These genres not only sprang from ASCII but were also delimited by restrictions of specific computer systems and the Web's coding base. Even more fascinating were the activities of ASCII artists, who compared their efforts to hobbies and crafts such as crocheting – learn the stitching rules,

[24] Ibid., 194.
[25] Ibid., 210.

then practice, practice, practice.[26] These artists played within ASCII's purview,[27] adding exotic symbols for embellishment, utilizing letters without regard for their meaning to forge full images such as trees,[28] novel fonts,[29] and even adding decorative borders around email signatures.[30] They also exploited the scrolling aspect of computer pages – the so-called "infinite canvas" – to produce images without interruption.

Danet illustrates an ancillary idea to Peters' articulation of the digital: that once information has been indexed – fixed by comprehensive rules – those very standards circumscribe experimentation and play. He asserts that digital media is "indexed" through sign systems by which information is stored: "a finger, like digital media, can point to anything, which means that what we point to is probably meaningless – and at best probabilistically meaningful – most of the time."[31] Because of this, three criteria are essential in the creation of an index: First, the index itself requires an (inherently) inexact digital representation of a real-world phenomenon; second, the representation must be an abstraction that reduces natural qualities of the occurrence to code; third, a set of rules must be constituted in order to explain (or even justify) how the abstraction connects to the thing it represents. Simply, an index institutes arbitrary rules, the hallmark of games. For instance, chess, a game that serves as a representation of real-world rivalries, is also a digital index, where war strategy is abstracted into a set of random and discrete movements on a patterned board. Once prescribed, rules may instill a sense of safety and familiarity within the time and frame of the game so that play can occur freely. Paradoxically, such rules also lay the groundwork for tinkering, experimentation, and modification. There are, for instance, no shortage of modifications to traditional chess, such as monochromatic chess, where players must only stay on one color square.

Similarly, the standardization of digital text cleared a pathway for experimentation with both entrenched and newly created technical and social rules. During the 2000s, artists and researchers demonstrated this with their numerous neologisms for text consumed through digital media. Espen Aarseth proposed the term "cybertext" to define emerging formats "perceived as outside of … the field of literature – or even in opposition

[26] Ibid., 230.
[27] Ibid., 255.
[28] Ibid., 220.
[29] Ibid., 221.
[30] Ibid., 212.
[31] Peters, "Digital," 101.

to it" – particularly interactive, digital, and online narratives.[32] Cybertext represented a shift in the relationship between reader, author, and text. For Aarseth, "The reader's pleasure is the pleasure of the voyeur. Safe, but impotent. The cybertext reader, on the other hand, is not safe.... The cybertext reader is a player, a gambler; the cybertext is a game-world or world-game; it is possible to explore, get lost, and discover secret paths in these texts...."[33] Each role is put in play and debated. How has the relationship between reader and author changed through cybertext? The reader can play with or even forge their own narrative, which gives them new power over the text. Consequently, who "writes" a digital or cybertext remains questionable. Writers no longer shape the "rules" when the audience can move, reuse, and remix the words so easily. Thus, ASCII and cybertext not only brought unexpected opportunities to creators and consumers, but also broke down the distinction between the distribution and production of text, as well as that between readers and authors.

The rise of postmodern theory in literary studies complemented scholarship that judged digital text as a reconfiguration of traditional literature. These theories stipulate a playful relationship between writers, their output, and readers. Derrida's "bricolage" alluded to the notion of "freeplay" with the structure and sign of the word,[34] an idea Turkle and Papert related explicitly to programming. In his history of binary code,[35] Kien compared the origination of coding to Lyotard's concept of the "language game" based on who holds power over the users.[36] Computers provided an apt testing ground to challenge presumptions about text, programming, and play.[37]

These philosophies later surfaced in a few core concepts that gained prominence in the 2000s: hypermedia, which manifested the playful theories of and experimentation with texts; "remix culture," an outgrowth of the reconsideration of authorship; and efforts at bottom-up digital preservation. An array of imagined and actual creations formed

[32] Espen Aarseth, *Cybertext: Perspectives on Ergodic Literature* (Baltimore, MD, and London: JHU Press, 1997), 18.

[33] Ibid., 4.

[34] Jacques Derrida, "Structure, Sign, and Play in the Discourse of the Human Sciences," in *A Postmodern Reader*, ed. Joseph Natoli and Linda Hutcheon (Albany, NY: SUNY Press, 1993), 223–242.

[35] Sherry Turkle and Seymour Papert, "Epistemological Pluralism and the Revaluation of the Concrete," *Journal of Mathematical Behavior* 11.1 (1992): 3–33.

[36] Kien, "The Digital Story," 18.

[37] Using new media to reappraise the old is not a new concept. For analysis, see Adam Hammond, *Literature in the Digital Age: An Introduction* (Cambridge: Cambridge University Press, 2016), 24.

the basis for hypermedia. Vannevar Bush's "Memex," a reading device conceptualized in 1945, presupposed the Internet's linking functions and warehouse of information; "Xanadu," Ted Nelson's proposed alternative software to the World Wide Web, begun in 1960, was designed to embody his interpretation of "hypertext," or electronic texts linked by references, or "hyperlinks." The theory came to define the disjointed nature of digital texts. Other benchmarks revolved around the interactive nature of digital media. Joseph Weizenbaum's 1964 experimental ELIZA program was an automated therapist into which users typed their thoughts and emotions; the 1976 text adventure computer game *Adventure* is considered the forebearer of interactive fiction and online multi-user dungeons (MUDs), role-playing games that enable all players to co-construct the narrative. By the 1990s, full-fledged hypertext fiction flourished. Kirschenbaum recognizes these early works, including William Gibson's *Agrippa* and Michael Joyce's *afternoon: a story*, as examples of what he calls "first-generation electronic objects" with "no material existence outside of the electronic environment of a computational file system."[38] Several other assumptions accompany such text: It is consumed in a referential manner, where citations and other writings are directly connected and easily retrieved;[39] it is variable and variant,[40] able to change and iterate rapidly. Further, hypermedia is spatial, exemplified by the map-like design of Shelley Jackson's classic *Patchwork Girl*,[41] or the equally cartographic Twine interactive fiction program.[42] Finally, a "feedback loop" exists by which readers can reflect on the changes their choices exert on the artistic object – which in turn directly influences the manner in which it is consumed.

These qualities are inherently playful. Feedback, design, and spatial thinking are integral to gamemaking, and hypermedia stimulate play with literary conventions. Kirschenbaum dismisses this playfulness as only being "screen deep"[43] and asserts that it does not accommodate the artifacts (computers, smartphones, etc.) that display hypermedia. However, from a literary point of view, this playfulness epitomized the artistic and

[38] Matthew G. Kirschenbaum, "Editing the Interface: Textual Studies and First Generation Electronic Objects," *Text* 14 (2002): 20.

[39] For a detailed review of these features, see Hammond, *Literature in the Digital Age*, 11.

[40] Kirschenbaum, "Editing the Interface," 40.

[41] Shelley Jackson, *Patchwork Girl*, CD-ROM, Eastgate Systems Inc. (1995).

[42] Jane Friedhoff, "Untangling Twine: A Platform Study" (paper presented at DiGRA 2013: DeFragging Game Studies, Georgia Institute of Technology, Atlanta, 2013): www.digra.org/wp-content/uploads/digital-library/paper_67.compressed.pdf (accessed July 15, 2023).

[43] Kirschenbaum, "Editing the Interface," 26.

philosophical milieu of the time as digital text and online media matured and reached mass appeal.

Playfulness also influences and challenges traditional perceptions of authorship. Diakopoulos and colleagues propose two historical renditions of the author, as a "lone creative genius,"[44] fostered by the Romantic ideal that came into being with the novel's popularity, and as a "collaborator," who builds a body of work on citing others, "reworking their ideas and contributing to an intertextual web of ideas and media."[45] The collaborative interpretation better fits digital text, which disrupts notions of "originality" and "attribution," hallmarks of copyright and compensation. Digital media is both ephemeral – it can be changed, iterated upon and published – and "intertextual" – it creates a network of links and associations. Such attributes alter the "authority" of the author, in that it recontextualizes the uniqueness of the text and "supports less authorial control."[46] Instead, creativity emanates from the ability to reconfigure existing formats, content, and ideas. New narrative formats also reinforce these conditions: They include video games, with the absence of a single "auteur" or creative voice, and online fan-fiction, which conflates original and mutually created texts. Such emerging genres further illustrate how digital texts open up uniquely "liquid" relationships between authors and audiences.

However, perhaps nowhere are these liquid relationships more prominent than in remix culture, or the burgeoning of mash-ups, derivative work, and other forms of quoting via digital media in the 2000s. Textual remixing, according to Lessig, grew from three sources: easily accessible publishing tools (in the form of blogs), metadata to connect texts (via tags and rankings), and indexes to track preferences, all of which stand as the bedrock of digital text production. Remix culture profoundly impacted authorship.[47] Stein and Busse recount a flurry of playful activity from communities of fan-fiction writers, who reworked existing intellectual property to their own ends, for example in remix challenges where website coordinators devised competitions among participants to remake another fan's work. This led to "radical re-conceptualizations" of the text,[48] including

[44] Nicholas Diakopoulos, Kurt Luther, Yevgeniy Medynskiy, and Irfan Essa, "The Evolution of Authorship in a Remix Society," in *Proceedings of the Eighteenth Conference on Hypertext and Hypermedia* (New York: ACM, 2007), 133.

[45] Ibid., 133.

[46] Ibid., 134.

[47] Lawrence Lessig, *Remix: Making Art and Commerce Thrive in the Hybrid Economy* (New York: Penguin Press, 2008).

[48] Louisa Stein and Kristina Busse, "Limit Play: Fan Authorship between Source Text, Intertext, and Context," *Popular Communication* 7.4 (2009): 199.

alterations to major plot points of the original story or even the fictional characters' universes. Within remix culture, multiple sources, rather than a single narrative voice, frequently lay claim to the material. It is also shaped by playing with the "possibilities of the interface to create a multilayered, multimedia story world."[49]

The time period also upended preconceptions about readership. There remains a pervasive concern that digital text's fragmentary nature may promote more superficial engagement and effortless distraction, requiring less mental effort to comb through snippets of information.[50] However, literary critics such as Hayles challenge this apprehension. She suggests the perusal of online text is merely different from the close reading prized in traditional humanistic scholarship and carries distinct research advantages, including the effortless juxtaposition of ideas.[51] Further, because readers can easily play with, remix, and reproduce interactive media, the boundaries between them and authors "may well be reaching a cumulative point in which the distinctions between these two collapse usefully and productively."[52]

As Hammond notes, the inclusion of readers in the process of interpreting literary forms precedes digitization to the era of mass production.[53] However, online media has extended the agency readers exert. This can be seen in digital preservation efforts such as Project Gutenberg and the Internet Archive. Founded in 1971 by University of Illinois student Michael S. Hart, Project Gutenberg volunteers have collected 54,000 books in the public domain and preserved them in ASCII for replication in a wide variety of formats, even audiobooks.[54] Similarly, the Internet Archive runs partially on the labor of volunteers who can enter links into the "Wayback Machine" to save a snapshot of the page in perpetuity, along with web crawlers that perform this process automatically. While both projects have origins in academia and are underwritten by official channels – the Internet Archive is housed in part at the Bibliotecha Alexandrina – preservation also encompasses unsanctioned and playful channels.[55] In their study of "peer preservation," Tenen and Foxman discuss one of the world's largest

[49] Ibid., 204.

[50] Adrianna Van Der Weel, "Feeding Our Reading Machines: From the Typographic Page to the Docuverse," *Digital Studies/Le Champ Numérique* 6.6 (2017): https://doi.org/10.16995/dscn.15.

[51] Katherine N. Hayles. "How We Read: Close, Hyper, Machine," *ADE Bulletin* 150, no. 18 (2010): 74.

[52] Chartier, "Languages, Books, and Reading," 155.

[53] Hammond, *Literature in the Digital Age*, 30.

[54] Borsuk, *The Book*, 213.

[55] Ibid., 220.

"shadow libraries," which makes use of a distributed architecture and ad hoc rules to save multiple and partial copies of over a million pirated books across thousands of computers.[56] These preservation efforts are sustained by a series of conventions imposed by users, who compete for status in the community by accumulating larger and larger personal collections to share. Without any institutional backing, an informal game motivates readers to act as peer preservers of their library.

Hypermedia, remix culture, and digital preservation demonstrate the myriad ways in which formal rules established around digital text permitted "play" with norms and conventions. Each exhibited new types of authors, authorship, producers, and readers who manipulated and contested long-held traditions of literature. Rather than conforming to a formal or static structure, they assumed what might be called a "lusory" or playful attitude toward the text.[57] This manifests most acutely in Danet's account, where interactivity, hacker culture, and relative anonymity permitted users to play with identity, verbal and visual puns (e.g., ASCII art), hypertext books, and computer games. This lusory behavior creates a "liminal [cyberspace] … freed from the rules and expectations that normally govern daily life."[58] In other words, it created an index of abstract rules that facilitate play.

3 Manipulating: Issues of Power and the Future of Digital Text

> Digits, like fingers, can wag, curl, clench, and deliver crushing blows. The spread of digital computing is no unmitigated good for all, and especially for the disenfranchised many.[59]

As much as rules establish boundaries of play, they also consolidate power. Who sets the rules dictates how the game is played. Similarly, some of the world's largest corporations are shaping the future of digital text and how it is accessed and experienced, a concern that dominates popular and academic discussion of the medium. One repeated apprehension is the sway Google has over literature owing to the Google Books project. Started in 2004, the project had scanned 30 million books as of 2015 in partnership

[56] Dennis Tenen and Maxwell Henry Foxman, "Book Piracy As Peer Preservation," *Computational Culture* 4 (2014): http://computationalculture.net/book-piracy-as-peer-preservation/ (accessed July 15, 2023).

[57] Katie Salen and Eric Zimmerman, *Rules of Play: Game Design Fundamentals* (Cambridge, MA: The MIT Press, 2003).

[58] Danet, *Cyberpl@y*, 8.

[59] Peters, "Digital," 102.

with libraries and universities from around the world, including Harvard, Oxford, and the University of Michigan.[60] Borsuk has detailed the scale and depth of the project, which has involved developing open-source scanning technology, donating $3 million to the Library of Congress, and employing scores of workers to scan pages by hand on Google's campus.[61] The company only makes "snippets" of books available when searched through their website to circumvent copyright restrictions. However, this also dictates the ways and means to encounter books; users are prevented from freely browsing content, but must instead peruse it through Google's proprietary algorithms and the material it highlights, which may only be a few sentences or a paragraph of text. Plainly, Google Books focuses primarily on searching through text rather than reading it: Borsuk notes that unlike Project Gutenberg and the Internet Archive, Google has built its entire catalog around "indexing, searchability, and easy access."[62] In so doing, it acts as a de facto gatekeeper, leading to "lawsuits … claims of copyright infringement … [and] concerns over Google building a monopoly on information…"[63] An ongoing struggle persists over how to own and who owns digital texts. Key battlegrounds in this fight involve Digital Rights Management (DRM), open access, copyright, and even the software and devices used for everyday reading.

The conventional concept of ownership, synonymous with the possession of physical objects, is understandably complicated by the immateriality of fluid and ephemeral digital text. However, it is important to remember that it does have materiality, which Matthew Kirschenbaum and Lisa Gitelman have long advocated should be at the forefront of research. Kirschenbaum rejects the scholarly fixation on the purportedly chaotic and fragmentary nature of digital text,[64] and seeks to shift attention to forcefully material considerations such as "multiple versions and releases, data standards, platforms, and file formats, all of which contribute to the textual composition of electronic objects."[65] Simply, the very software, operating systems and equipment on which digital communication relies deeply affect how it is experienced.

60 Jon Bath, Scott Schofield, and Leslie Howsam, "The Digital Book," in *The Cambridge Companion to the History of the Book*, ed. Leslie Howsam (Cambridge: Cambridge University Press, 2014), 181–196.
61 Borsuk, *The Book*, 226.
62 Ibid., 229.
63 Bath et al., "The Digital Book," 184.
64 Kirschenbaum, "Editing the Interface," 24.
65 Ibid., 43.

One digital-textual tangible construction that *has* received academic scrutiny is the e-reader, starting with the Sony Data Discman in the 1990s.[66] Part of the fascination with these devices stems from their ability to provide readers "an entire library … on the go,"[67] and to include features not found in the traditional codex, such as text-to-speech reading, the incorporation of video, and the ability to learn new words through immediate access to dictionaries.[68] A more current example is Amazon's Kindle, which uses electronic ink to simulate a traditional page.[69] Indeed, simulation defines the e-reader, which has historically emulated the codex. This replication extends to the platform level, as the most successful e-readers possess proprietary formats, so that only a single copy of a text can be purchased and owned like a traditional book. Ironically, this convention ties ownership to the devices themselves; "to change e-book device brand is in most cases to lose one's e-library."[70]

Consequently, as digital media and cultural content are further platformized,[71] the materiality of e-books takes on particular saliency. Controversy persists over how behemoth corporations, such as Amazon, Google, and Apple, monopolize the future of text through their hardware. If proprietary devices and software remain dominant, they will exert inordinate influence on how to apprehend and obtain multitudes of digital text. E-readers' proprietary formatting additionally allows publishers and authors to retain rights and ultimately income from their work. This is a cornerstone of copyright, which simultaneously established the rights of the author and the public domain – in which all texts eventually reside for future public consumption and use. In his study of e-books, van der Weel argues that publishers implemented DRM to manage and enforce copyright and retain control over the distribution of electronic texts.[72] The software encrypts downloaded versions of books to prevent illegal distribution, which confers power to publishers and distributors (such as Amazon and Google). Critics allege that such encryption will "deprive readers and buyers of privacy protection and

[66] Adriaan Van Der Weel, "E-Roads and I-Ways: A Sociotechnical Look at User Acceptance of E-Books," *Logos* 21.3–4 (2010): 47–57.

[67] Borsuk, *The Book*, 231.

[68] Randall Boone and Kyle Higgins, "Reading, Writing, and Publishing Digital Text," *Remedial and Special Education: RASE* 2.3 (2003): 132–140.

[69] To read more on this, see Borsuk, *The Book*, 230.

[70] Van der Weel, "E-Roads and I-Ways," 49.

[71] David B. Nieborg and Thomas Poell, "The Platformization of Cultural Production: Theorizing the Contingent Cultural Commodity," *New Media & Society* 20.11 (2018): 4275–4292.

[72] Van der Weel, "E-Roads and I-Ways."

undermine established owner rights to lend or sell books or to take copies for private use or safekeeping."[73]

Furthermore, DRM represents a regulatory regime for digital text that extends beyond encrypting to the privilege of ownership. For instance, the Terms of Service for Kindle explicitly state that Amazon's content is simply "licensed, not sold."[74] No Kindle owner truly owns their library; instead, they rent it in perpetuity from publishers. DRM is just a starting point for how contemporary platforms can maneuver and retain control of content. In essence, they frame who gets to play with digital text, as well as how and why.

However, power in digital text production is still up for grabs by publishers, authors, and the public at large. At the other end of the rights spectrum, calls for open access (OA) and creative commons (CC) licensing aim to expand the use of intellectual property. While CC concentrates on granting a variety of copyright licenses for easy sharing of text,[75] the mission of OA is to make literature "digital, online, free of charge, and free of most copyright and licensing restrictions."[76] Based primarily in academia, researchers who share their findings through OA bypass the traditional financial and legal hurdles of publishing, which is particularly valuable in a profession where citation count matters more than financial gain. Suber attests to the "nonrivalrous" nature of knowledge consumption that has allowed for this iconoclastic ownership regime.[77] At its extreme, OA defaults works to the public domain,[78] and advocates that knowledge housed online should not be thought of "as a commodity to meter out to deserving customers" and instead as "a public good, especially when it is given away by its authors, funded with public money, or both."[79] These two legal theories flatten authorship and readership. For instance, CC licenses permit easy remixing of material and support the idea of digital text as something collectively owned. There is almost an expectation of free play, that rules of usage should be commonly decided upon rather than imposed from elsewhere.

[73] Hillesund, "Digital Text Cycles."

[74] "Kindle Store Terms of Use," Amazon: www.amazon.com/gp/help/customer/display.html/ref=hp_200699130_storeTOU1?nodeId=201014950&tag=w050b-20 (accessed February 24, 2020).

[75] To read about the philosophy behind CC licensing, see Lawrence Lessig, *Free Culture: How Big Media Uses Technology and the Law to Lock Down Culture and Control Creativity* (New York: Penguin Press, 2004).

[76] Peter Suber, *Open Access* (Cambridge, MA: The MIT Press, 2012), 4.

[77] Ibid., 46.

[78] Ibid., 69.

[79] Ibid., 116.

As typified by the e-reader, new devices, new digital rights management encryption standards, and proprietary formats ultimately affect the future consumption of digital texts. In contrast to the ASCII general standard, if Kindle should decide to abandon its KPF format, or if users abandon the Kindle, how or if they can transfer their texts is uncertain. Furthermore, as Hillesund argues, the multimedia features of digital text "will give rise to new text genres with new linguistic styles, element types and element structures, many of which are incompatible with print."[80] As such, obsolescence and compatibility of digital text must be addressed.

Describing porting – or the means "by which software and electronic objects are migrated from one platform and operating system to another" – Kirschenbaum makes it clear that compatibility is a "messy business" in which varied systems, code bases, and eccentric software behavior ultimately restrict how text appears on different devices.[81] Much is inevitably changed – and lost – in the process of porting, and the same is true even of platform upgrades. New functions and prerogatives of developers and companies may alter texts and, eventually, the reading experience. This often happens without the consent of consumers, who, because of the proprietary nature of platforms, cannot opt to have their software revert back to an older version.

Comparable business decisions permeate contemporary computer technology industries. Fitzpatrick argues that obsolescence aligns with one of the great buzzwords of the digital age, "innovation," in that both are based around the notion of moving beyond the "now." Obsolescence is "a designed component of the product life cycle, intended to spur consumption not just through the production of the new but through the manufacture of oldness."[82] By making older versions of text "obsolete," digital innovations also remove the means by which they can be preserved. Digital text is becoming ephemeral not only at a theoretical level, but also materially so, simply wiped out in the inevitable next version. When it comes to the materiality, legal infrastructure, and even longevity of digital texts, those with power over distribution increasingly have the greatest influence to referee how and for how long readers and authors can play within textual spaces.

[80] Hillesund, "Digital Text Cycles."
[81] Kirschenbaum, "Editing the Interface," 41.
[82] Kathleen Fitzpatrick, "Obsolescence and Innovation in the Age of the Digital," in *The Routledge Companion to Media Studies and Digital Humanities*, ed. Jentery Sayers (New York: Routledge, 2018), 330.

4 Conclusion

In a series of historical snapshots, this chapter exposes critical issues surrounding the inception, proliferation, and future of digital texts. Peters' initial concept, that the digital inherently "counts" or translates phenomena into code, forms the foundational relationship between text and the digital: Digital technology has and continues to be a process by which natural phenomena are rendered into the symbolic.[83] Throughout this history, influential actors have circumscribed the means by which this occurs. They have created sets of rules and standards, some arbitrary and some not, with which users, readers, and authors alike have continuously played. This play has instigated perspectival shifts. Text itself has become more ephemeral, multimodal, and porous. Authorship continues to be a collaborative process, with fans, users, and writers able to remix and alter media, while at the same time trying to preserve ownership over their creations. Readership is also shared, and struggles persist over who, how, and in what ways texts can be kept and preserved when their very nature lends to malleability and play.

When considering the playfulness of digital text, it would be naïve to imagine that literature is now in a state of free play, enacting a turn-of-the-century utopian vision. Control, consolidation, and management remain particularly relevant in a contemporary environment where the few, as opposed to the many, increasingly configure the rules of digital text. Although their dictates lean toward codification and standardization, who and how they are constructed ultimately shape the medium. Consequently, authors, readers, and scholars must understand these explicit and implicit directives so they can navigate the textual environment around them and continue to play within it.

[83] Peters, "Digital Text."

PART II

Developments

CHAPTER 8

Prostheses

Alice Hall

In Flannery O'Connor's short story, "The Lame Shall Enter First" (1965), Rufus Johnson – a juvenile delinquent with a clubfoot – visits a shop "lined and stacked with the equipment of affliction": "Wheel chairs and walkers covered most of the floor. The walls were hung with every kind of crutch and brace. Artificial limbs were stacked on the shelves, legs and arms and hands, claws and hooks and straps and human harnesses and unidentifiable instruments for unnamed deformities."[1] The shopping trip is part of a broader program of physical and moral rehabilitation imposed on Johnson by his guardian, Sheppard, who seeks to "correct" his gait through the purchase of an orthopedic shoe, just as he tries to reform his behavior and offer him scientific enlightenment through another form of prosthesis, a telescope. However, Johnson refuses the shoe and resists the program of moral correction, and the story ends with him being arrested for burglary and Sheppard's own son committing suicide, hanging from the rafters just below the telescope.

O'Connor's story intertwines a meditation on the spiritual dimensions of disability with an individual and highly physicalized representation of prostheses. The so-called equipment of affliction is a recurring feature of O'Connor's fiction and life writing; from the frequent representation of spectacles, artificial limbs, and glass eyes in her fiction, to her letters that document reactions to the crutches that she herself used as a result of lupus.[2] In this chapter, a close reading of another O'Connor story, "Good Country People" (1955), alongside William Faulkner's "The Leg" (1934), provides a starting point for a broader examination of prostheses in literary, cultural, and disability theory. There is a long-standing tradition of writing about prostheses in literary writing, particularly in Gothic

[1] Flannery O'Connor, *Collected Works* (New York: Library of America, 1988), 620.

[2] Jess Libow, "Prosthesis Repurposed: Gender and Rehabilitation in Flannery O'Connor's Fiction," *Journal of Literary and Cultural Disability Studies* 11.4 (2017): 391.

traditions right up to the very contemporary, but O'Connor and Faulkner serve as important examples because their stories are set in a period of rapid change in the history of prostheses: Their narratives reflects a huge growth in the availability and rapid technological advancement of prosthetics in the United States and Europe after the two World Wars. Both O'Connor and Faulkner probe the normalizing "integrationist ideals" associated with prostheses early in the twentieth century; from the desire to integrate wounded soldiers back into communities, to assimilating diverse female bodies into a single "integrable" version of femininity as complete, whole, and "natural."[3] But Faulkner's and O'Connor's stories also go beyond registering historical shifts in relation to prostheses; they challenge normalizing discourses and help us to think about what literary representations of technology can offer and why narrative representations of disability are important.

Critical disability theorists have frequently suggested that disability sparks imagination and narration. Michael Bérubé states simply that disability "demands a story."[4] For David Mitchell and Susan Snyder, it is disability's "very unknowability that consolidates the need to tell a story about it."[5] This "demand for explanatory narrative" works on a crude level in everyday life, as people with disabilities are often expected to describe and even explain their bodies and histories in ways that those perceived as normal are not: "the scar, the limp, the missing limb, or the obvious prosthesis – calls for a story."[6] Some scholars suggest that literary narratives provide a space in which this demand for stories can be satisfied. Mitchell and Snyder's account of metaphor suggests that modern literary narratives tend to follow an inherently conservative trajectory: "Our notion of narrative prosthesis evolves out of this specific recognition: a narrative issue to resolve or correct – to 'prostheticize' ... a deviance marked as improper to a social context."[7] Disability not only demands a story, they argue, but it also demands an explanation that will make it disappear or cover it up; disability symbolizes a threatening form of bodily and social disorder, which can be temporarily explored in a narrative but must then be removed to

[3] David Mitchell, "Foreword," in *A History of Disability*, ed. Henri-Jacques Stiker (Ann Arbor: University of Michigan Press, 1999), xii.

[4] Michael Bérubé, "Disability and Narrative," *PMLA* 120.2 (2005): 570.

[5] David T. Mitchell and Sharon L. Snyder, *Narrative Prosthesis and the Dependencies of Discourse* (Ann Arbor: University of Michigan Press, 2001), 6.

[6] G. Thomas Couser, "Disability, Life Narrative and Representation," in *The Disability Studies Reader*, ed. Lennard J. Davis (New York: Routledge, 2017), 457.

[7] Mitchell and Snyder, *Narrative Prosthesis*, 6.

ensure a return to established social and bodily norms at the end of the story. In this view, narrative itself corresponds with a view of prosthesis as covering-up – what Robert McRuer describes as a "rehabilitative contract,"[8] which stipulates that "in return for integration, no complaints will be made, no suggestion for how the world, if not the disabled body or mind, might be molded differently. No complaints will be made even if the contract in effect relegates disabled people to the margins."[9]

Writing about physical disability, prosthetics, and rehabilitation certainly has the potential to serve a "prosthetic" function in the sense described by McRuer, Mitchell, and Snyder: propping up normative discourses through traditional bodily and narrative forms, stock characters, and reductive metaphors. However, as the examples from O'Connor and Faulkner suggest, fiction can also challenge the "rehabilitative contract" by placing disability center stage. "Good Country People" and "The Leg" focus on the physical difficulties and possibilities of living with a prosthetic leg. Instead of hiding away difference and disability, these are stories about exposure: They examine the boundaries between human and machine, organic and artificial, literal and metaphorical, spiritual and material. "Good Country People" and "The Leg" can be read as examples of a modernist tradition that used fiction to go against the grain, employing experimental forms and open-ended narrative structures to resist homogenizing discourses that construct disabled bodies in terms of deficit. As Davidson argues, the increasing influence of the technologies of "statistics, comparative anatomy, and racial science" early in the twentieth century directly paralleled the emergence of a modernist artistic aesthetic that, in contrast to the quantification and regularization of bodies, "shattered ideas of sculptural integrity, single-point perspective, narrative coherence, and tonal harmony."[10] The experimental forms, fragmented language, and representations of disabled bodies in O'Connor and Faulkner's short fiction challenge models of knowledge and self-perception predicated on quantification and regularization.

These examples are important because they demonstrate how fiction can not only reflect and record historical shifts, but also act as a powerful site for reimagining relationships between the body and technology. Faulkner and O'Connor's works engage with a particularly significant moment in

8 Robert McRuer, *Crip Theory: Cultural Signs of Queerness and Disability* (New York: New York University Press, 2006), 121.

9 Ibid., 13.

10 Michael Davidson, *Concerto for the Left Hand: Disability and the Defamiliar Body* (Ann Arbor: University of Michigan Press, 2008), xvii.

this history of prostheses, but they also remind us that literature across the ages has provided a space in which fraught questions about the relationship between human and machine, and fantasies of bodily enhancement and dismemberment, have been both represented and renegotiated. As David Punter argues, citing examples from Charles Dickens, Victor Hugo, Henry James, Mary Shelley, and Charles Maturin, "the history of [literary] dealings with the disabled body runs through the history of the Gothic, a history of invasion and resistance, of the enemy within, of bodies torn and tortured, or else rendered miraculously, or sometimes catastrophically whole."[11] In the twentieth and twenty-first centuries, prostheses such as voice synthesizers and other assistive technologies have revolutionized the process of writing itself for some people with disabilities; platforms such as YouTube and online publishing have opened up new audiences and create alternative forms of representation. Prosthesis has also become a potent metaphor for cultural theorists, from Donna Haraway's feminist reimagining of the possibilities of female empowerment through technology in her "Cyborg Manifesto" (1985) to Vivian Sobchak's semi-autobiographical critique, "A Leg to Stand On" (2006). This chapter seeks to give readers a sense of some of the rich and complex theoretical work in this area, but also, through the examples of the short stories by O'Connor and Faulkner, to argue that literary writing from the past is an important resource for rethinking our increasingly technologized lives in the present.

1 "The Leg": Rehabilitation and Masculinity

In his wide-ranging *History of Disability* (1999), Henri-Jacques Stiker argues that the 1920s marked an important turning point in the social and cultural history of physical disability. The end of World War I saw huge numbers of injured and physically impaired soldiers returning from battle and trying to reassimilate into their communities. This sudden increase in the visibility of disability in everyday life triggered, Stiker argues, a new conception of rehabilitation. This new integrationist ideal was distinct from existing medical conceptions of cure: "Cure is a removal and relates to health. Rehabilitation is situated in the social sphere and constitutes replacement for a deficit."[12] According to this deficit model of rehabilitation, disability is a lack that needs to be covered up and made to disappear.

[11] David G. Punter, "A Foot Is What Fits the Shoe: Disability, Prosthesis and the Gothic," *Gothic Studies* 2.1 (2000), 39.
[12] Stiker, *A History of Disability*, 124.

The widespread development of prosthetics in the same period represented a "technology of absorption" that was part of the same desire to restore injured men to an able-bodied ideal, or at least to sustain a fantasy of completion in the public sphere.[13] David Serlin argues that this expansion of the prosthetics industry sought to prop up both injured male bodies and a damaged national economy.[14] Gary Albrecht also emphasizes these interconnections between capitalist imperatives to be economically self-supporting and discourses of physical capability.[15] Katherine Ott casts this shift in distinctly gendered terms: "it is nearly impossible to avoid linking prosthetics with national recuperation, modernity and masculine redemption."[16]

These debates about rehabilitation, reintegration, and the complex role of prosthetics were also examined in a boom of fictional writing about disability after World War I. Disabled war veteran novels such as William Faulkner's *Soldier's Pay* (1926) and Dalton Trumbo's *Johnny Got His Gun* (1939) describe shattered bodies and minds using experimental, fragmented narrative forms. Faulkner's short narrative sketch, "The Leg" (1934), displays this fascination with war veterans through an engagement with prosthetics that is rendered in both highly visceral and richly symbolic terms. Like Trumbo's novel, "The Leg" begins with a wounded World War I soldier named David lying in a hospital bed in the darkness: "And my nights were filled too, with nerve- and muscle-ends chafed now by an immediate cause: the wood and leather leg. But the gap was still there, and sometimes at night, isolated by invisibility, it would become filled with the immensity of darkness and silence despite me."[17]

David conveys a powerful impression of disorientation and physical discomfort, related from a claustrophobic first-person perspective. Faulkner engages with the fear and anxieties of an individual protagonist within a wider social and cultural context. The wood and leather leg is an example of the prostheses developed in World War I and symbolic of the culture of rehabilitation that "figur[ed] disability as an anomaly to be made to disappear."[18] Yet in the story the narrator also hints at the multilayered

13 Ibid., 164.

14 David Serlin, *Replaceable You: Engineering the Body in Postwar America* (Chicago: University of Chicago Press, 2004).

15 Gary Albrecht, *The Disability Business: Rehabilitation in America* (Newbury Park, CA: Sage, 1992).

16 Katherine Ott, "Carnage Remembered: Prosthetics in the United States Military Since the 1860s," in *Materializing the Military*, ed. Bernard Finn and Barton Hacker (London: Science Museum, 2005), 48.

17 William Faulkner, "The Leg," in *Dr Martino and Other Stories* (London: Chatto and Windus, 1965), 311.

18 Stiker, *A History of Disability*, 137.

metaphorical significance of his prosthetic leg. This sense of the symbolic potential of prosthesis connects to the insistence in Stiker's historical account that "prosthesis is not only the pieces of wood, iron, now plastic that replace the missing hand or foot. It is also the very idea that you can *replace*.... Replacement, re-establishment of the prior situation, substitution, compensation – all of this now becomes possible language."[19] In "The Leg," Faulkner puts these assumptions about physical and linguistic substitution under scrutiny. Just as David describes the physical challenges of adapting to his prosthesis, the leg comes to symbolize the difficulties of narrating psychological loss and the impossibility of a return to his prior bodily or mental state. David's prosthesis becomes, paradoxically, a symbol for all that is absent and irreplaceable; in this surreal story he struggles to reimagine the presence of his missing leg and also to reconstruct his fragmentary memories of himself as a student and his dead companion, George.

The "new mental and social division,"[20] which was inaugurated by World War I, becomes incorporated into David's consciousness as the internal voice is split between himself and the imaginary presence of his dead friend, and into his own conception of his body as fragmented and unstable. For David, the missing leg also comes to symbolize the death of his friend George, a loss that refuses to be easily prostheticized or replaced: "I had lost them both."[21] Though the leg and his friend have both been lost in war, they are, however, powerfully and painfully present in the story. "The Leg" adopts a cyclical structure in which David's memory loops back to previous time periods and the reader becomes immersed in his sense of the blurring of "the line between truth and delirium."[22] The claustrophobic cyclical structure counters contemporary medicalized discourses of rehabilitation that, in the words of Dr. Howard Rusk, the "father of comprehensive rehabilitation," "takes the patient from the bed back to the job" ("Forgotten Casualty").[23] Like the raw, exposed "nerve- and muscle-ends" that Faulkner describes at the beginning of the narrative,[24] "The Leg" is an open-ended story that resists linear narratives of cure or overcoming. It ends as it begins, with David in a recumbent position, physically inactive

[19] Ibid., 123–124.
[20] Ibid., 125.
[21] Faulkner, "The Leg," 312.
[22] Ibid., 311.
[23] Howard Rusk, "Rehabilitation: Forgotten Casualty: The Disabled Civilian," *New York Times*, May 12, 1946, 94.
[24] Faulkner, "The Leg," 311.

yet engaged in an ongoing process of trying to reimagine his body and himself, in ways that are uncomfortable, hallucinatory, unstable, yet also highly creative. In Snyder and Mitchell's terms, "The Leg" is a story that refuses to "remove the unsightly from view."[25]

2 Enforcing Normalcy and Femininity

Like Faulkner's "The Leg." O'Connor's "Good Country People" was also written in the aftermath of conflict, this time World War II, at a moment when many disabled veterans were returning home and prostheses were becoming increasingly available and affordable. O'Connor is concerned, however, with how this technology also draws attention to the precarity of normative expectations about femininity. Hulga, the central protagonist in the story, wears a prosthetic leg following a hunting accident. In the first part of the story, O'Connor seems to use Hulga's prosthesis as a metaphorical shortcut: Her wooden leg can be read as a straightforward figure for the intellectual limitation that she feels, trapped in a claustrophobic domestic setting with her mother, the small-minded Mrs. Hopewell. Hulga's physical immobility and her domestic entrapment are aligned with a form of willful sensory deprivation; her eyes are "icy blue, with the look of someone who has achieved blindness and means to keep it."[26]

Yet, in a characteristic narrative twist, O'Connor offers readers this reassuring metaphorical crutch only to pull it away in the final moments of the story. In the climactic scene in the barn, Hulga's icy, ascetic intellectualism gives way to sexual desire for the Bible salesman, Manley Pointer. Like the raw, chafing nerve endings and the heavy wooden leg in Faulkner's story, the boundary between Hulga's flesh and her prosthesis is a focus of the narrative, and a source of fascination for Pointer, who asks Hulga repeatedly to show him where her "wooden leg joins on."[27] At this pivotal moment of exposure, the prosthesis is transformed from an easy metaphor for domestic and social limitation into a highly individual material object – an "artificial limb, in a white sock and brown flat shoe … bound in a heavy material like canvas and ended in an ugly jointure where it attached to the stump."[28] The boundary between the flesh and prosthesis is the crux of the story: When Hulga allows Pointer to touch and to remove her wooden leg, he steals it and places it out of her reach. In this climactic

[25] Mitchell and Snyder, *Narrative Prosthesis*, 8.
[26] O'Connor, *Collected Works*, 281.
[27] Ibid., 280.
[28] Ibid., 297.

scene, Pointer's religious rhetoric is replaced by the revelation that he is an atheist; he opens his Bible to reveal that it is hollowed out to allow space for whiskey and pornographic playing cards. Hulga's leg, which until this point she has taken "care of it as someone else would his soul, in private and almost with her own eyes turned away," is exposed, scrutinized, and sexualized as a highly personal material object.[29] In a story loaded with biblical imagery, the epiphany, then, is not a form of spiritual or sexual transcendence, but rather a return to the body.

Lennard Davis argues that ideas of racialized, gendered, ableist "normalcy" are "enforced" in a series of public venues; two of the most important, he argues, are technologies such as prostheses and forms of cultural production such as the novel. For Davis, the idealizing fiction of the "normate," a physically and economically self-supporting individual, highlights the way in which disability is socially constructed through a relationship between a person and their environment. For him,

> the very structures on which the novel rests tend to be normative, ideologically emphasizing the universal quality of the central character whose normativity encourages us to identify with him or her. Furthermore, the novel's goal is to reproduce … the middleness of life, the middleness of the material world, the middleness of the normal body, the middleness of a sexually gendered, ethnically middle world is created in symbolic form and then reproduced symbolically.[30]

"Good Country People" and "The Leg" are, I argue, more radical. They represent bodies that are not easily prostheticized: They imagine specific examples of the use of prosthetics in everyday life as sometimes painful, embarrassing, difficult to use, and always temporary. Hulga is not represented as a straightforward victim or a stereotypical tragic disabled figure; instead she is rendered as a complex character, strong-willed, stubborn, intelligent, vulnerable, manipulative, sexually aware, strong, and highly changeable in just a few pages. O'Connor seems to register the sensationalist fascination with prosthetics that the story itself could be accused of through Pointer's final proud revelation that he has stolen other personal objects on his travels, including a glass eye. The story invites us as readers to scrutinize the details of her body, but also warns of the dangers of reading surfaces, of taking words and metaphors at face value.

[29] Ibid., 297.

[30] Lennard J. Davis, "Constructing Normalcy: The Bell Curve, the Novel, and the Invention of the Disabled Body in the Nineteenth Century," in *The Disability Studies Reader*, ed. Lennard J. Davis (London: Routledge, 2006), 11.

On a structural level, by rejecting stereotypical cultural scripts such as the heroic progress narrative, these stories also refuse to be "prostheticized." Both stories have open endings that create a sense of ongoing emotional and physical rawness. After floundering alone without her wooden leg in the barn, Hulga returns to the oppressive stasis of the kitchen to face yet more of her mother's hollowed-out aphorisms and bubbling resentment. Faulkner's wounded soldier remains incapacitated and alone in the darkness and silence at the end of the story. Both O'Connor and Faulkner use the intense focus of the short story form to draw attention to the details of individual bodies, but also to depict ongoing situations: lives in flux, unresolved questions, "incomplete" bodies, and shifting metaphorical meanings. They engage with the social and political shifts in relation to prostheses in this period, but also try to imagine a personal perspective. In doing so, they engage with the paradoxical situation described by Simi Linton, in which postwar rehabilitation provided "better medical care and more effective treatments than people with mobility impairments had ever had" and yet also made the error of "speaking for disabled people which undermined the autonomy they claimed to promote."[31] Linton's work, which fuses autobiography with disability rights activism, insists that the voices of people with disabilities are heard and that physical differences are seen and celebrated, rather than covered up or normalized, in public spaces: "We have come out, not in those brown wool lap robes over our withered legs, or dark glasses over our pale eyes, but in shorts and sandals … straightforward, unmasked, and unapologetic."[32] These stories by Faulkner and O'Connor also focus on moments of exposure and place physical disabilities center stage. Crucially, they resist any urge toward stable order, whether narrative, social, or bodily. At once viscerally material and richly metaphorical, O'Connor and Faulkner depict the everyday lives of people with physical disabilities whose bodies refuse to be easily "corrected," covered, or removed from the narrative frame.

3 Prosthesis as Metaphor in Contemporary Cultural Theory

This interplay between material and metaphorical, central to the short stories by Faulkner and O'Connor, is also a key concern of recent cultural theory in which prosthesis features as a recurring trope. Tim Armstrong,

[31] Simi Linton, *My Body Politic: A Memoir* (Ann Arbor: University of Michigan Press, 2007), 80–81.
[32] Ibid., 6.

for example, puts forward the concept of "Prosthetic Modernism."[33] Marquand Smith and Joanna Morra's collection explores the "point of prosthetic contact – and the dialectic of the edges in such contact" in order to think about ways in which the prosthetic is integral to understandings of the human.[34] Donna Haraway, in her "Cyborg Manifesto," suggests that "Prosthesis is semiosis … the making of meaning and bodies, not for transcendence but for power-charged communication."[35] In these studies, prosthetics are considered in largely metaphorical terms as a means of theorizing the relationship between modernity, technology, and the body, and in order to explore shifting definitions of the human.

In cultural disability studies scholarship, this figurative use of prosthetics has often been criticized for the ways in which it fetishizes prosthetics and distances discussions from embodied, material experiences of disability. Tobin Siebers, for example, criticizes postmodern cultural theorists such as Haraway who, he says, invoke prosthesis as a straightforward metaphor for empowerment without giving any thought to the physical challenges of living with prosthesis. In this context, he argues, people with disabilities are caricatured as technologically enhanced "supercrips" as prosthesis enters a problematic level of theoretical abstraction:

> Pain is most often soothed by the joy of conceiving the body differently from the norm. Frequently, the objects that people with disabilities live with – prostheses, wheelchairs, braces, and other devices – are viewed not as potential sources of pain but as marvellous examples of the plasticity of the human form or as devices of empowerment … Rare is the theoretical account where physical suffering remains harmful for very long. The ideology of ability requires that any sign of disability be viewed exclusively as awakening new and magical opportunities for ability.[36]

Vivian Sobchack echoes this call for a "new realism" of the body in disability studies. Like Siebers, she denounces the "scandal of the metaphor" of prosthesis as an "unfleshed-out" catchword in contemporary cultural theory.[37] She suggests that she is both "startled" and "amused" by the prominence

33 Tim Armstrong, *Modernism, Technology and the Body: A Cultural Study* (Cambridge: Cambridge University Press, 1998), 4.

34 Marquand Smith and Joanna Morra, eds., *The Prosthetic Impulse: From a Posthuman Present to Biocultural Future* (Cambridge, MA: The MIT Press, 2006), 7.

35 Donna Haraway, *Simians, Cyborgs and Women: The Reinvention of Nature* (New York: Routledge, 1991), 277.

36 Tobin Siebers, *Disability Theory* (Ann Arbor: University of Michigan Press, 2008), 62–63.

37 Vivian Sobchack, "A Leg to Stand on: Prosthetics, Metaphor and Materiality," in *The Prosthetic Impulse: From a Posthuman Present to a Biocultural Future*, ed. Marquand Smith and Joanna Morra (Cambridge, MA: MIT Press, 2005), 21.

of prosthetics in contemporary cultural criticism, and she challenges the notion that prosthetics should be read as "sexy" or "exotic."[38] Sobchack's work takes a first-person perspective in order to explicitly challenge the tendency for prosthetics to be narrated from an external perspective, as a rhetorical or poetic figure "located *elsewhere*"; instead, she suggests that these "parts" become, in her experience, incorporated into an individual's body.[39] Like many of the recent works on prosthesis in disability studies scholarship, Sobchak's work fuses various genres and draws upon her own autobiography, in this case her experience of using a prosthetic leg, as a means of introducing and complicating her critical insights.

David Wills also blurs the lines between autobiography and theoretical writing. But, in contrast to Sobchack, Wills revels in the fluid movement between literal and metaphorical understandings of prosthesis. His lyrical, playful and experimental writing is at once highly personal – "a narrative of a father's stance" – and highly theoretical: a "critical posture."[40] Wills begins with his father's experience of using a prosthetic leg, but then broadens this to use prosthesis as a means of thinking about processes of linguistic substitution. For Wills, the act of writing itself reminds us of our prosthetic relationship to language and to technologies: "One cannot simply write about prosthesis when one is automatically, just by virtue of writing, writing prosthesis, entering into prosthetic relations, being prosthetic."[41] Wills's highly metatextual, self-reflexive theoretical writing therefore paradoxically returns readers to the materiality of their own bodies, reading or writing in the present moment.

Wills conceives of the act of writing itself as a prosthetic relationship: In the substitution of an idea or an object with a word, pens, typewriters, computers, tablets and phones become extensions of our bodies. Representation is always shaped by, and subject to, the material, physical capabilities and conditions of our bodies. But, as Siebers argues, focusing on disability foregrounds the physical dimensions of writing and requires an innovative, often experimental approach:

> Blind hands envision the faces of old acquaintances. Deaf eyes listen to public television. Tongues touch-type letters home to Mum and Dad. Feet wash breakfast dishes. Mouths sign autographs. Different bodies require and create new modes of representation. What would it mean for disability studies to take this insight seriously? Could it change body theory if it did?[42]

38 Ibid., 19; 32.
39 Ibid., 20.
40 David Wills, *Prosthesis* (Stanford, CA: Stanford University Press, 1995), 9.
41 Ibid., 30.
42 Siebers, *Disability Theory*, 54.

In a twenty-first-century context, the creative possibilities of these new modes of representation are extended through the increasing availability of new technologies of reading and writing. These prosthetic technologies have also revolutionized access to reading and writing for people with disabilities: from talking books and electronic reading machines developed for blind populations over the course of the twentieth century to rapidly advancing computerized assistive technologies such as voice synthesizers for those who are nonverbal in the present day. For example, internationally acclaimed young autistic authors such as Tito Mukhopadhyay and Naoki Higashida, who use computerized alphabet grids to compose their works, simply would not have been able to write their poems, short stories, or memoirs in an earlier age. Digital technologies enable the wider distribution of disability narratives, but have also led to the production of new genres and forms of writing. For example, these forms bring together words, images, and physical performances in new configurations, such as in sign language poetry or Amanda Baggs's autobiographical "In My Language" (2007), accessible on YouTube. In turn, critics and cultural theorists need to find new ways of thinking about the ways in which all of our bodies are increasingly involved in prosthetic relationships with technology.

4 Dismodernism, Disability, and Bodily Enhancement

Faulkner and O'Connor, writing in the first half of the twentieth century, represent prostheticized bodies that are disabled and exceptional; these are narratives of exposure that both build toward a climactic moment at which the boundary between human flesh and artificial prosthesis is revealed. By contrast, cultural theorists such as Slavoj Žižek and Lennard Davis argue that in the twenty-first century, prosthetics are becoming increasingly normalized and invisible, incorporated into all bodies. Žižek describes a sense of loss that

> jeopardizes our most elementary perception of "our own body" as it is related to its environs.... On the one hand, inside is always outside: with the progressive implantation and replacement of our internal organs, techno-computerized prostheses (bypasses, pacemakers...) function as an internal part of our "living" organism; the colonization of the outer space thus reverts to the inside, into "endolocolonization," the technological colonization of our body itself. On the other hand, outside is always inside: when we are directly immersed in VR, we lose contact with reality – electro-waves bypass the interaction of external bodies and directly attack our senses.[43]

[43] Slavoj Žižek, *Plague of Fantasies* (London and New York: Verso, 1997), 134.

Žižek argues that this "colonization of the body" by technology reconfigures the relationship between interior and exterior spaces. He describes a state in which "I rely less and less on my proper body; my bodily activity is more and more reduced to giving signals to machines which do the work for me (clicking on a computer mouse, etc.)," and yet, "on the other hand, my body is strengthened, 'hyperactivated' through body-building and jogging, pharmaceutical means, and direct implants."[44] For Žižek, therefore, the modern citizen exists in a paradoxical state in which they risk becoming at once a "hyperactive superman" *and* a "cripple who can move around only by means of prostheses regulated by a computer chip (like the Robocop)."[45] Žižek highlights how prosthetics are at once medical aids, designed to enable and often "correct" disabled bodies, but also part of growing fitness and cosmetics industries aimed at modifying and enhancing able bodies.

A Wellcome Trust exhibition, entitled "Superhumans" and launched to coincide with the 2012 Paralympic Games in London, exemplified these connections between disability and body enhancement through a focus on prostheses. The exhibition displayed technologies designed for people with disabilities from across the ages such as ancient Egyptian prosthetic toes or early hearing aids, alongside modern-day items that visitors might not usually consider to be prostheses, such as reading glasses, lipsticks, sex aids, and the latest iPhone. This everyday aspect of prostheses is theorized by Davis as a form of "Dismodernism": the idea that all bodies in the twenty-first century are dependent on technology and are deemed incomplete without consumer products from deodorant and hair gel to contact lenses, hearing aids, breast implants, pacemakers, and birth control implants. "The contemporary body," he argues, is always conceived of as deficient: "[it] can only be made complete by means of consumption."[46] Dismodernism is, therefore, a subject position that is closely connected to postmodernism: a new category that acknowledges the partial, incomplete nature of human subjects and focuses on dependency and interdependence rather than autonomy.

The examples discussed in this chapter, which range from the Southern Gothic of Flannery O'Connor and Faulkner to the twenty-first-century Wellcome Trust exhibition in London, suggest some of the ways in which

[44] Žižek, 135.
[45] Žižek, 135.
[46] Lennard J. Davis, *Bending over Backwards: Disability, Dismodernism, and Other Difficult Positions* (New York: New York University Press, 2002), 27.

approaching prosthetics from an arts and humanities perspective can help us to reflect upon, but also to challenge, established paradigms of ability, disability, beauty, and dependency. Language and storytelling are important to our understanding of prosthesis because anxieties, hopes, and fantasies about enablement, modification, and enhancement, as well as the powerful fiction of the "normate," are reinforced but also renegotiated in literary and cultural spaces: novels, comics, magazines, films, and the media.[47] O'Connor and Faulkner go against the grain and use processes of storytelling to expose rather than cover up difference; their short fiction interrogates voyeurism, sexuality, loss, and the boundaries of the body. Thinking about prosthesis through narrative draws us into rich, complex histories of technology and medicine, but also of gender and disability, and helps us to recognize their fundamental interdependency. As a material, daily reality for growing numbers of people around the world, and a deeply embedded critical metaphor, prosthesis shapes our bodies and the stories that we tell about our identities.[48]

[47] Rosemarie Garland-Thomson, *Extraordinary Bodies: Figuring Physical Disability in American Culture and Literature* (New York: Columbia University Press, 1997), 8.

[48] This chapter draws on material from my book *Literature and Disability: Contemporary Critical Thought* (Abingdon and New York: Routledge, 2016) and my chapter "Disability and the Short Story," in *The Edinburgh Companion to the Short Story in English*, ed. Adrian Hunter and Paul Delaney (Edinburgh: Edinburgh University Press, 2019).

CHAPTER 9

Clocks

Scott Lightsey

> Suddenly, towards the middle of the fourteenth century, the mechanical clock seized the imagination of our ancestors. Something of the same pride which earlier had expended itself in cathedral building was now diverted to the construction of astronomical clocks of astounding intricacy and elaboration. No European community felt able to hold up its head unless in its midst the planets wheeled in cycles and epicycles while angels trumpeted, cocks crew, and apostles, kings, and prophets marched and countermarched at the booming of the hours.[1]

Lynn White's colorful description of the clock's proliferation inextricably binds the technologies of the mechanical clock and lifelike *automata* through the pride and prestige that catalyzed their adoption.[2] This relationship limns a distinction between matters of time-telling and the visual symbolic regimes that drove the adoption of these early clocks. Sometimes the embrace of a technology seems so rapid that it appears on the long scale of history to be almost instantaneous, and the mechanical clock was one such technology. In the scant decades of a medieval lifespan, the device unleashed an energetic pattern of adoption that flung these machines across the European continent.[3] Within a few score years of their invention, as clocks found purchase amid church towers and town centers, they also began to appear in vernacular writing by figures from disparate

[1] Lynn White, *Medieval Technology and Social Change* (Oxford: Clarendon, 1962), 124.

[2] Despite this colorful and deceptively casual formulation, White seems nevertheless to have arrived somewhat presciently at what subsequent analysis confirms. Some of his claims have been tested, in, for example, Bert Hall, "Lynn White's *Medieval Technology and Social Change* after Thirty Years," in *Technological Change: Methods and Themes in the History of Technology,* Studies in the History of Science, Medicine, and Technology 1, ed. Robert Fox (Amsterdam: Harwood, 1996), 85–101, and their utility confirmed in works such as Alex Roland's excellent "Once More into the Stirrups: Lynn White Jr., *Medieval Technology and Social Change,*" *Technology and Culture* 44.3 (July 2003): 574–585, and Shana Worthen's "The Influence of Lynn White, Jr.'s *Medieval Technology and Social Change,*" *History Compass* 7.4 (July 2009): 1201–1217.

[3] Indeed, between 1371 and 1379, the proliferation of clocks was most rapid; the shape of this adoption-curve is discussed thoroughly in Gerhard Dohrn-van Rossum, *The History of the Hour: Clocks and Modern Temporal Orders*, trans. Thomas Dunlap (Chicago: University of Chicago Press, 1996), 157–162.

areas of court life, such as Christine de Pizan, Philippe de Mézières, Jean Froissart, and Geoffrey Chaucer. These authors inscribed clocks into a variety of regimes of meaning, engaging the clockwork in moral and political discourses far afield of keeping time.

The rapid spread of clocks during the fourteenth century has been characterized as a move from natural to artificial reckoning, as Europeans began to mark time according to the machine. Amid the *annales*-school-influenced readings of the evolving role of medieval European merchant capital, scholars of the mid-twentieth century sought to explain the rapid spread of the device by focusing on the development of middle-class interests.[4] Perhaps most influentially, Jacques Le Goff, following Gustav Bilfinger, addressed the effects of this new timekeeping technology in terms of a shift in qualitative human relations to time, characterized as a turn from "church time" to "merchant time."[5] Le Goff's early and influential formulation of "merchant time" was intentionally provisional and has been subject to critique and emendation,[6] but that striking notion – that the advent of the mechanical clock initiated a wholesale reconditioning of time-perception in medieval Europe – has remained durable.[7] This body

[4] Thus began the formulation of "clock time" in the work of Jacques Le Goff, "Temps de l'Église et temps du marchand," *Annales* 15.3 (1960): 417–433; Dohrn-van Rossum, *The History of the Hour*, 230–231; Paul Glennie and Nigel Thrift, *Shaping the Day: A History of Timekeeping in England and Wales, 1300–1800* (Oxford: Oxford University Press, 2009), 43–53; Jonathan Martineau "The Origin of Clock Time and the Origin of Capitalism," in *Time, Capitalism, and Alienation: A Socio-Historical Inquiry into the Making of Modern Time* (Leiden: Brill, 2015), 47–106, and his critique of Glennie and Thrift in "Making Sense of the History of Clock-Time, Reflections on Glennie and Thrift's Shaping the Day," *Time & Society* 26.3 (March 2015).

[5] Gustav Bilfinger, *Die mittelalterlichen Horen* (Stuttgart: Verlag von W. Kohlhammer, 1892); see also Jacques Le Goff, *Time, Work, and Culture in the Middle Ages*, trans. Arthur Goldhammer (Chicago: University of Chicago Press, 1980), 29–52.

[6] Matthew S. Campion, *The Fullness of Time: Temporalities of the Fifteenth-Century Low Countries.* (Chicago: University of Chicago Press, 2017), 8–9; see also Carlo M. Cipolla, in *Clocks and Culture, 1300–1700* (London: Collins, 1967), 42–43; Dohrn-van Rossum, *The History of the Hour*, 226–231; A. J. Gurevich, "Time as a Problem of Cultural History," in Louis Gardet et. al., *Cultures and Time* (Paris: UNESCO Press, 1976), 239–241; Steven A. Epstein, "Business Cycles and the Sense of Time in Medieval Genoa," *The Business History Review* 62.2 (1988): 243–244; Chris Humphrey "Time and Urban Culture in Late Medieval England," in Chris Humphrey and W. M. Ormrod, eds., *Time in the Medieval World* (Woodbridge: York Medieval Press, 2001), 105–118, esp. 105–108.

[7] The idea appears as a general reference for premodern time in works as disparate as, among others, those of Keumsoo Hong, "The Geography of Time and Labor in the Late Antebellum American Rural South: Fin-de-Servitude Time Consciousness, Contested Labor, and Plantation Capitalism," *International Review of Social History* 46.1 (2001): 1; and Keletso E. Atkins, "'Kafir Time': Preindustrial Temporal Concepts and Labour Discipline in Nineteenth-Century Colonial Natal," *The Journal of African History* 29.2 (1988): 229–244. For a more nuanced introduction to the ways that emergent technical practices and market forces affected time-perception, see Otto Mayr, *Authority, Liberty, and Automatic Machinery in Early Modern Europe*, Johns Hopkins Studies in the History of Technology, new series no. 8 (Baltimore, MD: Johns Hopkins University Press, 1986).

of work focused largely on the adoption of the timekeeping mechanism, and maintains a firm if often tacit link between the mechanical device and the idea of time-telling as such.

Although the hour-striking clock eventually brought changes to European culture, including the beginnings of change in the matter of telling time,[8] the technical development of the mechanical clock often has become too closely associated in scholarly analysis with the quotidian business of signaling the time of day. This is a natural enough association for moderns looking back from the perspective of a world governed by the mechanical hour. However, an understanding of the cultural role of clocks in the years of their earliest diffusion can be enhanced by separating clocks from time to distinguish their use in ordinary timekeeping from the symbolic discourses in which these devices first figured.[9] While it may seem counterintuitive to suggest that clockworks and the abstract idea of time should be considered separately, doing so illuminates separate paths that have been obscured by the too-easy fusion of time with the mechanism,[10] pointing to the significant symbolic and ideological forces that accompanied the early development of mechanical clocks, as European thinkers spread complex ideas associated with clocks independently of their slowly growing role in the work of keeping time.

Looking to the effects these mechanisms generated within social discourses, not just as machine qua machine or as transparent temporal indicators, we find in the clock an agent force at play in the semantic fields of the period. This symbolic aspect of early clockworks registers through their use as metaphors in texts that emerged during the height of their diffusion, and the force of these metaphors operated definitively outside the discourses in which timekeeping held primacy, instead focusing on moral qualities and the regulation of the desiring body in courtly writing. These discursive representations of clocks were literary and political, and anchored not in the interest of marking time, but in the same set of prestige-based social mores that drove civic and elite acquisition of clocks in the first place.

8 Dohrn-van Rossum, *The History of the Hour*, 108–113, esp. plate 28.

9 For revisions to the singular relation between device and time, see L. R. Mooney, "The Cock and the Clock: Telling the Time in Chaucer's Day," *Studies in the Age of Chaucer*, 15 (1993): 91–109 for the myriad ways time was told, suggesting the clock didn't dominate time sense; see also Martineau, "Making Sense of the History of Clock Time"; for a model breakdown of the multiplicity of temporalities in late medieval and early modern perceptions of time, see Campion, *The Fullness of Time*, 3–12 et passim.

10 Derek J. de Solla Price notes that clockworks only slowly came to be associated with quotidian timekeeping in "On the Origins of Clockwork, Perpetual Motion Devices and the Compass," *Contributions from the Museum of History and Technology*, Bulletin 218 (Washington, DC: Smithsonian, 1959), 81–112, esp. 82–83.

This division between the textual representation of clocks and their role as timekeeping mechanisms is inspired by Derek De Solla Price's suggestion that the mechanical clock was not at all a culmination of technological advancement for the purpose of keeping quotidian time, but rather "nought but a fallen angel from the world of astronomy," a device whose practical marking of daily time was a by-product devolved from the great astronomical devices whose complexity features so vividly in White's quote that heads this chapter,[11] perhaps best exemplified in the surviving example of the Prague astronomical clock, with its moving statues, hourglass-turning skeleton, and elaborately shifting calendrical and planetary surfaces, or by the Strasbourg clock, upon which cherubs spin an hourglass and Death rings out the hour with a hammer, while an iron rooster from the earliest version of this clock spread its wings to crow through a reed and bellow each noon. Although the possession of clocks was ultimately motivated by prestige, display, and symbol as much as by practical time-telling, this symbolic environment had very practical relationships with the sensory experience of time measurement as it occurred in the lives of medieval clerics, workers, and elites; these effects had to do with the work of marking time, and with the assimilation of new, mechanically enabled *techne* and technique into already-extant patterns of marking the Christian cosmology that regulated medieval European culture's understanding of time. We must begin, simply, with the sound of bells.

1 Aurality, Liturgical Time, and Labor in Medieval Clocks

Central to a fuller understanding of the incipient cultural impact of the mechanical clock is the work of signaling – from the Latin *signum*, to ring a bell – the means by which an indication of the specific time, holy office, or work activity was transmitted by a timekeeping device to a given population. The very words we use to describe mechanical timekeeping devices derive not from the devices themselves but from the preexisting means of signaling onto which these complex mechanisms were grafted. The English word *clock* derives from the Old French *cloche*, or *bell*, from the Latin *clocca*, a term privileging the means of signaling the time rather than the timekeeping device itself. In fact, the mechanical clock in its early development had no visual indicator of the passing hours, which were

[11] Derek J. Price, "Clockwork before the Clock," *Horological Journal* 97 (1955): 814 and 98 (1956): 31. See also John North, *God's Clockmaker: Richard of Wallingford and the Invention of Time* (New York: Hambledon and London, 2005), 164–165.

signaled by bells.[12] This aural sequence, in which the means of timekeeping, whether human or mechanical, must find its way to a distant and perhaps unassembled group of hearers, is a critical link for understanding the effect of a given device on a subject population. Tracing the connections between how time was measured and how it was perceived complicates any unqualified notion of the general impact and significance of nascent mechanical "clock time."[13]

To take but one example: In a 1371 stonemason's *regula* from York cathedral, the masons are directed that "till itte be hegh none smytyn by þe clocke … all yer tymes and houres sall by reweled bi a bell ordayned yarefore" or "until the clock strikes high noon … all your time and hours shall be [accounted] by a bell [designated for that purpose]"[14] While it may be natural to interpret the edict through a direct association between the mechanical timekeeping device and the masons' work, it is easy to forget that the pace of the masons' day derived not from the clock itself but from the sonic intermediary lying between the means of timekeeping and the work spurred by the signal of the bell. Here is the crux: In places where clocks emerged and were first adopted, the regimes of timekeeping did not suddenly shift from silence to a measured ringing of bells driven by mechanisms; rather, the aural world of medieval towns and cities had been rife with a cacophony of overlapping auditory regimens,[15] rung out on a variety of bells large and small, rung hard or softly, in straight counts and patterns that communicated to hearers who had to register the meaningful pattern of a given bell amid the competing sounds of other bells.[16]

These bells had been rung in England since the time of Bede, signaling birth and death, worship and work, natural events such as storms, and singular events such as divine *mirabilia*.[17] When mechanical clocks arrived in England in numbers during the fourteenth century, bell-founders had been at work for centuries in York, Gloucester, Nottingham, and London, and the market was so glutted by the mid-fifteenth century that protections were

12 See, for example, North, *God's Clockmaker*, 145–146.

13 See Bertrand H. Bronson, "Concerning 'Houres Twelve'," *Modern Language Notes* 68.8 (December 1953): 519.

14 John Britton, *The History and Antiquities of the Metropolitical Church of York, Illustrated by a Series of Engravings of Views, Elevations, Plans and Details of the Architecture of that Edifice, with Biographical Anecdotes of the Archbishops* (London: Longman, Hurst, Rees, Orme, and Brown, 1819), Appendix, no. VII, 80–81.

15 Glennie and Thrift, *Shaping the Day*, 138; Dohrn-van Rossum, *The History of the Hour*, 213–215.

16 Evelyn Welch, *Shopping in the Renaissance: Consumer Cultures in Italy, 1400–1600* (New Haven: Yale University Press, 2005), 117–121.

17 Bonnie Young, "A Medieval Bell," *The Metropolitan Museum of Art Bulletin* 11.10 (1953), 293–294.

enacted against the importation of foreign bells.[18] Medieval clocks tolled the time with these bells – first rung by an intermediary such as a monk and only later by a chiming drive-train – but inasmuch as the *signal* related to and therefore governed work, it remained aural, still functioning at a distance, with no visual indicator of the hour. To the receiver, such aural signaling needed only to fit a predetermined configuration that signified the labor to be accomplished. The ultimate origin of the auditory signal need not have been a mechanical clock at all, and whether the signal was sent by such a device was a matter about which the hearer would have no knowledge.[19]

The simple fact is that the advent of the mechanical clock was not closely aligned with the advent of a shift in time-telling for most people, whose work and days were measured in relation to liturgical time, remaining dependent upon enduring affiliations with centuries-old practices of ecclesiastical timekeeping governing the canonical hours, prayer, and other devotional activities. From the Cluniac reforms of the eleventh century, the Benedictines had practiced a rigid observance of the divine offices, and the development of lectionaries and breviaries that eventually birthed the Franciscan *Breviarium Curiae* signals this significance of liturgical time. This focus on specific increments of time for prayer also found parallel expression in the ordering of more worldly work among religious communities; this was not only because of the development and spread of the Benedictine doctrine of *ora et labora* that linked scheduled prayer and work, but also the aural nature of monastic time-signaling with bells.

Indeed, the Latin term *horologium* and derivative vernacular vocabulary for the clock itself derives from the Greek "ὡρολόγιον" or "hour teller," referring to the monastic worker whose labor – counting, chanting, observing celestial phenomena – would yield a reasonable estimate of the span of canonical hours, which he would signal to his peers by ringing a bell to indicate the time for prayer. The relative rigidity of monastic practice, not to mention its influential financial and moral authority in a given locality, found traction in the secular working communities whose awareness of the hours was governed by the Church.[20]

18 "History of Bells," *Scientific American* 81.7 (1899): 106.

19 In Le Goff's discussion of "merchant time" in *Time, Work, and Culture*, 35–37, the single example cited "among many" elides the importance of weighing the significance of the signal as separate from the marking of regular hours, an effect noted in Glennie and Thrift's evaluation of the importance of signal versus the importance of regular hours, characterized as an "unintended consequence," *Shaping the Day*, 138.

20 For the importance of time as emanating from monastic structures of prayer and work, see David Landes, *Revolution in Time: Clocks and the Making of the Modern World* (Cambridge, MA: Harvard University Press), 61–67; critical is Martineau's expansion on Landes in *Time, Capitalism, and Alienation*, 68–72.

For the population of medieval Christian Europe, then, the arrival of the mechanical clock did not augur a wholesale change in the way time was experienced. The passing days had been reckoned for centuries on a flexible hour that corresponded loosely to a daylight cycle divided into twenty-four hours, and time on the longer scale was reckoned according to the liturgical calendar, which measured out the celebrations, seasons, and ordinary time of the liturgical year. This way of conceiving of and recognizing the passing of time, in which the passing day was a cycle of light and dark embedded within the closely attended cycles of daylight and the natural seasons and of the carefully marked seasons of the Church, continued to dominate the reckoning of time for most of medieval Europe until the eighteenth century.

Traditional modes of perceiving time were not replaced with methods of mechanically reckoning time but instead gradually aligned with the mechanism, as the *regula* of devotional and civic life gradually synchronized with the improving reliability of mechanically regulated hours. Mechanical clocks were effectively layered into an existing aural frame of reference and all that was associated with it,[21] as work and prayer continued, decade after decade, while monastic and later secular technicians slowly improved the clock's ability to signal accurate time.[22] Yet amid the ongoing discussion of the work of mechanical clocks in the development of "merchant time" – a concept more lately morphed into "capitalist time" – it should never be forgotten that the technical pursuit of accurate measurement initially served the long-standing desire for more accurate scheduling of prayer within the prolonged arc of medieval Christian salvation history. Despite the enduring power of the idea that labor became structured by the clock as hypothesized by E. P. Thompson,[23] the alignment between the advent of what Le Goff called "clock time" and emergent early modern proto-capitalism is less useful when projected back upon the preindustrial world of the Middle Ages, a period so thoroughly structured by monastic practice and time discipline.

21 Evelyn Welch, *Shopping in the Renaissance: Consumer Cultures in Italy, 1400–1600* (New Haven: Yale University Press, 2005), 118–119.

22 Even Wallingford's great clock at Salisbury could only maintain time if constantly manually corrected for the friction loss; see Francis C. Moon and Preston D. Stiefel, "Coexisting Chaotic and Periodic Dynamics in Clock Escapements," *Philosophical Transactions: Mathematical, Physical and Engineering Sciences*, 364.1846 (2006): 2539–2563, esp. 2540; Froissart's close description too carries the admonition to frequently adjust the mechanism; see "The Tower Clock of the Palais De Justice at Paris," *The Illustrated Magazine of Art* 2.7 (1853): 50–52.

23 E. P. Thompson, "Time, Work-Discipline, and Industrial Capitalism," *Past and Present* 38 (1967): 56–97.

A lesson in how we have come to think about the work of timekeeping is embedded in the historical sematic shift around tolling bells, wherein the work of medieval human timekeeping is elided. Here a reattribution of agency was effected in early modernity, transferring the work of ringing the bell from the human to the machine. One may therefore reasonably harbor a false etymology associating the tolling bells with counting – a notion rooted in the Latin *telonium*, for toll-house,[24] giving us "toll" as in a tax. However there was no semantic transfer from counting money to counting the ringing of bells. Rather, in the later Middle Ages, ringing a bell was work, for a man would "*toilen*" at the bell,[25] laboring to both count and to pull the bell-rope.[26] As the self-regulating mechanism of the mechanical clockwork came to dominate ideas about time-telling devices during later centuries, the semantics of agency shifted even as the vocabulary calcified, and the toil of ringing came to be attributed to the clock itself, which would "toll" the hours, seemingly autonomously. Modern semantics thereby performs an erasure of medieval labor, obscuring what in the fourteenth century was the very important human endeavor of the maintenance and signaling of time.

A passage from the eleventh-century monastic reformer Peter Damian, in which the *signficator horarum* is not yet a mechanical clock but a person whose work is to keep time, characterizes timekeeping without benefit of mechanisms such as water-driven clepsydra or mechanically regulated devices:

> He could not find time for idle fables, nor hold long conversations, nor finally could he trouble himself about what was done by the laity, but always intent on the duties of his office, always provident, always anxious, he felt a desire to construct a voluble sphere that should never stop, should show the passage of the stars and the flight of time. He also had a custom of singing to himself whenever he wished to have a notion as to the quantity of time; that, whenever the brightness of the sun or the position of the stars

[24] Charlton T. Lewis and Charles Short, *A Latin Dictionary*, "tĕlōnĭum (-nĕum), ii, n., = *τελώνιον*," www.perseus.tufts.edu/hopper/text?doc=Perseus%3Atext%3A1999.04.0059%3Aentry%3Dtelonium (accessed July 15, 2023).

[25] OED: toil, *V.*, I. Senses relating to violent action or strife. 1. *Transitive.* To pull, drag, tug (someone or something) about in a violent or hostile manner.

[26] An alternate etymology in Middle English "*tolen*" (to draw or allure in the pejorative or negative senses) I find unconvincing given the vast and overwhelmingly positive cultural approbation of church bells, weighed against the semantic range of early English compounds in which the cognate term (*tillan*, to pull or draw) is inflected with a sense of deception, as in *fortyllan* (seduce, lead astray, etc.) or *betyllan* (to lure or decoy). Given that aural signaling was an action understood as labor, the root in *toilen* is far more convincing; this notion is supported by the extensive and positive semantic range of Old English *tilian*/*telian*/*teolian*/*tiolian*, and further buffered by European cognates such as the Middle Dutch *tuylen*, designating work, labor, or tilling.

> was obscured by the weather he might form a certain time-measurer by the quantity of psalmody he had accomplished.[27]

Timekeeping was encompassing work indeed, and the advent of the mechanical clock dreamed of in this passage formed only the earliest stage in the development of a reliable timekeeping mechanism; it would be decades before hour-striking clocks could offer a reliable means of quotidian timekeeping that could operate independent of the corrective human intervention that remained the work of the fourteenth-century horologer, and in fact the spread of the mechanical clock shows no demonstrable relationship to advances in timekeeping accuracy.[28]

The transference by which human labor is attributed to the machine is nowhere more clearly visible than in the name for the earliest forms of Western medieval *automata*, the mechanical "Jacks" or clockwork-driven human figures fabricated to perform the role of ringing church bells. This name was applied "to a man, or to the figure of a man arranged to do something automatically, and in particular to a figure designed to strike a bell,"[29] as in the case of Jack Blandifer, the fourteenth-century mechanical man who struck the bell at Wells Cathedral. In this way the human work of ringing bells was transferred to a machinic representation of the human element, personified figuratively with the generic nickname "Jack" for the human-shaped automaton.

These early jacks elaborated into complex machine-driven displays with the spread of early public clocks. The myriad mechanical figures – angels, kings, knights, magi, animals – were the main visual component of clockworks before the arrival of the first visual time-indicators, such as dials, whose operations still carry the semantic trace of our anthropomorphizing tendencies; even today we direct our eyes to the clock whose "face" looks back to "tell" the time by signaling with its "hands." These *automata* joined celestial indicators as the earliest visual aspect of clockwork devices.[30] The

27 John Beckmann, *A History of Inventions, Discoveries, and Origins*, Vol. I., 4th ed., trans. William Johnston (London: Henry G. Bohn, 1846), 345.

28 See Dohrn-van Rossum, *The History of the Hour*, 129–133, esp. 133.

29 R. P. Howgrave-Graham, *Peter Lightfoot, Monk of Glastonbury and the Old Clock at Wells* (Glastonbury: Avalon Press 1922), 38; cf. the dating in *OED* of "Jack" N.2, I.1.a, the late medieval usage indicating a hypothetical or generic common man, and II.5, wherein a mechanical device is personified through the name of the laborer, "Jack," which by the later medieval period becomes the common name for any mechanical bell ringer.

30 Glennie and Thrift, *Shaping the Day*, 38–39. For a discussion of the development of medieval *automata* from jacks to complex clock-driven devices, see ch. 2, "Art and the Marvelous: Magicians and Automata," in Michael Camille, *The Gothic Idol: Ideology and Image Making in Medieval Art* (Cambridge: Cambridge University Press, 1989), 244–258.

notion of a "clock" in this early period is therefore part of a broader semantic field finding material expression as a range of devices, from the suddenly ubiquitous bell or *cloche* timed through and for monastic labor to a variety of timekeeping machines. These operated with and without drive-trains for bells, hands, and fantastic performing *automata* driven by clockworks in public displays, such as the colorful jousting knights circulating on the clock at Wells, and including the clock-driven astronomical displays of the period, such as the first Strasbourg clock with its gilded rooster and three magi *automata*, and Giovanni de' Dondi's astronomical wonder, the fantastically complex clockwork *Astrarium* in Lombardy. This latter was described by contemporaries as a fantastically dizzying array of complex mechanical workings displaying the planetary movements as well as its own internal mechanism, displayed by the Visconti dukes in their library to impress visitors – who in turn wrote of its aura of wonder.

All of these clocks were in essence performances, displays eliciting a response accruing prestige to the owners of these marvelous machines, the elites whose *magnificentia* was confirmed by the device. Clockworks did eventually bring time measurement into the visual dimension, but in the period of their early adoption during the fourteenth century, they primarily offered the innovation of bringing into dimensional experience the static marvels and wonders heretofore known only in stories, and they did so to the reification of elite identity.

2 Clocks as Metaphors in Courtly Literature

Over and above any practical use in time-telling, the significance of the animated marvels driven by these early clocks must be acknowledged. Even the technicians who fashioned these clocks saw their visual impact as a most significant quality, for example when Peter Lightfoot of Wells described the clock there as *magnum horologium processionibus et spetaculis insignitum* – "a great clock distinguished by shows and figures in motion."[31] Lightfoot's description affirms White's suggestion that in terms of symbolic force, medieval Europeans looked to astronomical clocks and their *automata* less for quotidian timekeeping than for the projection and affirmation of social identity that accompanied their sudden proliferation. The presence of clockworks in the social imagination of the fourteenth century speaks to the reach of these machines, which took up habitation within the culture not just as new and absolute arbiters of temporal certainty, but

[31] Howgrave-Graham, *Peter Lightfoot*, 21.

as networks of mechanical, temporal, and social forces. Their function as social performance is the connection between these devices and the literary and epistolary representations of clockworks by writers such as Christine de Pizan, Jean Froissart, and Philippe de Mézières, which explains better than a concern with time the sudden appearance and social valences of these devices in literary expression.[32] The mechanisms' very presence and the manner of their representation in literary and moral works shows clearly that the clock participated in regimes of meaning in which time was secondary to symbolic notions related to elite governance of the body, personal and politic: the self as locus of personal and by extension political stability.

In this way, clocks in the fourteenth century could be said to have borne complex burdens of meaning in discourses ranging far from marking the passing hours; rather, in most instances the social and emotive qualities elicited through representations of clockworks employ the striking new technology as an adjunct to already-extant – and culturally and psychologically deeper – wells of story and habits of ideological projection. Representations of clockworks contemporaneous with their early technological adoption therefore spurred effects beyond timekeeping, as the devices were layered into considerations at the deepest roots of chivalric, courtly, and therefore human morality. It was through this role that the evolving technology made its way into the politics of self-presentation at the highest levels of the culture. All of these texts work to project elite identity, fashioning the courtly self by engaging the symbolic possibilities of the fashionable new technology of the clock, seemingly independent of revised considerations of time.

Although the clock is metaphorized in the early fourteenth-century Latin of Heinrich Seuse's *Horologium Sapientiae*, the Hainault chronicler and poet Jean Froissart's poem *Li Orloge Amoureuse* is among the earliest vernacular metaphorical representations of the new mechanical device.[33] The work is an extended metaphorical comparison between the lover's heart and the recently innovated escapement clock, fashioning the metaphor on the central theme of courtly discourse. Froissart is thought to have acquired his intimate technical knowledge of clockworks in Paris,[34]

[32] Scott Lightsey, *Manmade Marvels in Medieval Culture and Literature* (New York: Palgrave Macmillan, 2007), 81–86.

[33] Earlier works such as Heinriche Seuse's *Horologium Sapientiae* neither require nor reliably indicate mechanical escapement clocks; see Dohrn-van Rossum, *The History of the Hour*, 94.

[34] See "The Tower Clock of the Palais De Justice at Paris," *The Illustrated Magazine of Art* 2.7 (1853): 50–52.

but the dating of the poem to the 1360s, when he was based in England in service to Philippa of Hainault, Queen of England as the wife of Edward III, suggests he may have garnered at least some of his technical knowledge in England given the early presence of mechanical clocks in the court of Edward III. However, Jean traveled frequently, visiting the courts of Charles V, the Lombard Visconti, and the Low Countries; whatever the source of his own knowledge, there can be no question that his work influenced another servant of the English court, Geoffrey Chaucer, whose earliest known poem opens with an imitation of Froissart's *Paradis d'Amour*, written shortly after *Li Orloge*.[35]

Froissart engaged in the period's most extended metaphorical treatment of the clock, subsuming the tropes of love poetry to that end by extensively comparing the lover to the device, beginning "Je me puis bien comparer a l'orloge," or "I may profitably compare myself to a clock."[36] *Li Orloge Amoureuse* privileges the poet's technical understanding of the *horologium* as an intricate technological apparatus per se, to the point that it is widely conjectured that he knew Heinrich Von Wiek, horologer of Paris. Nevertheless, he familiarizes it through metaphor to the traditional aspects of the lover's body as represented in contemporary French love lyric. The poet-narrator equates each part of the device with aspects of a courtly self, held in the tension between desire and self-control until his conclusion, in which the lover encompasses the device completely:

> Car je sui la chambre et la maison / ou mis est li orloges amoureus.
>
> For I am the chamber and house / wherein lies the clock of love.[37]

Although the poem extends the clock metaphor, Jean finds his foundation in the traditional mores of courtly poetry: The parallels drawn between the parts of the clock and the lover's selfhood reinforce the common tropes of self-fashioning required for courtly prestige, privileging the metaphorized self in the clock over any meaningful engagement with time. Throughout, he subsumes the representation of *techne* to social purposes, hardly engaging with time except to reference the profit to be had from knowing the hours during the night. The implications of Froissart's metaphor lie in its implied audience: readers and auditors who were at familiar with the

[35] Susan Crane, "Froissart's *Dit dou Blue Chevalier* as a Source for Chaucer's *Book of the Duchess*," *Medium Ævum* 61.1 (1992): 59ff.

[36] Julie Singer, "L'horlogerie et la mécanique de l'allégorie chez Jean Froissart," *Médiévales* 49 (Autumn 2005): 155–172.

[37] Jean Froissart, *Le paradis d'amour; L'orloge amoureus*, ed. Peter F. Dembowski (Geneva: Librairie Droz, 1986), ll. 1147–1148, my translations.

workings of the clock, and who could accept the metaphorical parallels pervading the poem, as well as the tacit notion that time could be considered separately from the social import of the clock.

The degree to which a court environment could engage with and therefore demonstrate the viability of a clockwork metaphor is indicated by another notable example deployed in the courts of Charles V of France, in which the clock was metaphorized to describe the world itself. To serve the learned king's court as a kind of vernacular *summa* of astronomical knowledge, Nicole Oresme, an adviser to Charles and "a scholar at the center of European intellectual life,"[38] produced a French translation and commentary on Aristotle's *De Caelo et Mundo*, which had been translated into Latin by William of Moerbeke a century before.[39] Titled *Le Livre du Ciel et Du Monde*, Oresme's work explained the Aristotelian model of the universe through the metaphor of the new self-regulating mechanical clock, likening the world to "when a person has made an *horloge* and sets it in motion, and it then moves by itself."[40] Although his book was introduced in 1377, Nicole had already addressed the *De Caelo* in dialogue form two decades earlier without reference to the clock, suggesting that his metaphor linking cosmic and human time became established only during the subsequent decades, as clocks began appearing in a variety of vernacular court writing. Here again the social context of the work, in which the author's choice of metaphoric vehicle is gauged to find meaning among a broad courtly audience, shows that an understanding of the clock was growing among European courtiers to the point where it worked as a metaphor for the world and one's place in it, even when time was not directly involved.[41]

This interest in mechanical clocks among prestigious French-speaking courts helps to explain the striking presence of the clock in a moral allegory

38 Susan M. Babbitt, "Oresme's *Livre de Politiques* and the France of Charles V," *Transactions of the American Philosophical Society* 75.1 (1985): 1; see also 2–8 and 147–148.

39 Edward Grant, "Nicole Oresme, Aristotle's *On The Heavens*, and The Court Of Charles V," *Texts and Contexts in Ancient and Medieval Science: Studies on the Occasion of John E. Murdoch's Seventieth Birthday*. Edith Sylla and Michael McVaugh, eds. *Brill's Studies in Intellectual History*, vol. 78 (1997), 187–207, at 188.

40 Nicole Oresme. *Le Livre du ciel et du monde*, ed. Albert D. Menut and Alexander J. Denomy; trans. Albert D. Menut (Madison: University of Wisconsin Press, 1968), 289; Arno Borst, *The Ordering of Time* (Chicago: University of Chicago Press, 1983), 97.

41 Nicole's metaphor may bear further analysis, for while its surface appears to turn simply upon the clockwork's motive power, the implied hierarchical relationship between the creator and his creation suggests at least the possibility of a submerged metaphorical mobilization of the secondary mechanisms driven by the primary wheel; God creates the clockwork world as an extension of His will, wherein the reader of the metaphor is driven along a preordained path mapped by foreknowledge.

by Christine de Pizan. Christine, through her father's work for Nicole Oresme, was a habitué of the court of King Charles throughout her life and came to employ the clock as a metaphor for moral virtue in her *Epistre d'Othea*, a piece of moral instruction for princes composed in about 1400. In the poem, Christine figures the Clock of Temperance as a purely metaphorical symbol of human moral virtue, drawing on a familiar trope while reinvigorating it with the concrete image of a clock escapement.

Here the abstract allegorical use of the clock focuses on morality and the body, using reference to the *techne* involved in maintaining a clock; she must have known a good deal about how the regulating mechanism worked, for her innovation was in locating moral governance in the tension between internal measure, represented by the mechanical escapement, and a feminized external governance represented by the clockmaker's need to adjust the still-inaccurate devices – a need understood only by those with at least a modicum of knowledge about the techniques behind the use of the device. Her use of the clock in this metaphor further testifies to her audience's general understanding of the clock; this was represented in detailed renderings in surviving manuscripts of her work, which feature some of the most accurate extant technical representations of clocks from the period.[42]

Another contemporary of these authors who circulated among the transalpine French-speaking courts was Philippe de Mézières, perhaps the fourteenth century's most well-known advocate of chivalry and crusade, who encountered the early proliferation of clocks in the many centers of court life he visited during the latter half of the century. One clockwork marvel – the fantastic *Astrarium* of Giovanni de' Dondi, installed in the Visconti library in Pavia, near Milan – drew his particular attention, and he inscribed it in the *Songe du Vieil Pèlerin*, where in addition to touching upon its complexity and the mastery required to fashion it, he refers to the prestige for which the Visconti dukes had installed it in their library; it was "such a great marvel that the solemn astronomers come from far regions to see in great reverence the said Master John and the work of his hands," noting that those who experienced the device felt that there had never been recorded such a "subtle or so solemn an instrument."[43]

For Philippe, the clock, already becoming well known among European courtiers for its symbolic associations, gathered its meaning primarily from

[42] Charity Cannon Willard, "Christine De Pisan's 'Clock of Temperance,'" *L'Esprit Créateur* 2.3 (1962): 152–153, proposes her father's experience in Italy as an avenue by which Christine may even have known of the de' Dondi *Astrarium*.

[43] Silvio Bedini and Francis R. Maddison, "The Mechanical Universe: the Astrarium of Giovanni De' Dondi," *Transactions of the American Philosophical Society*, New Series, 56.5 (1966): 20.

possession of the device, rather than what it could accomplish as an instrument; despite the multiplicity of complex temporal and astronomical indicators of de' Dondi's *Astrarium*, for Philippe this most fantastically complex of clockworks was primarily an assertion of the taste and influence of its patrons, and an invitation to share in the glory reflected in appreciation of the marvelous *engin*. Its meaning derived as much from the prestige involved in the situation of the device as from what it could indicate about temporal orders; as with the others who figured the clock in their writings, his expression of the importance of the device has little to do with time and everything to do with prestige, self-presentation, and fame, finding the clock's meaning in the projection of the owner's identity and the effects generated by the reception of that message.

Why did these authors from across the spectrum of high European courts – Picard diplomat de Mézières, Low-Countries poet and chronicler Froissart, Italo-French lady of the court de Pizan – seek to write about clocks in ways closely attuned to moral identity, consistently subsuming the device to the self? The answer lies in the intersections among lives lived amid the courts of the trans-European axis along which the clock first spread. These were persons with access to elite audiences, and it seems clear that they were invested in a social premium that came with the metaphorization of the clock as an adjunct to elite identity. These writers engaged the clock as part of the common grounding upon which effective metaphors are built, employing them as tools for establishing moral authority and social status. That the metaphorized object must be fairly well known for the symbolism to do its work says a great deal about how clocks were understood and shared as meaningful objects among the class for which all of these authors wrote. Although they use the image of the clock in different ways, each of them employs the device in an already developed discourse where issues of telling time, never mind contemplations of temporality, were secondary or irrelevant to the purpose of the discourse through which each engaged their audience. They were not seeking out the clock to say something about clocks or time, but instead to serve their own metaphorical or analogical purposes by drafting in some qualitative associational signal carried by the mechanical device. In short, the clocks in their writings were not the objects of their endeavors any more than time was, but rather formed a familiar bridge-point to their main ideas because of a commonly understood quality.

This extension into metaphor helps to explain how the importance of the clock reverberated through the culture from the top down, as ruling elites and those who wrote for them expanded the symbolic range of a device intended by its makers simply to keep time. Although White characterized clockworks as having "seized the imaginations" of contemporaries, one could perhaps characterize the intersection of the clockwork with literary and epistolary endeavor as an insinuation or interpolation of the machine into the moral dimension of being through surface metaphorization, as demonstrated by their seemingly natural adoption as symbols in social and moral discourses like *amor*, *temperantia*, and diplomatics. Clocks had indeed seized their imaginations, but rather than representing a new disciplinary regime of timekeeping or a profound reconceptualization of abstract temporality, the mechanical clock was itself disciplined to the human heart.

3 Chaucer's Ambivalent Engagement with Clocks

A sense of life lived in proximity to these devices may be understood through attention to the career and writings of a messenger and functionary in the outer edges of court life: the English poet Geoffrey Chaucer. His career offers a fitting site of engagement with the clock's projection of meaning, for his employment in the logistical apparatus of the English court allowed Chaucer wide latitudes of both experience and expression; his career as a soldier, messenger, and bureaucrat under the extended family of King Edward III situated him amid the burgeoning growth of clockworks' presence in European culture during the time and in the places of their most rapid proliferation. He appears, paradoxically, to both engage with and resist the device, and his ways of associating it with time are telling.

The many travels of Chaucer's early years, together with his later professional appointments during the reign of Richard II, brought him into contact with some of the greatest clockworks of his day. In addition to his work for the family of Edward III and his many travels in France, Chaucer's civic appointments exposed him to Wallingford's clock at St. Albans; St. Paul's in London, surmounted by an automaton angel; at least four contemporary clocks installed in royal households by Edward III; as well as the Parisian clocks that inspired Christine de Pizan and Froissart. Further, he accompanied a diplomatic mission to the Visconti in the summer of 1378, his time in Milan overlapping with that of de' Dondi himself.[44] Chaucer also served as Clerk of the King's Works for two years, working closely with master mason Henry Yvele, who had maintained the

[44] Bedini and Maddison, "The Mechanical Universe," 14–18; Lightsey, *Manmade Marvels*, 67–68.

structures wherein Edward III's several clocks were installed,[45] and with William Hannay, who had served as clerk for King Richard II's coronation, which included the fantastic *automata* of the Goldsmiths' pageant.[46] The appointment also put Chaucer directly in charge of the maintenance of Edward III's clocks at Windsor, Langley, and Westminster, although his authority may not have extend to the remaining clock at Queenborough.[47]

Rather than risk attempting to gauge the extent to which Chaucer might have recognized the far-flung implications of the newly developing technology, I would instead look to his quotidian understanding of the *techne* behind the emergent device as he experienced it, asking in what extant registers this technology might have been understood by a man whose working life involved not only a detailed understanding of fine mechanics, but also exposure to all manner of engineering techniques.[48] This line of inquiry yields clues from a life engaged with a variety of technologies that included the clock, but Chaucer was not possessed of some inordinate form or quantity of technical knowledge, and need not have had an understanding of the emerging implications of that technology; rather, what his works and life reveal is that a man of his position and experience would have had to know a good deal about how things worked in order to get things done for the people for whom he worked. Unlike many of his contemporaries for whom knowledge of clockworks was not endemic to their daily lives, Chaucer was in a position to understand the devices from a technical standpoint. That he makes reference to this knowledge in verse in quotidian ways that resist the internalization of the clock prevalent in his contemporaries shows the balanced view of a man of two worlds.

Despite his demonstrably broad experience of the range of medieval clockworks, the perspective inscribed in his poetry appears practical and inflected with class-based views rooted in his working life. When in the *Parliament of Fowls* he describes a rooster as "orloge ... of thorpes lyte,"

[45] Derek Pearsall, *Geoffrey Chaucer: A Critical Biography* (Cambridge: Blackwell, 1992), 211; Donald R. Howard, *Chaucer: His Life, His Works, His World* (New York: Ballantine, 1987), 455.

[46] *Chronicon Angliae, ab anno domini 1328 usque ad annum 1388, auctore monacho quodam Sancti Albani*, ed. Edward M. Thompson, Rolls Series No. 64 (London: Longman and Company, 1874), 153–156; *Anonimalle Chronicle, 1333 to 1381*, ed. V. H. Galbraith (Manchester: Manchester University Press, 1970), 107–108.

[47] Martin M. Crow and Clair C. Olson, eds. *Chaucer Life Records* (Austin: University of Texas Press, 1966), 402–403.

[48] Bertrand H. Bronson makes reference to this issue in his critique of Skeat's note on the ringing of bells at the end of Chaucer's *Book of the Duchess*, in "Concerning 'Houres Twelve,'" *Modern Language Notes*, 68.8 (December 1953): 515–521. Chaucer's extensive knowledge of the *techne* of various fields including alchemy and astronomy, as well as in his professional appointments, has been extensively documented elsewhere.

characterizing the bird as a village clock,[49] he reflects the biases of a life lived in London and among European capitals where mechanical clocks signified noble and civic status. Further, Chaucer's discernment of the difference between the clock as a machine and as accurate marker of time is confirmed by his more direct references to clocks in the prologues of the *Man of Law's Tale* and the *Parson's Tale*, both of which only casually reference the "clokke" while pointedly avoiding the use of the device to measure time. In both cases the difference between form and method is telling, for Chaucer is at pains to delineate the actual work of accurate time-telling through dense descriptions of the precise measurement of shadow-lengths and astronomical cues, as when in the introduction to the *Man of Law's Tale* the Host takes note of the sun's arc, the lengths of the trees' shadows, the degree of the sun, and the latitude and date until tossing in the clock only as a marker: "It was ten of the clokke, he gan conclude." Similarly in the *Parson's Prologue*, the sun is measured at "Degees nyne and twenty as in highte" and a proportional division of shadows' lengths carefully performed in order to estimate that "Foure of the clokke it was tho, as I gesse."[50] Even supposing a clock is implied by the bell that awakens the dreamer of the *Book of the Duchess* as it "smyten houres twelve,"[51] the poet embeds this reference in an elaborate symbolic exposition on the castle of John of Gaunt, Duke of Lancaster, which would once again associate the clock with prestige and the representation of dreams rather than with time.

For Chaucer, fourteenth-century clocks were mechanical devices whose semantic reach far exceeded both the accuracy of their delicate workings and the auditory reach of their signaling mechanisms. As clocks rose to prominence in the fourteenth century, then, the nature of these machines as social performances and displays was every bit as integral to the reach of the devices as their ability to keep time, which remained until the fifteenth century largely nominal. As he made abundantly clear in reference to the rather silly cock Chaunticleer, technical innovation was no match for the old ways of telling time:

> Wel sikerer was his crowing in his logge
>
> Than is a clokke or an abbey orlogge.[52]

[49] Geoffrey Chaucer, *The Parliament of Fowles*, l. 350; all references to Chaucer's poetry are from *The Riverside Chaucer*, ed. Larry D. Benson, 3rd ed. (Boston: Houghton Mifflin, 1987).

[50] *The Man of Law's Tale*, l. 14; *The Parson's Tale*, l. 5.

[51] *The Duchess's Tale*, l. 1323.

[52] *The Nun's Priest's Tale*, ll. 2853–2854; on the inaccuracy of the early clocks, see Dohrn-van Rossum, *The History of the Hour*, 133.

This suggests that Chaucer understood the imprecision of early mechanical clocks enough to make it the object of humor. Fourteenth-century clocks, ringing out the hours, were mechanical devices whose semantic reach far exceeded the limited ambit of their delicate workings and signaling mechanisms.

4 *Automata*, Narrative, and the Normalization of Mechanical Time

The clock is a material instrument for binding human experience *to* time, and is therefore differentiated *from* time. This distinction between the instrument and the purposes in which it was enlisted is especially evident in these discourses from the dawn of the self-regulating mechanical clock.[53] Technologies rarely remain entirely within the imaginative horizons of their creators, and so clockworks, spreading across late medieval Europe at a rate seldom seen in the proliferation of technology in premodern societies, entered secular elite discourses as prestige objects invested with symbolic weight and meaning, idealized objects in discourses about the self – about courtly love and temperance and prestige – within which the notion of a self-regulating mechanism provided a concrete, exteriorized image as a symbolic analogy to the inner self, signaling status and inspiring wonder.

Time, during this period of the clock's rapid adoption, was still limned by the concentric rings of rigid traditional temporalities: the canonical hours, the liturgical calendar, and the arc of Christian salvation history from *In principio* onward. Each of these maintained connections to mystical religious experience, but quotidian time, in finding expression through the mechanism of the late medieval clock, was bound to medieval human temporality, elite symbolism, and the human body – not only by the ringing bells of a hidden mechanism, but also through the symbolic associations conjured by hidden clockworks.

So it seems fitting to return to the claim in White's quote at the opening of this chapter, in which he indicates that witnesses to the public clock's projection of meaning through spectacular clockwork *automata*

[53] John North offers a capsule discussion of the motivations driving the development of the clock metaphor, *God's Clockmaker*, 164–169; see also van Rossum's outline of the relationship between technology and portrayals of *Temperantia* in *The History of the Hour*, 6–7; for a discussion following on the above reference in Dohrn-van Rossum, see Nancy Mason Bradbury and Carolyn P. Collette, "Changing Times: The Mechanical Clock in Late Medieval Literature," *The Chaucer Review* 43.4 (2009), 358ff.

experienced pride and wonder. White referred to the Strasbourg clock, built in the mid-fourteenth century, upon which "angels trumpeted, cocks crew, and apostles, kings, and prophets marched and countermarched" at the hours. This clock's innovative displays of *automata* expressly enacted traditional narratives that underscored the connection between the movements of the heavens and frail human existence. The symbolism of its *automata* plays specifically on the body as it relates to Christian eternality: the Annunciation of the angels, the Embodiment of Christ adored by the magi, the cock that symbolized Peter's betrayals – all moving above a rendering of *homo signorum* or zodiac man, the representational embodiment of the heavenly spheres' direct effect on corporeal existence.[54] Those who beheld this marvelous machine may have possessed varying degrees of understanding of the *techne* underlying the performance, but as medieval Christians they uniformly understood the deep well of story-background that performed for witnesses a mechanical representation of their being with far more certainty than it may have prompted abstract consideration of the hours.[55]

Even in a culture whose passing day had been marked by the centuries-long habit of marking the "crowings" of the Roman watch as it partitioned the periods of day and night,[56] and since time out of mind by the quite literal cocks'-crowing that marked time in their agrarian world, the meanings carried by the rooster automaton at Strasbourg were for the medieval audience derived from the long arc of Christian salvation history. Here the motions of the celestial spheres were linked through the symbolic images driven by the clock with the corporeal experience of medieval lives, fixing the movements of the heavens to the human body – the locus of religious experience and the self.

This is evident in the links medievals made between the ubiquitous church weathercocks and the body of the faithful. Durandus in the thirteenth-century *Rationale Divinorum Officiorum* casts the bird in a pastoral role,[57] and centuries before it was automated the cock had been designated the primary church-top symbol by that great reformer of the

[54] The *homo signorum* encapsulated the medieval inheritance of classical ideas about the relationship between macrocosm and the body as microcosm; see Charles West Clark, *The Zodiac Man in Medieval Medical Astrology* (dissertation: University of Colorado at Boulder, 1971), 2–7; 283–355.

[55] For a contrasting view figuring the Strasbourg clock as an avatar of "the new, abstract, quantified hours of clock time," see Bradbury and Collette, "Changing Times," 370.

[56] Bilfinger, *Die mittelalterlichen Horen*, 10–13.

[57] John Mason Neale and Benjamin Webb. *The Symbolism of Churches and Church Ornaments: A Translation of the First Book of the Rationale Divinorum Officiorum by William Durandus, Sometime Bishop of Mende* (Cambridge: T. Stevenson, 1843), 27–28; 199.

calendar, Pope Gregory I, because the bird had signaled Peter's denials of Christ.[58] The cock thus became a crucial visual symbol figuring human frailty as the link between the bedrock of the Church, Simon-Peter, and the divine: between the duration of quotidian lives marked out by bells and the deep history of the Church, and therefore a fitting subject for wonder-inspiring *automata* with the introduction of the mechanical clock.

Acknowledging that the Strasbourg clock signaled the time, I would suggest that the range of meanings projected by the device had far more to do with the motive power of the clockwork driving the displays of *automata* and the elite and religious narratives within which their meanings were anchored, as separate from both quotidian day-marking time and abstract considerations of time. This gulf between the narrative meanings binding these *automata* to their audience, on the one hand, and abstract considerations of time on the other, is confirmed by the later addition of a simple hour-clock in the early fifteenth century, attesting to separate regimes of meaning for quotidian timekeeping and complex symbolic *automata*.[59] In a similar example, the *automata* of charging knights and religious figures at Wells Cathedral were supplemented only later by an exterior dial, which marked visually the passing time of day.[60] In all of these cases, the prestige object, saturated in narrative meaning and projected with the awe-inspiring power accompanying any innovation not yet fully understood, was marked as separate from the mundane business of quotidian timekeeping until the end of the Middle Ages.

The mechanical clock that ruled the streets and stalls of Renaissance Europe had first gained traction through late medieval innovations and awe-inspiring installations – not only through the astronomical efforts of churchmen, but also through the social influence of the nobility, whose prestige-driven prerogatives inaugurated the place of mechanical clocks in late medieval discourse.[61] And then, almost as precipitously as they arrived, these fantastic clockworks became subject to the same demystifying mechanisms that accompany the adoption of any marvelous new technology: Clocks became ubiquitous and then normalized, and in the process they lost that sheen of rarity and wonder that had propelled them across the continent and deep into late medieval discourses of the self. The prestige

58 John 13: 37–38; Luke 22: 54–57; Matthew 26: 31–35; Mark 11: 27–31.

59 See also Dohrn-van Rossum, *The History of the Hour*, 133.

60 See Karen Elaine Smyth, *Imaginings of Time in Lydgate and Hoccleve's Verse* (New York: Routledge, 2016), 26–28.

61 Dohrn-van Rossum, *The History of the Hour*, Introduction, 1–4, and his recapitulation of Bilfinger, *Die mittelalterlichen Horen*, 127.

object had become everyday, and the regulating force of the mechanism naturalized as it was improved, enabling it to carry on the dispensation of time without a great deal of expert human oversight.[62] Consequently, clocks became common, mechanical time became regular, and eventually, under expanding mercantile prerogatives, the secular patterns of tightly regulated human endeavor came to be the primary organizing principles of Renaissance time.[63]

[62] Dohrn-van Rossum, *The History of the Hour*, ch. 5, "From Prestige Object to Urban Accessory," 128–159.
[63] Linda Elaine Neagley perfectly encapsulates this movement in her analysis of mid-fifteenth-century civic adoption of the clock in *Disciplined Exuberance: The Parish Church of Saint-Maclou and Late Gothic Architecture in Rouen* (University Park: Pennsylvania State University Press, 1998), 108–110.

CHAPTER 10

Compasses

Chris Barrett

1 A Pair of Compasses

In Book 7 of John Milton's epic poem *Paradise Lost* (1667, 1674), the angel Raphael describes to the yet-unfallen Adam and Eve how their world came to be. The archangel explains that on the first of six days of creation, the Son of God engaged in a generative process of encompassing and bounding all that exists:

> He took the golden Compasses, prepar'd
> In Gods Eternal store, to circumscribe
> This Universe, and all created things:
> One foot he center'd, and the other turn'd
> Round through the vast profunditie obscure,
> And said, thus farr extend, thus farr thy bounds,
> This be thy just Circumference, O World.
> Thus God the Heav'n created, thus the Earth,
> Matter unform'd and void... (7.225–233)[1]

For Milton (1608–1674), the making of the universe begins with a pair of compasses.

A pair of compasses (also known simply as a "compass," but for clarity here referred to in the plural) consists of two rigid legs connected at a joint; when one leg is planted at a point, the other leg can be rotated around it to etch or draw – depending on the inscriptive implement at the end of the leg – an arc or a circle, the degree or radius of which is determined by the adjustable angle of the compasses' legs. Developed in antiquity, a pair of compasses is closely related to a similar instrument, the dividers, which is effectively a pair of compasses used to measure and calculate the distance

My thanks to Katharine Jensen (Louisiana State University) and Jeremy Cornelius (Bates College) for thinking about this chapter with me in its earliest stages.

[1] All references to the poem taken from John Milton, *Paradise Lost*, ed. Barbara K. Lewalski (Malden, MA and Oxford: Blackwell Publishing, 2007).

between two points, as on a map. Another related instrument, calipers, are dividers designed to measure distance between points on rounded surfaces or on different sides of an object.

This chapter offers a brief map of compasses in early modern contexts, especially in the literature of Renaissance England. Beginning with the pair of compasses, this chapter considers the multiplicity of tonally diverse references to this instrument amid the effects of the Cartographic Revolution in sixteenth- and seventeenth-century England. That revolution expanded the cultural imagination to include the technologies of mapping and navigation, and popular invocations of the pair of compasses proliferated, as did invocations of the magnetic compass, to which this chapter turns later. Primarily focusing on early modern writers, from Milton and Donne to Spenser and Shakespeare, this chapter concludes by considering twenty-first-century references to navigational technologies in today's literature in English, amid the world's grappling with the implications of a second, digital cartographic revolution.

Among the most iconic instruments of measurement in Renaissance England and Europe – especially in their geographical and navigational applications – pairs of compasses and dividers appear widely in the visual and textual culture of the period. Ever since Euclid incorporated the use of the compasses into his foundational text *The Elements*, the instrument had been virtually synonymous with geometry and its applications. Albrecht Dürer's immensely influential treatise on measurement (1525) offered instructions for measurement with compass and ruler, and early modern maps routinely featured an image of dividers stretched above the scale. The association between maps and compasses, too, made the latter a figure of celestial perfection. In his 1608 *Masque of Beauty*, Ben Jonson (1572–1637) describes "eight [female] *Figures*, representing the *Elements* of *Beauty*," including Perfectio, who appears "In a Vesture of pure *Gold*, a wreath of *Gold* vpon her head. About her body the *Zodiack*, with the *Signes*: In her hand a *Compasse* of gold, drawing a *circle*." The margin note to the 1608 printing of the masque's text adds importantly that the zodiac "& the *Compasse* are known ensignes of *perfection*."[2] This privileged, elevated association of the compasses and dividers with the representation and negotiation of space was commonplace by the time Milton placed one such object in the hands of the divine; consider a painting roughly contemporary to *Paradise Lost*, Johannes Vermeer's *The Geographer* (1668–1669), in which

2 Ben Jonson, *The characters of two royall masques The one of blacknesse, the other of beautie…* (London: by G. Eld for Thomas Thorp, 1608), D3^{r}.

the title subject leans over a sea chart, a globe in the background, dividers in his right hand.

For Milton's Raphael, the movement of "the golden Compasses" sets the "Circumference" of creation, and thus makes heaven and earth by bounding their limits in "the vast profunditie obscure." The image echoes a biblical one, the reference to creation in Proverbs 8.27 rendered by the 1611 King James Bible as "when he set a compass upon the face of the depth." Milton's verse itself here mimics the shape of the instrument in use: A caesura splits the line describing the use of the golden compasses, inserting a comma between the foot that was "center'd" and the foot that "turn'd," as though to joint the verse in ways similar to the supernatural device it posits. Two lines later, "extend" appears at the metrical center of the line, suggesting the separating of the compasses' jointed legs as it traces the boundaries of creation.

The appearance of a pair of compasses at the genesis of the world points to early modern English literature's fascination with the technologies of the spatial arts. Europe's Cartographic Revolution was the product of a confluence of factors: the need for more precise topographical information as cannonry improved, the evolution of mathematical techniques (such as advancements in trigonometry), the development of technological innovations (copperplate engraving, for example), and the refinement of practical arts (including surveying). Together, they led to a golden age of cartographic production – and, as a result, a new era in European navigational practice. This revolution crested in England in the sixteenth century, dramatically transforming numerous aspects of daily life.

While a person in England might, in the early sixteenth century, have gone her whole life never seeing a map, by the end of that century, maps appeared on the backs of playing cards. Advancements in mathematics and technologies produced a sudden flourishing of geographic, cartographic, and navigational techniques and materials. The proliferation of these techniques and materials altered everything from land use (surveyors sometimes worked under armed guard, since their appearance usually signaled to tenant farmers that a hike in fees was imminent) to governmental affairs (Elizabeth I's chief adviser William Cecil amassed a large collection of maps and charts, some of which he would annotate with the locations of goods requisitionable in an invasion or of suspicious recusants to monitor) – and even to home décor. John Dee noted in 1570 that "some, to beautifie their Halls, Parlers, Chambers, Galeries, Studies, Libraries ... loveth, gatteth and useth, Mappes, Chartes, and Geographicall Globes." The famous 1533 Hans Holbein painting *The Ambassadors* includes, on the shelves between the two men who are the painting's ostensible subjects, globes, a sundial, a quadrant, and other instruments of location- and wayfinding.[3] The material and instruments of navigation became newly precise and newly familiar in the cultural imaginary, as both professionals and laypeople embraced access to them. Familiarity with geography, navigation, and their technical components became so widely expected by the early sixteenth century, even among those without professional need of that literacy, that it could be compared unfavorably with travel itself. In Thomas Heywood's 1633 play *The English Traveler*, Dalavill remarks to his friend Geraldine, lately returned from travel, that:

> A Scholler in his study…
> …can decipher Seas,
> And give each severall Land his proper bounds;
> But set him to the Compasse, hee's to seeke,
> When a plaine Pilot can, direct his course
> From hence unto both th'Indies; can bring backe
> His ship and charge, with profits quintuple.
> I have read Ierusalem, and studied Rome,
> Can tell in what degree each City stands,
> Describe the distance of this place from that,
> All this the Scale in every Map can teach,
> …but what I
> Have by relation onely, knowledge by travell
> Which still makes up a compleat Gentleman,
> Prooves eminent in you. (Act 1, Scene 1, A4)

So familiar would Heywood's audience have been with compasses, maps, degrees of latitude, and scaled representation that Dalavill's conceit can sustain such length and appeal.

Yet of the changes wrought in England by this revolution, the sea change in conceptions of the world's geography – and its relationship to worldly powers – might be among the most remarkable. This efflorescence of the geospatial arts in mid to late sixteenth-century England was popularly linked to England's new colonial projects. Though later than other European nations to the transoceanic colonial project – by 1550, no

[3] For more on attitudes about, and threats to, surveyors see G. A. Hayes-McCoy, ed., *Ulster and Other Irish Maps, c.1600* (Dublin: Stationery Office for the Irish Manuscripts Commission, 1964), xii–xiii, and R. A. Skelton, "The Military Surveyor's Contribution to British Cartography in the 16th Century," *Imago Mundi* 24 (1970): 77–83. For William Cecil's use of maps, see John Rennie Short, *Making Space: Revisioning the World, 1475–1600*, 1st ed. (Syracuse, NY: Syracuse University Press, 2004), 87–89. John Dee's remark quoted by Walter Gibson in *The Mirror of the Earth: The World Landscape in Sixteenth-Century Flemish Painting* (Princeton: Princeton University Press, 1989), 51.

account of the New World nor of the voyages of figures such as Columbus or Magellan had been printed in English – England launched its overseas endeavors with what contemporary accounts described as a newfound skill in navigation. Indeed, navigation was, for the Renaissance English, definitionally a maritime endeavor. In his *c.* 1590 *A new and necessarie Treatise of Navigation...*, for example, the humanist scholar and wide-ranging writer Thomas Blundeville defines navigation as "an Arte which teacheth by true and infallible rules, how to governe and direct a ship from one port to another safely, rightly, and in shortest time..."[4] George Best, chronicling the voyages of famed seaman Martin Frobisher, with whom he sailed, celebrates the development of English navigational skill in 1578, declaring that "it commeth to passe, that Nauigation, whiche in the time of King Henrie the 7. was very rawe, & toke (as it were) but beginning (and euer since hath had by little and little continuall increase) is now in hir Maiesties [Elizabeth I's] raigne, growen to his highest perfection."[5] That refinement of navigational power attended the expansion of England's paper empire, and the literature of the sixteenth and seventeenth centuries grappled with the implications of navigation's "highest perfection."

Renaissance English poets and writers seized on the instruments of navigation as subjects for inclusion and figures for incorporation into their works. Maps, globes, mariners' compasses, quadrants, sextants, and other technologies all appeared in sixteenth- and seventeenth-century texts. Navigational materials had not been strangers, prior to the English Renaissance, to literature: Geoffrey Chaucer, while working on *The Canterbury Tales*, had also drafted *A Treatise on the Astrolabe*. Addressed to his son, the text explains the use of the sophisticated device for finding the latitude of any place, for determining direction, and so on. Even so, the instrument and objects of wayfinding nonetheless found their way into literature with unprecedented frequency in the early modern wake of the Cartographic Revolution.

John Milton was himself intrigued by navigation and the spatial arts. Throughout his life, and even after he completely lost his eyesight, he was an avid collector of maps and atlases, and he enthusiastically declared the necessity of navigation as part of the instruction of the young.[6] In his "Of Education,"

[4] Thomas Blundeville, *A new and necessarie Treatise of Navigation containing all the chiefest principles of that Arte...* Printed in *Blundeville, His Exercises* (London: Iohn Windet, 1597). Quotation from Ss2[r].

[5] George Best, dedicatory epistle to *A true discourse of the late voyages of discouerie, for the finding of a passage to Cathaya, by the Northvveast, vnder the conduct of Martin Frobisher ...* (London: Bynneman, 1578).

[6] For more on Milton's relationship to geographic and cartographic materials, his references to or uses of them in his works, and on Satan's trouble with navigation, see Chris Barrett, *Early Modern English Literature and the Poetics of Cartographic Anxiety* (Oxford: Oxford University Press, 2018), ch. 3.

he proclaims the importance of teaching students geography and navigation, as well as "the practical knowledge of sailing and of Sea-fight."[7] In *Paradise Lost*, before Adam and Eve hear of the "golden Compasses," the reader meets Satan, a figure who seems part Odysseus, part conquistador, whose relentless wanderings seem to capture the romance of navigational possibility. And yet, for all his journeys and global travel, Satan turns out to be a terrible navigator. He (twice) gets lost and has to ask for directions en route from hell to the newly created earth, and no matter how far he hurls himself, he never actually goes anywhere: The narrative persona explains that "within him Hell / He brings, and round about him, nor from Hell / One step no more then from himself can fly / By change of place" (4.20–23). Acknowledging this navigational perplexity, Satan himself cries, "Which way I flie is Hell; my self am Hell" (4.75). Satan's abject failures of navigation heighten the reader's attention to the "Compasses" with which the world is created. A demonic lostness contrasts with a divine ordering of the universe, the round bounding of the cosmos. Invoking one of the essential tools of navigational labor, Milton suggests that the essential act of creation is the drawing of an arc.

The golden compasses wielded in *Paradise Lost*, a work of the late English Renaissance, are preceded by many earlier literary employments. The poetry of John Donne (1572–1631), remarkable for its swiftly shifting and vital imagery, offers one of the most famous cameos of the pair of compasses in English literature – as well as numerous treatments of maps, globes, navigational materials, and navigational endeavors.[8] Donne's image of the pair of compasses in "A Valediction: Forbidding Mourning," however, might be among his most memorable invocations of the paraphernalia of navigation. The poetic persona, the lover, forbids the beloved to grieve his absence, explaining that their souls "endure not yet / A breach" with their separation, "but an expansion, / Like gold to ayery thinnesse beate" (ll. 22–24).[9] The poem comprises nine four-line stanzas, the last three of which develop the poem's dominant conceit. In a move licensed by the gold – which is beat to foil thinness in the preceding stanza, but which was also among the metals used to produce fine instruments – the lover compares his and the beloved's soul to the legs of a pair of compasses:

[7] "Of Education," in *Complete Prose Works of John Milton*, gen. ed. Don M. Wolfe, revised ed. (New Haven: Yale University Press, 1980), vol. 2, 389–392.

[8] Consider the complicated references to maps, for example, in "The Good-Morrow," "Goodfriday, 1613. Riding Westward," and "Hymne to God My God, in My Sicknesse." All Donne citations from *The Complete Poetry and Selected Prose of John Donne*, ed. Charles M. Coffin (New York: Modern Library, 2001). For the named poems, see 8, 257–258, and 282–283.

[9] Ibid., 38–39.

If they be two, they are two so
As stiffe twin compasses are two,
Thy soule, the fixt foot, makes no show
To move, but doth, if the'other doe.

And though it in the center sit,
Yet when the other far doth rome,
It leanes and hearkens after it,
And growes erect, as that comes home.

Such wilt thou be to mee, who must
Like th'other foot, obliquely runne;
Thy firmnes drawes my circle just,
And makes me end where I begunne. (25–36)

Donne's poem imagines the beloved as one leg of the pair of compasses, and the travel of her lover as the act of "draw[ing] my circle," made perfect or "just" by the compasses' movement. The poet Christopher Harvey (1597–1663) makes similar use of the simultaneous fixed and moving quality of the compasses' legs, though to different effect, in "The Church-Gate" segment of his *The Synagogue*, a collection of verses in imitative homage to Donne's contemporary, George Herbert, author of *The Temple*. Here, the church gate's movement – easily open or shut while "constant in its center" and "fetching a wide compasse round about" – mirrors the behavior of "He that the gates of righteousnesse would enter," who must "fix himselfe in God as in his center," the divine taking the place occupied by the beloved in Donne's analogy of the compasses.[10]

Donne's poem poetically mobilizes the pair of compasses by exploiting the use of the word "legs" to describe the physical shape of the instrument. If the pair of compasses' jointed components are "legs" with a fixed foot and a running foot, it is possible to imagine the respective stationary waiting and ambulatory travel of the beloved and lover. The printing of the lines, as well as their enjambment, underscore this literalization of the compasses' legs: The A-rhyme lines are justified differently from the B-rhyme lines, as though to mirror on the page the inability of the fixed and running feet to rest together, while the predominance of fully end-stopped lines in the B-rhyme lines nonetheless sonically connects the fixed and running feet of the A-rhyme and B-rhyme lines.[11]

[10] Christopher Harvey, *The synagogue, or, The shadow of the temple Sacred poems, and private ejaculations. In imitation of Mr. George Herbert* (London: John Legat for Phil. Stephens and Chrystopher Meredith, 1640) 3–4.

[11] I am grateful to Jonathan Dick (University of Pennsylvania) for this reading.

The image in Donne's poem is complicated by the very pair of compasses' movement that creates this arresting image: Insofar as the movement of the compass legs involves the drawing of a circle, the two legs of the compass will never be together. The unfixed foot rotating around the centered foot will indeed, in the drawing of a circle, "end where I begunne" – but that starting and ending point is the distance of the circle's radius from the beloved who is the fixed foot at the circle's center. The "lean[ing] and hearken[ing]" of the fixed leg toward the "rome[ing]" of the other might figure longing, but of the endless sort: The variable leaning of the fixed leg (a product of extending the compass feet apart) might happen if a curve is being described, but not the circle prescribed by the poem. If the lover and beloved as compass feet are reunited, it is because the use of the instrument has concluded: Ending "where I begunne" or "com[ing] home" in the poem requires abandoning the pair of compasses' use – the use subtending the entirety of the conceit. For all the felicity of the metaphor, marking the just circle with the compasses nonetheless involves a kind of loss. If Milton imagines creation as drawing the compasses' circle, Donne before him imagines that drawing as separation.

2 The Varieties of "Compass" Experience in Early Modern Literature

By the time Milton attributed golden compasses to the world's creator, the figurative senses of the word "compass" had become widespread in English. The word expanded beyond its literal sense of an instrument and came to describe also the circumference of an area, or the area so circumscribed. In the language of the *OED*, "compass" as a noun can suggest "Bounds, limits, as in within, beyond the compass of (sight, knowledge, power, ability, etc.)," and, as a verb, to encircle, or to comprehend – that is, to get one's mind around something.[12] Lucy Hutchinson (1620–1681) invokes this sense of encircling when in *Order and Disorder* – her own contemporary-to-*Paradise Lost* hexameral verse account of the creation of the world – she reports on the third day of creation that "Where Earth, fixed in the centre, was the ground, / A mantle of light air compassed it round" (2.73–74).[13]

[12] See, respectively, "compass, n.1, adj., and adv.," and IV.10 in "compass, v.1.," *OED*, online edition. March 2018. Oxford University Press: www.oed.com/view/Entry/37466?rskey=VDtOrL&result=1&isAdvanced=false (accessed May 27, 2018).

[13] Lucy Hutchinson, *Order & Disorder*, ed. David Norbrook (Oxford and Malden, MA: Blackwell Publishers, 2001).

The etymology of "compass" in English is itself densely intricate and somewhat vexed, but its dual association with, on the one hand, the making of measurement and line, and, on the other, the literal or figurative encircling of some place, thing, or idea, is as old as Middle English. When Milton's Raphael seeks to explain the creation of the world to Adam and Eve, he is forced to use metaphor, because "Immediate are the Acts of God, more swift / Then time or motion, but to human ears / Cannot without process of speech be told." The angel must thus rely on narrating these stories in ways "earthly notion can receave" (7.176–79), accommodating the limits of human understanding by supplying an imprecise but evocative analogy. By choosing the already polysemous compass, Milton's poem exploits the sense of the compass as instrument of generative bounding and as figure of comprehension, at precisely a moment when the poem wrestles with the impossibility of understanding itself. By putting the golden compasses in the hands of the world's creator, Milton's angel suggests that to know the world is to draw an arc around it. There is something of the enclosing circle that makes the universe comprehensible – even if (and here the paradox of the compasses in Donne's "Valediction" reasserts a sense of veiled loss) that comprehensibility simultaneously signals the inaccessibility of an ineffable, inexpressible truth.

That sense of the compasses as agent of the comprehensible and expressible can be found, too, in the allegorical romance epic *The Faerie Queene*, published in two parts in 1590 and 1596, by Edmund Spenser (1552–1599), to which Milton makes occasional reference in his own works.[14] In Book 4, the narrative persona seeks to describe, through personification, the marriage of two rivers, the Thames and Medway, and the rivers from around the world who attend the fluminous nuptial event as numerous guests. The narrator acknowledges the challenging nature of this geopoetic task, rhetorically asking

> But what doe I their names seeke to reherse,
> Which all the world haue with their issue fild?
> How can they all in this so narrow verse
> Contayned be, and in small compasse hild? (4.11.17.1–4)

In admitting the difficulty of this representational project, the poem deploys the "compasse" – with perhaps a gentle pun on its instrumental nature, given the geographic quality of the conceit – to suggest both the narrative space enclosed by the unavoidably insufficient verse, and the

[14] All citations of the poem taken from Edmund Spenser, *The Faerie Queene*, ed. Thomas P. Roche, Jr. (London and New York: Penguin Books, 1978).

intelligibility of the personification of global rivers as guests gathering at one English location. The "small compasse" here maintains the coherence of an event that otherwise strains intelligibility: Encompassing these rivers poetically makes them apprehensible to the reader, and the compass delivers a world at least partially comprehensible.

Milton also knew the works of William Shakespeare (1564–1616), whose plays triumphed on stages in the years before Milton's birth in 1608 and into Milton's adulthood. The later poet might indeed have noted how frequently the related senses of compassing as encircling and as understanding appear in Shakespeare's plays and poems. Preferring these senses of "compass" to its technical senses, Shakespeare's works offer more than four dozen instances of the word and its variants describing, in the noun form, a limit or bounded area (Aaron in *Titus Andronicus* says that "Few come within the compass of my curse" at 5.1.126), a range (Hamlet tells Rosencrantz and Guildenstern that they "would sound me from my lowest note to my compass" at 3.2.339–40), a moderate measure (Falstaff says that he once "lived well and in good compass" in *Henry IV, Part 1* 3.3.16), or the scope of comprehension ("To do this is within the compass of man's wit" says the Clown in *Othello* 3.4.18); and in the verb form, accomplishing (Joan in *Henry VI, Part I* rebukes those who "judge it straight a thing impossible / To compass wonders but by help of devils" at 5.5.47–48), or surrounding (also in *Henry VI, Part I*, a messenger relates how the unfortunate Talbot "By three-and-twenty thousand of the French / Was round encompassèd and set upon" at 1.1.113–14).[15]

Despite the denotative variety of "compass" and its connotative richness in Shakespeare's works, there are relatively few instances of technical navigational instruments and materials in that corpus. There are no sextants, quadrants, astrolabes, or cross-staffs. There are figurative invocations of maps, and a literal map does appear onstage in both *King Lear* and in *Henry IV, Part I*, though in both cases it signals disaster for those who seek to use it – suggesting a pattern of anxiety that attaches to the labor and equipment of navigation. That anxiety surfaces in the plays' several invocations of navigation itself, often in extended metaphors involving a pilot, whose seafaring endeavor is wildly dangerous, full of perils only narrowly avoided by skill and luck. In these cases, the work of navigation is the work of survival. Consider, for example, the martial Margaret's remarks in

[15] All citations from Shakespeare's plays taken from *The Norton Shakespeare*, 3rd ed., gen. ed. Stephen Greenblatt (New York and London: Norton, 2016). See David Crystal and Ben Crystal, *Shakespeare's Words: A Glossary and Language Companion* (New York: Penguin Books, 2002), 87, for a robust listing of the senses of "compass" in Shakespeare's works.

Henry VI, Part III, when she rallies her troops against Edward, Clarence, and Richard by imagining Henry as just such a pilot, while underscoring the certain dangers the pilot is charged with averting:

> What though the mast be now blown overboard,
> The cable broke, the holding-anchor lost,
> And half our sailors swallowed in the flood?
> Yet lives our pilot still. …
> …
> We will not from the helm to sit and weep,
> But keep our course, though the rough wind say no,
> From shelves and rocks that threaten us with wreck.
> As good to chide the waves as speak them fair.
> And what is Edward but a ruthless sea?
> What Clarence but a quicksand of deceit?
> And Richard but a ragged fatal rock?
> All these the enemies to our poor bark.
> Say you can swim: alas, 'tis but awhile;
> Tread on the sand: why, there you quickly sink:
> Bestride the rock: the tide will wash you off
> Or else you famish – that's a threefold death. (5.4.3–6, 21–32)

Margaret implicitly describes the work of the pilot as preserving the ship from dangerous sea conditions, quicksand, and rocks, the existential threats to the sailor. In a conceit so commonplace as to be universally clear, Margaret conjures the harm to which a ship may come, and sets them opposite the "keep[ing] our course." To navigate here is to endure. It is a project Romeo, by contrast, abandons in his last moments. In an echo of his earlier, happier pilot metaphor in the balcony scene, in which he pledged Juliet that even though "I am no pilot, yet wert thou as far / As that vast shore washed with the farthest sea, / I should adventure" to reach her (2.1.124–126), Romeo returns to his would-be navigator's identity, this time emphasizing not the success of travel but the disaster (literally, the star-crossing) that navigation strives to avoid. Crying, "Thou desperate pilot, now at once run on / The dashing rocks thy seasick, weary bark!" (5.3.117–118), he drinks the fatal poison. Keeping a ship on course reveals itself, over and over in the plays, as evidence of the ship's vulnerability to wreck.

In this sense, navigation and its technologies become acknowledgements of the disaster that navigating only inconsistently prevents. This twinning of navigation and wreck might be just audible, in the infinite depths of Shakespeare's punning, in Prospero's assurances to Miranda that the shipwrecking storm Ariel produces in *The Tempest* is harmless. "The direful spectacle of the wreck, which touched / The very virtue of compassion in thee," he says, "I have with such provision in mine art / So safely ordered," such that no one was injured by the titular tempest (1.2.26–29). "Compass" and "compassion" have distinct etymological histories, but their orthographic proximity allows the compass to flicker briefly in Miranda's compassion, as she wishes a successful navigation on the yet-unknown travelers she believed she saw swallowed by the storm. Their wreck, or failure of navigation, is greeted by compass-ion.

3 The Magnetic Compass

The compass qua instrument does appear, though, at least once in the corpus of Shakespeare's works – though it is a different instrument than the golden compasses Milton imagines for the creation of the world. In *Coriolanus*, a citizen suggests that the opinions of the so-called "many-headed multitude" (2.3.15) are so diverse that "they would fly east, west, north, south, and their consent of one direct way should be at once to all the points o' th' compass" (2.3.19–21). The citizen's hypothetical compass is the magnetic compass, which consists of a magnetized metal needle free to move in the direction of magnetic north, set over a card showing directional points at various degrees of specificity (the four cardinal directions, or the eight, sixteen, thirty-two, or sixty-four more specific directional points), all within a containing box or bowl.[16] Developed centuries earlier in China, the first mention of the magnetic compass appears in Europe in the twelfth century. It came into regular use sometime in the thirteenth century, and its refinement around 1300 transformed seafaring and commerce, first in the Mediterranean and then in the waterways of northern Europe and beyond. With the era of European exploration (and its associated colonial projects), the compass became virtually synonymous, for professional pilots and laypeople alike, with navigation – and wonder. As John Seller notes in his 1669 *Practical navigation…*, "This marvellous and most useful Instrument, called the Marrinars Compass," is "justly ranked

[16] For more on the origins of the eight, sixteen, thirty-two, or sixty-four points of the compass card, see Alan Gurney, *Compass: A Story of Exploration and Innovation* (New York and London: W.W. Norton & Co., 2004), 41–55. The magnetic compass turns up in early modern literature across Europe, though this chapter is focused on early modern literature in English. For example, for an account of the compass's appearance in Dante's *Paradiso* as a metaphor for that which draws the poet's attention, like a needle to the polestar, to the voice of Saint Bonaventure, see Amir D. Aczel, *The Riddle of the Compass: The Invention That Changed the World* (New York, San Diego, and London: Harcourt, Inc., 2001), 34–36.

amongst the greatest Wonders that this World affords, and deserves well to be understood by all that are Students and Practitioners in the Art of Navigation."[17]

Shakespeare's citizen in *Coriolanus* invokes the directional possibility embodied by the magnetic compass to suggest a kind of ineluctable confusion of populist voices. This rhetorical gesture points not just to the compass's broad footprints in the popular imaginary, but also to the susceptibility of the compass – and, by extension, the navigational project for which is was often emblematic – to error. Though the citizen is not thinking of the compass's technical limitations, the compass's availability as a symbol of the diffusion of consensus underlines the vulnerability of navigation to dissent or lostness. For the magnetic compass, there was an acute problem, one well known by the sixteenth century. The movement of the earth's magnetic north, and magnetic north's distinctness from geographical north, cause the phenomenon of magnetic variation, in which compass readings might be inaccurate or show multiple headings as north. This variation of the compass was dangerous for sailors and the subject of extensive treatment by mathematicians, geographers, cartographers, and others.[18]

No surprise, then, that the compass would sometimes appear in early modern English literature as an unreliable instrument, a tool of last resort, despite its allure and potential. In Book 2 of his massive *Faerie Queene*, Spenser compares Guyon, a knight separated from his sidekick Palmer, to a pilot who is forced to the use of a compass when preferred celestial navigation is not an option:

> As Pilot well expert in perilous waue,
> That to a stedfast starre his course hath bent,
> When foggy mistes, or cloudy tempests haue
> The faithfull light of that faire lampe yblent,
> And couer'd heauen with hideous dreriment,
> Vpon his card and compas firmes his eye,
> The maisters of his long experiment,
> And to them does the steddy helme apply,
> Bidding his winged vessell fairely forward fly. (2.7.1–9)

[17] The quotation begins a section on "The Original Discovery and Invention of the Mariners Compass, and the Excellency thereof," in John Seller, *Practical navigation...* (London: J. Darby and John Wingfield, 1669), 164.

[18] Consider, for example, William Borough's 1581 *Discourse concerning the Variation of the Compass.* For efforts to address magnetic variation, see Lesley B. Cormack, *Charting an Empire: Geography at the English Universities 1580–1620* (Chicago: University of Chicago Press, 1997), 93–96.

More explicit about her refusal to trust or use the compass is Britomart, the knight of Book 3, who proudly declares that she will "hunt out perils and aduentures hard, / By sea, by land, where so they may be met," but without navigational instruments to assist her. "For such intent into these parts I came, / Withouten compasse, or withouten card, / Far from my natiue soyle..." (3.2.7.6–8).[19] However far her travels, she will undertake them without the compass.

Margaret Cavendish (1623–1673) similarly takes the compass as a starting point for natural philosophical reflection and imaginative comparison, rather than as an object sufficient unto itself. In her *Observations upon Experimental Philosophy*, she dedicates a chapter to the properties of the lodestone and its capacity to magnetize the compass needle. But that compass is swiftly set aside by the denizens of *The Blazing World*, a proto-science-fictional text published with *Observations* in 1668.[20] Having been a passenger aboard a ship swept to the North Pole (where, of course, magnetic compasses are useless), *The Blazing World*'s heroine finds herself crossing over into another world, a pole of which meets the earth's. The denizens of this world are

> Very good Navigators ... and though they had no knowledg of the Loadstone, or Needle, or pendulous Watches, yet (which was as serviceable to them) they had subtile observations, and great practice; in so much that they could not onely tell the depth of the Sea in every place, but where there were shelves of Sand, Rocks, and other obstructions to be avoided by skilfull and experienced Sea-men: Besides, they were excellent Augurers, which skill they counted more necessary and beneficial then the use of Compasses, Cards, Watches, and the like... (7)

Here the magnetic compass, the hydrographic charts, and the clocks involved in estimating (alas, incorrectly until the eighteenth century) longitude, all pale beside the esoteric augury of these seafarers, whose navigational skill signals their technological superiority. As marvelous as the compass was, it sometimes signaled, too, the limits (or compass, one might say) of knowledge.

19 For more on the resistance to maps in *The Faerie Queene*, see Barrett, *Early Modern English Literature*, ch. 1.

20 Properties of the lodestone discussed in ch. 6 of Margaret Cavendish, *Observations upon Experimental Philosophy to which is added, The Description of a New Blazing World, Written by the Thrice Noble, Illustrious, and Excellent Princesse, The Duchess of Newcastle*, 2nd ed. (London: Printed by A. Maxwell, 1668), 17–20, and in ch. 5 of *Observations upon the Opinions of Some Ancient Philosophers* (London: Printed by A. Maxwell, 1666), 381.

4 Navigating Literature

The pair of compasses and the magnetic compass – along with the map and globe – might be the most famous navigational materials in early modern England, and the most frequently adopted for literary use, but they are not the only ones. The aforementioned astrolabe, for example, appeared intermittently in Renaissance English literature, too, and not only (though most often) in the sort of technical guides and instructional manuals – for lay and professional users – that Chaucer piloted for his son. References to the astrolabe arrested readers' attention in passages from imported writers. In John Florio's landmark 1603 translation of "Apology of Raymond Sebond," Michel de Montaigne (1533–1592) declares that "We are no nerer heaven on the top of Sina mount, then in the bottome of the deepest Sea: Consider of it, that you may see with your Astrolabe." In the influential *Divine Weeks* of Guillaume de Salluste Du Bartas, the astrolabe exemplifies mathematical and astronomical excellence. The 1655 English translation of Luís de Camões's (1524–1580) Portuguese epic *The Lusiads* describes the adventurers' use of "The ASTROLABE, a modern Instrument: / Which with sharpe Judgment SAGES did invent" (5.25.7–8).[21] Elsewhere, the astrolabe had something of a profile in religious texts, in part because of its intricate use and the delicate precision of its measurements, easily miscalculated or misinterpreted by an inexpert user. In the correspondence of late sixteenth- and early seventeenth-century religious scholars and theorists John Aynsworth and Henry Aynsworth, John warns of the stakes of religious debate: "And I showed you here as erring a little in some mathematical instrument, makes a mans sight and judgment quite contrarie as appeareth in the vse of the Astrolabe or crosse staffe: So I say the least error in any of these transcendental doctrinal points doth shake the whole body of beleef."[22] That cross-staff (used for estimating latitude based on the sun's angle of elevation above the horizon), along with the quadrant or sextant (both of which make angular measurements of celestial objects for purposes of calculating position), and other specialized instruments make occasional appearances in literature of the period, but they tend to surface

[21] Michel de Montaigne, *Essays vvritten in French by Michael Lord of Montaigne…done into English, according to the last French edition, by Iohn Florio…* (London: Printed by Melch. Bradwood for Edward Blount and William Barret, 1613), 297. Guillaume de Salluste Du Bartas, *Du Bartas his deuine weekes and workes translated: and dedicated to the Kings most excellent Maiestie by Iosuah Syluester* (London: Humfrey Lounes, 1611), 374. Luís de Camões, *The Lusiad, or, Portugals historicall poem…and now newly put into English by Richard Fanshaw, Esq* (London: Humphrey Moseley, 1655).

[22] John Ainsworth, *The trying out of the truth begunn and prosequuted in certayn letters and passages between Iohn Aynsworth and Henry Aynsworth* (Amsterdam: Printed by Giles Thorp., 1615), 113.

less in imaginative literature than in practical works, their specialized uses perhaps contracting their broader appeal as figurative vehicles or subjects of popular treatment.

5 The New Cartographic Revolution

The literary appropriations described here of navigational technologies are drawn from the early modern period, focusing on the sixteenth and seventeenth centuries when the Cartographic Revolution flooded popular and professional contexts with the newly precise and newly affordable materials of the spatial arts. It is worth considering, too, though, the new cartographic revolution in the midst of which this volume appears. In the late twentieth and now into the twenty-first century, the era of digital cartography is fundamentally altering the way we imagine navigation. Geographic information systems (GIS) and global positioning systems (GPS) – largely built on military satellite infrastructure – have transformed the project of navigation in its everyday instantiations. Intriguingly, the adventure and possibility of earlier navigational technologies persists: While the availability of real-time, precise locational data has turned mobile phones into virtuosic pilots, the compass "app" persists, so that a smartphone screen can, at a touch, become a handheld magnetic compass, pointing the user in one of those thirty-two directions.

And if the compass persists from bowl and card to preloaded app on iPhone, so does literature's interest in exploring and interrogating the possibilities and limitations of the navigational technologies of this second cartographic revolution. Literature in English – in diverse fields ranging from fine art to memoir to novel – continues to foreground the technical nature of navigation and its technologies. The map itself becomes an aesthetic medium, the navigational strategies of which enable new modes of expression in works such as Katharine Harmon's *The Map as Art: Contemporary Artists Explore Cartography*.[23] Similarly, Denis Wood's *Everything Sings: Maps for a Narrative Atlas*[24] makes of the map a technology for navigating not just space but place, experience, and memory. Reif Larsen's novel *The Selected Works of T. S. Spivet*[25] centers on a protagonist whose making of a variety of kinds of maps likens the work of narrative to the process of spatial representation. This is an undertone, too, of Andrew DeGraff's *Plotted:*

[23] (New York: Princeton Architectural Press, 2009).
[24] (Los Angeles: Siglio, 2010).
[25] (London: Penguin, 2009).

A Literary Atlas,[26] which offers nineteen maps spatially interpreting the stories and settings of nineteen literary works, effectively turning the work of reading into a navigational project. Meanwhile, Trevor Paglen's *Blank Spots on the Map: The Dark Geography of the Pentagon's Secret World*[27] and the 2010 *Invisible: Covert Operations and Classified Landscapes*[28] highlight the ways navigational (especially digital) technologies are interrupted or frustrated in order to preserve state security apparatuses.

Unsurprisingly, the new powers of visualization at work in the digital cartographic revolution undergird much literature in online platforms. The *Strange Maps* blog, for example, visualizes geographic data in innovative and surprising ways, while the digital magazine *Atlas Obscura* offers short-form articles connecting place and story for the imagined reader, for whom the wandering of an ever-surprising world is newly possible in the online environment. Digital humanities initiatives exploit GIS data while crowd-sourcing its navigational interpretation: Consider the *Placing Literature* effort, which allows participants to map locations from literary works onto online maps for use by other readers and scholars. And the *Map of Early Modern London* returns would-be navigators of its streets to the seventeenth-century city by way of an annotated and interactive map.[29] The preoccupation of literature in English with the technologies of navigation is far from exhausted.

[26] (San Francisco: Zest Books, 2015).

[27] (New York: Penguin, 2009).

[28] (New York: Aperture, 2010).

[29] The *Strange Maps* blog: https://bigthink.com/strange-maps/ (accessed July 15, 2023); *Atlas Obscura*, www.atlasobscura.com (accessed July 15, 2023); Placing Literature, www.placingliterature.com (accessed July 15, 2023); the Map of Early Modern London, https://mapoflondon.uvic.ca/ (accessed July 15, 2023).

CHAPTER 11

Telescopes

Peter C. Herman

When Galileo Galilei published *Sidereus Nuncias* (The Sidereal Messenger) in 1610, he described the instrument he used to observe the heavens, later named "the telescope," as the original disruptive technology. Galileo did not claim to have invented this instrument. As he says toward the start of the *Sidereus*, "About 10 months ago a rumor came to our ears that a spyglass had been made by a certain Dutchman by means of which visible objects, although far removed from the eye of the observer, were distinctly perceived as though nearby."[1] In fact, in 1608 several people applied to the States-General in the Hague for a patent, but the Dutch government denied the request on the grounds that the technology was too simple and too easily copied. For example, little telescopes were sold at the Frankfurt fair.[2] Before Galileo got his hands on one, they were considered toys. But Galileo did get his hands on one, improved it, and then did what nobody had thought to do before. He looked up – and, with one glance, instantly rendered the Ptolemaic universe obsolete while ushering in a new era of technologically enhanced observations.

Galileo proposes, at the start of *Sidereus Nuncias*, to present "great things for inspection and contemplation by every explorer of Nature," and they are "great" both because of "their newness ... and also because of the instrument with the benefit of which they make themselves manifest to our sight" (37). Shortly after the book's publication, the English ambassador to Venice, Sir Henry Wotton, included a description of Galileo's discoveries in a letter to King James's right-hand man, Robert Cecil, Earl of Salisbury, and he seems to echo Galileo's belief that this invention changed everything:[3]

[1] Galileo Galilei, *Sidereus Nuncius: Or, The Sidereal Messenger*, 2nd ed., trans. Albert Van Helden (Chicago: University of Chicago Press, 1989), 39. All further references are parenthetical.
[2] Van Helden, "Introduction," *Sidereus Nuncias*, 4–5.
[3] As quoted in Charles Coffin, *John Donne and the New Philosophy* (New York: Humanities Press, 1958), 84. In 1610, Thomas Harriot also observed the moon with a telescope. However, he kept his observations to himself, and so they had no impact on the larger culture. See Massimo Bucciantini,

> Now touching the occurrents [*sic*] of the present, I send herewith unto his Majesty the strangest piece of news (as I may justly call it) that he hath ever yet received from any part of the world; which is the annexed book [*Sidereus Nuncius*] (come abroad this very day) of the Mathematical Professor at Padua, who by the help of an optical instrument (which both enlargeth and approximateth the object) invented first in Flanders, and bettered by himself, hath discovered four new planets rolling about the sphere of Jupiter, besides many other unknown fixed stars; likewise, the true cause of the *Via Lactea* [the Milky Way], so long searched;[4] and lastly, that the moon is not spherical, but endued with many prominences, and, which is of all the strangest, illuminated with the solar light by reflection from the body of the earth, as he seemeth to say. So as upon the whole subject he hath first overthrown all former astronomy—for we must have a new sphere to save the appearances—and next all astrology. For the virtue of these new planets must needs vary the judicial part, and why may there not yet be more? … By the next ship your Lordship shall receive from me one of the abovenamed instruments, as it is bettered by this man.

Wotton's sense that the telescope constituted an utterly revolutionary technology, one that had "overthrown all former astronomy," set the path for how later historians of science and literary critics would understand the effect of the telescope in early modern culture. Charles M. Coffin, for instance, quoted approvingly an earlier critic's sense that the telescope instigated "the break-up of a whole system of thought"; Alexandre Koyré asserted that "not only astronomy, but science as such, began with Galileo's invention"; and Marjorie Hope Nicolson described Galileo's book in apocalyptic terms: "The sound heard in 1610, with the publication of Galileo's *Sidereus Nuncius,* was less Aaron's bell than the first note of Gabriel's trumpet.… Now for the first time a 'new astronomy' of new stars, new planets, a new moon, a new universe came home to men's business and bosoms."[5] And more recently, Andrew Fleck has observed that John Donne "lived through a revolution in human understanding of the [heavens]."[6]

Michele Camerota, and Franco Giudice, *Galileo's Telescope: A European Story,* trans. Catherine Bolton (Cambridge, MA: Harvard University Press, 2015), 129–135.

4 As Galileo says, the question, "what is the Milky Way … has always been a controversy among the philosophers" (19).

5 Coffin, *John Donne and the New Philosophy*, 5; Alexandre Koyré, *From the Closed World to the Infinite Universe* (Baltimore, MD: Johns Hopkins University Press, 1957), 90; Marjorie Hope Nicolson, *The Breaking of the Circle: Studies in the Effect of the "New Science" upon Seventeenth-Century Poetry* (repr. New York: Octagon Books, 1985), 119.

6 Andrew Fleck, "'None Ends Where He Begun': Astronomical and Polemic Revolutions in John Donne," in *The Book of Nature and Humanity in the Middle Ages and the Renaissance*, ed. David Hawkes and Richard G. Newhauser (Turnhout: Brepols, 2013), 273.

But we need to distinguish between the effects of the telescope as we, today, understand them, and how the telescope was perceived at the time – at least, how it was perceived in early modern English literary culture. Did the telescope have the immediately revolutionary, disruptive effect an earlier generation of scholars ascribed to it? And do we find this revolution reflected in the period's poetry and fiction? The answer is actually more complicated than most allow.[7] Some writers, such as John Donne, no doubt understood the potentially destabilizing effects of replacing one cosmology with another. As he famously put it, "The new philosophy calls all in doubt, / The element of fire is quite put out … / 'Tis all in pieces, all coherence gone" (ll. 205–206, 213).[8] But many responses were more equivocal. As we will see, the majority of authors responded to the telescope by using the device to reinforce whatever argument the author wanted to make rather than reacting to the telescope as a fundamental break with the past.

Let's start with Wotton's letter. The quote in the previous paragraph reproduces exactly what Charles Coffin uses in his seminal book, *John Donne and the New Philosophy*, and so it set the terms for generations of later critics. But crucially, Coffin leaves out several sentences that follow the quoted passage, which imply a more distanced, differently prioritized view of Galileo's book and instrument. The full passage reads as follows, with the sentence Coffin deleted in italics:

> For the virtue of these new planets must needs vary the judicial part, and why may there not yet be more? These things I have been bold thus to discourse unto your Lordship, whereof here all corners are full. And the author runneth a fortune to be either exceeding famous or exceeding ridiculous. By the next ship your Lordship shall receive from me one of the above-named instruments, as bettered by this man. *Now to descend from these superior novelties to these below, which do more trouble the wise men of this place.* (my emphasis)[9]

First, it is not clear from the letter whether the reference to astrology is meant seriously or as a joke, especially since the early modern period was

[7] Both Thomas S. Kuhn and Albert Van Helden note that the telescope's effect on astronomy and thinking generally was gradual, and that the geocentric universe had adherent well into the seventeenth century. See Thomas S. Kuhn, *The Copernican Revolution: Planetary Astronomy in the Development of Western Thought* (Cambridge, MA: Harvard University Press, 1957; repr. 1985), 185–228, and Albert Van Helden, "The Telescope in the Seventeenth Century," *Isis* 65.1 (1974): 53.

[8] Donne, "First Anniversary," in *John Donne's Poetry*, ed. A. L. Clements (New York: Norton, 1966), 73.

[9] Quoted in Logan Pearsall Smith, *The Life and Letters of Sir Henry Wotton* (Oxford: Clarendon Press, 1907), vol. 1, 487–488.

notoriously inconsistent on the topic.[10] Nor is Wotton sure if Galileo's book will make him famous or look like a fool. But most importantly, at the passage's end, Wotton brackets the controversy as a distraction – interesting, to be sure, worthy of note, and worthy of sending along both the book and a telescope, but a distraction nonetheless from the more serious issue of whether the French king and the Duke of Savoy will "assail the Dukedom of Milan."[11] In other words, philosophy and astronomy are all very nice, but foreign affairs are of much more immediate consequence, and so that's what troubles "the wise men" of Venice.

There is one further important qualifying factor for understanding how early Modern English literature responded to the telescope: Despite Wotton's enthusiasm, the evidence suggests that Galileo's *Siderius Nuncius* did not circulate widely in England. According to Early English Books Online, several decades had to pass before Galileo's book would find an English publisher; in 1653, Jacob Flesher brought out a near-exact reprint of the Venice edition of the *Siderius* (he changed the publisher information at the bottom of the title page), and Flesher appended the *Siderius* to his edition of Pierre Gassendi's *Institutio Astronomica.*[12] There is no English translation in this period, and there would not be one until 1880.[13] Furthermore, Private Libraries of Renaissance England, which documents the contents of hundreds of private libraries until 1653, does not contain a single reference to the *Siderius*, even though many of the lists detail the books owned by scholars at Oxford and Cambridge.[14] While some copies

[10] For example, Shakespeare's Edmund notoriously states that the stars have no influence on our behavior, "as if we were villains on necessity, fools by heavenly compulsion" (*King Lear* 1.2.110; in *The Norton Shakespeare: Later Plays and Poems*, ed. Stephen Greenblatt et al. [New York: Norton, 2016]. All references to Shakespeare's plays will be to this edition, and cited parenthetically). Yet in the early modern period, it was considered treason to cast the monarch's horoscope (J. G. Bellamy, *The Law of Treason in England in the Later Middle Ages* [Cambridge: Cambridge University Press, 2004], 126). See also Johann P. Somerville's web page on the matter: https://faculty.history.wisc.edu/sommerville/367/367-121.htm (accessed July 15, 2023).

[11] Ibid., 488.

[12] Jacob Flesher seems to have inherited his father, Miles Flesher's, thriving publishing business in 1649 along with his position as printer to the city of London. His first publication was *Fifty sermons. preached by that learned and reverend divine, John Donne*, and he also published *Letters to severall persons of honour written by John Donne* (1651). Before Galileo, he printed Latin translations of medieval Latin and Persian astronomical texts: Mahmud Shah Khulji (1436–1469), *Astronomica quaedam ex traditione Shah Cholgii Persae una cum hypothesibus planetarum* (1650) and Nasir al-Din Muhammad ibn Muhammad Tusi (1201–1274), *Binae tabulae geographicae una Nassir Eddini Persae altera Vlug Beigi Tatari* (1652). Interestingly, Tusi's criticisms of Ptolemy anticipate those of Copernicus. See F. Jamil Ragep, "Tūsī and Copernicus: The Earth's Motion in Context," *Science in Context* 14.1–2 (2001): 145–163.

[13] Van Helden, "Preface," *Siderius Nuncius*, xviii.

[14] See the project description at: http://wmpeople.wm.edu/site/page/rjfehr/purposeanddesign (accessed July 15, 2023).

of the *Siderius* no doubt circulated in early modern England (John Donne alludes in a marginal note to the "*Nuncius sydereus*" at the start of his 1611 *Ignatius his Conclave*),[15] the book evidently had very few owners, meaning very few people had firsthand knowledge of Galileo's discoveries.

Even so, for some, Galileo's telescope and his astronomical discoveries demonstrated the power of objective observation to fundamentally change knowledge.[16] In the *Pseudodoxca Epidemica*, Sir Thomas Browne alludes to Galileo's undermining of "the great Climactericall yeare, that is sixty three." Previously, the heavens were supposed to be governed by the numbers seven and nine – "but it is now demonstrable unto sense, that there are many more [planets], as Galileo hath declared in his *Nuncius Sydereues*, that is two more in the orbe of Saturne, and no lesse than foure more in the sphere of Jupiter...."[17] Similarly, in a 1646 letter, the polymath John Selden argued that Protestant theologians needed to take into account newly available ancient Jewish texts in exactly the same way that everyone should take into account the telescope and all that Galileo revealed. In both cases, newly revealed knowledge fundamentally changed understanding, and so could not be ignored: "Once the use of the telescope has been transmitted [to us], we ourselves perceive the very same thing as those Messengers, although otherwise we would be ignorant of it. The same applies to the use of oriental [i.e. rabbinical] doctrines, whence the whole of Christianity arose: without it, we are often deceived in our judgments of sacred matters...."[18] But others used Galileo's discoveries as a useful metaphor for very different purposes. In *The Duchess of Malfi* (1613–1614), John Webster uses Galileo to signify the impossible when the Cardinal subjects his lover, Julia (whom he will later kill), to a misogynistic tirade: "We had need go borrow that fantastic glass / Invented by Galileo the Florentine, / To view another specious world i' th' moon, / And look to find a constant woman there" (2. 4.16–19).[19] For the Royalist poet, George Wither, writing in 1649, the disruption of the new astronomy provides a handy metaphor for the execution of Charles I and upending of England's political

15 John Donne, *Ignatius His Conclave*, ed. T. S. Healy (Oxford: Clarendon Press, 1969), 7.

16 For an excellent survey of English responses to Galileo, see Judy A. Hayden, "Introduction: 'Faln Systemes' and 'Dead Chimaeras,'" in *Literature in the Age of Celestial Discovery: From Copernicus to Flamsteed* (New York and Basingstoke: Palgrave Macmillan, 2016), 1–21, and Bucciantini et al., *Galileo's Telescope*, 129–154.

17 Thomas Browne, *Pseudodoxia Epidemica* (London: 1646), sig. Dd2v.

18 Quoted in G. J. Toomer, *John Selden: A Life in Scholarship* (Oxford: Oxford University Press, 2009), 845. I owe this reference to Jason Rosenblatt.

19 John Webster, *The Duchess of Malfi*, in *English Renaissance Drama*, ed. David Bevington et al. (New York: Norton, 2002).

structure: After first comparing Cromwell et al. to the giants who sought to overthrow Jove, Wither, lumping Copernicus and Galileo together, hopes that "these *Youths* finde / The self-same Fate; whose Villanies have hurl'd / Earth from her *Center,* and unhing'd the World."[20]

In sum, there is no one response to the telescope. For some, such as Donne and Wither, it represented disorder; for others, such as Selden and Browne, the telescope and what it revealed constituted a firmer basis of knowledge. In the remainder of this chapter, I want to look in more detail at three very different literary responses to the telescope and the challenges it represented. As we will see, Francis Godwin has fundamental doubts about the moral probity of technology; John Milton, in *Paradise Lost*, associates the telescope with Satan; and both Aphra Behn and Margaret Cavendish use the telescope to demonstrate how easily our senses can be tricked. Far from issuing in a new era of objective observations, at least some regarded the telescope in particular, and technological advancement in general, as a metaphor for how one ultimately cannot know anything with certainty.

1 *The Man in the Moone*

Bishop Francis Godwin's *The Man in the Moone* (1638) takes the new approach to knowledge – that is, empiricism or what we call today "the scientific method" – and fictionalizes it in the form of a travel narrative to the moon and then, upon the narrator's return, to China.[21] The epistle to the reader, written by one E.M. (whose identity is unknown) announces the concatenation of science and travel by bringing together Columbus and Galileo, the New World, and the telescope:[22]

> thou hast here a new discovery of a new *world*, which perchance may finde little better entertainment in thy opinion than that of *Columbus*. ... That there should be *Antipodes* was once thought as great a *Paradox* as now that the *Moon* should be habitable. But the knowledge of this may seeme more properly reserv'd for this our discovering age: in which our *Galilaeusses* can by advantage of their spectacles [telescopes] gaze the Sunne into spots, & descry mountains in the *Moon*. (67–68)

[20] George Wither, *Vaticinium Votivum* (London: n.p., 1649), sigs. C1r–C2v.

[21] The book is occasionally called the first example of science fiction. See Catherine Gimelli Martin, "Sailing to the Moon: Francis Bacon, Francis Godwin and the First Science Fiction," in *Literature in the Age of Celestial Discovery*, ed. Judy Hayden, 109–132.

[22] Francis Godwin, *The Man in the Moone*, ed. William Poole (Peterborough, ON; Broadview Editions, 2009). All further references are to this edition, and cited parenthetically.

In this proto-novel, the protagonist, Domingo Gonsales, following several adventures on the European continent, finds himself shipwrecked on an island. After numerous experiments, he figures out that by harnessing a group of birds, he can fly to various parts of the island. A ship that rescues him runs aground to escape an English fleet, and so, to save his life, Gonsales rounds up his birds and flies upward. To his shock, the birds continue to rise until he reaches the moon, where he discovers a morally (but not technologically) advanced civilization. Along the way, Gonsales not only confirms the Copernican theory of a heliocentric universe, but also puts into practice the epistemological shift announced by both Galileo and Sir Francis Bacon.

Galileo stresses over and over again in the *Sidereus* the primacy of what Shakespeare, in *Othello*, calls "ocular proof" (3.3.357) over textual authority: "Anyone [looking through a telescope] will then understand with the certainty of the senses that the Moon" is not smooth (38). The same instrument, Galileo claims, will "put an end to the debate about the Galaxy or Milky Way and to have made manifest its essence to the senses as well as the intellect" (38): "with the aid of the spyglass, [the Milky Way] may be observed so well that all the disputes that for so many generations have vexed philosophers are destroyed by visible certainty, and we are liberated from wordy arguments" (64). Bacon puts forward much the same points. In *The Advancement of Learning* (1605), he criticizes those "intellectualists" who "have withdrawn themselves too much from the contemplation of nature and the observations of experience, and tumbled up and down in their own reason and conceipts."[23] In *The Great Instauration* (1620), he expands on the primacy of experience over book learning, proposing "a true and lawful marriage between the empirical and the rational faculty" (309) that will alter how one creates knowledge: "Now what the sciences stand in need of is a form of induction which shall analyse experience and take it to pieces, and by a due process of exclusion and rejection lead to an inevitable conclusion" (315). Bacon further asserts that those "who aspire not guess and divine, but to discover and know … to examine and dissect the nature of this very world itself, must go to facts themselves for everything" (318), and he is absolutely clear as to how one gains access to these facts: "Further, in the selection of the relations and experiments I conceive I have been a more cautious purveyor than those who have hitherto dealt

[23] Bacon, *The Proficiencie and Advancement of Learning*, in *Francis Bacon: A Selection of his Works*, ed. Sidney Warhaft (New York: Macmillan, 1982), 233. All references to Bacon's works, unless otherwise noted, will be to this edition and cited parenthetically.

with natural history. For I admit nothing *but on the faith of eyes*..." (320; my emphasis).

Godwin, in *The Man in the Moone*, portrays Domingo Gonsales as putting into (fictional) practice Galileo's and Bacon's theories. When he sets himself the project of creating a flying machine using wild swans (or "gansas") he proceeds, as Bacon would want, through exclusion and rejection leading to an inevitable, that is to say, successful, conclusion: "In this cogitation having much laboured my wits and made some triall, I found *by experience*, that if many were to put the bearing of one great burthen," then he would have to find some means of having the birds all rise at the same time (78; my emphasis). Like Galileo and Bacon, Gonsales admits nothing but on the faith his eyes, and using his eyes, he proves the accuracy of the New Philosophy. As he flies toward the moon, Gonsales notices that the earth "little and little did change every hower. The reason thereof I conceive to be this, that whereas the Earth, according to her naturall motion (for that such a motion she hath, I am now constrained to join in opinion with *Copernicus*), turneth around upon her own Axe every 24. howers from the *West* unto the *East*" (92).

After describing how the moon is illuminated by light reflected off the earth, Gonsales declares (again, echoing Galileo): "How ill this agreeth with that which our *Philosophers* teach in the schools I am not ignorant. But alas, how many of their Errours hath time and experience refuted in this our age" (97). For example, "as for that Region of Fire our *Philosophers* talke of, I heard no newes of it; mine eyes have sufficiently informed me that there can be no such thing" (98).

It would seem that Godwin intends his fable to demonstrate the superiority of Galilean and Baconian empiricism; except that Godwin gives his "hero" a nationality and a backstory that would cause any contemporary reader to regard him with the utmost suspicion, if not utter loathing.[24] First, Gonsales is a dwarf ("I must acknowledge my stature to be so little, as no man there is living I think lesse" [71]), and therefore (to those in the early modern period) deformed. More importantly, to state the obvious, Godwin makes

[24] Virtually all previous treatments of *The Man in the Moone* assume that this book unqualifiedly celebrates the new science, and that there is nothing problematic about the narrator. See, for example, Sarah Hutton, "*The Man in the Moone* and the New Astronomy," *Etudes Epistéme* 7 (2005): 3–13; Mary Baine Campbell, "Speedy Messengers: Fiction, Cryptography, Space Travel, and Francis Godwin's *The Man in the Moone*," *The Yearbook of English Studies* 41.1 (2011): 190–204; and David Cressy, "Early Modern Space Travel and the English Man in the Moon," in *Literature in the Age of Celestial Discovery*, ed. Judy A. Hayden, 62. Godwin's editor, William Poole, notes that "Gonsales is carefully placed among real contemporaries engaged in the grueling wars of independence" (Godwin, *Man in the Moone*, "Introduction," 27), but draws no conclusions from this.

his "hero" *Spanish*, not English. Critics have suggested that Godwin does so in order to associate Gonsales with Columbus and with the picaresque, yet this seems to me entirely too naïve, given the reputation of the Spanish in the early seventeenth century.[25] The title of a 1623 book by Thomas Scott warning James not to trust Spain gives a flavor of their reputation (a title that tantalizingly seems to conflate propaganda and Baconian empiricism): *An Experimentall Discovery of Spanish Practices, ... Wherein is Manifested from Known Experience, Both the Cruelty and the Policy of the Spaniard, to effect his own ends* (London, 1623). While Gonsales is not a monarch, he certainly exemplifies the early modern reputation that Spanish had for pride. For instance, Domingo (anticipating our own history of space travel), first uses an animal to test his flying device, a lamb, and he is unhappy that the poor beast has the honor of being the first: "whose happiness I much envied that he should be the first living creature to take possession of such a device" (79).

Even more damning, Gonsales tells us that he served with "Don Fernando, the noble and thrice-renowned Duke of Alva, [who] was sent into the Low Countries, viz. the year of Grace 1568" (70) – and that "The first expedition I was in was against the Prince of Orange" (70). This association, I suggest, would have had the same force for Godwin's readers as stating that someone today fought for the Taliban in Afghanistan or joined ISIS in fomenting terrorist plots. The English were fascinated by the Dutch revolt (Sir Philip Sidney, we might remember, died in the Netherlands), and the Duke of Alba quickly became the face of Spanish oppression. According to Thomas Churchyard's account, after the Netherlands "fell in a marvellous mislike" of their Spanish overlords, King Philip "appointed straight lawes and severe Governoures. And among the rest of cruelties, the inquisition was thought a necessarie curb or plague, to persecute the heads that were thrust out too farre. And with this inquisition was sent from Kyng Philip the Duke of Alva," whom Churchyard depicts as a kind of early modern Terminator.[26] Nothing, Churchyard writes,

> could plucke him from his purpose, that came for a pretenced persecution and Scourge ... And the Duke of Alva minding the matter he came for, and forgetting no advantage that might be taken in time, beganne roughly, and

[25] A. G. H. Bachrach, "*Luna Mendax*: Some Reflection on Moon-Voyages in Early Seventeenth Century England," in *Between Dream and Nature: Essays on Utopia and Dystopia*, ed. Dominic Baker-Smith and C. C. Barfoot (Rodopi: Amsterdam, 1987), 75; Mary Baine Campbell, *Wonder and Science: Imaging Worlds in Early Modern Europe* (Ithaca, NY: Cornell University Press, 1999), 156.

[26] Thomas Churchyard, *A Lamentable and Pitiable Description of the Woefull Warres in Flanders* (London, 1578), sig. E.iiv. According to Pieter Geyl, "Never was a nation subjected to a reign of terror with more calculated deliberation or more systematic persistence" (*The Revolt of the Netherlands 1555–1609*, 2nd ed. [repr. London: Ernest Benn, 1966], 104). For a slightly more sympathetic view, see Henry Kamen, *The Duke of Alba* (New Haven: Yale University Press, 2004), 106–135.

> with some rigor, to shew the power and commission he had, sparing neyther purse, cunning, nor practice, to accomplish hys desire, and bring to full effect by sword and policie the substance of a plotte and grounde… (sig. E.ii.r)

Godwin thus associates Gonsales Domingo, avatar of Baconian empiricism and Galilean astronomy, with a man widely considered a monster. This cannot be good, especially given that Godwin was a zealous reformer, an exponent of a new national, meaning Protestant, history of England who also wrote a history of bishops in England in which he sharply criticized the Marian (Catholic) bishops Stephen Gardiner and Edmund Bonner.[27] Godwin, in other words, was not a man who would invoke Catholicism and mean it positively. Spain, for him and for the majority in Protestant England, was an aggressive military empire that regularly threatened to invade England (they tried once in 1588, the Spanish Armada; it didn't work), and replace its monarch with a Catholic.

Godwin's highly ambivalent treatment of Domingo has its roots, I think, in the deep-seated religious resistance by both Protestants and Catholics to the new paradigm represented by telescopes and the new astronomy. The Catholic Church's antipathy to the new astronomy is well known. John Milton recounts in *Areopagitica* (1644) how he "visited the famous Galileo grown old, a prisner to the Inquisition, for thinking in Astronomy otherwise then the Franciscan and Dominican licencers thought."[28] It is less well known that the architects of Protestantism were equally opposed to Copernicus and the idea of a heliocentric universe. Martin Luther reportedly called Copernicus a "fool"; in a 1556 sermon, John Calvin called the opinion that the earth moves "monstrous" and that "when we see such minds [who hold this view] we must indeed confess that the devil possesses them."[29] Furthermore, as Thomas Kuhn reminds us, Galileo's observations "met initially with even greater opposition" than those held by Kepler and Copernicus;[30] greater because while Copernicus and Kepler

[27] H. W. Lawton, "Bishop Godwin's *Man in the Moone*," *Review of English Studies* 7 (1931): 33; Daniel Woolf, "Godwin, Francis (1562–1633)," *Oxford Dictionary of National Biography*, Oxford University Press, 2004.

[28] Milton, *Areopagitica*, *The Milton Reading Room*, ed. Thomas H. Luxon: https://milton.host.dartmouth.edu/reading_room/areopagitica/text.html (accessed July 15, 2023). Some critics have disputed this account, but they are convincingly refuted by Catherine G. Martin, *Milton's Italy: Anglo-Italian Literature, Travel, and Religion in Seventeenth Century England* (New York: Routledge, 2017), 54–56.

[29] Quoted in Robert White "Calvin and Copernicus: The Problem Reconsidered," *Calvin Theological Journal* 15 (1980): 233, 236; also "Calvin, Copernicus, and Castello" *Calvin Theological Journal* 21.1 (1986): 5–31.

[30] Kuhn, *The Copernican Revolution*, 225. On paradigms generally, see Kuhn's subsequent book, *The Structure of Scientific Revolutions*, 2nd ed. (Chicago: University of Chicago Press, 1970).

posed theoretical challenges, Galileo's physical observations threatened the "cosmology that for centuries had been the basis of everyday practical and spiritual life."[31] There is every reason to assume, in other words, that a conventional Protestant cleric in the early seventeenth century would approach the telescope, Galileo, and Copernicus with at least a modicum of suspicion, and we see that skepticism in Godwin's depicting his avatar of the new science as a Spanish dwarf who served with a man we would call a war criminal.

Yet at the same time, we cannot deny Godwin's interest in the new science – he also wrote a book on telegraphy – and the gleeful manner with which his hero punctures the old astronomy with firsthand evidence, following Galileo and Bacon. The book therefore reflects the ambivalence of the telescope's reception. The paradigm, as we know, was shifting, and people in the early to mid-seventeenth century found themselves between the old and the new. Readers today are on the other side of this shift. We take for granted that the earth revolves around the sun and that things change in the universe. Consequently, contemporary readers of Godwin's fiction have remained largely deaf to the contrary elements in his text: They assume that Godwin unproblematically and unqualifiedly applauded the new science. But Godwin lived and wrote at a time when both the old and the new had their adherents, and many looked at the new with deep wonderment and suspicion. His fiction embodies that ambivalence.

2 Paradise Lost

It would not be an exaggeration to say that Galileo loomed especially large in Milton's imagination. As noted earlier, Milton cited the Catholic Church's oppression of Galileo for his astronomical views in *Areopagitica*. He alludes to Galileo twice in *Paradise Lost*, once by name (5.261), once by an epithet ("the Tuscan artist" [1.288]) – the only contemporary so honored – and to the telescope three times, which he calls an "an optic glass" (1.288), a "glazed optic tube" (3.590), and "the glass / Of Galileo" (5.260–261).[32] In addition, Milton invents two extensive discussions about cosmology (4.660–87; 8.66–178). All of this has led critics to argue for the

[31] Kuhn, *The Copernican Revolution*, 225.

[32] "[I] visited the famous Galileo grown old, a prisoner to the Inquisition, for thinking in astronomy otherwise than the Franciscan and Dominican licensers thought," *Areopagitica*, in *The Complete Poetry and Essential Prose of John Milton*, ed. William Kerrigan, John Rumrich, and Stephen M. Fallon (New York: Modern Library, 2007), 950. All references to Milton's works are to this edition.

crucial importance of astronomy to Milton's themes.[33] However, while Milton's references to the telescope certainly demonstrate the degree to which Galileo's invention and discoveries had penetrated the English imaginary by the late seventeenth century, Milton does not invoke them to endorse the new astronomy. Instead, Milton uses them to create interpretive problems and to forward his revisionary account of the Fall.

When, for example, Milton alludes to the telescope, two out of three times Milton connects Galileo with Satan, which cannot work to Galileo's credit.[34] The first compares the size of Satan's shield to the moon:

> He scarce had ceased when the superior fiend
> Was moving toward the shore, his ponderous shield
> Ethereal temper, massy, large and round,
> Behind him cast, the broad circumference
> Hung on his shoulders like the moon, whose orb
> Through optic glass the Tuscan artist views
> At evening from the top of Fesole,
> Or in Valdarno, to descry new lands,
> Rivers or mountains in her spotty globe. (1.283–291)

The second alludes to Galileo's discovery of sunspots: "There lands the fiend [on the sun], a spot like which perhaps / Astronomer in the sun's lucent orb/ Through his glazed optic tube yet never saw" (3.588–590). The third compares Raphael's unobstructed view of stars:

> Not unconform to other shining globes,
> Earth and the gard'n of God, with cedars crowned
> Above all hills. As when by night the glass
> Of Galileo, less assured, observes
> Imagined lands and regions in the moon (5.259–263)

All three allusions undermine the accuracy of Galileo's observations. For if the *Sidereus Nuncius* announced a new means of achieving greater precision of observation, each of Milton's allusions to Galileo tells us absolutely

33 See, for example, Marjorie Nicolson, "Milton and the Telescope," *ELH* 2.1 (1935): 1–32; Neil Harris, "Galileo as Symbol: The Tuscan Artist in *Paradise Lost*," *Annali dell'Istituto e museo di storia della scienza di Firenze* 10 (1985): 3–29; Judith Scherer Herz, "'For Whom This Glorious Sight?' Dante, Milton, and the Galileo Question," in *Milton in Italy: Contexts, Images, Contradictions*, ed. Mario A. Di Cesare (Binghamton, NY: MRTS, 1991), 147–157; Amy Boesky, "Milton, Galileo, and Sunspots: Optics and Certainty in *Paradise Lost*," *Milton Studies* 34 (1996): 23–43; Catherine Gimelli Martin, "'What if the Sun be Centre to the World?': Milton's Epistemology, Cosmology, and Paradise of Fools Reconsidered," *Modern Philology* 99.2 (2001): 231–265; and Maura Brady, "Galileo in Action: The 'Telescope' in *Paradise Lost*," *Milton Studies* 44 (2005): 129–152.

34 Harris, "Galileo as Symbol," 12. Nonetheless, Harris (unpersuasively) tries to dissociate the term, "Tuscan artist," from Galileo, arguing that it applies to "Florentine scientists in general" (13).

nothing concrete. As Stanley Fish pointed out long ago, after finishing Milton's description of the size of Satan's shield, we still have no idea of its actual dimensions any more than we know the size of Satan's spear.[35] We have the appearance of accuracy and certainty, but in the end, that perception is undone. The same happens in the sunspot metaphor, which comes wrapped in qualifications. A superficial reading suggests that Satan, landing on the sun, looks like one of the sunspots revealed by Galileo's telescope. But in fact we have no certainty. Satan *may* look like one of the sunspots – "like which *perhaps*" – but maybe not. Then, Milton concludes the metaphor by upending expectation and stating that Galileo saw nothing at all like Satan on the sun: "through his optic tube *yet never saw*." Galileo's telescope, as Fish rightly says, represents "the furthest extension of human perception."[36] That is exactly how Galileo depicts the telescope. But instead of a finer-grained image, Milton's allusions using the telescope undermine perception by telling us nothing certain about the objects compared.

In the third allusion, Milton is most explicit in undermining the accuracy of Galileo's observations. The force of the metaphor is to emphasize the greater clarity of Raphael's perceptions. Galileo, looking through his glass at night, is "less assured" than the angel, no doubt because Galileo is a fallen human being. But Milton then goes further by discounting Galileo's lunar observations as "Imagined." We should remember that Galileo has no doubts about what he sees, and his observations constitute irrefutable proof that he is right and everybody else is wrong: "By oft-repeated observations of them we have been led to the conclusion that we certainly see the surface of the Moon to be not smooth, even, and perfectly spherical, as the great crowd of philosophers have believed about this and other heavenly bodies" (*Sidereus Nuncias*, 42). Yet with a single word, Milton erases Galileo's certainty: "Imagined," meaning, a product of the mind, a fantasy, a chimera – not physical, objective reality. In Milton's metaphor, Galileo does not see "lands and regions in the moon"; rather, he *thinks* he sees them, thereby implicitly undermining the reliability of both the telescope and the new approach to knowledge it represents.

Things become even stranger in the two cosmological discussions Milton includes in *Paradise Lost*. In Book 4, after Eve seems to disclaim intellectual curiosity ("God is thy law, thou mine: to know no more / Is

[35] Stanley Fish, *Surprised by Sin: The Reader in "Paradise Lost,"* 2nd ed. (Cambridge, MA: Harvard University Press, 1997), 27.

[36] Ibid., 28.

woman's happiest knowledge and her praise" [637–638]), she asks Adam a crucial question: "Wherefore all night long shine these [stars]"? (4.657). Adam responds by "mansplaining" the structure of the universe: "These [stars] have their course to finish, round the Earth, / By morrow evening, and from land to land /…/ they set and rise" (4.660–664). Adam of course errs by describing a Ptolemaic, not Copernican universe; in his flawed account, the stars circle the earth and the earth stays still. While in a sense Adam's mistake is explicable, Milton suggests the limits of Adam's perceptions by having him answer Eve's question with an outmoded, disproved cosmology.

But then, in Book 8, once again something profoundly odd happens. After Raphael finishes his narration about the war in Heaven and the creation of the universe, Adam asks the angel a question. When Raphael compares the earth and the stars "that seem to roll / Spaces incomprehensible (for such / Their distances argues and their swift return / Diurnal)" (8.20–22), Adam asks why God created the stars. They seem to be "useless" (4.25), so Adam wants to know why "nature wise and frugal could commit / Such disproportions" (8.26–27), and he repeats the Ptolemaic notion that the earth is "sedentary" (8.32). It should be noted that Adam asks Raphael the same question Eve asked (which I will return to in a moment), and which Adam pretended to answer. Milton thus seems poised to have Raphael correct Adam and endorse the Copernican universe. But that's not what happens. Instead, Raphael says that it just doesn't matter whether the sun goes around the earth or the earth goes around the sun. In fact, God laughs at our attempts to figure out the universe, and what's more, Adam shouldn't even think about it:

> … Whether heav'n move or Earth,
> Imports not, if thou reckon right; the rest
> From man or angel the great Architect
> Did wisely to conceal, and not divulge
> His secrets to be scanned by them who ought
> Rather admire; or if they list to try
> Conjecture, he his fabric of heav'ns
> Hath left to their disputes, perhaps to move
> His laughter at their quaint opinions wide (4.70–78)
>
> … What if the sun
> Be center to the world, and other stars
> By his attractive virtue and their own
> Incited, dance about him various rounds? (4.122–125)

> ... What if that light
> Sent from through the wide transpicuous air,
> To the terrestrial moon be as a star
> Enlight'ning her by day, as she by night
> This Earth? (4.140–144)
>
> ... joy thou
> In what he gives to thee, this Paradise
> And by fair Eve; heav'n is for thee too high
> To know what passes there; by lowly wise:
> Think only what concerns thee and thy being;
> Dream not of other worlds, what creatures there
> Live, in what state, condition or degree,
> Contented that thus far hath been revealed
> Not of Earth only but of highest Heav'n. (4.170–178)

It would seem that Raphael's dismissal of all astronomical speculation, whether by Galileo, Copernicus, or Ptolemy, constitutes an orthodox warning against all intellectual ambition. Except that the primary speaker of *Paradise Lost,* conventionally associated with John Milton, refuses Raphael's injunction to be "lowly wise." In the first proem, he invokes the Muse's aid "to my advent'rous song, / that with middle flight intends to soar / Above th'Aonian mount, while it pursues / Things unattempted yet in prose or rhyme" (1.13–16). And in Book 7, Milton is even more explicit about both his ambition ("I soar / Above the flight of Pegasean wing" [7.4]) and about his access to "other worlds" and the "creature there": "Up led by thee / Into the Heav'n of Heav'ns, I have presumed, / An earthly guest, and drawn empyreal air" (7.12–14). In other words, while Raphael enjoins Adam to cease all speculations, especially about the nature of the universe, neither the narrator of *Paradise Lost* nor John Milton himself – who, in *Areopagitica,* warns against becoming a "heretic in the truth" (952) if you do not confirm for yourself the validity of your beliefs – follows Raphael's advice. So what is going on here?

In short, the answer is that Milton's treatment of Galileo, the telescope, and investigations into the nature of the universe constitute examples of what I have elsewhere called the poetics of incertitude.[37] Milton's undermining treatment of Galileo in his epic similes follows the way in which Milton's epic similes generally conclude without a conclusion. For example, the Norwegian Pilot metaphor (in which a sailor moors to a whale)

[37] These two paragraphs generally draw on my *Destabilizing Milton: "Paradise Lost" and the Poetics of Incertitude* (New York: Palgrave, 2007).

ends without telling us what happened: He "Moors by his side under the less, while night / Invests the sea, and wished morn delays" (1.207–208). The description of Satan's standoff with Gabriel and his companions is equally suspended. They surround Satan "With ported spears, as thick as when a field / Of Ceres ripe for harvest waving bends / Her bearded grove of ears, which way the win / Sways them; the careful plowman doubting stands / Lest on the threshing floor his hopeful sheaves / Prove chaff" (4.980–985). Comparing the angelic spears to wheat suggests that the angels, not Satan, will be cut down, and again, the metaphor concludes with uncertainty, the plowman not knowing the outcome of his harvest. Milton's skeptical treatment of Galileo and the telescope thus form part of *Paradise Lost*'s more general pattern of pushing against expectation and undoing certainty.

Finally, the underlying purpose of Adam's question to Raphael – which repeats Eve's question to him – is not knowledge. Adam already thinks he knows why God created the stars. Instead, Adam asks Raphael about the stars because he wants to continue his conversation with the angel. As Adam says after he invites Raphael to stay and hear his origin story, "thou seest / How subtly to detain thee I devise, … / For while I sit with thee, I seem in Heav'n, / And sweeter thy discourse is to my ear / Than fruits of palm-tree pleasantest to thirst" (8.207–212). The crucial subtext in this passage is Adam's dissatisfaction with Eve as an intellectual companion, since "All higher knowledge in her presence falls / Degraded, wisdom in discourse with her / Looses discount'nanced, and like folly shows" (8.551–553), and his turning to Raphael for the "rational delight" (8.391) he cannot find in Eve. Even worse, Eve is completely aware of Adam's low opinion of her: As she says to Adam, "I chiefly who enjoy / So far the happier lot, enjoying thee / Preeminent by so much odds, while thou / Like consort to thyself canst nowhere find" (4.445–448). In sum, Milton's use of cosmology not only illustrates the ambivalence and anxiety caused by the telescope, but also one of the chief causes of the Fall: Adam's poor opinion of Eve's intellect and Eve's keen awareness that Adam thinks she's not smart enough for him.

3 *The Emperor of the Moon* (1687)

When Galileo composed the *Sidereus*, he evinced an almost naïve faith in ocular proof. All someone had to do, he implied, was look through the telescope, and "Anyone will then understand with the certainty of the senses that the Moon" is not smooth (38). Similarly, looking at the Milky

Way through the telescope makes "manifest its essence to the senses as well as the intellect" (38), that is, that the Milky Way consists of an infinitude of stars. After peering through the telescope at Jupiter for several nights in a row, he "arrived at the conclusion, entirely beyond doubt, that in the heavens there are three stars wandering around Jupiter, like Venus and Mercury around the sun" (68). All people had to do was use their eyes, and they would see the truth. But as Galileo quickly discovered, what you see is not necessarily what you get. You see what you want to see; or, to use Thomas Kuhn's terms, you see what the paradigm governing your thought processes allows you to see, as the paradigm "provides rules that tell the practitioner of a mature specialty what both the world and his science are like…"[38]

In 1609, while traveling back to Padua from Tuscany, where he had gone to demonstrate his "glass" to the Florentine court, Galileo visited his fellow astronomer, Giovanni Antonio Magini, and things did not work out well. In a letter to Kepler, Magini's assistant, Martin Horky, recounts:

> Galileo Galilei, the mathematician of Padua, came to us in Bologna and he brought with him that spyglass through which he sees four fictitious planets. On the twenty-fourth and twenty-fifth of April I never slept, day and night, but tested that instrument of Galileo's in innumerable ways, in these lower [earthly] as well as the higher [realms]. On Earth it works miracles: in the heavens it deceives, for other fixed stars appear double. Thus, the second evening I observed with Galileo's spyglass the little star that is seen above the middle one of the three in the tail of the Great Bear, and I saw four very small stars nearby, just as Galileo observed about Jupiter. I have as witnesses most excellent men and most noble doctors, Antonio Roffeni, the most learned mathematician of the University of Bologna, and many others, who with me in a house observed the heavens on the same night of 25 April, with Galileo himself present. But all acknowledged that the instrument deceived. (quoted in *Sidereus*, 94–95)

Horky ends his account observing that the "wretched Galileo," "full of himself," left in a huff, after trying to "[hawk] a fable" (95). One can only imagine Galileo's frustration. Still, the point is clear enough: The visual image does not interpret itself. It must be interpreted, and the preconceptions one brings to the image will determine what one sees.

That is exactly the point that Margaret Cavendish makes in *The Blazing World* (1666), in which the Empress commands her "bird-men" to use their telescopes to discover whether their world "was joined to the world

[38] Kuhn, *The Structure of Scientific Revolutions*, 43.

she came from, and try whether they could perceive any stars in it" (141).[39] Instead of certainty, the Empress receives a bundle of contradictory responses and observations. Faced with their inability to agree on what they see, the Empress declares, "I do plainly perceive that your glasses are false informers, and instead of discovering the truth, delude your senses; wherefore I command you to break them, and let the bird-men trust only to their natural eyes" (141).[40] Like Galileo's antagonists, the Empress thinks that it is the instrument, the telescope, that deceives – and so, she demands they get rid of it.

Aphra Behn goes even further in her final play, a three-act farce called *The Emperor of the Moon*, loosely adapted from Nolant de Fatouteville's *Arlequin, Empereur dans la lune* (Behn adds the focus on the telescope and the Doctor's retraction at the play's end).[41] In *The Emperor of the Moon*, Dr. Baliardo is so obsessed with his lunar-gazing that, rather than arrange their marriages to their lovers, Don Cinthio and Don Charmante, he keeps his daughter, Elaria, and his niece, Bellemante, confined. To shock the Doctor out of his self-involved fantasies, Cinthio and Charmante concoct an elaborate ruse in which the "Emperor of the Moon," along with servants playing Kepler and Galileo, gives his permission for two of his subjects to marry Elaria and Bellemante. The play ends with the Doctor realizing he has been tricked. As Judy A. Hayden has pointed out, Behn's play satirizes the increasingly widespread notion that the moon is inhabited.[42] But the play also illustrates how the telescope, pace Galileo and Bacon, does not neutrally present objective reality, but rather an image

[39] Margaret Cavendish, *The Blazing World and Other Writings*, ed. Kate Lilly (New York: Penguin, 1992). All further references are cited parenthetically.

[40] Cavendish's thorough critique of Restoration science has been widely noted. See, for example, Line Cottegnies, "Utopia, Millenarianism, and the Baconian Programme of Margaret Cavendish's *The Blazing World* (1666)," in *New Worlds Reflected: Travel and Utopia in the Early Modern Period*, ed. Chloë Houston (Burlington, VT: Ashgate, 2010), 71–91, and Todd Andrew Borlick, "The Whale under the Microscope: Technology and Objectivity in Two Renaissance Utopias," in *Philosophies of Technology: Francis Bacon and his Contemporaries*, ed. Claus Zittel, Gisela Engel, Romano Nanni, and Nicole C. Karafyllis (Leiden: Brill, 2008), 231–249.

[41] Judy A. Hayden, "Harlequin Science: Aphra Behn's *Emperor of the Moon* and the Plurality of Worlds," *English* 64 (2015): 171.

[42] Behn also alludes to Godwin's *The Man in the Moone*, suggesting that she, unlike most contemporary readers, understood that Godwin's narrator, Gonsalo, needs to be read skeptically. Elaria blames her father's "infection" with the belief that the moon has its own civilization "with reading foolish books," including "an heroic business called *The Man in the Moone*, if you'll believe a Spaniard, who was carried thither, upon an Engine drawn by wild geese" (1.1.94, 95–98). Hayden, "Harlequin Science," passim. See also Al Coppola, "Retraining the Virtuoso's Gaze: Behn's *Emperor of the Moon*, The Royal Society, and the Spectacles of Science and Politics," *Eighteenth-Century Studies* 41.4 (2008): 481–506; and Oddvar Holmesland, *Utopian Negotiation: Aphra Behn and Margaret Cavendish* (Syracuse, NY: Syracuse University Press, 2013), 207–226.

that is vulnerable to manipulation. We see, in other words, what we want to see – or what others want us to see.

Even though Behn's play draws on *commedia dell'arte* conventions, the telescope that Scaramouche, Dr. Baliardo's servant, drags onstage is distinctly realistic. The stage direction for 1.2 states that he brings "a telescope twenty (or more) feet long."[43] One might assume that a telescope of this length would be part of the satire, but in fact it's rather small. By 1660, the average length was about 25 feet; by 1670, 40 or 50 feet.[44] Behn's refusal to exaggerate focuses our attention, I think, on how easily a serious telescope (as opposed to a parodically long one) can be manipulated, which is exactly what happens. Charmante (disguised as an ambassador from the moon) tells the Doctor that if he purges himself "from vice, the optics of your sight will be so illuminated, that glancing through this telescope, you may behold one of those lovely creatures, that people the vast region of the air" (1.2.71–74). The Doctor of course says he will do so, and Charmante instructs him to "keep your eye fixed and open" (1.2.76). Scaramouche then "*takes a glass with a picture of a nymph on it*" (stage direction; 1.2.77; italics in the original), shows it to the audience, and asks the Doctor what he discerns. He responds: "Methinks I see a kind of glorious cloud drawn up – and now – 'tis gone again" (1.2.78–79). Charmante then "*puts the glass* [with the image of a nymph] *into the mouth of the telescope*" (stage direction; 1.2.85; italics in the original) and tells the Doctor to look again, and of course, mistaking fantasy for reality, he is "Astonished, ravished with delight" (1.2.85). Behn thus enacts a version of Horky's assumption that the "instrument deceived." Only in Behn's comedy, it is not the instrument that is at fault, but unscrupulous servants and a gullible viewer. But the point remains the same. The telescope does not automatically reveal the truth. The image it presents must be interpreted.

One might assume that the play would conclude with the Doctor learning to be more discerning, but in fact he takes his lesson to a surprisingly extreme end. At first, addressing the women and their future husbands, the Doctor says: "Come, all, and see my happy recantation of all the follies fables have inspired till now. Be pleasant to repeat your story, to tell me by what kind of degrees you cozened me" (3.3.227–230). But rather than stating that he has learned the proper use of the telescope, Behn has the

[43] Aphra Behn, *The Emperor of the Moon* in *The Rover and Other Plays*, ed. Jane Spencer (New York: Oxford University Press, 1995). All further references are to this edition and cited parenthetically.

[44] Van Helden, "The Telescope in the Seventeenth Century," 46–47; Hayden, "Harlequin," 177.

Doctor change his tone, speak to himself, and state that he has learned to doubt *everything*:

> (*Gravely to himself*) I see there's nothing in philosophy.—Of all that writ, he was the wisest bard, who spoke this mighty truth:
>
> He that knew all that ever learning writ,
> Knew only this: that he knew nothing yet. (3.3.230–234)

The telescope, for Behn, does not represent the promise of science, or the collapse of an old cosmology, but the fallibility of all human knowledge.[45] It is a dark conclusion for such a seemingly light play.

On the one hand, then, Donne was clearly right to say that the "new philosophy" puts all into doubt. As the century progressed, the Ptolemaic universe became less and less tenable, the Copernican universe gained ascendancy, and knowledge of the natural world progressed exponentially, thanks to such inventions as the telescope. Yet as I hope this survey shows, even as Galilean and Baconian epistemology pushed out other forms of knowledge, literary uses of the telescope were surprisingly varied. For Bishop Godwin, science was haunted by the specters of early Protestant rejections of Copernicus' theories; Milton was surprisingly equivocal about which cosmology was right, and he appropriated the debate for the purpose of revising Genesis, and Margaret Cavendish and Aphra Behn focused on how easily perception can be tricked, especially if you are tempted to see what you want to see. In a sense, the literary treatment of the telescope does what literature tends to do best: push against received wisdom, inviting readers to think a little harder about something they may have taken for granted.

[45] Barbara M. Benedict argues in *Curiosity: A Cultural History of Early Modern Inquiry* (Chicago: University of Chicago Press, 2001), 62. that Behn's farce "mocks the Royal Society's solemn assertions of disinterred perception"; Doctor Baliardo's pessimism about human cognition, however, seems a more general statement than specific to one group.

CHAPTER 12

Steam Engines

Nicola Kirkby

> Steam-Engine is the name of a machine which derives its moving power from the elasticity and condensibility [*sic*] of the steam of boiling water. It is the most valuable present which the arts of life have ever received from the philosopher. The mariner's compass, the telescope, gunpowder, and other most useful servants to human weakness and ingenuity, were the productions of chance and we do not know exactly how and to whom we are indebted for them; but the steam-engine was in the very beginning, the result of reflection, and the product of a very ingenious mind; and every improvement it has received, and every alteration in its construction and principles, were also the results of philosophical study.[1]

As introductions go, *Encyclopaedia Britannica*'s 1818 entry on "steam engines" is more concerned with the invention's cultural significance than its mechanisms. Throughout the 1760s and 1770s, inventor James Watt had patented a series of improvements to the compressor element of the engine that rendered the machine more fuel-efficient. These improvements mobilized steam engines away from coalfields where earlier models had worked in close proximity to fuel and water sources, and into physical and cultural circulation across and beyond Britain. While the impact of steam power on production and mobility throughout the long nineteenth century can hardly be overstated, what is striking about the *Encyclopaedia*'s far-from-comprehensive introduction is its interest in the engine's metaphysical implications, rather than mechanical specifics. Before setting the material conditions of the Industrial Revolution into motion, the steam engine offered the solution to a philosophical question that verged on alchemy. How might a substance as ephemeral and diffusive as steam be harnessed and transformed into power?

[1] John Robinson and James Watt, *The Articles Steam and Steam-Engines Written for the Encyclopaedia Britannica with Notes and Additions by James Watt* (Edinburgh: The Hope Trust, 1818), 46.

At their simplest, steam engines work by heating water into its more expansive form, steam, and channeling that steam to propel a moving component. They convert chemical energy (coal) into heat, and then harness this as kinetic energy.[2] One of the more significant precursors to Watt's designs, Thomas Newcomen's engine (1712), houses the moving component within an airtight cylinder: Steam pushes a piston within the cylinder forward, then a counterweight draws the piston back into its original position. Watt's addition of a condenser and an insulated cylinder to house the piston enhanced the engine's output to near-continuous action. With its main mechanism insulated, Watt's engine acquired a somewhat mysterious aspect to the uninitiated, yet its workings were very apparent to those regularly laboring alongside the engine: stoking the fire, maintaining a particular temperature in the boiler, monitoring the steam's pressure to avoid explosions, and servicing the machines while in use or dormant.

It is no surprise, then, that steam engines occupy an odd vanishing point that falls somewhere between ubiquity and obscurity, material presence and absence, in literary culture through and beyond the long nineteenth century. The works considered here rarely grapple with the mechanical specifications of steam technology, but they nevertheless offer acute insight into the invention's imaginative significance. As with other contributions to this volume, this chapter examines steam engines in conceptual terms, rather than comparing and contrasting machines with literary representations. The force of steam engines within the nineteenth-century literary imagination is visible in poetic meditations on what locomotion meant for the boundary between man and machine, and also in literary form itself, where steam power becomes a means of driving and disrupting plots in fiction.

Steam engines were not a single invention, and they cannot be conceptualized as such. Watt's mechanism was reworked to expedite a wide array of activities, in the form of power looms in cotton factories (Cartwright), steam hammers in iron works (Nasmyth), locomotives on the rails, steamboats on the seas (Trevithick, Stephenson), and calculation in Charles Babbage and Ada Lovelace's Difference and Analytical Engines. Inventors and engineers modified the invention for seemingly limitless purposes. As one anonymous biographer of steam engines writes, "To assign limits

[2] For a far more detailed account of the engine's development from within the steam age, see *The Steam Engine, Familiarly Described, with a Brief Account of Its History and Uses* (London: Cradock and Co., 1848).

to the power and application of steam is impossible."[3] Yet nowhere were steam engines more readily adaptable than on the page, where precise engineering gave way to imaginative flexibility and abstraction.

1 Steam, Ecology, and the Romantics

Steady integration of steam power into production and transport in the early decades of the nineteenth century contrasted with the picturesque, preindustrial landscapes often associated with steam's contemporary literary movement, Romanticism. William Wordsworth introduces such perceived incompatibility in his sonnet "Steamboats, Viaducts, and Railways" (1833), which sets poetry and steam in conflict from the opening lines: "Motions and Means, on land and sea at war / With old poetic feeling."[4] The phrase "Motions and Means," replaces conventional iambic meter with a more hurried, driving rhythm reminiscent of an engine at full speed. Wordsworth positions steam technology as an unseen presence that cannot be captured or contained by verse. While the poem eventually concludes that the natural world should accommodate "Her lawful offspring in Man's art" "with cheer sublime," its form suggests a slightly more awkward fit:

> In spite of all that beauty may disown
> In your harsh features, Nature doth embrace
> Her lawful offspring in Man's art; and Time,
> Pleased with your triumphs o'er his brother Space,
> Accepts from your bold hands the proffered crown
> Of hope, and smiles on you with cheer sublime.[5]

Rhyme gets ahead of itself in the final three lines as "Time" "triumphs o'er his brother Space." Rather than echoing the pattern of the previous tercet, the penultimate line skips ahead (D-E-F, becomes E-D-F), leaving the impression that technology has rushed the author to a less poetically balanced conclusion than he might have liked. Indeed, enjambment of "crown / Of hope" further exacerbates the effect. In the abstract, Wordsworth arrived at a truce with steam technology, but he was far more outspoken when faced with proposals to build a railway line through his beloved Lake District in 1844. The laureate took to the press to voice his concerns "On

[3] Ibid., 2.

[4] William Wordsworth, "Steamboats, Viaducts, and Railways," in *The Complete Poetical Works of William Wordsworth* (London: Edward Moxon, 1869), 357.

[5] Ibid.

the Projected Kendal and Windermere Railway" in verse, asking, "Is there no nook of English ground secure / From rash assault?"[6] Read in light of the contemplative verse I have quoted, Wordsworth's poetic plea reads as an early iteration of "not in my back yard." Yet twentieth- and twenty-first-century eco-critics have reframed this seemingly reactionary verse as a prescient environmental defense. As Jonathan Bate has argued in *Romantic Ecologies*, it was the "*rash*" policy of industrial expansion that concerned the poet the most, rather than railway construction in general.[7] In his attempts to situate steam engines both in verse and in the landscape, Wordsworth highlights a fear that machines, which – thanks to Watt's improvements – could operate anywhere, might foolishly be built everywhere.

But Wordsworth's poetry does little to address the steam engine directly as an object, or creatively interrogate its mechanisms. Writing while watching his nephew assemble a model steamboat, Percy Bysshe Shelley reflects on his own inner-workings: "And here like some weird Archimage sit I, / Plotting dark spells, and devilish enginery, / The self-impelling steam-wheels of the mind."[8] References to "dark spells, and devilish enginery," reminiscent of infernal works by Blake or Milton, contrast starkly with the diminutive toy steamboat. Shelley equips even the smallest of engines with the potential to undo humanity's moral autonomy, contributing to a literary and artistic mode since defined as the "technological sublime."[9] Arcane imagery aside, Shelley's mirroring of self and machine in this stanza reflects a wider movement to interrogate the impact of steam-powered technology on individual will, and what it means to be human.

Mechanism, Mind

In his 1829 essay "Signs of the Times," Thomas Carlyle declares, "Men are grown mechanical in head and in heart, as well as in hand."[10] Carlyle's remarks have since served as a touchstone in how writers and critics of the nineteenth century conceptualize any technology that falls under the umbrella term "machine." He universalizes the relationship between

6 William Wordsworth, "On the Projected Kendal and Windermere Railway," in *The Complete Poetical Works of William Wordsworth* (London: Edward Moxon, 1869), 217.

7 Jonathan Bate, *Romantic Ecology: Wordsworth and the Environmental Tradition* (London: Routledge, 2013), 50. Emphasis in original.

8 Percy Bysshe Shelley, "Letter to Maria Gisborne," in *Shelley's Poetry and Prose: Authoritative Texts, Criticism*, ed. Donald H. Reihman and Neil Fraistat, 2nd ed. (New York: Norton, 2002), 332.

9 David E. Nye, *American Technological Sublime* (Cambridge, MA: MIT Press, 1996), xvi.

10 Thomas Carlyle, "Signs of the Times," in *Selected Writings*, ed. Alan Shelston (London: Penguin Classics, 2015), 37.

humanity and steam engines, musing, "We war with rude Nature; and, by our resistless engines, come off always victorious, and loaded with spoils."[11] Amid his concerns about machine erosion of intellect and morality, then, Carlyle aligns "resistless engines" with unnatural human ambition. However peripheral to daily life, for Carlyle, the presence of steam engines had brought about a fundamental shift in the interface between people and their world. Imaginative entanglements between the categories of human and machine in the nineteenth century invite us to question how literature extends this link beyond direct invocations of steam technology.

Steam-powered computers were imaginatively plotted, if not materially realized, in Victorian Britain by Charles Babbage and Ada Lovelace in the Difference and Analytical Engines. These intricate, hypothetical machines were designed to mechanize complex calculations and reduce the incidence of error compared with calculations performed by humans. As Henry Colebrooke noted in 1824, unlike other engines, which "substituted machines for simpler tools or bodily labour," the proposed inventions harnessed "mechanical performance for an intellectual process."[12] Simon Schaffer has since pushed Colebrooke's emphasis on "intellect" further, arguing that "[t]o make machines look intelligent it was necessary that the sources of their power, the labour force which surrounded and ran them, be rendered invisible."[13] In this sense, Babbage and Lovelace's machines looked far cleverer on paper than they might have in practice, where the human labor and coal fuel that sustained them would undermine their apparent intelligence. Babbage's contemporaries suggested that the main impediment to realizing the inventor's designs was one of belief: "It transcended the imagination of the public in general to conceive its possibility; and the sentiments of wonder with which it was received were only prevented from merging into those of incredulity, by the faith reposed in the high attainments of its projector."[14] Difficulties in conceptualizing the relationship between humanity, machinery, and intelligence continue to preoccupy critics of technological history and culture. While Mark Seltzer's study remains central in its survey of Western literature that "couple[s] the body and machine," more recent scholarship has proposed a

[11] Ibid., 35.

[12] Henry Thomas Colebrooke, "On Presenting the Gold Medal of the Astronomical Society to Charles Babbage," *Memoirs of the Astronomical Society* 1 (1825): 509.

[13] Simon Schaffer, "Babbage's Intelligence: Calculating Engines and the Factory System," *Critical Inquiry* 21.1 (1994): 204.

[14] Dionysius Lardner, "Babbage's Calculating Engine," *The Edinburgh Review, 1802–1929; Edinburgh* 59.120 (July 1834): 204.

far closer entanglement.[15] Tamara Ketabgian suggests that binary comparisons between human and machine have limited mileage, arguing that "we must reread and rehistoricize Victorian culture in ways that do not merely pit people against machines but that instead examine their close mingling and identification."[16] Pursuing an artificial intelligence line, meanwhile, Megan Ward reads human fictional characters as "machines meant to *seem* human," and integrates the potential for adaptation, learning, or modulation into the steam engine's self-perpetuating mechanism.[17]

Blurred boundaries between human and steam-powered consciousness continue to pervade literary works throughout the long nineteenth century, oscillating between sober expressions of concern about human development and satire. In his industrial fantasy *Erewhon* (1872), Samuel Butler asks in earnest "who can say that the vapour engine has not a kind of consciousness? Where does consciousness begin, and where end? Who can draw the line?"[18] Yet Butler carries such parity between steam-powered thinking and human ingenuity to a farcical extreme, musing that "[e]ven a potato in a dark cellar has a certain low cunning about him which serves him in excellent stead."[19] However satirical, Butler's "cunning potato" highlights Victorian parallels between ecocritical conceptions of intelligence and artificial intelligence that have since converged in the late twentieth- and twenty-first-century revival of pan-physicist inquiry. Steam puts pressure on the question of what counts as consciousness, and intelligence becomes a matter of perspective, rather than a property exclusive to humanity and steam engines. If we want to understand how literature entangles the relationship between humanity and steam engines, we need to search beyond abstract references to unspecified engines invoked by Carlyle and think through more substantial examples of steam power at work on the page.

Productivity and Steam

For many Victorian workers, daily life operated around the steam engine's rhythms and ability to labor relentlessly, rather than diurnal, seasonal, or

15 Mark Seltzer, *Bodies and Machines* (London and New York: Routledge, 1992), 4.

16 Tamara Ketabgian, *The Lives of Machines: The Industrial Imaginary in Victorian Literature and Culture* (Ann Arbor: University of Michigan Press and University of Michigan Library, 2011), 1.

17 Megan Ward, *Seeming Human: Artificial Intelligence and Victorian Realist Character* (Columbus: Ohio State University Press, 2018), 2.

18 Samuel Butler, *Erewhon: Or, Over the Range* (London: Trübner and Co., 1872), 190.

19 Ibid., 191.

agricultural patterns.[20] In factories, novelty soon gave way to monotony, with workers putting in long hours to maximize production, while exposed to the dull yet constant danger of accidents on the steam-factory floor. Using a pseudonym that was popular among anonymous industrial poets, "A Factory Girl" muses:

> While my hands are employed, there's amusement for me
> To think of the power of the steam,
> That pow'r so gigantic, so quickly subdued,
> By uses so simple and mean.
>
> I muse on the wheels as they quickly go round,
> Admiring the genius of art;
> The metal, so useless a short time before,
> Now actively taking its part.[21]

This worker's fast-paced lyric echoes the clacking rhythm of a power-loom in full swing; her focus oscillates between abstract musings ("pow'r so gigantic" and "the genius of art"), and materials at hand (the "wheels" and "metal"). Though framed as "amusement," this verse questions the perceived neutrality of the "gigantic" force harnessed by engines, with the term "mean" ambiguously hovering between the senses of meagre and cruel. We need to be wary of approaching such verse as an authentic account of workers' attitudes to steam technology, since, as Kirstie Blair notes, the "Factory Girl" pen name was ventriloquized by several writers with varying connections to industrial labor.[22] Nevertheless, our assessment of steam engines as they operate in literature must take into account the conditions of labor and social factors that shaped literary production. Recent research into literary culture and the industrial workplace led by Blair highlights this as a particularly pressing area for critical expansion.[23] However emblematic of disembodied, nonhuman action, steam engines cannot be conceptually isolated from the social and financial cultural conditions in which they operated.

For the most part, then, our current critical assessment of steam industries in literary culture depends heavily on canonical middle- and

[20] For examples of work-time being organized around steam machinery, see E. P. Thompson, "Time, Work-Discipline, and Industrial Capitalism," *Past & Present* 38 (December 1967): 56–97.

[21] A Factory Girl, "To a Friend Who Came to the Factory," in *Poetic Thoughts in Working Hours* (Derby: Richard Keene, 1853), 2.

[22] See Kirstie Blair, *Working Verse in Victorian Scotland: Poetry, Press, Community* (Oxford: Oxford University Press, 2019), 138.

[23] Kirstie Blair, Mike Sanders, Oliver Betts, Lauren Weiss, and Duncan Hotchkiss, "Piston, Pen & Press – Literary Cultures in the Industrial Workplace, 1840–1918," Arts and Humanities Research Council: www.pistonpenandpress.org/ (accessed February 21, 2020).

upper-class writers without firsthand experience of operating engines. Elizabeth Gaskell reflects on worker strife in *Mary Barton* (1848), presenting steam machinery as a direct source of worker unrest and suffering. Her fictional Manchester laborers criticize the technology, with anonymous voices shouting, "Machines is th' ruin of poor folk."[24] Far from presenting a clear-cut antagonistic relationship between worker and machine, Gaskell's industrial novel offers a multifaceted social commentary. Yet in her use of steam as a social simile, Gaskell runs the risk of reducing the working-class characters in her fiction to an undifferentiated mass whose immense ability to shake things up is coupled with a lack of individual conscience.

While steam engines could increase output, demand did not always keep pace, with tragic consequences for factory workers whose well-being depended on stable employment. Gaskell's narrator withdraws from describing a trade union meeting to muse, "Combination is an awful power. It is like the equally mighty agency of steam; capable of almost unlimited good or evil."[25] "Combination" here is the collective bargaining power leveraged by trade unions. Unlike a self-controlled group of workers acting with shared social values, this secretive union operates as a destructive force in Gaskell's novel. The pressure of hardship builds, propelling the group toward extreme ends and setting the narrative on a catastrophic trajectory. In *The One vs. the Many* (2009), Alex Woloch suggests that such characterization is representative of a broader pattern in canonical nineteenth-century novels, including *Mary Barton*. He asserts that there are "two types of minor characters that structure the omniscient, asymmetric novel, the functional automaton and the deviant eccentric."[26] However sweeping his assessment of narrative structure, Woloch's "functional automaton" category is particularly suggestive in its mechanistic language. Steam technology exacerbates the polarity between these categories, aligning the former with unfeeling monomania and endowing the latter with accelerated and accentuated destructive potential.

If Gaskell examines steam technology in relation to a human workforce, Charles Dickens avoids direct parallels between humans and engines, even in his industrial fiction. *Hard Times* (1854) opens with an unusual townscape:

[24] Elizabeth Gaskell, *Mary Barton*, ed. Shirley Foster (Oxford: Oxford University Press, 2006), 85.
[25] Ibid., 168.
[26] Alex Woloch, *The One vs. the Many: Minor Characters and the Space of the Protagonist in the Novel* (Princeton: Princeton University Press, 2009), 162.

> It was a town of machinery and tall chimneys, out of which interminable serpents of smoke trailed themselves for ever and ever, and never got uncoiled. It had a black canal in it, and a river that ran purple with ill-smelling dye, and vast piles of building full of windows where there was a rattling and a trembling all day long, and where the piston of the steam-engine worked monotonously up and down like the head of an elephant in a state of melancholy madness.[27]

Entangling industrial and organic imagery, Dickens presents a steamscape that complicates the relational tension between human, engine, and nature that underpins earlier literary invocations of machinery. However "interminable" and "monotonous" the patterns established by these smoke plumes and piston heads, their serpent and elephantine characteristics threaten that continuity, with both animals suggesting subversion, whether subtle or rampageous. Ketabgian offers a particularly detailed reading of Dickens's engine-as-elephant, "Through its sheer range of symbolic connotations, this creature condensed a diverse blend of ideas about industrial labour, colonial power, mechanical behavior, and impenetrable forms of psychology."[28] For Ketabgian, the elephantine engine's melancholy aspect presents the most pressing line of inquiry because psychological suffering can link the human and ecological impact of industrialization across and beyond the British Empire. Without directly examining the complex links between British factories and global supply lines, Dickens implicitly situates the affective and imaginative limits of repetitive labor in *Hard Times* within a wider context of international trade, conquest, emotional hardship, and indenture.

Attending to product rather than labor, Harriet Martineau's essays for *Household Words* were directly instructive and provided detailed, nonspecialist accounts of modern industry. "The Wonders of Nails and Screws" describes a steam-powered nail factory in minute detail, from "the smallest screws required for putting together the nicest philosophical instruments, to the heavy bolt-screws which sustain the wear and tear of mighty steam-engines."[29] Such essays contribute to an emergent mid-nineteenth-century literary form, the "process article," which Catherine Waters defines as an "industrial tourist tale which held the promise of demystifying the commodity and restoring awareness of the labour involved in its production."[30]

[27] Charles Dickens, *Hard Times*, ed. Paul Schlicke (Oxford: Oxford University Press, 2006), 26.
[28] Ketabgian, *The Lives of Machines*, 48.
[29] Harriet Martineau, "The Wonders of Nails and Screws," *Household Words* (November 1851): 140.
[30] Catherine Waters, *Commodity Culture in Dickens's Household Words: The Social Life of Goods* (Aldershot: Ashgate, 2008), 17.

By inviting readers to imagine the material history of even simple objects, such writers could help those unfamiliar with steam engines to understand the invention's extraordinary impact. Indeed, steam engines made possible the mass production and circulation of *Household Words* and similar publications, lending the process article a self-reflexive critical dimension. Through her focus on the production of "nails and screws," Martineau recalls the economist Adam Smith's meditation on the "Division of Labour," which takes pin-makers as an illustrative example of processes applicable to a far broader range of industries and contexts.[31] Like Smith, Martineau goes beyond the object at hand, tracing the material journey of a single nail to address the imaginative challenge of scaling the vastly increased output attainable through steam-powered production: "If the same number were produced the old way," Martineau writes, "it would take half the nation to accomplish the work."[32]

2 Steam-Powered Transport

Populations that were geographically or financially isolated from the manufacturing scenes described earlier were nonetheless likely to encounter steam engines on the railways. George Eliot fictionalizes railway construction as a source of consternation among residents in her "study of provincial life," *Middlemarch* (1871), which is set in 1829–1832 in the midst of railway development in the English provinces. "In the absence of any precise idea as to what railways were," Eliot writes, "public opinion in Frick was against them."[33] Whether fixed or locomotive, steam engines demand an extensive infrastructure. Such technology could therefore have a profound impact even on communities distanced by time and space from the machines themselves. Like Eliot, many canonical authors – including Dickens, Gaskell, Hardy, and Thoreau – introduce railway lines into their fiction not just as a synecdoche for industrial development but also as a technological and geographic framework that helps define the stakes of the work as a whole. Railway infrastructure serves as a potent signifier in literature, whether or not we see any trains in motion.

Hyperbolic accounts of steam-powered transport bringing about "the annihilation of time and space" echoed through nineteenth-century

[31] Adam Smith, *An Inquiry into the Nature and Causes of the Wealth of Nations*, vol. 1 (London: W. Strahan and T. Cadell, 1776), 5–15.

[32] Martineau, "The Wonders of Nails and Screws," 139.

[33] George Eliot, *Middlemarch: A Study of Provincial Life*, ed. David Carroll (Oxford: Oxford University Press, 1997), 520.

journalism, poetry, and fiction.[34] Scholarly attention has largely followed this line of inquiry, taking its cue from Wolfgang Schivelbusch's emphasis on the phrase in his enduring cultural history, *The Railway Journey* (1977).[35] Steam engines could drive novels even where railways were not adopted as an extended metaphor within the text. Inspired by the fast-paced journalism that circulated on the rails, sensation novels including Ellen Wood's *East Lynne* (1861) and Mary Elizabeth Braddon's *Lady Audley's Secret* (1862) and *John Marchmont's Legacy* (1863) all introduce plots contingent on characters' varying knowledge of the pace and procedures of steam travel. Pushing this coupling of genre and technology further, Nicholas Daly suggests that "in the 1860s the sensation novel trained its readers to live within the temporality of the railway age."[36] Far from adapting to reflect steam engine culture, then, literature could provide readers with a psychosomatic inoculation to the impact of railway travel on the nervous system.

No study of literary steam engines would be complete without reference to Charles Dickens's *Dombey and Son* (1848), which serves as a key literary coordinate in the railway imaginary despite its relatively limited depiction of the technology. Where locomotives are concerned, Dickens presents a somewhat occluded perspective of a train tearing through the countryside: "with a shriek, and a roar, and a rattle, from the town, burrowing among the dwellings of men and making the streets hum, … the remorseless monster, Death!"[37] We may not directly see how the locomotive engine operates, but its destructive force is keenly felt through a particularly noisy soundscape. Throughout *Dombey and Son*, Dickens closely aligns fleeting but poignant railway perspectives either with individual characters' perspectives or with community attitudes toward a novel technology. Later Dickensian engagement with steam locomotion addresses the complex material and social infrastructure built up around the railways in more nuanced ways. Examples appear frequently throughout Dickens's journalism, but converge most prominently in his coauthored Christmas collection of short stories, *Mugby Junction* (1866). With each story assigned to a particular branch or main line, this collection proposes narrative

[34] "Railroads: Their Past History, Present Condition, and Future Prospects," *Fraser's Magazine for Town and Country, 1830–1869; London* 18.103 (July 1838): 47.

[35] Wolfgang Schivelbusch, *The Railway Journey: The Industrialization of Time and Space in the 19th Century* (Berkeley: University of California Press, 1986), 33.

[36] Nicholas Daly, *Literature, Technology, and Modernity, 1860–2000* (Cambridge: Cambridge University Press, 2004), 50.

[37] Charles Dickens, *Dombey and Son*, ed. Alan Horsman and Dennis Walder (Oxford: Oxford University Press, 2001), 311.

delineation rather than annihilation as an alternative response to steam technology, and Dickens and his coauthors explore this in form and content. The narrator muses, "But there were so many Lines. Gazing down upon them from a bridge at the Junction, it was as if the concentrating Companies formed a great Industrial Exhibition of the works of extraordinary ground-spiders that spun iron."[38] Unlike the runaway locomotive in *Dombey and Son*, then, the intricate yet materially delineated infrastructure in *Mugby Junction* remains connected to wider technological development and associated with a broadly delineated place.

However central steam acceleration was to the railway imaginary, any complete "annihilation of time and space" was undermined by the extent of the tracks themselves, which stretched across countries and continents. Tackling different challenges in perspective and perception, North American literature grappled with the sheer scale of railways coupled with the project of western expansion. Henry David Thoreau encapsulates this in his transcendentalist novel *Walden* (1854):

> When I meet the engine with its train of cars moving off with planetary motion – or, rather, like a comet, for the beholder knows not if with what velocity and with what direction it will ever revisit this system … when I hear the iron horse make the hills echo with a snort like thunder, shaking the earth with his feet, and breathing fire and smoke from his nostrils, (what kind of winged horse or fiery dragon they will put into the new Mythology I don't know,) it seems as if the earth has got a race now worthy to inhabit it.[39]

Observed from the trackside, this unpredictable steam engine is unbound by the vectors and timetables usually associated with railway travel; it is shaken loose from earthly realism through simile. By depicting the engine as a fantastic cosmic event and a rarity, Thoreau presents railways in North America as an intrusive and unfamiliar system, and one not yet embedded into everyday life through reiteration and practice. In an enduring study of technology in American literature, Leo Marx argues that "the ominous sounds of machines, like the sound of the steamboat bearing down on the raft or of the train breaking in on the idyll at Walden reverberate endlessly in our literature."[40] Marx's comments on noisiness might equally apply to Dickens's deathly caricature of the railway, but he emphasizes the recurring trope of contrasting the natural and technological sublime as particular to North American literature.

38 Charles Dickens, *Mugby Junction*, ed. Robert McFarlane (London: Hesperus, 2005), 11.
39 Henry David Thoreau, *Walden* (London: Penguin, 2016), 108–109.
40 Leo Marx, *The Machine in the Garden: Technology and the Pastoral Ideal in America* (Oxford: Oxford University Press, 1967), 15–16.

A less geographically determined railway novel, Nathaniel Hawthorne's parody *The Celestial Railroad* (1843), depicts a narrator journeying by rail as an allegory for industrial and moral improvement. Attempting to use Bunyan's *A Pilgrim's Progress* (1678) as a railway guide, the narrator is surprised to find the hardships encountered by his predecessor "smoothed over" by new technology:

> The engine at this moment took its station in advance of the cars, looking, I must confess, much more like a sort of mechanical demon that would hurry us to the infernal regions, than a laudable contrivance for soothing our way to the Celestial City. On its top sat a personage almost enveloped in smoke and flame, which – not to startle the reader – appeared to gush from his own mouth and stomach, as well as from the engine's brazen abdomen.[41]

Through an allegorical mode, Hawthorne elevates the steam engine to become a stock figure in nineteenth-century morality. He combines Miltonic infernal imagery with the erasure of human bodies and labor that Schaffer describes as central to techno-development. In an exploded invocation of the technological sublime, broken human bodies fuel the engine, but remain subject to its emissions, "enveloped in smoke." Self-consciously antipastoral, Hawthorne's unusual novel invites us to question the morality of steam acceleration in Babylonian terms, particularly when driven by capitalist ideology and used to expedite expansionist projects such as manifest destiny and imperial conquest. Steam-boats and locomotives accelerated journeys, but in Hawthorne's dystopia they also prevent a society from taking stock of its own trajectory. Exponentially increasing coal consumption, and accumulating smoke and smog, steam engines were unsustainable as the primary technology driving mass mobility and production. As Jesse Oak Taylor argues, "industrial … modernity is haunted, and its ghost leaves carbon footprints."[42]

The Afterlife of Steam

With the turn of the twentieth century, steam engine use decreased in favor of ventures powered by electricity and petrol, sources that once again distanced machinery from its fuel source. Steam locomotives were replaced by electric trains, and the internal combustion engine uncoupled acceleration on land from rails in the form of private motor cars. In

[41] Nathaniel Hawthorne, *The Celestial Railroad* (London: Houlston and Stoneman, 1846), 6.

[42] Jesse Oak Taylor, *The Sky of Our Manufacture: The London Fog in British Fiction from Dickens to Woolf* (Charlottesville: University of Virginia Press, 2016), 4.

1901, George A. Wade declared that the motor car "has an immense future before it, for it fills a place in the local requirements of modern life that even the railway-train cannot fill."[43] But early twentieth-century literature was reluctant to leave steam and its connotations entirely in the past. Poised between the steam age and the rise of the motor car, E. M. Forster's *Howards End* (1910) depicts the legacy of steam in affective terms: "he is a chilly Londoner who does not endow his stations with some personality, and extend to them, however shyly, the emotions of fear and love."[44] Motor car travel in *Howards End* offers comparatively little scope for such reverie. Forster describes how the scenery "heaved and merged like porridge," from the vantage point of a speeding car.[45] By 1910, Britain's railway networks were somewhat "lived-in"; passengers had grown familiar with and personalized the rails through regular, habitual journeying. Forster's railwayscape therefore also contrasts markedly with the alienating depictions of steam technology examined earlier in this chapter. By the beginning of the twentieth century, steam engines were so embedded in literary culture that they attained a nostalgic dimension.

While steam technology continued to operate well into the 1900s, breaking land-speed records, transporting millions of migrants across the world, and enabling mass production, its cultural significance remains closely entangled with Victorian innovation. Steampunk is a speculative mode that ponders what life could have looked like if inventors had continued to adapt and repurpose steam engines as *the* primary technology beyond the nineteenth century. William Gibson and Bruce Sterling's *The Difference Engine* (1990) exemplifies the genre, imagining a universe in which Babbage and Lovelace's inventions have become mainstream information systems. However technologically advanced Gibson and Sterling's imagined machines are compared with nineteenth-century systems, they have not resolved one of the most destructive consequences of steam techno-history: pollution: "The gloom of the day was truly extraordinary. It was scarcely noon, but the dome of St Paul's was shrouded in filthy mist. Great rolling wads of oily fog hid the spires and the giant bannered advertisements of Ludgate Hill. Fleet Street was a high-piled clattering chaos, all whipcracking, steam-snorting, shouting."[46]

[43] George A. Wade, "The Story of the Motor-Car," *English Illustrated Magazine* 218 (November 1901): 127.
[44] E. M. Forster, *Howards End*, ed. Oliver Stallybrass (London: Edward Arnold, 1973), 9.
[45] Ibid., 195.
[46] William Gibson and Bruce Sterling, *The Difference Engine* (London: Gollancz, 2014), 180.

While steampunk writing offers much closer attention to imagined technical details than its nineteenth-century predecessors, it also maintains long-standing emphasis on the by-products of steam engine activity. A deadly "oily fog" later chokes the city altogether, while the meaningful "clacking" of the difference engines loses coherence amid the uncontainable "chaos" of widespread noise pollution. Rather than invoking an alternative future framed by Edwardian nostalgia for a world organized around the engine, then, neo-Victorian authors such as Gibson and Sterling depict unlimited innovation and industry reliant on steam power as a shortcut to social and environmental catastrophe. From philosophical puzzle to a widely adopted mechanism, the steam engine casts a long and imaginatively charged shadow into the twenty-first century, given its centrality in shaping carbon culture.

CHAPTER 13

Wires

Aaron Worth

As John Durham Peters has observed, it is virtually *de rigueur* for modern discussions of the history of telecommunications to invoke, somewhere, the opening of Aeschylus' *Agamemnon*, with its account of the chain of beacon-fires carrying the news of Troy's fall to Argos.[1] In doing the same here, I can only offer the excuse that my purpose is to historicize this particular connection – to look, if only for a moment, at its origins in the Victorian period.[2] But with the invention of the electric telegraph in the 1830s – and especially in the wake of its explosive growth toward the end of the 1840s – the conceptualization of Aeschylus' "beacon-telegraph" took firm root.[3] Early to mid-Victorian verse translations of the play incongruously blended an archaic, sub-Shakespearean idiom with modern terminology (descriptions of "telegraphic fire," for instance). But I am interested here in Arthur Woollgar Verrall's 1889 prose translation and, more particularly, in his lengthy critical introduction to the play. Here, Verrall elaborates a curious interpretation centered on certain plot-holes, whose absurdity he highlights by "translating" Aeschylus's scenario into nineteenth-century terms:

> Scene: A room in London. Time: Early morning. Servants discovered preparing the room. From their conversation it appears that the master of the house has been for some time in Africa, and that the conduct of his wife, in relation to a person too often received, is causing them much anxiety and a strong desire for their master's return. … A telegram arrives for the lady, who presently appears and informs them that it is from her husband, who was despatched last night from Lake Nyanza. Being asked by a servant

[1] John Durham Peters, *The Marvelous Clouds: Toward a Philosophy of Elemental Media* (Chicago and London: University of Chicago Press, 2016), 238.

[2] In fact, the association between the beacon-fires of *Agamemnon* and contemporary information systems predates the Victorians: One finds Greco-Roman "telegraphy" (with implied reference to the *optical* telegraph) discussed in connection with *Agamemnon* in the *Asiatic Journal*, for instance, in 1831.

[3] See, for example, "Blew's Translation of the *Agamemnon* of Aeschylus," *Spectator Supplement* (February 2, 1856): 140–142.

> whether there is a telegraph at the Lake, she explains that the wires have just been extended so far by the result of her husband's enterprise. He intends to return forthwith. … [T]here is a ring at the bell. Enter the husband's courier, who announces that his master is detained for a few minutes at the terminus, but is coming immediately. He dilates upon the discomforts of the Overland route and the breaking-down of an Italian train. The husband follows accordingly. … In conversation with him she says nothing of the telegram, nor he to her. And so ends the first scene.[4]

Putting to one side the interesting figurative by-products of Verrall's extended conceptual metaphor (Lake Victoria as fallen Troy, exploration as conquest, etc.), this passage vividly illustrates his chief complaint: Namely, how absurd it is that Agamemnon's herald – and, subsequently, Agamemnon himself – should arrive almost immediately after the "telegram" from the Troad. Writing fully half a century into the age of electric media, and rather blithely conflating the late Victorian theatergoer and the spectator at the Dionysia in 458 BCE, Verrall simply refuses to believe that the latter would have swallowed such a plot, with its lack of teletechnological verisimilitude, or that a playwright of Aeschylus' skill and stature would have attempted to foist it upon them. From this conviction grows Verrall's "reconstruction" of the dramatist's "real" plot, which involves the surprising claim that *there was no beacon system* – only a single signal-fire, used to trigger a conspiracy, its existence explained away by Clytemnestra's monstrous lie of a trans-Hellenic network.

To be sure, Verrall's reading of the play was hardly a mainstream one (he had something of a reputation for overingenious interpretations of classical texts). What is striking for our purposes is the way in which Verrall's understanding of the play, its author's intentions, and its reception by an Athenian audience are determined by a historically specific relationship to media – one that he ahistorically projects back onto the classical past. Nor is this all that he is projecting onto that past. Nineteenth-century genre conventions, too, enter into his thinking, as he imputes to Aeschylus' audience not only an acute consciousness of issues involving the instantaneous transmission of data over distance, but also a set of expectations appropriate to the consumption of a Victorian novel (in dramatic form):

> Now at this point of the story we might either know the key to the riddle (if the author were dramatizing a popular novel) or we might wait for the solution in the sequel. But what would be the bewilderment and the dismay of the audience if it should prove that there was no solution, and that the

[4] A. W. Verrall, *The "Agamemnon" of Aeschylus, with an Introduction, Commentary, and Translation* (London: Macmillan and Co., 1889), xxiv–xxv.

> mysterious telegram, introduced with so much circumstance, had no bearing on the story whatever![5]

The type of "popular novel" that best fits the bill in this context is surely the sensation novel of the 1860s and 1870s, a genre also centering upon themes of adultery, secrecy, and murder. But the central role accorded in this scenario to modern networks of communication provides an unmistakable conceptual link to that genre as well.[6] What we have here, then, is a case of a novelistic genre decisively inflected by Victorian developments in communications technology, invoked by a scholar in the course of an interpretation of a classical drama – an interpretation that is itself powerfully shaped by those same Victorian cultural and technological forces.

This may seem an unnecessarily recursive example with which to begin. But I mean it to serve a double purpose. What follows is a discussion, necessarily highly selective, of the immense impact that the wired teletechnologies of the nineteenth century, the telegraph and telephone,[7] had upon literary production in the Victorian and modernist periods, with examples drawn chiefly from British and American fiction.[8] As examples of that impact, both the "telegraphization" of Aeschylus and the egregiously networked genre of the sensation novel serve to broach the subject. But there is also something like a cautionary tale to be discerned here – one of particular relevance to those of us who write about old media and their figuration within literary artifacts. To this topic and theme (*De nobis fabula narratur*) I will return, briefly, at the end of this chapter.

1 Telegraphic Fictions

There is a type of novel that stirs a special kind of interest in the media-minded literary critic. These texts are fascinated not merely with a particular

5 Ibid., xxv.

6 As Henry James put it in his review of Braddon's *Aurora Floyd*, the typical heroine of the sensation novel is "not a picturesque Italian of the fourteenth century, but an English gentlewoman of the current year, familiar with the use of the railway and the telegraph." Henry James, "Miss Braddon," in *Notes and Reviews* (Cambridge, MA: Dunster House, 1921), 112–113.

7 Historically, these two wired technologies are bookended, so to speak, by wireless ones, though at first glance this might not seem the most salient distinction to make: After all, both the telegraph of the 1790s and that of the 1890s (Chappe's and Marconi's, respectively) were "tele-technologies" as well, being not only media of transmission but also (initially at least in the case of the "wireless telegraph") "point-to-point," as opposed to "broadcast," technologies (on this distinction, see, for example, Robert Friedel, *A Culture of Improvement: Technology and the Western Millennium* [Cambridge, MA: The MIT Press, 2007], 515). Lines, however, must be drawn somewhere, and the case can be made for a distinctive poetics of the wire.

8 I am primarily interested, too, in the wire's appearance within the field of representation (insofar, in other words, as it appears as symbol, trope, device, etc.).

information technology (cinema, radio, telephone, etc.), but with multiple media and their interaction – with the "media ecology" itself, as it is called among such critics. I am thinking, for example, of works such as Bram Stoker's *Dracula* (1897), Thomas Mann's *The Magic Mountain* (1924), Thomas Pynchon's *The Crying of Lot 49* (1966), and Koji Suzuki's *Ringu* trilogy (1991, 1995, 1998). Such texts often demonstrate a striking awareness of their existence within an interlinked system of multiple technologies, a system that exposes their authors' own medium to new influences, forces, and pressures.

One of the first, and finest, examples of this species of "multimedia novel" is surely Nathaniel Hawthorne's *The House of the Seven Gables* (1851), a novel concerned fundamentally with emergent technologies of representation.[9] Hawthorne's treatment of the telegraph in particular is remarkable for its economy as well as its prescience: Little more than half a decade after Samuel F. B. Morse's ambivalent "What hath God wrought!" had sped from Baltimore to Washington, the novel articulates *en germe* a broad spectrum of telegraphic themes and connections to which writers would return throughout the second half of the nineteenth century. The setting for this episode is, appropriately, a speeding train, where the formerly reclusive Clifford Pyncheon is waxing visionary with a humbugging "old gentleman" for a foil – first about mesmerism and spirit-rapping, and then about the new technology so often associated with both of these:

> "Is it a fact—or have I dreamt it—that, by means of electricity, the world of matter has become a great nerve, vibrating thousands of miles in a breathless point of time? Rather, the round globe is a vast head, a brain, instinct with intelligence!..."
>
> "If you mean the telegraph," said the old gentleman, glancing his eye toward its wire, alongside the rail-track, "it is an excellent thing;—that is, of course, if the speculators in cotton and politics don't get possession of it. A great thing, indeed, sir; particularly as regards the detection of bank-robbers and murderers."
>
> "I don't quite like it, in that point of view. ... An almost spiritual medium, like the electric telegraph, should be consecrated to high, deep, joyful, and holy missions. Lovers ... might send their heart-throbs from

[9] See also, for instance, John Limon, *The Place of Fiction in the Time of Science: A Disciplinary History of American Writing* (Cambridge: Cambridge University Press, 1990); E. L. McCallum, "Hawthorne and Pynchon on the Line," *Arizona Quarterly* 56.2 (2000): 65–96; Sam Halliday, *Science and Technology in the Age of Hawthorne, Melville, Twain, and James: Thinking and Writing Electricity* (New York: Palgrave Macmillan, 2007); Paul Gilmore, *Aesthetic Materialism: Electricity and American Romanticism* (Stanford, CA: Stanford University Press, 2009).

> Maine to Florida, with some such words as these,—'I love you for ever!—My heart runs over with love!'—'I love you more than I can!'. … Or, when a good man has departed, his distant friend should be conscious of an electric thrill, as from the world of happy spirits, telling him,—'Your dear friend is in bliss!' Or, to an absent husband, should come tidings thus,—'An immortal being, of whom you are the father, has this moment come from God!'"[10]

It would be an exaggeration to characterize (channeling Whitehead on Plato) all subsequent literary treatment of the telegraph as a series of footnotes to this exchange. But Hawthorne, through these two interlocutors or antagonists, does cover a lot of ground here. For Clifford, the wire is self-evidently to be associated with love (both *agape* and *eros*), the spiritual, and the otherworldly.[11] For his part, the hard-headed and -hearted "old gentleman," just as self-evidently, envisions the telegraph as a financial, political, and disciplinary tool. As both a literary device and an aid to thought, the telegraphic wire would be put to many uses in the decades to follow – far too many to be covered in anything like a comprehensive fashion here.[12] But anyone trying to impose a rough kind of order on the innumerable depictions of the technology in nineteenth-century literature might do worse than to bear in mind these two contrary, yet equally adumbrative, visions of the wire: on the one hand, Clifford's centrifugal exuberance, his fantasies of infinite connectivity and boundary-crossing; on the other, the "gentleman's" carceral enthusiasm, his conception of new media as agents of punishment and control.

[10] Nathaniel Hawthorne, *The House of the Seven Gables* (Harmondsworth: Penguin, 1981), 264–265.

[11] "Media – as things that come in between – are liminal objects par excellence, and they deal not only with information but with birth, sex, love, and death." John Durham Peters, *Speaking into the Air* (Chicago: University of Chicago Press, 1999), 147.

[12] I do not consider here, for instance, many "canonical" telegraph fictions (if I may put it that way), such as Anthony Trollope's "The Telegraph Girl" (1877), Ella Cheever Thayer's *Wired Love* (1880), Thomas Hardy's *A Laodicean* (1881), and Henry James's *In the Cage* (1898); those new to scholarship on the subject will certainly want to read, in addition to other critical work I cite here: Laura Otis, *Networking: Communicating with Bodies and Machines in the Nineteenth Century* (Ann Arbor: The University of Michigan Press, 2001); Jay Clayton, *Charles Dickens in Cyberspace: The Afterlife of the Nineteenth Century in Postmodern Culture* (Oxford and New York: Oxford University Press, 2003); Richard Menke, *Telegraphic Realism: Victorian Fiction and Other Information Systems* (Stanford, CA: Stanford University Press, 2008); Jill Galvan, *The Sympathetic Medium: Feminine Channeling, the Occult, and Communication Technologies, 1859–1919* (Ithaca, NY: Cornell University Press, 2010); Mark Goble, *Beautiful Circuits: Modernism and the Mediated Life* (New York: Columbia University Press, 2010); and Christopher Keep, "Touching at a Distance: Telegraphy, Gender, and Henry James's *In the Cage*," in *Media, Technology, and Literature in the Nineteenth Century: Image, Touch, Sound*, ed. Collette Colligan and Margaret Linley (Farnham: Ashgate, 2011), 239–255.

To be sure, those fantasies of connection themselves took a seemingly infinite number of forms: spiritual, fraternal, racial, and erotic, to name just a few. In America in particular, the telegraph had been associated with projects of national unification and assimilation from its earliest days. Morse himself anticipated, in 1838, that "the whole surface of this country would be channeled for those *nerves* which are to diffuse, with the speed of thought, a knowledge of all that is occurring throughout the land; making, in fact, one *neighborhood* of the whole country."[13] The development of submarine telegraphy only spurred the imagination of ever-expanding "net-works" of insulated wire. In 1856, as the New World side of the telegraph network took its first tentative steps toward bridging the Atlantic, stretching under the Gulf of St. Lawrence to Newfoundland, Walt Whitman used the nascent network to "poetically [embrace] planet earth":[14]

> Such joined unended links, each hooked to the next!
>
> Each answering all, each sharing the earth with all...
>
> What do you see, Walt Whitman? ...
> I see the electric telegraphs of the earth,
>
> I see the filaments of the news of the wars, deaths, losses,
> gains, passions, of my race.[15]

By the mid-1860s, the Atlantic had been fully conquered. In the following decades, as tentacles of wire stretched out to embrace more and more of the earth's surface, such exuberant yawps as Whitman's (and Clifford's) came to seem almost quaint; paeans to global connectedness became as clichéd as the formulaic statement that the telegraph had "annihilated space and time." Then, in a series of bestselling novels (which Queen Victoria, it was said, eagerly devoured), the British writer Marie Corelli out-Heroded all those whose paltry imaginations extended no further than the idea of merely global communion, recasting the universe itself as the scene of the greatest drama of all: the Christian narrative of salvation. According to Corelli's "Electric Theory of Christianity," union

13 Quoted in Jill Lepore, *A Is for American: Letters and Other Characters* (New York: Knopf, 2002), 10.

14 Stefan Schöberlein, "Tapping the Wire: A Telegraphic Discourse," *American Literature* 88.2 (2016): 275.

15 Quoted in Schöberlein, 275–276. Schöberlein sees a moment of stark rupture in American figurations of the wire, precipitated by the Civil War as well as technological setbacks; he juxtaposes early examples of technological exuberance such as Whitman's (and John Greenleaf Whittier's) with Emily Dickinson's 1863 poem, "They put Us far apart –," telegraphic in choice of metaphor as well as style, reading it as emblematic of "death and disunion in times of severed transmission" (278).

with God is quite literally a matter of (wireless) telegraphic connection; if you are estranged from the divine "Electric Circle" and its "telegraphic ray," you don't need a theologian, you need an electrician. In keeping with the metaphor of a Christian communications system, Corelli's sage Heliobas, in his "Electric Creed," likens the Son of God himself to a length of gutta-percha-coated copper wire: "this Earth and God's World were like America and Europe before the Atlantic Cable was laid. Now the messages of goodwill flash under the waves, heedless of the storms. So also God's Cable is laid between us and His Heaven in the person of Christ."[16] Disconnection from God, it would seem, is very like disconnection from the Crown.

By the time these words were written, in Corelli's *A Romance of Two Worlds* (1886), Britain possessed a global communications network, a tool or weapon of crucial importance to the administration and control of its imperial possessions. It is significant, then, that Corelli likens "God's Cable" not to the wire to Calcutta or Khartoum, but to Britain's link with a former colony of shared blood. This points to the central role played by the late Victorian web in facilitating both fantasies and anxieties of Empire. The telegraphic wire, long conceptualized as a nerve, became a vein or artery as well – a metaphorical carrier not only of information but also of blood. Global connectivity, after all, cut both ways, and it was thought increasingly important to spell out precisely whose blood was flowing, so to speak, through what channels. J. Henniker Heaton, perhaps the most fervent advocate for imperial cables and a global penny post, called these "the nerves and arteries of the whole" British Empire, and a number of works of popular literature drew upon the same metaphor in imagining the preservation, or potential contamination, of a far-flung Commonwealth linked by language and blood.[17] Whitman had sung, thirty years earlier, of "the wars, deaths, losses, / gains, passions, of my race." But what had he meant by "race" – the "human race," or the "Anglo-Saxon"? The latter, almost beyond doubt – but the egalitarian Whitman, writing in

[16] See Aaron Worth, *Imperial Media: Colonial Networks and Information Technologies, 1857–1918* (Columbus: Ohio State University Press, 2014), ch. 2.

[17] Heaton quoted in Kate Thomas, *Postal Pleasures: Sex, Scandal, and Victorian Letters* (Oxford and New York: Oxford University Press, 2012), 168–169. As Thomas demonstrates, this master metaphor – postal and telegraphic networks as global delivery systems for Anglo-Saxon blood – signaled not only a desire to bind Britain more securely to her existing system of colonies, scattered across the world. It also fed fantasies of racial reunification with the lost jewel in her first imperial crown, as in Conan Doyle's first Sherlock Holmes story, "A Study in Scarlet" (1887), which Thomas reads in relation to contemporary discourses of Anglo-American reunion.

the 1850s, still leaves some room for ambiguity.[18] There would be less and less ambiguity on this point, however, as the age of imperialism approached its climax.

2 Telephony and Literature

In August 2017, one of James Campbell's "NB" columns in the *Times Literary Supplement* sparked an extended debate about the first literary appearance of the telephone. A Charing Cross Road browse had turned up a £4 copy of Robert Louis Stevenson's 1892 *The Wrecker*, coauthored with his stepson Lloyd Osbourne.[19] This is turn prompted Campbell's speculation that the novel "contains what is perhaps the earliest occurrence in literature of that polite inquiry: 'May I use your telephone?'"[20] *TLS*'s readerly hive mind was more intrigued, however, by the larger question of when the technology itself made its first appearance in fiction, pointing to earlier references in Conan Doyle's *The Sign of the Four*, Gilbert and Sullivan's *H.M.S. Pinafore*, and even a fragmentary George Eliot manuscript.[21] Other commentators would subsequently point out that Mark Twain has, almost certainly, the best claim to have written the first telephonic fiction.

There are, then, several possible entry points into our discussion of the literary impact of Bell's "speaking telegraph" during the first half-century of its existence. It does seem likely that Stevenson's (and Osbourne's) flawed potboiler represents the first work of *British* literature in which the telephone figures in a significant way.[22] Where the technology is invoked only in passing in *The Sign of the Four*, it plays a substantial role in Stevenson/Osbourne's own attempt, two years after Doyle's novel had appeared, to produce something in "that very modern form of the police novel or mystery story."[23] To begin with, the telephone is actually important to the plot,

[18] See Heidi Kathleen Kim, "From Language to Empire: Walt Whitman in the Context of Nineteenth-Century Popular Anglo-Saxonism," *Walt Whitman Quarterly Review* 24.1 (2006): 1–19.

[19] Robert Louis Stevenson and Lloyd Osbourne, *The Wrecker* (London, Paris, and Melbourne: Cassell & Company, 1892).

[20] "JC," "False Friends," "NB" column, *TLS* (August 16, 2017), www.the-tls.co.uk/articles/false-friends-nb/ (accessed July 16, 2023).

[21] John Picker, who detects early glimmerings of the telephonic idea in her 1876 novel *Daniel Deronda*, writes: "With vanishing Victorian grace, Eliot in this fragment finally allied her fiction with the technology it augured." John M. Picker, *Victorian Soundscapes* (Oxford and New York: Oxford University Press, 2003), 109.

[22] Though Osbourne's collaboration makes it an American one as well.

[23] Robert Louis Stevenson and Lloyd Osbourne, *The Wrecker* (London, Paris, and Melbourne: Cassell & Company, 1892), 425–426.

and serves as a device to generate mystery and suspense. At the auction at which the protagonist, Loudon Dodd, and his partner, Jim Pinkerton, acquire the wreck of the *Flying Scud*, their rival bidder – the "shady lawyer" Bellairs – desperately and repeatedly "beg[s] the favour of three moments at the telephone" to consult the absent party whom he represents – a request the auctioneer denies. After the sale, Bellairs hastens to the nearest functioning telephone-box to "communicat[e] with his principal"; Dodd first listens in, then instructs the uncannily unpresent operator ("a phantom central") to ring up the same number again, putting an "impertinent question" to the "tiny sing-song English voice" on the other end of the line, which causes him to flee in terror. Stevenson and Osbourne are thus helping to establish a nascent connection between the telephonic wire and an emergent type of fiction. For, much as the sensation novel had had the electric telegraph as its circulatory system, so would twentieth-century crime and mystery fiction develop in close symbiosis with telephonic networks (one need only think of the novels of Raymond Chandler).

The Wrecker also – precisely insofar as it is *not* typical of Stevenson – clearly helps us to perceive the decided *Americanness* of the telephone in the literary and popular imagination, particularly in the first years of its existence. The chief city of Dodd's Midwestern state of "Muskegon" is described as having "hundred-fold wires of telegraph and telephone matting heaven above [his] head," while San Francisco is conceived and figured as a telephonic city. The very background noise of the telephone network, in the absence of conversation, metonymically invokes the metropolis as a whole ("No answer came. The telephone vibrated and hummed in miniature with all the numerous talk of a great city") even as that network eagerly seeks to extend its reach even to ships entering the city's harbor ("'Have you a telephone laid on to the *Tempest*?' asked Pinkerton. 'Laid on yesterday,' said the clerk").[24] The seeds of these associations had been planted twelve years earlier, when Stevenson, summoned by a telegram, had made his way halfway across the world to be with his beloved, the still-married Fanny Osbourne, in California. There, "among desolate hills" in Napa Valley, the writer first put his ear to his fellow Edinburghian's celebrated invention, an experience he recorded in *The Silverado Squatters*.[25]

[24] Stevenson, *Wrecker*, 161, 152, 166.

[25] "But it was an odd thing that here, on what we are accustomed to consider the very skirts of civilization, I should have used the telephone for the first time in my civilized career. So it goes in these young countries; telephones, and telegraphs, and newspapers, and advertisements running far ahead among the Indians and the grizzly bears." Robert Louis Stevenson, *The Amateur Emigrant and The Silverado Squatters* (New York: Charles Scribner's Sons, 1911), 132.

But it is not, in fact, precisely an irony that Stevenson should have left the nerve center of a global empire (at exactly the same time, as it happens, that London's first telephone exchange was coming online), to encounter the phone for the first time at "Cheeseborough's Hotel," in Calistoga. Rather, Stevenson's experience highlights the important fact that America was not only the scene of the telephone's invention but also, among nations, the technology's prime "early adopter,"[26] a fact that inevitably affected its patterns of diffusion with respect to literary representation as well.

It is fitting, then, that America's most emblematic writer should himself have been an early adopter of the telephone, as well as the first to explore its possibilities as a literary device. Mark Twain – who also owned one of the first Remington typewriters, and met with Thomas Edison in hopes of writing *A Connecticut Yankee in King Arthur's Court* by phonographic dictation – was one of the very first people, and almost certainly the first writer, to have a phone installed in his home, in 1877. And he did not just invent "telephone literature" – he also wrote quite a lot of it. Indeed, an anthology of respectable size might be made from Twain's fiction about the technology, beginning with "The Loves of Alonzo Fitz Clarence and Rosannah Ethelton" (1877), a story fusing melodrama with science fiction that traces a courtship begun, conducted, and consummated (in matrimony) over the telephone. It is remarkable how much Twain foresees in this story: long-distance telephony, the portable phone, telephonic hacking, the eroticism of the absent body.[27] The 1880 sketch "A Telephonic Conversation" represents another first: the gendering of the telephone wire, with the Twain-narrator listening to one end of a gossipy discussion of cookery, children, and church between two women (he has had to place the call, as members of "the gentle sex" "shrink" from the technical side of the phone's operations). The dominant mode of Twain's writing about the telephone remains science fiction, however. In *A Connecticut Yankee* (1889), the time-traveling engineer Hank Morgan establishes a telephone network in Camelot (his daughter is named "Hello-Central"). Twain's description a futuristic system of interlinked telephones in "From the *London Times* of 1904" (1898) has earned him a twenty-first-century reputation as prophet of the Internet.[28]

[26] Paul Starr, *The Creation of the Media: Political Origins of Modern Communications* (New York: Basic Books, 2004), 191–192.

[27] Sam Halliday discusses the story as an adumbration of phone sex, in which "low fidelity communications become freighted with erotic or romantic energies." Halliday, *Science*, 91.

[28] Twain imagines a "telectroscope … connected with the telephonic systems of the whole world. The improved 'limitless-distance' telephone was presently introduced, and the daily doings of the globe made visible to everybody, and audibly discussable, too, by witnesses separated by any number of leagues." *The Science Fiction of Mark Twain*, ed. David Ketterer (Hamden, CT: Archon, 1984), 128.

The science-fictional mode similarly dominates the 1870s portion of Edith Wharton's *The Age of Innocence* (1920). When conversation turns to the rumored "new dodge for talking along a wire," Wharton's characters – Newland Archer, Julius Beaufort, and the Countess Olenska – speculate about

> the fantastic possibility that they might one day actually converse with each other from street to street, or even—incredible dream!—from one town to another. This struck from all three allusions to Edgar Poe and Jules Verne, and such platitudes as naturally rise to the lips of the most intelligent when they are talking against time, and dealing with a new invention in which it would seem ingenuous to believe too soon; and the question of the telephone carried them safely back to the big house.[29]

By the end of the novel, however, the fantastic has become the quotidian, as Archer, a quarter-century later, takes a phone call from his son in Chicago:

> The telephone clicked, and Archer, turning from the photographs, unhooked the transmitter at his elbow. How far they were from the days when the legs of the brass-buttoned messenger boy had been New York's only means of quick communication! ... Dallas seemed to be speaking in the room: the voice was as near by and natural as if he had been lounging in his favourite arm-chair by the fire. ... long-distance telephoning had become as much a matter of course as electric lighting and five-day Atlantic voyages. But the laugh did startle him ... across all those miles of country—forest, river, mountain, prairie, roaring cities and busy indifferent millions.[30]

Here, as throughout the novel, media technologies, particularly wired ones, serve not only as historical markers but also as potent figures for such favorite Wharton themes as modernity, communication and its failures, and the clash of residual and emergent social structures.[31] In *Age of Innocence*, the telegraphic network of Old New York – as both metaphoric stand-in for the ubiquitous, code-bound networks of Society and the powerful information system that serves it – had been no friend to Archer's illicit relationship with Ellen, twenty-six years before. Now, however, he

The telephone has thus had a place in modern science fiction since the beginning (it also plays a role, along with the gramophone, in Villiers de l'Isle Adam's pioneering novella containing the first "android," *L'Ève future* [Paris: M. de Brunhoff, 1886]).

29 Edith Wharton, *The Age of Innocence*, ed. Carol Singley (Boston, MA, and New York: Houghton Mifflin, 2000), 121.

30 Ibid., 275–276.

31 For a discussion of both novels, as well as *The House of Mirth*, see Aaron Worth, "Edith Wharton's Poetics of Telecommunication," *Studies in American Fiction* 36.1 (2008): 95–121.

manages to feel something like nostalgia for the age of the "brass-buttoned messenger boy" – the more so, perhaps, because despite the "natural" sound of his son's voice coming from the receiver, Archer cannot *quite* naturalize the instrument or its operation, any more than he can *quite* normalize the prospect of Dallas Archer's coming marriage to one of "Beaufort's bastards" – the subtext of their long-distance conversation. If the dissolution of the old codes of propriety is a symptom of modernity, the telephone is its symbol.

This particular trope – phone as emblem of the Modern – was far from unique to Wharton. It was, rather, a commonplace upon which authors would ring a variety of changes, on both sides of the Atlantic. Significantly, the British writer perhaps most fascinated with the technology and its potential as a literary device during the period of literary modernism was that most cantankerous of antimodernists, Evelyn Waugh. "I think I can claim," Waugh would write in a later preface to *Vile Bodies* (1930), "that this was the first English novel in which dialogue on the telephone plays a large part."[32] Certainly it is the novel containing Waugh's best-known depiction of the technology, an entire chapter consisting entirely of telephone dialogue between Adam Symes and Nina Blount. In an essay centering upon a close reading of this conversation, Bronwen Thomas notes that "the medium appears especially suited to exposing the shallowness of the Bright Young Things."[33] Telephones appear, and function to similar effect, in such novels as *Decline and Fall* (1928) and *A Handful of Dust* (1934), as well as the London portions of *Black Mischief* (1932).[34] But Waugh's writing from the same period based on his travels in Ethiopia should be mentioned as well; here the phone frequently appears, in the company of the gramophone, cinema, telegraph, wireless, and photograph, as a prominent component of a modern, Western media ecology imperfectly grafted onto a colonial space.[35]

Certainly Waugh's writing of the 1920s and 1930s shows him to have been acutely conscious of media ecology, even if he lacked (and would doubtless have ridiculed) our modern critical jargon. He was equally sensitive to the question of literature's place within such a system. In the 1932 story "Excursion in Reality," the novelist Simon Lent is summoned

[32] Evelyn Waugh, *Vile Bodies: A Novel* (New York: Little, Brown and Company, 2012).

[33] Bronwen Thomas, "'It's Good to Talk'? An Analysis of a Telephone Conversation from Evelyn Waugh's *Vile Bodies*," *Language and Literature* 6.2 (1997): 107.

[34] Evelyn Waugh, *Decline and Fall* (London: Chapman and Hall, 1928); *A Handful of Dust* (London: Chapman and Hall, 1934); *Black Mischief* (London: Chapman and Hall, 1932).

[35] See Evelyn Waugh, *Waugh in Abyssinia* (London: Longmans, Green, and Co., 1936).

over the telephone by a moving-picture magnate, and hired to modernize Shakespeare's language for a screenplay. Immersion into the world of film production – a world depicted as a multimedia system, one characterized above all by incessant telephoning – convinces Lent, paradoxically, that he has "come into contact with Real Life," leading him to proclaim (sounding very like a McLuhanite *avant la lettre*), "I'm going to give up writing novels. It was a mug's game anyway. The written word is dead – first the papyrus, then the printed book, now the film."[36] Lent's experience prompts the reader to ask: Would (or "could," or even, perhaps, "should") literature survive in the age of telephone, gramophone, and cinema? And if so, what might it become?

Waugh was not the first to pose such questions. Indeed, in posing them, he had a good deal in common with those contemporaneous purveyors of (in his words) "absolute gibberish" and "great rot" whose experiments in literary form he abominated. The modernist project, as has come to be recognized with ever greater urgency, simply cannot be understood in isolation from the increasing saturation of society by modern media technologies, the process of conceptual consilience by which the idea of a media *system* came to take hold, and the formulation of highly reflexive questions concerning the status of literary production within such an environment. Interestingly, the origin of each of these elements can be traced, at least in part, to the belated adoption of the telephone in late Victorian Britain. Richard Menke's reading of British telephonic fiction in the 1890s – such as existed – suggests that this belatedness led to the technology's being always-already (as it were) conceived as a synecdochic stand-in for something else, namely an emergent technological *Gestalt*. These texts, which include Kipling's "The Finest Story in the World" (1891), are interested in the telephone less on its own terms, than as a kind of shorthand for "an entire complex of media," an entity that poses a potential threat to the modern author.[37] By the early twentieth century, of course, such developments had only accelerated, helping to drive a dynamic process of reciprocal engagement between art and technology from which the former would emerge radically transformed.[38]

36 Evelyn Waugh, *The Complete Stories of Evelyn Waugh* (Boston, MA: Little, Brown and Company, 1998), 78.

37 Rudyard Kipling, "The Finest Story in the World," *The Contemporary Review* LX (July 1891): 9–31; Richard Menke, "The Medium Is the Media: Fictions of the Telephone in the 1890s," *Victorian Studies* 55.2 (2013): 213–214.

38 Julian Murphet goes so far as to call modernism itself the product, or an expression, of the modern media ecology: "the entire system of the arts, in the critical years 1910–1914, [would] refashion itself as a 'media system' proper, both in order to accommodate itself to the congeries of newer

If we seem to have wandered some little distance away from the wires, strung tidily in parallel, of Bell's speaking telegraph, it is because, in turning to the modernist period proper, the telephone becomes increasingly difficult to disentangle from larger systems of enmeshed technologies and networks. It also becomes increasingly ubiquitous as a presence within popular and "literary" forms alike – increasingly likely, too, to be implicated in matters of form as well as content. Key authors and landmark texts of high modernism are "telephonic" in important ways. Well before the current boom in media-oriented criticism, scholars noted the importance of the phone to Kafka (*Amerika*, *The Trial*, *The Castle*, "The Neighbor"), Proust (*Le Côté de Guermantes*, *La Prisonnière*), Fitzgerald (*The Great Gatsby*, *Tender Is the Night*), and Joyce (*Ulysses*). Authors who have been discussed more recently in connection with the technology (or deserve to be) include Virginia Woolf, Ford Madox Ford, Elizabeth Bowen, Samuel Beckett, George Bernard Shaw, Ralph Ellison, John Dos Passos, P. G. Wodehouse, Muriel Spark, Jean Toomer, Nella Larsen, Henry Green, Richard Wright,[39] and William Faulkner.[40] In short, at this point in our narrative, potential branch lines radiate in all directions.

3 Reach Out and Touch Me

And our time has expired, or nearly, in the disconcertingly Donnean idiom of the payphone operator. In that spirit, then, let us end in the grave, where subterranean telephonic networks have been laid, in imagination, since at least 1898. In the German statesman Walter Rathenau's "Die Resurrection Co.," published that year, a necropolitan exchange installed as a safeguard against premature burial leads unexpectedly to communication with the dead.[41] A better-known example comes from the "Hades"

mechanical media, and to protect the gamut of its own practices." Julian Murphet, *Multimedia Modernism: Literature and the Anglo-American Avant-Garde* (Cambridge: Cambridge University Press, 2009), 5.

39 I am thinking, for instance, of the episode in *Native Son* in which Bigger and Gus use "imaginary telephone transmitter[s]" to "play 'white.'"

40 There are far too many studies of individual authors to name here; recent books on the intersection of media and literature during this period include Murphet's *Multimedia Modernism*, Goble's *Beautiful Circuits*, and David Trotter's *Literature in the First Media Age: Britain between the Wars* (Cambridge, MA: Harvard University Press, 2013).

41 Walter Rathenau, "Die Resurrection Co.," *Die Zukunft* 24 (July 9, 1898): 72–78. See Louis Kaplan, "Walter Rathenau's Media Technological Turn as Mediated through W. Hartenau's 'Die Resurrection Co.' An Essay at Resurrection," *New German Critique* 62 (1994): 39–62 and Friedrich A. Kittler, *Gramophone. Film, Typewriter*, trans. Geoffrey Winthrop-Young and Michael Wutz (Stanford, CA: Stanford University Press, 1999), 12.

episode of *Ulysses* (1922), in which Leopold Bloom reflects on the wisdom of "a telephone in the coffin."[42] But I am more interested here in a text almost exactly contemporaneous with Joyce's, the pulp horror story "The Statement of Randolph Carter" (1920), by H. P. Lovecraft. The story, which indeed takes the form of a direct "statement" to the police, begins with its speaker having been brought, like Kafka's contemporaneous Josef K., before the Law. As in *The Trial*, too, the telephone is responsible for bringing Carter here, though not through a direct summons. To put it in Lacanian terms, he has been on the phone, not with the Symbolic Order, but with the Real, and the experience has destroyed his mind – more particularly, his memory, which Lovecraft figures as an inscriptive sound technology.[43] Enough remains of Carter's recollection, however, to present a tolerably complete narrative of "that awful night" when he had accompanied his friend Harley Warren, a dabbler in necromancy, to an "ancient cemetery" in search of a never-specified "*thing*" (italics Lovecraft's). As Carter tells it, the two seek out a particular tomb, clear away earth and vegetation, and raise a great granite slab, revealing steps of stone descending into charnel mystery. Then, the hard work done, Warren gently suggests that Carter – a nervous wreck at the best of times – should remain above ground. Not to worry, though – Warren, who has brought "a portable telephone outfit," with "enough wire … to reach the centre of the earth and back," will provide updates.[44] Into the ground he goes, paying out wire for "more than a quarter of an hour" while Carter sits anxiously perched on a tombstone, clutching the receiver: "I was alone, yet bound to the unknown depths by those magic strands whose insulated surface lay green beneath the struggling beams of that waning crescent moon." At last, there is a clicking on the line, and a "shaky whisper" is transmitted from the earth's bowels; Warren has found what he was seeking – but it is *not* what he was expecting. It is worse – unimaginably worse; whatever the *thing* is, it cannot be described – even approximately, even over the

[42] James Joyce, *Ulysses*, ed. Hans Walter Gabler (New York: Vintage, 1986): 6.868–9. As Steven Connor, among others, has noted, Bloom, or Joyce, is surely confounding or conflating two technologies here: "It is easy to miss the strangeness of what occurs to Bloom here. What occurs to him is the idea, not of a gramophone record, but of a gramophone, kept in every grave. Bloom seems to regard the gramophone as much as a means of communication as of reproduction." Steven Connor, *Dumbstruck: A Cultural History of Ventriloquism* (Oxford and New York: Oxford University Press, 2000), 391.

[43] "And now for the first time my memory records verbal discourse, Warren addressing me at length in his mellow tenor voice." H. P. Lovecraft, *The New Annotated H. P. Lovecraft*, ed. Leslie Klinger (London and New York: Norton, 2014), 14.

[44] Ibid., 13–14.

telephone: "*I dare not tell you – no man could know it and live – Great God! I never dreamed of THIS!*"[45] With more than usual obtuseness for even a Lovecraft character, Carter remains on the line for ages, while Warren screams at him to flee. Eventually, long after the wire has fallen ominously silent, "there [is] a further clicking in the receiver," and...

> Again I called down, "Warren, are you there?", and in answer heard the *thing* which has brought this cloud over my mind. I do not try, gentlemen, to account for that *thing*—that voice—nor can I venture to describe it in detail, since the first words took away my consciousness and created a mental blank which reaches to the time of my awakening in the hospital. Shall I say that the voice was deep; hollow; gelatinous; remote; unearthly; inhuman; disembodied? What shall I say? It was the end of my experience, and is the end of my story.[46]

Soon after, Lovecraft delivers what is supposed to be the sting in the tale, as a reply ("*YOU FOOL, WARREN IS DEAD!*") issues from the receiver; but the line is anticlimactic – even redundant, or something like it (a simple "*Who's there?*" would have been at least as effective). In any case, Carter makes clear that it is the voice itself, rather than the message, that has erased his mind.

There has been a good deal of criticism written about the uncanniness of the telephonic voice, and much of it would seem salient here, beginning with Michel Chion's famous conception of the "acousmatic voice," the voice without a visible origin – a conception that is frequently invoked in connection with the telephone within sound studies, psychoanalytic criticism, and elsewhere.[47] The tangible quality of the Thing's voice, or the voice-as-Thing, puts one in mind, too, of Steven Connor's discussion of the early twentieth-century séance, with its indebtedness to contemporary sound technologies, which Carter's phone conversation strikingly recalls.[48] Alternatively, one might venture a "classic" media-studies reading, as Lovecraft seems to intuit McLuhan's famous characterization of the phone as a "cool" (low-definition, high-participation) medium,[49]

45 Ibid., 15–16.

46 Ibid., 17.

47 In the context of Proust and his grandmother specifically, see, for example, Mladen Dolar, *A Voice and Nothing More* (Cambridge, MA: The MIT Press, 2006), 63–65 and Slavoj Žižek, *Less than Nothing: Hegel and the Shadow of Dialectical Materialism* (London and New York: Verso, 2012), 672–676. As this episode also shows, in amputating voice from body, the technology defamiliarizes both.

48 Connor, *Dumbstruck*, 392.

49 "As we read, we provide a sound track for the printed word; as we listen to the radio, we provide a visual accompaniment. Why can we not visualize while telephoning?" McLuhan, *Media*, 267.

and to exploit that property in the way it recruits the reader's imagination, simultaneously encouraging and frustrating our ability to visualize an unvisualizable horror. We might go on and on, no doubt, diligently working out how quintessentially "telephonic" Lovecraft's horror-tale is, how perfectly the voice of the unseen "Thing" resonates with emergent anxieties about this particular technology, at this particular historical moment.

And yet – listen to the "hideous voice" of the dead-alive Monsieur Valdemar, as recorded by Edgar Allan Poe seventy-five years earlier:

> I might say, for example, that the sound was harsh, and broken and hollow; but the hideous whole is indescribable, for the simple reason that no similar sounds have ever jarred upon the ear of humanity. There were two particulars [which] convey some idea of its unearthly peculiarity … the voice seemed to reach our ears—at least mine—from a vast distance, or from some deep cavern within the earth … it impressed me (I fear, indeed, that it will be impossible to make myself comprehended) as gelatinous or glutinous matters impress the sense of touch.[50]

Poe's and Lovecraft's descriptions – Valdemar's voice and the Thing's – are all but identical; both are "hollow" and "unearthly," associated with depth and remoteness, "indescribable" (which does not prevent either narrator from attempting description) and "inhuman";[51] both, too, are specifically termed "*gelatinous*," blending sound and touch, rendering sound as touch. Direct influence is certainly possible, perhaps even likely.[52] But then … how is it that a story from 1845 can exert a "telephonic" influence on a 1927 text? It will not really do here to say that the idea of the telephone was "in the air" in Poe's case, though precursor technologies and schemes can certainly be identified.[53] But perhaps we don't have to. Adam Frank has persuasively argued that "Valdemar" should be understood as a *telegraphic* fiction, with the dead man's "quivering," "vibratory" tongue figuring the "clattering tongue" of the telegraph key, a figure the story defamiliarizes in order "to render telegraphy's acoustic experiences as a manipulative, violent touch."[54] For Poe, the telegraph also has

[50] Edgar Allan Poe, *Poetry, Tales, & Selected Essays* (New York: The Library of America, 1996), 839.

[51] If by implication in Poe's case: "no similar sounds have ever jarred upon the ear of humanity."

[52] Lovecraft's later story "Cool Air" (*Tales of Magic and Mystery* 1.4 [March 1928]: 29–34) is a grotesque tale of unnatural preservation that essentially rewrites "Valdemar."

[53] During this same decade, for instance, Antonio Meucci was in Havana, healing the sick with a mixture of mesmeric and proto-telephonic treatments, uncannily paralleling the case of M. Valdemar.

[54] Adam Frank, "Valdemar's Tongue, Poe's Telegraphy," *ELH* 72.3 (2005): 635–662.

a voice, and a palpable one; it, too, participates in the "hapto-sonorous," to uncanny effect.[55]

No doubt it is bad form to conclude by offering a reading of a text, only to undermine it a moment later. But what I want to stress in closing is that there is much more to be learned, and to be said, about the multifarious figurations of the wires of the past within the popular and literary imaginations – and that *which* figurations we perceive, and how we perceive them, are determined by our own experiences within an ever-changing media ecology. Just as the nineteenth century invented "Aeschylus' telegraph," so did the widespread conceptualization of "Victoria's Internet,"[56] at the end of the twentieth, help to shape a generation of critical accounts of Victorian technology, which often privileged figures and themes of connection, transmission, (mis)communication, far-flung networks, and so on. To be sure, this critical picture was never a monolithic or mechanistic one. And today, as Amy Wong has recently discussed in the context of Victorian media studies specifically, a host of new approaches and paradigms has emerged, often signaling a shift away from models of transmission and toward figures of immersion and virtuality. Wong discusses, too, the growth of media archaeology and Victorian sound studies, with the increased attention these have brought to sonic and haptic registers and modalities.[57] Similar intellectual currents have influenced modernist studies as well, with exciting results. Again, such shifts are clearly related to our understanding of our own continually evolving media environments. And since that process of evolution shows no signs of deceleration, it will be fascinating to see what new knowledge is generated – what "new" wires are discovered, or constructed – by and within future critical engagements with the texts of the past.

55 Other critics have begun to give more attention to telegraphic sound as well, as in Christopher Hanlon's reading of Whitman's "A Word Out of the Sea" (later retitled, and better known as, "Out of the Cradle Endlessly Rocking"). See Christopher Hanlon, "Whitman's Atlantic Noise," *Nineteenth-Century Literature* 70.2 (2015): 194–220.

56 To modify slightly the title of Tom Standage's popular 1998 history of the telegraph.

57 Amy R. Wong, "Victorian Media Studies, History, and Theory," *Literature Compass* 15 (2018): n.p. See also the introduction to (and essays in) Colligan and Linley, eds., *Media, Technology, and Literature in the Nineteenth Century*, which Wong draws upon here.

CHAPTER 14

Cameras

Beci Carver

When photography first became possible in the mid-nineteenth century, it was heralded as an opportunity to make the world visible, not just to the forgetful eye of memory but to everyone whose curiosity stretched beyond her means of travel and her immediate visual range. Photography made distant wonders such as the Grand Canyon visible in the 1870s to those who would otherwise never see them, while also revealing what has always been under our noses. Walter Benjamin coins the term "optical unconscious" to describe elements of our experience we feel but cannot see.[1] He explains, by reference to the act of walking: "Whereas it is a commonplace that … we have some idea of what is involved in the act of walking (if only in general terms), we have no idea at all of what happens during the fraction of a second when a person actually takes a step."[2] Photography has allowed us to catch up with our bodies, to see our limbs act.

In the years following its invention, photography made the visible world tangible to the imagination. When Louis Daguerre discovered in 1839 that he could record light onto a silver-coated photographic plate, he exclaimed "I have captured the light and arrested its flight,"[3] as though he had caught an until-now elusive bird. For the inventor of the photographic negative, Henry Fox Talbot, "the eye of the camera" embodied a new superhuman avenue of sight; he writes, reflecting on the "*invisible rays* which lie beyond the violet, and beyond the limits of the [human] spectrum," that "the eye of the camera … see[s] plainly where the human eye would find nothing but darkness."[4] In this chapter,

[1] Walter Benjamin, "Little History of Photography," in *Selected Writings, 1927–1934*, trans. Rodney Livingstone, ed. Michael W. Jennings, Howard Eiland, and Gary Smith (Cambridge, MA: Harvard University Press, 1999), 511.

[2] Ibid.

[3] Quoted in Roger Watson and Helen Rappaport, *Capturing the Light: The Birth of Photography* (London: Macmillan, 2013), v.

[4] Henry Fox Talbot, *The Pencil of Nature,* repr. in *Henry Fox Talbot: Selected Texts and Bibliography,* ed. Mike Waver (Boston: G. K. Hall, 1993), 91–92. Emphasis in original.

I understand cameras not only to make the visible world familiar, as early inventors hoped they might do, but also to make it *strange*. Footsteps are odd to an eye that has never been able to examine them, as Edward Lear gleefully suggests in a limerick of 1871:

> There was an Old Person of Deal.
> Who in walking used only his heel;
> When they said, "Tell us why?" – he made no reply;
> That mysterious Old Person of Deal.[5]

1 Specimen

The "specimen of a building" in William Empson's poem of 1930, "Description of a View," is wholly bizarre until we suspect it of being a photograph:

> Well boiled in acid and then laid on glass
> (A labelled strip) the specimen of a building,
> Though concrete, was not sure what size it was,
> And was so large as to compare with nothing.[6]

Photographic negatives are not boiled, but they are bathed in acid in the volcanic red light of a darkroom, elevated, laid out to dry on a screen, and "labelled." They are "specimens" in the double sense that they are examinable extracts from a larger whole, and visual objects; "specimen" comes from the Latin *specěre*, meaning "to look."[7] In the second line quoted above, the absence of an 'I' to govern Empson's predicate, "was not sure what size it was," makes us wonder *who* is looking – whether the specimen is itself prompted to ask "what size it was," like Lewis Carroll's Alice in *Alice in Wonderland* wondering whether she is being shrunk: "I must be growing small again."[8] Not only do we not know who is looking here – just as photographs do not show us an onlooker – but we also have no way of solving the mystery of size. The building in the image is "so large as to compare with nothing," meaning both that it has been removed from its original environment (as specimens always are) and that it has been photographed at sufficient distance to be seen whole. The photographer has been obliged to make the building small so that its full proportions were visible

[5] Edward Lear, *The Complete Nonsense and Other Verse* (London: Penguin, 2006), 331.
[6] William Empson, *The Complete Poems*, ed. John Haffenden (London: Penguin, 2001), 54.
[7] *OED*, online edition.
[8] Lewis Carroll, *Alice's Adventures in Wonderland and Through the Looking Glass* (London: Penguin, 1998), 18.

in the shot. By a sequence of paradoxes, the building has been made small to be seen big, with the result that its size has become enigmatic.

Empson suggests that poems and photographs have a similar capacity to make the known world strange. His title, "Description of a View," is a synonym for "specimen of a building," whose central component, "-script," invokes "photography's" suffix, from the Latin for "writing."[9] Photographs make the world unfamiliar from the moment an aperture is made to manipulate an object's size. What the eye does naturally, the camera achieves by artificial means. For early photographers, this artifice was pushed to the fore by the novelty and extreme delicacy of the procedures in which it became necessary for them to train themselves. Saved from all this fiddle by new technology, members of Empson's generation could Kodak, a verb since 1890,[10] and, as the slogan ran, leave it to professional developers to "do the rest."[11] Yet Empson himself knew enough about cameras in 1930 to be able to visualize a darkroom's weird red twilight.

The oddity of the camera's recreated worlds seemed to Empson worth insisting upon, as it did to film theorist Jean Epstein, who in an essay of 1921 on the cinematic close-up, "Magnification," compares the ripple of emotion across actors' faces on the silver screen to "seismic shocks."[12] Photographed bodies were not people; they were monstrous enlargements of visual data. At the other extreme, the era's inventors sought to make photography seem natural. In the 1920s in New York, the inventor of the photobooth, or as it was then called, the "Photomaton," Anatol Josepho, debuted a machine that carried a tiny darkroom around in its gut, and could produce portraits within minutes of its subjects' having posed for them.[13] The end-products could be disconcerting; Roland Barthes complained sixty years later: "the Photomat turns you into a criminal type."[14] But the intention at least was to make photography as natural as looking. At midcentury, the first Polaroid cameras achieved on a practical level the spontaneity that photography has always feigned, enabling their operators to activate a self-developing dye in the paper onto which their images fell. But the results were and still are

9 *OED*, online edition.

10 Ibid.

11 Quoted in Elizabeth Brayer, *George Eastman: A Biography* (Rochester, NY: University of Rochester Press, 2006), 69.

12 Jean Epstein, "Magnification," trans. Stuart Liebman and Richard Abel, ed. Richard Abel, *French Film Theory and Criticism, a History/Anthology, 1907–1939* (Princeton: Princeton University Press, 1988), vol. I, 236.

13 Näkki Goranin, *American Photobooth* (New York: Norton & Company, 2008), 18.

14 Roland Barthes, *Camera Lucida*, trans. Richard Howard (London: Vintage, 2000), 12.

dreamily adrift from anything our eyes see: fuzzy, blanched, either golden or too pale, somehow emphatically rectangular.

In its second two stanzas, Empson's poem wanders away from the subject of photography, but returns again in the last line to the heart of the matter. Writing of the sky above the building, he now pictures "A dome compact of all but visible stars."[15] Empson's phrase "all but visible" here paradoxically restricts photography's domain to that of the invisible, as there is still no way for machines to arrive at what real eyes see. Photography stops at almostness, and in the space of illusion it opens up between seeing and not seeing, writers of the last two centuries have sketched alternative forms of visual encounter with the world.

2 Realism

Ironically, one sense in which photographs may seem to depart from reality is by making it *too* real. When in the 1850s, John Ruskin sought a word to describe the effect of excessive vividness he found so discomfiting in the sixteenth-century paintings of Agnola Bronzino, he chose "realism,"[16] which by then had come to suggest "photographic."[17] *Everything* is shown in Bronzino, with an accuracy that looks like excess. Writing of Bronzino's treatment of the "grotesque," Ruskin concludes that "the grotesque seems better to be expressed merely in a line, or light and shade, or mere abstract colour, so as to mark for a thought rather than a substantial fact."[18] It was not simply the case that more was less for Ruskin but that absolute fidelity was untrue – enough was too much. The single "line" that Ruskin proposes as an alternative to Bronzino's lavish detail here implies the opposite of "substantial fact," since, as Roger Fry would write in 1919, painterly lines rely for their success on the contradiction between their own bareness and the "infinite complexity and fullness of matter."[19] Lines succeed as art by the same measure that they depart from material reality, or more precisely, they succeed as art by remaining evocative of reality while simplifying it.

Part of what made realism's "resemblance to what is real" unsightly for critics in the 1850s was the huge and expanding popularity of cameras in the period.[20] For, undeterred by the formidable weirdness of darkrooms,

[15] Empson, *The Complete Poems*, 54.
[16] John Ruskin, *Modern Painters* (New York: John Wiley, 1863), vol. III, 102.
[17] *OED*, online edition.
[18] Ruskin, *Modern Painters*, 102.
[19] Roger Fry, *A Roger Fry Reader* (Chicago: University of Chicago Press, 1996), 329.
[20] *OED*, online edition.

the immense lists of equipment, from squeegees to tripods, the practical inconvenience of even a single photograph's creation, and the near-certainty that most photographs would be duds, Victorian amateur photographers multiplied in their thousands. Magazines on photography in their turn proliferated, houses were fitted with little gloomy cubicles, and the silhouette of the hopelessly overburdened portraitist became a familiar one. In this era, the word "photograph" was used synonymously with "sun picture,"[21] which, though it does no more than translate the Greek and Latin pantomime horse of "photo-" and "-graph," more distinctly conveys the idea of an outflow of script from the sun. That almost anyone seemed able to achieve solar miracles of this type (equipment permitting) ironically made them cheap. In an essay of 1967, John Berger snapshots the first, frantic theoretical endeavors to dissociate painterly portraits from photographic ones as follows: "Only a man, not a machine (the camera), could interpret the soul of the sitter. An artist dealt with the sitter's destiny: the camera with mere light and shade. An artist judged: a photographer recorded. Etcetera, etcetera."[22] Berger here makes the distinction between paintings and photographs seem tenuous by stressing its defensiveness, and a similar air of insecurity haunts the complaints of nineteenth-century reviewers whose reading matter now increasingly faced comparisons with photography. When in a review of 1850, George Eliot snorts that her rival, Charles Dickens's, novels are mere "sun pictures,"[23] the clear injustice of her comment hints at an anxiety on behalf of her own reputation. Novels and paintings alike were under pressure in this period to explain how human artistic vision improved upon mere fidelity, or how fidelity could either be too much (as in Bronzino's case) or too little (as with the sitter whose soul goes unappreciated). The poet-critic Alfred Austin wrote in 1870: "No realistic writer can by any possibility be a great writer. He may be amazingly clever, remarkably entertaining, and even overwhelmingly popular; but the gods know him not."[24] Like Berger's skeptics, Austin here hurts his argument by exposing its reactionary nature. At the same time, his concept of art as an act witnessed by God betrays its origin in a camera-crowded age, when the ultimate proof of being was to be seen.

The reflex of snobbish dissociation between literary mimesis and photograph-like realism continued into the twentieth century. Virginia

21 Ibid.

22 John Berger, *Selected Essays*, ed. Geoff Dyer (London: Bloomsbury, 2001), 98.

23 Quoted in David A. Novak, *Realism, Photography and Nineteenth-Century Fiction* (Cambridge: Cambridge University Press, 2008), 63.

24 Alfred Austin, "Charles Dickens," in *Charles Dickens: The Critical Heritage*, ed. Philip Collins (London: Routledge, 2005), 148.

Woolf chortled at the puny craft of Winifred Holtby's *South Riding* in 1940: "I think she has a photographic mind,"[25] having herself, for years, been reassured by obsequious critics that "there [was] 'nothing 'photographic' about Mrs Woolf's characters,"[26] or that her fiction was "not, of course, photographic."[27] In literary criticism of the last decades, too, "realism" has slowly been cordoned off from photographic fidelity as its own self-contained, superior aesthetic mode. Nancy Armstrong insists in her seminal study: "As I use this term, realism does not indicate a genre or mode of writing that strives to document actual social conditions by means of visual description … By 'realism', I mean the entire problematic in which a shared set of visual codes operated as an abstract standard."[28] In Armstrong's view, for an author simply to invoke the visual as a touchstone may be a realist gesture, meaning that a fictional character's exaggerated description of a fantasy may be just as realistic as an author's faithful description of a street scene. According to this logic, Empson's building from the last section may be realistic in spite of its birth in boiling acid, since in Armstrong's words it offers "a visual definition of the real."[29] Going even further than Armstrong, David A. Novak invents an "alternative version of Victorian … photographic realism" whereby authors consciously *include* "figures that [would] seem out of place in the realist novel."[30] Novak's realism turns traditional realism upside down in order to make a home for the novel's fugitives, among whom were those whose defiance of social and aesthetic convention rendered them "grotesque" to the Victorian gaze.[31] We may wonder at this point whether we have come full circle. Would Bronzino's excessive fidelity be welcome in Novak's realism?

3 "Shy" Photography

In his preface of 1909 to *The Golden Bowl*, Henry James suggests that one way for photography to protect itself against attack from critics is to appear "shy …."[32] Having chosen to illustrate his own novel with his friend Alvin

[25] Virginia Woolf, *The Letters of Virginia Woolf* (London: Hogarth Press, 1975), vol. 6, 382.

[26] Louis Kronenberger, review for *New York Times* (May 8, 1927), in *Virginia Woolf: The Critical Heritage*, ed. Robin Majumbar and Allen McLaurin (London: Routledge, 2003), 197.

[27] Raymond Mortimer, article in *The Bookman* (February 1929), in *Virginia Woolf: The Critical Heritage*, 242.

[28] Nancy Armstrong, *Fiction in the Age of Photography* (Cambridge, MA: Harvard University Press, 2002), 11.

[29] Ibid.

[30] Novak, *Realism*, 31.

[31] Ibid.

[32] Henry James, *The Golden Bowl* (Ware: Wordsworth, 2000), xxi.

Langdon Colburn's photographs, James was convinced that the images in the book had found their own distinctive and compelling "way ... not to keep, or to pretend to keep, anything like dramatic step with their suggestive matter."[33] This absence of harmony between text and picture, achieved through a continuous "discrete disavowal of emulation,"[34] develops in the book into a steady rhythm of disagreement without rupture: a friendly, loveless, yet successful marriage – notably unlike any of the marriages on which the novel focuses. The photographs "plead their case for relevance with some shyness,"[35] and with an inbuilt acknowledgment that, where written language has an immense repository of effects at its disposal, photographs may only be "optical symbols or echoes."[36] Berger would write in 1968 that "photography has no language of its own,"[37] and James preempts him here with a theory of the photograph as art's shyly dependent sibling, incapable of the autonomy that makes art art. In Berger's more positive view, the photograph's status as a referent to scenes beyond itself may potentially bring it closer to our own reality. For the fact that we do not "expect [it] to be as conclusive as a painting" may seem to capture the essential spirit of modern life as a thing of loose ends.[38] But for James in 1909, art was most successful when complete in itself.

When James associates photography with the creation of "optical symbols," he at once points to the medium's tentacular dependence on external sources and articulates a persistent irony of the photographic image: that, for all its granular precision, it may not specify the unique. Based on visual events that are themselves so unique as to be unvisitable by the eye ever again, photographs nonetheless confer generality onto everything they show. A photograph of a street becomes a typical street, a photograph of an elephant a typical elephant. The growing popularity of photographic portraits in the mid-nineteenth century when James was a child would have sensitized him to the flattening impact of writing with light. It was during this period too that the prevalence of the "type" qua cultural phenomenon led to the birth, in 1887, of a new "-type" suffix. From now on, one could enjoy claret of a "Burgundy type" while feasting on a "California-type barbecue" in a "Dutch-barn-type building."[39]

33 Ibid.
34 Ibid.
35 Ibid.
36 Ibid.
37 Berger, *Selected Essays*, 217.
38 Ibid., 102.
39 *OED*, online edition.

In my opening paragraph, I alluded to the photographs taken of the Grand Canyon in the 1870s that introduced those who saw them to a region hitherto almost unknown; but photographs introducing new sights were far outnumbered in this period by those confirming preconceptions. The freedom of photographers to move around at all was then still novel, following the invention of the photographic "dry plate" in 1871, on which the previously "wet" chemical coating of the camera's equivalent of the retina was applied in advance. Roving photographers who had long been saddled with liquid chemicals now had their burden marginally lightened. Yet these pioneers continued to haul after them a "large, view camera, tripod, ... heavy glass plates" and a "portable darkroom,"[40] even across the canyon's crags. Portable, adventurous photography thus remained far from being fashionable. The form of photography that everyone knew of, whose products everyone had seen, and which Ruskin, Eliot, Austin, and James were most likely to have in mind when distinguishing between photographs and art, was that which belonged to the portraitist's studio: a place of choreographed gestures and planned costumes.

Dickens was likely to have connected cameras with portraiture, especially toward the end of his life, when his customary look of windblown exhaustion achieved household fame. In keeping with this probability, one of the few outright references to photography in his work is to a portrait. In his novel of 1865, *Our Mutual Friend*, he writes of the cherubic Reginald Wilfer:

> If the conventional Cherub could ever grow up and be clothed, he might be photographed as a portrait of Wilfer. His chubby, smooth, innocent appearance was a reason for his being always treated with condescension when he was not put down. A stranger entering his own poor house at about ten o'clock P. M. might have been surprised to find him sitting up to supper. So boyish was he in his curves and proportions, that his old schoolmaster meeting him in Cheapside, might have been unable to withstand the temptation of caning him on the spot.[41]

Dickens could be said to court comparisons between his method of characterization and photography here, although he does so *not* by establishing Wilfer's life-likeness or indeed his more nuanced mimetic qualities, but by insisting on the blond's collapse into a type. Whatever he does, Wilfer

[40] David Nye, "Visualising Eternity: Photographic Constructions of the Grand Canyon," in *Picturing Place: Photography and the Geographic Imagination*, ed. Joan M. Schwartz and James M. Ryan (London: I.B. Tauris, 2003), 80.

[41] Charles Dickens, *Our Mutual Friend* (Oxford: Oxford University Press, 1998), 32.

is, and cannot help but remain, a cherub. Throughout his career, Dickens had been accused – both sternly by his detractors and affectionately by his admirers – of reverting to stock characters, either in pursuit of laughter or out of an aversion to psychological depth. Wilfer is a stock character whose status as such is announced as loudly as the blush on his cheeks, while Dickens, in the act of knowingly conforming to his own believed tendency, becomes a type himself. Wilfer is a cherub-type so that Dickens may be a Dickens-type. And this outcome in a sense keeps everyone happy; Wilfer's "old schoolmaster" may continue to divert himself with fantasy punishments and Dickens's critics may go on punishing him for the same flaws. The only downside (in the novel) is that Wilfer develops a complex about being the person he is; he is "shy, and unwilling to own the name of Reginald, as being too aspiring and self-assertive a name."[42] Dickens suggests by this that the espousal of types may lead to a loss of the distinctions that make identity possible. What would Wilfer, what would photography be, if they were granted characters of their own?

4 Kodakers and Kinema

As time wore on, photography strengthened its claim to lifelikeness by getting up and leaving the studio. In his poem of 1937, *Letters from Iceland*, W. H. Auden snapshots a crowd of modern tourists "Massed on parade with Kodaks or their Leicas."[43] The two cameras identified here – the Kodak, cheap and easy to use, and the Leica, expensive and intricate – mark a division in the expectations brought to them by their different operators, who ranged from the artless to the earnest to the playfully avant-garde. Auden was himself among the avant-gardists, and contributed an array of whimsical snaps to the first edition of the text, including that of a horse's bottom.

Everyone seemed to become fixated on capturing their lives on photographic film in the modernist period. In a poem of 1929, "ANAGRAMMAGIC," Robert Graves mockingly follows the example of Kodak's founder George Eastman, who had famously hit upon Kodak's name during an anagram game, when "trying out a great number of combinations of letters that made words starting and ending in 'k.'"[44] Graves's poem blames Kodak and Eastman for afflicting the British "nation"

[42] Ibid.

[43] W. H. Auden, *Letters from Iceland* (London: Faber & Faber, 2002), 50.

[44] Elizabeth Brayer, *George Eastman: A Biography* (Rochester, NY: University of Rochester Press, 2006), 63.

at once with an artificial new temperament, "lustalgia," and with an alliterative disease.[45] In the last stanza, Graves balances one Kodakian concocted word upon another; he ends by responding to the challenge with which he opens; namely, to "anagrammatis[e] / TRANSUBSTANTIATION":[46]

By such anagrammagic
And masturbantiation
They fathered then this tragic
Lustalgia on the nation,
And after that, and after that,
ON A TIN SIN TUB ART SAT.[47]

The miracle of the Catholic Eucharist is here caricatured by the capitalized anagram of the last line, which achieves intelligibility only by a whisker. Graves thus accuses Kodak and Eastman of writing bad poetry and encouraging the writing of bad poetry, and even of writing Graves's own bad poem. Art sits on a "SIN TUB" defaced by the monstrous words of an ingrained Kodak mindset.

Could good Kodak-era poems be photographic? Empson's "Description of a View" comes to mind here, although Empson avoids entangling himself with the newly mobile photographers of the period by insisting on his photograph's stillness. On the other hand, in 1917, Thomas Hardy's brilliantly weird poem "The Photograph" embraces the modern notion of the moving photograph, bringing it into dialogue with the macabre dimensions of early cinema. Where the Kodakers freed photography from the studio and (to an extent) from what James calls "optical symbolism," Hardy sets out in his curious poem to repurpose the photograph as a kind of weapon. The following stanzas eroticize a woman's paradoxically animating destruction:

The flame crept up the portrait line by line
As it lay in the coals in the silence of night's profound,
    And over the arm's incline,
And along the marge of the silkwork superfine,
And gnawed at the delicate bosom's defenceless round.

Then I vented a cry of hurt and averted my eyes;
The spectacle was one that I could not bear,
    To my deep and sad surprise;

[45] Robert Graves, *The Complete Poems*, ed. Beryl Graves and Duncan Ward (London: Penguin, 2003), 307.
[46] Ibid.
[47] Ibid.

But, compelled to heed, I again looked furtivewise
Till the flame had eaten her breasts, and mouth, and hair.

"Thank God, she is out of it now!" I said at last,
In a great relief of heart when the thing was done
        That had set my soul aghast,
And nothing was left of the picture unsheathed from the past
But the ashen ghost of the card it had figured on.[48]

Hardy's invented word "furtivewise," whose first syllable etymologically stems from the Latin for thief,[49] is an attempt to snapshot in sound an act of spectatorship that is at once greedy, guilty, ruinous, harmless, and irrevocable. On one level this is a poem about the reanimation of an ex-lover in flames that progressively reveal her "delicate bosom," moving with a lover's curiosity from her breasts to her mouth and hair. She seems "defenceless," as no mere image can be, as if brought to life by the curl of scorched paper and the consciousness of threat. It is one of the persistent oddities of photographic portraits that they cannot return our gaze in the way that painted ones do, but Hardy creates a woman who looks back and sees him burn her. With the opening line's metatextual allusion, "The flame crept up the portrait *line by line*," an inverse relation is established between the poem's composition and the desired body's decomposition, between the upward-creeping flame and the author's writing hand as it moves downward line by line. To write is to set fire to by photographing.

Laura Marcus provides a lovely account of the first film the Lumière brothers exhibited, on March 22, 1895, in which workers at a photographic plate factory (by then manufacturing modern dry plates with their built-in chemicals) peer into a camera that records their peering.[50] Viewers of the film watched the animated eyes of the workers, who in a sense really did look back, though not at the viewer herself but at their own mirrored faces. One of the permanent weirdnesses of cinema manifested itself at this early moment, in the disillusionment of the viewer whom instinct is trained to expect reciprocation from live eyes. In the act of confronting their own desire to see their look acknowledged, audiences of *La Sortie de l'Usine Lumière Lyon* – like Hardy's killer in "The Photograph" – saw only ghosts. Hardy's poem may be read as protocinematic in the macabre dimension of its gaze, although it remains more photographic than

48 Thomas Hardy, "The Photograph," in *Selected Poems*, ed. Tim Armstrong (Abingdon: Routledge, 2014), 211–22.
49 *OED*, online edition.
50 Laura Marcus, *Dreams of Modernity: Psychoanalysis, Literature, Cinema* (New York: Cambridge University Press, 2018), 178.

cinematic in its final insistence on the ultimate stillness of the woman in the still, whose life is as much a conceit as the poem's own words are conceits of real utterance. In 1927, Alexander Bakshy wrote that "The only real thing in the motion picture is *movement*,"[51] a statement that aims to remind us of the conjury whereby cinema's illusions fool us but may also indicate a decaying scene all around the forlorn vibrancy of the film reel. What was sometimes called "kinema" may have looked, in Marcus's suggestive phrase, like "progress being made in photography";[52] but the new medium also reasserted and added to the limitations of photography's experiments with the lifelike.

5 "Wishing Rose"

In a poem of 1934, "Easily, my dear," Auden pictures the tightening circle of a camera's aperture as a rosebud making a wish, whose pink plea then in itself evokes an upturned mouth waiting to be kissed. The last line in the extract below offers up its lips at the line-break, pursing them to make a full stop:

> Easy for him to find in your face
> The pool of silence and the tower of grace,
> To conjure a camera into a wishing rose.[53]

In the automatic apertures of our own twenty-first-century cameras in smartphones, computers, and tablets, the pursed lips that Auden imagines are now either invisible or understated. And so among the shocks of the Covid era has been the mismatch between our cameras' view of us and our vision of ourselves. For the first time ever, perhaps, we have wondered about the location of the aperture on our screens. But if Auden's analogy seems remote to us now, the association of cameras with wishing remains robust. We have never stopped wanting cameras to recreate life as we see and know it, or to stand in for lives we cannot see or know. Photography has always been shaped by the irrational weight of the expectations brought to it, gaining definition through its failures as much as through its progress.

From the late nineteenth century through to the early twentieth, the ripple of new inventions associated with recording differed in their legacy from other scientific advances in that rather than promoting rationalism they seemed to confirm visual superstitions. Late Victorian journalist

[51] Quoted in ibid.
[52] Ibid. Emphasis in original.
[53] W. H. Auden, *Selected Poems*, ed. Edward Mendelson (London: Faber & Faber, 1979), 34.

W. T. Stead credited them with "mak[ing] psychic phenomena thinkable,"[54] while photography in particular lent itself to accommodating belief in the otherworldly through those of its effects that appeared unnatural. In 1903, early color photographer John Cimon Warburg dyed the naturally white dandelions in his photograph of 1903, "Fairy Clocks," an ethereal pale gold, letting the darkroom's interspace between visual fact and photographic representation enchant them. Photography was for Warburg a site of wishful thinking, perfectly complemented by the dandelion's fairy clock, that not only measures time but also grants wishes. In the same period, his fellow photographers experimented with double exposure to create ghosts.

In 1869, Lewis Carroll accompanied his amateur interest in photography with a poem on wanting to see ghosts. "Phantasmagoria" is a playful poem about the demand among new homeowners for residential ghosts, as exemplified by a single, male homeowner, and endowed with inevitability by a heavy terminal rhyme between "haunted" and "wanted":

"That Spectre left you on the Third –
Since then you've not been haunted:
For, as he never sent us word,
'Twas quite by accident we heard
That anyone was wanted.

"A Spectre has first choice, by right,
In filling up a vacancy;
Then Phantom, Goblin, Elf, and Sprite –
If all these fail them, they invite
The nicest ghoul that they can see."[55]

Photograph-like, Carroll's "ghoul" is a product of light and writing, "Seen in the dim and flickering light" *while* written into existence by the poem's words. The creature is apparently afraid of light too, and announces to Carroll's homeowner that "Ghosts have just as good a right, / In every way, to fear the light, / As Men to fear the dark."[56] This fear sends a continuous tremor through his body in the poem, as though the same double exposure that created him made his existence unsteady. Carroll here presents the human fear of the dark as the equivalent of the ghost's photophobia,

[54] Roger Lockhurst, *The Invention of Telepathy, 1870–1901* (Oxford: Oxford University Press, 2002), 139.

[55] Lewis Carroll, *Selected Poems*, ed. Keith Silver (Manchester: Carcanet Press, 2002), 41.

[56] Ibid.

which may also explain why his company is "wanted." It as if he were photographed to soothe the fears of an inverted ghost (the homeowner).

Just as photographs generate and invigorate wishes, they also draw attention to the facilitative work of the imagination in accepting the camera's partial untruths or complete fantasies. Writing in 1945 in his short story "Time and Ebb" of the perennial oddity of human flight, Vladimir Nabokov opines: "it is not easy to imagine airplanes, particularly because old photographic pictures of those splendid machines in full flight lack the life which only art could have been capable of retaining."[57] To see a stationary plane in the air is to witness what technology cannot achieve: the mere suspension of a heavy object without the help of propulsion. The fragility and danger of aerial suspension was a fresh issue at the time of writing; a decade before Nabokov's story appeared in the *Atlantic Monthly*, the word "jettison" had begun to be used to describe the urgent disposal of planes' fuel tanks in the event of an imminent break in momentum.[58] Nabokov's suggestion is that it is the artist *in us* who makes the plane move, responding to the photograph by contradicting its assertion of stillness. Jean-Paul Sartre had made a similar point in 1940 in *L'Imaginaire*, in relation to a photograph of a man named Pierre: "if [a] photo appears to me as the photo 'of Pierre' … it is necessary that the piece of card is animated with some help from me, giving it a meaning it did not yet have. If I see Pierre in the photo, *it is because I put him there*."[59] In Sartre's example, the philosopher's own reflex of "animat[ing]" Pierre is echoed by ours in imagining a hypothetical figure (Pierre) as a real man within a hypothetical photograph. Sartre animates Pierre and then we do, the irony being that Pierre does not exist for either of us (not even for Pierre). Our imagination thus goes further than a photograph ever could, in not only compensating for the partial unreality of a photograph but also providing the whole reality of one: creating Pierre *ex nihilo*.

Sartre here may seem to conclude as Nabokov does that fiction, in its capacity as imagination's equal rather than its parasite, is superior to any photograph. But what if an alternative artistic achievement may be understood to reside not in granting viewerly wishes but in exposing and threatening them? What if it may be aesthetically more compelling to discover with a shock that photographs are still?

57 Vladimir Nabokov, *The Stories of Vladimir Nabokov* (New York: Vintage, 2008), 585.
58 *OED*, online edition.
59 Jean-Paul Sartre, *The Imaginary*, trans. Jonathan Webber (Oxford: Routledge, 2010), 19. Emphasis in original.

6 "Night Photograph"

Bernard Stiegler sees as the defining feature of modern late-capitalist society "a rhythm of constant innovation,"[60] in which the instillment of consumerly habit is offset by "the evolution of the technical system."[61] In Stiegler's prognosis, our modern temporal consciousness is reduced to a thin hyperawareness of the future, because only the future has meaning in an environment of constant novelty. We are never satisfied, yet we never lose our faith in the prospect of satisfaction. An adherence to the principle that the grass is greener or *will* be greener robs us of the present. Stiegler's argument belongs very much to its 1990s moment, a time of widespread technological optimism when cultural theorists were obliged to work harder than ever to incentivize critique. But there is still – in 2022 – truth to his broad premise that new technological innovations are never enough for us, and that we would prefer to project ourselves into the future (looking ahead, say, to the more densely "megapixelated" cameras of forthcoming iPhones) than to coexist with our disappointments in the present. This predicament applies especially well to cameras, whose promise to show us ourselves and the world as we see them, or might see them, or would like to see them, is impossible to keep. If it is the task of the inventor to adapt his device to the demands of a declared wish, photography's innovators fail from the start by harnessing themselves to a shooting star.

But at the same time that our consumerly eagerness compels us to think ahead, photography's cat and ball games with our wishes may still inspire inquiry. We do not only live in the future, as Stiegler would have us believe. In a poem of 1992, "Night Photograph," Lavinia Greenlaw turns her back on two decades of photographic advances – the invention of the digital camera in 1975 and of the color-capable digital camera in the 1980s – in describing a Polaroid photograph taken at night:

> Crossing the Channel at midnight in winter,
> coastline develops as distance grows,
> then simplifies to shadow, under-exposed.
>
> Points of light – quayside, harbour wall,
> the edge of the city –
> sink as the surface of the night fills in.

[60] Bernard Stiegler, *Technics and Time: The Fault of Epimetheus*, trans. Richard Beardsworth and George Collins (Stanford, CA: Stanford University Press, 1998), 17 and 43.

[61] Ibid., 39.

Beyond the boat, the only interruption
is the choppy grey-white we leave behind us,
gone almost before it is gone from sight.

What cannot be pictured is the depth
with which the water moves against itself,
in such abstraction the eye can find

no break, direction or point of focus.
Clearer, and more possible than this,
is the circular horizon.[62]

The ambiguity of Greenlaw's "we" in the third stanza permits us to imagine not only two pairs of eyes but also two ways of seeing: that of the speaker on her boat and that of her Polaroid camera. The scene "we leave behind us" is thus visible on two retinas at once, whose different mechanisms are woven together by the mutually descriptive technical language of the second lines: "coastline develops as distance grows, / then simplifies to shadow, under-exposed." In the first and second stanzas, the interchangeability between human and Polaroid vision establishes a harmony between them. In the third, conversely, the hairbreadth's time lapse between "sight" and visual fact in the statement "choppy grey-white we leave behind us, / gone *almost before* it is gone from sight" evokes two different processes of obscuration. Where the Polaroid's eyes go blind in the overexposed image, those of the speaker move out of range of the white water. Finally, in the last stanzas, the two visual perspectives are abruptly tugged apart, then combined with a jolt like agitated flotsam, when the depth of the unlit water becomes too much for any camera ("What cannot be pictured"). Then almost immediately afterward, the "circular horizon" is clear and bright for both. At this point, the relationship between the two perspectives subtly acquires the depth of a human emotional intimacy, in which the immersive darkness seen by one observer and not the other threatens to end their closeness, while their glimpse of the horizon's beacon is an ice-breaker. Greenlaw finds a lovely, lived, ongoing complexity in the competitions of eyes.

In our own more recent present, the disparity between real and virtual vision has been less inclined to seem romantic than frustrating, and even heartbreaking when, in the depths of lockdown, "abstraction" – to borrow Greenlaw's paradox – has set the conditions of our sight. In May

[62] Lavinia Greenlaw, *Night Photograph* (London: Faber & Faber, 2016), 54. Emphasis added.

2021, Tiana Clark published a wonderfully arresting poem in the *New Yorker*, "First Date during Social Distance," in which vision forfeits its old role as the primary medium of sensory vividness. For Clark, it is touch, taste, smell, and sound that convey reality most effectively, rather than sight. Mimesis is impossible without these. When vision is introduced, it achieves efficacy only by the oblique route of taste: "the sky dimmed from spring / and wet-paint blue to sherbet / shades of pink fruit juice."[63] In the 2010s, the quick rise of Instagram and the emergence of TikTok made virtual images in all their manifold Photoshopped falsity seem as though they defined our modern moment. However, in the 2020s, we have become unsure of what we want from visual media. Imagining a camera and a literary discourse of the camera suited to our own era may in the future involve a recognition that photography's limitations and permissions may be doing us damage, while its accustomed functions may, with benefit and pleasure, be outsourced to our other virtually recreated senses. It is tempting to hope for a modern camera based on Clark's tongued eyesight, that tastes sherbet in a sky's fizzy pink.

[63] Tiana Clark, "First Date during Social Distance," *New Yorker*, May 10, 2021, online edition.

CHAPTER 15

Phonographs

Jason Camlot

The phonograph, a media technology for recording and reproducing sound, was an object that evoked both immediacy and hypermediacy from the moment of its introduction in the late nineteenth century: immediacy, since it suggested a direct, unmediated experience of events from the past; and hypermediacy, since it drew attention to how the material limitations of this media technology worked to shape the real-time sonic events it recorded, and thus revealed how indebted our sense of reality is to mediating factors.[1] Thomas Edison's early expository speculations upon the import of his inventions, the 1877 tinfoil phonograph, and the 1888 "perfected" wax cylinder phonograph, posited a technology that realized the ascendancy of presence over distance, speech over writing, voice over print, and listening over reading.[2] As the argument went, by means of the phonograph, Edison's phonograph cylinders did not need to be "deciphered" (as with written text) but could "speak for themselves."[3] Freeing its users from "the drudgery of the pen,"[4] the phonograph evoked a new kind of reality capture medium, making possible "a spoken literature" rather than "a written one" and enabling authors to communicate "with all the living reality of the present moment."[5] Such were some of the suggestions from the earliest notional and promotional discourse that asserted this technology's realization of a new kind of immediacy in communication. This discourse of unmediated or transparent access to literature via the author's voice was paralleled by a fascination with how the technology worked,

[1] Jay David Bolter and Richard Grusin, *Remediation: Understanding New Media* (Cambridge, MA: MIT Press, 2000), 6–19.

[2] Thomas Edison, "The Phonograph and Its Future," *North American Review* 126 (1878): 530.

[3] Thomas A. Edison, "The Perfected Phonograph," *North American Review* 379 (June 1888): 645.

[4] Frank Andrews, *The Edison Phonograph: The British Connection* (Rugby: The City of London Phonograph and Gramophone Society, 1986), xv.

[5] "Julian Hawthorne in *America*," *The Phonograph and Phonograph-Graphophone* (New York: Russell Bros., 1888; repr., London : London Phonograph and Gramophone Society, 1973), 24; J. Mount Bleyer, "Living Autograms," *Phonogram* 1 (1893): 16.

what it could do, and by a developed awareness of the phonograph as a media technology with its own affordances for shaping reality, and of vocal performance as a technical practice in its own right.

The term medium (and its plural, media), comes from the Latin term *medius*, or middle, evoking something working in between a real, live event and its mechanical reproduction. In the case of our specific topic, the real, live event is a sound, and that something working in the middle is the media technology of the phonograph. Early phonograph demonstrations not only underscored the phonograph's reproduction capacities, but flaunted "the fact of mediation" that sound recording entailed, by playing records backward and at different speeds, in effect showing off how the medium worked and what it could do to shape and reshape real, recorded sounds.[6] The term phonography (*phono*: voice/sound, *-graphy*: writing) held multiple historical meanings in the nineteenth century when phonographs first appeared, referring both to written systems of phonetic transcription (shorthand scripts) and applications of new phonographic media for the recording of sound. This chapter provides an account of the phonograph as a literary technology by considering (1) historical (and ongoing) metaphorical continua between writing, print and sound, inscription and aurality;[7] (2) the conceptual and practical implications of such concepts as media, format, performance, and production; and (3) recent literary critical ideas about the historical nature of the "literary" sound recording, and what "the literary" sounded like in early phonograph recordings. The first area of focus reveals how early sound recording technologies were often understood in terms of earlier writing and print publication media, and how the phonograph has served as an important metaphor for interpreting print-based works of literature since the technology was introduced. Next, by considering the way phonographs were used to produce recordings of literary works according to the affordances of the technology and material record formats, we can understand how the medium influenced and shaped the kinds of recordings that could be made. Finally, by considering these early recordings in generic and formal terms, we can begin to understand the audible features that defined a spoken recording as a literary artifact. Together, these points of focus explain the ideological and material significance of the phonograph for literature.

6 Matthew Rubery, "Thomas Edison's Poetry Machine," *19: Interdisciplinary Studies in the Long Nineteenth Century* 18 (2014): 7. See also Patrick Feaster, "'A Compass of Extraordinary Range': The Forgotten Origins of Phonomanipulation," *ARSC Journal* 42 (2011): 163–203.

7 Lisa Gitelman, *Scripts, Grooves and Writing Machines: Representing Technology in the Edison Era* (Stanford, CA: Stanford University Press, 1999).

1 Writing and Sound in Literature

Ideas about how literature sounds were discussed and written about long before the phonograph was invented, particularly in the study of prosody. Literary prosody, or metrics – whose study dates to classical antiquity and has a long history in English literary studies – can refer either to analysis of the sonic features of a written work (scanning the meter or rhythm of a printed line, tracing assonance, consonance and rhyme schemes, etc.) or to analysis of the audible features of a text when it is read or spoken out loud. By contrast, prescriptive prosody, or elocution, provides practical rules and principles for the oral delivery of a literary work. It was founded as an English subject of study in the eighteenth century, and formed a prominent part of literature pedagogy and literary interpretation into the first half of the twentieth century. Both literary prosody and prescriptive prosody represent early methods of conceiving of the sonorous elements of literature from the perspective of print-based media. The analysis of sound and voice in modern literary criticism goes back to the New Criticism at least, when reference to voice shifted from the audible utterance of an interpretive reader to an abstract hermeneutical category deployed for analysis of the silent, printed word. Beyond these formidable critical legacies, we may further distinguish between (1) the *phonographic reading*, which interprets a literary work whose thematic or formal features seem to respond to phonograph recording technologies; (2) the *phonographic text*, which features the technology as an explicit element of theme or narrative; and (3) the *literary audiotext*, a sound recording that represents a technological and sonic remediation of the literary. As an example of the first category, a *phonographic reading*, Ivan Kreilkamp develops an illuminating interpretation of Joseph Conrad's *Heart of Darkness* as a narrative exploration of what an invention that allows speech to sound without a human body might mean for humanity, and for the future of storytelling. Arguing that the phonograph is the informing figure that lies behind "the synechdocal representation of 'voice'" in Conrad's novella,[8] Kreilkamp reads Marlow's description of Kurtz as "A Voice … very little more than a voice" to represent the newly possible mechanical separation of speech from embodied voice as a horrifying challenge to authentic human presence – and consequently to identity, meaning, and a stable sense of reality. However, as Kreilkamp's reading suggests, where Marlow the narrator depicts this

[8] Ivan Kreilkamp, "A Voice Without a Body: The Phonographic Logic of *Heart of Darkness*," *Victorian Studies* 40.2 (1997): 229.

model of the storyteller (Kurtz) as bodiless voice to be horrifying, Conrad seems to hear and see in this mechanical technology for the reproduction of voice possibilities for new modes of literary representation.[9] Many late Victorian and early modernist texts are suggestive for such media-focused hermeneutical interpretations, which reveal the ways in which new communication technologies were explored by literary authors and woven into the fabrics of their texts.

A wide array of *phonographic texts* appeared after Edison's tinfoil phonograph, well into the modernist period. These ranged from early phonograph dramas and burlesques that enacted farcical fantasies of what this new technology would mean for human communication in the future,[10] to science fiction stories such as Edward Bellamy's "With the Eyes Shut" (1889), a dream vision (or rather, *audit*ion) of a world in which the phonograph, sound, and listening have replaced writing and textuality as the dominant discursive media; to novels such as Jules Verne's *Le Château des Carpâthes* (*The Castle in Transylvania*) (1892), which identifies a phonographic device as the scientific explanation behind the seemingly supernatural phenomenon of a deceased singer's voice that, hauntingly, had continued to be audible after her death. Bram Stoker's *Dracula* (1897), the next phonographic novel after Verne's to explore Transylvania in a gothic narrative, has been the source of numerous critical readings in relation to the history of phonographic media.[11] Friedrich Kittler's "Dracula's Legacy" (1982/1989) analyzes the significance of communications media ranging from the newspaper, typewriter, shorthand, and the phonograph to demonstrate how the novel is as much concerned with technologies of information processing as with gothic horror.[12] Kittler's media-historical approach to literature and culture stresses how sound recording technology has had a transformative impact upon our relationship to the past. He argues that the emergence of time-based preservation media technologies such as the phonograph and gramophone capture, preserve, and reproduce temporality in a dramatically new way, allowing us to bypass syntactical systems associated with language and writing, so that, for the first

9 Ibid., 237.

10 For example, Charles While, *The Bogus Talking Machine* (New York: Dramatic Pub. Co., 1876); A. C. Fraser Wood, *The Phonograph: Comedietta* (Walsall: St George's Hall, Walsall, 1989); Frank Hockenberry, *Professor Black's Phunnygraph, or, Talking Machine* (Chicago: T.S. Denisen, 1882).

11 Edward Bellamy, "With the Eyes Shut," *Harper's New Monthly Magazine* 79.473 (October 1889): 736–745; Jules Verne, *Le Château des Carpâthes* (Paris: Hetzel, 1892); Bram Stoker, *Dracula* (London: Archibald Constable and Company, 1897).

12 Friedrich Kittler, "Dracula's Legacy," trans. William Stephen Davis, *Stanford Humanities Review* 1.1 (1989): 143–173.

time in history, "the real takes the place of the symbolic."[13] He states this idea with dramatic flair, arguing that, with phonographs, "[t]he dream of a real … audible world arising from words has come to an end," and a new "reality" medium has emerged in its place.[14] The identification of the phonograph as a new "reality" medium, another articulation of phonographic immediacy, is importantly qualified when we think of the phonograph in media-historical and sociological terms. It is qualified because an understanding of how the media technologies and formats worked reveals the ways they shaped and produced this new, historically specific sense of what was "real."

2 Technology, Media, and Format

The technology and media formats of the phonograph had a strong material influence upon the nature and kinds of literary sound recordings that could be made and how they were used. Just as printing media technologies helped establish recognizable visual formats for poetry, novels, and essays in magazine and book formats (such as the three-volume novel popular in the mid-nineteenth century in connection with circulating libraries such as Mudie's), the limited storage capacity of early cylinders and discs, and the limited sensitivity of acoustic recording mechanisms, influenced the kinds of texts that could be recorded, how they were recited into the phonograph horn, and how and where they could be played back for listening and use.

Lisa Gitelman usefully defines media as "socially realized structures of communication, where structures include both technological forms and their associated protocols."[15] Protocols surrounding the use of a media technology can allow us to see and explain connections between such elements as the announcement of a performer, sketch title, and record label heard at the start of an early commercial phonograph cylinder recording; the materials and designs of phonograph cylinder cases; and the distribution systems put in place to lease (and later sell) phonograph machines. Jonathan Sterne notes that a format associated with a media technology "denotes a whole range of decisions that affect the look, feel, experience, and workings of a medium," establishing the rules by which

[13] Friedrich A. Kittler, *Gramophone, Film, Typewriter*, trans. Geoffrey Winthrop-Young and Michael Wutz (Stanford, CA: Stanford University Press, 1999), 24.

[14] Ibid., 14.

[15] Lisa Gitelman, *Always Already New: Media, History and The Data of Culture* (Cambridge, MA, and London: The MIT Press, 2008), 7.

it operates.[16] In the case of phonographs and gramophones, the implications of media format were played out in the competition between cylinder (phonograph) and flat disc (gramophone), protocols of use (for recording and replay), arguments about sonic fidelity resulting from the cutting format (vertical versus lateral stylus inscription), duplication potential (flat discs could be pressed from a master whereas cylinders, initially, could not), the possibilities or limitations of playing records produced by different companies, visual presentation styles of the record player within the playing environment and of storing records – and in a whole host of other ways.

Acoustic recording, as employed with phonographs and early gramophones, is a purely mechanical process of capturing and reproducing sound. A conical horn captures or picks up the sound of a voice or instrument by responding to the fluctuations in air pressure that it generates. The air pressure vibrations captured with the wide end of the horn are directed to a framed diaphragm membrane with a needle attached to it that is situated at the tapered end of the horn. The vibrating diaphragm transfers the patterns of air pressure to the stylus or needle that then inscribes indentations (in accordance with variations in air pressure) upon the surface of a cylinder or flat disc that is spinning or turning at a constant speed. This is how sound is recorded with the "acoustic" process. To reproduce a sound, one simply reverses the process by placing the stylus at the beginning of the spinning record. The stylus vibrates in accordance with the inscribed patterns previously produced and sets the diaphragm vibrating, thus replicating (transducing) the air pressure patterns inscribed on the records surface during the recording process. The conical horn attached to the diaphragm works in this instance to amplify the vibrations as audible sound.[17]

During the acoustic era, records were either cylindrical or flat round discs. Each media format has its own affordances for sound storage and use. Early cylinder phonographs were designed for recording and reproducing. The cylinders could be shaved to erase the indentations that had been recorded and reused. Gramophone flat discs were produced of harder substances and were not designed for recording but only for the reproduction of commercial records. The storage capacity of a cylinder or disc was

[16] Jonathan Sterne, *MP3: The Meaning of a Format* (Durham, NC: Duke University Press, 2012), 7.

[17] For an extended explanation of the process in the context of a history of the development of the technology, see Jonathan Sterne, *The Audible Past: Cultural Origins of Sound Reproduction* (Durham, NC: Duke University Press, 2003), 31–85. For a detailed account of the components of various models of Edison phonographs, with instructions for use and illustrations, see *The Phonograph and How to Use It* (London: National Phonograph Company, 1900).

determined by the material nature of the media format, combined with the application of the technology, specifically in terms of the speed of play (expressed in revolutions per minute, rpm). The implications of the great variety of storage formats and reproduction speeds were significant for the nature of the materials that could be delivered on record. The limited storage capacity of early records would often demand excerpting and/or textual compression, and prohibited the recording of some kinds of materials altogether. Poems for recitation had to be trimmed and timed in accordance with the phonographic media format used to make a record. For example, Edgar L. Davenport released eight commercial dramatic recitation recordings of the cowboy poem "Lasca" between 1905 and 1920. These recordings were made for three different record companies (Edison, Victor, and Columbia) in six different media formats, and varied in length from two minutes and thirteen seconds at the shortest to four minutes and forty seconds at the longest, with versions of the excised recitation text that ranged from 359 to 740 words, and reading speeds that varied from 151 to 174 words per minute. Some of the Davenport recordings of "Lasca" had extensive musical accompaniment whereas others had just sparse orchestration. Comparative observations about such recordings of the "same" poem by the "same" reader can raise interesting questions about the relationship between differential media formats, the treatment of the recitation text, and the nature of the performer's delivery of that text. Each recorded version of this poem represents a unique literary artifact with its own content, tempo, and sound.

Novels could not be reproduced in their entirety until well into the electrical era of recording, namely in the 1940s when the Library of Congress introduced LP records that played at $33\frac{1}{3}$ rpm, to reproduce novels as part of the Books for the Blind project.[18] Even within the limited number of examples of early short-form adaptations of fiction into sound, we find variation in approach and cultural signification. Often, early adaptations of literary fiction into sound consisted of the selection of a dramatic, transformative scene, already well known to readers and stage audiences from the longer novel or stage adaptation of the novel. Recording artist Len Spencer displays his skills as a monopolylogist – someone capable of doing many different voices – in his recordings of scenes dramatized from novels such as *Uncle Tom's Cabin*

[18] For a history of the modern, full-length audiobook, which begins in earnest with an account of the Library of Congress Books for the Blind project, see Matthew Rubery, *The Untold Story of the Talking Book* (Cambridge, MA: Harvard University Press, 2016).

"(Flogging Scene)" (1904), in which he performs the voices of both Uncle Tom and Simon Legree, and the transformation scene from *Dr. Jekyll and Mr. Hyde* (1905) performed in imitation of the scene as it was acted onstage by actor Richard Mansfield.[19] Herbert Beerbohm Tree's recording, "Svengali Mesmerizes Trilby" (1906),[20] functions as a sonic memento of this actor's renowned performance of the role of Svengali in Paul Potter's stage adaptation of George Du Maurier's novel, *Trilby*. Alternatively, the numerous early recordings derived from the novels of Charles Dickens by the likes of Bransby Williams, Mortimer Kaphan, and William Sterling Battis focused primarily on photogenic realizations of the distinctive traits of favorite Dickens personages, delivered in monologues and touted as "life portrayals" of characters from fiction.[21] The earliest recorded effort to transcend the limitations of the single-record format – which encouraged brief recorded scenes of transformation or the verbal ticks of foreshortened characters – can be heard in Bransby Williams's Scrooge recordings made for Columbia in 1912, in which he pursued the moral narrative arc of Dickens's *A Christmas Carol* in a set of three records, "Before the Dream," "The Dream," and "The Awakening."[22]

3 Performance

It is commonly said of the artists who made early sound recordings that they included either speakers "with little or no stage experience and stage performers with no recording experience."[23] Tim Gracyk underscores the importance of distinguishing between the stage performer and the recording artist, since during the first two decades of the recording industry, stage celebrities often could not afford the time in the recording studio necessary to cultivate recording careers.[24] There are certainly exceptions to this rule. In the American context, while white recording artists rarely had careers

[19] "*Uncle Tom's Cabin* (Flogging Scene)," Len Spencer, performer, Edison Standard 8656, 1904; "*Dr. Jekyll and Mr. Hyde*," Len Spencer, performer, Edison Standard 8879, 1905.

[20] "Svengali Mesmerizes *Trilby*," Herbert Beerbohm Tree, performer, The Gramophone Company, 10-inch disc, 1313, 1906.

[21] See, for example: "Micawber (from *David Copperfield*)," William Sterling Battis, performer, 12-inch disc, Victor 35556-B, 1916; and "*David Copperfield* (Charles Dickens)–Wilkins Micawber's Advice," Bransby Williams, performer, Edison cylinder 13508. March 1906.

[22] "*A Christmas Carol*–Scrooge–The Dream," Bransby Williams, performer, Columbia "12-inch disc", 6276–2, 1912/1924.

[23] David J. Steffen, *From Edison to Marconi: The First Thirty Years of Recorded Music* (Jefferson, NC, and London: McFarland & Company, 2005), 35.

[24] Tim Gracyk, *Popular American Recording Pioneers, 1895–1925* (New York: Routledge, 2008), 18.

in live performance, most black recording artists did.[25] The British context also suggests a different trend, with fewer cultivated recording artists and more recordings by stage personalities in the earliest years of recording.[26]

The performance of a recording artist is a specific kind of mediated speech act. The performer may have selected and treated (cut and condensed) his text, or even have written it in preparation for the recording, making sure that it would fit within the limited storage capacity of an early cylinder or disc. In most cases the text would have fulfilled certain generic expectations of the emerging market for spoken recordings – reenactments of historical speeches (e.g., "Lincoln's Speech at Gettysburg"),[27] recitations of poetic works or speeches from plays, comedic stories, dialect sketches – and the performing artist would have aimed to fulfill the expectations associated with the genre of speech act he recorded in his performance. For some of the more popular texts prepared for recording, a performer would not only have to perform an already familiar text, but perform it in a manner that was expected, based on the success of previous recordings made by other performers. In these instances, it may not have been the voice signature of the recording artist that mattered so much as his replication of the voice signature associated with the recording personality he was performing.[28] Further, some recordings were presented as a performer's imitation of a style of performance that was associated with a different well-known or deceased actor, the recording thus functioning as a performative interpretation not only of a well-known text, but of an entire manner of performance. Bransby Williams's "imitations" of the melodramatic performance mode of Henry Irving,[29] first on the London music hall stage, and then on Edison cylinder,

[25] Tim Brooks, *Lost Sounds: Blacks and the Birth of the Recording Industry* (Urbana, Chicago, and Springfield: University of Illinois Press, 2005), 8.

[26] Susan Schmidt Horning, *Chasing Sound: Technology, Culture, and the Art of Studio Recording from Edison to the LP* (Baltimore, MD: Johns Hopkins University Press, 2013), 18.

[27] William F. Hooley, speaker, "Lincoln's Speech at Gettysburg," Berliner Gramphone 6012 (New York: September 21, 1898). Cited in Paul Charosh, *Berliner Gramophone Records in America: A Discography* (Denver, CO: Mainspring Press, 2012), 101.

[28] For example, Joe Hayman's successful recording of the comic monologue "Cohen on the Telephone" (recorded for Regal Records in London and as Columbia Record A1516 in the USA) in 1913, was re-recorded by Monroe Silver in 1914, Barney Bernard (Victor matrix B-17337) and George Thompson (Edison Record 4285) in 1916, and others afterward. Information on the Bernard record is from *Discography of American Historical Recordings*, s.v. "Victor matrix B-17337. Cohen at the telephone / Barney Bernard": http://adp.library.ucsb.edu/index.php/matrix/detail/700002364/B-17337-Cohen_at_the_telephone (accessed May 24, 2022). Information about the Thompson recording can be seen, and the recording heard, at the UCSB Cylinder Audio Archive: www.library.ucsb.edu/OBJID/Cylinder1040 (accessed May 24, 2022).

[29] Bransby Williams, "An Imitation of Sir Henry Irving in the Murder Scene from *The Bells*," Edison Gold Moulded Record, 13348 (1907) was listed in the "Talking Records Miscellaneous" section of an *Edison Gold Moulded Records British-American List* (July 1907), 20.

represent an example of such imitative performance, and, can be classed in the same family as other examples of "impersonation" performances.[30] Early phonograph speech recordings ranged from comic dialect sketches to formal recitations of well-known poems, but across this continuum of speech sounds we can discern certain elocutionary methods of recitation that were recognized to convey the elevated, artistic sounds of serious expressive interpretation and that were particularly resonant of literary value.

The phonograph presented a certain paradox of presence by having a voice sound in the absence of a speaker's body. With this status as an "acousmatic voice" – that is, the voice with no visible source, emanating as if "from an immaterial and non-localized body" – it evoked strange and magical powers.[31] Yet the fact remains that to analyze the performance heard in a spoken recording entails consideration of the performer's efforts to physically enact the elocutionary techniques considered relevant for the successful delivery of an audiotextual script. Analysis of a recorded performance also requires an understanding of the process of technical mediation applied to the voice that is recorded in the production of a record. We want to know why a performer delivered a text in a particular way, and how the technology used to make a recording may have shaped the way it was recited during the recording process.

The scenario of early acoustic recording was unforgiving, and the phonograph demanded the performer's attention in adjusting her vocal style, volume, and physical positioning in order to produce a usable acoustic phonograph record.[32] Depending on the natural pitch of the performer's voice and the nature of the text that was recited (as well as the kinds of vocal sounds it demanded), different physical maneuvers would be required to achieve a successful recording. Vocal performers might need to move their bodies significantly to achieve the correct proximity in relation to the recording horn for different moments in a song or recitation. Sometimes they would mark their positions with chalk on the studio floor to remember where to stand at any given moment as the recording cylinder turned during their process of recording a recitation.[33] In short, the way an early spoken recording sounds was strongly shaped by the performer's application of vocal techniques in response to how early recording technologies worked.

30 Eric Jones-Evans, "With Irving and *The Bells*: A Memoir," in *Henry Irving and The Bells: Irving's Personal Script of the Play*, ed. David Mayer (Manchester: Manchester University Press, 1980), 27.

31 Michel Chion, *The Voice in Cinema*, trans. Claudia Gorbman (New York: Columbia University Press, 1999), 24.

32 Horning, *Chasing Sound*, 21.

33 Ibid., 21.

4 Production

Most commercial spoken recordings were commissioned and produced by record companies. This process entailed scouting for talent and then developing the repertoire of a selected artist for adaptation to the medium. Producers, in this capacity, would play a role either in managing the larger process by which a stage performer's act was remediated to a cylinder or disc, or, they might commission an already proven recording artist to perform a text they felt would fulfill market demand. These figures would come to be known as A&R (artist and repertoire) experts, functioning as a new kind of specialist within the emerging recording industry.[34] At times, recording artists would double as A&R experts themselves, as was the case with Len Spencer. Spencer began in the industry as an announcer of other artists' records for Columbia,[35] then had a prolific career performing material that ranged from hymns and popular songs, historical speeches and recitations, to comedy sketches on his own. He also developed an entire repertoire of minstrel records by recruiting a performance troupe (comprising vaudeville performer Billy Williams, tenor singer Dan W. Quinn, and popular black recording artist George W. Johnson) and arranging the materials for his "Imperial Minstrels" for cylinder.[36] In some cases, the producer might be an industry "jobber" (a mercantile middleman) collecting information from clients (phonograph shops, schools who purchased machines and records in large quantities, etc.) and then applying that information to the development of specialized catalogs for which specific performance materials and recording artists would be sought and commissioned. In such cases, the production of a record entailed much beyond the recording process itself, including the location and shaping of material to be recorded, and the development of sales narratives and promotional documents that communicated the value of such commissioned material.

The nature and sound of acoustic recordings depended upon the significant technical knowledge of recording specialists. The more technical version of the producer was the sound recordist who oversaw the material production of the record, including the process of recording. Acoustic sound recordists needed to be familiar with the mechanics, acoustics, and chemical properties that recording media technologies and formats entailed. The experience recordists gained in such tricks as selecting

34 Steffen, *From Edison to Marconi*, 35–36.
35 Gracyk, *Popular American Recording Pioneers*, 314.
36 Brooks, *Lost Sounds*, 37.

recording horns, diaphragms, needles (of varying sizes and qualities), and in staging the performers during the recording session, were sometimes protected as valuable trade secrets from studio to studio.[37] Early recordists occupied a liminal yet crucial role within the industry, applying extensive technical knowledge combined with the necessary patience and interpersonal skills needed to manage artists at work in order to produce successful recordings. Employed by record companies, they often worked in competition with one another, hiding trade secrets rather than sharing technical knowledge – yet, as David L. Morton Jr. notes, they were such "highly prized employees" that they would frequently receive offers from competing companies.[38] The professional identity of the sound recording engineer would not be consolidated until the late 1940s when professional organizations such as the Sapphire Club, the Audio Engineering Society, and the Professional Group on Audio began to develop.[39]

The spaces and environments in which early recordings were produced represent another source of influence upon the recording process and the ultimate sound of the acoustic recording. The earliest recording studios did not necessarily take into account the acoustic features of space in any significant detail, but were extensions of the experimental laboratory spaces and machine shops used in developing the technology, identifying recording as an ongoing process of testing and experimentation. The first point of material focus in the acoustical recording setting, once the studio as a space dedicated to sound recording emerged, was the nature and location of the static horn that directed the sounds the performers made to the diaphragm, stylus, and cylinder or disc. Even in the earliest recording rooms, methods of separation between the machine and the performer were developed by installing a wooden barrier between the technician working the machine and the performers producing the sounds.[40] Horns of different shapes and reach were developed and experimented with for use in recording different kinds of sounds. Platforms of different levels were built to situate distinct performers and the kinds of sounds they generated in relation to each other for capture on the recording medium. Rooms of different kinds were treated with the aim of generating different acoustical effects. As David Morton notes, "Edison's studio had thick, soundproof walls insulated with

[37] Horning, *Chasing Sound*, 22.

[38] David L. Morton Jr., *Sound Recording: The Life Story of a Technology* (Baltimore, MD: Johns Hopkins University Press, 2004), 58.

[39] Horning, *Chasing Sound*, 73–77.

[40] Andre Millard, *America on Record: A History of Recorded Sound*, 2nd ed. (Cambridge: Cambridge University Press, 2005), 258.

seaweed or cow hair, but Victor's recorders preferred a 'livelier' room with more reverberation, which gave Victor records a distinctive sound."[41] For the most part, these early recording rooms were spaces in factories or office buildings – rooms above shoe shops, office basements – retrofitted to fulfill the function of recording room. At the turn of the century, the term studio might refer to elaborately furnished *listening* studios, "talking machine establishments" that exhibited portraits of the recording artists who could be heard during the daily listening programs presented to audiences.[42] As custom-built *recording* studios were developed in the early 1900s, they became more comfortable for artists whose arduous work demanded stamina for repeated performances. Large rectangular rooms would be fitted with carpets, long draperies of different kinds were hung to control the acoustical effects of the space and to separate the machine and technician from the performer, and a red light was installed to signal the beginning of the recording process and the necessity of absolute silence from all but the performers.[43] Early recording studios would sometimes be heated to high temperatures to keep the wax blanks soft;[44] these elevated temperatures would prevent the stylus from skipping during the process of recording, but they could also make the recording artist sweat. This single example of the heated studio room illustrates how a recording environment that was developed to deal with the chemical properties of the recording medium (wax) might also influence the physical performance of the recording artist. Another key material object in the studio was a stopwatch or clock that would keep the recordist and performers alert to the necessity of pacing the performance to fall within the two or three minutes of storage capacity that an early recording cylinder or disc would allow.[45] To assuage the pressure that the recording process placed upon performers, some studios developed "Artists' Rooms" furnished with armchairs, plants, and natural light, where the performers could relax between takes.[46]

Owing to the relative simplicity of voice recording as compared with the recording of musical ensembles, spoken records were also sometimes produced out of the studio in different, uncontrolled environments. Examples include the early noncommercial recordings made in the homes

41 David Morton, *Off The Record: The Technology and Culture of Sound Recording in America* (Piscataway, NJ: Rutgers University Press, 2000), 20.

42 "Artistic Talking Machine Studio," *The Talking Machine World* 1 (November 15, 1905): 6.

43 "Why Grand Opera Artists Are Heard at Their Best through Talking Machine Records," *The Talking Machine World* 14 (March 15, 1918): 29.

44 Morton Jr., *Sound Recording*, 58.

45 Millard, *America on Record*, 262.

46 "The Aeolian Co. Announces the Vocalion Record," *The Talking Machine World* 15 (May 15, 1918): 68.

of subjects or in the salon environment of George Gouraud's house; recitation records made at home by phonograph man William Lynd for sale at the Edison Bell Consolidated Phonograph Company shop in London; and field, amateur, and vernacular recordings of different kinds.[47] In all cases, the concrete material conditions of record production influences the remediation of literary texts into audiotexts.

5 Phonographic Audiotextual Forms

When we speak of the *audiotext*, we are referring to the discernible contours and qualities of the audible signal of the spoken recording. What would this sound signal look like if we visualized it? How would we name its generic features? Elements informing the reading format of early spoken recordings include (1) the speech formulae that preceded the performance on record, such as announcements, and any other para-audiotextual features that might have been recorded before or after a reading; (2) the acts of framing, compression, and adaptation that were often applied to the texts prepared for recording, thus altering significantly the form of the source text as it had been published originally; and (3) the enactment of elocutionary or performative protocols in relation to the text or partially improvised sketch that was being recorded. The reading format as a category sits in close proximity to conceptions of literary genre, and the points of overlap and productive difference between the two concepts are useful to consider. The formulaic and sometimes overdetermined nature of speech recordings can be understood as compensatory for the absence of an immediately identifiable situation justifying the speech heard; the generic qualities of the audiotext help orient the listener in placing a recorded speech within some identifiable and comprehensible context.[48] In the absence of quotation marks and other conventions of depicting speech and dialogue that had been developed as print conventions in the novel, without the visual aid of elocutionary gesture, and without the cues of costume, stage set, and a cast of characters to situate a particular three minute speech within a much broader dramatic context, new generic tactics and formulae were required to help the listener situate in meaningful ways speeches heard emanating from machines.[49]

[47] The recording activities of William Lynd, recording artist, are documented in his 1899 pocket diary. William Lynd, William Lynd's Diary, 1899, University of Exeter Archives, GB 29 EUL MS14.

[48] Patrick Feaster, "Framing the Mechanical Voice: Generic Conventions of Early Phonograph Recording," *Folklore Forum* 32.1/2 (2001): 59.

[49] Marjorie Garber, "" " (Quotation Marks)," *Critical Inquiry* 25.4 (1999): 657.

Traditional literary methods of generic designation, whether based on fixed outer forms (e.g., the metrical and rhyming characteristics of the sonnet), subject matter (funeral elegy, epithalamion), intended effect (horror), or inner tonal elements such as the piece's attitude or valence (satire, irony),[50] certainly inform an understanding of the generic format of an early literary sound recording. However, such aspects of the critical idiom surrounding literary genre will always be supplemented by the audiotextual codes and restrictions that work to inform the framing of a recorded speech with the aim of shaping the expectations of a listener. Patrick Feaster usefully identifies a few clear examples of such tactics of audiotextual formatting, ranging from the very explicit introductory announcements that would introduce, name, or describe the sounds to follow, to the regularization of formats that informed more complex audiotexts that combined multiple sonic elements. For example, "descriptive" and "minstrel" records are audiotextual formats that quickly developed generic meaning within the early culture of sound recording.[51] The meaning of "descriptive" as an audiotextual format, while wide-reaching, referred to a range of expected sonic elements, including the performance of multiple voices (sometimes by a single speaker) often of different speech dialects, enacting some kind of socially inflected scene (an auction, a journey, an encounter, a debate), with sound effects that both informed and were identifiable because of the framing scene. These speeches were also delivered in a manner that conveyed spatial movement and depth through the strategic uses of sonic amplitude. Such records might have very explicit verbal cues to situate the listener in the scene, or might rely upon sound effects to do that work for the recording. Many early recordings based upon literary content would have fallen within the broader "descriptive" audiotextual format category, yet not all of them would have been understood as "literary" in nature. The "dramatic recitation" was a phonograph genre that had many of the broad features associated with the descriptive sketch but that most obviously sounded the literary as an elocutionary, interpretive performance of poetry, delivered from the perspective of a situated speaker.

An audiotext is not an inherently social artifact, but becomes one through its implication in the different kinds of associations and activities that define it at different historical moment of production and use.[52] Take, for example, the numerous cylinder recordings of Bible recitations in the

[50] Heather Dubrow, *Genre* (London and New York: Methuen, 1982), 3–4.

[51] Feaster, "Framing the Mechanical Voice," 78–91.

[52] Bruno Latour, *Reassembling the Social: An Introduction to Actor-Network Theory* (Oxford: Oxford University Press, 2005), 5–17.

high elocutionary mode produced between 1890 and 1900. The scenarios of production, circulation, marketing, use, and meaning of these records varied drastically depending upon the context and the actors (individuals) working within different networks of social and cultural activity. While many of the audiotexts heard in such biblical recitations certainly emerged out of the repertoire performed at revival camp meetings of the late nineteenth century, the late Victorian demand for recorded gospel songs and recitations from sacred texts indicates that the story of the production and purpose of these records does not pertain to the history of denominational activity alone. Yes, there are accounts of recorded hymns and recitations being integrated into the regular liturgy, such as that of the New Jersey pastor who used the phonograph "to deliver all parts of his service besides the sermon," thus framing his own live contribution with recordings of a violin solo, a hymn, and recorded recitations of a psalm, prayer, and benediction.[53] And approximately one-third of the extant catalog discussed by Richard Martin consists of vernacular recordings – that is to say, recordings made by non-professional performers in the home, church, or in the field.[54] Each one of these vernacular recordings suggests a mystery of historical production, use, and meaning to be researched and accounted for. But beyond recordings that were in different ways artifacts of local social and spiritual use, there were a broad range of professional and celebrity recordings that indicate the emergence of the recitation of psalms as another form of phonographic entertainment that could be marketed for the qualities of the reader's voice and the poetic nature of the recited lines, as well as for their potential use in private spiritual reflection. Berliner recordings of popular evangelist Dwight Moody reciting "The 91st Psalm" (1898) and "The Sermon on the Mount" (1897), and of the ubiquitous professional recording artist Len Spencer reciting "The 23rd Psalm and The Lord's Prayer" (1897/1902),[55] while easily grouped together owing to their common subject matter, may have held very different meanings depending on the consumer. The Moody recordings represented the portable capture of a celebrity preacher's voice reciting passages that were already well associated (to those in the fold) with large revival meetings contemporaneous with the record release, whereas Spencer's enacted an exaggeratedly

[53] Richard Martin, Meagan Hennessey, and Michael Devacka, *Waxing the Gospel: Mass Evangelism & The Phonograph, 1890–1900* (Champagne, IL: Archeophone Records, 2016), 51.

[54] Ibid.

[55] "Reading of The 23rd Psalm and The Lord's Prayer," Len Spencer, performer, Edison Record 8155, brown wax concert cylinder (1902): www.library.ucsb.edu/OBJID/Cylinder14254 (accessed May 24, 2022).

heightened elocutionary performance that suggests that its primary selling point was his enactment of the sounds of the sacred voice itself – sounds that were strongly associated with literary performance.[56] Although we might have focused on more obvious literary examples, such as early adaptations of 900-page-long novels by Charles Dickens onto three minute wax cylinders, or recorded recitations of Victorian narrative poems with orchestral accompaniment, the example of the psalm encourages us to focus on the particular, grave sound of literary authenticity as it was performed and preserved on record during the early period of sound recording. Marit J. MacArthur has noted how the monotonous and slow cadence deployed to convey neutrality and sincerity typical of the Protestant liturgy came to inform a common and long-standing approach to reading poetry out loud, wherein the literary text is delivered as if to evoke a secular version of sacred ritual.[57] MacArthur calls this mode of reading "poet's voice," but we might just as easily identify it as one among several late Victorian sounds of "the literary" that can be heard on record to this day.

As the majority of early phonograph and gramophone recordings come to us today in the form of digital files, interfaces, and computational hardware, in studying the impact of the phonograph we need to be critically aware of the normalized and normalizing (digital) media technologies we use to pursue critical study in the present as we work to decipher strange technologies from the past. And, of course, archaic media technologies are only one element in a diverse assemblage of human techniques, practices, ideologies, and aesthetic positions that developed around this analog technology and that we must attend to in our critical engagement with audiotexts that were originally produced with phonographs.

[56] Martin et al., *Waxing the Gospel*, 211, 145.

[57] Marit J. MacArthur, "Monotony, the Churches of Poetry Reading, and Sound Studies," *PMLA* 131.1 (2016): 41–42, 59–60.

CHAPTER 16

Waves and Rays

Jennifer A. Janechek

The history of electric media is as much a story about overcoming distance to bring people closer together as it is about enforcing distinctions to police the boundaries between self and other. Modern communications technologies such as the telegraph, telephone, phonograph, and radio promised to resolve the troubling distance between bodies, while modern imaging technologies such as X-ray, ultrasound, and magnetic resonance imaging (MRI) endeavored to traverse the barriers presented by one's own body. The physical phenomenon driving all these technologies, which rely either on sound or electromagnetic waves, is vibration. Shelley Trower theorizes vibration as the "connection between the external world of objects in motion and the internal world of mental activity."[1] Julie Beth Napolin similarly defines it as "the shared physical property of sound and image as well as the shared physical substance between beings."[2] Sound and light are not static objects; rather, sensory organs receive the physical stimuli of vibrations from rays of light and sound waves and transduce them into electrical signals, which the brain interprets as sounds or images. Although both sound and light travel through the air, the former must be conducted by molecules, whereas the latter, as electromagnetic waves, can travel independently of matter. The electromagnetic spectrum distinguishes forms of radiation based on wavelength (in meters) and frequency (in Hertz) – from radio waves ($<3 \times 10^{11}$ Hz), which have the lowest frequency and longest wavelength; to microwaves (3×10^{11}–10^{13} Hz); to infrared light (10^{13}–10^{14}); to visible light (4–7.5×10^{14} Hz); to ultraviolet light (10^{15}–10^{17}Hz); to X-rays (10^{17}–10^{20} Hz); to gamma

[1] Shelley Trower, *Senses of Vibration: A History of the Pleasure and Pain of Sound* (New York: Continuum, 2012), 2.

[2] Julie Beth Napolin, "'A Sinister Resonance': Vibration, Sound, and the Birth of Conrad's Marlow," *Qui Parle* 21.2 (2013): 79: http://muse-jhu-edu.proxy.lib.uiowa.edu/article/504334 (accessed December 7, 2013).

rays (10^{20}–10^{24} Hz), which have the highest frequency and shortest wavelength.[3] Similarly, sound exists on a spectrum, with infrasound (<20 Hz) and ultrasound (2 to 15 MHz) existing outside the realm of audibility (20 to 20,000 Hz).[4] As the constituent element of both electromagnetic and sound waves, vibration is that "invisible" phenomenon that resists sound/image dichotomies while conveying both aural and visual sensory perceptions to the brain. It connects and penetrates, reaches outward and inward, expands and collapses bodily and spatial boundaries, and in its technologization creates a new means of formulating narrativity and subjectivity.

Through a focus on vibration as the constituent element of both waves and rays, authors in the late nineteenth and early twentieth centuries used technological innovation to reconceptualize the relationship between writer, reader, and text, ushering in a literary modernism predicated not on pure visuality or aurality, but rather on a subaural activity that simultaneously dissolves the boundaries between self and other and reaffirms these divisions in its homogenizing impulses.[5] Although many electric media shaped the development of the modernist phonotext, the telephone, radio, and X-ray contribute most directly to a narrative aesthetic distinctly modern in its attempt to reach beyond reporting and revealing toward a mode of direct presencing enabled by connective and imaging media.[6] Joseph Conrad's *Heart of Darkness* and *Lord Jim,* as well

[3] "The EM Spectrum," *The University of Tennessee-Knoxville*, The University of Tennessee-Knoxville: http://labman.phys.utk.edu/phys222core/modules/m6/The%20EM%20spectrum.html (accessed January 13, 2020).

[4] "Medical Ultrasound," *ScienceDirect*, ScienceDirect: www.sciencedirect.com/topics/neuroscience/medical-ultrasound (accessed January 13, 2020).

[5] The notion of vibrations as the matter of sound and image predated the invention of modern sound technologies. In a chapter of *The Ninth Bridgewater Treatise: A Fragment* (London: John Murray, 1837), Charles Babbage extends the work of Pierre Laplace and William Wollaston to postulate that the "pulses of air emitted by the voice" exist in diminished form in the atmosphere but may be inaudible to the human ears." See John M. Picker, *Victorian Soundscapes* (Oxford: Oxford University Press, 2013), 16. For Babbage, the air was a book of voices, a storehouse of all the utterances ever produced. His theory of aural permanence informed Victorian authors' narrative aesthetic, particularly that of Charles Dickens who, as Picker notes, paraphrases the ninth chapter of the *Treatise* in *Dombey and Son* in describing Sir Barnet Skettles as "like a sound in air, the vibration of which, according to the speculation of an ingenious modern philosopher, may go on travelling for ever through the interminable fields of space" (17). In addition, nineteenth-century theories of nerve energies posited vibrations in the nerves as being "conserved and converted into sensations of light, sound, and so on." See Trower, *Senses of Vibration*, 75.

[6] As David Trotter notes, "When literary historians speak of modernism's relation to new media, they usually have one medium in mind: cinema." See David Trotter, "Literature between Media," in *The Cambridge History of Modernism*, ed. Vincent Sherry (Cambridge: Cambridge University Press,

as Virginia Woolf's *The Waves*, are particularly useful for understanding the stakes of this vibratory narrative logic, as well as how it evolves with improvements in wave- and ray-based technologies. As these texts reveal, the modernist novel is vibrant matter that physically unites authors and readers through the medium of the text – not quite silent, as many would have it, sounding only through metaphor or mimesis, but actually channeling its frequencies through the body of the reader, who vibrates in response to it.[7] Beyond the reading voice – that inner voice so crucial for silent reading – we find, in the modernist novel, the voice of the text: the excess of language that exists before and beyond the written or spoken word, a continuous vibration that cuts through bodies to bind them together.[8] However, as we will see, this permeability occasions a sonic violence in its forced reconciliation with the other – the other conceived of in cultural, gendered, and racial terms, as well as the other existing at the core of selfhood.

1 "We Are Only Telephone Wires": Technologizing the Human Sensorium

Innovations in wave- and ray-based technologies both resulted from and contributed to advances in sensory research; the two domains of inquiry are so intimately and reciprocally bound that it is often impossible to discern whether modes of listening and looking shifted prior to or after the introduction of sonic and imaging technologies. Bell Labs, which would later become the communications giant American Telephone & Telegraph (AT&T), hired both physicists and engineers to study jointly and separately the mechanism of human hearing and the means of

2016), 386. In his recovery of modernism's telephonic inheritance, Trotter helpfully distinguishes between representational and connective media, the former (e.g., phonographs, photographs, cinema) recording and storing sensory impressions and the latter (e.g., telephones, radio, telegraphs) transmitting messages across a distance (391).

7 In his introduction to *Sounding Modernism*, Julian Murphet notes that literary modernism experiments with the auditized grapheme by moving beyond sonic description (representation) and onomatopoeia (mimesis), instead probing the audibility of the seemingly silent Real and referencing "sound that cannot be described, but which is Real." See Julian Murphet, "On Not Listening to Modernism," in *Sounding Modernism: Rhythm and Sonic Mediation in Modern Literature and Film*, ed. Julian Murphet, Helen Groth, and Penelope Hone (Edinburgh: Edinburgh University Press, 2017), 22.

8 Garrett Stewart locates the reading voice as the inner voice that sounds the text, registering the aural contours of the page. See Garrett Stewart, *Reading Voices: Literature and the Phonotext* (Berkeley: University of California Press, 1990), 11.

improving the quality and efficiency of telephonic transmission. Jonathan Sterne explains that "[t]elephonic transmission drove research into hearing for much of the century and, as a result, shaped both what it means to hear and the notion of the hearing subject that subtends most new audio technologies today."[9] The reverse is also true: Media-technological discursive shifts contributed the impetus and rationale for the invention of sound and imaging technologies.[10] In fact, much of the technological innovation in the late nineteenth and early twentieth centuries resulted from the reconceptualization of hearing following the development of physiological acoustics.

An epistemological shift can be traced back to the work of German scientist Hermann von Helmoltz, whose landmark 1863 treatise *On the Sensations of Tone as a Physiological Basis for the Theory of Music* contributed greatly to the new "organic physics," which revealed that "material bodies tended to function as sites of energy conversion," thereby dispelling the myth of difference between organic and inorganic matter.[11] Helmholtz isolated the tympanic function of the human ear, revealing it to be a resonant mechanism. By instrumentalizing the ear, he uncovered its incredible ability to parse the multiple vibrations in a single sound wave. No longer merely the basis for prosthetic augmentation, the human body itself could now be understood as a machine in its own right, with the ear "capable of registering material effects in the absence of a perceiving subject."[12] The discovery of the mechanical properties of the ear, particularly its ability to convert sonic vibrations into electrical impulses, enabled the development of modern sound technologies.

The earliest sound recording technology was Édouard-Léon Scott's phonautograph, a device that implemented principles of Helmholtzian acoustics to "write sound." Patented in 1857, the phonautograph converted

[9] Jonathan Sterne, *MP3: The Meaning of a Format* (Durham, NC: Duke University Press, 2012), 3.

[10] Friedrich Kittler's *Discourse Networks 1800/1900* resists the impetus of technological determinism. Similarly, Carolyn Marvin argues in *When Old Technologies Were New* that "the early history of electric media is less the evolution of technical efficiencies in communication than a series of arenas for negotiating issues crucial to the conduct of social life; among them, who is inside and outside, who may speak, who may not, and who has authority and may be believed." See Carolyn Marvin, *When Old Technologies Were New: Thinking About Electronic Communication in the Late Nineteenth Century* (Oxford: Oxford University Press, 1990), 5: http://site.ebrary.com/lib/uiowa/detail.action?docID=10087117 (accessed December 26, 2019).

[11] Hermann von Helmoltz, *Die Lehre von den Tonempfindungen als physiologische Grundlage für die Theorie der Musik* (Braunschweig: Verlag von Fr. Vieweg u. Sohn, 1863); Benjamin Steege, *Helmholtz and the Modern Listener* (Cambridge: Cambridge University Press, 2012), 68–69.

[12] Anthony Enns, "The Human Telephone: Physiology, Neurology, and Sound Technologies," in *Sounds of Modern History: Auditory Cultures in 19th- and 20th-Century Europe*, ed. Daniel Morat (New York: Berghahn, 2014), 48.

sound into its visual representation by funneling sound waves through a conical apparatus (simulating the external ear) that terminated in a diaphragm (imitating the tympanic membrane), which, vibrating, activated a pig's bristle stylus (replacing the middle ear ossicula) that would permanently inscribe the sound waves onto a piece of carbon-blackened glass.[13] Following in his father's footsteps by using sound technologies to teach deaf students standard English, Alexander Graham Bell saw in the phonautograph a means of accomplishing what his father's phonetic notation system, Visible Speech, could not: a reduction of the gap between spoken language and its graphic representation by enabling deaf students to see the shapes of their sounds and compare them to the "correct" shapes of normate speakers.[14] Bell describes the idea as "a machine to hear for them, a machine that would render visible to the eyes of the deaf the vibrations of the air that affect our ears as sound."[15] With the assistance of the American aurist Clarence Blake, Bell modified the phonautograph by replacing the diaphragm with the ear of a cadaver to transduce sound waves into writing.[16] In this way, Bell's 1874 "ear phonautograph" causes sound to be experienced as disembodied and "heard" through the amputated organ of the corpse. This sound-writing device cleared the way for the invention of other technologies that dislocate sound from the body in order to reproduce it.

Bell directly attributed his ability to invent the telephone to his experimentation with the ear phonautograph, for it "gave him the clue" to the ear's mechanical processing of sound.[17] With the help of Thomas Watson, Bell created a number of membrane diaphragm telephones in 1875 modeled on the human ear, including a "real ear telephone" that contained components of an actual human ear.[18] While functional, these devices lacked the sensitivity to sensory stimuli necessary for communication at

13 Ibid., 54–55.

14 Jennifer Esmail, *Reading Victorian Deafness: Signs and Sounds in Victorian Literature and Culture* (Columbus: Ohio State University Press, 2013), 184. Other inventors modified Scott's phonautograph before Bell, including Karl Rudolph Koenig (1859); Adam Politzer (1861), who himself experimented with attaching a human ear to the device, assisted by Bell's eventual collaborator, Clarence Blake; and Charles Morey (1874) – but none to the level of recording accuracy demanded by Bell. See Enns, "The Human Telephone," 55.

15 Quoted in Jonathan Sterne, *The Audible Past: Cultural Origins of Sound Reproduction* (Durham, NC: Duke University Press, 2003), 38.

16 Sterne, *Audible Past*, 35, 31.

17 Alexander Graham Bell, "The Telephone," *The Musical Standard* 13.698 (December 15, 1877): 375: http://search.proquest.com.proxy.lib.uiowa.edu/britishperiodicals/docview/7561048/652F4529A72469DPQ/8?accountid=14663 (accessed December 14, 2013).

18 Enns, "The Human Telephone," 58.

a distance, leading Bell and Watson to engineer an all-metal diaphragm magneto telephone in 1876.[19] This instrument could transmit the vibrations that constitute speech across a wire and reproduce them as sound at another location, as Bell and Watson discovered on March 10, 1876, when Bell transmitted the first telephonic message to a receiver positioned in a separate room of his Boston workshop. Electrically reproduced sound dramatically restructured the relationship between sound, bodies, and space. As Emily Thompson notes, "The telephone … was heralded for 'annihilating' space and time, by effectively eradicating the physical distance between people who wished to communicate, and by transmitting their communications across space virtually instantaneously."[20] The telephone's compression of space and time finds representation in much early twentieth-century literature, including Marcel Proust's *In Search of Lost Time*, in which the narrator describes telephony as "the admirable sorcery whereby a few moments are enough to bring before us, invisible but present, the person to whom we wish to speak, and who … finds himself suddenly transported hundreds of miles (he and all the surroundings in which he remains immured) within reach of our ear, at the precise moment which our fancy is ordained."[21] Telephony cultivated a sense of immediate intimacy that enabled direct communion with another individual while leaving bodily boundaries somewhat intact.

In addition to point-to-point communication, early iterations of the telephone often facilitated the unidirectional transmission of messages. Marvin refers to telephony as a "proto-broadcasting system," noting how it served as "a medium of multiple address for public occasions of music, theatre, and politics."[22] In 1881, a version of the telephone termed the theatrophone carried sounds from the Ópera and the Théâtre Français to two different rooms, each containing ten pairs of headsets, at the Paris Exposition Internationale d'Électricité. This capability excited the affluent portions of English society – the queen included – who by 1896 could pay a yearly fee to access various performances in London via private "electrophone" connections.[23] Communication engineers discussed the potential of wireless transmission, but "[a]s late as 1921, Walter Gifford" – who

[19] Ibid., 58, 64.

[20] Emily Thompson, *The Soundscape of Modernity: Architectural Acoustics and the Culture of Listening in America, 1900–1933* (Boston: The MIT Press, 2002), 235.

[21] Marcel Proust, *In Search of Lost Time*, trans. C. K. Scott Moncrieff and Terence Kilmartin (New York: The Modern Library, 2003), 3: 173.

[22] Marvin, *When Old Technologies Were New*, 209.

[23] Ibid., 209–10.

became president of AT&T in 1925 – "had difficulty visualizing separate roles for wired and wireless media in the twenty-first century" and referred to both technologies as simply telephony.[24] While not substantially different in purpose to these experiments in telephone diffusion, wireless technologies promised to make long-distance communication more accessible to the general public, who typically could not afford the steep subscription prices.

Heinrich Hertz's discovery of radio waves (also called Hertzian waves), electromagnetic radiation that could be generated and channeled, made wireless communication a practical reality. Initial experiments with radio waves led to the development of wireless telegraphy, which conveyed not voices but rather messages of an electric telegraph wirelessly. In 1895, Guglielmo Marconi, a student of Hertzian acoustics, broadcast the first radio signal – a distance of a little over a mile. In 1897, he successfully transmitted a message from the Isle of Wight to a ship in the English Channel. Beyond further leveling geographical, bodily, and spatial boundaries, Marconi's experiments generated a host of spiritual fantasies that contemporary authors explored in their fiction. Rudyard Kipling's short story "Wireless" (1902) captures many of the hopes and anxieties associated with radio waves, as well as their contributions to literary style.[25] In this tale, a consumptive chemist's assistant named Mr. Shaynor falls into a drugged trance and begins to write poetry, unknowingly penning fragments of a John Keats poem – much to the surprise of the narrator, who learns that Mr. Shaynor has never read Keats. At the same time, the chemist's shop is hosting long-range wireless experiments, presenting the question as to whether Mr. Shaynor is receiving his message from radio waves in the ether. Fascinated with emergent sound technologies, Kipling imagined the human body as in direct connection with the "nerve-wires" of the telecommunications network, leading him to tell Rider Haggard in 1918 that "[w]e are only telephone wires."[26] In "Wireless," Kipling muses on whether wireless telegraphy "will reveal to us the Powers – whatever the Powers may be – at work through space – a long distance away."[27] He depicts Hertzian waves as going "kick—kick—kick into space," a fragmentary transmission that suffuses not only Mr. Shaynor's poetic

24 Ibid., 231.
25 Rudyard Kipling, "Wireless," *Scribner's Magazine* 32.2 (August 1902): 558.
26 Rudyard Kipling, *Rudyard Kipling to Rider Haggard, the Record of a Friendship*, ed. M. Cohen (London: Hutchinson, 1965), 100.
27 Kipling, "Wireless," 558.

musings, but also the story itself, which adopts a telegraphic style.[28] Immediately after observing the "unknown Power," the narrator says he "caught the clear '*kiss—kiss—kiss*' of the halliards on the roof."[29] Significantly, the narrator doesn't "hear" this noise – he "catches" it, further linking perception with radiant energy. Kipling's short story thus reflects on the role of electric media in literary inspiration as well as modes of inscription and narration.

It was not until later that "wireless" moved beyond telegraphy into radiotelephony, or the wireless transmission of speech sounds – a feat enabled by Reginald Aubrey Fessenden, who had perfected Marconi's method of wirelessly transmitting Morse code. On December 23, 1900, he successfully replicated the sound of a human voice wirelessly across a distance. On Christmas Eve 1906, Fessenden produced the first true "radio broadcast," channeling a Christmas program to unsuspecting crews aboard United Fruit Company ships in the Atlantic Ocean and the Caribbean Sea.[30] Radiotelephony changed the landscape of telecommunications: No longer was electronically reproduced speech something that could be turned on and off; it was now a continuous stream of sound waves, a discovery that reconfigured notions of space, time, and subjectivity. Italian Futurist F. T. Marinetti recognized the liberatory potential of broadcast media, recommending authors use a "wireless imagination" to foster Deleuzian lines of flight in their texts, destroying syntax and making and unmaking meaning in assemblages of "words in freedom."[31] As with wireless telegraphy, the telephone and radio attracted spiritualist fantasies of connecting with the dead as well as completely merging one's body with the world around it. T. S. Eliot's wife Vivien was among those who experienced what she termed "telephone episodes" – auditory hallucinations of disembodied voices that she associated with the telephone.[32] And in *Memoirs of My Nervous Illness*, Daniel Paul Schreber charts his experience receiving messages from waves and rays without the use of his sensory organs. With nerve endings perpetually open to the sensory onslaught of the

[28] Ibid., 564.

[29] Ibid.

[30] Mervyn C. Fry, "Radio's First Voice … Canadian!" *The Cat's Whisker: Official Voice of the Canadian Vintage Wireless Association* 3.1 (March 1973): www.ieee.ca/millennium/radio/radio_birth.html (accessed December 26, 2019).

[31] F. T. Marinetti, "Futurist Sensibility and Wireless Imagination," *New England Review* 17.4 (Fall 1995): 30: www.jstor.org/stable/40243100 (accessed April 1, 2017).

[32] T. S. Eliot, *The Letters of T. S. Eliot*, ed. Valerie Eliot and Hugh Haffenden (New Haven: Yale University Press, 2011–2016), 3: 79.

universe, Schreber became a living telephone who mediated the "nerve-language" of the ether, which manifested as synesthetic experiences.[33] Trower explains that Schreber's description of the sun's rays emanating from "the nerves of God" and manifesting as human language blends old theories of solar power with new ideas about wireless transmission.[34] Schreber's experience taps into cultural fantasies inspired by nascent electric media that these technologies would enable direct sensory experience through an audiovisual nerve language.

The discovery of X-rays by Wilhelm Conrad Röntgen in 1895 also spawned spiritualist fantasies of the human body simultaneously emitting and receiving messages telepathically as a result of radiation. For instance, William Crookes, president of the Society for Psychical Research, imagined the ways in which atmospheric vibrations generate sensory impressions in humans, identifying 32 to 32,768 vibrations per second as the range for vibration's perception as sound.[35] According to Crookes, those higher-frequency rays – from heat, to ultraviolet, to X-rays – act directly on the human nervous center, where, he postulates, "these rays as the vocal chords use sound vibrations … and sends them out, with the velocity of light, to impinge on the receiving ganglion of another brain."[36] Beyond their imagined role in telepathy, X-rays fostered a fantasy of long-distance transmission because their penetrative power was so great. Nikola Tesla, inventor of the alternating current, explained this potential as follows: "Röentgen gave us a gun to fire … projecting missiles of a thousandfold greater penetrative power than that of a cannon ball, and carrying them probably to distances of many miles … without any hurtful consequences."[37] Tesla further predicted that high-frequency electromagnetic radiation would unite the globe in a "World System" of wireless communication and limitless energy generation.[38] Whether channeling sound waves or electromagnetic radiation, auditory and imaging technologies reshaped the soundscape of modernity; restructured the ways bodies related to each other, to sound, and to space; and gave modernist authors inspiration for a narrative aesthetic that resolves the gap between author, reader, and text while also permitting a more direct sensory experience of the text.

33 Trower, *Senses of Vibration*, 79.
34 Ibid., 87–88.
35 Ibid., 51.
36 Quoted in Trower, *Senses of Vibration*, 51.
37 Quoted in Trower, *Senses of Vibration*, 86.
38 Trower, *Senses of Vibration*, 88.

2 The Vibratory Narrative Logic of Conrad's Early Fiction

One of literary modernism's progenitors, Joseph Conrad, wrestled with the best means of creating a narrative aesthetic that transcended the seeming silence of the written word by generating acoustical images. In the famous preface to his 1897 novel *The Nigger of the "Narcissus,"* Conrad presents his aesthetic project as follows: "My task which I am trying to achieve is, by the power of the written word to make you hear, to make you feel – it is, before all, to make you *see*."[39] With its culminating emphasis on seeing, this sentence has earned Conrad the regard of scholars who attempt to place him in an ocularcentric modernist tradition.[40] However, beyond the likely metaphorical meaning of "seeing" as perceiving, it is clear that Conrad's aesthetic depends equally on sound and vision, for he writes elsewhere in the preface that "it is only through the shape and ring of sentences that an approach can be made to plasticity, to colour."[41] For Conrad, narrative transmission depends on its vehicle for communication and its remains, once emptied of semantic content – the sonorous materiality of language. Accordingly, Napolin identifies "an alternative aesthetic tension" in Conrad's modernism – "a vibrancy within the realm of the audible and visible" that structures narrative "in neither explicitly oral nor visual terms."[42] Emergent sound and imaging technologies would provide Conrad with the conceptual framework he needed to cultivate a literary aesthetic that permits a direct sensory experience of the text, where readers encounter neither discrete sound nor concrete image, but the vibrational properties driving both.

In 1898, in the midst of writing *Lord Jim* and about to begin work on *Heart of Darkness*, Conrad observed two technologies that kindled his

[39] Joseph Conrad, *The Nigger of the "Narcissus"* (Garden City, NY: Doubleday, 1897), 14 (emphasis in the original): http://archive.org/details/niggernarcissusooconrgoog/page/n7. (accessed December 11, 2013).

[40] Edward W. Said, for instance, argues that "Conrad's goal is to make us see, or otherwise to transcend the *absence* of everything but words, so that we may pass into a realm of vision beyond the words." See Edward Said, "Conrad: The Presentation of Narrative," in *Critical Essays on Joseph Conrad*, ed. Ted Billy (Boston: G. K. Hall, 1987), 33. In *The Political Unconscious*, Fredric Jameson similarly emphasizes seeing over hearing in Conrad's early fiction, arguing that it is only in Conrad's later works such as *Nostromo* (1904) that "the new idea of an auditory image" emerges. See Fredric Jameson, *The Political Unconscious: Narrative as a Socially Symbolic Act* (Ithaca, NY: Cornell University Press, 1981), 239. On the other hand, critics such as Stewart and Sam Halliday interpret the preface as underscoring the importance of aurality to the production of narrative. See Garrett Stewart, "Literary Writing and the Filmic Difference," in *Sound States: Innovative Poetics and Acoustical Technologies*, ed. Adalaide Morris (Chapel Hill, NC: University of North Carolina Press, 1997), 242; and Sam Halliday, *Sonic Modernity: Representing Sound in Literature, Culture and the Arts* (Edinburgh: Edinburgh University Press, 2013), 31.

[41] Conrad, *Nigger of the "Narcissus,"* 13.

[42] Napolin, "A Sinister Resonance," 71, 92.

interest in wave theories and transformed not only his narrative technique, but also the course of literary modernism. In a letter to his friend Edward Garnett, Conrad reports spending hours in a room with ship owners and a radiologist, toying with a phonograph and a Röentgen (X-ray) machine and talking about "*the* secret of the Universe" as being "in the existence of horizontal waves whose varied vibrations are at the bottom of all states of consciousness."[43] He further informs Garnett of his discovery that "the various vibrations of waves (electricity, heat, sound, light, etc.)" passing through "*all* matter" (both organic and inorganic alike) are what give birth to "our sensations—then emotions—then thought."[44] Following this physics lesson, Conrad's aesthetic becomes increasingly inflected with principles of vibration – so much so that in his autobiography, *A Personal Record*, he presents his maritime tales as attempts to accurately represent these "horizontal waves," saying, "I have tried with an almost filial regard to render the vibration of life in the great world of waters."[45] Both Conrad's fiction and nonfiction suggest that electric media provided a model for deconstructing textual sound and image into the same essential components: vibrations of matter and air that produce sensory impressions, which emerge into awareness before eventually dissipating into their environment.[46]

In *Heart of Darkness*, Conrad deploys a vibratory narrative voice that permeates inorganic and organic objects, texts and readers, in order to create shared multisensory perceptions. This vocal figure is theorized

[43] Edward Garnett, ed., *Letters from Joseph Conrad, 1895–1924* (Indianapolis, IN: Bobbs-Merrill, 1928), 142: http://archive.org/details/lettersfromjosep007757mbp (accessed December 7, 2013).

[44] Ibid.

[45] Joseph Conrad, *A Personal Record* (New York: Harper & Brothers, 1912), 9: http://archive.org/details/apersonalrecordooconrgoog (accessed December 7, 2013).

[46] While many Conrad scholars acknowledge the vibratory logic of *Heart of Darkness*, they disagree on the technology on which the narrative voice is modeled. Picker, Ivan Kreilkamp, and Geoffrey Winthrop-Young propose that *Heart of Darkness* operates based on a phonographic logic, while Napolin posits an X-ray logic, "a vibratory logic" that links sound to images in order to unite bodies across distances. See Picker, *Victorian Soundscapes*, 137; Ivan Kreilkamp, *Voice and the Victorian Storyteller* (Cambridge: Cambridge University Press, 2005), 183; Winthrop-Young, "'This Voice in the Darkness!': Technologies of the Tropical Talking Cure in Stefan Zweig's *Amok*," in *Stefan Zweig and World Literature*, ed. Mark H. Gelber and Birger Vanweesenbeek (Rochester, NY: Camden House, 2015), 56; and Napolin "A Sinister Resonance," 89. Owen Knowles intimates that the novella possesses a telegraphic logic when he suggests that Conrad makes readers "'hear' the spoken word" by "rel[ying] very heavily upon the implied centrality of a sensitive listener who … tends to fugitively *over*hear spoken words which are then impressionistically telegrammed to the reader" (Owen Knowles, "'To Make You Hear … ': Some Aspects of Conrad's Dialogue," *The Polish Review*, 20.2–3 (1975), 165). In my article "The Horror of the Primal Sound: Proto-telephony and Imperialism in *Heart of Darkness*," I identify a proto-telephonic logic in the text. See Jennifer A. Janechek, "The Horror of the Primal Sound: Proto-Telephony and Imperialism in *Heart of Darkness*," *The Conradian* 41.2 (2016): 8–27.

in his portrayal of the rogue agent Kurtz, whose voice retains primacy over his body in life as in death, and enacted in Marlow's narration. As Napolin aptly notes, there is a shift in narrative styles between the Marlow of "Youth" (1898) and that in *Heart of Darkness* (1899), with the former invested in verisimilitude and the oral mode of storytelling and the latter predicated upon "a subaural activity that permeates the apparent stability of entities."[47] In an added "Author's Note" prefacing the 1917 edition of *Youth, a Narrative, and Two Other Stories*, Conrad explains that the "sombre theme" of *Heart of Darkness* had to be given "a sinister resonance, a tonality of its own, a continued vibration that, I hoped, would hang in the air and dwell on the ear after the last note had been struck."[48] Thus is born a new mode of narration in the modernist novel, one whereby the vibrations of the narrative voice cut across time and distance to resonate with the body of the reader – even long after they have put down the text.

Conrad structures a diegetic space wherein the air is electrified by the vibrations from the voices of absent speakers – in particular, the voice of the seemingly bodiless Kurtz, the "first-class agent" who has barricaded himself in an ivory trading post somewhere in the heart of Africa and who is described by Marlow as "[a] voice … very little more than a voice," one famed for its "profound tone."[49] Marlow explains his understanding of Kurtz as pure voice – "I had never imagined him as doing, you know, but as discoursing.… The man presented himself as a voice" – and one that is technologically augmented at that.[50] As Marlow recalls, Kurtz's voice "sounded to me far off and yet loud like a hail through a speaking-trumpet," an amplifying technology used in early attempts at long-distance communication.[51] The idea of a disembodied voice that commands authority across distances fuels Marlow's obsessive desire to locate its site of production. The hunt for Kurtz becomes the search for an externalized voice whose quality does not diminish during the process of transmission but "[rings] deep to the very last."[52] It is the pursuit of a narrative voice that attains to "a continued vibration" that persists in readers' bodies.

This ideal narrative voice figured by Kurtz is noteworthy for its simultaneous materiality and immateriality. Its lack of referentiality paints it as acousmatic sound, or sound without a visible source, and yet it is the

47 Napolin, "A Sinister Resonance," 71, 72.
48 Joseph Conrad, *Youth/Heart of Darkness, The End of the Tether* (London: Penguin, 1995), 11.
49 Joseph Conrad, *Heart of Darkness* (New York: Norton, 2006), 48, 65.
50 Ibid., 47.
51 Ibid., 65.
52 Ibid., 67.

"external," extralinguistic features of the voice that linger in the air.[53] Echoing the language used in the preface to *The Nigger of the "Narcissus,"* Marlow praises "the shape and ring" of Kurtz's vocal emissions while also noting the disjuncture between these sounds and their supposed source: "The volume of tone he emitted without effort, almost without the trouble of moving his lips, amazed me. A voice! A voice! It was grave, profound, vibrating, while the man did not seem capable of a whisper."[54] Kurtz's "profound" voice – "profound" seemingly indicating its depth, its emergence from within a body – does not quite match his incapacitated bodily state. Further, it seems ventriloquized, as it manifests without Kurtz really moving his lips. This is not sound that has its origins within the body; rather, it is the technological voice recast as spatialized sound. For Marlow, Kurtz represents both the challenge and the ideal of storytelling – the potential for a narration independent of and not aiming toward physicality but with the same, or even enhanced, capabilities of inspiring communion as oral transmission. He challenges his audience to scrutinize their means of experiencing his tale: "[Kurtz] was just a word to me. I did not see the man in the name any more than you do. Do you see him? Do you see the story? Do you see anything?"[55] Rather than mental images, this vibratory aesthetic binds its audience together by virtue of its materiality, which explains why the frame narrator "listen[s] on the watch for the sentence, for the word, that would give [him] the clue to the faint uneasiness inspired by this narrative."[56] Here, the figure of speech "listened on the watch" is defamiliarized, through its connection with the disembodied voice, to highlight the multisensory nature of Conrad's resonant prose. Beneath and beyond sight and voice is vibration, a subaural activity that generates sensations rather than discrete perceptions – the novel "erasing its own status as writing" in an attempt to become pure connectivity.[57]

Kurtz's technologized voice serves as a model for Marlow's storytelling, as the latter searches out a means of replicating the "shapes" of Kurtz's sounds by attending to their "tone" and "vigour."[58] Embracing a

[53] In *Audio-Vision*, film theorist Michel Chion theorizes the acousmatic voice to account for a voice detached from a body that, when returned to the body, doesn't exactly fit it. He notes that precinematic technologies such as the telephone, "which transmit sounds without showing their emitter, are acousmatic media by definition." See Michel Chion, *Audio-Vision: Sound on Screen*, trans. Claudia Gorbman (New York: Columbia University Press, 1994), 71.

[54] Conrad, *Heart of Darkness*, 60.

[55] Ibid., 27.

[56] Ibid.

[57] Napolin, "A Sinister Resonance," 89.

[58] Conrad, *Heart of Darkness*, 60, 65.

vibratory mode of address that renders him bodiless – the frame narrator describes Marlow's tale as "shap[ing] itself without human lips" – he ensures that after Kurtz's death, the latter's "words will remain," lingering in the air.[59] Marlow adopts the same storytelling strategies in *Lord Jim*, as the narration issues from the "outside," speaking him into existence: "with the very first word uttered Marlow's body ... would become very still, as though his spirit had winged its way back into the lapse of time and were speaking through his lips from the past."[60] The syntax of this sentence, with its missing preposition "by" between "word" and "uttered," marks the voice as occasioning the body's emergence and bridging spatiotemporal divides. The subject no longer receives its selfhood from the voice but rather is supplanted by an external force whose mediality causes an ontological crisis – as with Jim: "his voice spoke"; "[h]is voice sounded reasonable."[61] Dislocated from his body in an alienating manner – "[i]t was very loud" and "rang startling in his own ears" – Jim's mechanized voice searches for "a meticulous precision of statement [that] would bring out the true horror behind the appalling face of things."[62] This truth can be accessed only outside language – in the vibrations that provide the text material substance and yet exceed vision and hearing. Like Kurtz's resounding final condemnation, the truth of the *Patna* (and thus Jim's truth) is disclosed by the electrified diegetic space of the novel, with the ship's destruction "haunt[ing] the surface of the image as a residual acoustical force."[63] Indeed, Conrad portrays the *Patna* as "quiver[ing] in response" to a "faint noise as of thunder ... less than a sound, hardly more than a vibration," sailing along "a narrow belt of vibrating water and humming air," and "trembl[ing]" within a noctural scene "vibrat[ing] like a bass string."[64] Like *Heart of Darkness*, *Lord Jim* searches out a mode of storytelling that most accurately represents life in both its individuality and its totality. As Marlow learns, this "truth" exists outside language in the physical forces that render humans porous and cause them to sympathize bodily with each other.

With his post-*Youth* Marlow tales, Conrad develops a narrative mode that unites authors and readers through the essential materiality of sound and image – vibrations that motivate distant bodies to attune themselves

59 Ibid., 27, 122.
60 Joseph Conrad, *Lord Jim* (New York: Norton, 1996), 33.
61 Ibid., 80.
62 Ibid., 21, 23.
63 Napolin, "A Sinister Resonance," 84.
64 Conrad, *Lord Jim*, 21, 55.

to the frequency of the collective. Rather than championing the written word for its sound or image storage capabilities, Conrad privileges the excess of language – its tenor and shape that exist beyond signification – as that "continued vibration … that dwell[s] on the ear after the last note ha[s] been struck."[65] However, in his anxiety about the threat to selfhood presented by the electrified voice's mediality and its susceptibility to interference, his aesthetic stops short of completely dissolving the boundaries between reader and author, self and other. Emerging from the Victorian tradition that assigned the seat of subjectivity to the voice and its self-presencing, Conrad worries about the destabilization of selfhood occasioned by a voice existing in between, rather than within, bodies that no longer speak, but are spoken.

Of all the communications technologies, the telephone best figures the voice's mediality and virtuality as the by-product of language. The telephone elicited apprehension about the voice's integrity and its vulnerability to foreign elements as it passed from node to node in the wired network. As Trotter notes, in the early telephone system lines were often crossed and callers had to speak quite loudly to be understood, making it easy to overhear others' private conversations.[66] Telephony makes manifest the voice's occupation of the interstices between self and other, revealing that the voice is hardly the interiorized breath of life, conjoined with, and inseparable from, the soul; instead, it is always structured by and through an other. As a signal, it can never be "pure sound," for as Steven Connor explains, only noise is capable of purity: "Signal, a product of traces and difference, is always impure, always shot through with the impurity of the other."[67] Trower remarks that the "extended nervous system" engendered by telephony "suggests that distance is annihilated, that self and other are in intimate contract, virtually identical – between them, though, is interference on the line."[68] This other, though kept at a physical distance, always haunts the telephone, threatening the line with its potential vocal returns.

Although not a sound technology, the X-ray similarly forces a confrontation with an inaudible sonic violence. Tesla cautions on the dangers of X-rays extending beyond exposure burns to include the Röentgen bulb's generation of a "violent extrasensory sound":

65 Conrad, *Youth*, 11.

66 David Trotter, *Literature in the First Media Age: Britain between the Wars* (Cambridge, MA: Harvard University Press, 2013), 42.

67 Steven Connor, "Photophonics," *Sound Effects* 3, no. 1 (2013): 150: www.soundeffects.dk/article/view/15645 (accessed March 6, 2016).

68 Trower, *Senses of Vibration*, 81.

> Exactly the same sensation is produced when working for some time with a noisy spark gap, or, in general, when exposing the ear to sharp noises or explosions. Since it seems impossible to imagine how the latter could cause such a sensation in any other way except by directly impressing the organs of hearing, I conclude that a Röentgen or Lenard tube, working in perfect silence as it may, nevertheless produces violent explosions or reports and concussions, which, though they are inaudible, take some material effect upon the bony structure of the head.[69]

In liberating bodily boundaries, X-rays occasion an extra-auditory noise that marks the sublimity and the violence of bodily union – and, for that matter, a porous subjectivity. In *Heart of Darkness*, this inaudible sonic violence is the primal sound, the repressed voice of the other, that inhabits the voice from the inside.[70] As Claude Maisonnat argues, "[V]oices in *Heart of Darkness* carry the inhumanity (the horror) that lies at the core of all human voices."[71] It is this voice that shatters Kurtz's notion of self-presence, leading to his final condemnation of life as "The horror! The horror!"[72] Marlow alludes to this when he suggests that the wilderness "had whispered to him things about himself which he did not know, things of which he had no conception till he took counsel with this great solitude – and the whisper had proved irresistibly fascinating."[73] This realization discourages Marlow from producing a narrative of pure voice that would dissolve the bounds of fiction and life into a totalizing sensory motility. While not achieving the status of pure resonance, Conrad's early fiction develops a model for the modernist novel whereby the narrative voice, figured as vibrations, mediates sound and image in order to inspire direct impressions in the reader, who is no longer watching or listening to the text, but experiencing its sensations.

3 Storytelling as Subaural Event in Woolf's *The Waves*

Conrad's vibratory aesthetic reaches maturity in the sensory experimentation of Virginia Woolf, particularly in *The Waves* – her own novel that wrestles with the "truth" of a life and the reverberations of death on the

[69] Quoted in Trower, *Senses of Vibration*, 87.

[70] This is also the Lacanian *objet a*, the void in the field of audible that structures subjectivity.

[71] Claude Maisonnat, "The Voice of Darkness," in *Conrad's Heart of Darkness and Contemporary Thought: Revisiting the Horror with Lacoue-Labarthe*, ed. Nidesh Lawtoo (London: Bloomsbury, 2012), 165.

[72] Conrad, *Heart of Darkness*, 69.

[73] Ibid., 58.

lives of others.[74] Leveraging the decades of technological advancement since the publication of Conrad's Marlow tales – mostly notably, wireless – Woolf infuses this novel with a fully immersive narrative logic that embeds the reader within its vibratory network. Connor explains that "[t]he telephone offers a quasi-controlled collapse of boundaries," but "the technology of the 'wireless' apparently [does] away even with this material mediation, as sound became the enacted form of electromagnetic fluctuation itself."[75] Although "suspicious of broadcast media" throughout her career, especially during World War II, when radio became a vehicle for fascist ideology and British propaganda, Woolf draws on radiotelephony as a model for a literary aesthetic in which the self can fully dissolve in the collective, reveling in the pain and pleasure of sensation as well as physical communion.[76]

Many early twentieth-century British intellectuals, particularly those in the Bloomsbury Group, were attracted to the medium of radio because of the opportunities it presented to shape the wider English culture. Todd Avery suggests that "the Bloomsbury writers saw radio as a potential partner in the advancement of a utopian internationalism grounded in the tenets of their ethical aestheticism."[77] Debra Rae Cohen and colleagues argue more broadly that the "writers and poets of the Modernist period … found their very sense of the artist's mission reshaped by the cultural project of radio."[78] Beyond its solidification of a British national and cultural consciousness, radio promised to reinvigorate Britain's literary and cultural tradition by introducing a revolutionary way of conceptualizing sound, space, and bodies.

Woolf herself gave three radio talks during her life – two in the late 1920s and one in 1937 – and her husband, Leonard Woolf, frequently delivered broadcast lectures in the 1930s and sporadically thereafter.[79] In addition, she was very interested in the new physics that contributed to the discovery and elaboration of notions of wireless sound reproduction. Arthur Eddington's *The Nature of the Physical World* (1928) and *Science*

[74] Virginia Woolf, *The Waves* (London: Hogarth Press, 1931).

[75] Steven Connor, "The Modern Auditory I," in *Rewriting the Self: Histories from the Middle Ages to the Present*, ed. Roy Porter (London: Routledge, 2002), 206, 208.

[76] David Trotter, "e-Modernism: Telephony in British Fiction," *Critical Quarterly* 51.5 (April 2009): 27: doi: 10.1111/j.1467-8705.2009.01843.x.

[77] Todd Avery, *Radio Modernism: Literature, Ethics, and the BBC, 1922–1938* (Farnham: Ashgate, 2006), 36.

[78] Debra Rae Cohen, Michael Coyle, and Jane Lewty, eds., *Broadcasting Modernism* (Gainesville: University Press of Florida, 2009), 3.

[79] Avery, *Radio Modernism*, 59–60.

and the Unseen (1929) were popular reading materials of the Bloomsbury Group, and Virginia Woolf was known to have read the work of physicist James Jeans while writing *Between the Acts*.[80] Such texts argued that all matter is traversed by electromagnetic waves, diminishing the distinction between self and other, mind and matter, and internal and external "realities." In *The Nature of the Physical* world, for example, Eddington contends that "all knowledge of our environment from which the world of physics is constructed, has entered in the form of messages transmitted along the nerves to the seat of consciousness.... We are acquainted with an external world because its fibers run into our consciousness; it is only our ends of the fibers that we actually know."[81] All sensory impressions thus reach the brain through broadcast signals, a notion that the discovery of radio waves in the late 1880s and the invention of radio communication at the turn of the twentieth century made manifest in the realm of audition. Beer explains that "[b]y the late 1920s ... waves in motion were – according to the new physics – all the universe consists in."[82] Particularly interested in broadcast technologies and the way they restructured language, Woolf often describes speech in her fiction using the rhetoric of wireless. In "Kew Gardens" (1919), a work that powerfully captures the modern soundscape, words are often depicted as raining down upon people from a single source, an image of radiotelephonic transmission also common in her first novel, *The Voyage Out* (1915). An elderly woman in "Kew Gardens" "look[s] through the pattern of falling words at the flowers ... letting the words fall over her, swaying the top part of her body slowly backwards and forwards."[83] As evident in Woolf's fiction, wireless created two contradictory experiences of sound: on the one hand, "invisible" waves that permeate all matter and create a diffusive, fluid soundscape; on the other hand, a very material transmission that can be seen and touched.

As in *Heart of Darkness* and *Lord Jim*, the diegetic space of *The Waves* is electrified, reverberating with vibrations that resound through the characters. The six characters tell their stories in a narrative mode that radiates more than it shows or tells: One perspective takes over from another,

80 Gillian Beer, "'Wireless': Popular Physics, Radio and Modernism," in *Cultural Babbage: Technology, Time and Invention*, ed. Francis Spufford and Jenny Uglow (London: Faber & Faber, 1997), 161.

81 Arthur Eddington, *The Nature of the Physical World* (Cambridge: Cambridge Scholars, 2014), 275–276.

82 Gillian Beer, "Physics, Sound, and Substance: Later Woolf," in *Virginia Woolf: The Common Ground: Essays by Gillian Beer* (Edinburgh: Edinburgh University Press, 1996), 115.

83 Virginia Woolf, "Kew Gardens," in *The Complete Shorter Fiction of Virginia Woolf*, 2nd ed., ed. Susan Dick (Orlando, FL: Harcourt, 1989), 93.

throbbing with emphasis before eventually dissipating into the boom of another voice. For instance, one of Neville's fragments concludes quietly with "I begin to wish for firelight, privacy, and the limbs of one person."[84] A new paragraph then opens with "'I begin to wish,' said Louis, 'for night to come.'"[85] The interruption of Louis's sentence after "I begin to wish" not only highlights the repetition; it also enhances the emphasis on the first part of the line. Louis himself acknowledges the pulsating nature of their story, saying, "We shall not always give out a sound like a beaten gong as one sensation strikes and then another."[86] Susan, too, recognizes the gong-like nature of their narration, saying of Bernard as she chimes in, "Now you trail away … making phrases."[87] The trailing off is not a complete cessation like that required by the telephonic relay in *Heart of Darkness*, where the vibrations constituting Kurtz's voice are transmitted to Marlow, relayed to the frame narrator, and then finally channeled to the reader. Instead, as Louis's statement indicates, the narration takes the form of electromagnetic waves. Bernard even describes his body as "trembling with strange oscillations and vibrations of sympathy," a statement that alludes to the oscillating currents, which propagate radio waves, as generative of the resonance that causes bodies to vibrate in unison.[88] This current courses through the characters, uniting them across the divide of space – and even, one might argue, time, as it binds them together with their deceased friend, Percival. Rhoda alludes to this motivating current when she presents a theory of life that mirrors its literary mode: "With intermittent shocks … life emerges heaving its dark crest from the sea. It is to this we are attached; it is to this we are bound."[89] Narrative transmission, figured as electromagnetic radiation, promises a story that does not conclude when the narrator stops speaking but persists in the air "after the last note ha[s] been struck."[90]

This narrative aesthetic invites the complete dissolution of bodily boundaries, both those separating characters and those separating readers and authors. Louis explains, "I am all fibre. All tremors shake me."[91] Bernard says of Susan, "[W]e melt into each other with phrases."[92] Jinny

84 Virginia Woolf, *The Waves* (New York: Harcourt, 1931), 52.
85 Ibid.
86 Ibid., 39.
87 Ibid., 18.
88 Ibid., 114.
89 Ibid., 64.
90 Conrad, *Youth*, 11.
91 Woolf, *Waves*, 12.
92 Ibid., 16.

adds, "[O]ur senses have widened. Membranes, webs of nerve that lay white and limp, have filled and spread themselves and float round us like filaments, making the air tangible and catching in them far-away sounds unheard before."[93] In this novel, the air is thick with vibrations that enable bodies to experience multidimensional sensations directly rather than as discrete sound or image. For example, Bernard references "words [that] beat a gong in the space which I have so laboriously cleared with half a dozen telephone messages and post cards, give off ring after ring of sound, booming, sonorous: and pictures rise."[94] The ringing of the telephone translates into the echoic nature of his speech, which generates both "tremendous and sonorous words" and visual impressions.[95] This ringing erupts through the "silent" page in moments as when Neville accuses Bernard of being "like a *dangling* wire, a broken bell-pull, always *twangling*."[96] Rather than merely recording or transmitting sound and image, Woolf's narration depends on the subaural event of vibration to transcend bodily limitations, as well as the supposed auditory restrictions of the graphic medium of literature.

While Woolf invites a complete surrender to the current, she acknowledges both the pain and pleasure that such a submission involves. Louis reflects on the satisfactory nature of having "fused [his] many lives into one" with the help of telephonic technologies.[97] While it allows him to reconcile his various selves into one identity, radiotelephony also necessitates a dissolution of the self, which involves its own sort of violence. Bernard describes how a "smoke ring issues from [his] lips ... and circles [a fellow train passenger], bringing him into contact. The human voice has a disarming quality – (we are not single, we are one)."[98] While Bernard ultimately finds pleasure in this, Neville comments on its unsettling nature: "Yet how painful to be recalled, to be mitigated, to have one's self adulterated, mixed up, become part of another."[99] The violence of union finds its ultimate figuration in the dissipation of all strands of narration into Bernard's voice, who continues, rather than replaces, their dialogue. He reflects: "I have been talking of Bernard, Neville, Jinny, Susan, Rhoda and Louis. Am I all of them? Am I one and distinct? I do not know."[100]

93 Ibid., 135.
94 Ibid., 210.
95 Ibid., 32.
96 Ibid., 19, emphasis mine.
97 Ibid., 168.
98 Ibid., 68.
99 Ibid., 83.
100 Ibid., 288.

Figuring the homogenization of frequencies required by resonance as a sort of death, Bernard looks for a medium beyond language to retain and communicate the truth of his life. Finally done with "making phrases," he turns to the voice drained of semantic content – "I need a howl; a cry" – and then to silence.[101] The truth of a life, he discovers, is in the motivating force before and beyond language – "the chain whirling round, round, in a steel-blue circle beneath" – the subaural physical force on the underside of language that constitutes and deconstructs subjectivity.[102] In *The Waves*, storytelling is understood as most penetrative when the narrator, rather than succumbing to the "wild music" and "false phrases" of realism, channels this undulating current as radiant energy that can be processed by the reader.[103]

4 Modern Literature as Connective Technology

With the invention of sound reproduction technologies in the nineteenth century, literature lost its monopoly on sound storage. Many studies that examine the relationship between literature and technology in this period take an agonistic approach, positioning literature in competition with other, "more modern" technologies. Julian Murphet, Mark Wollaeger, Trotter, and others have sought to treat the evolution of art and technology as more of a dialectic, whereby the model of influence becomes multidirectional rather than driven purely by scientific advancement.[104] While it is certainly true that technological innovation inspired new modes of literary experimentation, it is equally valuable to approach aesthetic and scientific advancements as intertwined and embedded within a larger system. Doing so directs attention toward the discourses that motivated both – shifting understandings of perception, including the need for sensory augmentation.

The development of narration from Conrad to Woolf can be productively located within a larger cultural system in which the discourses of vibration and radiation transformed how humans understood their place in the world as well as their relationship to themselves and each

101 Ibid., 69.
102 Ibid., 137.
103 Ibid., 295.
104 See Julian Murphet, *Multimedia Modernism: Literature and the Anglo-American Avant-Garde* (Cambridge: Cambridge University Press, 2009); Mark Wollaeger, *Modernism, Media, and Propaganda: British Narrative from 1900 to 1945* (Princeton: Princeton University Press, 2006); and Trotter, "Literature between Media," 386–389.

other. Contextualizing an emergent vibratory narrative aesthetic in this way reveals the modernist novel not as trying to allegorize or simulate electronic transmission, but rather as taking advantage of the principles already energizing it. The discovery of waves and rays and their technological manipulation revealed all matter – inorganic and organic – to be traversed by vibrations, enabling bodies to be enlarged beyond their material boundaries. As time and space are "annihilated" by connective and imaging technologies, collapsing divisions between the self and other, modernist authors explored the potential for a narrative mode that could more accurately represent the impressions of life while also inspiring a collective subjectivity. No longer beholden to the representation of reality, the novel could conceivably foster direct sensory experience, becoming a connective technology in its own right.

CHAPTER 17

The Bomb

Ann Larabee

By the mid-1980s, a severe decline in bachelor's degrees awarded in the humanities and a depressed job market (especially in literature and languages) alarmed the profession. At the worst moment of the perceived crisis, a solution was proposed: The humanities should find their mission in fighting the Bomb. In 1984, *Diacritics* – a "forum for rethinking the aims and methods of the humanities" – published its now famous issue on "nuclear criticism," including an essay by Jacques Derrida. The editors defined nuclear criticism as a twofold project: reading literary and critical works to uncover their "unconscious nuclear fears" and showing how an understanding of the workings of language could illuminate nuclear policy debates. It called on critical theory to make a "more important contribution to the public discussion of nuclear issues," examining the "psychology of the arms race," analyzing apocalyptic horror, and critiquing nuclear policy.[1] Derrida defended the role of an "incompetent humanities" – without expertise in state diplomacy or "nuclear techno-science" – to "concern ourselves seriously with the nuclear issue" by engaging with the arms race as discourse.[2]

By the early 1990s, nuclear criticism had fizzled out as a movement in literary studies, unable to achieve its ends of saving the humanities or ending nuclear weapons production. The stand nuclear critics took against "techno-science" proved problematic within the institutional realm, as the STEM fields (science, technology, engineering, and mathematics) ascended and interdisciplinary science, technology, and society studies (STS) became less overtly critical of technological systems – as represented in the work of Albert Borgmann, Jacques Ellul, and Langdon Winner – and more interested in social studies of knowledge. Derived from Martin

1 "Proposal for a *Diacritics* Colloquium on Nuclear Criticism," *Diacritics* 14.2 (1984): 2–3.

2 Jacques Derrida, "No Apocalypse, Not Now (Full Speed Ahead, Seven Missiles, Seven Missives)," *Diacritics* 14.2 (1984): 22.

Heidegger, the oft-used term "techno-science" was an attempt to describe scientific thought and practice and their use in technological development as a seamless, tacit system of destructive social power and dominance that required strong resistance. As used in nuclear criticism, the term was highly abstract and ill-defined, infused with deep suspicion, and oblivious – if not antagonistic – to the scientists next door. As the humanities have reached toward STEM in recent years with the rise, for example, of digital humanities, its traditional moral stance toward the scientific disciplines and technological development – predicated on distance – has eroded. Nevertheless, nuclear proliferation and nuclear war remain key issues of our time. The question now is whether new critical and creative forms might emerge that bring the humanities and the sciences together to address threats such as nuclear weapons development and deployment. The humanities can move away from their traditional role as antagonists of the sciences while still providing effective moral contemplation, judgment, and potential intervention across the old divides. For literary studies, that means getting beyond the highly specialized textual analysis advocated by nuclear criticism, which has had little effect in fulfilling its aims.

1 A Fabulously Textual Nuclear Criticism

The brief rise and precipitous fall of nuclear criticism is a cautionary tale for the humanities. The desire for a self-sustaining political and moral efficacy was undermined by a combination of self-defensiveness, wild speculation, and esoteric writing combined with didacticism and passionate overstatement. In 1990, *Papers on Language and Literature* (*PLL*) ran its own special issue on nuclear criticism, which set forth a full-throated defense of the humanities. Invoking Martin Luther's declaration defying Church and empire, "Here I stand, I can do no other," William Scheick's introduction described nuclear criticism as "a polymorphous ethical mode of critical inquiry" that could be applied "to the study of human cultural myths, structures, and artifacts."[3] Scheick suggested that the nuclear criticism's humanistic moral "stand" was a spiritual mission to generate "positive enlightenment," to confront death, and ultimately to transform and save humanity from its "negative, self-destructive impulses."[4] Nuclear critics would stand above and apart to create "the *nucleus* of a renewed or new ethical sensibility."

[3] William Scheick, "Nuclear Criticism: An Introduction," *Papers on Language and Literature* 26.1 (1990): 4.

[4] Ibid., 8.

As it emerged, nuclear criticism veered between long passages of dense poststructuralist jargon and brief, urgent invocations of "the total extinction of all life."[5] The most convoluted writing came with the apparent urgency of imagining "total annihilation," as in this passage on the "nuclear sublime": "The notion of the sublime is continuous with the notion of nuclear holocaust: to think the sublime would be to think the unthinkable and to exist in one's own nonexistence."[6] Military strategist Herman Kahn's infamous charge to the public to face up to the possibilities of a nuclear war – to "think the unthinkable" – haunted nuclear criticism, caught up with notions of both the overstated "unthinkable" and the unwritable. In his opening salvo to nuclear criticism, Derrida had raised the stakes, offering that literature as a written archive could be wiped out in a total nuclear war and therefore carried its complete annihilation within it. As part of that archive, nuclear planning was a "fabulously textual" realm that was always pondering its own end.[7] The obsessiveness of the question – whether total annihilation could be thought and written – intellectually froze the nuclear critics, offering little possibility, but spiraling ever further inward.[8]

The "total extinction of all life," along with the erasure of the written archive, became a metaphor for the extinction of the humanities, especially literary studies. In a manifesto excoriating humanities professors for ignoring the "nuclear predicament," Dan L. Zins explicitly related nuclear criticism to a revitalization of literary studies "in the doldrums" and suggested that the literary canon be "exploded" to confront the nuclear threat.[9] He quoted English professor Marion K. Richards's recollection of the Cuban Missile Crisis: "I was faced with the real possibility that I was teaching my last class, *everyone's* last class."[10] By 1990 when *PLL*'s issue appeared, humanities majors were enjoying a brief rebound, but a perceived crisis in the humanities disciplines remained. In 1988, the president of National Endowment for the Humanities under the George H. W. Bush administration, Lynn

5 Ibid., 5.

6 Frances Ferguson, "The Nuclear Sublime," *Diacritics* 14.2 (1984): 7.

7 Derrida, "No Apocalypse," 23.

8 Other literary scholars have noted the problem. Daniel Cordle writes that nuclear criticism was caught between two contradictory impulses in literary studies: to provide readers with moral improvement through studies of literature and to oppose value judgments and humanistic explanations (Cordle, "Cultures of Terror: Nuclear Criticism During and Since the Cold War," *Literature Compass* 3.6 [2006], 1191). Even as he offered an overview of nuclear criticism in 1993, K. K. Ruthven had already declared it in danger of becoming rarefied and obsolete (*Nuclear Criticism* [Melbourne: Melbourne University Press, 1993], vii).

9 Daniel L. Zins, "Exploding the Canon: Nuclear Criticism in the English Department," *Papers on Language and Literature* 26.1 (1990): 13.

10 Marion K. Richards, "The Examined Life of a Humanities Professor," *College Teaching* 36.4 (1988): 135.

Cheney, had, in a widely read report, relayed the news that students were choosing "vocational" paths, leading to an alarming decline in English, philosophy, and history majors over a twenty-year period.[11] "My last class" was on many humanities educators' minds as they observed the rapid ascendancy of vocational programs and the STEM fields, a different sort of end.

Refuting the argument by Cheney and others that the humanities save themselves by returning to canon and tradition, Zins sympathized with English educational expert Alan C. Purves, who remarked during the Vietnam War that the humanities – having become overly fascinated with "intellectual specialization" over moral values – should be destroyed and recreated with "a function of preserving the human race by any means necessary."[12] No less than all life itself was at stake in the teaching of "nuclear texts: plays, poems, novels, and short stories, to be sure, but also a wide variety of 'non-literary' nuclear texts."[13] Zins went so far as to repeatedly suggest that English teachers, by not taking up the subject, were as complicit in a banality of evil (in this case, a "nuclear Holocaust") as Berlin professors who had offered no resistance to the Nazis.[14]

Of the many problems with nuclear criticism, the greatest was this operatic hyperbole. In an escalating rhetoric, nuclear war became the end of civilization as we know it, the complete destruction of the written archive, of all humanity, of all life. These predictions went beyond scientifically modeled, worst-case scenarios of nuclear winter, in which biologists have long ruled out the possibility of human extinction.[15] But nuclear criticism's urgency frequently came to depend on imagining the worst of the worst. As Jacqueline R. Smetak wrote in a discussion of eschatological narratives, "We can [now], all by ourselves, bring about the end of the world and stop time forever."[16] What these nuclear critics failed to realize was how productive they were of an apocalyptic paralysis themselves.

[11] Lynn Cheney, *Humanities in America: A Report to the President, the Congress, and the American People* (Washington, DC: National Endowment for the Humanities, 1988), 11.

[12] Alan C. Purves, "Life, Death, and the Humanities," *College English* 31.6 (1970): 558, 564.

[13] Zins, "Exploding the Canon," 13.

[14] Ibid., 21.

[15] Alan Robock, "Nuclear Winter" *WIREs Climate Change* 1 (May–June, 2010): 424. Nuclear winter is the hypothesis – originating with the Union of Concerned Scientists – that a global thermonuclear war would throw up so much soot as to block out the sun and annihilate all life. In *Papers on Language and Literature*'s special issue, J. Fisher Solomon tried to ground the discussion of the complete destruction of all life – the "nuclear referent" – in the cautious acceptance of nuclear winter's probability. J. Fisher Solomon, "Probable Circumstances, Potential Worlds: History, Futurity, and the 'Nuclear Referent,'" *Papers on Language and Literature* 26.1 (1990): 71.

[16] Jacqueline Smetak, "'So Long Mom': The Politics of Nuclear Holocaust Fiction," *Papers on Language and Literature* 26.1 (1990): 46.

In his study of the post-Cold-War Los Alamos National Laboratory, anthropologist Joseph Masco observes that national attitudes about the nuclear project have veered between terror and banality, between overstimulation and psychic numbing, between fears of apocalypse and tacit acceptance of technological progress.[17] Both attitudes, he suggests, work in tandem, feeding on each other, making it impossible to adequately think through the everyday scientific, technical, economic, and social complexities of nuclear weapons production and national security. Even the discourses of vulnerability and insecurity that fuel antinuclear and environmental movements promote "a specific apocalyptic vision" that obscures "impacted everyday lives."[18] For Masco, the answer to the "unthinkable" is a turn to "everyday life": ethnographic study of particular bodies and voices in particular social spaces throughout the chain of nuclear production facilities.[19]

Masco critiques "public discourse about the bomb" as caught in a debilitating cultural imaginary that both produces terror and refuses to face technological dangers. Masco refers to Gertrude Stein's 1946 prose poem "Reflection on the Atomic Bomb," which begins, "They asked me what I thought about the atomic bomb. I said I had not been able to take any interest in it." In his criticism of Stein, Masco asserts that she inverts the usual "apocalypticism of the bomb not to mobilize for or against the nuclear complex but simply to banalize it."[20] The problem with such public discourse about nuclear war (including fiction) is that it is, indeed, caught in the unthinkable – caught between terror and banality – that freezes any useful response to nuclear weapons. Following Derrida's impossibility of thinking or writing past the final event, Masco agrees that in the realm of public discourse, this highly imaginative thinking about the nuclear weapons complex has been a form of denial. As an anthropologist, he counters that the consequences of nuclear technology can be better faced through observation of systems of production and decision-making that occur in the realm of everyday life. As it was practiced in the 1980s and 1990s, nuclear criticism circulated what Masco calls "the phantasmagoria, a spectral fascination that distracts attention from the ongoing daily machinations of

[17] Joseph Masco, *The Nuclear Borderlands: The Manhattan Project in Post-Cold War New Mexico* (Princeton: Princeton University Press, 2006), 14.

[18] Masco, *Nuclear Borderlands*, 4–5.

[19] Ibid., 11.

[20] Ibid., 13.

the U.S. nuclear complex."[21] Well-intentioned but unsuccessful efforts to revive nuclear criticism and extend it to environmental issues such as global warming have perpetuated the negotiation between this spectral fascination with nuclear war and other species-threatening disasters and the highly technical expositions of poststructuralist literary criticism.[22] Because of their high degree of abstraction, both of these modes contribute to what Masco calls the Bomb's "incomprehensibility" in the "cultural imaginary."[23] Nuclear criticism's avowed political purpose to end, or at least manage, human-made risks flounders in these shoals. However, in his promotion of an ethnographic approach as a better way to understand everyday life in and around the nuclear complex, Masco's assessment of a cultural imaginary driven by "anesthetic comfort" forestalls the possibility of imaginative transformation.[24] The question remains as to whether the humanities might also offer a way of thinking that escapes the tendency of public discourse to fall into apocalyptic cliché.

In his contribution to the two cultures problem (the oft-debated historic divide between the sciences and the humanities), the sociobiologist Edward O. Wilson takes up the moral conundrum of nuclear weapons, arguing that the solution lies in both the sciences and the humanities: "Science owns the warrant to explore everything deemed factual and possible, but the humanities, borne aloft by both fact and fantasy, have the power of everything not only possible but also conceivable."[25] Calling for a "third Enlightenment," Wilson argues that the humanities must expand beyond their anthropocentrism and recognize their relationship with the sciences as "a single continuum of creative thought."[26] As the traditional seat of moral contemplation, the humanities have had a seemingly obvious claim to deliberation on technological developments such as nuclear weapons, but have also been hampered by this perceived distinctiveness. Nuclear criticism set itself up as a corrective opposition to "techno-science" – a world it did not attempt to understand – rather than fully facing the extent to which the humanities are a part of that "single continuum of creative thought."

Limited by his own immersion in the sciences, Wilson has an ill-defined idea about the range and depth of creativity in the humanities

[21] Ibid., 14.
[22] Dan Cordle, "Cultures of Terror: Nuclear Criticism During and Since the Cold War," *Literature Compass* 3.6 (2006): 1186–1199.
[23] Masco, *Nuclear Borderlands*, 2.
[24] Ibid., 14.
[25] Edward O. Wilson, *The Origins of Creativity* (New York: Liveright, 2017), 70.
[26] Ibid., 80.

and the arts, reducing music, for example, to the invocation of emotional responses and art criticism to "deep intuitive wisdom."[27] He argues that it's up to the humanities to leave behind their alleged limitations and create a road to the sciences by forming alliances with paleontology, anthropology, evolutionary biology, psychology, and neurobiology. However, rather than representing the humanities as the intellectually impoverished handmaidens to the wealthy sciences, we can reconceive them as a richly imaginative and intellectual terrain where the sciences can also reconceive projects that have profound human impacts. Reconceiving the relationship between the sciences and the humanities as a "single continuum of creative thought" is a worthy and demanding challenge with great intellectual and life-enhancing benefits.

2 The Nuclear Project's Soundworld

Caught on the seesaw of banality and apocalypticism, and setting itself up as a didactic critic of an abstracted "techno-science," nuclear criticism was unable to imagine such a terrain. That vision, however, can be found in an unexpected place: contemporary musical works that take the nuclear complex as their subject, combining literary and historical narrative, archival documents and sounds, and live performance. These works offer an answer to Wilson's charge that the humanities are unknowingly caught within an anthropocentric "audiovisual bubble."[28] Instead, they meditate on the soundworld, especially the perceptible and imperceptible technological soundworld that emanates from and shapes modern human (including scientific) endeavors, including endeavors with highly destructive real and potential consequences.

Since the Second Industrial Revolution, many musical compositions have consciously and unconsciously reflected the audio transformation of the world, including the sounds – real and imagined – of science and its instrumentation. For example, Edgard Varèse's *Ionisation*, first performed in 1933, creates an audio metaphor for the collision of particles within a star. Of all the arts, music is most partnered to scientific understanding: through the biological effects of music on the body, the physics of sound, and the mathematics of composition. Composer John Adams has written that "music is organized sound, and sound is, after all, nothing more than molecules banging against one another in the

[27] Ibid., 83.
[28] Ibid., 53.

atmosphere."[29] But he has also critiqued the early European avant-garde composers for treating musical pitches as "mere data … made to obey arbitrary laws of combinatoriality, models of mathematical perfection, expressive of nothing except their own interrelationships."[30] Musical composition that sees itself as mathematical modeling is, for Adams, too far from humanistic concerns with meaning-making, and his own often controversial operatic works combine arts and humanities – music and history, creative expression and critical analysis – as a collective reflection on culture, very broadly conceived.

Musical works of the twentieth century combined scientific fascination with an effort to capture the discordance, atonality, thrumming, harshness, and percussive hammerings of the modern instrumental soundworld, including the sounds of war and devastation. Though inspired by physics, Varèse's *Ionisation* is no mere data: An urgent, relentless siren blares through a clattering timbre of the sound particles, invoking the familiar twentieth-century sound of attack and emergency. Ross Lee Finney based his 1962 choral work *Still Are New Worlds* on what he called a "principle of complementarity" derived from physics, a theory introduced by physicist Niels Bohr and embraced by the Manhattan Project director Robert Oppenheimer.[31] Finney's work ended with a loud combination of orchestra and recorded sound in, as one reviewer put it, a *fortississimo* portrayal of "total nuclear destruction," accompanied by these lines from Milton: "He … with ambitious aim … the Almighty Power / Hurled headlong flaming from the ethereal sky / With hideous ruin and combustion, down / To bottomless perdition."[32] These compositions don't preach to the audience or demand analysis to uncover secret designs, but rather explore how psychologically, physically, intellectually, and socially embedded we are in a technologically mediated, multisensory lifeworld that produces unprecedented weapons by design.[33] Human experience in such a world stretches across poetry, physics, and music.

While these works archived and artistically transformed the abrasive and often brutal sounds of the twentieth century, more recent works have expanded this project to incorporate the visual archive. Composed between

[29] John Adams, "John Adams on Steve Reich" 1997: www.stevereich.com/articles/John_Adams.html (accessed October 9, 2018).

[30] Ibid.

[31] Paul Cooper, "The Music of Ross Lee Finney," *Musical Quarterly* 53.1 (1967): 2; Ray Monk, *Robert Oppenheimer: A Life Inside the Center* (New York: Anchor, 2012), 141–142.

[32] Wayne C. Hobbs, "Review of *Still Are New Worlds, for Speaking Voice, Mixed Voices, and Orchestra*," *Notes* 25 (1968): 336.

[33] For the concept of the technologically mediated lifeworld, see Don Ihde's post-phenomenological explanation in *Technology and the Lifeworld: From Garden to Earth* (Bloomington: Indiana

1998 and 2002, Steve Reich and Beryl Korot's video opera *Three Tales* engages its audience in a contemplation of three controversial scientific projects, combining choral work, storytelling, and historical documentary. *Three Tales* uses Reich's characteristic minimalist sound, combining looped recorded and live voice with archival photographs and videos, one showing a scientist working out a topography of blast waves. One of the "tales" is the nuclear testing in the Bikini Atoll which weaves together the recorded voices of naval officers and radio announcers, text fragments from Genesis, and a chorus of three tenors witnessing a "gigantic, a gigantic shimmering mushroom ever changing, ever changing its form and color, ever changing."[34] The composition features a visual and aural countdown (including chimes) in an ever-unresolved, phased repetition, accompanied by video of a ticking metronome, revealing the implications of musical rhythm for scientific and technological endeavors, including the most destructive. The audience is immersed in a somber meditation on these endeavors through the combination of instrumentation; synthetic sound; documentary; manipulated visual and audio perceptions of time and space; and human poetic, religious, scientific, and journalistic voices. The nuclear bomb is not just a phantasm in an apocalyptic cultural imaginary and not just a product of a research complex, but a broad, complex recorded experience of an "expanding technological environment."[35] Reich and Korot have said that they avoided showing images of atomic mushroom clouds to avoid "bombast," thus providing ethical reflection while escaping nuclear criticism's apocalypticism.[36] Nevertheless, the evolutionary biologist Richard Dawkins publicly objected to his representation in the piece: a repeated, roboticized clip of him saying that "We, and all other animals, are machines created by our genes." An atheist, Dawkins also rejected the religious overtones of the work, as evidenced in the display of lines from Genesis, and suggested that Reich was unintelligent.[37] *Three Tales*'s obvious criticisms of science and scientists, obtained through editing of interview footage, may have undermined a wider reach.

University Press, 1990). Ihde writes specifically of the scientific and technological transformation of our soundworld in *Listening and Voice: Phenomenologies of Sound* (Albany: State University of New York Press, 2007) and *Acoustic Technics* (New York: Lexington, 2016).

34 Steve Reich and Beryl Korot, *Three Tales* Libretto, Steve Reich website: www.stevereich.com/threetales_info.html (accessed 30 September 2019).

35 Ibid.

36 Quoted in Peter Culshaw, "How Everything Changed," *Telegraph,* September 17, 2002: www.telegraph.co.uk/culture/art/3582800/How-everything-changed.html (accessed September 30, 2019).

37 Adam Shatz, "A Fighting Man's (and Woman's) Work," *New York Times*, October 13, 2002: www.nytimes.com/2002/10/13/arts/music-a-fighting-man-s-and-woman-s-work.html (accessed December 28, 2019).

A more successful effort at reaching the scientific community has been John Adams's and librettist and director Peter Sellars's opera *Doctor Atomic*, which also provides a meditation on nuclear weapons without falling into the apocalyptic or the banal. Like *Three Tales,* it composes the complex multimodal world from which nuclear weapons arose. Whereas *Three Tales* contains an overt criticism of scientists, *Dr. Atomic* tells the operatic story of a very well-known scientist, J. Robert Oppenheimer, in a momentous event, the Trinity test of the first atomic bomb, engaging history and biography, poetry and drama, music, science, religion, and cosmology in a complex, resonant soundworld. A work of both musical composition and historical scholarship, *Doctor Atomic* may be described as a work of socially engaged, creative nuclear criticism. Audiences bear witness to the Trinity Test while immersed in its soundworld and while participating in a meditation on a cosmology that provides a foundation for the nuclear project. *Doctor Atomic* offers a sustained ethical reflection on that project, showing how the bombast of apocalypticism can give way to the quietude of compassion.

Doctor Atomic has been somewhat loosely described as a *Gesamtkunstwork*, the ideally comprehensive art form, derived from German aesthetics and associated with Richard Wagner. As one critic wrote of its 2005 San Francisco Opera (SFO) world premiere, "[It is] a true Gesamtkunstwerk, a mostly superb marriage of music, text, production, melding elements of history, philosophy, politics, poetry, mass- and individual-psychology, fear, and hope – against hope."[38] To that list, one could add science. Heavy with the thrills and anxieties of scientific discovery, the opera takes place in a laboratory, features scientists and technicians, and transcribes historical documents that include scientific papers on nuclear physics. All of these are transformed by the soundworld. The single continuum of creative thought might here be described as a sonic web transmitting across a wide range of motion, activity, understanding, and expression.

The key figure of *Doctor Atomic* is Oppenheimer, head of the Manhattan Project, whose iconic presence in a vast body of literary and journalistic works serves as a touchstone for understanding and negotiating the nuclear age.[39] Of great interest to scientists who admire his brilliance, Oppenheimer's biographies often describe him as an expansive intellect, crossing the sciences and the humanities: a physicist who read literary

[38] Janos Gereben, "John Adams' *Doctor Atomic* at San Francisco Opera," David Gregson's Opera West: www.operawest.com/2004/08/ (accessed May 10, 2022).

[39] Lindsey Banco, *The Meanings of J. Robert Oppenheimer* (Iowa City: Iowa University Press, 2016), 2.

works in several languages. In popular accounts, his interest in poetry is often aligned with moral meditations on the consequences of nuclear weapons. In an interview with *Physics Today*, composer Adams explained that because Oppenheimer was "relatively cultured" he stood out from the "technocrats," a theme important to Adams, who seeks to transcend the abstract, technocratic modernism of much twentieth-century musical composing.[40] As the head of the Institute for Advanced Study at Princeton after the war, Oppenheimer himself was interested in the creative continuum, providing community and research support for physicists, mathematicians, philosophers, psychologists, literary critics, economists, historians, artists, archaeologists, and writers (including T. S. Eliot). Oppenheimer's ambitious effort at "a multidisciplinary understanding of the whole human condition" is apparent in *Doctor Atomic*.[41] The opera interweaves the humanities (history, music, art, dance, poetry, religion) and the sciences (nuclear physics, the physics of sound, scientific method) into a spectacle of an expansive but bounded and blind collective consciousness.

As a collective marking of time and remembrance and judgment of the past, history is central to *Doctor Atomic*'s recreation of the Manhattan Project. The libretto incorporates historical and literary texts: meeting minutes, government documents, scientific papers, memoirs, and poetry. Librettist Sellars operated like a scholar, combing through archival texts, clipping quotations, and reassembling them. With a historian's enthusiasm, he focused on declassified documents such as physicist Leo Szilárd's petition, signed by seventy Manhattan Project scientists, urging President Harry S. Truman to warn Japan of an impending nuclear strike and allow it to surrender. Sellars also included Oppenheimer's words from a declassified June 1945 science committee report: "We cannot give the Japanese any warning.... We should seek to make to a profound psychological impression on as many inhabitants as possible."[42] Once "quietly discarded," Sellars said, these documents are "now set for singers and orchestra for all the world to hear."[43] If historiography provides one kind of glue for reassembling snipped archival materials, opera provides another, repositioning texts in an audiovisual world with its own embodied, aesthetic, and intellectual modes of feeling and understanding.

40 Mark Wilson, "Doctor Atomic to Premier in San Francisco," *Physics Today*, September 1, 2005: 29.

41 Kai Bird and Martin J. Sherwin, *American Prometheus* (New York: Vintage, 2005): 377.

42 Scientific Panel of the Interim Committee on Nuclear Power to G. L. Harrison, "Recommendations on Future Policy," June 16, 1945: http://blog.nuclearsecrecy.com/wp-content/uploads/2015/03/1945-06-16-Scientific-Panel-of-Interim-Committee-recommendations.pdf (accessed October 9, 2018).

43 Mark Swed, "Explosively Original," *Los Angeles Times*, September 11, 2005, E64.

Capturing the voices of Manhattan Project scientists involved more than physics and governmental policy. Like many of his colleagues, Oppenheimer's interests extended beyond purely scientific pursuits. Sellars creates the multidisciplinary mind and world by extensively incorporating poetry, from the traditional "Cloud Flower Lullaby" sung by Robert and Kitty Oppenheimer's Tewa nursemaid, Pasqualita, to John Donne's "Batter my heart, three-person'd God," one of Robert Oppenheimer's favorite poems. Heightening emotional tension, the poetry's dream-like, even hallucinatory presence in the arias swells from the more prosaic conversations among the scientists and military strategists making decisions about experimental design and test times. The physics, too, is sung in choral verse, offering a creative continuum of human expression from science to poetry. As the chorus intones:

> We believed that
> "Energy can be neither
> created nor destroyed
> but only altered in form."
> But now we know that
> energy may become matter,
> and now we know that
> matter may become energy
> and thus be altered in form.

The libretto of Kitty Oppenheimer comprises Muriel Rukeyser's verse, which blended poetry and physics. A childhood schoolmate of Oppenheimer's brother, Rukeyser worked in the Graphics Department of the Office of War Information creating World War II propaganda posters. In 1942, aspiring to a conceptual system for poetry inspired by scientific ideas, she wrote a biography of physicist Willard Gibbs, who made major contributions to the study of thermodynamics. As Peter Middleton has explained, Rukeyser was inspired by Gibbs's notion of "phase space": a mathematical structure for ideally representing the phases or states of molecules enclosed in gas. Rukeyser applied this to interrelationships, transliterations, and changing conditions of elements in a poem, seen as a closed system.[44]

Called "the best poet of her exact generation" by Kenneth Rexroth, Rukeyser was as embedded in the swirling ideas of her time as Oppenheimer was, coming from an intellectual milieu that encouraged an ecumenical interest in the sciences and the humanities for creative thought. Rukeyser

[44] Peter Middleton, *Physics Envy: American Poetry and Science in the Cold War and After* (Chicago: University of Chicago Press, 2015), 137–138.

was known for her documentary voice, grounded in witnessing and imaging, a voice fitting to *Doctor Atomic*'s confrontation with – and creative transformation of – history. For example, on the evening before the first plutonium bomb explodes on the Jornado del Muerto desert, Kitty sings Rukeyser's *Easter Eve 1945*, as if to herself, "Now I say that the peace the spirit needs is / not lack of war, but fierce continual flame." Temporally poised a few months before the atomic bombing of Hiroshima and Nagasaki, this ambiguous verse offers a troubled and troubling state of national consciousness that may harbor the destructive flames of war and conflict, or ideological passions, or the peace flame.

Poetry doesn't save anyone onstage from participation in this conflicted consciousness: It is part of the weave and warp of a complex worldview concentrated in the microcosm of Los Alamos. After discussions of the device's potential defects and unintended consequences, targets in Japan, bad weather reports, Leslie Grove's struggle with his diet, and moral dissent among the scientists, Oppenheimer sings John Donne's Holy Sonnet 14, "Batter my heart, three-person'd God." Oppenheimer was famously known for having mentioned this sonnet as inspiration for naming the Trinity Test. Nuclear critics, especially those in religious studies, have made much of Oppenheimer's attraction to this work, offering that it reflected various personal pathologies: his need for consolation after personal tragedy, the overcoming of his fear and doubt, his desire for external authority, his obedience to duty, his placing of the bomb in Christian eschatology, his death wish and creation of a death cult.[45] Donne scholars have seen Oppenheimer as engaging deeply with the poet: Donne biographer John Stubbs writes, "The God of [Holy Sonnet 14], to whom we can only turn to be battered by atrocities of conscience, may be the only realistic deity to have survived the snows of fallout in Japan."[46] A Christian poet, Donne was another sweeping intellect, interested in alchemy and cosmology. In his public speeches, Oppenheimer was fond of quoting from Donne's *An Anatomy of a World,* which reflected on the Copernican revolution: "'Tis all in pieces, all coherence gone; all just supply, and all relation."[47]

[45] See, for example, Bird and Sherwin, *American Prometheus,* 11; Susan B. Thistlethwaite, "God and Her Survival in a Nuclear Age," in *Shuddering Dawn: Religious Studies and the Nuclear Age,* ed. Ira Chernus and Edward Tabor Linenthal (Albany: State University of New York Press, 1989), 140; James A. Aho, "'I am Death … Who Shatters Worlds': The Emerging Nuclear Death Cult," in *Shuddering Dawn,* 55; Darrell Fasching, *The Ethical Challenge of Auschwitz and Hiroshima: Apocalypse or Utopia?* (Albany: State University of New York Press, 1993), 101–102.

[46] John Stubbs, *John Donne: The Reformed Soul* (New York: Norton, 2006), 477.

[47] See, for example, Robert J. Oppenheimer, "To Live with Ourselves," in *Uncommon Sense,* ed. N. Metropolis, Gian-Carlo Rota, and David Sharp (Boston: Birkhäuser, 1984), 178.

The Donne aria is an antique lament marked by a familiar descending tetrachord, a form used as an operatic climax with high emotional intensity, traditionally expressing the central character's desperate negotiation with fate.[48] The most well-known baritone to perform *Doctor Atomic*'s Oppenheimer, Gerald Finley, under Sellars's direction, embodies Donne's words by gazing up, slamming his fist to his chest with "batter my heart," and falling to his knees with "shine and seek to mend." The exaggerated embodiment of the words is accompanied by a rising and falling orchestra with irregular timpani: the sound and feel of a stressed heart. At the end, ringing bells suggest a sacrament, a repeated ritual marked by expected sound. The amplified words are ultimately impersonal, a recitation – an automatic repetition – of a remote seventeenth-century poem in the clichéd operatic lament. The aria suggests that the wholly familiar pathways of artistic expression – caught in the eschatological and the clichéd – can't accommodate the moment: the decision to go forward with the final test of the most fearsome weapon ever devised. Physics, military strategy, familial relationships, news reporting, history, and poetry are all part of that project.

Offering a wide range of human intellect, these collected, amplified voices of the Manhattan Project are woven through a web of instrumental music that offers the sounds of physics and engineering, of twentieth-century science and science fiction. In the opera's prelude, Adams digitally splices together recorded archival sounds of power tools and humming engines, which gives the impression of a particle accelerator's sound. The result is uncanny, moving between the workshop and laboratory, the physical and mental labors of war. This opening sequence also includes a plane taking off and a skipping recording of Jo Stafford's nostalgic "The Things We Did Last Summer," interrupted by clarion from the orchestra's brass section, pounding the human voice momentarily into silence. As Alice Cotter points out in her study of Adams's compositional methods, the music borrows from Igor Stravinsky's *Symphony in Three Movements*, which Stravinsky later said was inspired by war documentaries and newsreels that featured goose-stepping soldiers marching to the "grotesque" sound of military bands.[49] Adam's music also has roots in musical Minimalism, which he sees as a "response to the precise, regular, periodic behavior of

[48] Ellen Rosand, *Opera in Seventeenth-Century Venice: The Creation of a Genre* (Berkeley: University of California Press, 1991), 361–386.

[49] Alice Miller Cotter, "Sketches of Grief: Genesis, Compositional Practice, and Revision in the Operas of John Adams," (PhD dissertation: Princeton University, 2016), 332.

machines, and particularly of electronic machines."[50] Those technological sounds, completely new in human experience, grew ever louder through the twentieth century. In its ambition to capture a precise world, *Doctor Atomic* heightens attention to its white noise, the uncanny background of modern life, and to the unheard musical rhythms of atoms and clocks.

This soundworld not only shapes our emotional responses to science and technology, but also carries deeply embedded rhythms, a sense of time that allows the invention, building, and testing of the device. Accompanied by harp, celesta, antique cymbal, and glockenspiel, an otherworldly chorus sings the description of a plutonium core, transcribed almost directly from Richard Rhodes's annotation to *The Los Alamos Primer*, physicist Robert Serber's series of lectures inaugurating the Manhattan Project:

> We surround the plutonium core
> from thirty two points
> spaced equally around its surface,
> the thirty-two points representing the centers of the
> twenty triangular faces
> of an icosahedron
> interwoven with the
> twelve pentagonal faces
> of a dodecahedron.[51]

The shimmering sound is familiar to science fiction fans as heralding the mysteries – such as previously unknown forces or beings – revealed by advanced technologies. Throughout the opera, including in this passage, a subtle presence of ticking clocks, with bells marking time, weaves through the sound. The subdued presence of the glockenspiel invokes the intricate mechanical clock in the town square that performs an animatronic "bells play" (the English translation of *glockenspiel*). *Doctor Atomic* is, in a sense, a bells play: a mechanism for a technological age, ringing the time of collective memory.

As musicologist Yayoi Everett has observed in her study of *Doctor Atomic*'s "temporal flow," the historical time of the Trinity test is juxtaposed with the timelessness of poetry and the audience's psychological time that dilates and constricts through the musical experience. The second act is especially notorious for its languorous pace, as the play ineffably slows

[50] John Adams, *Hallelujah Junction: Composing an American Life* (New York: Farrar, Strauss, and Giroux, 2009), E-book, 200.

[51] Robert Serber, *Los Alamos Primer: The First Lectures on How to Build an Atomic Bomb*, ed. Richard Rhodes (Berkeley: University of California Press, 1992), xvii.

and stretches out when, according to the expected Aristotelian dramatic structure, the action should be briskly rising toward the climax. Sellars has pointed to the influence of the *Bulletin of the Atomic Scientists'* Doomsday Clock, always poised at minutes before nuclear midnight, but never yet arriving, time always dilating beyond the Newtonian absolute time.[52] The opera's last scene extends a two-minute countdown for the Trinity explosion to more than six musical minutes and catapults out of the Aristotelian unities through space-time, as the atomic bomb on the New Mexican desert merges with the one at Hiroshima. The music's imaginative manipulations of time and space are traces of the physicist's mathematically observed, abstracted, and counterintuitive understandings of space-time. But because the opera is a finite spectacle, its cosmology is bounded by beginning and end, a mechanism and myth to be contemplated.

The end of *Doctor Atomic* is an elongated countdown to the atomic bomb explosion, incorporating *musique concrète* that echoes the prelude: crying voices, an intruder alarm, humming machines. It culminates in twenty timepieces, each played by different instruments – brass, woodwinds, strings, percussion, and voice – each marking an independent count. To play with clock time against stage time and historical time, Adams composed this sequence on a MIDI platform.[53] The stage fate of the atomic bomb blast – which everyone knows will come – is represented musically rather than visually with a discordant loudspeaker blast of live and recorded sound, including baby screams and agitated wordless choral music. *Doctor Atomic* is a self-destructing opera, demolishing its own device.

Through this sound comes harp, celesta, and tuned gongs sounding like a tolling bell, reminiscent, as Mathieu Duplay writes, of the Hiroshima Peace Bell.[54] Adams describes this sound as "a light shower of clock fragments."[55] The opera goes quiet, with only the bell and a woman's voice speaking in polite Japanese: "Please, water." The words are taken from journalist John Hersey's profoundly moving, bestselling *Hiroshima,* an account of the atomic bomb's immediate aftermath, based on interviews with survivors.[56] This popular work, more than any other, opened Americans' eyes to the unbearable, deeply identifiable human suffering of the bombing, partly represented in desperate thirst. Adams and Sellars

52 Alex Ross, "Countdown," *New Yorker*, October 3, 2005: www.newyorker.com/magazine/2005/10/03/countdown-4 (accessed October 25, 2018).

53 Cotter, "Sketches of Grief," 350–351.

54 See Mathieu Duplay, "Événement et trauma dans *Doctor Atomic* de John Adams," *Transatlantica* 2 (2010), n.p.

55 Adams, *Hallelujah Junction*, 291.

56 John Hersey, *Hiroshima* (New York: Bantam, 1948).

had meant for the culmination to generate a revelation. As the entire cast gazes out at the audience, Adams has suggested, "The audience gradually realizes that they themselves are the bomb."[57] The audience is fully implicated in the world generated onstage: in its apprehension of the various strands of human thought and experience and in its response to the rhythms and tones that tie these together. The final Japanese spoken word breaks through this world of a mesmerized involvement in Oppenheimer's world, obsessed with intellectual achievement and grand revelation.

Peter Sellars often uses the word "cosmology" and "cosmic design" to describe opera, a "whole galaxy" and "total experience" of music, poetry, dance, and visual art.[58] Earlier in his career, he told *Opera News*, "Each time one goes to direct an opera, one has literally to set up cosmology, set up an existential level – where are these people, where are their lives placed in the context of human and divine existence? What is space, and what is time?"[59] For Sellars, this cosmology comprises "layers of reality" from the individual to the spiritual and suggests both scientific and religious understandings of the universe.[60] Sellars, through cosmology, and Adams, through myth, take an anthropological approach to opera, constructing the world of a specific group – in this case scientists in an intellectual, religious, political, institutional, technological, social, cultural, and sensual milieu – across these many dimensions. Masco's call for a sociological look at the everyday world of the nuclear complex is fulfilled and expanded through this creative understanding. To show that cosmology and myth are bounded and limited, they hint at other cosmologies and myths. In *Doctor Atomic*, these are presented through a Tewa dance onstage and a neon-lit, writhing, thundering chorus of the Bhagavad Gita. Twenty years after the Trinity Test, Oppenheimer, who read Sanskrit, claimed to have been thinking at the time of a passage from this Hindu scripture: "I am become Death, the destroyer of worlds."[61] Inspired by Donne's shattered and shattering vision, Oppenheimer's cosmology is an intellectual fusion generating affective intensities, ending in a massive detonation.

In 2018, Sellars directed a revival of *Doctor Atomic* at the Santa Fe Opera semiopen theater, overlooking the birthplace of the atomic bomb, Los Alamos, where scientists, engineers, and technicians still work in

57 Adams, *Hallelujah Junction*, 291.
58 PBS, Interview with Peter Sellars, The Question of God: Other Voices, 2004: www.pbs.org/wgbh/questionofgod/voices/sellars.html (accessed October 17, 2018).
59 Quoted in Thor Eckert, Jr., "Taking Issue," *Opera News*, July 1985: https://operanews.com/Opera_News_Magazine/2016/37__Taking_Issue.html (accessed May 11, 2002).
60 PBS, Interview.
61 Quoted in Bird and Sherwin, *American Prometheus*, 309.

laboratories that help update the US nuclear arsenal. The director could reasonably expect that these personnel might attend the opera, both as a cultural event and as an intervention in local perceptions of daily work, community concerns, and regional contributions to national history. As Cheryl Rofer, a retired chemist from Los Alamo National Laboratory, put it in her review in *Physics Today*, "Myths are stories we tell ourselves to learn about who we are. This myth has come back to its origin, the *sipapu* from which nuclear weapons emerged."[62] Rofer borrowed the Hopi word for a small hole in the floor of a Pueblo Indian *kiva*, near the fire pit, believed to be a link to an underworld region from which the tribal ancestors emerged. Rofer put the opera in the context of ongoing impacts of nuclear development, such as the continued proliferation of nuclear weapons and the lasting health impacts of radiation, hoping that it would "further the process of healing" through the community gathering at the historical source.[63] To emphasize the opera's goal of having the audience reflect on the ongoing consequences of their nuclear activities, a giant mirrored orb hung on the stage, like an alien object familiar in science fiction, in which the cast and the audience could see themselves. Sellars also invited area residents who had lived close to the Trinity explosion to perform, standing silently as witnesses to the end. These "downwinders" from the Tularosa Basin were in the process of petitioning the US Department of Justice for compensation for radiation exposure. Before the opera, members of the Santa Clara, San Ildefonso, and Tesuque Pueblos, representing a different cosmology, performed a ceremony of healing and cleansing. Onstage during the opera, Sellars writes, their "ritual prayer for moisture and the continuity of all life joined the ceremony of opera where communities come together to address larger questions of the future."[64] *Doctor Atomic*'s partial transformation into community-based theater further decentered its potential apocalypticism and acknowledged the limitations of its cosmology.

3 The Continuum of Moral Contemplation

The nuclear critics had an explicit goal of eradicating nuclear weapons through a moral critique from the humanities, held distant from the sciences. But as Sellars told *The Bulletin of the Atomic Scientists*, scientists "have a very

[62] Cheryl Rofer, "*Doctor Atomic* Is as Relevant as Ever," *Physics Today*, August 7, 2018: https://physicstoday.scitation.org/do/10.1063/PT.6.3.20180807a/full/ (accessed October 18, 2018).
[63] Ibid.
[64] Peter Sellars, Letter to Santa Fe Opera patrons, September 17, 2018.

refined moral sensibility" and "deep moral awareness" that must be brought to bear on such questions.[65] While *Doctor Atomic*'s initial reception, in 2005, was mixed among operagoers – mostly because of its dense, cryptic libretto – it has been well received by scientists and science historians and educators. It has been reviewed and discussed in *Physics Today*, *Nature*, *The Bulletin of the Atomic Scientists*, *Popular Mechanics*, and *Wired*. *Doctor Atomic*'s promoters and directors have worked with science and technology museums to host related exhibits on the Manhattan Project and have used scientists as commentators and consultants. During the San Francisco premier, the Exploratorium – the city's science museum, founded by Oppenheimer's brother – hosted an online exhibit, providing annotations of the libretto. Dedicated to preserving the Manhattan Project's history, the American Heritage Society's webpage provides a synopsis and discussion of the opera because it "does the important work of engaging with and inviting moral contemplation of history of the atomic bomb."[66] If human thought, for E. O. Wilson, is a creative continuum across the traditional disciplines, it also carries with it the opportunity for moral reflection across those disciplines.

As with the ongoing crisis in the humanities, *Doctor Atomic* appeared, as Robert Fink has written, in "the gathering gloom of what seems more and more like the extended twilight of Western art music."[67] A revitalization of these spheres depends, in part, on the recognition of the continuum of creative thought and moral contemplation in our technology-driven world. Offering inventive possibility, ambitious multimedia forms such as contemporary opera – with its great capacity to create complex sensual, human-made worlds with intellectual and emotional depth – can show the importance of the humanities and the arts to our understanding of scientific and technological projects. By revealing the continuum of thought and avoiding didacticism, apocalypticism, and quick judgment of entire fields of human endeavor, the humanities and the arts may encourage reflection on the whole – on what Sellars calls the "cosmology." Here, bringing intellect and emotion to bear, we can find the time and space to consider the creative possibilities and destructive consequences of technological development, without furthering false divisions that paralyze us.

65 John Rezek, Interview with Peter Sellars, *Bulletin of the Atomic Scientists* 64.1 (2008): 12.

66 Atomic Heritage Foundation, "*Dr. Atomic*," Manhattan Project Legacy, June 20, 2018: www.atomicheritage.org/history/doctor-atomic (accessed May 11, 2022).

67 Robert Fink, "After the Canon," *The Oxford Handbook of Opera* (New York: Oxford University Press, 2022), 1068.

CHAPTER 18

Networks

David Ciccoricco

1 Picture Worth a Thousand Nodes

Picture a network. In one sense, the task is impossible; networks are abstractions that serve to represent or visualize a dataset, without which there is no picture. If we accept that we are picturing a picture, then our network may take many forms. Adopting the language of graph theory, which underpins the logic behind network science, *nodes* might be anything from people to computers, economies, airports, or terrorist cells. Our *links* (or *edges*) might be social relations and connections, computer cables and electromagnetic waves, trade routes and flight paths, or encrypted emails and cell phone conversations. Networks are equally subterranean and atmospheric, suffusing the skies by way of planes, drones, satellites, and waves, just as they burrow the ground by way of transportation tunnels or communication fiber optics. The very process of imagining a network inevitably draws on a network, or more specifically the biological network of our modular mind that we mobilize with each act of cognition.

There are, however, yet other pragmatic challenges when it comes to picturing networks. In many cases, their connections and associations are invisible until graphed or diagrammed. Even after they are instantiated, in the form of one-way (directed) or bidirectional links, the complexity of possible pathways and permutations they create can exceed human apprehension. Experientially, that is, networks can transcend human scale quite easily, a problem compounded by their inherent extensibility. Expansion, formally and ideologically, is only a matter of adding an associative link, in contrast to cumbersomely building new levels at the top or the bottom of a hierarchy, the network's conceptual rival and putative antagonist. In fact, critical discourse pivots on the question of whether or not the notion of a total, totalizing, or purely distributed network is even possible outside the theoretical ideal, even though we must grant that some networks are indeed bounded by their physical context. (A bus network on a small Pacific island, for instance, would be extensible only in certain limited ways.) Nevertheless, most theorists on the topic readily position both hierarchies and wholes in opposition to the network. As Caroline Levine notes, some critics "consider wholeness to be a myth that networks helpfully shatter," while "others adopt wholeness as troubling reality that can and should be violated by networked extension" – and "still others want to hold onto the older form of the rooted community as a safeguard against global capital and the homogenization of linguistic and cultural experience worldwide."[1] Clearly, in theory, the network remains among the best weapons against (hierarchical, totalizing) systems of domination, oppression, and control – both despite and because it too can be weaponized in practice.

If networks elude us in their invisibility, complexity, and scale – which is also to say in their spatial quality – then they also elude us in time. Networks are mutable, and graph theory, in the words of Alexander Galloway and Eugene Thacker, remains "diachronically blind" to this fact: "Paradoxically, the geometrical basis (or bias) of the division between 'nodes' and 'edges' actually works against an understanding of networks as sets of relations existing in time."[2] For the same reason, it is productive to make a distinction between topological networks and topographical ones, especially when describing and defining computer networks. In computer science and mathematics, the field of topology is all about connection rather than location; it indexes data arrangements, computer infrastructures, and is concerned with intrinsic properties of spatial configurations independent of their location and shape (and is often called "rubber sheet geometry" for that reason).[3] The same formulation is apparent in some of the earliest theorizing on networked society and informational capitalism, namely what Manuel Castells has described as the more local and locatable "space of places" and the comparably globalizing and now predominant

[1] Caroline Levine, *Forms: Whole, Rhythm, Hierarchy, Network* (Princeton: Princeton University Press, 2015), 117. Compare Alexander R. Galloway and Eugene Thacker's observation that "often the discourse surrounding networks tends to pose itself both morally and architecturally against what it sees as retrograde structures like hierarchy and verticality" (*The Exploit: A Theory of Networks* [Minneapolis: University of Minnesota Press, 2007], 25). And perhaps the best-known catalyst for the political mobilization of the network is found in the philosophy of Gilles Deleuze and Félix Guattari and their trope of the rhizome, which muses on root-like figures in opposition to hierarchies (*A Thousand Plateaus: Capitalism and Schizophrenia* [Minneapolis: University of Minnesota Press, 1987]).

[2] Galloway and Thacker, *The Exploit*, 33.

[3] For a discussion of an expressly narratological application of topology in digitally networked environments and its implications for reading, see David Ciccoricco, *Reading Network Fiction* (Tuscaloosa: University of Alabama Press, 2007), 45–46.

"space of flows."[4] Topology places more investment in movements than distances; it puzzles over flexible rubber doughnuts rather than rigid grid-based metrics. The distinction illuminates not only the radical nature of networks in a formal sense but also in a sociopolitical one. Networks are, more specifically, sociotechnical phenomena that carry political affordances that are both potentially empowering and oppressive.

In its simplest definition, a network is a configuration of nodes and links.[5] It is not a technology per se; rather, it is enabled by technologies and potentially – voraciously – subsumes them as it connects them. Furthermore, the computer network, more than any other instantiation, has subsumed not only earlier technologically mediated networks (from radio and television to mail and telecommunications), but also earlier *conceptions* of the networked form. For example, since the spread of so-called neural networks in artificial intelligence computing at the end of the twentieth century, the digital and computational conception of the network has overwritten the neurobiological one. Similarly, at the start of the twenty-first century, the ascendancy of digitally mediated social networking, replete with (now archaic-sounding) synchronous and asynchronous textual messaging systems and "real-time" audio and video links, has effaced the very notion of a predigital social network. That shift has even forced its own acronym of FTF (face-to-face) communication to signify the act of human communication without technical devices. In short, through curious historical inversions, *neural networks* and *social networks* have become increasingly digital by default – their artificial, digital, computerized, and technological modifiers dropping off as these metaphors take on a life of their own.[6]

If digital culture is responsible for runaway metaphors, then perhaps literary culture is responsible for reeling them in, or at least providing a set of critical checks and balances that allow us to reflect on the "proliferation of the network" – what Patrick Jagoda has described as "the principal architecture and most resonant metaphor of the globalizing world."[7] This chapter advances the project of examining how literary engagements

[4] Manuel Castells, *The Rise of the Network Society* (Cambridge, MA: Blackwell, 1996).

[5] The fact that networks are always multiple, always a grouping, and always potentially changeable or extensible is implied in the term *configuration* (as opposed to *structure*, which – though common to network science definitions – is comparably static). *Figuration*, moreover, is itself rich in connotations that apply across the arts and sciences, at once encompassing literary figures such as metaphors and scientific ones such as diagrams or graphs.

[6] We can see the shift reflected in the definite article deployed in the popular film *The Social Network* (2010). In this sense, there are no longer social *networks* – there is only Facebook.

[7] Patrick Jagoda, *Network Aesthetics* (Chicago: University of Chicago Press, 2016), 3.

with technologies have shaped our sense of society and ourselves. More specifically, after marking some literary-theoretical contributions to our understanding of network aesthetics, I examine literary appropriations of the network as figure and form that allows us to reimagine, for better and worse, the relations between mind and machine, self and other. I draw on two texts to illustrate: One is a print novel about networks, the other is literally – which is also to say digitally – a networked fiction. William Gibson's *Pattern Recognition* follows Cayce Pollard, a marketing consultant caught up in a mission to find the origins of "the footage," a set of entrancing film clips published anonymously on the Web. Her search is bankrolled by marketing tycoon and head of the Blue Ant agency, Hubertus Bigend, who wants to exploit it for advertising profit.[8] If we shift focus away from the cryptically networked film footage, however, and on to Cayce's own at once extraordinary and debilitating propensity for pattern recognition, we reveal much more about the force and frailty of the embodied neural networks in play. In Porpentine's digital fiction *With Those We Love Alive*, readers take on the role of servant for an evil insectoid Empress who hunts humans for sport.[9] Here, the ideology, ambivalence, and potential violence of socially networked masses manifests as a mob, which you must decide whether or not to join – with inevitable risk to your principles or your person. Both texts help us picture the links, nodes, and networks that matter to us most. Moreover, both texts cultivate conceptions of sociotechnical networks that keep them alive to their human peculiarities, even as they interface with and flow through the materiality of digital media.

2 Nervous Nets

Networks have always been intrinsic to literary form (both narrative and poetic), whether that means connecting plot points, characters, allusions, or symbols.[10] Literary texts also propagate wider networks of their own: In his description of intertextuality, Foucault refers to a book as a "node within a network."[11] Critical focus on a distinct mode of network aesthetics, however, arose in the late twentieth century, not surprisingly in

[8] William Gibson, *Pattern Recognition* (New York: G.P. Putnam's Sons, 2003).

[9] Porpentine, *With Those We Love Alive* (2014), http://slimedaughter.com/games/twine/wtwla/ (hereafter *WTWLA*) (accessed July 16, 2023).

[10] Spoiler alert: This section contains revealing plot details in William Gibson's *Pattern Recognition.*

[11] Michel Foucault, *The Archaeology of Knowledge and the Discourse on Language* (New York: Vintage, 1982), 23.

tandem with the rise of the programmable and networked computing that saturates all manner of social and commercial transaction, locally and globally. The notion of network aesthetics is diffuse, enveloping works that frame the problem of connectedness thematically; embody networks in their form; make use of the network for their distribution; invite critical methodologies that rely on computational networks in their analysis; or indeed some combination of all of these.[12]

Nevertheless, a necessary first step is weighing up the relationship between network and narrative, itself a cultural form that, by some accounts, is antithetical to the "database logic" of networked media.[13] After all, narratives possess seriality and linearity; they instill an ordered logical progression and (logocentric) rationality, much like that other conceivably inimical form, the hierarchy. Of course, based on the wealth of literary and cultural production that populates the field of digital art and literature, along with the immense commercial and indie success of story-driven videogames, we know that these two cultural forms actually play quite well together in practice. In fact, in a more theoretical vein, narrative takes on a vital role in articulating what networks inevitably leave out; or, put another way, narrative reincorporates and contextualizes the negative – the missing or failed connections – amid the propagation of positive linkages.[14]

Furthermore, if network aesthetics index the ways in which networks might be artful – from the most sublime data visualization to the most mundanely color-coordinated subway map – then we must avoid willfully neglecting their politics (as one adopting a more traditional and aspiringly apolitical mode of aesthetics might do). If aesthetic forms are inherently political, then perhaps networks are exceptionally so. As Jagoda observes,

[12] Jagoda's *Network Aesthetics* is the most comprehensive and insightful treatment of that topic to date, moving across the narrative media of novels and films to video games and alternate reality games. Jagoda argues that "the problem of global connectedness cannot be understood, in our historical present, independently of the formal features of a network imaginary" (3). In order to do so, we must also adopt a broadly inclusive conception of the network in all of its material and figurative forms.

[13] See, most notably, Lev Manovich's claim that narrative and database are natural enemies: "As a cultural form, database represents the world as a list of items and it refuses to order this list. In contrast, a narrative creates a cause-and-effect trajectory of seemingly unordered items (events). Therefore, database and narrative are natural enemies. Competing for the same territory of human culture, each claims an exclusive right to make meaning out of the world." Lev Manovich, "Database as a Symbolic Form," *Millennium Film Journal* 34 (1999): www.mfj-online.org/journalPages/MFJ34/Manovich_Database_FrameSet.html (accessed July 16, 2023).

[14] With recourse to the work of N. Katherine Hayles on systems theory, Phillip Gochenour makes this point in an illuminating article that historicizes and theorizes the discourse on "nodes": "Nodalism," *Digital Humanities Quarterly* 5.3 (2011): 27: www.digitalhumanities.org/dhq/vol/5/3/000105/000105.html (accessed July 16, 2023).

"network aesthetics, as they play out in narrative art forms like the novel and procedural art forms like the videogame, marks both the dominating and emancipatory dimensions of networks." He adds that *politics* is "not a term reserved for negotiations, elections, campaigns, or ideologies"; rather, it can serve more broadly to describe a "field of sensibility" that can render certain lives or certain ways of living – especially those that transpire outside of digital networks – invisible.[15]

In William Gibson's *Pattern Recognition* (2003), Nora Volkova works just out of sight of the many networks – institutional, informational, social – that would otherwise include or even identify her. Her work involves creating minimalist yet profoundly alluring film segments and disseminating them individually and anonymously on the Web. She has the help of her twin sister, Stella, and a regimen of video editors who render her clips in a kind of privatized prison on the outskirts of Moscow. The entire operation is even more remarkable given that Nora is not able to speak and barely able to move after suffering a severe injury in the politically motivated bomb attack that killed her parents. She is left with a T-shaped fragment of shrapnel from the bomb lodged permanently in her brain, and it is the same T-shape, employed as a watermark image on one frame of footage (and originally mistaken as the pattern of a city streetscape), that leads the novel's protagonist, Cayce Pollard, to Russia and to Nora.

If the footage gains its aura and mystique through the network form, it is in turn analyzed by another network, that of the cult-like online forum called F:F:F (for Fetish:Footage:Forum), which aims to demystify it. On a metadiegetic level, the varied forum posts construct a parody of the academic tension between what is portrayed as a heady hermeneutics on the one hand and an overly subjective affective response on the other; that is, some "footageheads" are attacked on the forum for citing French philosophers while others are attacked for their overly emotional and uncritical response. There are, nonetheless, formalist concerns that any foray into network aesthetics must confront – for those in the forum or outside it. For instance, at one stage Hubertus Bigend, the head of the Blue Ant advertising agency intent to solve the footage mystery, debates with Cayce:

> "...if he ever assembles them, then they can be reassembled."
> "'He'?"
> "The maker." She shrugged.
> "You believe that the segments are parts of a whole?"

[15] Jagoda, *Network Aesthetics*, 18–19.

"Yes." Zero hesitation.
"Why?"
"It doesn't feel so much like a leap of faith as something I know in my heart." Strange to hear herself say this, but it's the truth.[16]

Bigend proceeds to correct her, insisting that specific location where she "knows" is not in her heart but in her "limbic brain," the "seat of instinct," which "spreads continent-wide beneath it, mute and muscular, attending its ancient agenda. And makes us buy things."[17] The discussion taps into the same analytical context present on the forum, and foregrounds central questions of commercializing art. But it also underscores the challenge of cognitively mapping Nora's [net]work with any kind of coherence. The order in which the segments are released is not necessarily the order that they occupy in a larger whole or, for that matter, the order in which they are experienced – and no one is certain that there is a completed whole to begin with. Cayce eventually learns that a "Completist" understanding of the footage is mistaken: Upon the invitation of Stella, she is taken into the bowels of the production facility outside Moscow to the room where she witnesses the artist with her work *in progress* (although, ironically, the work itself will not necessarily continue to creatively *grow* given that Nora's previous project saw her editing three of her films to a single frame).[18] The task of locating narrative, however, continues to elude Cayce and, unable to escape the force of confabulation, she finds herself imposing one – literally superimposing the image of her father, who went missing in New York on September 11, 2001, on a grainy figure in Nora's footage.[19] Ultimately, her search for the footage and her father run parallel in that they culminate only in the realization that closure, in both cases, must remain indeterminate.[20]

Topologically, the novel might be visualized as a set of nested networks: These radiate outward from the nebulously interconnected footage, which is nested within the online cult-forum. These are both nested within the multinational capitalist networks that confound borders as its players transition seamlessly, physically and virtually, between New York, London, Tokyo, and Moscow (save the occasional disjunctions that Cayce intuits as "mirror

16 Gibson, *Pattern Recognition*, 68–69.
17 Ibid., 69.
18 Ibid., 304.
19 Ibid., 305. A dreaming Cayce earlier conflates the image of a similar figure – whose body language she knows unmistakably from "uncounted viewings of seventy-eight segments of footage" – with that of her father (226).
20 For an incisive and more detailed reading along these lines, see also Katharina Donn's *A Poetics of Trauma after 9/11: Representing Trauma in a Digitized Present* (New York: Routledge, 2017).

world" moments). Finally, ever present as a kind of haunting ambient backdrop is the terrorist network responsible for the attacks on September 11, 2001. By something akin to a strange loop, however, we might also move from the novel's outermost networks and return to another network: that which has its rhizomatic roots in Cayce's own neurology.

Indeed, if the network of video art – what Cayce calls the "headwaters of the digital Nile"[21] – is something of an originary force in the narrative, then so too is Cayce's uncanny aptitude for recognizing cultural patterns. Her quasi-telepathic talents make her among the most sought after "cool-hunting" marketing consultants in the game (she apparently has a hand in tracking down the first man to sport a baseball cap backward).[22] But the aptitude is in equal part allergy, and certain brand logos in particular trigger a panic response that she must mitigate and manage throughout her day – her documentary director friend Damien describes it as a "morbid and sometimes violent reactivity to the semiotics of the marketplace."[23] As Fredric Jameson notes in his review of the novel:

> Now it is a little easier to see the deeper meaning of the footage for Cayce: its utter lack of style is an ontological relief, like black-and-white film after the conventional orgies of bad technicolour, like the silence of solitude for the telepath whose mind is jammed with noisy voices all day long. The footage is an epoch of rest, an escape from the noisy commodities themselves, which turn out, as Marx always thought they would, to be living entities preying on the humans who have to coexist with them.[24]

While predatorial commodities may not make for the most harmonious coexistence, Cayce's condition also highlights our relation to a different kind of "living" entity, albeit one alive in the conspicuously artificial sense of neural networks. After all, Gibson's title plays directly on the dual connotation of pattern recognition as a function of both human and (so-called) machine intelligence. Artificial neural networks are at the forefront of many of the scientific advances in AI and ethical controversies in posthumanist discourse, especially given their characteristic ability to *learn* through repeated iterations of their algorithms. With a few initial instructions, and many repeated attempts, an artificial neural network can learn to recognize, for example, a particular face in the crowd on a video

[21] Gibson, *Pattern Recognition*, 305.
[22] Ibid., 32.
[23] Ibid., 2.
[24] Fredric Jameson, "Fear and Loathing in Globalization," *New Left Review* 23 (September–October, 2003), https://newleftreview.org/II/23/fredric-jameson-fear-and-loathing-in-globalization (accessed July 16, 2023).

feed. Compared with experimental models common to classical cognitive science, which attempt to simulate propositional logic in a serial fashion, artificial neural networks, in the field of connectionism, are designed to produce more faithful simulations of the structure and function of the human brain by emulating their parallel circuitry and recursive learning.[25]

However, in the same way that we adopted the classical computer-processing paradigm to understand everything from the language of consciousness to the mechanics of perception and memory, we now also risk an uncritical and reductive conflation of artificial neural networks and biological ones.[26] Moving from a notion of mind as computation to one of mind as network is by all means an improvement for which we credit contemporary cognitive science. But contemporary cognitive science is also quick to point out the chasm in understanding that the neural network analogy creates, such as the fact that in practice, unlike human minds, artificial neural networks are dedicated to discrete single tasks only.[27]

N. Katherine Hayles yokes pattern recognition to her discussion of "nonconscious cognition," the mental operations that transpire outside – but not necessarily "below" or secondary to – higher consciousness.[28] Using examples that range from text analysis to high-frequency stock trading, she points out that nonconscious cognition, which we have long shared with so-called lower organisms, we now share with computers. If Hayles's theory encourages us

[25] Gochenour succinctly explains the logic behind connectionism: "the mechanism that governs the relation between neurons and generates thought out of their individual states … establishes an analogy between structure and function that can be replicated technologically; if thought (defined as the working out of propositions in Boolean logic) is the product of interaction between neurons that function as yes/no on/off switches, then it should be possible to replicate thought through electronic circuits that function in the same way" ("Nodalism," n.p.).

[26] It is possible to claim that this conflation is already past tense: A Google Image search for "neural network" yields dozens of directed graphs before the first models of gray matter appear down the page; popular websites that "explain stuff" note up front that "we're going to use the term 'neural network' throughout and always use it to mean 'artificial neural network'" (www.explainthatstuff.com/introduction-to-neural-networks.html). The history of cognitive science suggests a more convoluted chain of events. For example, father of modern computing and figurehead of cybernetics John von Neumann wanted to model the human brain in order to create a digital computer. Yet subsequently the operations of the computer become the dominant model for understanding the mind. Philosopher of mind Gualtiero Piccinini explains the same circularity with reference to the creators of connectionism, Warren McCulloch and Walter Pitts, who "made many of their simplifying assumptions about networks of neurons in order to solve the mind-body problem by using logic and Turing Machines as descriptions of the nervous system, but after their theory was formulated, their theory was used as evidence that the brain is indeed a computing mechanism." See Gualtiero Piccinini, "The First Computational Theory of Mind and Brain: A Close Look at McCulloch and Pitts's 'Logical Calculus of Ideas Immanent in Nervous Activity,'" *Synthese* 141.2 (2004), 205.

[27] For more on the points of disjunction, see Andy Clark, *Mindware: An Introduction to the Philosophy of Cognitive Science* (New York: Oxford University Press, 2001).

[28] N. Katherine Hayles, *Unthought: The Power of the Cognitive Nonconscious* (Chicago: University of Chicago Press, 2017).

to come to terms with our newly decentered planetary place in relation to natural and technical environments, then Gibson's novel allows us to see some of the implications. As *Independent* reviewer Pat Kane rightly suggests, "too much reliance on 'pattern recognition' is rendered by Gibson as bogus knowledge,"[29] and the most pathological if not paranoid emblem of such in the story is Cayce's mother. Long obsessed with "Electronic Voice Phenomena," in which often supernatural or paranormal messages are detected in audio recordings, Cynthia Pollard is convinced that her deceased husband is addressing her and her daughter directly. Also at stake, however, is not merely how much pattern recognition is too much, but what exactly happens when we surrender so much of it to the machine.

It is notable that even though the film footage undergoes a computational process in its composition, its reception is processed humanly – and indeed humanely, at least by the protagonist of this story (Cayce even has to outsource computational – that is, nonhuman – analysis of the digital watermark that leads her to Nora).[30] Perhaps unsurprisingly for an author with a penchant to portray the loathsome and lonely side of technoculture, Gibson's hero reminds us that pattern recognition has a distinctly human downside: the tormented overdose of connectivity called apophenia, which results in the experience of seeing patterns where there are none. At the same time, we find something redemptive in the doubly deferred closure of the search for a missing father and for a completed artwork – or at least we feel something familiar in Cayce's need to indulge indeterminacy. While some lament what they perceive as Gibson's retreat into the present with *Pattern Recognition*, away from his more familiar science fiction worlds,[31] such claims overlook the more pervasive acceptance that the twenty-first century has caught up with science fiction anyway. Moreover, sometimes art simply goes where art is needed, and the mixed and all too often invisible effects of computational networks are a pressing and present reality. Algorithms do not have anxiety, and despite the discomfort of a sympathetic nervous response for an enfleshed system, our anxieties do tend to play an indispensable, affective role in our calculations. Early on in the analysis of the segments, an email from (username) Parkaboy, one of the prominent "footageheads" (and Cayce's eventual love interest), succinctly observes: "Homo sapiens is

[29] Pat Kane, "*Pattern Recognition* by William Gibson," *Independent* (May 3, 2003), www.independent.co.uk/arts-entertainment/books/reviews/pattern-recognition-by-william-gibson-103040.html (accessed July 16, 2023).

[30] There is perhaps a further irony to note here: Nora initially sources her raw material from another network, the closed-circuit security cameras operating in the hospital where she is convalescing.

[31] Kane, "*Pattern Recognition*," n.p.

all about pattern recognition … Both a gift and a trap."[32] Clearly, it is a gift we now share with artificial, algorithmic, and machinic networks. And we still have much more to learn about its traps.

3 The Antisocial Network

With Those We Love Alive (2014) is both a narrative about networks and a digitally networked fiction. The self-published text was created by Porpentine Charity Heartscape (who goes by and publishes as Porpentine) using the open-source hypertext authoring software Twine. In recent years, works authored in the Twine platform have drawn critical and popular attention for their innovative incorporation of gameplay and interaction and focus on "questions of love, gender, sexuality, body awareness, and mental illness – using the text-dominance and intimacy afforded by hypertext to explore deeply personal topics that mainstream gaming rarely addresses."[33] Porpentine's *With Those We Love Alive* is in these respects a highly representative Twine work. In the story, you take on the role of servant for an evil insectoid Empress who hunts humans for sport. Most of your time is spent exploring the palace gardens, building things for the Empress, and generally trying to stay safe.

There are moments in the text when we (the reader, playing as the nameless servant) are faced with the prospect of joining a mob about to initiate a hunt for humans at the behest of the Empress. Granted, there is a fine line between mass protest and mass riot, and much depends on the ideas that serve as the engine for action. For example, juxtaposing images of, say, the 2017 Gaza protests against moving the US embassy to Jerusalem with those of the Canucks ice hockey team losing the Stanley Cup final in Vancouver in 2011, reveals a striking if not disturbing compositional likeness: the colorful flags, the flames, the angry young males, and so on. There are also certain scenarios whereby some decide to join a group or a cause for reasons of coercion or even personal safety. These observations provide context for Porpentine's intensely claustrophobic and indeed strictly binary scenarios in a form perhaps more conventionally associated with unencumbered multiplicity, movement, and freedom. In turn, *With Those We Love Alive* starkly illuminates the darker side of social networks and the ways in which digitally mediated networks sustain them, especially in light of the blatantly binarized sociopolitical moment more broadly.

[32] Gibson, *Pattern Recognition*, 22.
[33] Astrid Ensslin and Lyle Skains, "Hypertext: Storyspace to Twine," in *The Bloomsbury Handbook of Electronic Literature*, ed. Joseph Tabbi (London: Bloomsbury, 2017), 302.

In the first scenario with the mob, when it comes time for the Empress to initiate her rapturous hunt, we find that we are in fact powerless to intervene. There are no linked options available and the narration simply progresses: We have no choice but to remain silent, and perhaps complicit in the slaughter. Everyone is simply afraid to challenge the ruling authority and the system, and afraid of the Empress, who you see rise "from the water, dragging her train of leaves and ichor"; "Her larval skin floats across the lake like the carcass of a pale leviathan. Her aides pick wet plant matter from her skull."[34] While this encounter forces a sense of powerlessness and complicity, the second encounter works quite differently. Later in the story, readers *must* choose whether or not to join the same murderous mob, when they are murdering not humans, but soft, pink, kitten-like "princess spores" that have spawned from the Empress. (Although the prospect of killing her children is perhaps initially baffling, it turns out that she is so evil that each year, when the spores spring forth, all the subjects of this empire join a wild drunken ritualistic hunt to destroy them so that they do not grow up to challenge the Empress for power.) This decision, however, is not presented in any kind of straightforward way. Two hyperlinked choices are anchored by phrases contained in the question (each highlighted here in bold): Are you **part of the world, one with others, a person**, or **are you alone and apart?**[35] On the one hand, we do not want to kill; however, we also do not want to go against the mob, the Empress, or even have one of the spores grow up to become an even worse Empress. On the other hand, we do not want to be alone, alienated, and possibly in danger (the latter stages of the story involve an intimately fraught reunion with an estranged companion); however, that might mean going against our values and principles. When we think of "community," we tend to adopt a primarily positive and prosocial notion, but as Emily Short notes in her exceptional review of the text, there are risks of the collective: "any collective group, any economy, any community of principle, risks falling victim to itself, the rules becoming a weapon against the people."[36] In Porpentine's text, we cannot avoid the violent militancy of the collective; the network oppresses, and its links enchain rather than liberate.

More generally, if Porpentine's work serves as an embrace of network aesthetics, it also serves – reflexively and reflectively – as its critique. More

[34] The *ichor* in the description provocatively evokes the celestial and corporeal – both the fluid that flows through the veins of gods in Greek mythology and the watery discharge from a wound.

[35] Porpentine, *WTWLA*, n.p.

[36] Emily Short, "IF Comp 2014: *With Those We Love Alive* (Porpentine, Brenda Neotenomie)" (October 16, 2014): https://emshort.blog/2014/10/16/if-comp-2014-with-those-we-love-alive-porpentine-brenda-neotenomie/ (accessed July 16, 2023).

specifically, we can trace narratological continuities as we move from the earliest experiments with narrative in digital environments, such as the hypertext fiction created in the Storyspace platform in the 1990s, to the popular proliferation of Twine fiction.[37] For example, works in both the Storyspace and Twine platforms exploit flows of digital networks to reinvigorate the poetics of repetition. As I have previously suggested in relation to early hypertext fiction, digitally networked narratives "rely on reiteration for their iteration; that is, *re-reading* can no longer be thought of as an epiphenomenon of *reading* in a network text since the re-reading of textual elements, via the recycling of nodes, is fundamental to (hyper)textual comprehension."[38] The same general effect plays out in emphatic fashion in Twine and certainly in Porpentine's work. What comes next is often what comes before; in order to advance, there are seemingly incessant narrative returns. *With Those We Love Alive* forces readers into repetitive actions: Again and again we "sleep," "do our meditations," and return to our "worktable."

Nonetheless, the points of departure from that earlier sense of network aesthetics are perhaps more telling. Porpentine, for example, does not deploy textual networks to their full extent: Narrative returns ultimately lead readers along strict linear rails toward a singular conclusion. The design underscores the fact that some kind of Platonic networked form whereby all choices are available and interconnected is itself a fiction, especially when we think of idealized treatments of the network in the earlier ideologically charged discourse of hypertext theorists and poststructuralist theorists alike. Admittedly, devoutly formalist readings will reveal the degree to which the solely text-based and parser-driven interactive fiction has inflected Twine's form while the gaming industry has colored its rhetoric. In fact, it is entirely possible that Twine writers are politically responding to the commercial game industry; genealogically influenced by the fringe tradition of interactive fiction; and serendipitously producing something akin to networked fiction. That said, we can still intuit a general pattern: Twine fiction often uses starkly oppositional pathways and outcomes along with alienating disconnections as a counterpoint to the conspicuous connectivity of an idealized network. In Porpentine's work, links are deployed coercively in order to make readers see how it feels to be trapped by binary choice.

[37] With regard to comparing Storyspace to Twine, I grant that much of the current focus falls on discontinuity, and the move from a predominantly academic and wholly proprietary model to an open-source and countercultural one that challenges mainstream forms of gameplay (see also Ensslin and Skains, "Hypertext: Storyspace to Twine").

[38] Ciccoricco, *Reading Network Fiction*, 23.

All the coercion, claustrophobia, and kitten-like spores are still not necessarily cause for despair. Even though the choices you make in the text have little actual bearing on the story outcome (there is only one ending), consideration of paratext in *With Those We Love Alive* does open the possibility for morally sanctioned choice. The title is derived from the Bhagavad Gita, at a point when the protagonist Arjuna accepts his position as disciple of Lord Krishna and asks him for advice on how to remedy his lamentation and grief: "Better to live on beggar's bread / with those we love alive, / than taste their blood in rich feasts spread, / and guiltily survive!"[39] Another (potentially extradiegetic) paratextual prompt appears at the start of the narrative: "nothing you can do is wrong."[40] The direct address lifts the text out of poststructuralist relativism and the reader out of repetitive malaise – at least if you read it as absolving your guilt in advance if, out of fear, you opt to join the mob.

Picture a network through the lens of literary imagination. The result may not always be a pretty or comforting one, but it will allow for a recognition of patterns across the many material and figurative instantiations of networks. As *readers* of networks – not just producers and consumers of them – we can learn to leverage the structural analogies across these domains, keeping them discrete as we interconnect them. In connecting the networks of the world to those of the mind, moreover, literary figurations reveal the ambivalence of the metaphors we use to describe them. Just as metaphor itself relies on distance between source and target, figurations of networks are vital to the project of maintaining a critical distance from the social and political networks that we propagate and that in turn interpenetrate our experience. Perhaps the fullest expression of network aesthetics would also present us with an opportunity to cultivate a more compassionate criticism, nourished in intimate fashion by the "alone-togetherness" of twenty-first century networked culture.[41] What if an emergent network of sentiment were somehow intrinsic to digital literary studies not despite but because of our paradoxically detached interconnectivity? One can hope.

[39] *The Bhagavad Gita*, trans. Sir Edwin Arnold (New York: Heritage Press, 1965), 4.

[40] Porpentine, *WTWLA*, n.p.

[41] Jagoda, *Network Aesthetics*, 18–19. Compare Leisa Reichelt's earlier notion of "ambient intimacy," which originated as a kind of vernacular criticism from a blogpost: "Ambient Intimacy," *Disambiguity*, March 1, 2007: www.disambiguity.com/ambient-intimacy/ (accessed July 16, 2023).

PART III

Applications

CHAPTER 19

Distant Reading

Natalie M. Houston

A variety of technological shifts in the twenty-first century have transformed the questions, objects, tools, and methods of humanities scholarship. Today, even those who do not perceive the methods or objects of their research as having anything to do with digital technology are likely to consult digital library catalogs and reference databases, read secondary or primary source materials from digital surrogates, and manage some of their personal research materials as digital files. Although in recent years the idea of distant reading has largely become associated with computational analysis performed with large textual datasets, when Franco Moretti first coined the phrase "distant reading" in the year 2000, he was referring to comparative studies that synthesize data from a number of sources to enable analysis of literary history on a grander scale. His subsequent work with the Stanford Literary Lab, the increased availability of digitized texts, and the developing field of digital humanities has led to the current understanding of distant reading as "the computational processing of textual information in digital form" or "using digital tools to 'read' large swaths of text."[1]

In distant reading, Moretti suggests, "distance … *is a condition of knowledge*: it allows you to focus on units that are much smaller or much larger than the text: devices, themes, tropes – or genres and systems."[2] As the Google Library Project began scanning the contents of university library shelves in 2004, followed by the formation of the Hathi Trust Digital Library in 2008, the possibilities for large-scale literary

[1] Johanna Drucker, "Why Distant Reading Isn't," *PMLA* 132.3 (2017): 629; Matthew K. Gold and Lauren F. Klein, "Introduction. Forum: Text Analysis at Scale," in *Debates in the Digital Humanities*, ed. Matthew K. Gold and Lauren F. Klein (Minneapolis: University of Minnesota Press, 2016), open access edition: https://dhdebates.gc.cuny.edu/projects/debates-in-the-digital-humanities-2016 (accessed April 22, 2022).

[2] Franco Moretti, *Distant Reading* (London: Verso, 2013), 48; emphasis in the original.

history evoked by Moretti's bold claims began to emerge.[3] At the same time, researchers and general internet users alike became accustomed to searching digital text, from web pages to scholarly databases. As Ted Underwood suggests, algorithmic search has been "invisibly naturalized" over the past two decades, obscuring the technological sophistication of search processes and the impact of relevance ranking of search results.[4] Full-text search and open access digital archives have expanded the kinds of research questions literary scholars could pursue, at both the very large and very small scales.

But even as these developments have made computers and digitization very familiar, the integration of computational analysis into humanities scholarship has been slow and sometimes controversial.[5] This chapter situates the methodological approach known as distant reading within the technological changes of the last twenty-five years by highlighting key examples of exploratory, generative, and predictive modeling applied to humanities research questions and showing how web-based tools now make such models available even to those without computer programming experience.

1 Defining Distant Reading

The rhetorical power of the phrase "distant reading" has persisted in part because of the way Moretti set it in opposition to the close reading methods enshrined in Anglo-American literary criticism after the New Criticism. Moretti argues that "the trouble with close reading (in all of its incarnations, from the new criticism to deconstruction) is that it necessarily depends on an extremely small canon … you invest so much in individual texts *only* if you think that very few of them really matter."[6] Moretti thus linked his argument for changing the scale of writing literary history to a critique of the literary canon as overly restrictive. He acknowledges that studying literary form and cultural processes at other scales means

[3] "About the Library Project," Google Books: https://support.google.com/websearch/answer/9690276 (accessed April 22, 2022); "Welcome to Hathi Trust!," Hathi Trust Digital Library: www.hathitrust.org/about (accessed April 22, 2022).

[4] Ted Underwood, "Theorizing Research Practices We Forgot to Theorize Twenty Years Ago," *Representations* 127.1 (Summer 2014): 64.

[5] See, for example, Katie Trumpener, "Paratext and Genre System: A Response to Franco Moretti," *Critical Inquiry* 36 (Autumn 2009): 159–171 and Alexander R. Galloway, "Everything Is Computational," *Los Angeles Review of Books* (June 27, 2013): https://lareviewofbooks.org/article/franco-morettis-distant-reading-a-symposium/ (accessed April 22, 2022).

[6] Moretti, *Distant Reading*, 48; emphasis in the original.

that "between the very small and the very large, the text itself disappears": Distant reading is not at all the same thing as reading.[7]

Working with a very large corpus of texts requires new kinds of analysis, as he suggests in a later study: "we are not doing the same thing, 1,000 times bigger; we are doing a different thing. The new scale changes our relationship to our object, and in fact it changes the object itself."[8] Although the rationale for selection is not always made explicit in traditional literary studies, scholars inevitably focus on a selection of texts: texts chosen because they exemplify certain patterns, genres, or themes; because they were produced under certain historical conditions; or because they were written by certain authors. Selecting and preparing texts for computational analysis requires explicit justification for numerous decisions made throughout the process. As Moretti points out, "no one writes corpora; they are not 'communicative events' – they are not events at all, they are artificial objects created by a researcher."[9] Even for those with good institutional support and resources, researchers must decide whether they will work within the selection biases and technological constraints of already-digitized materials, or instead put significant time, money, and labor into digitizing other texts.[10] By changing the scale at which texts are analyzed, whether breaking a text down to individual parts of speech or examining the developments of genres over many decades, distant reading transforms the object of study and thereby the kinds of questions that can be explored.

Ted Underwood traces the intellectual origins of distant reading in fields like "book history, sociology, and linguistics," which "pose broad historical questions about literature, and answer them by studying samples of social or textual evidence."[11] Adopting an experimental approach requires distinguishing among the stages of knowledge production: forming a research question, developing a hypothesis, selecting appropriate data, conducting analysis, and formulating an argument for its significance. Importantly, this experimental methodology "separates the construction of the sample

7 Ibid., 49.

8 Franco Moretti, "Patterns and Interpretation," *Pamphlets of the Stanford Literary Lab* 15 (September 2017), 1: https://litlab.stanford.edu/LiteraryLabPamphlet15.pdf (accessed April 22, 2022).

9 Ibid., 2.

10 Mark Algee-Hewitt and Mark McGurl, "Between Canon and Corpus: Six Perspectives on 20th-Century Novels," *Pamphlets of the Stanford Literary Lab* 8 (January 2015), 1–8: https://litlab.stanford.edu/LiteraryLabPamphlet8.pdf (accessed April 22, 2022).

11 Ted Underwood, "A Genealogy of Distant Reading," *DHQ: Digital Humanities Quarterly* 11.2 (2017), para. 3, para 10: www.digitalhumanities.org/dhq/vol/11/2/000317/000317.html (accessed April 22, 2022).

from the process of historical inference."[12] The distinctions among these steps are often only implied in literary criticism. As Matthew Jockers points out, experimentation "offers a method through which competing observations and conclusions may be tested and ruled out," which runs counter to the traditional emphasis on debate and subjective interpretation in literary studies.[13]

2 Models

In statistics, a model is a "high-level, global description of a data set" that identifies its important features, and uses them either to summarize and describe the data (known as descriptive modeling); to hypothesize about the distributional processes that generated the data (in generative modeling); or as the basis for learning about the data in order to predict aspects about other data points (in predictive modeling).[14] A model can be understood as "a general scheme, or template" that represents both "components of the information (features of texts, images, numbers, etc) and their relations to each other."[15] The purpose of the analysis would determine the choice of model, which would then guide the selection of specific features of the data.

A library's catalog, for example, can be understood as a model for representing the books that sit on its shelves. Most library catalogs for general circulating collections represent each book with its bibliographical information, such as author name, book title, publication year, and publisher name and location. A catalog can thus generate different summary descriptions of the library's holdings: The same collection could be described as containing 500 books; books by 200 different authors; books published from 1705 to 1999; or books published in London, New York, and Paris. A slightly more complex descriptive model would analyze how those different features relate to each other, by counting the number of books held by each author or looking at the distribution of publisher location in different decades.

Models are always constructed for a specific purpose and involve numerous decisions about which aspects of the object of study will be represented. For example, circulating library catalogs rarely represent the

[12] Ibid., para. 11.

[13] Matthew L. Jockers, *Macroanalysis: Digital Methods and Literary History* (Urbana: University of Illinois Press, 2013), 6.

[14] David Hand, Heikki Manilla, and Padhraic Smyth, *Principles of Data Mining* (Cambridge: MIT Press, 2001), 165; David Foster, *Generative Deep Learning: Teaching Machines to Paint, Write, Compose and Play* (Sebastopol: O'Reilly, 2019), 1–2.

[15] Drucker, "Why Distant Reading Isn't," 629.

material aspects of their holdings in detail, such as the paper composition or binding materials. But rare book libraries may choose to represent those features in their catalog records, because they are considered more relevant to understanding or classifying rare books. As Andrew Piper suggests, even though the language of modeling may seem alien to the domain of literary studies, literary critics nonetheless represent texts in a kind of descriptive model, by quoting passages from the text and producing historical, biographical, or formal descriptions of it.[16]

In order to prepare texts for statistical modeling, words and other features of the text must be represented by numeric values. This can be either a binary representation (1 if the word is present, 0 if it is not) or a count of the word's frequency in the text. Nonword features of a text can also be represented in the model, through categorical variables describing features of the text such as genre, form, or authorship, or through discrete or continuous numeric variables recording information such as dates, line counts, or formal elements of the text.

3 Descriptive Modeling

Descriptive models offer new understanding of a dataset by changing the scale at which its observations are understood. For example, transforming a literary text into a list of all of its words with their frequency counts shifts the meaningful unit of interpretation from the book, paragraph, or sentence down to the level of the word. Bypassing theme, plot, or other narrative conventions to examine patterns at the level of the sentence, vocabulary, or genre system changes what counts as evidence, as well as what kinds of questions can be pursued.

Even very simple measures of word frequency can reveal interesting patterns when examined in a large corpus of texts. Type-token ratio (TTR), for example, is a standard measure of lexical variety: the ratio of word types (distinct words) in a text to the number of its tokens (all words, including repeated ones). A 100-word text containing 100 distinct words would have a TTR of 1, and very high lexical variety; a 100-word text containing 25 distinct words, would have a TTR of 0.25, indicating more word repetition. Examining TTR in a large corpus of over 1,000 canonical and noncanonical nineteenth-century novels, Algee-Hewitt et al. found that the canonical texts tended to have lower TTRs, corresponding to their emphasis on realistic depictions of oral speech. Although the less-canonical novels also

[16] Andrew Piper, "Think Small: On Literary Modeling," *PMLA* 132.3 (2017): 652–653.

included passages of dialogue, "their 'spoken' passages have a decidedly 'written' quality … formal tirades that sound closer to a written disquisition than to an oral exchange."[17] They found that the noncanonical novels use more nouns and adjectives than do the canonical ones, which contributes to this discrepancy in register. Exploratory analysis thus provides a picture of the larger context of novelistic language against which specific examples can be compared.

Some experiments in distant reading transform works by a single author, or even a single work, by changing the scale of observation. In her research, Sarah Allison created a descriptive model of George Eliot's novel *Middlemarch* by selecting every third sentence, totaling 4,400.[18] This practice of selection strategically disrupts typical narrative reading practices, and her analysis of their syntactical structure reveals important patterns in Eliot's writing. Allison identifies a frequent grammatical construction that she calls the "commentative clause": a sentence that links the narrative's past tense with a generalizing present tense by means of the relative pronoun "which."[19] Allison demonstrates how the novel uses this clause to multiply and diffuse critical judgments in its description of characters and events, pointing out that "a major philosophical problem in *Middlemarch* is how to see others clearly but without contempt: the many facets of this problem and the partial solutions to it that *Middlemarch* proposes are most clearly seen not in its plot but at the level of the sentence."[20]

Andrew Piper similarly uses descriptive modeling to resist the force of plot in narrative theory, focusing on "words in the distributional sense, as a larger set of patterns."[21] Working with German, French, and English novels, Piper calculates the vocabulary distribution for each chapter within a given novel and then measures their similarity to one another. Using these measurements, he identifies a set of novels in which chapters in the second half of the text are more similar to each other than those in the first half. Examining the vocabularies used in the first and second halves of these "contractive" novels points to shifts in the use of characters' proper names and the resolution of the marriage plot as connections between the social world reflected in modernist fiction and the vocabularies used

[17] Algee-Hewitt, Mark, et al., "Canon/Archive: Large-Scale Dynamics in the Literary Field," *Pamphlets of the Stanford Literary Lab* 11 (January 2016), 10: https://litlab.stanford.edu/LiteraryLabPamphlet11.pdf (accessed April 22, 2022).

[18] Sarah Allison, *Reductive Reading: A Syntax of Victorian Moralizing* (Baltimore, MD: Johns Hopkins University Press, 2018), 63.

[19] Ibid., 61–63.

[20] Ibid., 80.

[21] Andrew Piper, *Enumerations: Data and Literary Study* (Chicago: University of Chicago Press, 2018), 42.

in its writing: "There is an implicit argument being made here about the relationship between marriage, lexical constraint, and semantic surplus. As we move into the interior space of marriage, the linguistic world collapses even as the semantic resonance of that world increases."[22] His descriptive model adds new insight to the far-reaching effects of marriage, not only at the level of plot, but also of language in the novel.

Descriptive modeling builds on the pioneering work of John Tukey, who offered methods for "looking at data to see what it seems to say."[23] These methods included using quartile and mean measures to describe the spread of values in a dataset (now enshrined in most statistical software packages as a "five number summary" or "Tukey summary" function) and using simple visualizations to reveal patterns within the data. Tukey's book contains instructions on creating stem and leaf plots and box plots by hand; today, data visualization techniques are widely available in spreadsheet software and online tools as well as in different programming languages. Exploratory analysis focuses on identifying trends and patterns in the data, which can often be better understood through graphical representation than in data tables alone.

For example, Moretti compiles bibliographic data and performs an exploratory analysis of changes in novel titles over the course of a century.[24] He presents twenty-one scatter plots and bar graphs that allow the reader to examine changes in title length, and how they relate to the numbers of novels published per year; the use of proper names in short titles; and a comparison of the use of definite and indefinite articles in novels from different genres. These data visualizations provide the overall view of the corpus, juxtaposed with Moretti's discussion of illustrative examples. Because most of the titles he mentions come from what Margaret Cohen called "the great unread," it is the visualizations that allow readers to compare his findings to what they already know about literature from the period and to make sense of the patterns in the data for themselves.[25] In exploratory analysis, data visualizations help construct the argument, rather than merely illustrating it.

Another example of exploratory modeling in literary studies is Matthew Wilkens's map of geographical references found in a collection of 100 nineteenth-century American novels that were digitized as part of the

[22] Ibid., 56.

[23] John W. Tukey, *Exploratory Data Analysis* (Reading, MA: Addison-Wesley, 1977), 2.

[24] Moretti, "Style, Inc.: Reflections on Seven Thousand Titles (British Novels, 1740–1850)," *Distant Reading*, 179–210.

[25] Margaret Cohen, *The Sentimental Education of the Novel* (Princeton: Princeton University Press, 1999), 23; Moretti, *Distant Reading*, 180.

Wright American Fiction Project.[26] Although one could simply analyze the number of references to each major city, Wilkens also chose to visualize the data on a world map. Exploring this data by mapping those locations reveals that "the imaginative landscape of American fiction in the mid-nineteenth century appears to be pretty diversely outward looking" when "our standard model of the period is that its fiction is strongly introspective … concerned largely with American identity and belonging."[27] In other words, when visualized, the data tells a different story than what literary critics have assumed to be true.

4 Generative Modeling

Topic modeling, a kind of generative modeling, is also widely used in distant reading to explore the semantic contents of large corpora. Generative models create a probabilistic model of how a set of data came to be distributed, and then use that model to describe the structure of the dataset or to generate new data instances. As David M. Blei explains, topic models "reverse the imaginary generative process to answer the question 'What is the likely hidden topical structure that generated my observed documents?'"[28] The most commonly used form of topic modeling in the humanities is Latent Dirichlet Allocation (LDA) topic modeling, which assumes that documents in a corpus are made up of topics, each of which are present in every document in varying proportions.[29] The model also assumes that topics are made up of words, which are also described by a probability distribution. It is as if "first, the writer picks a 'mixture' of topics to write about; then the writer constructs the text word-by-word by first randomly choosing a topic from the mixture and then picking a word based on the probability table for that topic."[30] Even though this does not sound like the way authors actually write texts, this model enables the algorithm to discover sets of co-occurring terms.

[26] Matthew Wilkens, "Canons, Close Reading, and Evolution," in *Debates in the Digital Humanities*, ed. Matthew K. Gold (University of Minnesota Press, 2012), open access edition: http://dhdebates.gc.cuny.edu/debates/text/17 (accessed April 22, 2022).

[27] Ibid.

[28] David M. Blei, "Topic Modeling and Digital Humanities," *Journal of Digital Humanities* 2.1 (2012): http://journalofdigitalhumanities.org/2-1/topic-modeling-and-digital-humanities-by-david-m-blei/#topic-modeling-and-digital-humanities-by-david-m-blei-n-3 (accessed April 22, 2022).

[29] David M. Blei, Andrew Y. Ng, and Michael I. Jordan, "Latent Dirichlet Allocation," *Journal of Machine Learning Research* 3 (2003): 993–1022.

[30] Jeffrey M. Binder, "Alien Reading: Text Mining, Language Standardization, and the Humanities," in *Debates in the Digital Humanities*, ed. Matthew K. Gold and Lauren F. Klein

The algorithm uses an unsupervised iterative process by which it assigns each word in a document to a topic, gradually refining the assignments to correspond to the co-occurrence patterns it finds in the corpus. This iterative process gradually uncovers distinctions between different meanings of the same word through their collocations. For example, imagine a corpus in which the word "bats" appears 100 times. On a first pass, all of the "bats" might be grouped together in one topic; after several iterations through the documents, some instances of the word "bats" will be sorted into a topic about baseball and others into one about mammals.

Although these lists of co-occurring words output by the LDA algorithm are called "topics" in the scientific literature, they do not exactly resemble the phrases or sentences that human readers and writers would call themes or topics. They are simply lists of co-occurring words, which reveal different kinds of textual relationships. For example, in their examination of several different topic models of articles from over eighty years of the journal *PMLA*, Andrew Goldstone and Ted Underwood demonstrate how the algorithm identifies the presence of different national languages within the corpus, broad subject categories, and discursive patterns that reflect both critical methodologies and also more subtle linguistic "habits": "A topic model doesn't just show you what people are writing about (a list of 'topics' in our ordinary sense of the word). It can also show you how they're writing … topic modeling can identify discourses as well as subject categories and embedded languages."[31] As they suggest, words in LDA topics do not necessarily mean what we might think they mean, "forcing us to attend to concrete linguistic practice" rather than assuming that texts fit with our preconceived ideas about their contents.[32]

The benefits of topic modeling are perhaps best seen in its applications to very large corpora that could not feasibly be interpreted by a single human reader. In an influential early study, Sharon Block modeled 82,000 newspaper articles and advertisements from the eighteenth-century *Pennsylvania Gazette*, exploring "how print discourses operated to marginalize particular groups in early America" and demonstrating the utility of topic modeling for examining discursive trends over time.[33] Two years

(Minneapolis: University of Minnesota Press, 2016), open access edition: https://dhdebates.gc.cuny.edu/projects/debates-in-the-digital-humanities-2016 (accessed April 22, 2022).

31 Andrew Goldstone and Ted Underwood, "What Can Topic Models of *PMLA* Teach Us about the History of Literary Scholarship?," *Journal of Digital Humanities* 2.1 (2012): http://journalofdigitalhumanities.org/2-1/ (accessed April 22, 2022).

32 Ibid.

33 Sharon Block, "Doing More with Digitization," *Common-place* 6.2 (2006): http://commonplace.online/article/doing-more-with-digitization/ (accessed April 22, 2022).

after their study of *PMLA*, Goldstone and Underwood used topic modeling to explore long historical trends in the field of literary studies, represented by 21,367 full-length articles published in seven scholarly journals over 120 years.[34] Lauren Klein constructs a topic model of 224,160 North American newspaper articles published between 1827 and 1865 in order to analyze the impact of particular editors in shaping abolitionist discourse.[35]

The LDA algorithm creates two kinds of outputs that can be used to explore and assess the model's results: a list of topics in each document, ranked by probability, and a list of the words in each topic, ranked by probability. Researchers tend to focus on the top-ranked topics and top-ranked words, as that is where meaningful semantic distinctions can be observed. In the 2003 paper that introduced the LDA algorithm, Blei et al. displayed four lists of top-ranked words from a topic model of 16,000 articles from the Associated Press, labeling the topics as "Arts," "Budgets," "Children," and "Education."[36] This practice of labeling topics with simple one- or two-word names based on domain knowledge has become widespread in subsequent topic modeling research, in part because it helps make broad semantic distinctions clear. As Block notes, "Readers may quibble over the exact topic label, but should be able to see the relationship between the words listed in each topic."[37] Yet this practice is not without controversy, particularly when applied to literary, rather than journalistic or critical writing.

Matthew Jockers presents selected results from his 500-topic model of a corpus of 3,346 nineteenth-century novels by displaying the top-ranking words for each topic as word clouds, with the words sized by their probability rank, and a companion website to the book allows viewers to explore data visualizations for all 500 topics.[38] The word clouds allow the viewer to situate any particular word among "the much larger company of other words that the model returns," and to explore how each word functions differently in the context of each topic.[39] But because Jockers also applies a label to each topic, such as "Native Americans" and "Ireland," the reader is guided to understand the results as perhaps more cohesive than any topic

[34] Andrew Goldstone and Ted Underwood, "The Quiet Transformations of Literary Studies: What Thirteen Thousand Scholars Could Tell Us," *New Literary History* 45.3 (Summer 2014): 359–384.

[35] Lauren F. Klein, "Dimensions of Scale: Invisible Labor, Editorial Work, and the Future of Quantitative Literary Studies," *PMLA* 135.1 (2020): 37.

[36] Blei et al., "Latent Dirichlet Allocation," 1009.

[37] Block, "Doing More with Digitization."

[38] Jockers, *Macroanalysis*, 126. The companion website is: www.matthewjockers.net/macroanalysisbook/macro-themes/ (accessed April 22, 2022).

[39] Ibid., 127.

model actually can be. Jeffrey Binder cautions against trying to interpret the words output in a topic model as if they hold meaning in the same ways that words do in an individual text, because each is an "abstract composite" representing numerous different, though semantically related, uses of the word.[40]

Jockers discusses in detail the steps he took in preparing his corpus of novels for topic modeling, including the "controversial step" of modeling only the nouns in the novels, in order to produce "highly interpretable and thematically coherent topics."[41] The clarity and elegance of Jockers's results are usefully balanced by his thorough technical discussion, which explains how each step in selecting and preparing the data, and configuring the parameters of the model affects the coherence of the results. As he points out, literary critics discuss "the specific elements of a text that we consider to be the interpretable elements"; the advantage of topic modeling is that it always also shows us what does not fit into our assumed interpretive framework.[42]

In her groundbreaking work on topic modeling poetic language, Lisa M. Rhody points out that the fundamental relationship between word and meaning is configured differently in poetry than in informational texts, because "the use of highly figurative speech actually increases the scope of the language one might expect to see in a document."[43] The expectation that co-occurring words relate to the same semantic topic could be confounded by metaphor and other devices that expand the signification of poetic texts.

In keeping with this interpretive caution, Rhody consistently refers to topics in her model by numbers, rather than by assigning her own interpretive labels to them. In her sixty-topic model of a corpus of 4,500 poems, she finds four types of topics: those relating to OCR errors or other linguistic variations, such as the presence of foreign languages or dialect; topics corresponding to very long, repetitive poems; "semantically evident" topics; and "semantically opaque" topics. Even in those that appear "semantically evident," she warns that "the illusion of thematic comprehensibility obscures what is actually being captured by the topic model," arguing that rather than being simply "about night," poems such as Anne Sexton's "The Starry Night" "participate in discourses surrounding 'night' and 'natural

[40] Binder, "Alien Reading."
[41] Jockers, *Macroanalysis*, 131.
[42] Ibid., 130.
[43] Lisa Rhody, "Topic Modeling and Figurative Language," *Journal of Digital Humanities* 2.1 (2012): http://journalofdigitalhumanities.org/2-1/ (accessed April 22, 2022).

landscapes.'"[44] Examining the poems associated with more opaque topics reveal the subtle discourses of poetry's history: "To say that Topic 2 is about 'death, loss, and internal turmoil' is overly simplistic ... to say that Topic 2 draws from the language of elegy would be more accurate."[45] As Rhody demonstrates, topic modeling can be valuable for exploring literary corpora only if used with an awareness of the methodological and linguistic assumptions that underlie the method.

5 Predictive Modeling

In supervised machine learning, one of the most widely used techniques in predictive modeling, a machine learning algorithm is trained with a portion of the dataset in which each instance has been labeled according to two or more predefined categories. The model is then tested against the remaining portion of the dataset to see how accurately it can predict the category labels of those instances. A successful model may then be used to predict the labels for additional, similar data. Predictive models are commonly used in situations where the prediction itself is of value, such as an algorithm that examines the words used in an email to guess the likelihood of its being spam.

Although the scientific literature refers to disagreements between the model's label assignment and the actual label as misclassifications, in computational humanities scholarship they are often seen as a valuable source of insight, rather than treating them as errors. In distant reading, the predictions made by such models are used to better understand critical categories such as gender, genre, and historical period. As Andrew Piper suggests, "Predictive models allow us to say with how much certainty we can identify texts that belong to a specific group and under what criteria."[46] Because the model estimates the likelihood of each label it assigns, it offers a way to compare different categorizations of the same data.

An influential early example was Matthew Jockers's use of predictive modeling with a dataset of 106 nineteenth-century novels from twelve different fiction subgenres, such as historical, religious, silver-fork, Gothic, and industrial novels. Jockers demonstrates that the model could accurately predict the genre of a text 67 percent of the time using the relative frequency counts of only the highest-frequency word and punctuation

[44] Ibid.
[45] Ibid.
[46] Piper, *Enumerations*, 101.

features from the novels, such as articles and pronouns, rather than words that are directly tied to theme or setting.[47] Jockers argues that when dealing with classes such as genre, which "are human inventions that are not always clearly delineated," researchers ought "to consider both the first- and the second-place assignments when assessing the overall performance and value of the model," noting that in some cases these two probabilities may be very close.[48] If two novelistic genres are frequently labeled as each other, for example, he suggests there might be a "stylistic affinity" between those genres that further research could uncover.[49] A frequent misclassification might also indicate that there are confounding factors in the experiment. Texts are not only produced as examples of genres; they are written by particular authors, in particular historical moments, in particular places. Each of these factors might produce a stronger textual signal than that of genre.

In a second experiment with the same dataset of 106 novels, Jockers compared how successful predictive models were in predicting the authorship, author gender, publication decade, genre, or specific novel title for segments of the texts. Jockers found that the models for author signal were significantly more accurate than those for other categories, suggesting that "classifications based on loosely defined genres produce comparatively poor results when viewed next to the results for a more objectively defined category."[50] In a dataset of only 106 novels spread over twelve genres, authorship would significantly overlap with the genre categories, making them difficult to distinguish.

In their study of English-language haiku, Hoyt Long and Richard So use predictive modeling to examine "whether the machine recognizes a haiku over and against a text that is nonhaiku and if so, what statistical evidence it uses to make that decision."[51] To do this, they compiled a corpus of 400 English haiku, both translations and adaptations, and 1,900 short poems published in periodicals during the early twentieth century, and ran a series of experiments that trained the classification model with different language features from the poems. A model that included syllable counts and excluded function words was able to correctly identify haiku translations 91 percent of the time and haiku adaptations 86 percent of

47 Jockers, *Macroanalysis*, 72.
48 Ibid., 73.
49 Ibid., 73.
50 Ibid., 92.
51 Hoyt Long and Richard So, "Literary Pattern Recognition: Modernism between Close Reading and Machine Learning," *Critical Inquiry* 42.2 (Winter 2016): 252.

the time. But like Jockers, Long and So are more interested in examining the misclassifications. Another model that ignored syllable counts and included function words increased the number of nonhaiku poems that the model classified as haiku. Long and So examine the 202 poems that were most frequently misclassified by the model as haiku, organizing them into three groups: "haiku in waiting," "potential haiku," and "machine haiku," suggesting that rather than simply defining these misclassifications as errors, critics can productively use them to "reconsider our own interpretive biases."[52]

Ted Underwood suggests that "a mode of inquiry founded on models can study relationships rather than isolated facts," allowing researchers to connect sociocultural phenomena with textual change.[53] Genre is a key focus of his study, in part because its defining features change over time. What readers in the 1890s recognized as detective fiction is different from what readers in the 1990s expected in detective fiction. Among the many examples discussed in his book, two exemplify Underwood's thoughtful deployment of predictive models and experimental thinking.

He shows that a useful way to test the validity of specific genre models is to test them on different corpora. For example, he tests a model trained on detective fiction to see if it can identify works of science fiction. If the model is truly identifying something distinctive in the texts it identifies as detective fiction, one would expect that experiment to fail, and indeed it does. He calls this "the method of mutual recognition," as it can be run in both directions to show how distinctive different subgenres of fiction are.[54]

To test critical assumptions about genre and literary history, Underwood develops a method he calls "perspectival modeling": a "strategy that gets leverage on cultural history by comparing models trained on different subsets of the evidence."[55] Because a supervised model "describes one set of texts through their relation to another," he examines changes within a specific genre such as science fiction by asking a model trained on early texts to classify texts from later decades, and vice versa.[56] Underwood's experiments suggest that although traditional critical accounts of fictional genres such as detective fiction, Gothic fiction, and science fiction emphasize change and discontinuity, in part because they focus on the influence

[52] Ibid., 262–265.
[53] Ted Underwood, *Distant Horizons: Digital Evidence and Literary Change* (Chicago: University of Chicago Press, 2019), xii.
[54] Ibid., 46–47.
[55] Ibid., 36.
[56] Ibid., 61–65.

of individual authors, a distant reading approach using predictive models with large corpora shows more continuity within genres over the nineteenth and twentieth centuries.

6 Tools for Distant Reading

In the early to mid-2000s, AJAX (Asynchronous JavaScript and XML) programming fostered the development of what became known as Web 2.0, which allowed for user interactivity, including user-generated content on blogs and wikis, social media, and the creation of web-based software applications.[57] These technologies emphasized participation and leveled the technological playing field: "Users could 'write' the Web in the browser itself, rather than using separate tools that required additional technical knowledge."[58] As these technologies have continued to develop, the ability to combine clientside data with serverside processing has allowed users to explore, analyze, and remix text, audio, and visual data. A large number of digital humanities tools, including both installed software packages and web-based applications, have been developed for text analysis, geospatial analysis, network analysis, and data visualization.[59] Although most of the scholarship cited earlier was performed in programming languages such as R or Python, today there are several robust toolsets that allow scholars and students without programming backgrounds to begin experimenting with distant reading. Toolsets such as Voyant Tools, Lexos, and Orange can be used as a low-stakes way to learn about its methods and insights and contribute to new knowledge. All three of these toolsets can be used for analyzing large text corpora and for data visualization (exploratory modeling); Voyant and

[57] Susannah Fox and Mary Madden, "Riding the Waves of 'Web 2.0.'" Pew Internet Project, October 5, 2006: www.pewresearch.org/internet/2006/10/05/riding-the-waves-of-web-2-0/ (accessed April 22, 2022).

[58] Doug Belshaw, "A Unified 20-Year History of the Radically Changing Way We Relate to the Web," *Washington Post*, December 3, 2014: www.washingtonpost.com/news/the-intersect/wp/2014/12/03/a-unified-20-year-history-of-the-radically-changing-way-we-relate-to-the-web/ (accessed April 22, 2022).

[59] Unfortunately, a number of these tools have since suffered the effects of terminated funding or have simply become technologically obsolete. Even some of the major directories of tools, including DiRT and Project Bamboo, have met the same fate; a current directory as of this writing is TERESAH, the Tools E-Registry for E-Social science, Arts and Humanities. See Quinn Dombrowski, "What Ever Happened to Project Bamboo?" *Literary and Linguistic Computing*, 29.3 (September 2014): 326–339: https://doi.org/10.1093/llc/fqu026 (accessed April 22, 2022); "DiRT: Digital Research Tools Wiki," last modified 1 September 2012: https://digitalresearchtools.pbworks.com/w/page/17801672/FrontPage (accessed April 22, 2022); and "TERESAH: Tools E-Registry for E-Social science, Arts and Humanities," Data Service Infrastructure for the Social Sciences and Humanities (DASISH): http://teresah.dariah.eu/ (accessed April 22, 2022).

Orange offer workflows for LDA topic modeling (generative modeling); and Orange offers workflows for text classification (predictive modeling).[60]

Finally, an extensive array of resources exists for users interested in learning enough programming in R or Python to analyze texts in the ways surveyed in this chapter. In addition to general-audience books, courses, and online tutorials, some are specifically targeted at humanities scholars and students.[61]

Before the 1980s, humanities computing was largely restricted to those with access to university mainframe computing resources, and data storage limits and the necessity of hand-keying textual data imposed significant constraints on the creation of textual corpora. Today, open access archives of digital texts combine with powerful personal computers and online tools to put distant reading within reach of anyone with an experimental mindset.

[60] Stéfan Sinclair and Geoffrey Rockwell, "Voyant Tools," version 2.5.4, February 11, 2022: https://voyant-tools.org/ (accessed April 22, 2022); "Lexos," Wheaton Lexomics, 2019: http://lexos.wheatoncollege.edu/upload (accessed April 22, 2022); "Orange," University of Ljubljana: https://orangedatamining.com/ (accessed April 22, 2022).

[61] Taylor Arnold and Lauren Tilton, *Humanities Data in R: Networks, Geospatial Data, Images, and Text* (Cham: Springer, 2015); Matthew L. Jockers, *Text Analysis with R for Students of Literature*, 2nd ed. (Cham: Springer, 2020); and Folgert Karsdorp, Mike Kestemont, and Allen Riddell, *Humanities Data Analysis: Case Studies with Python* (Princeton: Princeton University Press, 2021).

CHAPTER 20

Visualization

Daniel Carter

Visualization has become a representative technique for literature scholars who use digital tools. Charts, graphs, and maps allow scholars to perform analysis in new ways and at new scales, and they often serve as highly visible symbols of digital humanities work. As Elyse Graham points out, however, "the humanities are a latecomer to the field" and are only now working to "reconcil[e] the young age of data analysis with the rich texture of research that humanities scholarship emphasises."[1] As Graham implies, recently introduced digital visualization tools alter processes of knowledge production that have long histories. Terms such as "distant reading,"[2] or "machine reading,"[3] indicate this transition from practices such as close reading that have defined literary studies for centuries to methodologies that, while sometimes reminiscent of earlier approaches, are distinct in important ways. While visual representation and statistical analysis are far from new, the recent availability of large datasets and computational techniques encourages literature scholars to adopt new tools and work practices and to reflect on how these tools and practices can be used to produce knowledge in distinctly humanistic ways.

Digital visualization tools offer literature scholars compelling affordances, particularly in relation to scale: They hold out the possibility of analyzing 1 million pages of manga through a single scatterplot,[4] for example, or of locating otherwise imperceptible patterns of repetition within

[1] Elyse Graham, "Introduction: Data Visualisation and the Humanities," *English Studies* 98.5 (July 4, 2017): 449.

[2] Franco Moretti, *Distant Reading* (London: Verso Books, 2013).

[3] N. Katherine Hayles, *How We Think: Digital Media and Contemporary Technogenesis* (Chicago: University of Chicago Press, 2012).

[4] Lev Manovich, "How to Compare One Million Images?," *Understanding Digital Humanities*, ed. David Berry (New York: Palgrave Macmillan, 2012).

Gertrude Stein's *The Making of Americans*.[5] At the same time, critical scholarship on the use of visualization in the humanities draws attention to the disciplinary histories of techniques that are most often developed and employed within the quantitative sciences. As Tanya Clement points out, "new methods in digital humanities such as statistical analysis, visualization and ethnography do not exist in a vacuum."[6] In order to bring these new methods into their work, Clement suggests that humanities scholars must articulate their processes of knowledge production and explicitly argue for why their work is aligned with humanistic norms and values.

1 Epistemologies of Visualization

Lauren Klein's scholarship has approached the problem of articulating specifically humanistic forms of visualization by returning to historical examples as objects of critique and reinvention. By tracing the connections between historical, analog forms of visualization and the epistemologies to which they are linked, Klein argues for how these connections could be reimagined and for how the affordances of digital tools can be used to support the work of literature scholars. In her essay "The Image of Absence: Archival Silence, Data Visualization and James Hemings," for example, Klein argues that Thomas Jefferson's analog visualization practices reinforced a worldview that traced a clear line from what could be observed to what could be visualized and from what could be visualized to what was unequivocally true.[7] As Klein argues, Jefferson's epistemology and related visualization practices were rooted in what he perceived to be a political need: for the citizens of a democratic society to accept a common set of facts. Accordingly, he presents his hand-drawn tables as isolated objects, cut off from commentary and implying a frictionless transition from observation to shared belief. As Klein argues, his analog visualization practices suggest the possibility of telling one story that can be true everywhere.

5 Tanya E. Clement, "'A Thing Not Beginning and Not Ending': Using Digital Tools to Distant-Read Gertrude Stein's *The Making of Americans*," *Literary and Linguistic Computing* 23.3 (September 1, 2008): 361–381.

6 Tanya E. Clement, "Where Is Methodology in Digital Humanities?," in *Debates in the Digital Humanities*, ed. Matthew K. Gold and Lauren F. Klein (Minneapolis: University of Minnesota Press, 2016).

7 Lauren F. Klein, "The Image of Absence: Archival Silence, Data Visualization, and James Hemings," *American Literature* 85.4 (December 1, 2013): 661–688.

Klein's own visualization work takes as its starting point Jefferson's representation of his enslaved chef, James Hemings. In a personal notebook in which Jefferson recorded information related to his various homes, including the people enslaved there, Hemings is given a single line in a simple, hand-drawn table: "Jemmy. 1765". Klein argues that Jefferson's inscription of Hemings reduces the intricacies of his life to a name and, furthermore, does so using a visual style that masks the assumptions and biases underlying its creation. That is, while Jefferson's observations are influenced by his specific position (as a white man, as a slave owner), the choices he makes in visualizing his observations suggest that they are complete and universal facts.

Citing Johanna Drucker's concern that visualization conventions used within the humanities "are cloaked in a rhetoric taken wholesale from the techniques of the empirical sciences that conceals their epistemological biases under a guise of familiarity,"[8] Klein sets out to use digital visualization tools in ways that would complicate Jefferson's analog visualizations by highlighting the roles Hemings played and also the ways the archive renders those roles invisible. In Figure 20.1, for example, Klein visualizes the connections between Jefferson and those to whom he wrote concerning Hemings. In describing her process for producing the visualization, she makes clear her theoretical commitment to highlighting the "ghostly presence" of Hemings in the archive and the ways this commitment influenced specific choices related to data collection and visualization.[9] She describes choosing to use an arc diagram, which places individuals' names prominently along the left axis, rather than a force-directed network graph, a more conventional choice but one that makes individuals less identifiable and comparable. And while Klein notes that she could have linked the arcs connecting individuals to the content of the letters exchanged between them, she argues for constraining her visualization in order to provide a view of the archive that draws attention not to Jefferson's words but to Heming's influence as well as his erasure. Contrary to Jefferson's approach, which used analog techniques to produce visualizations that portrayed individuals' observations as universal facts, Klein's digital approach suggests that she has purposefully produced one view of the archive, and that others are possible.

8 Johanna Drucker, "Humanities Approaches to Graphical Display," *Digital Humanities Quarterly* 5.1 (2011).

9 Klein, "The Image of Absence," 668.

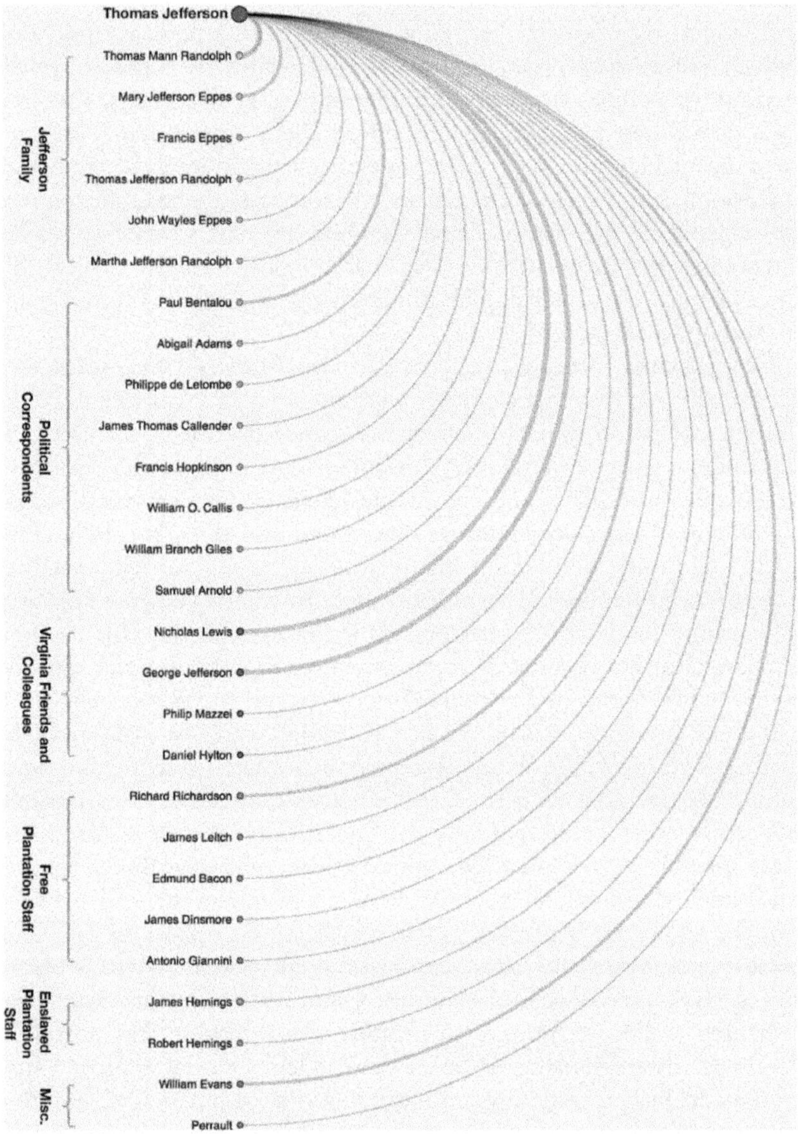

Figure 20.1 An arc diagram produced by Klein indicating with whom Jefferson communicated about Hemings. Arc width indicates the frequency of correspondence. Courtesy of Lauren Klein.

2 What It Truly Means to Know: Articulating Visualization within Literary Studies

Making a broad case for the potential of digital visualization for literary studies, Klein argues for an approach that reflects on and makes visible not just data but also the situated perspectives and choices of scholars working with data. The need for reflection is strongly tied to the features of recently developed digital tools, which, Klein argues, "by virtue of their technical nature, … highlight the position of the reader and his or her relation to the text. The critic's involvement in the design and implementation – or at the least, the selection and application – of digital tools demands acknowledgement of his or her critical agency."[10] Ultimately, Klein argues that digital visualizations and related tools do more than increase the scale or efficiency with which literary scholarship can be performed; the transition from analog to digital visualizations also calls for "a rethinking of what it truly means to know."[11]

In the remainder of this chapter, I explore questions around what it "truly means to know" in literary studies by focusing on the ways that digital visualization tools introduce new relationships into scholarly work: with new forms of data and new software objects, with scholars from outside literary studies, and with organizational structures that are not conventional within English departments. This focus on relationships is somewhat unusual in relation to the scholarship on visualization that has emerged from within literary studies, where a considerable bulk of the writing takes a normative approach to sorting out how visualizations should be produced or how they might advance scholarship.[12] Rather than adopting this normative approach, in this chapter, I instead focus on describing the visualization practices enacted by literature scholars. Following science and technology studies scholars who have focused primarily on the role of visualization and similar forms of evidence in scientific labs and related settings,[13] I approach visualization as a phenomenon that is socially and

[10] Ibid., 667.

[11] Ibid., 665.

[12] See, for example, Martyn Jessop, "Digital as a Scholarly Activity," *Literary and Linguistic Computing* 23.3 (September 1, 2008): 281–293; Stéfan Sinclair, Stan Ruecker, and Milena Radzikowska, "Information Visualization for Humanities Scholars," *Literary Studies in the Digital Age* (New York: MLA Commons, 2013); Manovich, "How to Compare One Million Images?"

[13] For example, Lorraine Daston and Peter Galison, *Objectivity* (Brooklyn: Zone Books, 2007); Michael Lynch, "The Externalized Retina: Selection and Mathematization in the Visual Documentation of Objects in the Life Sciences," in *Representation in Scientific Practice*, ed. Michael Lynch and Steve Woolgar (Cambridge, MA: MIT Press, 1990); Bruno Latour and Steve Woolgar, *Laboratory Life: The Construction of Scientific Facts* (Princeton: Princeton University Press, 1986).

materially constructed – or, as Chiaro Ambrosio argues, as an "epistemological relation" that is "*discovered* through processes and practices that are historically grounded."[14]

Casting visualization as a relation draws attention to the technical tools, data structures, and social roles that surround graphs, maps, and other visual forms. And casting visualization as a relation that is *discovered* draws attention to visualization as a process that is situated historically as well as materially in the ways that people work to produce knowledge. As scholars within literary studies produce digital visualizations, they come into contact with databases, programming languages, software packages, interactive displays, printed graphs and literatures, and colleagues from other disciplines. In order to take advantage of the affordances of digital visualizations, scholars negotiate these new relations and work out how to align new tools with existing processes for performing scholarly work. This is the process of discovery to which Ambrosio refers: not a simple path from observation to graph or map but an ongoing struggle with the materials with which scholars interact. Reflecting on "what it truly means to know" therefore requires acknowledging these relations and exploring how, within literary studies, scholars preserve conventional processes of knowledge production while introducing new tools and affordances into their work.

In order to write this chapter, I interviewed thirteen scholars who currently produce digital visualizations as part of their work. I focus, in the following sections, primarily on two projects discussed in these interviews, but draw on others in order to provide context and draw attention to larger patterns present across scholars' work. These scholars range in their level of experience from doctoral students to full professors. Their work focuses largely, but not exclusively, on literature and spans a diverse array of techniques, from machine learning to social network analysis and 3D modeling. Interviews included here took place between 2015 and 2017, and participants' titles, affiliated institutions, and other information reflect their status at that time.

The scholars with whom I spoke make clear that visualization practices, like other practices such as close reading, are material and social – material because scholars' projects reveal the role that data formats, software

[14] Chiara Ambrosio, "Objectivity and Representative Practices across Artistic and Scientific Visualization," in *Visualization in the Age of Computerization*, ed. Annamaria Carusi, Aud Sissel Hoel, Timothy Webmoor, and Steve Woolgar (London: Routledge, 2014), 119, emphasis in original.

packages and even physical spaces play in the construction of knowledge, and social because scholars learn how to produce visualizations and integrate them into their work processes through interactions with colleagues both inside and outside literary studies and by consulting a relatively stable canon of key texts. Indeed, one of the most interesting patterns to emerge from discussions with these scholars is that few learn to produce visualizations by reading articles or books published by scholars within literary studies or the broader humanities. More often, the literature they reference comes from other disciplines: John Tukey's *Exploratory Data Analysis*, for example, or the works of Edward Tufte.[15] In contrast, the sources they reference within the humanities are often informal publications such as blog posts by Miriam Posner or Benjamin Schmidt, or study groups affiliated with a center or graduate program. Nora Benedict, a postdoctoral fellow at the Center for Digital Humanities at Princeton University, for example, works in a social context in which techniques for producing visualizations are shared in formalized ways, with code made available on Github and working groups gathered around specific techniques. The resulting projects, as she describes them, share a family resemblance: They draw on a common set of tools and techniques, and are influenced by a set of shared commitments.

Similarly, the tools with which humanities scholars produce visualizations are for the most part borrowed from other disciplines and professions, but the specific scholarly practices around their use vary widely. At times, humanities scholars use tools to produce visualizations in ways that are consistent with the conventions of other disciplines such as statistics or computer science. Lauren Tilton, an assistant professor of digital humanities at the University of Richmond, works closely with Taylor Arnold, a statistician, and notes that over time she has come to see exploratory data analysis – a conventional methodology in statistics – as very much in line with the values of the humanities. "I think in some ways there's an assumption that the divide's larger than it is," Tilton says of the relationship between the humanities and statistics. However, at other times, literature scholars' practices are highly idiosyncratic, as are the visualizations produced. Ryan Heuser, a doctoral candidate at Stanford University, uses machine learning techniques drawn from the field of natural language processing but prefers to visualize their results using network graphs rather than visual forms that are more conventional in the machine learning

[15] John Tukey, *Exploratory Data Analysis* (Reading, MA: Addison-Wesley, 1977); see, for instance, Edward Tufte, *The Visual Display of Graphic Information* (Cheshire, CT: Graphics Press, 2001).

community. In justifying his unconventional decision, Heuser draws connections between the form of a visualization and how scholars are able to use that form to generate insights: "There's a continuousness to [visualizations conventional in machine learning]. There's just a sea of data, and wherever you are, there's really nothing that distinguishes where else you could be. Whereas for me, networks have this angularity that's really interesting, that's like, 'You're right here, and where can you go from here?' There's just a different topology to it." As Heuser implies, data availability, statistical techniques, and digital visualization tools afford new ways of thinking about literature – but what matters is how these elements are brought together and the choices that scholars make along the way.

In the following sections, I zoom in on two projects, highlighting the relations that surround digital visualizations and the ways that scholars negotiate these relations. In the first section, I argue that although the statistical techniques underlying many digital visualizations are developed in fields with processes of knowledge production that often align poorly with those in literary studies, literature scholars use visualization as a way to produce objects that are amenable to interpretive processes that are conventional within their own field. In the second section, I consider ways in which scholars use digital visualizations to make visible their distinct processes and interpretations so that they can be shared, critiqued, and compared.

3 Making Objects Interpretable

As Johanna Drucker argues, many of the processes surrounding visualization are not developed within the humanities and, consequently, may be out of step with the epistemological commitments or work practices of scholars such as those in literary studies.[16] Topic models provide a representative example of this influx, as they are widely used in literary studies but were originally developed for use in information retrieval tasks such as search and summarization. Topic modeling applies a collection of statistical techniques that attempt to identify abstract topics present in a collection of texts and to describe each text as composed of a mixture of those topics. For example, a topic model might describe *Moby Dick* as composed of a topic associated with seafaring, a topic associated with marine mammals, and a topic associated with food and cooking. As with many statistical techniques

[16] See Drucker, "Humanities Approaches to Graphical Display."

used for similar tasks, topic models can quickly process a large number of texts, allowing scholars to ask otherwise insurmountable questions such as how a specific topic is distributed across centuries of texts.

While topic models were developed outside literary studies and the broader humanities, in many ways they have become representative of the work produced under the label "digital humanities." As Meeks and Weingart argue, "The rapid pace of communication about topic modeling, the focus on workshops and gray literature and snippets of code, the mixed methods invoked and used, are an ideal introduction to what it means to be a digital humanist in a networked world."[17] In describing topic models' representativeness as a digital humanities technique, Meeks and Weingart also begin to suggest the variety of relations required to import a technique from another discipline and align it with the conventions of literary studies. Literature scholars who use techniques such as topic modeling are not only networked because they talk to one another but also because they use new software tools and exchange work and collaborate with colleagues in new ways. As scholars form these diverse relationships, they must also negotiate with new processes of knowledge production and norms for performing scholarly work.

Techniques for visualizing topic models play a key role in this negotiation by producing objects that can be interpreted or discussed in ways that are fairly conventional to literature scholars. While the numerical results of topic models and other statistical techniques might feel foreign in a literary studies publication, existing projects suggest that producing visualizations based on these techniques translates their results into a form that is interpretable in largely conventional ways. For example, scholars have used topic models to understand the themes present in nineteenth-century literature;[18] to study the social and political life of the city of Richmond during the Civil War, as seen through the topics present in the local paper;[19] even to visualize the development of software,[20] and the whaling routes written about by sailors.[21]

[17] Elijah Meeks and Scott B. Weingart, "The Digital Humanities Contribution to Topic Modeling," *Journal of Digital Humanities* 2.1 (April 9, 2013).

[18] Matthew L. Jockers and David Mimno, "Significant Themes in 19th-Century Literature," *Poetics*, 41.6 (December 1, 2013): 750–769.

[19] Robert K. Nelson, "Mining the Dispatch," Digital Scholarship Lab, the University of Richmond, n.d. http://dsl.richmond.edu/dispatch/pages/intro (accessed July 16, 2023).

[20] Michael L. Black, "A Textual History of Mozilla: Using Topic Modeling to Trace Sociocultural Influences on Software Development," *Digital Humanities Quarterly* 9.3 (December 23, 2015).

[21] Benjamin M. Schmidt, "Words Alone: Dismantling Topic Models in the Humanities," *Journal of Digital Humanities* (April 5, 2013).

Andrew Goldstone's work with topic models demonstrates the potential of visualization for producing interpretable objects, as well as the tensions that are introduced to that work by new relationships. Goldstone, now an associate professor of English at Rutgers University, first discovered topic models when he was on a postdoctoral appointment at Stanford. He was drawn to the technique as part of his interest in the history of literary studies, and he hoped that by modeling a large collection of academic articles, he would be able to identify broad patterns in that corpus. In order to analyze over one hundred years of scholarship, Goldstone, working with Ted Underwood, produced a series of line charts, each showing the prominence of a given topic over time (Figure 20.2). This process is highly standardized among literature scholars who work with topic models – but Goldstone notes that producing such line charts is highly unconventional outside literary studies and related fields, noting, "It's the thing that pretty much everyone else in English or History has done who has fiddled with topic models, which is incredibly weird because it's not even what they were designed for. But we all did it because that's the thing that seems interpretable."

As Goldstone's comment implies, objects amenable to interpretation are not simply *found*; they are actively *constructed.* Among literature scholars, the numerical results of topic models are typically not thought to be an especially useful base for interpretation until they are visualized – and some processes for producing visualizations are more likely to lead to interpretable objects than others. Producing visualizations of topic models is not only a way to access the affordances they provide with respect to efficiency and scale but also a way of shaping those affordances in order to align with the specific needs and habits of literature scholars.

Describing ways that he and colleagues would share and discuss these line charts, Goldstone indicates what it means for a visualization to be "interpretable" in this context. When discussing series of line charts such as those represented in Figure 20.2, for example, he says he would note of a particular topic, "This looks interesting" or "This topic seems historically meaningful. What can we do about that?" Here, the visual affordances of line charts are clear, as are the ways these affordances align with processes that Goldstone finds familiar. Line charts condense information, but still give scholars visual features that are detailed enough to isolate and discuss. They're also highly comparable, allowing scholars to identify patterns or aberrations for further attention. And, when constructed with time along the x-axis, they speak to core concerns of literature scholars with an interest in history.

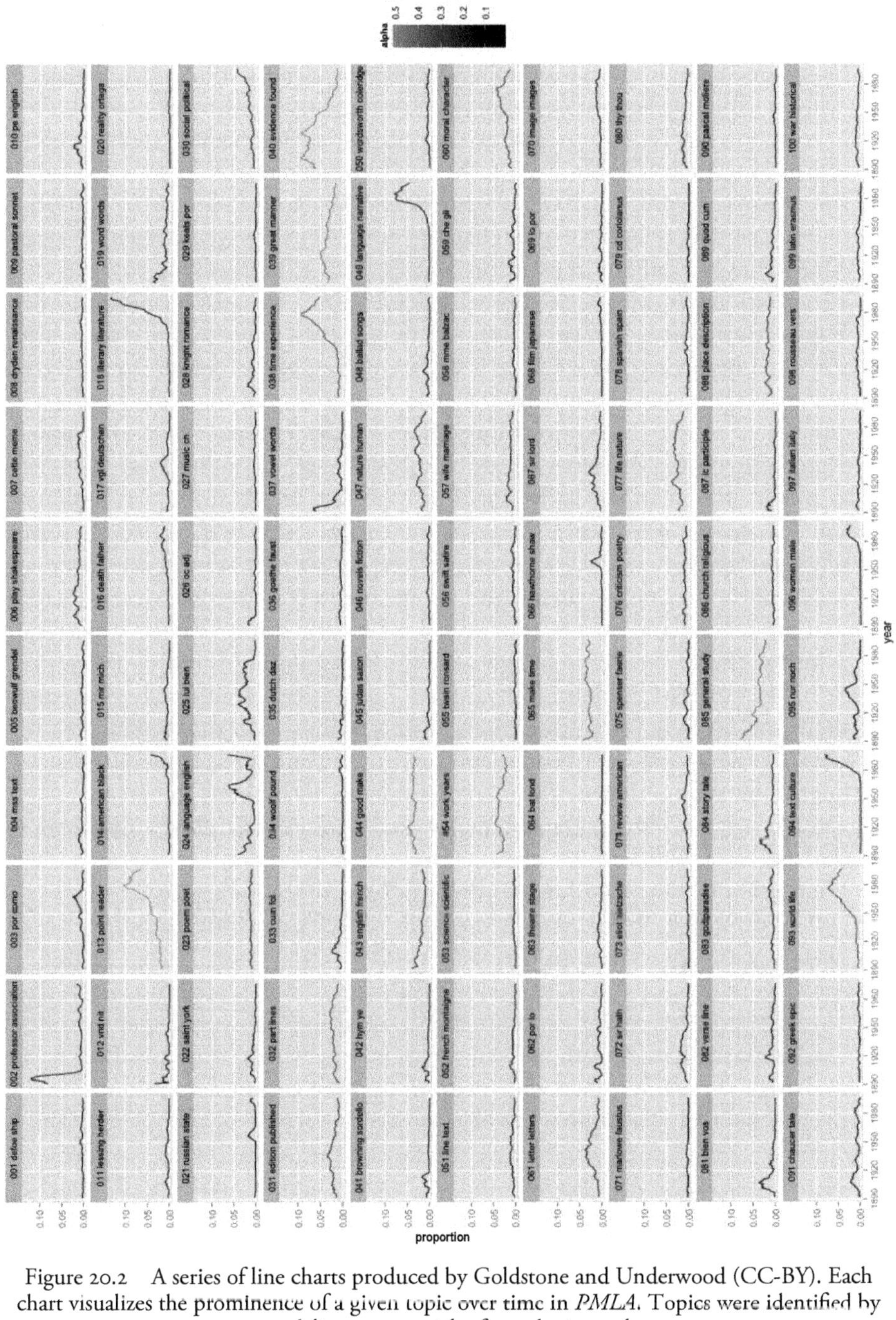

Figure 20.2 A series of line charts produced by Goldstone and Underwood (CC-BY). Each chart visualizes the prominence of a given topic over time in *PMLA*. Topics were identified by modeling 5,940 articles from the journal.

Perhaps owing to these affordances, line charts are frequently employed in digital literary studies. As background for his own work, for example, Goldstone cites Franco Moretti's *Maps, Graphs and Trees*,[22] which incorporates similar visualizations. But he also suggests that the pull toward line charts showing change over time cannot be tied to specific predecessors, speculating that "there's some rather mysterious cultural logic that made [literature scholars] gravitate to wanting to visualize a time series." Indeed, in separate interviews for this chapter, both Matthew Jockers and Mark Algee-Hewitt similarly remark on how normal it has become to produce visualizations in this specific form. Algee-Hewitt, an assistant professor of English and Director of the Stanford Literary Lab, refers to line charts that place history along the x-axis as the "favorite graph" of literature scholars who use digital tools. Similarly, Matt Jockers, Dean of the College of Arts and Sciences and Professor of English and Data Analytics at Washington State University, describes producing line charts of topics over time as especially suited to the early stages of a project in which he was looking for "low-hanging fruit and whatever was easiest to do first." Further, both scholars describe similar processes of interpreting these line charts, noting the importance of comparison and being able to pick out individual charts that are interesting or provocative. Algee-Hewitt, for example, describes printing charts showing change over time and taping them to the walls of his lab so that students working on the project could easily compare them and identify interesting cases. "The ways in which the students made sense of the graphs very much replicated their training as humanities students," he says: "That is, they were interested in looking for those outliers." As with Goldstone and Underwood's line charts, the visualizations that Algee-Hewitt and his students produce construct objects that can be interpreted in ways that he describes as distinctly humanistic.

The ubiquity of line charts showing topics over time indicates how visualization practices in literary studies are standardized through social relationships and shared workflows. When collaborating with Underwood, for example, Goldstone describes how the pair would work separately, using their own datasets, but would then produce and exchange visualizations in what came to be a consistent document format that combined line charts and lists of words related to each topic. This common visual format afforded the kind of interpretive acts described earlier; but it also standardizes the pair's work across space and divergent datasets. Similarly, Jockers's example of producing line charts of topics

[22] Franco Moretti, *Maps, Graphs, and Trees* (London: Verso, 2005).

over time as part of an emerging collaborative relationship indicates the perceived utility of this visual form and the expectation that it would lead to valuable moments of interpretation, but his comment about "low-hanging fruit" also suggests the momentum provided by existing software tools and workflows. While he might make small adjustments to established processes for a specific project, his experience producing and interpreting line charts of this kind provides a kind of roadmap that is easily followed.

These social and material relationships facilitate the movement from a statistical technique to a form of visualization that aligns with the interpretive needs of those working within literary studies. Scholars negotiate between the scale and efficiency of topic models, for example, and the close attention to specific objects that often characterizes the work of literary studies, allowing large numbers of texts to be analyzed without removing the individual scholar from the process of generating insights. As Goldstone puts it, the processes for interpreting visualizations described here still very much revolve around the scholar's vision and the patterns and divergences that they are able – or predisposed – to identify.

However, Goldstone's more recent work illustrates that processes for interpreting visualizations within literary studies are not wholly standardized and that techniques such as topic modeling and visual forms such as line charts might exist within what Ambrosio refers to as "a plurality of relations."[23] That is, while Goldstone's practices, described earlier, represent a set of relations for producing visualizations that are interpretable within literary studies, this is only one of many possible sets of relations. Goldstone says that he has become wary of the kind of visual interpretation described here and has begun to explore alternative processes. Although he began by looking at series of line charts and focusing on individual topics that seemed to be interesting or to provide some momentum for further thought, he has also come to question this tendency:

> It just seemed clear to me that digital humanities, in particular, was characterized by overinterpretation of visualizations ...: an inability to make any principled distinction between artifacts of visualization and meaningful features of the data. And I had been doing that myself, and I feel that at least as an English literature scholar, I'm trained in overinterpretation. What I'm really good at is looking at some slice of text and making as much as I can out of it, but it's really dangerous to do that with visualization because you just don't have the same sense of the whole that the visualization represents, which is to

[23] Ambrosio, "Objectivity and Representative Practices," 138.

> say the dataset, that you do when you are talking about a passage from a novel or something, in which case you have a sense of the whole and a sense of the world around it that you can use to kind of validate what you're doing.

Goldstone began to address these concerns by searching for techniques and visual forms that would allow him to judge more easily whether observed patterns were meaningful and not quirks or "artifacts" of the statistical model underlying the visualization. If he notices and "makes as much as [he] can" out of a visual feature, is he really talking about a historically meaningful pattern or just an accidental bump produced by the topic modeling process? In discussing his attempts to construct this process, Goldstone also suggests alternative relations (with different software objects, different skills, and different collaborators) that might form around visualizations. In the past, he has taken statistics courses and attempted to collaborate with colleagues in other disciplines, working to construct processes of interpretation that are less conventional in his field. At the same time, his work demonstrates the diversity of practices that might exist around visualization, even within literary studies.

4 Making Interpretation Visible

Goldstone's earlier work illustrates how digital visualizations can align statistical techniques that are foreign to literary studies with processes of knowledge production that are conventional in that area. One way in which visualization functions, for Goldstone and others, is by giving the scholar something to interpret. In this section, I focus on the work of a group of scholars who use digital visualization techniques to make data visible and interpretable – but also to make their own choices and processes of interpretation visible to other scholars. As with Goldstone's work with topic models and line charts, these scholars use visualization techniques in order to align objects that are foreign to literary studies with conventional processes of knowledge production, but they also use them to purposefully enable their own distinct interpretations to be seen and compared. In this way, they demonstrate both how the affordances of digital visualizations are brought into the work of literature scholars and the ways those scholars self-reflectively push back against tools' assumptions.

Since 2013, Alex Christie, Katie Tanigawa, Stephen Ross, Jentery Sayers, and other contributors to the Z-Axis project have been distorting 3D maps in order to produce new perspectives on modernist novels. The resulting maps attempt to represent the spatial experience depicted in novels, allowing cultural or political features to warp the geographies of 2D maps. As

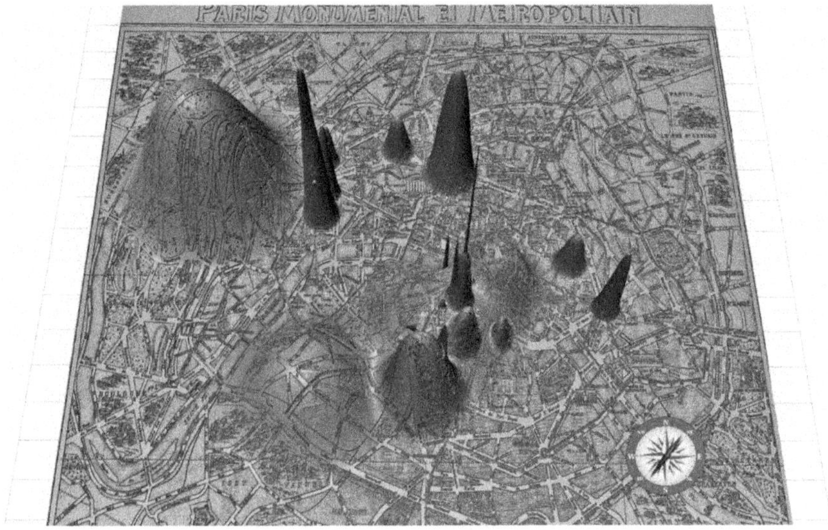

Figure 20.3 A distorted map of Djuna Barnes's *Nightwood* produced by Christie as part of the Z-Axis project. Courtesy of Alex Christie.

Christie explains, the project is strongly influenced by the argument that producing visualization is an interpretive process – that maps, for example, do not directly represent events or the relationships between places but actively construct one view of them. A consequence of this perspective, for members of the Z-Axis team, is that they assumed from the project's outset that conventional mapping software would be poorly aligned with their goals. Christie, for example, references a character in Djuna Barnes's *Nightwood* who, when narrating his actions, misremembers or misrepresents where they took place (Figure 20.3).[24] In pushing back against conventional mapping techniques and attempting to foreground the interpretive quality of maps, the Z-Axis team hoped to create forms of digital visualizations capable of representing misremembered places and the other deformed geographies of modernist novels. Christie's map, for example, highlights the "warping" of Paris's Left Bank – a distortion that, Christie and Tanigawa argue, "[is] both characterized by and produces the conditions for fluid and unstable identifications."[25] The choice to model spatial

[24] Djuna Barnes, *Nightwood* (London: Faber and Faber, 1936).

[25] Alex Christie and Katie Tanigawa, "Mapping Modernism's Z-axis: A Model for Spatial Analysis in Modernist Studies," in *Reading Modernism with Machines*, ed. Shawna Ross and James O'Sullivan (London: Palgrave Macmillan, 2016), 93.

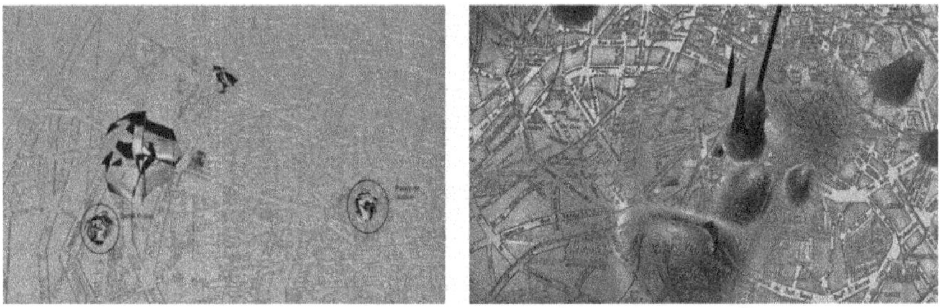

Figure 20.4 Distorted maps of Paris produced by Tanigawa (left) and Christie (right) illustrating visual choices that correspond to individual interpretations and reading processes. Where Christie's map emphasizes the connections between places by blending the hill shapes into each other, Tanigawa's emphasizes isolation and distance with a more fragmented visual representation. Courtesy of Katie Tanigawa and Alex Christie.

distortion using bulges points to geometric qualities such as radius and height, but, as Christie and Tanigawa argue, the radii here indicate not flat geometry but zones of possibility and freedom for the novel's characters.

From the outset, the team also had the goal of making their own interpretive practices visible:

> The maps themselves are meant to model interpretation and are themselves open to interpretation. So, the maps we make, we show them to someone, and what we're really modeling are interpretive processes. That doesn't mean that the reader has to agree with us. We see them as very open-ended in that way, and part of sharing our workflow involves inviting people to make their own maps, or to even make their own versions of the same maps we made.

Rather than seeing visualizations, first, as objects that can be interpreted, members of the Z-Axis team see them as representations of individual interpretive processes. These processes begin with scholars reading novels and encoding information about the locations in them and continue through the choices made when transforming their encodings into maps using Autodesk Mudbox, a 3D painting and sculpting tool conventionally used by artists and designers. Within this broad workflow, the team assumes that different readers will produce different maps of the same novel and that the visual features of these maps will reflect individual interpretive processes (Figure 20.4).

As Christie describes, the team's practices when using Mudbox to deform maps are highly idiosyncratic:

> We're using Mudbox in a very particular way, for a very particular [purpose]. One of the things that I think is so interesting about digital humanities or

digital literary studies is that literature offers a test case for the technology, so we're reading the literature on the technology, but we're also seeing where the literature we're trying to model pushes against the edges of the technical frameworks we have in hand. Part of our exploration with Mudbox is also an exploration of how 3D modeling software is suited or not suited to the ways of expressing knowledge that we're interested in.

Part of "pushing against" Mudbox, for the Z-Axis team, includes experimenting with the different effects the software makes available for distorting shapes. In part because the software is not intended to be used for warping maps based on encoded data, it does not include a dedicated tool or effect for this task, nor even suggest a workflow. The team thus explored effects intended for other purposes, ultimately producing a variety of visualizations ranging from maps that look like bar charts to a form that members refer to as a "data tornado." "We might come in and open Mudbox and just sort of explore," Christie says of the team's process. "In the same way that people talk about serendipity in a library, it was almost like serendipity in a production environment." Following their early commitment to using digital visualization tools in order to highlight their own interpretive processes, team members do not attempt to standardize their explorations or production choices, instead discussing the ways that different effects represent different approaches to the novels. In line with Klein's argument that digital tools place increased focus on the position of the reader or the critic with respect to the archive or the text, the Z-Axis team embrace the fact that they each approach texts differently. Rather than standardizing their visualization processes so as to make different objects comparable, they highlight their individual choices in order to make their positions as readers comparable.

While Christie and other members of the Z-Axis team base much of their work on the assumption that existing mapping tools are unsuitable for their project, other humanities scholars working with geographical data use conventional tools in largely conventional ways, demonstrating the diversity of relationships that surround visualization. Like members of the Z-Axis team, Jen Jack Gieseking, an assistant professor of geography at the University of Kentucky, uses digital visualization tools to tell alternative stories about place, focusing in his Queer New York project on lesbian and queer spaces. Gieseking's maps are valuable for making visible a diversity of spaces collected through interviews with lesbian and queer women, as well as documents from the Lesbian Herstory Archives (Figure 20.5). "My participants' stories are already so sliced and diced," Gieseking says. "That's the fragmented quality of queer experience; LGBTQ people don't sit around

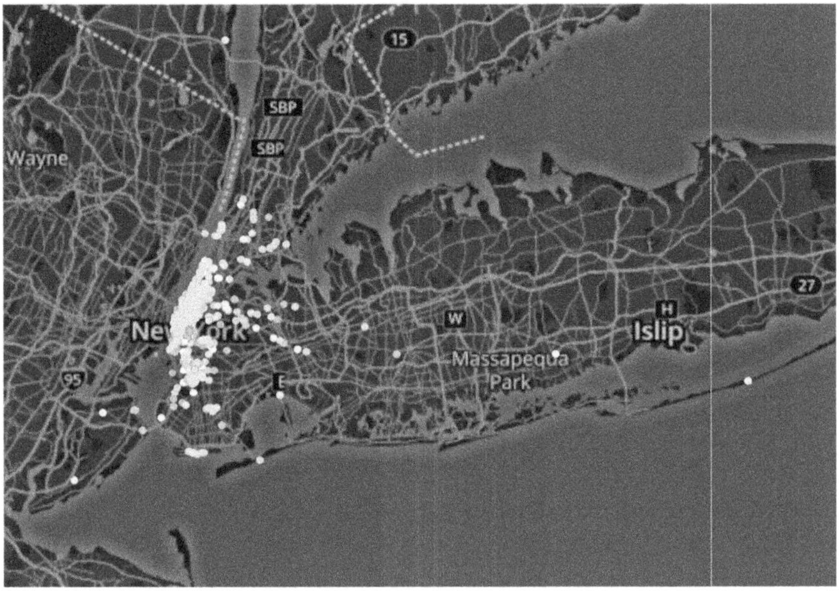

Figure 20.5 A map of lesbian and queer spaces produced by Jen Jack Gieseking (CC-BY) for his Queer New York project.

and tell one another all of their stories, especially about the harder things they face. So making the data visualization really bridges these stories."

Gieseking produced the maps for his Queer New York project using fairly conventional software tools, such as QGIS and MapBox. While he elsewhere critiques the standardization of software for visualizing geographic information,[26] arguing that producing queer histories should entail choosing and producing new tools designed for this objective, he also demonstrates that alternative mappings are possible using tools in largely standard ways. Rather than relating differently to software, as the Z-Axis team does, Gieseking introduces unconventional relationships and archival processes into otherwise standard mapping work. The resulting maps present an interpretation of the city, a view that reduces some features while foregrounding others. These maps do more than enable scholars to analyze phenomena that might otherwise be too large or diffuse to grasp; they also make individual analyses visible to other scholars or community members and encourage social processes of knowledge production.

[26] Jen Jack Gieseking, "Operating Anew: Queering GIS with Good Enough Software," *Canadian Geographer* 62.1 (August 25, 2017): 55–66.

5 Conclusion

Digital visualization techniques allow literature scholars to perform conventional work in new ways – to analyze hundreds or thousands of texts or to produce 3D maps that bend and twist in response to textual features. They also enable new ways of making scholarly work visible and sharing it with others. Scholars produce and distribute charts and maps, but they also use visualizations to make explicit their own positions or processes of analysis. Digital tools foreground the diverse ways in which data can be manipulated, analyzed, and represented. In part because they foreground nontrivial technical choices (between various effects or forms of visualization), they allow scholars to suggest that a visualization is only one view into the data and to indicate how that view was produced. From tweaking effects in 3D sculpting software to choosing how to structure documents that include visual forms such as line charts, scholars who use digital visualization techniques consciously negotiate between the many ways a visualization could appear and their distinct values and needs.

This negotiation is especially clear within literary studies because scholars are forced to reconcile established processes of knowledge production with new tools that are developed in other fields and are often intended for other uses. The choices scholars make and the relationships they form around their visualization work take on special relevance in this context; as Klein argues, the nature of digital tools and the choices they force on scholars present valuable opportunities to foreground the situated role of the scholar and to reconsider knowledge production in a changed technical environment. In this way, digital visualization acts as a bridge, allowing scholars to access provocative new tools but also translating the results of those tools into objects that can be used in scholarly work that remains distinctly humanistic.

CHAPTER 21

Digital Editions

Susan Brown

Digital editions are inextricably bound up with fear for the book. Well into the digital turn, reports of the demise of print appear to be greatly exaggerated, although independent bookstores are on life support.[1] Still, virtually all literary publications are now emitted electronically as a matter of course, and digital editions have superseded print ones entirely in some cases. As commercial forms remain bound to print paradigms, a gulf divides standard digital publication formats from experiments by artists, writers, and academics. Digital affordances have transformed textual scholarship in theory and practice, and scholarly editions are being recast profoundly despite major infrastructural challenges.

The *OED*'s entry for "edition" illustrates the extent to which print still dominates our conception of the term: "A particular form or version of a book or other published text issued at one time...."[2] The definition seems capacious, but despite cross references to *first edition*, *pocket edition*, and *railway edition* the *OED* is mute on the digital edition. This is ironic, since the *OED Online* itself contributed to the shift from the bound text to the networked one for major academic publications.[3] Digital editions occupy

I would like to acknowledge the assistance of Sam Peacock in the preparation of this manuscript, as well as the support of the Canada Research Chairs Program.

[1] E-book sales constituted 10.6 percent of the total trade sales in the United States in December 2021. "AAP March 2021 Statshot Report." *Association of American Publishers*, January 26, 2022: https://publishers.org/news/%ef%bf%bcaap-december-2021-statshot-report-publishing-industry-up-2-8-for-month-and-12-2-calendar-2021/ (accessed July 16, 2023). Perri Smith, "The Viability of E-Books and the Survivability of Print," *Publishing Research Quarterly*, 37.2 (2021): 264–277: https://doi.org/10.1007/s12109-021-09800-1 (accessed July 16, 2023). Alex Shephard, "Is This the End of the Indie Bookstore?" *The New Republic*, April 16, 2020: https://newrepublic.com/article/157315/end-indie-bookstore (accessed July 16, 2023).

[2] "edition, *n.*," in *Oxford English Dictionary* (online), 3rd ed., ed. John Simpson et al. (Oxford: Oxford University Press, 2020). Fully revised for the 3rd edition, and last revised June 2021.

[3] Not only did the *OED* online establish early on the technical advantages and financial viability of large-scale digital reference works, but it also produced an innovative web search technology that led to the founding of one of Canada's major software companies, OpenText Corporation. Tom Doerner and Margaret Dobbin, "KM at Open Text: Practicing What We Preach," in *Leading with*

an evolving space in which material, economic, and cultural factors reinforce a perception of the relationship between print and digital as a zero-sum game in which "the book" will be lost. However, as D. F. McKenzie argued, "Whatever its metamorphoses, the different physical forms of any text, and the intentions they serve, are relative to a specific time, place and person. This creates a problem only if we want meaning to be absolute and immutable."[4] Editions vary vastly from one context to another and evolve within the broader context of technological and socioeconomic change.

1 The Future of the Book

Changes in media – starting with Plato's response to the invention of writing – have typically produced both social panic and futuristic euphoria about the prospect of earlier forms being supplanted. Vannevar Bush noted in 1945 that publishing, along with information storage and retrieval, was ripe for an update.[5] Douglas Adams made an e-book the eponymous focus of his prescient sci-fi romp *The Hitchhiker's Guide to the Galaxy* (1978); the spin-off of novels, plays, films, comics, and games from the original radio show anticipated a transmedia future in which new and old forms cross-fertilize rather than replacing one other.[6]

Yet predictions about the future of the book proliferated in the late twentieth century, spurred by the hype surrounding the emergent Web as well as hypertext software developed for newly available personal computers. Eastgate Systems' Storyspace and Apple's HyperCard (both 1987) hypermedia authoring systems supported not only text but also graphics and sound. A strong connection between emergent digital textuality and literature was evident from the start in the simultaneous launch of Storyspace with codeveloper Michael Joyce's now canonical *afternoon, a story*.[7] A DIY ethos emerged in which formal experimentation accompanied both creative and academic writing, including fledgling digital

Knowledge: Knowledge Management Practices in Global Infotech Companies, ed. Madanmohan Rao (New Delhi: Tata McGraw-Hill, 2003), 363–379.

4 D. F. McKenzie, *Bibliography and the Sociology of Texts* (Cambridge: Cambridge University Press, 1999), 60–61.

5 Vannevar Bush, "As We May Think," *The Atlantic* 176.1 (July 1945): www.theatlantic.com/magazine/archive/1945/07/as-we-may-think/303881/ (accessed July 16, 2023).

6 Henry Jenkins, *Convergence Culture: Where Old and New Media Collide* (New York, New York University Press, 2006).

7 *afternoon, a story* was launched at the first conference on Hypertext in 1987 to demonstrate the Storyspace software. Jay David Bolter and Michael Joyce, "Hypertext and Creative Writing," *Hypertext '87: Proceedings of the ACM Conference on Hypertext* (New York: ACM, 1987), 41–50.

editions.[8] HyperCard creator Bill Atkinson described it as a "software erector set that lets non-programmers put together interactive information."[9] HyperCard both presaged developments in desktop publishing that made the Internet a global publishing platform and paved the way for Web applications, by preparing "a generation of developers who knew what [the early web browser] Netscape was *for*" by teaching them to think through hypertext.[10]

"The book has lost its privilege," pronounced Michael Joyce in 1991, one year after the first web browser was introduced, invoking the remainder sale and library deaccessioning as the morgue and mortuary of the book respectively. Joyce saw "constructive hypertext" in which readers play a determining role as "the first instance of what we will come to conceive as the natural form of multimodal, multi-sensual writing: the multiple fiction, the true electronic text, not the transitional electronic analogue of a printed text like a hypertextual encyclopedia."[11] Sven Birkerts lamented the book in *The Gutenberg Elegies* just as Robert Coover announced "The End of Books," even as he flagged the difficulties of sustaining hypertext systems.[12] Early digital editions are thus intimately linked not just to questions about the future of books but also to computing history, especially the PC revolution and the rise of the Web.

Traditional books are far from supplanted.[13] Their persistence has much to do with their materiality – physical structure, texture, smell, heft – as does their ability to be sold, loaned, resold, and inherited. The industrialization of

[8] Storyspace was used for teaching writing. When Mark D. Larsen used HyperCard to produce a quite full-featured teaching anthology of Latin American poetry, complete with annotations and bibliography, he not only "'stretched' the book to allow more room for the text" but also expanded it conceptually by incorporating elements of what we would now call courseware. Larsen could stretch the book because Storyspace let users create visual pages with text, tables, images, interactive buttons, and links to other pages. Mark D. Larsen, "Dealing Your Own Hand with HyperCard." *Hispania* 71.2 (1988): 454.

[9] Matthew Lasar, "30-plus years of HyperCard, the missing link to the Web," *ArsTechnica*, 25 May 2019: https://arstechnica.com/gadgets/2019/05/25-years-of-hypercard-the-missing-link-to-the-web/ (accessed July 16, 2023).

[10] Ibid.

[11] The first text-only web browser was introduced by Tim Berners-Lee in 1990. James Gillies and Robert Cailliau, *How the Web Was Born: The Story of the World Wide Web* (Oxford: Oxford University Press, 2000), 192. Michael Joyce, "Notes Toward an Unwritten Non-linear Electronic Text, 'The Ends of Print Culture' (a Work in Progress)," *Postmodern Culture* 2.1 (1991).

[12] Sven Birkerts, *The Gutenberg Elegies: The Fate of Reading in an Electronic Age* (London: Faber and Faber, 1994); Robert Coover, "The End of Books," *New York Times*, June 21, 1992: https://archive.nytimes.com/www.nytimes.com/books/98/09/27/specials/coover-end.html (accessed July 16, 2023).

[13] North America dominates the e-book market. E-books constituted only 20 percent of U.S. 2018 book sales, and apparently lost market share in the COVID-19 pandemic, even though sales and library borrowing of e-books increased. Cliff Guren, Thad McIlroy, and Steven Sieck, "COVID-19 and Book Publishing: Impacts and Insights for 2021," *Publishing Research Quarterly* 37.1 (2021): 1–14.

print saw the introduction of "gift books," markers of cultural and material capital and objects of exchange.[14] Even now, as much as a third of works of fiction are sold as gifts.[15] Much can be learned from considering the materialities of different types of editions and their economic implications.

2 Comparative Materialities: Print and Digital Editions

"A book is a machine to think with," says I. A. Richards.[16] The book is a highly naturalized technology, making it hard to disentangle digital editions from print conventions solidified over hundreds of years. With respect to literary production, new text technologies have been both extremely transformative – in the shift from pen to keyboard or touchscreen, for instance, to the extent that prestige manufacturers of writing instruments such as Mont Blanc and Lamy produce styli for tablets – and minimally disruptive as far as the distribution of literature is concerned, consolidating the concentration of formal publication in a few multinational corporations that continue to mimic print conventions. E-books still sell one by one rather than via subscription services like music and movies.

Mainstream e-books are skeuomorphic in design, invoking the materiality of print books in size and attempting to reproduce affordances that evoke the look, layout, and mechanisms of the page. As Jessica Pressman says, "Though e-readers could have developed in multiple ways, they adopted the visual and linguistic semiotics of the codex."[17] There are beneficial differences from print books: The storage and search capacities of devices and cloud services blur the line between e-books and ultra-portable digital libraries, making vast quantities of text available through a single material object.[18]

Other advances over print are limited, however.[19] E-reading platforms address some accessibility needs, but screen reader and navigation support

[14] Lorraine Janzen Kooistra, *Poetry, Pictures, and Popular Publishing: The Illustrated Gift Book and Victorian Visual Culture, 1855–1875* (Athens: Ohio University Press, 2014).

[15] Luís Leitão, Suzanne Amaro, Carla Henriques, and Paula Fonseca, "Do Consumers Judge a Book by its Cover? A Study of the Factors that Influence the Purchasing of Books," *Journal of Retailing and Consumer Services* 42 (2018): 88–97.

[16] I. A. Richards, *Principles of Literary Criticism* (London: Routledge, 2001), vii.

[17] Jessica Pressman, *Bookishness* (New York: Columbia University Press, 2020).

[18] Amaranth Borsuk, *The Book* (Cambridge, MA: MIT Press, 2018).

[19] Anastasia Salter finds considerably greater potential in iBook than in e-book design. She and others cited here recognize the complexity of the book as a social artifact, and resist simplistic oppositions between print and digital forms. Salter, *What Is Your Quest? From Adventure Games to Interactive Books* (Iowa City: University of Iowa Press, 2014); Simon Peter Rowberry, "The Ebook Imagination," *DHQ* 16.1 (2022); Andrew Klobucar, "Against Information: Reading (in) the Electronic Waste Land," *Electronic Book Review* (2013); Andrew Piper, *Book Was There: Reading in Electronic Times* (Chicago: University of Chicago Press, 2012).

are often unavailable.[20] Highlighting and notetaking are typically minimal and the results difficult or impossible to extract. Multimedia features are underutilized except for children's literature, where sounds, textures, and interactive features have long been a staple, so cultural producers wanting to go beyond text and illustration migrate to other media such as video games. E-books support basic navigation, "bookmarks," and word look-ups. However, the index, a crucial technology for scholarly reading, is typically missing or won't work in mainstream e-readers because of flowing pagination. Indexes are clunky even within the interfaces for books and journals from major academic publishers. Some devices and interfaces give a nod to social reading in displaying passages others have highlighted, but considering the potential for intertextual connections, e-book affordances are woefully impoverished.

The opportunity to recreate the book beyond the material limitations of printed text has been curtailed, foremost by corporate interests. Because the book is a highly naturalized machine, simulating it closely and ensuring that enhancements supported traditional reading practices allowed the e-reader industry to build on an existing market, whereas more disruptive approaches to delivering digital text would demand new literacies. Arnand Nourry, then head of the Hachette Livre publishing group pronounced, "The ebook is a stupid product. It is exactly the same as print, except it's electronic. There is no creativity, no enhancement, no real digital experience."[21] Nourry believes publishers' attempts to deliver content digitally through apps and websites fell flat, literally, because of the magnitude of the shift in medium:

> I'm convinced there is something we can invent using our content and digital properties beyond ebooks but I reached the conclusion that we don't really have the skills and talents in our companies because publishers and editors are accustomed to picking a manuscript and creating a design on a flat page. They don't really know the full potential of 3-D and digital. So we acquired three video game companies in the last two years to attract talent from different industries and see how we can nurture one another and how we can go beyond the ebook on digital. We need to offer different experiences to our consumers.[22]

[20] Seth Ketron and Kelly Naletelich, "How e-Readers Have Changed Personal Connections with Books," *Qualitative Market Research* 19.4 (2016): 433–452; Mark O. Pendergast, "Evaluating the Accessibility of Online University Education," in *Accessibility and Diversity in Education: Breakthroughs in Research and Practice* (Hershey, PA: IGI Global, 2020), 19–33.

[21] Harsimran Gill, "'The Ebook is a Stupid Product: No Creativity, No Enhancement,' Says the Hachette Group CEO," *Scroll.in*, February 17, 2018: https://scroll.in/article/868871 (accessed July 16, 2023).

[22] Ibid.

Just a few tech companies and publishers control the materiality of the digital edition, which is increasingly read on customized devices. While print on paper is relatively stable, the fragile materiality of digital texts requires more infrastructure.[23] In the age of apps and e-readers, text technologies require both software and hardware development, including significant material science and complex manufacturing processes, as well as their ongoing maintenance. Such factors undermine the ability of small presses, for instance, to translate a commitment to fitting form to content into the production of digital editions. Despite their differences, the Big Five publishers and Amazon share an understanding of texts as property, which inevitably pushes toward proprietary apps and platforms that lock down their properties and, with them, most of the potential of networked textuality.[24]

3 Moving Text beyond the Page

Digital editions crafted by writers, designers, developers, or artists beyond the publishing industry bear no resemblance to the faux pages of e-books. Designer Ben Fry's compact and dynamic visualization of 190,000 words from all six editions of *The Origin of Species* vividly demonstrate how dynamic and interactive display can provide insight into processes of revision.[25] Bespoke e-lit sidesteps conventional platforms in the service of independent creativity, offering the opportunity to play with form more radically than is possible in other publishing contexts. E-lit constitutes a vibrant tradition of experimentation with the possibilities of digital media. These have been theorized variously, but always with a strong emphasis on dynamic and interactive features. George P. Landow stressed early on the empowerment of readers as they moved through and among texts, while N. Katherine Hayles sees digital texts themselves as performative, reinstantiated with each appearance on a screen.[26] The procedural aspect of digital interactivity, identified by Janet Murray and extended by Ian

[23] Matthew G. Kirschenbaum, *Mechanisms: New Media and the Forensic Imagination* (Cambridge, MA: MIT Press, 2012).

[24] John W. Maxwell provides a fine contextualization of the e-book in relation to struggles over digital media control between traditional publishers and other corporations, particularly Amazon: "E-Book Logic: We Can Do Better," *Papers of the Bibliographic Society of Canada* 51.1 (2013); Amazon controls at least 50 percent of online book sales and 75 percent of e-book sales (Guren, "COVID-19").

[25] Ben Fry, "The Preservation of Favoured Traces," Fathom (2009): https://benfry.com/traces/ (accessed July 16, 2023).

[26] George P. Landow, *Hypertext 2.0: The Convergence of Contemporary Critical Theory and Technology* (Baltimore, MD: Johns Hopkins University Press, 1997); N. Katherine Hayles, *Writing Machines* (Cambridge, MA: MIT Press, 2002).

Bogost,[27] creates space for a new "procedural" rhetoric that joins words, images, and other aspects of representation to the affordances of specific programs or platforms. The borderline between interactive multimedia literature and video games is consequently blurred in exciting ways.[28]

Yet doing the book differently in ways that have broad appeal and reach a critical mass of readers has to date proven elusive. All the resources – imaginative, financial, social – available to J. K. Rowling, the richest author in the world, one whose initial refusal to allow her work to appear in e-books undoubtedly spurred paper sales of the most successful literary series in history, were insufficient to translate the magic of Harry Potter to the computer screen in the Pottermore website, which promised "an online reading experience unlike any other," with a stress on participatory and interactive elements.[29] Launched in 2012, the site allowed users to travel through moments from the book, "designed as an immersive experience that also enabled particular forms of interactivity: each scene's artwork could be zoomed into, with sound effects and collectible items embedded into the images."[30] However, after several reworkings the site was replaced entirely in 2019 by the "Wizarding World" fan site tied into the Universal Studios theme parks. Harry Potter is now available in standard e-books.

Small presses dedicated to the aesthetics of artisanal literary production have been sites of both innovation in and opposition to digital editions. Even artisanal presses dedicated to hand production often participate in what Alan Galey has called "technological hybridity," serving as reminders that "rigid oppositions between print and digital technology are of little use in the complex world of modern book production."[31] Coach House Books was on the vanguard of digital publishing: In 1984, it introduced *SwiftCurrent*, the first online literary magazine and writers' network, helped establish standards for electronic text, and spawned the first commercial editing software for the descriptive text markup that undergirds complex

[27] Janet Murray, *Hamlet on the Holodeck: The Future of Narrative in Cyberspace* (Cambridge, MA: MIT Press, 1998); Ian Bogost, *Persuasive Games* (Cambridge, MA: MIT Press, 2007).

[28] Gonzalo Frasca, "Ludologists Love Stories, Too: Notes from a Debate That Never Took Place," in *DiGRA '03 – Proceedings of the 2003 DiGRA International Conference* (Utrecht: DiGRA, 2003), 92–99.

[29] J. K. Rowling, speaking in "Pottermore Announcement" video, YouTube. Comment by "The Art Moose" with 266 likes: www.youtube.com/watch?v=sEu6fNbjbO4&ab (accessed July 16, 2023).

[30] In addition to contributing much original content to the Pottermore site, Rowling personally invested close to £8 million in the venture. Cassie Brummitt, "Pottermore: Transmedia Storytelling and Authorship in Harry Potter," *Midwest Quarterly* 58.1 (2016): 114 et passim.

[31] Alan Galey, "The Enkindling Reciter: E-books in the Bibliographical Imagination." *Book History* 15 (2012): 221.

digital publications and best practices for scholarly editing. The press also experimented early with copyleft licensing and innovative formats, taking the unprecedented step of "putting its entire frontlist online in unexpurgated form," not as downloadable PDFs but as free "mini-Web sites that [made] full use of animation, sound, plugins such as Flash, Javascript programs and so on."[32] Coach House editor Darren Wershler noted in 2002 that "One of the problems with electronic publishing now is that anyone interested in engaging in it also has to be willing to engage in the construction of the infrastructure to support it."[33] The model was not sustainable, and those mini-websites vanished into standard e-book formats.[34]

An absence of standardizing infrastructure means that author-driven e-texts tend to be one-offs, and often feel like incunabula, texts from when the "machine" of the book was still evolving. E-lit reminds us that it took more than half a century from the invention of the press in the West to establish de facto standards – pagination, tables of contents, indexes – of the codex as a highly effective text technology.[35] New forms of writing challenge readers: Espen J. Aarseth coined the term *ergodic* to evoke the work required to navigate multiple pathways through a text.[36] Indeed, the parallels Pressman draws between e-lit and modernist writing flag how tensions between high and low culture play out in digital space. Bespoke forms and incompatibility with mainstream platforms – and literacies – have limited the impact of e-lit, which demonstrates both the ability of digital literary texts to go beyond underwhelming e-reading formats and the challenges of doing so given scarce options for monetization. However, engagements with digital textuality within other industries with digital infrastructure demonstrate the potential for broader appeal. For instance, John Branch's *New York Times* feature "Snow Fall" won a Pulitzer Prize

32 Frank Davey, "SwiftCurrent returns," *border/lines* (Spring 1990), 15–16; Susan Brown, "Remediating the Editor," *Interdisciplinary Science Reviews* 40.1 (2015): 78–94; Darren Wershler, *FREE as in Speech and Beer: Open Source, Peer-to-Peer and the Economics of the Online Revolution* (London: Financial Times/Prentice Hall, 2002); Maxwell, John, "Coach House Press as a Digital Pioneer," *Amphora* 161 (2012): 7–14. The work of Abigel Lemak informs my understanding of e-books in the Canadian publishing industry.

33 Wershler, 102.

34 An attempt to archive the sites was made through Library and Archives Canada, and also in CD-ROM form: Coach House Books, *Y2oK*: www.chbooks.com. CD-ROM (Toronto: Coach House Books, 1998). The Wayback Machine of the Internet Archives preserves some elements of the site: https://web.archive.org/web/20230000000000*/www.chbooks.com (accessed July 16, 2023).

35 Cristina Dondi, "The European Printing Revolution," *The Oxford Companion to the Book* (Oxford: Oxford University Press, 2010).

36 Espen J. Aarseth, *Cybertext – Perspectives on Ergodic Literature* (Baltimore, MD: Johns Hopkins University Press, 1997).

for its riveting long-form narrative of a fatal avalanche.[37] Games engage with writing in a host of ways, including by transmediating books directly or intertextually, incorporating significant amounts of text into gameplay and incorporating literary techniques.[38] Through such widely distributed creations, a sense of the possibilities of digital storytelling is slowly expanding and literacies are shifting.

Just as indie games can be written for major platforms, authors can adopt social media sites as publishing infrastructure. Instapoetry is the most prominent example of popular e-lit to date; the term indicates publication on Instagram, but extends to other social media platforms including Tumblr, Twitter, and TikTok.[39] Although Instapoetry arose in English, there are parallel phenomena in other languages, not least the popular cell phone novel from Japan that has spread within and beyond Asia.[40] Instapoets including Atticus, Rupi Kaur, Lang Leav, Amanda Lovelace, Warsan Shire, and Najwa Zebian publish substantial bodies of work, building up large followings that help to drive sales of print publications. Books are often initially self-published, some are taken up by publishers after initial success, and some have become bestsellers. Kaur's *Milk and Honey* has sold more than 3.5 million copies and been translated forty times.[41] Deplored as "the poetry of capitalism" and celebrated for having ignited interest in poetry among the young, Instapoetry tends to consist of short poems with strong elements of visuality – sketches, photos, and video – and of identity performance, in keeping with social media.[42] Instapoets "disrupt the assumptions that poetry is an elitist form,"[43] highlighting questions about literary value,

[37] John Branch, "Snow Fall," *New York Times*, December 20, 2012: www.nytimes.com/projects/2012/snow-fall/index.html#/?part=tunnel-creek (accessed July 16, 2023); David Dowling and Travis Vogan, "Can We 'Snowfall' This? Digital Longform and the Race for the Tablet Market," *Digital Journalism* 3.2 (2015): 209–224.

[38] Steven E. Jones, *The Meaning of Video Games: Gaming and Textual Strategies* (London: Routledge, 2008); Astrid Ensslin, *Literary Gaming* (Cambridge, MA: MIT Press, 2014); Salter, *What Is Your Quest?*; James O'Sullivan, *Towards a Digital Poetics: Electronic Literature & Literary Games* (New York: Springer, 2019).

[39] Anne Kiernan, *Writing Cultures and Literary Media: Publishing and Reception in the Digital Age* (London: Palgrave Macmillan, 2021), 45–57; Faith Hill and Karen Yuan, "How Instagram Saved Poetry," *The Atlantic*, October 15, 2018: www.theatlantic.com/technology/archive/2018/10/rupi-kaur-instagram-poet-entrepreneur/572746/ (accessed July 16, 2023).

[40] Gabriella Lukacs, "DREAMWORK: Cell Phone Novelists, Labor, and Politics in Contemporary Japan," *Cultural Anthropology* 28.1 (2013): 44–64.

[41] Hill and Yuan, "How Instagram Saved Poetry."

[42] Soraya Roberts, "No Filter," *The Baffler*, January 24, 2018: https://thebaffler.com/latest/instapoetry-roberts; Maria Manning, "Crafting Authenticity: Reality, Storytelling, and Female Self-Representation through Instapoetry," *Storytelling, Self, Society* 16.2 (2020): 263–279. I am indebted for my understanding of social-media-based literary writing to the work of Kiera Obbard.

[43] Manning, "Crafting Authenticity," 265.

authenticity, and neoliberalism as they relate to digital media. Many are young women of color who thereby evade literary gatekeeping to build an audience for self-representations grounded in more diverse voices, stories, and audiences.[44] The work of these poets raises profound questions about the place of literature in the digital age and its complex relationship with affect and relatability.[45] It also exists in a medium that could and almost certainly will disappear in ways that print has not.

4 The Precarity of Digital Editions

Novelist Stephen Marche proclaims that "Literature is not data," but e-books are as certainly data as they are also forms of property instantiated in material objects. No less data are authors' digital files wending their way through publishers' production queues. The shift to word processing radically changes literary history, as tracked by Matthew G. Kirschenbaum; different modes of production leave different traces.[46] Kirschenbaum's insistence that literature is data, and no less valuable for that, highlights the falsity of fetishizing books as material objects. Marche opens with a scare, "Big data is coming for your books,"[47] that equates print with culture and invites us to save both, reflexively. But in practical terms, at this point in history, digital text is at greater risk than print. Marche's own modest foray into e-lit – the choose-your-own-adventure story "Lucy Hardin's Missing Period" in the online edition of *The Walrus*, magazine – itself came to a temporary stop a few years after publication, and was later rescued by forces outside the market economy.[48]

The scale and cost of infrastructure constitute critical differences between the printing press and electronic publishing. Gutenberg adapted

[44] Ibid., 270; Kiera Obbard, "Feminist Humour's Disruptive Potential: Trevor Noah's *Born a Crime: Stories from a South African Childhood* and Rupi Kaur's 'I'm Taking Back My Body'." *Journal of Applied Journalism & Media Studies* 10.2 (2021): 169–182.

[45] Akane Kanai, *Gender and Relatability in Digital Culture: Managing Affect, Intimacy and Value* (New York: Springer, 2018).

[46] Matthew G. Kirschenbaum, *Track Changes* (Boston: Harvard University Press, 2017).

[47] Stephen Marche, "Literature Is Not Data: Against Digital Humanities," *Los Angeles Review of Books*, October 28, 2012.

[48] Stephen Marche, "Lucy Hardin's Missing Period," *The Walrus*, November 10, 2010: https://thewalrus.ca/lucy-hardins-missing-period/ (accessed July 16, 2023). The interactive story was unavailable for some time and then reappeared. *The Walrus* website notes: "The author would like to thank Steve Marks, Digital Preservation Librarian at the University of Toronto, for his work updating and preserving Lucy," perhaps inadvertently flagging the conflation in this story of digital experimentation with a rather reductive attempt to write "the reality" of a woman's relationship to her body that asks "How would she be seen? Who was she?"

an existing and established technology, the wine press, to invent mass printing in Europe, where paper and the codex were already in place, and the essentials remained largely unchanged for hundreds of years thereafter. Creating infrastructure for delivering electronic text, by contrast, involves software development and maintenance in a rapidly changing technological environment, and the material forms of both infrastructure and literary products are much less stable, making costs and risks considerably higher. The German-based tech startup Oolipo, inspired by the French Oulipo literary movement, produced an innovative social-media style app for authoring and publishing transmedia stories for smartphones, with the tagline "stop writing. START CREATING."[49] It delivered engaging serialized stories, including *Jellybone,* a psychological thriller by Kate Pullinger that used affordances such as alerts and vibrations, and incorporated a real Instagram account.[50] However, Oolipo's major financial backer, the publisher Bastei Lübbe, pulled support in November 2017, citing low user numbers, less than two years after its launch; the creative works disappeared with the app.[51] Oolipo's premature demise exemplifies the risks of developing innovative e-reading infrastructure. The persistence of creations by Tender Claws, the digital game studio behind the award-winning 2013 "cinematic novella" *Pry* by Danny Cannizzaro and Samantha Gorman, may point to a more feasible strategy for mass distribution and monetization of digital stories.

Considering such digital artifacts digital incunabula brings home their vulnerability. Whether on standalone websites, social writing sites such as Wattpad,[52] innovative apps, online newspapers, or social media platforms

[49] Oolipo, "Create Interactive Multimedia Stories with Our Storytelling Tool," YouTube, July 28, 2017: www.youtube.com/watch?v=jqTbiVco_HM&ab_channel=oolipo (accessed July 16, 2023).

[50] "Jellybone," *Turn On Literature.* August 2017: https://turnonliterature.eu/works/2017/08/07/jellybone/ (accessed July 16, 2023).

[51] Judging from rash of media stories in March of 2017 and the link on Twitter (@oolipo) to a statement that the startup's financial backer had pulled out on November 29, 2019, Oolipo was given an exceptionally short window in which to prove the value of an investment of more than 3 million Euros. "Unplanned Write-down at Subsidiary Oolipo AG Burdens the Result in the Second Quarter," Bastei Lübbe, November 11, 2017: www.luebbe.com/en/news/2017-11-07/bastei-luebbe-ag-unplanned-write-down-at-subsidiary-oolipo-ag-burdens-the-result-in-the-second-quarter/id_692a44d8d06583b7b403e8a4d4afeef3 (accessed July 16, 2023).

[52] Wattpad, a mobile-oriented user-generated content platform that began with high literary aspirations signaled by "Atty" awards named for Margaret Atwood (replaced by "Watty" awards), is now dominated by romance, teen fiction, and fan-fiction. Some texts published on such platforms extend into print publication (including by Wattpad itself) and have become bestsellers, and some self-published online authors are so successful they are declining traditional publishing contracts. Wattpad: www.wattpad.com (accessed July 16, 2023); Sarah Brouillette, "Romance Work," *Theory & Event* 22.2 (2019).

such as Instagram, digital texts are not only performative in Hayles's sense but also correspondingly precarious. Although libraries are increasingly stepping up and developing improved methods for archiving digital media, preservation let alone sustainability remain major challenges. E-lit is largely dependent for survival and preservation on academic and para-academic infrastructure, particularly through the Electronic Literature Organization.[53] Digital editions require conditions very different from printed books, which with few exceptions have remarkably similar requirements for persistence, unlike the myriad ones associated with digital objects.

To return to the affect surrounding material books, Instagram hosts a paradoxical fetishization of the materiality of the book that, according to Pressman, is "about class and consumerism. It is about constructing and projecting identity through the possession and presentation of books."[54] Nostalgia for the printed book naively ignores the complex interrelation of human creativity, economics, and technology that has always shaped literary form. Amazon built on the conflation of print books with a love for the literary to establish its identity as a "bookstore"; ironically, as the world's largest online retailer for which books constitute perhaps 10 percent of sales, Amazon has disrupted publishing and stunted e-book development.[55] Instagram paradoxically fosters both a parallel bourgeois sensibility of "bookishness" performed through feeds relishing the materiality of books,[56] and also fosters new forms of writing that undermine that fetishism along with narrow definitions of authorial identity and the literary. However, neither platform has any particular investment in the ongoing maintenance or preservation of the digital publications that it hosts, and e-literature broadly shares in this vulnerability.

5 Expanding Possibilities

One might expect both book fetishism and literary gatekeeping to be intense in the field of textual scholarship, dedicated as it is to the painstaking production of scholarly editions of past works by important authors,

[53] Electronic Literature Organization: https://eliterature.org/ (accessed July 16, 2023).

[54] Pressman, *Bookishness.*

[55] "Amazon garners almost 75% of e-book revenue, with the balance going to the Big Five publishing companies," note Henrich R. Greve and Seo Yeon Song, "Amazon Warrior: How a Platform Can Restructure Industry Power and Ecology," in *Entrepreneurship, Innovation, and Platforms* 37 (Bingley: Emerald Publishing, 2017), 312. See also Mark McGurl, *Everything and Less: The Novel in the Age of Amazon* (London: Verso, 2021); Brad Stone, *The Everything Store: Jeff Bezos and the Age of Amazon* (Boston: Back Bay Books, 2014).

[56] Pressman, *Bookishness.*

yet this is the most fertile context in which the digital edition is being remade. A symbiotic relationship emerged between theories of electronic textuality, editorial theory, and practices of scholarly editing that is a reworking of notions of authority, editorial control, sources, citations, notes, and completeness. Fittingly, the most controversial edition of the later twentieth century, Hans Walter Gabler's 1984 *Ulysses*, was prepared entirely on a computer, although it was initially issued only in print.[57]

If editing is understood as the alteration of an existing text, record, or inscription, then digital editing now takes place on an unprecedented scale. Online banking, video games, posting to social media, texting, writing emails, revising novels with word processors, and producing authoritative scholarly editions all draw on the ability to modify the charges of electrons and thereby change a field, record, document, sound file, image, or video. This fundamentally dynamic quality of electronic textuality marks a key difference between it and "paper knowledge."[58] Notably, the way in which the portability of devices would make digital texts accessible was heralded in the name Dynabook, an early notebook computer prototype.[59] Editorial theorists embrace the text as processual, with Jerome McGann characterizing editions and translations as "deformances," repetitions with a difference that productively deform, in the sense of reshaping or reorganizing, an earlier textual performance.[60] As for e-books and e-lit, platform, software, and interface are inseparable when considering digital scholarly editions.

Hypertext hugely influenced notions of the digital edition. Building on Landow and others, Jay David Bolter saw hypertext as epitomizing postmodernism and deconstruction, thereby decentering the author.[61] Nonlinear texts were celebrated for both solving thorny editorial problems and empowering the reader. An edition of Emily Dickinson's poetry, whose ordering is controversial, for instance, no longer demanded definitive decisions with respect to order, allowing readers to generate new interpretations from the path they chose through digitized manuscripts, contextual materials, and editorial context, and making it possible to expose "the

57 J. C. C. Mays, "Gabler's *Ulysses* as a Field of Force," *Text*, 10(1997): 1–13. A digital version of Gabler's edition appeared online in 2018, though at press time is available only in archived form. James Joyce, *Ulysses: A Digital Critical and Synoptic Edition*, prepared by Hans Walter Gabler with Wolfhard Steppe and Claus Melchior, eds., Ronan Crowley and Joshua Schäuble, http://web.archive.org/web/20220317010925/http://ulysses.online/index.html (accessed September 8, 2023).

58 Lisa Gitelman, *Paper Knowledge* (Durham, NC: Duke University Press, 2014).

59 Susan B. Barnes, "Alan Kay: Transforming the Computer into a Communication Medium," *Annals of the History of Computing*, 29 (2007): 18–30.

60 Jerome McGann, *Radiant Textuality: Literary Studies after the World Wide Web* (New York: Springer, 2016).

61 Jay David Bolter, *Writing Space: Computers, Hypertext, and the Remediation of Print* (New York: Routledge, 2001).

processes of knowledge at work in the assemblage of an edition."[62] Sarah Humphreys argues that a playable edition of Mourning Dove's *Cogewea* created using the Twine platform can reflect the novel's decolonization of the Western, in Maori theorist Linsa Thuiwa Smith's sense that it works to "to demystify, re-center, and rewrite to re-right the place of Indigenous peoples in history, culture, and politics."[63] Digital editions focused on user agency share the same philosophy, if not the high-resolution graphics, as the 3D open world of Tracy Fullerton's *Walden: A Game*, where players encounter notes, texts, and letters during a year spent with Thoreau.[64]

Though digital editions are not typically immersive, they are increasingly characterized by multimediality that allows for rich contextualization. Zoomable images of art and manuscripts distinguish the Blake, Rossetti, and Whitman archives, and meticulous metadata and encoding provide access to features such as annotations, revisions, additions, deletions, and image components.[65] The Touch Press/Faber and Faber app *The Waste Land* made a splash beyond academia by augmenting the poem with manuscript views, images, explanatory notes, commentary by luminaries including Seamus Heaney and Jeanette Winterson, and readings by Eliot and other famous writers and actors, attracting praise for its interactivity, touch navigation, and typography.[66] The *New York Times*'s "Close Read" series employs a more standardized format to dramatize visual and textual analysis, including of Elizabeth Bishop's "One Art" and W. H. Auden's "Musée des Beaux Arts," with similarly high production values, demonstrating how digital editions can mobilize intertextual and contextual relationships in ways a codex cannot.[67]

[62] Martha Nell Smith, "The Human Touch Software of the Highest Order: Revisiting Editing as Interpretation," *Textual Cultures* 2.1 (2007): 12.

[63] Sara Humphreys, "Creating a Playable Academic Edition of Mourning Dove's *Cogewea* or How Games can Decolonize," *KULA: Knowledge Creation, Dissemination, and Preservation Studies* 3 (2019): 2.

[64] Tracy Fullerton, "Surveying the Soul: Creating the World of *Walden, a Game*," in *World-Builders on World-Building*, ed. Mark J. P. Wolf (New York: Routledge, 2020), 93–109.

[65] Morris Eaves, Robert N. Essick, and Joseph Viscomi, eds., *The William Blake Archive*: www.blakearchive.org/ (accessed July 16, 2023); Jerome J. McGann, ed., *The Complete Writings and Pictures of Dante Gabriel Rossetti*: www.rossettiarchive.org/ (accessed July 16, 2023); Matt Cohen, Ed Folsom, and Kenneth M. Price, eds., *The Walt Whitman Archive*: https://whitmanarchive.org/ (accessed July 16, 2023).

[66] See Hilary Kenna, "Touching the Text of TS Eliot's *The Waste Land*: A Critical Discussion of Interactive Design and Screen Typography for an iPad e-book," *Book 2.0* 1 (2011), 207–238. Klobucar, "Against Information."

[67] Close Read, series, *New York Times*: www.nytimes.com/interactive/2021/arts/close-read.html (accessed July 16, 2023); examples from the series include Dwight Garner and Parul Sehgal, "19 Lines that Turn Anguish Into Art," *New York Times*, June 18, 2021; Elisa Gabbert, "A Poem (and a Painting) About the Suffering That Hides in Plain Sight," *New York Times*, March 6, 2022.

More esoteric editorial conjuring is enabled by technologies that make damaged manuscripts and books newly accessible: Spectral imaging has recovered lost works of Archimedes that were overwritten by Christian religious texts, as well as faded portions of explorer David Livingstone's journals written with improvised inks made from substances such as berry juice.[68] A crucial benefit of digital editions generally is in making rare, fragile, and geographically remote resources available online, immeasurably increasing access to archival materials by scholars and the public while reducing the number of people who handle or travel to consult them.

Innovations in navigation can both distinguish and limit digital texts and their environments. Bespoke access points create silos of data; an interface may or may not allow for searching, viewing, copying, comparing, annotating, contributing, saving, or downloading. The Women Writers Project at Northeastern offers not only keyword search but also analytical tools and visualizations that work across multiple editions. The typically tight coupling of foundational scholarly collections, such as the Oxford Text Archive, the Text Creation Partnership, and Hathi Trust Digital Library, with discovery, access, and display interfaces, means that tools tend to be customized to work with single collections even though content may be open and theoretically interoperable.[69] Commercial content providers increasingly provide tools or "workbenches" for doing more with their digital content than searching and reading. The persistence of such silos, even large ones, which limit possibilities for working across multiple collections for all but the most technically skilled, remains a major shortcoming of online resources.

Capacious storage makes constellations of digital editions possible. Vannevar Bush anticipated the "memex" in the late 1930s as "a sort of mechanized private file and library … in which an individual stores all his

[68] Roger L. Easton, Keith T. Knox, and William A. Christens-Barry, "Multispectral Imaging of the Archimedes Palimpsest," in *Proceedings of the 32nd Applied Imagery Pattern Recognition Workshop, 2003* (New York: IEEE, 2003), 111–116; see also The Archimedes Palimpsest: http://archimedespalimpsest.org/ (accessed July 16, 2023); Stephen Davison, Adrian S. Wisnicki, and Elizabeth McAulay, "The David Livingstone Spectral Imaging Project," in *Proceedings of the 12th ACM/IEEE-CS Joint Conference on Digital Libraries* (IEEE, 2012), 411–412; Adrian Wisnicki, dir, Livingstone Online: https://livingstoneonline.org/ (accessed July 16, 2023).

[69] The Oxford Text Archive, https://ota.bodleian.ox.ac.uk/repository/xmlui/ (accessed July 16, 2023). Content is sometimes shared, in the sense of being ingested by other sites, as in the case of the Text Creation Partnership. See "FAQ," *Text Creation Partnership*: https://textcreationpartnership.org/faq/ (accessed July 16, 2023). The Hathi Trust offers tools for working with its collection, including tools for analysis and the Hathi Trust Bookworm. See "HTRC Collections and Tools," Hathi Trust Digital Library: www.hathitrust.org/htrc_collections_tools (accessed July 16, 2023).

books, records, and communications, and which is mechanized so that it may be consulted with exceeding speed and flexibility."[70] Just as the notion of the archive has been expanded, problematized, and reinvigorated by the digital turn, the understanding of the digital edition has expanded and its boundaries blurred; many editions now include reception materials, for instance, that might once have been published separately, and thematic research collections are a form of editorial activity that transcends single authors or texts. Digital media enables a strong relationship between text and collection, edition and digital environment, and digital editions formed parts of larger collections from the outset. Project Gutenberg began in 1971, before the graphical Web, when graduate student Michael Hart leveraged access to massive computing resources to demonstrate the value of downloadable, standardized, open access editions; it grew into an international, volunteer-staffed venture that is still extensively used by both academics and the public.[71] Project Gutenberg focuses on well-known texts, but numerous complementary efforts in the early days of the graphical Web were devoted to underrepresented groups: The Women Writers Project, A Celebration of Women Writers, The Charles Chestnutt Archive, and Voices from the Gaps survived the decades, but many sites associated with minority literatures did not as the canon reasserted itself.[72] The Internet Archive, with its aim to provide "universal access to all knowledge," including the entire web as well as digitized books, audio, videos, games, and software, provides primary and secondary materials for future digital editions.[73] The digital edition thus blurs into the archive.

The ability to interrelate vast amounts of content from multiple locations begs the question of the boundaries of the digital edition in relation to the wider information ecology of reference works, scholarly articles and monographs, educational resources, and other sources of information on the Web. Print authors from Laurence Sterne to Flann O'Brien and Jorge Luís Borges played with the encroachment of paratexts on the printed page. The unbounded digital text, particularly a critical or complete works

[70] Bush, "As We May Think."

[71] Michael Hart, "The History and Philosophy of Project Gutenberg," Project Gutenberg (1992): www.gutenberg.org/about/background/history_and_philosophy.html (accessed July 16, 2023); Rebecca J. Rosen, "The Legacy of Project Gutenberg Founder, Michael S. Hart," *The Atlantic*, September 8, 2011: www.theatlantic.com/technology/archive/2011/09/the-legacy-of-project-gutenberg-founder-michael-s-hart/244787/ (accessed July 16, 2023).

[72] Amy E. Earhart, "Can Information Be Unfettered? Race and the New Digital Humanities Canon," in *Debates in the Digital Humanities*, ed. Matthew K. Gold (Minneapolis: University of Minnesota Press, 2012), 309–318.

[73] Brewster Kahle, "Universal Access to All Knowledge," *The Internet Archive,* November 30, 2011, https://archive.org/details/brewsterkahlelongnowfoundation (accessed July 16, 2023).

edition, begs the question of where, or whether, the context relevant to a digital edition ends.

6 Preservation, Standards, and Innovation

Digital text does end, however, if not sustained. Preserving digital cultural artifacts is thus a matter of great concern, since some significant early collections have already been lost. Experimental, bespoke, and proprietary systems vastly increase the difficulty of preservation, which is why libraries and scholars in the digital humanities have become advocates of standards for digital publications, as well as of open-source code and open access content, all of which assist in sustaining digital editions. Text markup with Extensible Markup Language (XML) is the standard for producing digital editions. Commercial e-book publishers except Apple typically produce either the XML-based and accessibility-oriented EPUB format or the formerly proprietary but now open PDF standard. XML in particular supports highly customizable, domain-specific descriptive markup that systematically labels features of texts, such as their structure or content, to allow for information exchange, transformation, processing, and formatting. The semantic capacity of XML makes it more powerful as a base format than either PDFs or HTML, the language of Web pages, for both commercial and publishing applications.[74]

In a world in which, as Hans Walter Gabler observed, "editions realized in a digital environment still tend to remain largely imitative of scholarly editions in print," academic digital editions have embraced semantic markup, not only because it is preservation-friendly but also because the same underlying text can generate multiple outputs, support interoperability with other editions, and be processed with common tools, as well as reflecting the scholarly interpretation or model of a text in its structure.[75] The vibrant community of practice that has grown up around the Text Encoding Initiative's long-standing work on a shared XML schema has fueled debates and established practices for digital editions, and enabled acclaimed online scholarly editions of literature.[76] The separation of TEI

[74] Elliotte Rusty Harold and W. Scott Means, *XML in a Nutshell*, 2nd ed. (Beijing: O'Reilly, 2002).

[75] Hans Walter Gabler, "Foreword," *Digital Scholarly Editing: Theories and Practices*, ed. Matthew James Driscoll and Elena Pierazzo (Cambridge: OpenBook Publishers, 2016); Julia Flanders, "Text Encoding," in *Doing Digital Humanities: Practice, Training, Research*, ed. Constance Crompton, Richard J. Lane, and Ray Siemens (New York: Routledge, 2016), 104–122.

[76] James Cummings, "The Text Encoding Initiative and the Study of Literature," in *A Companion to Digital Literary Studies*, ed. Susan Schreibman and Ray Siemens (Oxford: Blackwell, 2007): 451–476.

markup from presentation means that a single base text can record multiple witnesses and therefore support flexible presentation of different versions of a work, including the production of multiple editions, as with the Piers Plowman Electronic Archive.[77] Semantic representations also underlie the standards for what is called linked open data, which enables digital editions to pull in images from other locations on the Web, as in the variorum edition of *Frankenstein* in the Shelley-Godwin Archive, or to link to details of images, so that *The Life of the Buddha* can be illuminated by interlinking specific areas on a long scroll with sections of narrative.[78]

Linked data has considerable potential for aggregating content and coordinating contributions from multiple sources, and since it creates a huge set of interconnected online resources referred to as the Semantic Web or global graph, it offers rich multifaceted contextualization.[79] Systems such as this may offer the best hope of overcoming the blocks that rights-protected materials pose to digital editions, since they leave web resources "in place" but link to them from porous interfaces. Indeed, scholar-developed platforms for scholarly editions and exhibitions, including Omeka S, Scalar, ResearchSpace, and the LEAF Linked Editorial Academic Framework, are increasingly incorporating linked data technologies to enable the creation, editing, curating, showcasing, interlinking, and contextualizing of both digitized and born-digital content. Their support of multimodal, collaborative, and pedagogical scholarship, and various strategies for customizing the display of content, has produced an array of experimental digital editions, artifacts, and collections that are nevertheless standards-based and supported by common infrastructure.[80] Networked textuality of the sort supported by linked open data involves less the divergent paths or tree structures associated with hypertext and more a set of interconnected data points that draw on and recombine multiple sources. Ed Folsom's and N. Katherine Hayles's claims that database and narrative are symbiotic forms

[77] Piers Plowman Electronic Archive: http://piers.chass.ncsu.edu/ (accessed July 16, 2023).

[78] "Web Annotation Data Model" *W3C* (W3C, 2017), www.w3.org/TR/annotation-model/ (accessed July 16, 2023); *International Image Interoperability Framework*: https://iiif.io/ (accessed July 16, 2023); *Frankenstein, or the Modern Prometheus*, gen. eds. Neil Fraistat and Raffaele Viglianti: http://shelleygodwinarchive.org/contents/frankenstein/ (accessed July 16, 2023); *The Life of the Buddha*, dir. Andrew Quintman and Kurtis R. Schaeffer: http://lotb.iath.virginia.edu/ (accessed July 16, 2023).

[79] Dominic Oldman, Martin Doerr, and Stefan Gradmann, "Zen and the Art of Linked Data: New Strategies for a Semantic Web of Humanist Knowledge," in *A New Companion to Digital Humanities*, ed. Susan Schreibman, Ray Siemens, and John Unsworth (Oxford: Wiley Blackwell, 2016): 251–273.

[80] Omeka S: https://omeka.org/s/; Scalar: https://scalar.me/anvc/scalar/; ResearchSpace: https://researchspace.org/; Linked Editorial Academic Framework: www.leaf-vre.org/.

is borne out by the ability to construct long-form arguments that incorporate highly structured linked data.[81]

Truly expansive understandings of the digital edition in editorial theory that depart from print-oriented notions of the fixed text include John Bryant's notion of texts as both fluid and culturally situated, and Marcello Vitali Rosati's concept of *éditorialisation* as an ongoing process whereby digital space is structured by actions both collective and individual.[82] However, intellectual property laws limit how expansive digital editions can be. The widespread piracy on the Web parallels the unauthorized editions of texts that preceded the introduction of international copyright laws, reflecting the limitations of legal regimes wedded to print paradigms. Copyright drastically limits experiments in digital editing. For instance, no edition can be created of the Edwin Morgan Scrapbooks, a collection of painstakingly organized ephemera that is both a performance of gay identity and a rich embodiment of recombinant textuality, for which Bridget Moynihan and Akmal Putra produced impressive digital prototypes: Tracking down and obtaining permission from copyright holders is simply not feasible.[83] Until legislation catches up with new media practices, many new-form digital publications will be hobbled. Indeed, Janneke Adema argues that only by moving beyond commodified models inherited from print can scholarly publishing arrive at open, dynamic "living books."[84]

Dynamic and participatory editions are radical experiments that seriously challenge print-legacy notions of authority. Wikipedia, the largest knowledge resource in human history, established a new paradigm for community editing and knowledge production that superseded the parent Nupedia project that foundered on traditional scholarly workflows.[85] Large scholarly editions have typically been collaborative and often multigenerational, but the Web's support for editing makes it possible to distribute the labor of creating digital editions broadly across geographically distributed teams of scholars. Some projects invite participation from

81 Ed Folsom, "Database as Genre: The Epic Transformation of Archives," *PMLA* 122.5 (2007): 1571–1579; N. Katherine Hayles, "Narrative and Database: Natural Symbionts," *PMLA* 122.5 (2007): 1603–1608.

82 John Bryant, *The Fluid Text: A Theory of Revision and Editing for Book and Screen* (Ann Arbor: University of Michigan Press, 2002); Marcello Vitali Rosati, "What Is Editorialization?," *Sens public* (January 19, 2016), para. 26: https://doi.org/10.7202/1043408ar (accessed July 16, 2023).

83 Bridget Moynihan and Akmal Putra, "Prototyping the Archival Ephemeral: Experimental Interfaces for the Edwin Morgan Scrapbooks," *Digital Studies/Le Champ numérique* 9.1 (2019).

84 Janneke Adema, *Living Books: Experiments in the Posthumanities* (Cambridge, MA: MIT Press, 2021).

85 Larry Sanger, "The Early History of Nupedia and Wikipedia: A Memoir," *Open Sources* 2 (2005): 307–338.

citizen scholars: The Bentham letters are being transcribed through public contributions, and Amanda Visconti's *Infinite Ulysses* experimented with online annotation of a digital edition, although the edition itself proved finite given the challenges of sustainability.[86]

Platforms and other infrastructural considerations are as crucial to academic digital editions as to commercial e-publishing. Textual scholars and curators of digital archives are fortunate that libraries are increasingly stepping up to address the challenges of digital archiving. Preserving interfaces is a huge challenge that is rarely undertaken, although it is extremely pressing when it comes to e-lit and editing experiments.[87] As Laura Estill notes "the loss rate for digital projects is high" – somewhere around 50 percent – indicating the extent to which the history of, as well as the knowledge produced by, early digital editions is in jeopardy.[88] Preserving complex Web resources is much more difficult than keeping books on shelves or in conservation boxes. Standard data formats such as XML facilitate preservation without markedly constraining interface options, although they increase production and publication costs. Interface standardization, however, is not only elusive but also inappropriate, since more formal experimentation is overdue. The persistence of codex conventions indicates how powerful normalized text can be, so evaluations of digital editions will need to engage in critical infrastructure studies along with other forms of analysis.[89]

7 Conclusion

Far from replacing printed books, digital editions will remain in dialogue with them for the foreseeable future. The convergence of software, hardware, and social factors means that e-reader interfaces are baked into platforms and devices. The naturalized affordances of books as technologies underpin the hailing of consumers through a mimicry of printed books

86 See the Infinite Ulysses project, created by Amanda Visconti: http://infiniteulysses.com/ (accessed July 16, 2023). It is now archived as a static website, necessarily if ironically given its exploration of interactive open editing.

87 The Electronic Literature Organization has made heroic efforts to preserve early e-lit in the multivolume *Electronic Literature Collection* (2006, 2011, 2016): https://collection.eliterature.org/ (accessed July 16, 2023); Stuart Moulthrop and Dene Grigar, *Pathfinders: Documenting the Experience of Early Digital Literature*, Scalar (2015).

88 Laura Estill, "Legacy Technologies and Digital Futures," in *Doing More Digital Humanities*, ed. Constance Crompton, Richard J. Lane, and Ray Siemens (London: Routledge, 2020), 8–9. Robert Camille Davis cites studies with even higher rates of "reference rot": "The Future of Web Citation Practices," *Behavioral & Social Sciences Librarian* 35.3 (2016): 129.

89 Alan Liu, "Toward a Diversity Stack: Digital Humanities and Diversity as Technical Problem," *PMLA* 135.1 (2020): 130–151; Critical Infrastructures Studies.Org: https://cistudies.org/ (accessed July 16, 2023).

and an adherence to "bookishness" that obscure the ways in which corporate publishers have shut down the potential for digital texts.

The "mechanization of the word," John Maxwell reminds us, starts prior to Gutenberg and is ongoing, yet the development of the digital edition constitutes a watershed moment in that process.[90] The form of the book has not been overturned by mainstream transmediation, but authorship and authority have undergone a sea change. Reading now happens in the context of increasing immersion in digital textuality, within which online marketing has embraced the notion of the "edit," a recognition of the value added by the curation, remix, presentation, and contextualization of commodities that invokes the creative possibilities of digital space.[91]

Digital editions demand analysis in terms that take content organization and appearance into account along with the shaping forces of interface, platform, software, infrastructure, and economics. It is simultaneously true that we are, in the words of Kate Pullinger, in a golden age of storytelling as artists and scholars explore the potential of new forms of multimodal representation, and that we are in the age of incunabula in establishing conventions and infrastructure to pry editions away from the legacy of print forms toward the wide range of affordances offered by digital instantiations of texts.[92] The best digital editions gesture not only, inevitably and skeuomorphically, back to the book, but also forward toward unbounded networked textuality.

[90] John W. Maxwell, "Text Processing Techniques and Traditions (or: Why the History of Computing Matters to DH)," in *Doing More Digital Humanities*, 70–83.

[91] Literary remix of course long precedes print. One of a host of examples of literary remixes of digital sources is Jordan Abel's *Injun* (Vancouver: Talonbooks, 2016), a decolonizing "edition" of Western novels. On remixing the scholarly book, see Janneke Adema, "Cutting Scholarship Together/Apart: Rethinking the Political Economy of Scholarly Book Publishing," in *The Routledge Companion to Remix Studies*, ed. Eduardo Navas, Owen Gallagher, and xtine burrough (New York: Routledge, 2014), 268–279; and Martin Paul Eve and Jonathan Gray, eds., *Reassembling Scholarly Communications: Histories, Infrastructures, and Global Politics of Open Access* (Cambridge, MA: MIT Press, 2020): https://mitpress.mit.edu/books/reassembling-scholarly-communications (accessed July 16, 2023).

[92] See Kate Pullinger, "Interview with Kate Pullinger: Writing and the Digital Age," *Litro Magazine*, October 30, 2019, www.litromagazine.com/usa/2019/10/interview-with-author-kate-pullinger-writing-and-the-digital-age/ (accessed July 16, 2023).

Index

Milton Keynes UK
Ingram Content Group UK Ltd.
UKHW021050280124
436838UK00001B/1